The Perils
of Proximity

THE PERILS
OF PROXIMITY

China-Japan Security Relations

RICHARD C. BUSH

BROOKINGS INSTITUTION PRESS
Washington, D.C.

Library of Congress Cataloging-in-Publication data

Bush, Richard C., 1947–
    The perils of proximity : China-Japan security relations / Richard C. Bush.
       p.   cm.
    Includes bibliographical references and index.
    Summary: "Explores the factors underlying the security dilemma confronting Japan
and China despite their positive economic interaction, including China's growing military
capability, the Japan-U.S. security alliance, and issues such as Japan's occupation of China
in the mid-twentieth century and rights in the East China Sea"—Provided by publisher.
    ISBN 978-0-8157-0474-4 (hardcover : alk. paper)
    1. Japan—Military relations—China. 2. China—Military relations—Japan. 3. National
security—Japan. 4. National security—China. I. Brookings Institution. II. Title.
    UA845.B88 2010
    355'.03109510952—dc22   2010029382

9 8 7 6 5 4 3 2 1

Printed on acid-free paper

Typeset in Minion

Composition by Cynthia Stock
Silver Spring, Maryland

Printed by R. R. Donnelley
Harrisonburg, Virginia

For my mentors

Contents

Acknowledgments

I have accumulated a large number of debts at every stage of the project that has culminated in the publication of *Perils of Proximity*. This brief acknowledgment does not do justice to those who have helped me, nor does it implicate them in the end result.

Generous financial support came from the Smith Richardson Foundation, the John D. and Catherine T. MacArthur Foundation, and another donor who prefers to remain anonymous.

Strobe Talbott, president of the Brookings Institution, Martin Indyk, director of the Foreign Policy Studies Program at Brookings, and his predecessor, Carlos Pascual, have all offered strong encouragement for my work. Kevin Scott, Aileen Chang, Jennifer Mason, and Jiyoung Song—my colleagues at Brookings's Center for Northeast Asian Policy Studies (CNAPS)— took on more program management responsibilities so that I would have more time for my scholarship. In addition, Jennifer was everything one could ask for in a research assistant. She worked tirelessly to track down information, translate Japanese materials, and ensure that I made sense. A series of CNAPS interns did special projects. Scholars from East Asia who have been CNAPS visiting fellows over the years provided useful insights on specific subjects. Chu Shulong, Guo Rongxing, Richard Hu Weixing, Iizuki Keiko, Iwashita Akihiro, Jin Linbo, Matsumura Masahiro, Pang Zhongying, James Tang, Taniguchi Tomohiko, Yamaji Hideki, and Yang Bojiang come especially to mind.

Other colleagues at Brookings, particularly Michael O'Hanlon and Jeffrey Bader, have been a source of inspiration. Mike, along with two anonymous reviewers, offered valuable suggestions on how to improve an early draft, and I appreciate their guidance. The staff of the Foreign Policy Studies

Program, notably Peggy Knudson, and the staff of the Brookings library have been consistently supportive. Once again, Eileen Hughes of the Brookings Institution Press was an outstanding editor.

In the course of this effort I have learned a tremendous amount from scholars in China and Japan who seek to understand the security environment that their respective countries confront and to clarify the choices that their governments and peoples face. Some I have had the privilege to interview personally, for which I am very grateful. All of them have taught me something. I have honored the desire of some of those with whom I spoke not to have their comments attributed to them. When I was doing interviews in China, the Brookings-Tsinghua Center in Beijing was especially helpful. In Japan, the Ministry of Foreign Affairs provided kind facilitation.

I have also learned a great deal, both over the years and during this current project, from America's cadre of outstanding scholarly talent on both China and Japan. The group is too large to try to name everyone, but Michael Green, Alastair Iain Johnston, Mike Mochizuki, Richard Samuels, and Michael Swaine stand out.

Officials in the Chinese, Japanese, and U.S. governments have helped clarify important details. John Hill of the U.S. Department of Defense and Michael Meserve of the U.S. Department of State were especially influential.

As she has for decades, my wife Marty indulged my desire to find answers to obscure questions.

Finally, I would like to express my deep gratitude to the individuals who have served as my mentors during my education and professional careers. Avoiding invidious distinctions is impossible, but the following deserve special mention: Chung-do Hah (Lawrence University, 1965–69), the late Michel Oksenberg (Columbia University, 1969–74), and Andrew Nathan (Columbia University, 1972–78), who were my principal professors; Robert B. Oxnam (The Asia Society, 1977–83), Stephen J. Solarz (U.S. House of Representatives, 1983–93); and Lee Hamilton (U.S. House of Representatives, 1993–95).

A note: in this book, I have followed the Chinese and Japanese practice of putting the family names of individuals first: for example, Koizumi Junichiro rather than Junichiro Koizumi and Hu Jintao rather than Jintao Hu. The only exceptions are for individuals who have rendered their names in Western fashion in a published source.

1
Introduction

In U.S. security policy, as would be expected, adversaries pose the greatest challenge. Whether with respect to the Soviet Union during the cold war or Iran, North Korea, or nonstate actors today, the relative paucity of information and absence of open channels of communication make it difficult to gauge the other side's intentions and underlying motivations. The temptation to read the worst into an adversary's capabilities and how it uses them is strong.

But there is a lesser though still significant challenge. It involves groups of countries with which the United States seeks to maintain good relations but that cannot get along with one another. The enduring conflict between Israel and the Arab states is one case; the dispute between China and Taiwan is another. Here, Washington has at least two options: one is to play its friends off against each other in order to get them to exercise mutual restraint; the other is to recognize that the countries may not be able to avoid conflict and that the United States might have to intervene militarily to defend one of the parties and its own credibility. Generally, the United States has chosen to minimize the chance of conflict rather than feed it.

The evolving security relationship between China and Japan creates another such dilemma for the United States. China's power in Asia is growing, and China's economy will soon pass Japan's as the leading economy in Asia. Although the capabilities of Japan's military, the Self-Defense Forces (SDF), are not trivial, those of the People's Liberation Army (PLA) are growing steadily. The PLA's budget grows by double digits each year, while the SDF's is essentially flat. Moreover, in China's modernization of its military, the emphasis is on power projection: the ability of its air and naval forces to stretch their reach to the east, encroaching on Japan. Japanese regard the PLA's growth and focus with deep ambivalence. How should they respond? With hopeful conciliation? With a military buildup of their own? Or—the traditional postwar answer—by relying on Japan's alliance with the United States?

Of course, current developments have a historical context. Japan invaded and occupied China in the 1930s, causing both human suffering and physical devastation. More than any other country, Imperial Japan exposed and exploited China's weakness, fostering a deep sense of victimization among the Chinese and leaving scars on the Chinese psyche. Those scars cause pain even today, as China returns to national health and its former status as a great power. In spite of joint efforts to reduce and manage tensions, China doubts that Japan will accommodate its expansion. For the Chinese, the shadow of the past darkens the future. Chapter 2 looks at a dimension of that tragic history, the military conflict between Japan and China in the 1930s.

Given that background, a good understanding of the strategic context of current relations between Japan and China is necessary. That understanding begins with the recognition that the two nations are caught in a security dilemma in spite of their positive interaction when it comes to economics and trade. That is, neither really wishes the other ill, but the steps that one side takes to promote its own security leave the other with a growing sense of vulnerability, which in turn causes it to take steps in response, and so on. This template for interpreting relations between the two is useful, but it does not appear to explain everything that is going on between China and Japan. So, in chapter 4, after reviewing postwar China-Japan relations in chapter 3, I seek to broaden the concept to make it more applicable. In particular, I argue that the conclusions that a country draws about another's intentions are based not only on the capabilities that the other acquires but also on their mutual interactions on sensitive issues.

This volume does not address the totality of Japan-China security relations, which is a large and complex subject. Instead it focuses on the nations' interaction in the East China Sea. The presence of the navy, air force, and law enforcement units of the People's Republic of China (PRC) is expanding toward the east, thereby moving into Japan's area of operations—and also that of the United States. Chapter 5 describes the growing interaction between Beijing and Tokyo in the East China Sea and explores why both regard it as strategically important.

There are, moreover, particular points of friction that, like magnets, draw the military forces of the two countries into close proximity. Specifically, they dispute ownership of the Senkaku/Diaoyu Islands north and east of

Taiwan, which are controlled by Japan. They argue over rights to exploit maritime oil and gas fields east of Shanghai, and they have competing views on the extent of China's undersea continental shelf and on the extent of their respective exclusive economic zones.

Finally, if the political dispute between Taiwan and China were to erupt in conflict and the United States were to come to Taiwan's defense, Japan, as a U.S. ally, could end up in a war with China. Since the chances of a Taiwan-China conflict have declined significantly since the 2008 change of government in Taiwan, the first two issues, which create some possibility of an accidental clash between Chinese and Japanese ships and planes in the East China Sea, are more worrisome. These issues are addressed in chapter 6.

As units of the two countries operate closer to each other, a number of institutional factors come into play that can increase or decrease the probability of a clash and affect the immediate aftermath. Those factors, which are discussed in chapter 7, include the autonomy that the nations' military and law enforcement units have vis-à-vis their civilian authorities, the degree of centralization of their command-and-control systems, and their views concerning the use of force. The discussion of civil-military relations exposes a contrast. In China, military officers adhere to norms that are quite consistent with those of the ruling Communist Party, but they both weigh in on policy issues that touch on their domain and enjoy broad discretion in implementing the policies adopted. In Japan, by contrast, officers appear to be more independent with respect to values and norms, but they are under relatively tight civilian control when it comes to policy and operations—though not necessarily in the East China Sea. Although military and law-enforcement organizations from both countries are tempted to operate independently and somewhat aggressively to carry out their missions, the problem is greater on the Chinese side.

Should there be a clash between Japanese and Chinese naval or air forces, civilian leaders and institutions would come into play. At issue would be whether those leaders and institutions have the skill and capacity to ensure that the clash did not become a crisis. To probe that question, it is necessary first to know more about how the Chinese and Japanese governments are structured, how they function in routine situations, and whether they have accurate information and analysis at their disposal. Chapter 8 looks at China and chapter 9 at Japan. The picture that emerges is of two systems in which leaders make tough decisions on a collective basis but often do not have the sort of information that they need; in which line agencies such as foreign and defense ministries put too much emphasis on protecting their turf and therefore are often ineffective in working together to shape coherent policy responses; and in which policy-coordination mechanisms do not always work well. These similarities in crisis response exist in spite of the differences in the political systems of the two nations: Japan is a special kind of democracy and China is an authoritarian regime. The discussion examines the points at which civilian officials and military officers, defense policy and operations, and security policy and domestic politics all come together and interact.

Complicating matters is the impact of domestic politics. Again, despite the differences between systems, the public in each country shapes the environment in which the leaders make decisions. Although Japanese opinion is not favorably disposed to China and competitive mass media can make that disposition even less favorable, ironically it is in nondemocratic but Internet-friendly China that a hard-edged, anti-Japanese nationalism is a vocal and influential force. Chinese leaders and officials are often reluctant to swim against that tide. To make matters worse, some members of the public have the ability to do damage in Japan through cyber warfare. Chapters 10 and 11 discuss those issues.

If decisionmaking is not necessarily effective in either country during times of routine interaction; if civil-military relations in China grant the PLA substantial policy and operational autonomy; and if domestic politics restricts civilian leaders, then the chances of the two governments responding to sudden tensions between them in a measured way are not great. That is the subject of chapter 12.

The book then returns to the question with which this discussion began: the consequences of the relationship between Japan and China for the United States, which seeks good relations with both and which must maintain its reputation for credibility. The United States is, after all, a treaty ally of Japan with a responsibility to come to Japan's defense in the event of external attack. The bedrock of that alliance is Japan's confidence that it will not be abandoned. On the other hand, how the two allies address the revival of China as a great power is a complex matter. Chapter 13 considers the implications of security interaction between Beijing and Tokyo for Washington.

I do not assume that conflict between a reviving China and a defensive Japan is inevitable. Far from it. Nor do I assume that either Tokyo or Beijing would deliberately seek war with the other. The leaders of both countries understand the interests that they share, particularly economic interests, and they know the costs of conflict. Recent Japanese governments—particularly the new Democratic Party of Japan government elected in August

2009—have pursued moderately accommodating policies toward China. But just because the probability of war is not very high does not mean that it is zero. Moreover, if a clash occurs, it is far from certain that the two nations could automatically avoid sliding off the cliff of conflict. In addition, the chance of conflict is not likely to decline as time goes on. The strategic reality in the East China Sea is unlikely to change; nor will domestic politics moderate in the short term. It is certain that although the possibility of conflict may be low, the consequences would be catastrophic for both countries.

For all those reasons, it is incumbent on China, Japan, and the United States to take steps to reduce the odds of clash and conflict; to achieve that end, chapter 14 offers a set of recommendations. It concludes that Tokyo and Beijing should start small with steps to restrain their forces in the East China Sea by creating a conflict-avoidance regime. Thereafter, they should pursue measures that address aspects of their security dilemma, institutions, and domestic politics. None of that will be easy. Nothing will happen without political leadership. But the results will have the salutary result of reducing the perils of proximity.

2

Prologue: Japan-China Military Conflict in the 1930s

The Chinese believe without question that Japan committed acts of aggression against China during the twentieth century. But different Chinese address that history in different ways. Formal, somewhat stern, official statements convey the views of the Chinese leadership.[1] Scholars' dry statistical inventories of losses sustained are compelling in their cumulative impact.[2] Museums and historic sites, which remind visitors of the horrors inflicted by Japan's Imperial Army, introduced a narrative of victimization that Chinese had not heard before.[3] The same is true of textbooks that seek to inculcate patriotic values in China's youth and fictional accounts that refract the past through their author's imagination. One of the best novels is Mo Yan's *Red Sorghum*, which is set in Shandong province and includes vivid stories of Japanese brutality.[4] Then there are the shrill emotional diatribes, brimming with righteous indignation at the victimization of China. A contributor to the Strong Nation bulletin board, a feature of the Communist Party newspaper *People's Daily*, wrote that Japan "butchered 35 million of our compatriots and robbed countless amounts of our wealth in the war of invasion against China between 1936 and 1945. . . . Therefore, we can conclude that Japan has relied on robbing the Chinese people to expand itself. Killers must pay with their lives. Debts must be paid with money. Heaven will settle all accounts. Japan should be incorporated into Chinese territory!"[5]

And then there is Chinese scholarship. A visit to a bookstore in Shanghai reveals a whole section of books on Japan's invasion of Manchuria in 1931 and expansion into North China thereafter. Even among serious studies, however, authors offer extensive detail on military operations but do not probe a key question: how exactly did the tiger of Japanese militarism slip its leash to inflict the horrors that Chinese now remember? They adopt the premise that Imperial Japan was a unitary actor and that aggression in China was its project.[6] The few treatments that probe more deeply do so allusively.[7] Thus, the content of Chinese historical memory, which animates much of popular sentiment about Japan today, is on the *consequences* of the Imperial Army's aggression. That is perfectly understandable, but it begs a question: why is there so little attention to its *causes*?

Japanese mainstream scholarship on the subject is quite sound. Indeed, it was mainly Japanese scholars after World War II who combed through archives to document how the China War came about.[8] Yet other Japanese seek to revise history, denying the factual record in order to assert that Japan bore no responsibility. As late as 2008, General Tamogami Toshio, the chief of staff of the Air Self-Defense Force, entered an essay in a magazine-sponsored contest that asserted that Japan was not the aggressor in China. He argued instead that Japan's military campaigns were a response to Chinese provocations that had a communist origin.[9] Tamogami won the contest but lost his job; he was drummed out of the military.

The causes of Japan's China War are not the subject of this volume, but they are relevant. A strong case can be made that institutional failings in both the Japanese and Chinese governments contributed significantly to Japan's aggression and to the death and destruction that ensued. Three turning points were crucial.

The first was Japan's takeover of the Manchurian northeast and the adjoining province of Rehe in late 1931 and early 1932. The driving force was Japan's Guandong (Kwantung) Army, a unit that had a modest geographic presence in China, deployed as it was on the Liaodong Peninsula and along the Southern Manchurian Railway. Its officers had both nightmares of peril and dreams of ambitious expansion. They believed that Japan faced adversaries in the capitalist West, in communist Russia, and in a resurgent Nationalist (and nationalistic) China. The Great Depression had shown the dangers of economic interdependence. Increasingly, the Japanese, including those army officers, came to believe that their country would be better served by self-reliance. The starting point was China's northeast, a land of agricultural and industrial promise.

The fact that the civilian government in Tokyo was pursuing a foreign policy of cooperation and arms control with the West plus a moderate approach to China did not sway the officers. If the government would not adopt a policy to seize Manchuria, they would begin the seizure and force the government to follow. The "right of supreme command" gave the military considerable power, making it accountable to no one but the constitutional monarch, who reigned but did not rule. That defective constitutional structure created a climate that made it easier for the headstrong Guandong officers to take independent action, and that is exactly what they did. In the Mukden incident of September 18 (Mukden is now known as Shenyang), they fabricated a Chinese attack on a railway train and used that as a pretext to begin the takeover. The officers correctly counted on receiving support from the national media and nationalistic public opinion, each feeding on the other, for their expansionist action. The Guandong Army would continue to create faits accomplis in China, and the civilian government capitulated at every turn, in part because of a real fear of assassination by radical right-wing groups.

Thus a field unit of the Japanese Imperial Army initiated a major change in Japanese foreign and security policy, usurping the authority of both the civilian government and the military high command in Tokyo. Mid-ranking officers started Japan's shift from a basically status-quo power to a revisionist power.

The second turning point was the beginning of the China War in July 1937. It is another story of flawed decisionmaking, but of a much different sort. Not all the details are known, but the main theme is that conflict could have been avoided or at least delayed had it not been for a game of "chicken" that occurred, fueled by limited information and misperceptions.

The trigger was an incident that stemmed from exercises conducted by Japanese military units during the evening of July 7 and the temporary disappearance of a Japanese officer. The episode occurred at Lugou Bridge (Lugouqiao), known as Marco Polo Bridge in English. The bridge is in the southwest of Beijing (then known as Beiping). It seems clear that this relatively minor incident was not a premeditated trigger for expansion of Japanese military control of North China, either by the Japanese high command or local commanders, as was the Manchurian case six years before. Indeed, the military conflict that ultimately resulted was at odds with Japan's fundamental security strategy of creating economic self-sufficiency in preparation for a war with the Soviet Union. The direction of Japanese policy during the last four months of 1936 and the first half of 1937 was to avoid conflict with China, not to foster it. Indeed, some improvement in Japan-China relations would serve Japan's basic security goals. China, on the other hand, had been moving toward a challenge of Japan ever since a Manchurian warlord had kidnapped Chiang Kai-shek in December 1936 to pressure him to resist Japan, after which Chiang had agreed to begin to form an anti-Japanese united front with the Communists.[10]

The Marco Polo Bridge incident escalated into a crisis in which both sides—or elements on both sides—were determined to show their resolve and gain predominance in the Beiping area. Based on reports from officials in North China, Chinese leaders in Nanjing, the capital of the Republic of China (ROC), concluded that the initial Japanese actions were a premeditated prelude to war and that a firm response was required. Chinese commanders were able to work out on the spot what they thought was an adequate termination of the incident, but Chiang Kai-shek rejected it. The decisions made in Nanjing had three bases. First, officials did not believe that their commanders in North China were fully trustworthy. Second, given their past experience with gradual Japanese encroachment, they believed that if they did not draw a line in the strategically important Beiping area, it would soon fall. And third, calls for resistance from an increasingly anti-Japanese public had reached unprecedented levels. Consequently, units of the central Nationalist army were moved toward Beiping.[11]

On the Japanese side, officers in the army's operations division had initially proposed to intervene after the incident, but the Cabinet rejected the idea. Policymakers vacillated on the central question of whether to mobilize forces in Japan for deployment to North China. At every point of progress toward a local agreement, the mobilization order was suspended or cancelled. On the other hand, Chinese moves at both the national and local level led the authorities in Tokyo to accept recommendations for troop reinforcements in the Beiping-Tianjin area. The spiral toward conflict was probably irreversible by July 25.[12]

Perhaps war would have come eventually. Perhaps there was no way to reconcile the interests of a resurgent, nationalistic China and a hegemonistic Japan, particularly a Japan that had created a puppet state in China's northeast region.[13] Yet the bulk of the evidence demonstrates that Japan did not intend to mount a major military expansion in China in July 1937 and that a minor incident at Lugou Bridge led to a much bigger and more dangerous game of chicken. Leaders with incomplete knowledge made miscalculations that meant that war came sooner rather than later.

The third turning point came with Chiang Kai-shek's decision in August 1937 to preemptively open a second front against the Japanese in the Shanghai area. He had several reasons for doing so.[14] He wished to draw enemy troops away from the north and so reduce the threat that they posed to the central Chinese city of Wuhan, which was the terminus of a military supply line from the Soviet Union. He had exaggerated confidence in the capabilities of the Chinese army, particularly those of his best-trained units. He accepted the strategic advice of his German military advisers, who told him that Shanghai should be held. He thought that a victory in the city would rally the Chinese public and elicit support from the Western powers. And because his forces in the Shanghai area vastly outnumbered the small Japanese marine contingent, he thought that they could "drive the Japs into the sea."[15]

So in mid-July, Chiang Kai-shek determined to expand a local war in the north into total war and to eliminate the Japanese presence in the Yangzi Valley.[16] On July 21, commanders from all over China met to pledge their loyalty to the country and to unite under Chiang's leadership. About a week later, when ROC defenses were collapsing in North China, Chiang moved two elite divisions to the Shanghai suburbs. On August 7, he made the decision to attack, and "the Chinese took swift, decisive, and well-coordinated action" when hostilities started on August 13.[17] The strategy was to encircle the Japanese settlement and blockade the coast against Japanese reinforcements. But it did not work as planned. Forward units did push the Japanese marines into an isolated position, but gunfire from Japanese ships in the harbor made it difficult for the ROC elite units to wipe out the enemy units. Then 75,000 Japanese troops landed, and within a few days they had eliminated half of the best Chinese units. The Chinese air force performed miserably. On September 1, the Japanese seized Wusong, which is located at the waterway that runs from the Yangzi River to Shanghai.

In early November 1937, after weeks of fierce fighting in which China committed half a million and Japan committed 200,000 troops, Japanese units landed at Hangzhou, outflanking the Chinese units at Shanghai to the north. Chiang's armies withdrew to the west. At first they tried to defend Nanjing at all costs but then suddenly abandoned the capital to the Japanese. The result was the Imperial Army's occupation of East and Central China.[18]

Again, the Japanese might have invaded the Yangzi River Valley sooner or later. But the "what ifs" of history go only so far. In any case, it is clear that Chiang Kai-shek's gamble in the summer of 1937 guaranteed both the loss of his regime's geographical and political base and the suffering of the people whom his retreating armies left behind. With Chiang's army confined to Sichuan in the west, the door was open for military units of the Chinese Communist Party to fill the power vacuum that had been created. Chiang's bold preemption became a disastrous miscalculation.[19]

The escalating military conflict between Japan and China in the 1930s demonstrates that the flawed decisionmaking of leaders and the dysfunction of institutions determine ultimate outcomes. As Chiang Kai-shek's brother, Song Ziwen, observed in August 1937: "The Japanese army underestimates the Chinese army, and the Chinese army overestimates itself."[20] Countries that engage in brinksmanship can fall off the brink. High-stakes gambles that go wrong can have devastating military outcomes and create profound civilian suffering. In 1931, unaccountable officers in Japan's Guandong Army took irreversible policy steps without their superiors' knowledge. In July 1937, Chiang Kai-shek took a firm stand after the Lugouqiao incident, provoking a game of chicken. And in August, a dominant, overconfident Chiang miscalculated his chances of driving the Japanese units into the sea. It is apparent, therefore, that in the study of international relations, the institutional mechanisms that govern—or misgovern—the use of military power deserve more attention than they receive.

3

China-Japan Relations: A Brief Review

The early 1970s was a time of hope for relations between China and Japan. Animated by their shared suspicion of Soviet expansionism, the two countries removed the cold war barriers that had divided them. Diplomatic relations were established in September 1972. The prospects for economic cooperation were good, even though Japan had a mercantilist capitalist economy and China a command system. There was hope that Chinese memories of past Japanese aggression would not fray the new ties. There seemed to be a tacit understanding that leaders in Beijing would raise history only at the right time and in the right way and that their counterparts in Tokyo would demonstrate proper contrition.

Fast forward to three-plus decades later, around 2005. The promise of the reconciliation begun in 1972 has waned. To be sure, economic ties have broadened and deepened, but each country worries that the other's growing military power will weaken its own security, if not right away then in the medium term. The two nations interact on a number of complex issues, thereby gaining an idea of the future intentions of the other. For China, the "history issue" heightens the sense of vulnerability. The shadow of the twentieth-century past darkens the twenty-first century future.

Postwar Sino-Japan Relations

In the immediate aftermath of World War II, there was little chance that Japan and China might emulate France and Germany and quickly work out some sort of reconciliation; China's memories of invasion, warfare, atrocities, and fourteen years of occupation were too bitter.[1] Moreover, once Japanese troops withdrew from the Chinese mainland, there ensued a train of events that reshaped the East Asian security order and created new obstacles to harmony and cooperation.

In China, Chiang Kai-shek's Nationalists and Mao Zedong's Communists fought a bloody civil war. The Communist Party won control of the mainland and established the People's Republic of China in October 1949. Chiang's Republic of China government retreated to Taiwan, which Japan had acquired in 1895 as the result of an "unequal treaty," according to the Chinese view of history, and gave up in 1945. China allied with the Soviet Union, and the treaty between the two named Japan specifically as a potential attacker. In June 1950, North Korea invaded South Korea, prompting U.S. intervention both on the peninsula and in the Taiwan Strait. Even before those setbacks for U.S. interests, Washington had begun to reverse its original postwar intention of imposing a pacifist, demilitarized future on Japan. After North Korea's invasion, Japan became a staging area for the U.S. defense of South Korea. With that quickly accomplished, United Nations forces marched north, causing the leadership of the People's Republic of China to fear that their newly won revolution was in jeopardy. By the end of 1950, the PRC had intervened. The cold war had arrived in East Asia, ideologically, politically, and militarily.

When in 1952, after seven years of U.S. occupation, Japan regained its formal sovereignty and an international legal personality, the country's leaders accepted alignment with the United States for practical rather than ideological reasons. Led by Yoshida Shigeru, Japan entered into a security bargain with the United States that granted the latter military bases in return for its commitment to defend Japan. Japan would be free to regain its economic power but would use the U.S.-imposed "peace constitution" as a means of avoiding entrapment in U.S. military adventures. Japan was therefore a reluctant partner in the economic and political containment of communism, particularly the containment of China. Yoshida, his successors, and the business community looked to the day that Japan could revive its economic presence in China, and they worked to expand ties incrementally in the meantime.[2]

Whatever variation occurred in Japan-China relations from 1952 to 1972 was a function of the cycles of moderation and radicalization in China's domestic and foreign policy.[3] Thus, ties improved marginally for a time after the end of the Korean War, deteriorated when the Great Leap Forward began in 1958, improved again in harmony with economic pragmatism in Beijing, and then sank once the Cultural Revolution started in 1966.

A fundamental improvement in Japan's policy relations with China could occur only after a strategic shift in the policy of its ally, the United States.

That came in 1971–72, when Richard Nixon and Henry Kissinger sought an opening with China to balance the power of the Soviet Union. Even though Sato Eisaku, Japan's prime minister at the time, had been a stalwart supporter of Washington, he was left in the dark until the last minute. As devastating as this "Nixon shock" was, it did free Sato's successor, Tanaka Kakuei, to normalize Japan's relations with Beijing. He did so in September 1972, more than six years ahead of the United States.

Key concerns for the normalization communiqué were the status of Taiwan and the history issue. With respect to Taiwan, Japan recognized the People's Republic of China as the sole legal government of China (thus negating the two-Chinas approach), expressing full understanding and respect for Beijing's stand that Taiwan was an "inalienable part" of the PRC.[4] With respect to history, Japan stated that it was "keenly aware of Japan's responsibility for causing enormous damage in the past to the Chinese people through war and deeply reproaches itself." In the communiqué the two countries declared that "the abnormal state of affairs" that had existed between them was terminated and pledged that they would work to conclude a treaty of peace and friendship.[5]

The rest of the 1970s was a period of foundation building, made possible because the countries' bilateral relationship was not tightly linked to the U.S.-PRC-U.S.S.R triangle.[6] The two sides concluded basic economic agreements on trade, civil aviation, maritime transport, and fishing. There was a break at mid-decade while the communist elite fought over the succession after Mao Zedong's death, but with the victory of the coalition led by Deng Xiaoping, who favored economic modernization, the pace resumed. A long-term trade agreement was reached in early 1978, and in the fall of that year the two countries signed and ratified a treaty of peace and friendship. In 1979 Japan made its first yen loan to China and provided substantial support to China's economic development thereafter.[7] But problems of various sorts began to surface in the 1980s:

—Faced in 1980 with an overheated economy and few tools to respond, the Chinese leadership reduced or canceled major contracts with Japanese companies.

—In 1982, Japan's Education and Culture Ministry softened the treatment of the wartime period in some textbooks, offending both the government and the public in China and other Asian countries that had suffered Japanese aggression.

—In August 1985, Japan's prime minister, Nakasone Yasuhiro, visited the Yasukuni Shrine, which is dedicated to those who gave their lives in battle for the emperor but at which the spirits of fourteen Class A war criminals were secretly enshrined in 1978. There were demonstrations in China against the visit and against a growing flood of Japanese imports.

—In February 1986, a Japanese court ruled that a Chinese student dorm near Kyoto belonged to the Taiwan government. Later that year, there was another textbook incident and Japan's defense spending breached the politically accepted limit of 1 percent of gross national product.

—After the Tiananmen Square incident, in June 1989, Japan joined Western countries in imposing economic sanctions on China.[8]

Yet those episodes did not throw the China-Japan relationship into a state of permanent hostility. Indeed, they reflected the kind of initial mutual testing to be expected of two nations that had different political and economic systems and that also shared a contentious history. Moreover, at the time the United States was encouraging Japan to play a more robust regional security role, raising concerns in China about the "revival of militarism." The textbook revisions and Yasukuni visits were symbolic acts by which Beijing measured Japan's broader intentions. Nonetheless, the two governments were able find either solutions to the immediate problems or ways to address them. Japan provided credits to allow the economic development projects that it had been funding to continue, and no Japanese prime minister visited Yasukuni for another decade. Japan took the lead internationally in dismantling the post-Tiananmen sanctions and facilitating the end of China's isolation.

On other issues, management rather than resolution was the norm, particularly when other government agencies or public opinion deprived the two foreign ministries of full control. In such cases, a kind of ritualized management often emerged, whereby diplomats worked in concert to accommodate the other forces at play but also ensured that the issue did not spin out of control.[9] The Senkaku/Diaoyu chain of islands close to Taiwan was a case in point. Claimed and controlled by Japan but claimed also by both Beijing and Taipei, the islands are the object of periodic action by patriotic groups in Taiwan, Japan, and Hong Kong (whose residents have more freedom than mainland Chinese to sail to the islands), actions that only inflame public opinion all around. The issue is taken very seriously for a while, but soon the mini-crisis winds down and remains dormant until the next time. As one scholar of China-Japan relations, Kokubun Ryosei, put it in mid-2005: "Back in the old days, when some incident occurred between Japan and China, various communications channels, including secret envoys, were mobilized" to resolve the problem.[10]

To refer to Tokyo's and Beijing's treatment of these issues as "ritualized" is not to trivialize them. It is, however, to suggest that the diplomats have learned over time the roles that different parties play—and expect to play—in such dramas and how to ensure that they receive recognition for their performance. Ming Wan reaches the same conclusion: "Previous dispute management has an impact on subsequent disputes, providing a script and parameters for pushing and pulling. On the other hand, repeated interaction ameliorates disputes by playing them out and allowing both sides to vent. And repeated interaction allows the two countries to quarrel over things within safe limits because they know each other and know the boundaries." He warns, however, that "repeated disputes keep old wounds open and can start a vicious cycle."[11]

Downturn

It was during the 1990s that the relationship began to deteriorate in a way that suggested that new factors were at work, something more than the frictions caused by system differences, Taiwan, and history in the 1970s and 1980s.

To be sure, economic ties continued to grow. Two-way trade grew from $18.2 billion in 1990 (right after the Tiananmen incident) to $57.9 billion in 1995, $85.5 billion in 2000, and $267.0 billion in 2005.[12] That is, the volume of trade increased by more than ten times over just fifteen years. Japanese cumulative foreign direct investment grew from $1.8 billion in 1990 to $8.3 billion in 1995, $15.1 billion in 2000, and $36.3 in 2005.[13] By the summer of 2008, China had replaced the United States as Japan's biggest export market.[14] The reason for the twentyfold increase in investment over a decade and a half was China's expanding role in global manufacturing and the emergence of a domestic market. And trade followed investment. A substantial segment of Japanese exports went to plants in China in which Japanese had invested; as a result, trade, previously skewed in China's favor, became more balanced. In return, China was sending people to a Japan in which the working-age share of the population was shrinking, making the country increasingly dependent on foreign workers. Indeed, in 2008 Chinese constituted the largest contingent of foreign residents (606,889).[15] In 2007, 4 million Japanese visited China and 1.2 million Chinese visited Japan. By 2009, there were 18,000 Japanese students studying in China and four times as many Chinese students in Japan.[16]

On the security side, however, several developments triggered concerns in each capital about the intentions of the other.[17] For Japan, the critical years were 1995 and 1996.[18] First, from May 1995 to July 1996, China exploded nuclear weapons in advance of signing the comprehensive test ban treaty. The tests produced a strong public and political reaction in Japan, and the government responded with a symbolic suspension of grant aid. Second, in June 1995, a month after the first explosion, Taiwan's president, Lee Teng-hui, made an unprecedented visit to the United States to give a speech at Cornell University. Because Beijing saw in Lee's action a trend toward separatism, over the course of the late summer and fall the People's Liberation Army conducted a series of exercises to deter future steps. China intensified its coercive diplomacy in March 1996 with a new round of exercises, most provocatively the firing of missiles near Taiwan ports, prompting the United States to send two carrier battle groups into the area. Along with other countries in the region, Japan was alarmed by Beijing's forceful response to Lee's political challenge. And third, later in the decade, there was increasing Japanese concern about Chinese military patrols in the Senkaku/Diaoyu area.

The principal Japanese response was to reduce assistance to China, partly because the government regarded aid as its major leverage over Chinese behavior and partly because politicians demanded some response to what they regarded as challenges to Japanese interests. Over time, Tokyo shifted from negotiating its aid packages with China on a multiyear basis to an annual basis, and the average yearly amount fell from almost 200 billion yen in the late 1990s to 86 billion yen in 2004. In 2005, Japan decided to end yen loans to China altogether by 2008.[19] More significant, Japanese leaders came to realize that aid no longer worked as a lever.[20]

China, for its part, saw itself as the target of Washington's and Tokyo's efforts to strengthen their alliance. In April 1996, President Bill Clinton and Prime Minister Hashimoto Ryutaro issued a joint declaration on security, and in September 1997 the two governments concluded guidelines for defense cooperation, which Japan's Diet enacted two years later. China's concerns arose from a clause in the guidelines that defined their scope to be situations in areas surrounding Japan as well as the Japanese home islands. It was actually the North Korea crisis of 1994 that had spurred the two countries to develop first the security declaration and then the guidelines. In preparing to defend South Korea, the Pentagon discovered that under the prevailing interpretation of Japan's constitution, its assumptions about the assistance that Japan would provide had been excessive. Although the Korean situation was the stimulus for broadening the alliance, the Hashimoto government would not exclude the possibility that Taiwan could be one of the situations that the guidelines would encompass. China drew the conclusion that

Taiwan was included and that in the event that it acted against Taiwan, it now had to plan for both U.S. intervention and Japanese involvement.

The two sides tried at various times to reduce tensions through dialogue between their respective security establishments.[21] Yet such exchanges were repeatedly overshadowed by repeated clashes over history and the growing proximity with which the military forces of each operated. In East Asia, the countries competed to dominate the emerging regional architecture.[22]

A telling clash over history came in November 1998, when China's president, Jiang Zemin, visited Japan. There was some expectation on the Japanese side that if Prime Minister Obuchi Keizo was more explicit than his predecessors had been in his expression of regret for past aggression (as he had recently been regarding South Korea), China might take his statement as the "final word." Yet Jiang was not prepared to accept the approach that Obuchi took toward Korea, and he stridently lectured a Japanese leadership already worn down by "apology fatigue" on the history issue. (There is retrospective evidence that before his visit, Jiang was unprepared to "take 'yes' for an answer."[23]) Concludes Michael Green: "In the end [the Jiang visit] would only reinforce the mistrust emerging between Beijing and Tokyo."[24]

Jiang's visit signaled another trend: the waning effectiveness of China's strategy of using history as a lever. Just as Japan was beginning to realize that perhaps aid was no longer a means of encouraging Chinese restraint, so China experienced growing frustration that it could no longer influence Japanese behavior by raising memories of the 1930s and 1940s.[25]

But the 1998 dispute over the past was only a prelude to the five-year period during which Koizumi Junichiro was president of the Liberal Democratic Party (LDP) and prime minister of Japan (April 2001 to September 2006). Koizumi brought an uncommon personal charisma and intuitive approach to politics that confounded his opponents and appealed to a changing public. His repeated visits to the Yasukuni Shrine reflected both his sentimental respect for the sacrifice of the common Japanese soldier and a stubborn insistence on continuing to visit in spite of the damage that it did to Japan's foreign relations. Along with other countries in East Asia, China read Koizumi's insensitivity to its feelings about Yasukuni as a sign of Japan's broader intentions. As one Chinese scholar wrote toward the end of the Koizumi era: "For Koizumi, visiting the shrine was neither a 'historical preference,' nor a religious belief. In today's Japanese society, the Yasukuni Shrine is a banner for the Greater East Asia Co-Prosperity Sphere, which stands for a political symbol for an attempt to restore the old dream of the great Japanese empire. Visiting the shrine as a Prime Minister, Koizumi aims to break away from the historical burden of its aggression war and head for a dream of being a political and military power."[26]

The turn of the new century was significant in other ways. First of all, the two militaries were becoming more capable. The modernization of the People's Liberation Army has been primarily a response to the situation with Taiwan. Although the Taiwan issue is not irrelevant to Japan, over time the trajectory of China's military buildup is likely to affect Japan's sense of its own security as well. Japanese public defense documents have begun to refer to China's "military expansion," an important signal of nonpublic assessments. There were more practical concerns as well. Chinese "research ships" began sailing through Japan's exclusive economic zone, and the Japanese government's inference was that the ships were exploring passages for submarines. For a while, there was an understanding that China would provide advance notice of such transits, but it stopped doing so in 2004.

China, on the other hand, could point to a number of worrisome trends. Japan already had a robust military capability. There was a serious effort brewing to revise article 9 of the constitution to remove its strictures on the use of Japan's armed forces for collective defense. Japan was deepening its alliance with the United States, including by cooperating on missile defense, which, if effective, would remove China's main offensive advantage against Japan. And after September 11, the Koizumi government secured Diet approval for unprecedented deployments of the Self-Defense Forces to support U.S. operations in Afghanistan and Iraq.

As Hu Jintao assumed Jiang Zemin's top party positions at the time of the Sixteenth Congress of the Chinese Communist Party in late 2002, apparently some in Beijing saw a chance for a change for the better and for "new thinking" on Japan policy; they believed that mutual fear and misunderstanding were promoting a vicious circle that was not in China's interests.[27] But their proposal to ignore history and focus on what the two countries had in common sparked a vigorous debate among scholars, and the public posted fierce attacks on it on the Internet.[28] Territorial disputes and energy exploration overlapped to roil bilateral ties. As China's share of global manufacturing grew, its search for new sources of energy—among them oil and gas fields in the East China Sea—expanded apace. But Tokyo and Beijing disagreed on the dividing line between their respective exclusive economic zones, and Chinese energy companies sought to steal a march on their Japanese competitors. In 2004, they began to drill in the East China Sea, and Japan worried that they would inevitably tap into and divert supplies on the Japanese side of the line, as Japan defined it. So Tokyo moved a year later to grant drilling rights to its companies. In this tit-for-tat process, military elements of the two countries were ultimately sent to the area to protect their interests.[29]

The end of 2004 and the first half of 2005 represented a tipping point of sorts. In November 2004, a Chinese submarine was discovered in Japanese territorial waters. Planes of Japan's Maritime Self-Defense Force (the Japanese navy) tracked it as it operated near Okinawa. The Japanese government acted with restraint, and Beijing eventually accepted responsibility for the incident and apologized, but there was a public outcry in Japan.

A growing mutual wariness can be read in the official statements of the two sides. A late 2004 PRC defense white paper warned that "complicated security factors in the Asia-Pacific region are on the increase. . . . Japan is stepping up its constitutional overhaul, adjusting its military and security policies and developing the missile defense system for future deployment. It has also markedly increased military activities abroad."[30] Around the same time, Japan was going public with its China concerns. The report of the semi-official Council on Security and Defense Capabilities (the so-called Araki Report) noted "security problems unique to [Japan's] location in East Asia, including a China with nuclear weapons, the possibility of armed clashes in the Taiwan Strait, and failure to resolve peacefully disputes over resource development."[31] The National Defense Program Outline, issued by the Cabinet two months later, noted specifically that China was modernizing its nuclear and missile capabilities plus naval and air forces and expanding its maritime operations. "We will have to remain attentive to its future actions," the report said.[32] In February 2005, the United States and Japan provoked China's ire by designating the peaceful resolution of the Taiwan Strait issue a common strategic objective. Beijing interpreted (or overinterpreted) that as a commitment on Japan's part to come to Taiwan's defense, which would complicate its campaign to stop separatism. Japan in turn joined the U.S. campaign to lobby Europe not to drop its arms embargo against the PRC.

Things went from bad to worse in April, when the Chinese public got into the act. Responding first to a new Tokyo campaign to become a permanent member of the UN Security Council and then to revisions in some Japanese textbooks, crowds in a number of Chinese cities demonstrated and rioted for several days. Japanese shops and offices were vandalized and the embassy and ambassador's residence were defaced. Asked for an apology, Chinese diplomats responded that Japan's "incorrect handling of history" had caused the riots and that China had no reason to apologize. The government soon brought the disturbances under control, but Vice Premier Wu Yi, on a visit to Japan in May, further offended Japan by canceling a scheduled meeting with Koizumi. Throughout that period, tensions over gas fields in the East China Sea festered, and Japan decided that China had become sufficiently developed to graduate from development assistance.

On October 17, 2005, following the Diet elections in September, when Koizumi led the LDP to an unexpected victory, he visited Yasukuni Shrine. At that point, China began to look to his departure from office in September 2006. It sought to cultivate elements of the political spectrum that were sympathetic to China's approach on Yasukuni. Yet if Beijing was hoping to help select a prime minister to its liking, it failed. In the end, Fukuda Yasuo, its likely favorite, chose not to run, ensuring that Abe Shinzo would be prime minister. Abe represented the rising generation of Japanese politicians, more nationalistic and more realistic about China. Meanwhile, Japanese opinion about China had sunk to a low level. Only 32 percent of respondents in October 2005 polls felt warmly toward China, down from 48 percent four years before.[33]

After defending Koizumi's Yasukuni visits as chief cabinet secretary, Abe surprised just about everyone once he became prime minister. He did not renounce worship at the shrine—he only declined to announce his future plans—but he moved quickly to repair relations with Beijing and Seoul by making those the first capitals that he visited after taking office. After having demanded an explicit pledge not to visit Yasukuni as a condition for the resumption of high-level meetings, the PRC government was willing to accept Abe's ambiguity in order to get back to a more normal relationship. When Abe, who visited Beijing in October 2006, soon after he took office, proposed that the two countries build a "mutually beneficial strategic relationship" (*zhanlue huhui guanxi* in Chinese) Beijing quickly agreed. It also apparently sought to create a momentum through reciprocal leadership visits that would make it difficult for Abe to visit Yasukuni because it might put those visits in jeopardy. Thus Premier Wen Jiabao made a successful trip to Tokyo in April 2007. Among other things, he adopted a softer stance on the history issue, which was welcome to the Japanese side: he balanced statements about the wartime disaster with others about the long positive past that preceded it (something Mao Zedong and Zhou Enlai had done) and expressions of gratitude for Japanese assistance and inspiration in the latter part of the twentieth century.

Abe Shinzo lasted only one year as prime minister before being replaced by Fukuda Yasuo in late September 2007. China regarded him favorably because he was willing to pledge not to visit Yasukuni. Moreover, he accelerated his predecessor's efforts to improve ties with Beijing, which he visited in late December. He made a statement concerning Taiwan that the PRC government had sought for some months—that Japan "did not support" Taiwan independence— and he gave a well-received speech at Peking University. He was a leader after China's liking. His tenure was marked by some successes—an exchange of visits by Fukuda and Hu Jintao and the conclusion in June 2008 of a political agreement on the East China Sea. But there also were setbacks, most notably a conflict over tainted dumplings produced in China and exported to Japan (which some in the Japanese media suspected had been deliberately poisoned) and the failure of the two sides to implement the East China Sea pact.

Fukuda lasted less than a year, and Aso Taro, an ally of Abe's, became prime minister. Although relations continued without significant problems, there was no significant progress. Nothing was done to implement the goals stated in the East China Sea agreement, and the China-led negotiations to restrain North Korea's nuclear and missile programs collapsed, to the detriment of Japan's security.

Then in August 2009, Japanese voters gave the Democratic Party of Japan (DPJ) a stunning victory in elections to the lower house of the Diet, ending the fifty-four-year dominance of the Liberal Democratic Party. The DPJ proposed to create a better balance between Japan's ties with the United States and those with Asia. That was not a new idea, as Fukuda Yasuo's China policy had demonstrated.[34] The DPJ has perhaps taken Fukuda's ideas further. Its prime minister, Hatoyama Yukio, spoke of "fraternity" as a guiding principle in Japan's relations with Asia. Yet the party's campaign policy statements emphasized the differences between Japan and China (human rights, the environment, lack of transparency regarding China's military buildup, and issues related to the East China Sea), not their commonalities, such as their economic interdependence.[35]

As of mid-2010, it was unclear how a DPJ government could improve on the warming of relations that the LDP's Abe and Fukuda had engineered. Only time will tell. But an exploration of the reasons for the 1995–2005 downturn in relations, the subject of the next chapter, suggests that forces are at play between the two countries that are immune to the good intentions of new leaders.

4 | *Explaining the Downturn*

Identifying the negative trend in relations between China and Japan from 1995 to 2006 and the issues involved is relatively easy, but explaining why it occurred is difficult. Possible reasons are leaders' decisions, public nationalism, domestic politics, and failure to communicate effectively. The prospects for the future hinge on the explanation.

Complicating the task of explaining the downturn are the many ways in which the two countries can and do cooperate. There is no question that they complement each other economically. Japanese companies bring investment and technology to their production and assembly operations in China, and China brings relatively inexpensive labor.[1] In addition, as Japan's population declines, one potential source of labor is immigration from China, assuming that Tokyo alters its current policy on foreign labor.[2] Officials and specialists on both sides can offer sound intellectual arguments for the mutual benefits of the relationship, and both sides understand the danger of conflict and the damage that it would bring.[3] But there are limits to countries' ability to keep politics and economics separate, and tensions have arisen nonetheless.

To be sure, leaders like Jiang Zemin and Koizumi Junichiro had their impact and public nationalism constrained the choices of the two governments. Yet it is difficult to avoid another reason for the tensions: that they are in some sense structural, driven by dynamics over which the two nations' leaders have limited control and bound up in the conflicting ways that China and Japan define themselves and each other. To ignore that explanation— even if relations have, at least superficially, improved—only increases the possibility of future trouble.

The most cogent case for structural causes comes from Michael Green. For the first time in more than a century, he argues, China and Japan have similar levels of national power and face unanticipated realities. Tokyo expected

Beijing to accept its leadership of Asia because of Japan's economic prowess and assumed that Japan would always have the larger economy. China assumed that Japan would remain an "economic power," not seek to be an Asian political or military power, leaving those roles to China. Each had to face the fact that the levers that they were accustomed to using—Japan's economic assistance and China's history issue—no longer had much pull.[4] Similarly, Christopher Hughes writes that "Japanese responses to China, as well as creating the possibilities for cooperation, carry the risk of over-stimulating Sino-Japanese competition and creating the very downward spiral of confrontation they are designed to obviate."[5] And both experts worried that Northeast Asia wasn't big enough for two major powers. As the Chinese say, "Two tigers can't lie on the same mountain" (*Yishan burong ehrhu*).

I, too, have concluded that the tensions have a structural basis and can be understood best through the concept of the security dilemma, as a growing number of specialists on Japan and China suggest.[6] This concept, from the defensive realism school of international relations theory, seems appropriate because it elucidates the dynamic between two actors who objectively have significant reasons to cooperate but whose relationship becomes dominated by mutual fear.[7] But I go beyond the tendency of most scholars to simply assert that a security dilemma exists. Instead, I explore whether the concept can be refined in a way that facilitates analysis and better clarifies what has been going on between Beijing and Tokyo.

I conclude that a narrow version of the concept—a general spiral of mutual fear regarding material power—is only moderately helpful in understanding the bilateral tensions between China and Japan.[8] Also important is a second factor—interactions for good or ill on specific points of tension, which inform each nation's conclusions about broader trends in the other. A third factor is how the two countries view the past, which shapes how they think about the present. Japan's aggression in the first half of the twentieth century colors how the Chinese think about Japan's military power today and how it might be used as well as their perception of Tokyo's actions on specific issues. China's long-term refusal to acknowledge that Japan's postwar record is fundamentally different from its prewar record shapes how the Japanese interpret both the growth of the People's Liberation Army and Beijing's behavior on matters like Taiwan.

The Defensive Realist Perspective

A defensive realist understanding of a security dilemma includes the following essential elements:

—In an anarchic international system, there exists the objective possibility that states can enjoy mutual security and cooperation but there is no hegemon that requires them to do so.

—Each state is unable to persuade the others of its peaceful intentions and must guard against the possibility of future aggression by another.

—Each state's efforts to prudently prepare to defend itself against aggression by another is likely to include the ability to threaten the other and the other will perceive it as such.

—The other state will acquire military capabilities and alliances as defensive measures and come to see the first state as hostile.[9]

In applying this approach to Japan-China relations, the first step is to examine how each country assesses the actions and intentions of the other. Various public statements provide a reliable indicator of private conclusions, because they are formulated through a systematic and periodic institutional process. Among them are statements by senior leaders and the analyses of foreign ministries, intelligence agencies, and defense establishments. Through the first half of the 2000s, the statements of both the Chinese and Japanese governments conveyed their growing concerns about security.[10] For example, a 2006 Chinese defense white paper noted that "the United States and Japan were strengthening the alliance." Specifically, Japan was seeking to relax the "peace clause" in its constitution to legitimize the Self-Defense Forces (SDF) and was shifting to a more externally oriented military posture, including development of theater missile defense (TMD). The white paper also highlighted "complex and sensitive historical and current issues in China's surrounding areas [that] still affect its security environment" (Taiwan is the principal issue). The Japan white paper of the same year speculated on the motives behind China's military modernization; dwelt on PRC actions to prepare for a war against Taiwan; asserted the need to judge whether "the objective of the modernization exceeds the scope necessary for Chinese defense"; and noted in particular possible reasons for the Chinese navy's growing maritime activities against Japan and the need to study them carefully.[11]

How did each country respond to the other's assessment? Here the situation is complicated. If one looks at the procurement of advanced equipment, which is probably the category of defense spending that best demonstrates that a government is responding to a perceived threat, China's expenditures grew substantially during this period but Japan's apparently were flat (see table 4-1). Japan's actually are somewhat deceiving because of reallocation of resources within a constant defense budget. For example, the defense budget proposed for 2008 was 0.5 percent less than the previous year's budget, but it included new funds for upgrading F-15 fighters, which defense officials said

Table 4-1. *Value of Japan's Acquisitions of Defense-Related Equipment and China's Import of Major Conventional Weapons, 1997–2006*
Constant 1990 U.S. dollars, in millions

Year	Defense-related equipment acquisitions and R&D (Japan)	Major conventional weapons imports (China)
1997	7,379	741
1998	6,598	292
1999	7,567	1,684
2000	7,283	1,874
2001	6,399	3,234
2002	6,093	2,636
2003	6,439	2,068
2004	6,729	2,906
2005	6,282	3,346
2006	5,746	3,719

Source: Stockholm International Peace Research Institute, Arms Transfers Database (http://arms trade.sipri.org/arms_trade/values.php [accessed March 31, 2009]); *Defense of Japan 2006*, Japan Ministry of Defense (www.mod.go.jp/e/publ/w_paper/pdf/2006/7-1-1.pdf); *Defense of Japan 2008*, Japan Ministry of Defense (www.mod.go.jp/e/publ/w_paper/pdf/2008/44Reference_1_80.pdf). Calculations were made using currency exchange information from Oanda (www.oanda.com) and the U.S. Bureau of Labor Statistics CPI Inflation Calculator (www.bls.gov/data/inflation_ calculator.htm).

was for the purpose of dealing with "the buildup of the Chinese military," particularly in air power.[12] Moreover, defense missions can change within a constant resource stream. Still, an absolute ceiling does impose limits. In 2004, the Japan Defense Agency announced that it would have to cut back procurement of destroyers and tanks in order to pay for missile defense.[13]

But the situation is even more complicated. Japan and China have not necessarily acquired military capabilities with each other in mind. In fact, much of China's acquisition of equipment has been designed to deter Taiwan from permanently separating from China. Similarly, Japan's primary motivation for developing missile defense capability is to defend itself against North Korea, which has sought both nuclear weapons and the means to deliver them.

On the other hand, even though Japan may not have been the primary reason for China's acquisitions, it may have been a secondary reason. The same is true of China with respect to Japan's acquisitions. On the other hand, the threat posed by each may have been the other's true justification, whatever the public rationale offered. Moreover, what is important is not so much why one side acquired the capabilities in question but what the other perceives to have been its motives. If Japan *believes* that China was acquiring power projection equipment with it in mind, or if China *believes* that the Japanese missile defense system has a Taiwan or anti-China mission, then the reality is immaterial. It is even more immaterial if time horizons are lengthened and today's problems are ignored.

Finally, China's sense of a Japanese threat stemmed less from the acquisition of new equipment by Japan's Self-Defense Forces than from the relaxation of controls on the use of their existing capabilities. Up to the 1990s, Beijing took comfort from the legal and policy constraints imposed on Japan's military. These included article 9 of the constitution, with its prohibitions on war, threats of force, and belligerency, and policies that allowed only a military strategy that is exclusively defensive, a defense budget of only 1 percent or less of gross domestic product, no collective self-defense (for example, coming to the aid of the United States), no nuclear weapons, no dispatch of troops overseas, and so on. China began to worry when it perceived that this structure was being dismantled and the scope for SDF activities expanded.[14]

This ambiguous situation has generated a debate among specialists. Christopher Hughes of Warwick University concludes that "Japan is in many cases engaged in something of a quiet arms race with China: matching Chinese growing air power with its own enhanced air defensive power, countering Chinese growing blue-water naval ambitions with its own more capable anti-submarine and carrier assets, and attempting to nullify Chinese ballistic and cruise missiles."[15] But a study by the RAND Corporation of the responses of six East Asian nations to China's military buildup found that "the concerns about China and associated military responses have been limited. Chinese military modernization has not sparked a regional military buildup." On balance, it appears that North Korea rather than China is the main driver of Japan's military procurements.

Of course, expanding one's own force structure is not the only way that a country can accumulate capabilities in response to a perceived threat; it may acquire allies or improve the alliances to which it is already a party.[16] In fact, throughout the period that China-Japan relations were deteriorating, Tokyo was tightening its alignment with Washington. Some Chinese strategists therefore concluded that the combination of U.S. military power in the western Pacific and Japan's already significant military establishment were a potential obstacle to China's rise. For example, Jin Xide of the Chinese

Academy of Social Sciences stated that "the United States and Japan feel that the realistic danger of war has increased, and China also poses a challenge to the U.S.-dominated East Asia order, and so strengthening the U.S.-Japanese military alliance to inhibit China has become an inevitable move in the chess game."[17]

So there are two trends that began in the mid-1990s. On one hand, the PLA increased its capabilities by acquiring equipment and strengthening the institutional functions—command and control, personnel, training, exercises, logistics, and so on— that turn equipment into capabilities. That caused concern in Tokyo, which tightened its security alignment with the United States, a trend that China duly noted.[18]

But there is a correlation-versus-cause problem here. Even though the U.S.-Japan alliance was deepening *at the same time as* China's military buildup was occurring, it is more difficult to treat it as *the cause* of the buildup—and vice versa—through some sort of security dilemma dynamic. Indeed, the reasons for deepening the alliance had very little to do with China. They had more to do with the North Korean threat and the George W. Bush administration's effort to transform regional alliances in a U.S. global security strategy.[19] The only exception was the Taiwan Strait issue, where alliance strengthening and China's acquisitions were related.

What is important, again, is not the actual motive for enhancing an alliance but what a potential adversary perceived the motive to be. If Beijing *believed* that Washington and Tokyo drew closer together in order to defend Taiwan even though the reason for their action was North Korea, its perception and its response are what counts. And one aspect of China's buildup concerning Taiwan has been to develop capabilities designed to keep the United States out of the fight.

In addition, the case can be made that *in the medium term* the security problem between China and Japan does not involve conventional military capabilities. A substantial body of water and the Korean peninsula provide each country with a strategic buffer against the other. If there is a problem in the medium term, it is China's nuclear capability. That is the one area in which Japan does not have an equivalent offensive or defensive capability. Here, however, Japan does not display excessive alarm.

To sum up so far, the interaction between China and Japan does not yet fully exhibit the dynamic of a security dilemma as commonly conceptualized by realist scholars. The two countries have exhibited worry about the future intentions of the other, as evidenced by the formal statements of their leaders and assessments in defense white papers. China is engaged in a systematic effort to build up its military power and acquire power-projection capabilities (the ability to conduct and sustain military operations far from the homeland). Japan is modernizing its military in selected areas and strengthening its alliance with the United States. Yet there is not a direct and strong connection between one country's perception of vulnerability in the face of the other's growing power and the decisions that it makes to strengthen its own capabilities.

The Second Cut: The View through the Lens of History

In a more constructivist vein, it is no surprise that the two countries view their security interactions through the lens of their historical experience. Each country's views of general trends and specific cases are refracted through a lens ground by its memories of the wartime past.[20] How Chinese policymakers regard what Japan does with respect to Taiwan and the East China Sea and the changes in SDF capabilities is skewed by recollections of the War of 1894–95, the invasion of Manchuria in the early 1930s, and the takeover and occupation of North and East China in the late 1930s. For example, a Chinese military commentator asserts that Japan's prewar seizure of the Ryukyu Islands drives its disagreement with Beijing on delineation of the East China Sea continental shelf.[21] A recurring theme in Chinese discussions of the past "is the need for China to remain strong to prevent a recurrence of such predations."[22]

How the Japanese view the revival of Chinese power and China's behavior at points of bilateral friction is biased by their own understanding of the conduct of the Imperial Army in China before 1945, how Japan regards its postwar role, and how it would like to be regarded in the future. They have been frustrated by long-term refusal of the Chinese to give Japan credit for its peaceful postwar development, by their lack of gratitude for Japan's contribution to Chinese economic development after 1972, and by their claim that Japan is unrepentant about the war.[23]

Using the "historical lens" to explain security outcomes is complicated. Sometimes it is clear that policymakers let that filter shape their security calculus. Thus, Jiang Zemin, China's former president, clearly dwelt on Japan's "path of militaristic aggression" against China, in part, no doubt, because he "personally experienced the anguish of seeing the country's territory being annexed and the nation's very survival hanging in balance."[24] Prime Minister Koizumi likely kept visiting the Yasukuni Shrine, with its fourteen Class A war criminals, both because he felt obligated to honor Japan's war dead and because he was determined not to let China dictate how Japan recognized its past.[25]

Usually, however, we do not know what is in leaders' minds. Issues of history and national identity are more often observable in the views and behavior of a nation's intellectuals and its public, which, though unofficial, are still relevant for the purposes of this analysis. In both China and Japan, elite and mass opinions do have an impact on foreign policy, if only by imposing restraints on policymakers. As previously mentioned, positive public opinions in each country regarding the other declined in the 1995–2005 period, and teasing out the possible impact of historical views on those opinions is at least instructive.

If the various and competing views at play are summarized, several identities can be delineated for China and Japan with respect to the past that shape how they look at the present. For China, there are three:

—*China as the victim of an evil Japan.* This identity predominates in Chinese thinking about Japan's aggression. Ironically, it came to the fore in the 1990s, likely as a part of a post–Tiananmen Square effort by the Beijing regime to relegitimize itself by playing up the Communist Party as the twentieth-century savior of China. This narrative required an enemy, and prewar Japan was the obvious choice. (In a conversation with me, a retired Chinese general likened Japan to a fierce tiger whose "teeth and claws" had been removed after the war. Why, he asked, was the United States now restoring the teeth and claws?)[26]

—*China as judge of Japan's sincerity with respect to atonement.* Japan has sought to find a way to address the history issue by apologizing for its wartime actions. The most convincing to the Chinese was probably the apology of Prime Minister Murayama Tomiichi in August 1995, which a senior Chinese scholar termed "a sincere expression, still a model for his successors."[27] Since then, other apologies have been more routine,[28] yet the question remains whether Beijing would be willing to accept a more clear-cut and concrete formulation. For example, in 1998, prior to Jiang Zemin's state visit to Japan, Tokyo appeared willing to go beyond what it had done before *if* there was assurance from China that the issue would be buried. The model was a similar arrangement with President Kim Dae Jong of South Korea.

In the end, however, Jiang refused to accommodate Japan. Fear that the public would attack the government for softness probably was a factor, but perhaps Beijing was unwilling to abandon the leverage afforded by taking the moral high ground. There may be a parallel with the regime's approach to criminals: "Lenience to those who confess, severity to those who resist." The regime, of course, reserves the right to judge when a criminal's confession is sincere and when the criminal is resisting.

—*China as the frustrated resurgent power.* China believes that it is regaining its rightful place in the world and that other powers should accept its return as a major power. Beijing interprets Washington's and Tokyo's actions as an effort to frustrate its rightful return. "Due to . . . the relatively strong [Japanese] feeling of vigilance over, and resistance to, China's rise . . . the Japanese government has evidently decided to generally refrain from taking the initial step in offering major concessions in Sino-Japanese political and strategic disputes, or even from offering any major concessions at all."[29]

These conceptions of what China *is* color how the Chinese view what Japan *does*. Supplementing them are Chinese assumptions about Japan: that it wishes to move beyond being an economic power to becoming a political power (through, for example, gaining a permanent seat on the UN Security Council) and even a military power again; that Japanese are psychologically disturbed by the prospect of becoming Number 2 in Asia; and that rightwing, nationalist political forces grew in strength in Japan during the 1990s.[30]

On the Japanese side are an opposite set of identities:

—*Japan as the World War II aggressor:* This view, which basically accepts the perspective of Chinese and other Asians on the past, apparently is widespread in Japan. Polls over the last two decades indicate that a significant majority (around 85 percent) take the view that "militarist Japan brought suffering and hardship to Asia."[31]

—*Japan as falsely accused defendant or World War II victim:* In its baldest form, this view rejects the idea that Japan was an aggressor at all and disputes the facts regarding specific wartime episodes. A recent and notorious example is an essay that Tamogami Toshio, the Air Self-Defense Force chief of staff, wrote for a contest sponsored by a conservative magazine. Tamogami asserted that Japan's entry into China was based on treaty rights and that it was a response to provocations by the Chinese government, which was influenced by the Communist International (Comintern), the external arm of the Soviet Communist Party. (Tamogami neglected to mention the Imperial Army's takeover of Manchuria).[32] When his essay became public, Tamogami was quickly fired. A corollary of this perspective is that the Tokyo war crimes tribunal rendered "victors' justice." In addition, however, there is also the sentiment that the Japanese people were themselves victimized, by both the Japanese military, which took the country to war, and the United States, which used inhumane means to secure its victory. "The only kind of death that is being discussed in this narrative is the death of Japanese civilians";

non-Japanese victims and even Japanese soldiers are ignored.[33] The implication is that Japan stands on the same moral level as China.

—*Japan as a civilian or middle power:* The core principle here is that Japan itself does not have to act on the implications of its security environment. Because the United States, for its own interests, has committed itself to protect Japan, Tokyo does not need to have a robust defense establishment, which would raise fears in the region about its intentions. Instead, it can devote itself to its own economic growth and the economic development and welfare of others. To the extent that Japan engages in security activities abroad, they occur either under the aegis of the United Nations or are subject to domestically derived limitations. This approach, it is argued, is consistent with the pacifist and antimilitaristic values that have dominated Japan's public consciousness since World War II and is not threatening to other powers.[34]

—*Japan as vulnerable island nation:* Because Japan has few natural resources, its economic prosperity and survival depend on access to international markets and on freedom of navigation. If sea lanes are obstructed, as they were in World War II, Japan faces a fundamental threat to its existence. A pamphlet issued by the Japan Defense Agency in 1970 put it this way: "The removal of threats against our sea lanes of communication is vital in securing survival of the nation. All threats, including the direct invasion of our homeland, could be more easily prevented in advance if the attack from the sea is stemmed or thwarted."[35] And note the prediction of the former chief of the Japan Maritime Self-Defense Force in the event that Taiwan unified with China: "The sea lanes would turn all red."[36]

These conceptions of what Japan *is* bias how Japanese people interpret what China *does*. Accompanying them are views about special features of the Chinese system—that it is not democratic and that its leadership cynically manipulates anti-Japanese nationalism in order to maintain its hold on power.[37] Yet the fact that Chinese identities work in one direction and Japan's work in several suggests that it would be easier for Japan to accommodate China than the other way around.

Obviously, the two sets of identities are at odds (and Japan's identities conflict with one another). Japan's wish to be accepted as a normal, even civilian, power conflicts with China's preference that it remain just an "economic power." For Japan to advance to the status of "military power" or even "political power" is contrary to the Chinese belief that it has not atoned sufficiently for its past aggression against the Chinese people. That sense of grievance conflicts with the Japanese feeling that Japan also was a victim;

that its virtuous behavior since the end of the war has wiped the slate clean; and that China is manipulating the history issue. Part of Japan's sense of virtue lies in its democratic system, which contrasts with China's authoritarian system. China's desire to shed the weakness of the past and to be recognized and accepted as a great power conflicts with Japan's concept of itself as Asia's most successful country.

The Third Cut: Interaction on Specific Issues

An alternative way of explaining China-Japan tensions is to consider the interactions between the two countries on *specific issues*. Such experiences, it is hypothesized, shape more general assessments of long-term intentions. In the context of a *general* and deepening sense of insecurity, disagreement and conflict over specific matters have occurred that cause each side to be more suspicious of the other's intentions. Each side interprets today's relations more negatively because of how the other addressed sensitive issues in the past.

Several such issues come to mind. Beijing and Tokyo have been at odds over how to rein in North Korea's nuclear program. They have argued over who has what rights to oil and gas deposits under the East China Sea, which each regards as important for maintaining its economic growth, and there is the Taiwan Strait dispute. The interaction here was regular, mutually disturbing, and increasingly intense over a whole decade. And like other issues, it led each side to conclude over time that the other's intentions were not benign. Through their interactions, Japan and China were inclined to expect the worst of the other.

Taiwan

Table 4-2 outlines the initiatives and interaction between Beijing and Tokyo over the 1996–2000 period, during which each learned negative lessons about the stance and intentions of the other. Japan saw a growing danger of conflict over Taiwan, one that would test its commitment to its alliance with the United States and threaten its economic lifeline. China viewed Japan's steps to strengthen its U.S. alliance, particularly its growing cooperation on missile defense, as a display of disregard for China's a core interest of national unification that encouraged those who would frustrate unification and make it more difficult for China to enforce its rights. Japan saw China's opposition to missile defense as insensitivity to the threat posed by North Korea.

After the election of Chen Shui-bian as president of Taiwan in March 2000, the primary focus of China-Japan relations was on politics; security

Table 4-2. *China-Japan Interactions Concerning Taiwan, 1996–2000*

Time	Initiative	Response
March 1996	PRC fires missiles in vicinity of Taiwan to influence outcome of Taiwan's presidential election; the United States responds by sending two carrier battle groups.	One missile lands not far from the Okinawa island group; Prime Minister Hashimoto contemplates evacuating residents if situation worsens. Incident "left a big scar on Japan's security psyche and led many Japanese to doubt the credibility of China's no-first-use nuclear pledge."[a] Japanese air travel and shipping in the area are disrupted.[b]
April 1996	President Clinton and Prime Minister Hashimoto issue a joint declaration that mentions "situations that may emerge in the areas surrounding Japan and which will have an important influence on the peace and security of Japan."	China views the declaration as a response to its missile launch and infers that it includes Taiwan within the scope of the alliance. China attacks it as "containment" and as an instrument of U.S. domination and Japanese militarism.
Fall 1997	New U.S.-Japan defense guidelines focus on "situations surrounding Japan"; some Japanese officials say Taiwan is included.	China attacks inclusion of Taiwan Strait in "sphere of Japan-U.S. security cooperation."
Fall 1998	In response to North Korean missile launch over Japan, Tokyo increases its cooperation with the United States on missile defense.	China views missile defense as negating the deterrent power of its missiles and mounts a sustained campaign of criticism.
November 1998	China mounts a campaign to get Japan to explicitly deny that Taiwan is covered under the new defense guidelines.	Japan refuses to deny that Taiwan is covered. Beijing's attacks cause Tokyo to question whether the Chinese government still has a basically positive view of the alliance.

Time	Initiative	Response
May 1999	Japan passes defense guidelines legislation.	China criticizes the legislation on the assumption that Taiwan is covered.
March 2000	Chen Shui-bian, candidate of the pro-independence Democratic Progressive Party, wins the Taiwan presidency, in spite of Chinese hints that his election would mean war. China later says that the United States and Japan together had "inflated the arrogance of the separatist forces in Taiwan, seriously undermined China's sovereignty and security, and imperiled the peace and stability of the Asia-Pacific region."	Japan is pleased at Taiwan's democratic transition but worries about getting drawn into a conflict pursuant to the guidelines. Foreign Minister Kono urges peaceful resolution of issues through PRC-Taiwan dialogue.

a. Kori J. Urayama, "Chinese Perspectives on Theater Missile Defense: Policy Implications for Japan," *Asian Survey* 60 (July-August 2000), p. 616.

b. Alessio Patelano, "Shielding the 'Hot Gates': Submarine Warfare and Japanese Naval Strategy in the Cold War and Beyond (1976–2006)," *Journal of Strategic Studies* 31 (December 2008), p. 878.

was secondary. The main issue was travel by former Taiwan president Lee Teng-hui to Japan and visits by Japanese political leaders to Taiwan, which Beijing claimed was encouraging Chen Shui-bian's separatist tendencies.[38] On the security side, Taiwan was eager to upgrade its ties with Japan to supplement those with the United States. Retired senior officers traveled both ways, sometimes to observe military exercises. China, of course, was critical of such developments.[39] Still, leaders' statements and defense ministry assessments were relatively mild, and China's rhetorical sense of alarm that the alliance and the component of theater missile defense in particular would encourage Taiwan to challenge its interests receded. The reason, it seems, was that Beijing gained confidence that if it supported Chen Shui-bian's opponents, they would be strong enough to defeat him in the March 2004 presidential election. Simultaneously, the PLA would build up its military power.

If that was Beijing's assumption, it proved to be mistaken. Through his formidable political skill, displays of which included some provocation of China, Chen won reelection by a narrow margin. When it came time for the authors of the PRC defense white paper to describe the Taiwan Strait situation later that year, they chose the word "grim" and portrayed the U.S. role in far more agitated terms than two years before.

All of this was prelude to a series of exchanges that deepened China-Japan suspicions over Taiwan. The policy context was the preparation of Japan's new National Defense Program Guidelines (NDPG), itself part of a larger process of reengineering the U.S.-Japan alliance. As later revealed by the media, in September 2004 the Self-Defense Agency, in contributing to the development of the guidelines, developed three scenarios under which China might attack Japan; one was a conflict between China and Taiwan. This internal study reportedly concluded that Beijing's imperative to defend China's sovereignty and territorial integrity might override its usual caution regarding the use of force. The NDPG, which was released on December 10, said this: "China . . . has been modernizing its nuclear and missile capabilities, as well as naval and air forces, and expanding its area of operations at sea. We will have to remain attentive to its future actions."[40] China responded to the NDPG with "strong dissatisfaction" and concern about "the great changes of Japan's defense strategy."[41]

Meanwhile, Chinese vessels conducted more oceanographic research and intelligence gathering in Japanese territorial waters, contrary to bilateral understandings and international law. In early November, Self-Defense Force elements discovered a People's Liberation Army Navy (PLAN) submarine submerged near Okinawa. The incident, which occurred just before Koizumi was to meet China's president, Hu Jintao, at the Asia-Pacific Economic Cooperation (APEC) meeting in Chile, caused a media firestorm and general public concern in Japan. It was perhaps no coincidence that in mid-December Tokyo approved a visa for Lee Teng-hui to visit Japan for sightseeing—a move that Beijing criticized in harsh language.[42]

Conservative scholars in Japan devoted considerable analysis to the maritime encroachment of PLAN surface and subsurface vessels, seeking strategic implications in activities such as undersea surveying. Hiramatsu Shigeo of Kyorin University was the most definitive:

China was convinced [after the Taiwan Strait crisis of 1996] that in order to prevent the United States from interfering in the event of an emergency in Taiwan, it must build a submarine-based defense system to keep U.S. aircraft carriers from being deployed near Taiwan. To this end, China is supposed to be conducting surveys for submarine navigations in the Pacific near Japanese waters.[43]

Hiramatsu, who worked for many years as an analyst in the National Institute of Defense Studies, the think tank of the Japanese defense establishment, was one of several scholars to stress the strategic value of Taiwan for Japan. As he put it: "If Taiwan unifies with China, East Asia including the sea lanes will fall entirely under the influence of China. The unification of Taiwan will by no means matter little to Japan."[44] Hiramatsu's views were echoed by Furusho Koichi, former chief of the Japan Maritime Self-Defense Force."[45] (Note that this anxiety exists even though China's proposal for Taiwan unification does not seem to contemplate having the PLAN operate out of Taiwan ports. Even if it did, Japanese ships could simply bypass the Taiwan Strait.)

The next step in the interaction between Japan and China over Taiwan came on February 19, 2005. As part of the process of deepening the U.S.-Japan alliance, which included Japan's completion of the NDPG, the United States and Japan announced several strategic objectives, one of which was "peaceful resolution of issues concerning the Taiwan Strait through dialogue."[46] Although that objective was stated in a benign way, China read it as a move to make explicit what had been implicit in the 1997 defense guidelines—that Japan would join Washington in coming to Taiwan's defense—which complicated its security task of opposing separatism. *People's Daily* questioned the motive behind and the effects of this move by the alliance to "interfere in China's internal affairs": "If the United States and Japan genuinely want to do something to preserve Asia-Pacific regional security and stability," the newspaper declared, "they should abide by their commitments on the Taiwan issue, resolutely uphold the one-China principle, do nothing that encourages the 'Taiwan independence' forces, and refrain from adding to the Taiwan Strait turmoil."[47] A month later, Premier Wen Jiabao reiterated China's criticism of the U.S.-Japan move, calling it interference in China's internal affairs by "foreign forces," in a press conference at the National People's Congress.[48]

Simultaneously, Beijing itself was deepening Japanese and U.S. concerns. The same National People's Congress passed an "anti-secession law" that asserted China's desire for a peaceful resolution concerning Taiwan but, more ominously, established a legal basis for military action. Tokyo issued a statement expressing its concern about the law because it "might exert a negative influence over peace and stability in the Taiwan Straits [sic] and also relations between the two sides of the Straits."[49] Then, to Beijing's annoyance, Japan joined the United States in lobbying European governments not to abandon their embargo on the sale of arms to China. For example, Foreign Minister Machimura Nobutaka told Javier Solana of the European Union that lifting the ban would "have a negative effect on security not only in Japan, but also in East Asia."[50] (In the event, the EU decided not to lift the embargo.)

Japan-China tensions over Taiwan then relaxed somewhat, even as they increased concerning the East China Sea. PRC president Hu Jintao made overtures to the leaders of the island's opposition parties and took other initiatives that improved China's image after the setback caused by the anti-secession law. But in 2006, Japan's *Diplomatic Blue Book* raised the Taiwan issue for the first time: "While China is expanding its economic interaction with Taiwan, it adopted the Anti-Secession Law. It is necessary to observe closely . . . cross-strait relations."[51] Around the same time, a leading Chinese government think tank, the China Institutes of Contemporary International Relations, drew a categorical conclusion from the U.S.-Japan 2 + 2 statement in February: "If there were a Taiwan conflict, Japan would act in cooperation with the United States."[52]

It is hard to avoid the conclusion that the Japan-China interaction regarding Taiwan over the 1995–2006 period left each country more suspicious of the broad intentions of the other. As each shaped the attitudes of the other on this and other issues, its sense of insecurity deepened.

Beyond 2006

Weaving these explanations together, I arrive at a generalized causal statement: each country's acquisition of capabilities (including strengthened alliances) and its behavior on specific issues work together to influence the other country's sense of vulnerability. So far, although Japan's general concern that China is closing the capability gap is real, the interaction between the two countries on specific issues like Taiwan and the East China Sea appears to have had more impact on their assessments than the mere acquisition of capabilities. Moreover, their perspectives on the past modify and intensify the lessons that they learn from specific interactions and their views of general trends.[53] At any point in time, those three factors (lessons learned from specific interactions, views of broader trends, and historical factors) work together in complicated ways to create future interactions. How they work together may change over time. It would be useful to have indicators for measuring relative impacts more precisely.

It is fair to ask whether this explanation for the 1995–2006 deterioration in relations between China and Japan applies to their relations after the departure of Koizumi Junichiro as Japan's prime minister. After all, bilateral relations improved under his successors from the Liberal Democratic Party. The Democratic Party of Japan, which won the lower house elections in August 2009, was even more favorably disposed to maintaining positive, stable relations with China. However, it seems likely that the more structural factors will persist.

During early 2008, just after Prime Minister Fukuda Yasuo made a successful visit to China, I did a series of interviews in Beijing with Chinese specialists on Japan. My principal questions were whether structural factors were indeed the cause of the deterioration in relations and whether the recent improvement has mitigated them significantly. Another was whether the decisionmaking mechanisms in each country reduce the structural problem or make it worse. All of my interlocutors took the view that structural factors had been at work since the end of the cold war, particularly during the Koizumi period, and that although Koizumi aggravated those problems, he did not create them. And most of the analysts took the view that what had changed in the interim was just the atmosphere—that there was no mitigation of structural contradictions. Some scholars assert that while relations have stabilized, the situation is not improving in any substantive sense and that Japan's goals have not changed. Discussions between the two governments are rhetorical and symbolic, and they engage in nothing more than "soft cooperation." There were optimistic exceptions to the mainstream. A couple of scholars believed that incremental improvements in the atmosphere between the two countries and soft cooperation could have a cumulative and transformative impact on structural contradictions.

The Japanese display a similar mistrust, even in the post-Koizumi period. American scholar Daniel Kliman conducted a survey of Japanese elites in the spring of 2009 about their views of China's Japan policy. Three perceptions stood out: China behaves badly; China's intentions are questionable at best; and Japan's influence in Beijing is low.[54]

Even after the DPJ took power, there was skepticism about the prospects for a significant improvement in relations. Kitaoka Shinichi, a mainstream scholar, understands the implications of China's military buildup for Japan's security ("We are absolutely worried about how the arms will be used") and Beijing's failure to move forward on issues like oil and gas deposits in the East China Sea ("China has not been particularly friendly toward Hatoyama's foreign policy"). Those concerns create uncertainty about whether China will become "a truly responsible member of the international community."[55] Kokubun Ryosei, another mainstream scholar, warns that the situation may change as China's power eclipses that of the United States: "Right now, Chinese leaders are cautious, telling people to keep their heads down. But sooner or later, their heads will rise. They will also speak up."[56]

Brad Glosserman, a Japan scholar, wrote: "The real obstacles to improved Japan-China relations defy any change in government and many require changes not in Tokyo, but in Beijing. . . . [The divisive issues] speak to a profound unease in Japan about China's rise."[57] Chinese Japan specialist Yang Bojiang observed that "contradictions" between the two countries would continue to exist, particularly over territorial issues, human rights, and the PLA buildup. The DPJ may focus less on history, but it does worry about strategic issues. It also possesses a number of factions, some of which "tend to pay more attention to disputes with Japan's neighbors" (that is, China).[58]

As if to confirm that the arrival of the Hatoyama administration did not spell the end of Japan-China tensions, two episodes in April 2010 raised anxiety in Tokyo at the time of PLAN exercises. First, a Chinese navy helicopter veered "provocatively close" to a Maritime Self-Defense Force destroyer that was monitoring the exercises. Second, PLAN vessels sailed through a narrow corridor in international waters but between Okinawa and another island in the Ryukyu chain. The Hatoyama government decided to disclose the incidents, said Chief Cabinet Secretary Hirano Hirofumi, in order "to send a message that the Japanese government is watching."[59]

Of the three explanations offered in this chapter for Japan-China tensions from 1995 to 2006—general competition for power, historical memories, and interaction on specific issues—this book focuses on the third. It explores the interaction of the two countries' armed forces and related organizations in an increasingly shared geographic space. It further examines the institutions that regulate—or try to regulate—that interaction. Any optimism that the interaction will be problem free is unjustified. And whatever happens, China and Japan each will draw conclusions from specific interactions about the other's broader strategic intentions. Moreover, their interactions will, for good or ill, be viewed through the prism of conflicting national identities and visions of history. In short, as naval vessels sail and jet fighters fly, they may well make the future.

5

Navies, Air Forces, Coast Guards, and Cyber Warriors

Since the 1970s, Japan's Self-Defense Forces have acquired naval and air capabilities that can not only mount a more robust defense of Japan but also patrol sea lanes of communication (SLOCs) far from the home islands. Recently Japan has added missile defense and its coast guard has been beefed up. Since the 1990s, China's People's Liberation Army has been securing naval, air, and missile assets to deter a separatist challenge by Taiwan and to prevent the United States from coming to the island's defense. China's Marine Surveillance Force also plays a role.

Both countries' military forces seek, in similar ways, to deny their adversaries access to or control of critical strategic areas. But the areas in question overlap significantly. Thus, China's long-term goal is to make it difficult or impossible for U.S. and Japanese military forces to operate in the zone west of the island chain formed by Japan (including the Ryukyu Islands), Taiwan, and the Philippines. And, as discussed in the next chapter, there are specific points of bilateral friction in the East Asian littoral. Consequently, the two navies and air forces now operate closer to each other than ever.

Japan

Several factors converged in the 1970s and 1980s to steer Japan's force structure in a regional direction. First was the growth of Soviet naval power, designed reduce the vulnerability of the Soviet Far East to an attack by sea. Second was U.S. pressure on Japan to contribute to security in East Asia during a period when U.S. military assets were stretched fairly thin. Third was the initiative of Nakasone Yasuhiro, who served as prime minister of Japan from 1982 to 1987. He worked vigorously to contribute in concrete ways to the U.S. security effort and to remove constraints on the SDF, such as the 1 percent limit on Japanese defense spending. In the air, the task was to constrain the operations of the Soviet air force. In the area of naval operations, the new missions were to defend the seas surrounding Japan out to several hundred miles and to protect SLOCs up to 1,000 nautical miles away.[1]

Prime Minister Suzuki Zenko, Nakasone's predecessor, had made the commitment to expand air and naval operations beyond the home islands to the United States as early as 1981, but his government delayed implementation. Nakasone energized the Japanese system to make good on Suzuki's pledge. His objective was to block Soviet submarines from passing through the straits that separate the islands of Japan and to defend sea lanes "between Guam and Tokyo and between the Strait of Taiwan and Osaka."[2] And Nakasone did more than make rhetorical commitments. He engineered a large and rapid acquisition of equipment for both the Maritime Self-Defense Force (MSDF) and the Air Self-Defense Force (ASDF) to enable them to carry out their missions. Spending for the Self-Defense Forces rose 36 percent between 1982 and 1987. The MSDF increased its fleets of destroyers, submarines, and minesweeping helicopters. The ASDF acquired advanced fighter interceptors. In 1987, Japan decided to acquire Aegis destroyers, which significantly reduced the danger of air attacks on surface ships and later became a missile defense platform.[3] Tables 5-1 and 5-2 show the changes in naval and air force structure over the 1999–2009 period.

The Maritime Self-Defense Force and the Coast Guard

The Japan Maritime Self-Defense Force has a significant fleet of vessels of various capabilities, divided into four destroyer groups, four submarine groups, one minesweeper group, and nine air squadrons.[4] Naval specialist Bernard Cole has called it "the most powerful Asian naval force on any given day."[5] Supplementing the MSDF in ensuring Japan's maritime security is the Japan Coast Guard (JCG). Previously called the Maritime Safety Agency, it has around 12,000 personnel and forty armed cutters. It also has helicopters plus fixed-wing aircraft for sea surveillance.[6]

The protection of sea lanes—one of the MSDF's missions—is not a small matter for an island nation without natural resources that depends on commerce for national success and survival. Since World War II, of course, Japan has relied on the U.S. Navy to ensure that trade continues to flow. But that does not eliminate an existential anxiety. As Rear Admiral Takei Tomohisa, director general of the operations and planning department of the Maritime Staff Office, writes:

Table 5-1.   *Evolution of Japan's Maritime Self-Defense Force Force Structure, 1999–2009*

Number

		1999	2009
Active duty personnel		43,800	44,100
Submarines	Total	16	16
SSK	Yuushio	7	. . .
	Harushio	7	6
	Oyashio	2	10
Principal surface combatants			
Destroyers	Total	36	42
DDG	Hatsuyuki	11	11
	Asagiri	8	6
	Murasame	4	9
	Takanami	. . .	5
	Tachikaze	3	1
	Hatakaze	2	2
	Kongo	4	4
DD	Haruna	2	2
	Shirane	2	2
Frigates	Total	19	8
FFG	Ishikari	1	. . .
	Yubari	2	2
	Abukuma	6	6
FF	Yamagumo	2	. . .
	Takatsuki	2	. . .
	Chikugo	6	. . .

Sources: International Institute for Strategic Studies, *The Military Balance 2000–2001* (London: Oxford University Press, 2001), pp. 200–01; and International Institute for Strategic Studies, *The Military Balance 2008* (London: Routledge, 2008), pp. 384–87.

Japan's national survival relies on unimpeded economic activities via SLOCs. . . . Protecting maritime interests and preserving shipping lanes in today's climate has become more challenging, . . . [and] mitigating factors such as proliferation of WMD, maritime terrorism, [and] piracy . . . compound the security problems surrounding maritime interests.[7]

Table 5-2. *Evolution of Japan's Air Forces Force Structure, 1999–2009*
Number

		1999	2009
Air Self-Defense Force			
Active duty personnel		45,200	45,600
Aircraft			
FGA	F-I	40	...
	F-4EJ	20	...
FTR	F-2	...	40
	F-4EJ	50	70
	F-15 series	160	150
	Total	270	260
Maritime Self-Defense Force, Naval Aviation Division			
Active duty personnel (estimated)		12,000	9,800
Aircraft			
MR	P-3C	90	80

Sources: International Institute for Strategic Studies, *The Military Balance 2000–2001* (London: Oxford University Press, 2001), pp. 200–01; and International Institute for Strategic Studies, *The Military Balance 2008* (London: Routledge, 2008), pp. 384–87.

Hence the MSDF conducts patrols and anti–surface ship, antisubmarine, minesweeping, and local air defense operations; escorts commercial vessels; and defends straits and harbors. An adversary vessel trying to attack Japanese ships "will be destroyed by using MSDF destroyers, submarines, and patrol aircraft."[8]

The other key mission of the MSDF and JCG, of course, is the maritime defense of the home islands. Operationally, that takes the form of an active program of intelligence collection, surveillance, and reconnaissance (ISR) in the air and on the surface of the water and below it. Defense of Japan also includes the seaborne part of missile defense through the Aegis platforms. ISR operations take the form of daily patrols by MSDF P-3C aircraft and "the flexible use of destroyers and aircraft as required."[9] The MSDF and the Ground Self Defense Force (GSDF) work together to monitor the key straits, such as the Tsugaru Strait between the Japanese islands of Honshu and Hokkaido. The most famous case of intrusion into Japanese territorial waters was the 1999 case of a North Korean spy ship, in which both the JCG and MSDF responded by firing on the vessel.

Japan's offshore islands also get attention. The most important of these are the Senkaku/Diaoyu islands, which Japan controls but China also claims. In normal times, defending the islands requires intelligence gathering and regular patrols by both the MSDF and the Japan Coast Guard. If the islands were threatened, the SDF would seek to prevent an invasion.[10]

In the event of an attack on the home islands, the MSDF, working with the other services, would work to obstruct the enemy's progress and deplete its strength through surface, subsurface, and air operations. Its vessels would patrol harbors and ports, and remove enemy mines. At the same time, mines would be laid in the main straits, and if enemy vessels sought to transit those areas "they will be destroyed."[11]

Finally, the MSDF engages in overseas operations. It conducted mine-sweeping in the Persian Gulf after the 1991 war; undertook refueling operations in the Indian Ocean after September 11 to provide support for allied actions in Afghanistan; supported a tsunami relief effort in Southeast Asia in 2005; and sent ships to the Gulf of Aden in 2009 to take part in an international campaign against Somali pirates.[12]

In an assessment of the MSDF's capabilities today, several stand out. First, the MSDF was the first Asian navy to acquire destroyers equipped with the impressive Aegis combat system (it has four); the system combines phased-array radars, computers, and weapons launchers, plus other weapons systems. Aegis ships serve several functions: maritime battle management, area air defense, and ballistic missile defense. With their superior air-defense capability, they provide essential support for warning and surveillance operations in the seas surrounding Japan, for sea control of Japan's important maritime areas, for defense of SLOCs, and for helping to establish air superiority in the event of an attack on the home islands. A retired MSDF admiral wrote tellingly of changes in the strategic environment that made Aegis valuable:

> Some people might question the deployment of powerful Aegis ships for these [peacetime] missions. However, *in view of the trend toward enhancement of surface ships in China* and other nations, it will become necessary, depending on the movements of the opponents, to deploy Aegis ships in sea areas surrounding Japan, particularly *in areas where competing maritime interests exist.*[13]

They will, he asserted, create a more effective deterrent and prevent "an error-induced situation from escalating."

Second, below water, the MSDF has nineteen conventionally powered submarines, with two more advanced ones under construction. Its force has developed gradually since the middle of the cold war; its vessels are better than anything Japan's neighbors have fielded so far, particularly with regard to noise reduction; and its personnel are highly trained professionals. In the mid-1970s, the submarine arm was responsible for surveillance and defense of Japan's three major straits (Tsugaru, Soya, and Tsushima), along with ISR operations. That was especially important because of the belief that under the U.S.-Japan security treaty, a Soviet attack on Japan's merchant ships would not oblige the United States to act. In the 1990s, with the end of the cold war, the submarine force adapted to the sharp decline of the Soviet/Russian navy and the incremental improvements of the Chinese one, but surveillance and defense of the straits continued to be its core missions. Surveillance and reconnaissance were extended to "the peripheries of the [Japanese] archipelago close to possible turbulent areas outside Taiwan and in the East China Sea," in shallower waters. That shift in orientation was only enhanced by the issuance in 2004 of Japan's National Defense Program Guidelines, which took account of increased Chinese naval activity. In view of the new, broader context, MSDF submarines would do less with respect to strait defense and engage in more ISR activities at "points of strategic importance in the East China Sea and the Sea of Japan." Their area of operations expanded to cover maritime crossroads in the East China Sea, down to the Taiwan Strait and the Bashi Channel, which separates Taiwan from the Philippines.[14]

Third, naval aviation is also a strong point of the MSDF, particularly with its ten minesweeping helicopters and more than eighty P-3C aircraft, which are used for antisubmarine warfare (ASW) but also are capable of conducting antisurface and electronic warfare. As noted above, through their daily patrols the P-3Cs are the workhorses of the ISR mission. And fourth, the mine warfare force is one of the best in the world, with more than thirty vessels; it effectively cleared mines in the Persian Gulf after the 1990–91 war. It has five ships from which helicopters can operate (in addition to the Aegis ships), and of those, three can handle vertical and short takeoff and landing aircraft. The majority of the surface ships are dedicated to antisubmarine warfare.[15]

The Japan Coast Guard is not part of the Self-Defense Forces bureaucracy; it falls under the Ministry of Land, Infrastructure, Transport, and Tourism. But its missions overlap with those of the MSDF. They are to enforce maritime laws and regulations, conduct maritime search-and-rescue operations, prevent maritime pollution, prevent and suppress criminal acts at sea, conduct criminal investigations and make arrests at sea, and regulate ship navigation. The vast majority of its 12,000-plus personnel engage in operations to protect Japan's territorial waters and exclusive economic zones. Thus it has both law enforcement and security missions.[16]

Richard Samuels goes further, defining the JCG as the "fourth branch of the Japanese military." Unlike the SDF, whose budget is either flat or declining, the JCG has seen its funding increase. As of late 2007, it had eighty-nine armed patrol ships that each exceeded 500 tons and fifty-six that exceeded 1,000 tons. The largest patrol ships have helicopter platforms. The JCG's total tonnage is more than half that of China's surface fleet, and its capabilities are far more advanced than those of its Chinese counterpart, the Marine Surveillance Force (MSF). Its aircraft have sophisticated equipment for maritime patrolling, including early warning radar. However, the JCG is constrained when it comes to firepower and long-range operations: "It has limited capacity to attack enemy targets, to support ground operations, to establish blockades, to launch amphibious assault operations, to protect sea lanes of communication, and to deter conflict."[17] Still, it brings significant capabilities to what it does, which includes protecting Japan's territorial waters, including those surrounding offshore islands.

Not only is the JCG gradually becoming a more robust force, its operational flexibility is expanding. When the Coast Guard Law was revised in October 2001, the Coast Guard gained the authority to use force to cope with maritime incursions and seaborne actions against the homeland; indeed, the JCG has more flexibility with regard to the use of force than the MSDF does. One month after the revisions were passed, JCG vessels received orders to fire on an intruding North Korean vessel. They first fired warning shots; then, as the vessel attempted to escape, they disabled the ship temporarily. The North Korean ship resumed its escape after the crew repaired the damage, whereupon JCG personnel forcibly boarded it and engaged in small-arms combat. After the North Korean crew fired a rocket at a JCG ship, the latter responded with cannon fire, sinking the intruding craft.[18]

The Japanese Air Self-Defense Force

The Air Self-Defense Force (ASDF) has a set of modern platforms, with F-15 interceptors as the leading system (see table 5-2), and an array of warning and anti-aircraft assets. An indigenously produced fighter, the F-2, is to be equipped with joint direct attack munitions, giving it enhanced defensive and also offensive capabilities.[19] The air force also is in charge of Japan's ballistic missile defense (BMD) system and is responsible for operating ground-based systems.[20]

Pursuant to the Suzuki-Nakasone commitments of the early 1980s, the ASDF's primary mission is air defense of Japanese territory, including offshore islands. In peacetime, that mission entails detecting unidentified planes that enter Japanese airspace, identifying the aircraft to ensure that they are not hostile, and, if they are, to intercept them and see that they retreat. On the issue of offshore islands, Hirata Hidetoshi, commander of the ASDF in 2009, stated: "If an island were invaded or occupied, we would need to get it back. First we have to work hard to ensure that such things do not happen. We have to watch our territory very closely, and then take proper action."[21] In wartime, the ASDF's task would be to destroy intruding enemy aircraft if appropriate.[22]

In peacetime, the ASDF maintains surveillance of Japan's territorial and adjacent airspace on a twenty-four-hour basis through ground-based and airborne early-warning aircraft, both E-2Cs and E-767s. Planes are on constant standby to be ready to intercept aircraft that appear to be challenging Japan's airspace. It is worth noting that Japan's air defense identification zone—which is the area that Japan designates as sensitive to its national security and within which ASDF planes may challenge foreign aircraft that do not identify themselves—is basically the same as Japan's exclusive economic zone and much larger than the space specified by most countries.[23]

Between 1998 and 2007, ASDF planes conducted between 150 and 300 intercepts a year against foreign aircraft incursions. Those incursions changed over time according to which country's planes were involved. Russian planes constituted at least half and rose to 83 percent in 2007, but the PLA air force accounted for about half in 2005, during the time of tensions over oil and gas drilling in the East China Sea.[24] The rules of engagement for intercept operations of the ASDF are reportedly very strict. Pilots may fire on intruding aircraft "only when Japan is in imminent danger."[25]

The geographical focus of ASDF operations has changed. Because the perceived threat from Russia has declined and that from China is growing, there has been a shift of assets and operations from north (Hokkaido) to south (offshore islands like Okinawa and the Senkaku Islands); more capable F-15s therefore replaced older F-4 squadrons on Okinawa.[26]

Aside from air defense, the mission of the ASDF expanded with the end of the cold war. Development of Japan's BMD capability, which has occurred in close cooperation with the United States, was a response to the emergence of North Korea's long-range ballistic missile program, demonstrated most graphically when Pyongyang flew a Taepodong-1 missile over Japan in a flight test. But hypothetically, missile defense is relevant to China as well. A second new mission is air transport to support international activities such as peacekeeping and U.S. operations in Iraq. The third is contributing to domestic disaster relief.[27] Because of the way that the constitution is interpreted, Japan possesses no long-range air assets, either bombers or missiles.

The ASDF will soon have to address the aging of its fighter fleet. Its F-4s will have to be replaced at some point, and the modernization of China's air force is reducing the quality differential that had given the ASDF its edge. It is looking at the U.S. F-22 as the replacement for an intercept aircraft, but U.S. law currently prohibits its acquisition by any foreign buyer (the ban was imposed for reasons that had nothing to do with Japan).[28]

China

For more than forty years, the People's Liberation Army Navy (PLAN) and the People's Liberation Army Air Force (PLAAF) played a distinctly second-ary role in China's defense posture. The ground forces that had won the revolution were the dominant service, and they still are. Army generals were not inclined to favor either the navy or the air force with robust budgets. Moreover, from the late 1960s to the late 1980s, the real threat was on land: the Soviet Union. Resources were so limited that the navy could serve only as a coastal defense force and the air force's mission was limited to defending China's borders and protecting the ground forces. During those four decades or more, the quality of ships and aircraft declined in relation to those of the U.S. Navy and Air Force and Japan's MSDF and ASDF.

In the early 1990s, strategic factors forced a dual change in China's force structure. On one hand, the Soviet Union collapsed, ending the land threat from the north and permitting serious attention to be given for the first time to China's sea and air vulnerability to the east and south.[29] On the other hand, the first Persian Gulf War exposed both the backwardness of the People's Liberation Army, whose force structure was similar to that of the Iraqi armed forces, and the strength and sophisticated assets of the U.S. military. The shock of that realization led to a set of decisions in 1993 on basic strategy that translated into the acquisition of advanced equipment, the reform of institu-tions, and the revision of doctrine.[30] Moreover, defense companies in the new Russia were looking for customers because their own government could no longer afford advanced systems, and China emerged as an eager customer.

The task of rectifying the PLA's weakness became urgent in the mid-1990s. The PRC leadership concluded, rightly or wrongly, that Taiwan's leaders intended to seek de jure independence and so challenge the funda-mental principle on which China's claim to Taiwan is based, which is that the island is a part of the state called China. Beijing had been prepared to wait patiently for Taiwan to "return to the embrace of the Motherland," but this new assessment made it necessary to give the PLA—and particularly the

Table 5-3. *Change in PLA Navy's Modern Force Structure, 1999–2009*
Number

		1999	2009
Active duty personnel (estimated)		230,000	215,000
Submarines	Total	10	31
SSN	Han class	5	4
SS	Kilo class (Type EKM 877 & 636)	4	...
	Song class	1	...
SSK	Kilo class	...	12
	Song class	...	13
	Yuan class	...	2
Principal surface combatants			
Destroyers	Total	18	27
DDG	Hangzhou class (RF Sovremenny-class)	...	4
	Luda class (Type-051)	16	15
	Luhu class	2	2
	Guangzhou class/Luyang class	...	4
	Luzhou class	...	2
Frigates	Total	35	49
FFG	Jianghu class	about 31	29
	Jiangwei class	4	14
	Jiangkai class	...	6

Sources: International Institute for Strategic Studies, *The Military Balance 2000–2001* (Oxford University Press, 2002), pp. 194–97; and International Institute for Strategic Studies, *The Military Balance 2008* (London: Routledge, 2008), pp. 376–80.

PLAN, the PLAAF, and the missile force (the Second Artillery)—the capabilities to deter "separatism" and inflict punishment if deterrence failed. If punishment was to be effective, PLA strategists also concluded, it would be necessary to deny access to the U.S. Navy and Air Force if they were ordered to come to Taiwan's defense. All three services therefore received increased budgetary allocations to gradually modernize their obsolete force structures. Their evolution is captured in tables 5-3 and 5-4, which focus only on relatively modern systems.

Table 5-4. *Evolution of Force Structure of Second Artillery and of PLA Air Force, 1999–2009*

		1999	2009
Second Artillery (strategic missile force)			
Active duty personnel		100,000+	100,00+
Intermediate-range ballistic missiles			
DF-21 (estimated)		8	Circa 33
Sea-launched ballistic missiles			
Xia SSBN with 12 CSS-N-3 (JL-1)		1	1
PLA Air Force			
Active duty personnel		220,000	300,000–330,000
Aircraft			
BBR	H-5 series	200+	. . .
	H-6 series	120	up to 82
FTR	J-7 series	700	504
	J-8 & J-8II series	250	432
	J-11/Su-27SK	52	116
FGA	Su-30MKK	. . .	73
	MiG-19 series	. . .	72
Total of J-8, J-8II, J-11/Su-27SK, and Su-30MKK fighters		302	621

Sources: International Institute for Strategic Studies, *The Military Balance 2000–2001* (Oxford University Press, 2002), pp. 194–97; and International Institute for Strategic Studies, *The Military Balance 2008* (London: Routledge, 2008), pp. 376–80.

The PLAN

Table 5-3 demonstrates the increase in numbers and classes of naval vessels, but it does not reveal the improvements in quality. The Luda class destroyer, deployed in 1999, was better than its Luhu and Luhai predecessors because it had better anti-ship firepower. The Russian-made Sovremennys came next, with anti-ship cruise missiles. But the Luyang and Luzhou classes were even better because they finally gave PLAN destroyers a defense against attacks from the air, not unlike that possessed by U.S. Aegis ships. Similarly, Jiang-kai class frigates are more capable than the Jiangwei class, of which there are several models, each better than the last.

Regarding submarines, the indigenous Songs and the Russian Kilos improved significantly on the cold war–era Romeos and Mings, and when their development is complete they will be equipped with anti-ship cruise missiles. And China's more advanced conventional submarines, like the Kilo class, are relatively quiet and can negate the antisubmarine warfare capability of even the U.S. Navy (it therefore is likely that Japanese submarines do not know the location of Chinese subs, and vice versa).[31] After decades of neglect, the PLAN is acquiring the means for amphibious warfare, which would be especially relevant for the security of the Senkaku/Diaoyu Islands. The indigenous vessels are produced by a shipbuilding industry that, according to one specialist, made "dramatic strides in capability."[32]

Equipment assets are distributed among the PLAN's five combat branches—submarine, surface force, naval aviation, coastal defense, and marine corps—which are formed into three fleets. The North Sea Fleet, which operates closest to the Japanese home islands, is located at Qingdao and has other major bases at Lushun and Xiaopingdao. The East Sea Fleet, which operates in the East China Sea and which would play a prominent role in a conflict over Taiwan or the Diaoyu Islands, is located at Ningbo and has additional major bases at Shanghai, Fujian, and Zhoushan, at the entrance to Hangzhou Bay. The South Fleet, based at Zhanjiang, is less relevant to Japan.[33]

Deterring Taiwan's independence is not the PLAN's only objective. According to a Chinese defense white paper, the PLAN's primary missions are to "guard against enemy invasion from the sea, defend the state's sovereignty over its territorial waters, and safeguard the state's maritime rights and interests."[34] It seeks to become a modern maritime force "consisting of combined arms with both nuclear and conventional means of operations" and gradually to "expand the strategic depth of its offshore defensive operations."[35] Hu Jintao echoed that general mission statement in speaking to the Tenth Navy Communist Party Congress in late December 2006. He emphasized that "China is a maritime power, and the navy's status is important and its mission glorious in defending our sovereignty and security and upholding our maritime rights and interests." He noted the importance of ideological work; readiness ("to ensure that we can effectively carry out missions at any time"); procuring modern capabilities; training personnel; and governing the military according to law.[36]

In 2007 Wu Shengli and Hu Yanli, commander and political commissar of the PLAN, respectively, provided their own, plausible statement of the reasons for naval missions: to "maintain the safety of the oceanic transportation and the strategic passageway for energy and resources, ensure the jurisdiction of our nation to neighboring areas, continental shelf, and exclusive economic zones, and effectively safeguard our national maritime rights." Morevoer, Wu and Hu attach numbers to missions:

more than 18,000 kilometers of oceanic coast line, more than 6,500 islands that are larger than 500 square meters, more than 3 million square kilometers of oceanic area, with sovereignty and jurisdiction and international exclusive exploitation rights for 75,000 square kilometers at the bottom of the Pacific.

To realize those missions, Wu and Hu said, the PLAN will gradually *"expand the strategic depth of its offshore defensive operations."*[37]

The last statement is telling. Michael McDevitt argues convincingly that the strategic vision behind the PRC's naval modernization is similar to that of another continental power that faced vulnerabilities from the sea: the Soviet Union. Especially in the 1980s, the Soviets "developed a defensive maritime strategy with spaced, roughly parallel sea lines of defense . . . at varying distances from the Soviet Union's coasts, with each succeeding line defended by weapon systems and tactical schemes appropriate to its location."

As it began to think about more ambitious missions than coastal defense, the PLA adopted a similar "layered" approach, with the Pacific island chains defining the boundaries of each defense zone. The first island chain runs from Japan's Kyushu Island through the Ryukyus Islands and Taiwan to the Philippines. The second runs from the east-central coast of Japan through Guam and down to Papua. The third runs down the middle of the Pacific through Hawaii. The objective was to create strategic depth for China by reducing the access of or denying access to adversary navies to deploy in each of the zones. As one Chinese security scholar noted, China had seas but not the ocean. "If a big power is not at the same time a maritime power, its position is not secure."[38]

Of special importance in that regard is the territory within the first island chain, which is where the PLAN would want to establish dominance if China had to act forcefully to punish Taiwan for unacceptable political initiatives. A key goal would be to block U.S. forces from intervening. It is also the area where the maritime energy resources that are most accessible to China exist.[39]

China was not, of course, the first power to think in terms of Pacific island chains. They formed the organizing principle for U.S. naval planning before World War II, for the U.S. advance across the Pacific during the war, and for U.S. security strategy during the cold war. No matter which states are competing for maritime space, the existence of island chains frames the competition. However, it now appears that Chinese military strategists are less inclined to use island chains as their organizing concepts. As Paul Godwin remarks, "It seems probable that offshore defense is now a strategic concept with no defined geographical limit." Nan Li suggests that if the PLAN employs a geographic lens, it is more likely to think in terms of "near coast," "near seas," and "far seas."[40]

Whatever the terminology, China's strategy for the East Asian littoral is an anti-access/area-denial strategy. That poses a problem for Japan, because China's push for strategic depth encroaches on Japan's traditional area of operations. As the Pentagon's annual report on the PLA puts it, "Current trends in China's military capabilities are a major factor in changing East Asian military balances, and could provide China with a force capable of conducting a range of military operations well beyond Taiwan."[41]

One aspect of the navy's modernization has been enhanced emphasis on training and exercises, which vary in terms of scale, level of the units involved, form, conditions, location, and objective.[42] These give the PLAN experience in the various tasks that an ocean-going navy might perform by practicing, for example, maneuvers and combat tactics.[43] In terms of specific campaigns, there are six in which the PLAN would play a key role: sea blockade, anti-SLOC operations, sea-to-land attack, anti-ship attack, sea transportation protection, and naval base defense.[44] Obviously some would be conducted by the PLAN alone; others would be conducted on a joint basis. Mounting a sea blockade, for example, would require participation of the air force to gain air superiority.

Japanese and U.S. officials have often complained that China's military buildup is "not transparent," that China's security goals are not obvious from the PLA's growing force structure. But Taylor Fravel argues that the force structure that the PLAN is acquiring is "roughly consistent" with the capabilities needed to block access and establish area denial around China's periphery, which in turn serves some of Beijing's strategic goals: territorial integrity, national unification, and maritime security (defending maritime rights and interests). The forces that China now has would permit it to attack Taiwan and to operate in maritime East Asia, "*into waters in which other navies already operate.*"[45]

Indeed, the PLAN is operating increasingly in the waters of maritime East Asia. In October 2008, MSDF P-3C patrol planes detected two PLAN submarines tailing the U.S. aircraft carrier *George Washington* in waters between Japan and Korea. Later in the month, four Chinese naval vessels, including a destroyer, went through the Tsugaru Strait between Honshu and Hokkaido. Though the transit was in international waters, it still caught the attention of the Japanese. In early November, four Luzhou missile destroyers were observed patrolling in the East China Sea off the coast of Okinawa, reportedly in Japanese territorial waters. In December, two PRC survey ships came close to the Senkaku Islands, into what Tokyo considers its territorial waters. And the Federation of American Scientists reported in February 2009 that Chinese attack submarines had done twelve patrols in 2008, up from seven in 2007, two in 2006, and none in 2005.[46]

China's other maritime actor is the Marine Surveillance Force (*haijian zongdui*). It is a part not of the PLA but of the State Oceanic Administration, which is subordinate to the Ministry of Land and Resources under the State Council. One of its core missions is to "uphold China's maritime rights and interests by administrative law enforcement means." The MSF inherits older ships from the PLAN as the latter acquires more sophisticated new vessels; thus the MSF fleet of more than 200 ships and nine planes is becoming increasingly modern, although it is not on a par with the Japanese or the U.S. Coast Guard. The MSF can thereby bring increasing firepower to its law enforcement mission: "These small and mid-sized vessels were themselves designed for naval combat, and therefore . . . are more suited to the new requirements involved in the buildup of China's maritime security forces. . . . They are robust vessels with good guns."[47]

The MSF deploys its forces in the North Sea, East China Sea, and South China Sea. In 2006 it began to patrol the East China Sea, including the Senkaku Islands, and it conducts daily sorties by sea and air. In 2009, the MSF dispatched its ships on 230 different missions and its aircraft on 540 sorties, monitoring 747 different targets.[48] In October 2008, one commentary noted specifically the MSF's activities regarding Japan.[49] And in September 2009, the head of the State Oceanic Administration wrote that

> China's marine surveillance patrols and law enforcement have changed from irregular to regular, and China has begun to carry out regular safeguarding rights patrol work in the Yellow Sea, the East China Sea, the northern . . . and southern part[s] of the South China Sea.[50]

The results of China's naval modernization effort should not be exaggerated. Ship for ship and sub for sub, the PLAN is still not a match for the MSDF, to say nothing of the U.S. Navy. Naval aviation is still rather weak. No conventional submarine is using air-independent propulsion, which permits longer submersion times. Antisubmarine warfare is still a challenge. Constraints exist concerning the quality of personnel, training, and maintenance—all keys to good performance—and logistical limitations reduce the time that vessels may remain at sea. The Department of Defense therefore estimated in 2008 that "China's ability to sustain military power at a distance remains limited."[51] On the other hand, the steady and systematic gains in quality, in both hardware and software, augur a Chinese navy that will be able to stay at sea longer and that will have more speed and offensive and defensive firepower than it has had. By 2017, Cole predicts, the PLAN will be "capable of denying command of the East and South China Seas to another power, and of commanding those seas for discrete periods." Whether it will dominate the MSDF depends on whether the latter itself modernizes.[52]

A big question for the future and for Japan's security is whether China acquires aircraft carriers. For at least three decades, Chinese naval planners have debated the pros and cons of basing the country's maritime defense on submarines or carriers. Subs are better for carrying out sea denial, such as denying access to the U.S. Navy in any confrontation related to Taiwan. Carriers are probably necessary to establish sea control, the PLAN's goal for the area within the first island chain and for which air superiority is a precondition. The advocates of submarines were long aided by resource constraints and by the technical difficulties associated with carriers, the need to assemble other vessels to defend them, and the need to develop the logistics capability to support them. Yet the proponents of carriers are gaining ground. One reason is the general belief in China that aircraft carriers are associated with great power status, which, of course, China seeks. Major General Qian Lianghua, director of the Foreign Affairs Office of the Ministry of National Defense, said in November 2008 that "having an aircraft carrier is the dream of any great military power." Moreover, the PLAN has noted that carriers are useful not only for projecting power, which may be threatening to nearby states, but also for more benign missions, such as conducting humanitarian operations and protecting sea lanes of communication. So, as General Qian said, "the question is not whether you have an aircraft carrier, but what you do with your aircraft carrier."[53]

Whenever the PLAN does acquire carriers, assuming that achieving sea control on China's littoral is one of their missions, they will increase the potential for friction with the Japanese navy and air force.[54] The institute connected to Japan's Ministry of Defense has offered this sober assessment:

> Taken together, the aircraft carrier development program, the emergence of a doctrinal framework for high-seas operation, the enhancement of blue-water supply capabilities, and the normalization of blue-water activity should be interpreted as signs that China has already started to establish a presence on the high seas. This trend should be closely monitored, not only because it represents a potential threat to

China's neighbors and a possible source of friction with such powers as the United States and India, but also because it will have an impact on sea lanes that are a lifeline for Japan.[55]

The PLAAF

Like the PLA Navy, the PLA Air Force is acquiring platforms that enable it increasingly to extend operational coverage toward Japan, to say nothing of the East China Sea. For example, the Sukhoi-27 fighters and Sukhoi-30 fighter-bombers that China acquired from Russia have the range needed to reach the Japanese home islands from bases in North China and Okinawa from bases in East China.[56] The older Hong-6 bomber has a range of 3,000 kilometers. In addition, the PLAAF has acquired fourth-generation air defense suites (sensors and missiles) from Russia that expand the area in which it can put intruding adversary aircraft at risk.

The PLAAF is no longer tasked just with defending China's borders and ground forces, as it was during and after the cold war. Its missions have changed. As stated in the PRC's 2008 defense white paper, the PLAAF is also

> responsible for such tasks as safeguarding the country's . . . territorial sovereignty. . . . [It] has begun its transition from territorial air defense to *both offensive and defensive operations*. . . . It now has strong capabilities to conduct air defensive and offensive operations, and certain capabilities to execute long-range precision strikes and strategic projection operations.[57]

Specifically, the emphasis of force modernization has been on "suppression of enemy air defenses and offensive counter-air operations."[58] Therefore it was declared at a meeting of the leadership of the PLAAF's Tenth Air Force in December 2008 that "the air force should have corresponding capability of creating a posture, controlling a crisis, and winning a war in our country's territorial air and in the areas that have relation with our national interests."[59]

As with the navy, the principal driver of this transition was concern that Taiwan's leaders were plotting to separate the island from China permanently. To deter them—and to coerce Taiwan if deterrence failed—the PLAAF would need systems that could ensure air superiority in the Taiwan Strait to pave the way for either a naval blockade or an amphibious invasion and to block U.S. intervention. (The anti-access/area-denial strategy discussed in relation to the PLAN requires joint operations with the PLAAF.) As early as 1990, the PLAAF set achieving air superiority as its highest priority.[60]

Beijing took advantage of the buyer's market that emerged with the collapse of the Soviet Union to purchase Sukhoi-27s and -30s and obtained the right to coproduce a version of the Sukhoi, the J-11, with the Russian manufacturer in China. It also acquired transports, tankers, and longer-range air defense systems. In addition, today China's indigenous aircraft industry is making technological strides after a long period of little progress. As important as improvements in hardware are, efforts to improve the education and training of personnel and to develop a doctrine appropriate for the air force's new missions are crucial.[61]

Beyond Taiwan, a proliferation of national interests has imposed new demands on the PLAAF. Among the current or future missions that the article identified were "maintain air surveillance over China's maritime interest, . . . protect China's national dignity, sovereignty, rights, and interests, provide air security for China's overseas investment, communication and transport, [and] scientific survey."[62] Xu Qiliang, the PLAAF commander, has stressed the link between the air and the sea: "Having control over the air and space means having control over the ground, the oceans, and the electromagnetic space and having the strategic initiative."[63] A key geographic area where those interests are at play is the East China Sea, and the PLAAF's modern platforms will allow it to conduct operations far from China's shores.[64]

To carry out those broad objectives, the PLAAF is acquiring the ability to carry out several operational missions or campaigns. The first is air deterrence, "the use of airpower as a means to coerce or deter an adversary short of large-scale military operations." The second is offensive air strikes, to establish air superiority and reduce the adversary's ability to mount a defense. The third is air blockades, to compel an enemy to surrender—for example, by shutting down its air and marine traffic.[65]

The 2006 defense white paper had this to say regarding the PLAAF's training and exercises:

> [The PLAAF] stresses mission-oriented and confrontational training, increasing combined tactical training of different arms and aircraft types, and conducts training in flying refitted new aircraft and using new weaponry and equipment in an active and stable way. Air Force pilot training is conducted at flying colleges, training bases and combat units in five phases, namely, basic education, primary flying, advanced flying, refitted combat aircraft flying and tactical flying. Aviation units mainly conduct training in counter-air operations, air-to-ground attacks and joint operations. Pilots fly training hours [that] are commensurate with the tasks assigned to pilots.[66]

The goal is to develop over time

a highly trained modern Air Force equipped with high-tech aircraft, advanced precision-guided munitions, support aircraft that serve as force multipliers, and networked command, control and intelligence capabilities that . . . could . . . undertake offensive strikes against ground and naval targets further away from China's borders.[67]

To achieve that goal China must make significant progress on airborne early warning systems and indigenous production of jet engines. More broadly, China's military leaders will face key trade-offs in deciding which services and branches should have which roles and missions and in deciding whether to emphasize foreign or domestic procurement, greater or lesser technological sophistication, and combat or support platforms.[68] The choices made will have an impact on the PLAAF's ability to project power. A key indicator for the future is whether it acquires advanced strategic bombers. If it did, that would spell "a major shift in the balance of power in Asia," including Japan.[69]

Taking the PLA's expanding complement of submarines, surface ships, modern aircraft, air defenses, and the accompanying ordnance together, China is on the way to reaching its goal of denying adversary navies and air forces the ability to deploy and fight within the first island chain. According to the 2009 report on Chinese military power by the U.S. Department of Defense, the PLA "present[s] and project[s] increasingly credible, layered offensive combat power across its borders and into the Western Pacific." It either has or is gaining "the ability to hold large surface ships, including aircraft carriers, at risk . . . deny use of shore-based airfields, secure bastions, and regional logistics hubs . . . and hold aircraft at risk over or near Chinese territory or forces." Precision strike capability is growing as sensors and targeting improves.[70] The PLA is still weak when it comes to conducting truly joint operations among the branches of its armed forces, which is something that it has never had to do but would have to do well to carry out an access denial campaign. But it is aware of that limitation and seeks to reduce it.[71]

Other Capabilities: Missiles and Cyber Warfare

To sum up, Japan's air and naval capabilities are significant and China's are growing. Supplementing the work of the two countries' navies are the Japan Coast Guard and China's Marine Surveillance Force. All these forces are operating in a geographic space that each nation deems a significant security interest.

In addition, there are two areas in which China has growing capabilities that can "touch" the Japanese home islands and in which Japan lacks corresponding assets. The first has to do with ballistic and cruise missiles. For example, the Japanese home islands are within the range of China's CSS-5 and CSS-2 medium-range ballistic missiles (1,750 and 3,000 kilometers, respectively) as well as the DH-10 land-attack cruise missile.[72] However, an assessment of long-range strike capabilities concludes that "there is little indication to date that [China's] conventional missile force possesses broader regional missions [such as Japan]. This force is strongly preoccupied with Taiwan scenarios."[73]

Cyber warfare is another matter. Parties in China conduct active information warfare attacks against foreign targets, including Japan. Joel Brenner, a former official of the U.S. Office of the Director of National Intelligence, described China as a "cyber-counterintelligence threat" that stands out because of the "pervasive and relentless nature of the attacks." A 2008 report of the U.S.-China Economic and Security Review Commission, which was established by Congress, found that "China is pursuing cyber warfare capabilities that may provide it with an asymmetric advantage against the United States."[74] Dennis Wilder, former senior director for Asia on the National Security Council staff, said at a Brookings Institution event in April 2009 that "today, the amount of cyber attacks coming out of China is astounding. . . .What we do know though is it's very persistent, sometimes pretty targeted, but it is wide and pervasive, and it [leaves] you with a very uneasy feeling."[75]

Japan shares the U.S. sense of vulnerability. In 2008, the Ministry of Defense's white paper reported that "China appears to have interest in the cyber warfare and they seem to have organized and are currently training a cyber warfare–specialized unit. China's interest in . . . cyber warfare can be attributed to the increasing reliance of information gathering and command and communication in the military sector, which are vital for swift and efficient exercise of military strength, on satellites and computer networks."[76] An Internet security specialist observed that Chinese hackers "used to just have fun with us, but now they have become more vicious and have a clear intent to do damage."[77] A former general in Japan's Ground Self-Defense Force predicted that a deliberate attack on servers associated with a major system, such as air traffic, "would result in unimaginable mass chaos throughout Japan."[78] Japan's National Police Agency publishes reports on trends in attempts to gain access to its computers, and China is the most prevalent source of attacks. As figure 5-1 indicates, the number of Chinese attacks is generally rising. There was a decline during and after the Beijing

Figure 5-1. *Unauthorized Attempts Originating in China to Access Japanese Servers and Websites*

Percent change in month-to-month access attempts per IP address per day

Number of access attempts per IP address per day

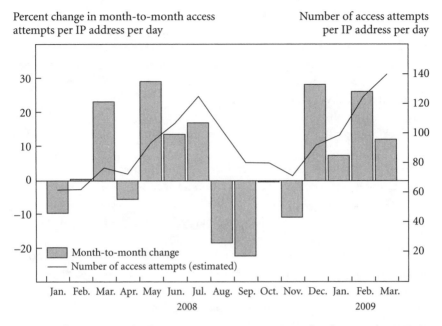

Sources: "Japan: National Police Agency Internet Security Report," various months, 2008–09, and estimates based on author's calculations.

Olympics, but the numbers resumed an upward path in December, with an average month-on-month increase of about 15 percent.[79]

The question, of course, is whether Chinese hackers are acting on their own or for agencies of the Chinese government. Brenner says that "some [attacks], we have high confidence, are coming from government-sponsored sites," either agency or contractor sites. An expert on Chinese cyber activities who has worked for both the U.S. Army and as a contractor for the U.S. intelligence community observes that "the relationship between citizen and state is fluid in China, and that the Chinese government tends not to prosecute hackers unless they attack within China. . . . The lack of supervision is tacit approval, and it constitutes a de facto partnership between civilian hackers and the Chinese government." A 2009 report prepared for the U.S.-China Economic and Security Review Commission found that there was evidence of "apparent collaboration between more elite individual hackers and the PRC's civilian security services.[80] James Lewis, a specialist at the Center for Strategic and International Studies, concludes that there is a range of relationships between the regime and the hackers: "The government at a minimum tolerates them. Sometimes it encourages them. And sometimes it tasks them and controls them."[81] Brenner says: "It's a kind of cyber militia" that is mounting attacks "in volumes that are just staggering."[82]

Unifying this dispersed capability is a strong sense of nationalism. According to a long-time Chinese hacker, "Unlike our Western counterparts, most of whom are individualists or anarchists, Chinese hackers tend to get more involved with politics because most of them are young, passionate, and patriotic." Consequently, hackers can become national heroes for their vigorous defense of the national honor.[83]

This volume returns later to the dangers of mixing nationalism and a transnational noncombat capability among actors who are not always—or not usually—under government control. But first it is necessary to examine why evolving military, paramilitary, and cyber capabilities matter. That they exist does not mean that they will be used. And Japan and China have good reasons to avoid war. The chance that either would initiate a war of choice seems miniscule, but wars are not always deliberate. In that regard, it is useful to examine the ways in which Chinese and Japanese military forces intersect over specific issues. That is the subject of the next chapter.

6

Points of Proximity and Friction

On March 8, 2009, Chinese vessels associated with China's Bureau of Fisheries harassed the USNS *Impeccable* in the South China Sea, engaging in dangerous acts such as trying to snag and presumably seize a towed sonar buoy. The clash became public knowledge and complicated China's effort to get off to a good start with the new Obama administration.

The incident occurred on the high seas, but under special circumstances. The *Impeccable*, a submarine surveillance vessel, was operating about seventy-five miles away from a new People's Liberation Army Navy (PLAN) base for nuclear attack and ballistic missile submarines, at Yulin on Hainan Island. It can be inferred that the *Impeccable* was collecting information about the movements of the subs, the better to conduct antisubmarine warfare in the event of conflict.

The harassing Chinese vessels did not belong to the PLAN, but they were probably under its direction. Moreover, other U.S. ships had been challenged during the previous week, including by being monitored by PRC marine surveillance aircraft. For example, a Chinese ship shining a high-intensity spotlight approached the USNS *Victorious* in the Yellow Sea about 1,500 miles away from and five days before the *Impeccable* episode. That suggests a level of coordination that only a government agency could achieve.[1]

Those encounters were not unprecedented, of course. They recalled the April 2001 case of a PLAN aircraft that harassed and collided with a U.S. EP-3 reconnaissance aircraft not far from Hainan. The Chinese plane and pilot were lost, and the damaged EP-3 had to make an emergency landing. In September 2002, planes of the People's Liberation Army Air Force (PLAAF) and reconnaissance vessels harassed the USNS *Bowditch*, a sister ship of the

Impeccable.[2] A Chinese Han class submarine had come very close to the USS *Kitty Hawk* in 2005 without being detected.

In the case of the *Impeccable*, evidently the Foreign Ministry was unaware of the harassing actions and their negative diplomatic impact. Two other things are clear. First, the Chinese and U.S. armed forces (or parties acting at their governments' behest) are operating in closer and closer proximity to each other. The United States collects intelligence about PLA activities not far from China's shores, and there are hints that U.S. monitoring has been increasing. Beijing dislikes the surveillance for understandable reasons and reportedly had demanded repeatedly through diplomatic channels that it cease.[3] The Chinese actions are also part of its broader anti-access strategy: to limit or eliminate the U.S. presence in the waters and airspace above the continental shelf.[4] China's Marine Surveillance Force (MSF) later revealed that "situations that are similar to the USNS *Impeccable* incident occur almost every month in the sea areas around China, and loud and silent struggles at sea that focus on our maritime rights and interests have never stopped."[5]

Second, Beijing and Washington have irreconcilable differences about how international law applies here, and that reinforces the geopolitical dispute. China believes that the UN Convention on the Law of the Sea (UNCLOS) forbids another power to conduct military surveillance anywhere in its exclusive economic zone. The United States, which has not ratified UNCLOS but observes its provisions, holds that the convention gives it broad freedom to do just that. Mutually reinforcing geopolitical and legal differences ensure that China and the United States will be at odds on a regular basis.[6]

In examining the navies and air forces of Japan and China, chapter 5 concluded that China's power is growing relative to Japan's and that increasingly their navies and air forces will operate east of China's coast, in a geographic space that each party believes is strategically important. Within this large territory (more than 3 million square kilometers, according to the Chinese estimate), there are specific points of friction. If conflict between China and Japan erupts, it is more likely to erupt over those points, and that is the subject of this chapter.

There are good reasons for this focus. Certainly, both China and Japan believe that maritime territorial issues are important. As shown in the last chapter, the PLAN's missions included "deterring Taiwan independence, defending the states' sovereignty over its territorial waters, and safeguarding the state's maritime rights and interests."[7] A Chinese military scholar put it more bluntly, identifying three "real threats" to the national interest: "The reunification of the motherland being obstructed [Taiwan]. . . . Islands being occupied [Diaoyu/Senkaku]. . . . Sea rights being invaded and seized."[8]

Meng Xiangqian, a scholar at the Strategic Studies Institute of the National Defense University, argues that the way for China to establish its maritime rights is to assert them through action. "We say that this sea area has historically been ours, but this alone is no use. It depends on whether we have actual control there. China's maritime monitoring must demonstrate its presence and express effective jurisdiction in the sea areas under its jurisdiction."[9] Indeed, because the Chinese government's policies regarding the East China Sea may impinge on its strategy of offshore defense, the People's Liberation Army Navy has an important stake in those policies—and it acts to protect that stake.[10]

For Japan's part, maintaining control over the Senkaku/Diaoyu Islands[11] and protecting its interests in the East China Sea are important priorities. The Japanese public appears to broadly support the idea that the islands belong to Japan. Experts point to the islands' strategic value and the need to assert Japan's interests. Takai Mitsuo, a former instructor with the Ground Self-Defense Force, warns that if China were to occupy the islands, "it would secure superiority in intelligence and control of the air and sea space in the southern sector of the East China Sea, . . . gaining definite control over energy and various maritime resources." Nakanishi Terumasa points to the island's strategic link to Taiwan: "If unification with China occurred, the areas surrounding the Senkaku Islands would immediately become China's seas completely" and Japanese air force and navy would be forced out of the area. If that happened, China's warships would be constantly conducting naval exercises in the East China Sea off the coast of Okinawa, and Japanese ships and airplanes would be pushed out of the area. Kayahara Ikuo advocates a firm response in the face of "illegal landings" in order to "demonstrate at home and abroad the real situation of effective control over the Senkaku Islands."[12]

Besides Beijing's and Tokyo's expressed concerns, there are theoretical reasons for paying attention to territorial issues, including maritime resource issues. First, as I argue in chapter 4, among the reasons for the deterioration in Japan-China relations that began in 1995 are specific disputes that can lead each party to suspect the other's intentions. This type of spiral can occur independently of a competition for capabilities, but it can also reinforce it. So it makes sense to examine the disputes that foster or may foster mutual fear between Beijing and Tokyo.

Second, scholars who study interstate conflict generally find that territorial disputes are an especially important causal factor. Paul Senese and John

Vasquez conclude that pairs of countries "whose relations are dominated by territorial disputes or who simply have recurring territorial disputes . . . are more apt to go to war than those that are not contending over territory." That is true in particular of countries that are neighbors. Although most territorial conflicts do not result in war, those in which the parties increase their capabilities (arms or alliances) and tactically emphasize toughness and resolve raise the chance of a fight.[13] Paul Huth and Todd Allee find that conflict over disputed territory is more likely when the territory is deemed to be of strategic value.[14]

Finally, Beijing's general approach to territorial disputes is relevant for disputes that are relevant to Japan. China has been more likely to compromise on land disputes than those at sea; on the latter, it bargains hard but prefers to delay resolution until its power position improves.[15] But that means that the disputes are allowed to fester. When it comes to competition for energy resources, there is some evidence that disputes are more easily resolved when the parties concerned have symmetrical power relations and trust each other's intentions. Those conditions do not apply in the case of Japan and China.[16]

This chapter looks at four points of friction. The first is the Diaoyu/Senkaku Islands, a true territorial issue. The second concerns rights to exploit oil and gas resources in the East China Sea. The third has to do with maritime straits. And the fourth is the Taiwan Strait issue. Reflecting Japan's concern on these issues, in 2004 the Japan Defense Agency examined conflict scenarios regarding the Senkaku/Diaoyu Islands, ocean resources, and Taiwan as part of a major defense-planning effort.[17]

Geography, Energy Resources, and International Law

Understanding the geography of the East China Sea, energy resources as a driver of competition, and some points of international law is relevant to understanding the political-military issues at play in the first three of the four specific points of friction.

First geography: from the coast of the Chinese mainland, the land mass extends eastward underwater, toward the Pacific Ocean. The gradient is moderate for about 500 miles, with the depth in this shallow area reaching no more than 200 meters (650 feet), until there is a sharp drop into much deeper waters at the Ryukyu Trench, which follows a line formed by the east side of Japan, the Ryukyu Islands, and Taiwan. Crossing the shallow land mass are a number of subterranean troughs. An important one is the Xihu depression, which is about 110 kilometers from the Chinese coastal province of Zheji-ang.[18] Closer to the Ryukyu chain is the much deeper Okinawa trough, which is more than 2,000 meters deep in many places. The Senkaku/Diaoyu Islands sit on the edge of the rim of the trough near the southern end.[19]

China and Japan began their relationship regarding energy on a com-plementary basis after 1972. Japan, as always, was highly dependent on oil imports and China appeared to have large supplies (coal was another resource that fostered complementarity). Moreover, Japan's aid program to China was geared to a significant extent to enhancing exploitation of China's resources. The situation today is different. China became a net oil importer in 1993, and the two countries now compete for energy resources. Moreover, while Japan's needs are large and constant, China's are large and growing. For example, imports are likely to constitute 60 to 80 percent of China's oil consumption by 2020.[20] Since the release of a UN report in 1969 that sug-gested that the Senkaku area has significant oil deposits, both countries have looked to the broader East China Sea area as a pillar of their future energy security. Although estimates are not necessarily reliable because little explo-ration has occurred, one Chinese estimate for the whole area is around 200 trillion cubic feet of potential gas reserves. Foreign estimates for potential oil reserves run as high as 100 billion barrels. The Xihu and Okinawa troughs are regarded as the prime areas for exploration and drilling.[21]

China and Japan disagree on just about everything with respect to who has rights to the oil and gas resources in the East China Sea. Their differences are self-serving, with each seeking to interpret international law in ways that accord with its desire to maximize its access to those resources.[22]

The dispute begins with the issue of what constitutes the continental shelf. China says it runs as far as the Okinawa trough, which, it claims, is deep enough at some points to meet the UNCLOS definition for the end of a con-tinental shelf.[23] Japan argues that despite the Okinawa trough, the shelf is one continuous formation that runs all the way to the Ryukyu chain and therefore is shared by both Japan and China.

A second issue is how the exclusive economic zone (EEZ) of each country should be delineated and defined. Here, each government relies on differ-ent, conflicting UNCLOS provisions. Drawing on article 76, China supports application of the principle of "natural prolongation" of the continental shelf, out to 350 nautical miles (nm), which would give it sovereign rights to exploit the resources on the ocean floor of the whole shelf. Japan bases its approach on UNCLOS's normal grant of 200 nm for EEZs and its principles of "equidistance" and "equitable solution." Given that the East China Sea is narrower than 400 nm, Tokyo argues for drawing a median line down the East China Sea, which would give China and Japan rights to the natural resources on their respective sides of that line.[24]

That Tokyo and Beijing disagree over the scope of their respective EEZs is significant because both Japan and China use those zones to define their airspace. China has consistently claimed that military and reconnaissance flights by the planes of a foreign military in the airspace of its EEZ are a threat to China's national security and that it has a right to intercept them.[25] Japan uses the boundary of its EEZ (as it defines it) to set the limits of its air defense identification zone (ADIZ), the area that it designates as sensitive to its national security and in which aircraft of the Air Self-Defense Force (ASDF) may challenge foreign aircraft that do not identify themselves. Thus, "the ASDF issues an order to scramble when unidentified planes enter an ADIZ. If such planes violate the nation's airspace, ADF fighters issue warnings and force them to land."[26] Japan's ADIZ is much larger than that specified by most countries.[27]

A third issue is whether the Senkaku/Diaoyu Islands actually are islands, in the UNCLOS sense of being able to support human habitation. China has not taken a position on this question, while Japan asserts that they are. Tokyo has good reason for its assertion because, if accepted, it would both justify a separate 200 nm EEZ and "pull" its claimed median line westward.[28]

Fourth is the question of whether some gas and oil fields lie on both sides of Japan's declared median line or only on China's side. Japan claims that the Chunxiao and Duanqiao fields extend over the line and that China is obligated to share data from its exploration and drilling in those areas, because Chinese exploitation will "suck out" resources from its side. China claims that the fields are completely on China's side of Japan's median line; there is no need, therefore, to provide data.

A fifth point of contention is whether the delimitation and territory issues should be resolved before resource development is considered. China has long argued that in areas in which sovereignty (broadly defined) is contested, the two sides should set aside their disputes and pursue joint development. Thus, joint development is appropriate for the Diaoyu/Senkaku Islands and for the part of the East China Sea that Japan claims as its EEZ but not for the part west of Japan's asserted median line. Japan has resolutely refused to discuss joint development of the Senkaku/Diaoyu Islands and has been ambiguous regarding the East China Sea.

A sixth issue is whether Chinese survey ships are doing scientific research or surveys of natural resources. UNCLOS states that when a state does

Table 6-1. *Chinese Research Vessels in Japanese Waters*

Year	Chinese research vessels	
	Confirmed total	Unsanctioned vessels
1994		
1995	7	3
1996	15	15
1997	4	4
1998	16	14
1999	33	30
2000	24	20
2001	13	5
2002	12	4
2003	11	9
2004	14	14
2005	2	0
2006	19	7
2007	11	1

Source: Japan Coast Guard, "Maritime Security Annual Report," 1998 through 2008 editions, available in Japanese at www.kaiho.mlit.go.jp/info/books/index.htm.

natural-resources surveys in the EEZ of another, it is required to secure prior consent of the EEZ state. Japan, which adheres to that position, has protested when Chinese ships appeared to be doing surveys in the area that it claimed for its EEZ. China has either ignored the protests, claimed that the ships were doing scientific research, or rejected Japan's EEZ claim. The number of cases involving Chinese research vessels peaked in 1999 at thirty-three and then dropped to the teens in the early 2000s. In 2004, when China failed to secure prior consent on any voyages, the two sides reached a bilateral agreement on prior notification, but it has not worked well, in part because of differences in interpretation (see table 6-1).[29]

Seventh is the question of what military activities are appropriate in a coastal state's EEZ. China believes that "military surveys, military maneuvers, and military reconnaissance are a form of battlefield preparation" and therefore inappropriate. Japan, the United States, and most countries argue that surveys and intelligence gathering are allowed.[30] In addition to EEZ regimes, with their contested norms, UNCLOS applies different rules to different kinds of maritime situations, as clarified in table 6-2.

Table 6-2. *Treatment of Various Bodies of Water by the UN Convention on the Law of the Sea*

Type of sea	Type of passage by foreign vessels	Specifics
Territorial Sea: the sea extending twelve miles from a state's coast, including that of offshore islands, unless the state chooses a limit of less than twelve miles.	*Innocent passage:* continuous and expeditious traversing though the coastal state's territorial sea, in a manner not prejudicial to the peace, good order, or security of the state.	Without the coastal state's permission, another may not collect intelligence, conduct research, or survey in the territorial sea. Submarines must navigate on the surface and show their flag.
International strait: a strait that connects the high seas or an EEZ with the high seas or another EEZ through a gap between two coastlines that is less that twenty-four miles in total (unless the state or states decide to create a high seas corridor through the strait).	*Transit passage:* continuous and expeditious passage in the normal mode of operation.	Submarines do not have to surface.
High seas: waters outside the twelve-mile limit of any coastal state, unless the coastal state reduces the limit.	*High seas freedoms:* no restrictions.	

Sources: Peter Dutton, "Scouting, Signaling, and Gatekeeping: Chinese Naval Operations in Japanese Waters and the International Law Implications," Chinese Maritime Studies Institute (U.S. Naval War College, February 2009); Euan Graham, *Japan's Sea Lane Security, 1940–2004* (New York: Routledge, 2006), pp. 241–43.

The Diaoyu/Senkaku Islands dispute is a case in which the law of territorial seas applies. The law governing innocent and transit passage is crucial to understanding the question of straits.

Senkaku/Diaoyu Islands

The Senkaku/Diaoyu are a group of islets that are located around 200 kilometers northeast of Taiwan, 300 kilometers west of Okinawa, and 300 kilometers west of the Chinese mainland. Geographically, they sit on the edge of the southern end of the Okinawa trough, on the China side. Japanese have harvested guano on the islands, and the highly valued blue fin tuna swims in the surrounding waters. The U.S. military used the islands as a firing range during its control of the Ryukyus from 1945 to 1972. Although they might support human habitation, they remain uninhabited.

The dispute over the Senkaku/Diaoyu is the only territorial dispute between Japan and China. Indeed, Taiwan also is involved, in that the governments in Beijing and Taipei both claim them for "China." None of the three governments took them seriously until 1968, when a UN survey indicated the promise of significant petroleum deposits in the area.[31] Which country "owns" the islands then became a matter of energy security for all concerned, even though there is little certainty that commercially viable oil fields exist. Who holds sovereignty over the islands for purposes of UNCLOS is also important, because it affects the size of Japan's exclusive economic zone.

China has two bases for its claim. One is the existence of references to the islands in writings and maps that date back to the fifteenth century, during the Ming dynasty. The other is the assertion that the islands were transferred to Japan under the 1895 Treaty of Shimonoseki, which concluded the Sino-Japanese War of 1894–1895, and that this "unequal" treaty and all its provisions became null and void with Japan's defeat in 1945. Chinese cite the Cairo Declaration of December 1943, in which Prime Minister Winston Churchill, President Franklin Roosevelt, and President Chiang Kai-shek announced that it was "their purpose that . . . all the territories Japan has stolen from the Chinese, such as Manchuria, Formosa, and the Pescadores, shall be restored to the Republic of China." In basing their claim on the Treaty of Shimonoseki, the Chinese ignore the fact that it does not mention the Diaoyu/Senkaku.

Japan bases its legal claim on several points. First, it says, the imperial government gained control of the islands along with the Ryukyus in 1879 and formally annexed them in 1895. Second, after World War II, the United States specifically included the Senkaku/Diaoyu in the territory covered by its trusteeship over the Ryukyu Islands. Third, Washington transferred administrative control over them to Japan pursuant to the Okinawa Reversion Treaty of 1971. But the United States takes no position on which state owns the Diaoyu/Senkaku, and the treaty does not speak to their legal status.[32] When Japan and China concluded a peace treaty in 1978, Deng Xiaoping declared that they should set aside the sovereignty issue concerning the islands and pursue joint development of energy resources.[33]

For decades, the Senkaku/Diaoyu were more a political irritant that a security concern. Self-styled patriots on each side of the issue would act to assert their country's claim, and the public in one or more capitals would get exercised. Groups from Hong Kong, China, and Taiwan repeatedly attempted to sail to the islands to plant the PRC or Republic of China flag. Japanese right-wing elements built lighthouses there in 1990 and 1996.[34] In order to preserve the two countries' shared interests, particularly in economic relations, Tokyo and Beijing did develop techniques for managing the matter. Indeed, as noted in chapter 3, a cyclical ritual emerged in which nationalists acted to assert their country's claim but diplomats worked in concert both to accommodate these shows of patriotism and to maintain basic control.[35]

Yet that history can be interpreted in more ominous tones. Political scientist Krista Wiegand demonstrates that China employed some level of coercive diplomacy in the series of episodes after 1978 in order to secure an advantage on other issues.[36] And as early as the mid-1990s, ritualized management gave way to something else. At that time, Chinese military ships and aircraft began operating near the islands, sometimes in a dangerous fashion.[37] In the summer of 2004, the Japanese Coast Guard (JCG) decided to deploy a larger patrol ship to the Senkaku/Diaoyu Islands in place of the smaller ships that had been operating there.[38] There were two likely reasons. One was continued landings by Chinese activists. After an episode in March 2004, the Security Committee of the Japanese Diet passed a resolution calling for greater coordination among government agencies "to have thorough countermeasures in place for vigilance and security of waters surrounding the islands so as not to invite a situation allowing further unlawful landings." The other reason was increased activity by Chinese research ships in the area, probably for mapping the ocean floor to facilitate the operations of PLAN submarines and antisubmarine warfare against the U.S. Navy.[39] Chinese observers soon expressed concern that Japan might establish military facilities on the islands. As one put it, "There are prospects of [the islands] becoming an important stronghold in Japan's strategy of 'annihilating the enemy [China] at sea,' greatly extending Japan's military defensive depth, and becoming a screen for preventing the Chinese Navy from entering the Pacific."[40]

Aside from occasional demonstrations by patriotic groups, the situation remained calm until early February 2007, when the JCG detected another Chinese research ship in the area and warned it to stop operations. The ship refused and the Japanese government protested, on the grounds that under UNCLOS, foreign survey or research activities and intelligence collection were not permitted in a country's territorial waters without its permission.[41]

The PRC government replied that notification was not necessary because the Diaoyu/Senkaku Islands were Chinese territory.

The pace picked up in 2008. In early June, the Japanese Diet enacted a law on foreign ship navigation in Japan's territorial waters. The act prohibited foreign vessels to remain in Japanese territorial waters without sufficient reason and authorized the Japan Coast Guard to do on-the-spot inspections of suspicious ships and issue expulsion orders in the event of illegal activity. The legislation strengthened Japan's heretofore weak authority for regulating the passage of foreign ships.[42] It applied mainly to the home islands but was relevant to the Senkaku/Diaoyu as well.

Almost immediately, there was a collision between a Taiwan sport fishing boat and a JCG ship. The incident was resolved diplomatically, with an apology from the captain of the Japanese vessel. But it revealed how easily potentially violent encounters could occur.

Then on December 8, 2008, the JCG spotted two ships of the Chinese Marine Surveillance Force (*haijian zongdui*), part of the PRC's State Oceanic Administration, in the Diaoyu/Senkaku area. They were relatively new and well equipped. One displaced 1,100 tons and the other 1,900. Based on a Chinese account of the episode, their operation was well planned. The ships left their ports (Shanghai and Ningbo) to rendezvous in the East China Sea. Receiving orders to proceed, they entered the twelve-mile limit of the Senkaku/Diaoyu Islands just at the time that JCG patrol craft were executing a shift change. After loitering at their initial stopping point for an hour, the Chinese vessels then proceeded to circle around the islands.[43]

To respond to challenges in the Diaoyu/Senkaku area, the Japan Coast Guard has created three zones. Within twelve nautical miles of the islands is an off-limits zone, from which it will expel foreign ships. Between twelve and twenty-four miles is a zone in which strict monitoring and control is conducted. The JCG identifies ships entering that zone and orders them to leave. Outside the twenty-four-mile limit the JCG monitors ships and may warn them to leave, depending on their place of origin. Reportedly, the JCG cooperates closely with the Maritime Self-Defense Force, as the Chinese Marine Surveillance Force does with the PLAN.[44]

According to a Chinese account, when the Chinese ships approached the Senkaku/Diaoyu Islands on December 8, a JCG patrol boat repeatedly ordered the Chinese ships to leave "Japan's territorial waters." The Chinese captains ignored the orders, whereupon the Japanese ship threatened to "squeeze out" and "crash" the intruders. It also sought to block their route. Soon, because of the "pressures" from the Chinese ships, the JCG boat backed off in order to avoid a clash. Nine hours after the Chinese ships arrived, they departed.[45]

The Japanese government filed a protest, and the Chinese Foreign Ministry responded as it had in 2004, stating that the area was Chinese territory. The incident had diplomatic implications, for Japan's prime minister, Taro Aso, was about to meet President Hu Jintao of China. Aso felt domestic political pressure to raise the issue, and the discussion reportedly was "heated."[46]

The incident had several consequences. Internet commentators in China swelled with pride. They called the ships "twin heroes" and the operation "a landmark achievement of China's safeguarding of maritime sovereignty." The Marine Surveillance Force announced plans to step up marine survey activities in the future. Deputy director Sun Shuxian declared that "in sea areas where there is a territorial dispute under international law, it is important to display presence in the sea area under jurisdiction and continue accumulating records of effective control." His remarks were a reference to the practice of reinforcing claims through state action: the more China maintains a presence in what Japan claims as its territorial waters, the stronger is China's claim to the Diaoyu/Senkaku Islands.

Other Chinese argued for increasing the MSF's capability because it was "inadequate to compete with quasi-maritime military forces of the Japan Coast Guard. . . . In the event of confrontation or armed conflict on the sea, China will likely be in a passive position."[47] An air force colonel argued in favor of displaying naval assets, particularly in China's territorial waters. "'Showing our might' in and above our territorial waters, like the tank groups charging in land exercises, may more effectively release messages of deterrence to those who are coveting China's maritime territory." A professor of strategic studies linked the Senkaku/Diaoyu issue to Taiwan: the crux of the Taiwan issue is Diaoyu Island, and the Diaoyu Island issue is a Japan issue. Therefore, grasping the "weakest link," Diaoyu Island, will solve half of the Taiwan issue, and solving the Taiwan issue will settle all sea issues of China.[48] A military scholar proposed a more cautious approach: Japan had strengthened its position in the Senkakus because a decline in U.S. power had provided the opportunity "to thoroughly occupy the . . . islands." China, he said, should focus on preparing for a "trial of strength" with the United States, not engaging in displays of force over small islands.[49] A civilian scholar took yet another view. It was premature for China to challenge the U.S. maritime hegemony, but it was imperative to "develop its sea power forces to safeguard its sovereignty."[50]

For its part, Japan enhanced its security operations. After the incident it increased the number of daily patrols from two to three and also increased flights by fixed-wing aircraft. Then in February 2009, it dropped back to two a day but deployed a bigger vessel equipped with helicopters that could monitor the area several times a day. The MSDF continued its regular surveillance flights, eliciting a stiff protest from China: Japan's actions to strengthen its control were "illegal and invalid and should be stopped immediately."[51]

The Japanese government considered but did not approve the JCG's proposal that in response to increasing Chinese and Taiwan incursions, it be given the power to arrest offending ships if warnings and inspections were of no avail. Even so, the JCG claimed that the enhanced enforcement was having a "deterrent effect."[52] Nonetheless, the face-offs continued: the Japanese press reported that one took place in August, and a source at the JCG headquarters said that "this type of occurrence has now become an everyday event." And the December 2008 episode happened after Hatoyama Yukio, the prime minister in the new Democratic Party of Japan government, declared that the East China Sea should be a "sea of fraternity."[53]

Several points about the December 2008 encounter are noteworthy. First, there is something of a capability race occurring with respect to the Senkaku/Diaoyu Islands. Each country's maritime surveillance authorities are gradually beefing up the ships that they deploy to the area. Second, although higher-level commanders were conducting the operation, the captain of each ship appeared to have a certain amount of discretion in handling the situation as it developed. The Japanese vessel acted rather aggressively until it met "pressure" from the Chinese side. Third, whatever the economic potential of the area, the contested facts of history—who used to own the islands and who had the right to transfer it under international law—have been key factors shaping behavior, along with the perceived imperative to protect national honor. Fourth, domestic politics was at play, limiting the actions of decisionmakers.

Finally, whether China or Japan is correct regarding sovereignty and whether PRC ships have a right to be in the area, the danger of some sort of clash remains. In 2009, a Japanese think tank warned that further expansion of PLA maritime activities in the East China Sea could escalate tensions with Japan into military clashes.[54] Escalation into a serious conflict could involve the United States by virtue of its mutual defense treaty with Japan, which Washington has indicated implicitly applies to the Diaoyu/Senkakus Islands.[55]

Oil and Gas Fields in the East China Sea

China and Japan both share an interest in energy security. As discussed above, however, they disagree on a number of points pertinent to the exploitation of oil and gas reserves in the East China Sea. For example, Japan wishes to push its EEZ as far to the west as possible and so insists that the Senkaku/ Diaoyu Islands are its sovereign territory. China claims an EEZ that reaches the Okinawa trough. The claims of each undercut those of the other. But more strategic issues also are in play. China likely wishes to preserve the largest possible operating area for its navy in case of a conflict.[56] Japan is concerned about the security of sea lanes of communication.

Their disputes retained an academic character through the late 1990s, as Chinese and various foreign oil companies pursued ways to cooperate on a commercial basis to exploit ocean floor resources. Reinhard Drifte makes the case that Japan was relatively restrained in asserting any legal rights in the East China Sea until 2003, when Chinese exploration set off alarms in Tokyo that Japan's energy interests were threatened.[57] Thus the matter became a foreign policy issue; by the middle of 2005, as detailed below, a military dimension had emerged as well.

It is the military dimension that is of concern. That is, as Chinese and Japanese military forces operate closer to each other to protect their nations' conflicting economic interests, the possibility of some sort of accidental clash increases. Observers have warned of the danger of such an occurrence if the dispute is allowed to fester. Li Ming of Peking University's School of Law warns that if the two countries "continue quarreling over the law, . . . it is very possible that bilateral relations will be harmed, even to the point of inadvertent hostilities being set off at sea and having clashes resulting from jurisdictional disputes."[58] Drifte predicts that "with China's increasing military power and willingness to protect its growing military and economic stakes in the East China Sea, the absence of an agreed maritime border could conceivably lead to a military conflict."[59]

The focus of the dispute is the Chunxiao oil and gas field, east and south of Shanghai. Japan believes that the field extends across its median line and that a Chinese "straw" would sip from its part of the pool. Japanese companies probably did not intend to transfer East China Sea energy resources back to Japan, which would have been an expensive venture, but they did wish to benefit financially if oil and gas was used in East China, which is much closer. (Chinese companies were also extracting natural gas from the Pinghu field west of Chunxiao and transmitting it through a pipeline to east coast cities like Shanghai, Hangzhou, and Ningbo.)[60]

It was in mid-2004, as bilateral relations were generally deteriorating over Koizumi Junichiro's visits to the Yasukuni, that the dispute over exploration and drilling for gas in the East China Sea surfaced. In late May, the Japanese press revealed that Chinese energy companies had begun building an exploration rig in the Chunxiao gas field. The Japanese government, facing pressure from members of the Diet and the press, sought to manage the issue through diplomatic means, but to no avail. Its ploy, which China rejected, was to request data on the exploration on the grounds that future Chinese drilling might draw gas from the Japanese side of the line. Beijing proposed joint exploitation of the gas fields, but Tokyo spurned the offer out of concern over its sovereignty claims. In July, Japanese companies began exploring the Japanese-claimed side of the median line. In October, working-level talks were held, but they made no progress on the issues in dispute. There were also rumors that the Chinese government had granted its companies exploration rights on the Japanese side of the median line, which Tokyo regarded as an escalation.[61]

On New Year's Day 2005, a Japanese newspaper reported that Chinese exploration was occurring on the Japanese side of its claimed demarcation line, and the government subsequently confirmed the report. Tokyo then demanded that Beijing cease the exploration and provide data on the activities, and China refused. On March 2, the opposition Democratic Party of Japan (DPJ) introduced legislation on exploration in the East China Sea calling for the Japanese Coast Guard to support Japanese companies in the area.[62] At the end of March, the China National Offshore Oil Company announced that production at the Chunxiao field would begin in five to six months. In mid-April, the Japanese government announced that it would begin accepting exploration applications from Japanese companies, a move that Beijing said was a "serious provocation." Working-level talks were held in May, and each side offered a proposal for joint development that the other quickly rejected. Even before the talks, Nakagawa Shoichi, the Japanese minister of economics, trade, and industry (METI)—a conservative even by Liberal Democratic Party standards (LDP)—spoke of Tokyo's weak negotiating position by comparing China's simultaneously exploring and drilling to a person's "shaking hands with someone with the right hand and striking with the left."[63]

Despite Japan's perceived disadvantage and the broader negative context, until mid-2005 the East China Sea was still only a diplomatic issue. That was about to change. As the Japanese government approved its first exploration licenses, to vociferous Chinese protests; as the two sides rejected each other's negotiating proposals; and as evidence mounted that Chinese production would soon begin at Chunxiao and had already begun at the Tianwai field further west, a military dimension emerged for the first time.[64] On September 9, right before parliamentary elections in Japan, five PLAN vessels were seen patrolling on the Chinese side of Japan's median line. Reportedly, gunners on one of them "locked on" to an antisubmarine patrol aircraft of the MSDF, a threatening gesture. After the Teikoku Oil Company completed the exploration license registration process in August, its president sought a commitment that the government would protect his workers if they were bothered by China. The METI minister pledged on September 21 that "Japan will do its duty."[65] In November, the LDP's special committee on maritime interests proposed legislation to protect exploration in Japan's EEZ. A key element of the plan was to establish a 500-meter zone around exploration platforms and forbid entry by unauthorized ships into safety zones. Clearly, some enforcement mechanism was contemplated. The LDP adopted the recommendations in December, and the Diet approved a version in March 2006.[66]

In the field, the military dimension took on greater salience as well. Even when Chinese entities were in the prospecting stage at Chunxiao, SDF planes and warships monitored their activities. After drilling began, small Japanese planes flew over the rigs, taking pictures.[67] The number of times that planes of the Japanese Air Self-Defense Force scrambled to address possible violations of territorial airspace jumped from 141 in fiscal year 2004 (which ended in March 2005) to 229 in fiscal year 2005. As *Defense of Japan 2006* explained, "The increase was mainly attributed to more scrambles against Chinese jet fighters."[68] Recall that the boundaries of Japan's air defense identification zone are the same as that of its EEZ.

In March 2006, the same month that the Diet passed its EEZ exploration legislation, the head of the China State Oceanic Administration, Sun Zhihui, held forth on Beijing's determination to safeguard its sovereignty over its claimed sea territory. He cited with approval South Korea's hardline approach toward its island dispute with Japan ("No compromise or surrender is possible"). Although Sun acknowledged the competing priority of development, he warned that if it were absolutely necessary, "China is determined to confront Japan."[69] In the same month, a Japanese Diet member who specialized in defense matters worried that "the government has made no decision on how to utilize the Self-Defense Forces in the event a military clash should take place around the gas fields in the Japanese EEZ."[70] Sometime during the desultory search to find a mutually acceptable solution through negotiations, Japan indicated that because of the lack of progress, it might start exploratory drilling. The Chinese reportedly replied, "In that case there will be a war; we will dispatch our warships."[71]

At some point in the first half of 2006, the military encounters declined. For example, although the number of ASDF scrambles was 239 in fiscal year

2006 (which ended in March 2007) and 307 in fiscal year 2007, they were increasingly directed more at Russian aircraft than Chinese.[72] Apparently, leaders on both sides had decided that a cooling-off period was necessary, and they redoubled their efforts to reach an agreement on the issue.[73] In mid-2006, during diplomatic negotiations on the dispute, Japan proposed and China accepted that a mechanism be established between the "relevant authorities" to address East China Sea contingencies. In 2007, it was agreed that the Japan Coast Guard and the Chinese State Oceanic Administration (the agency to which the Marine Surveillance Force reports) would meet. They did so, in July, but the talks stalled and did nothing to clarify the maritime "rules of the road."[74] Simultaneously, press reports in early 2007 that production had begun in the Chunxiao field reinforced Japan's anxiety that it was about to face a fait accompli.[75] In April, the Japanese Diet passed a law on ocean affairs that could be interpreted as authorizing the protection of Japanese exploration facilities.[76]

The key issue in the negotiations was the location and terms of "joint development." Japan succeeded in rebuffing Chinese demands that the Senkaku/Diaoyu Islands be included, in line with Tokyo's long-standing position that sovereignty over the islands had to be determined before economic cooperation was addressed. The negotiations tried to maximize the number of other areas where Japan and China would work together; in the end, however, the agreement reached in June 2008 was something of a disappointment to Tokyo. China held firm to the position that in Chunxiao—the trigger for the dispute—cooperation would not involve "joint development": "Chinese enterprises welcome the participation of Japanese legal persons [private Japanese companies as well as government-backed corporations] in the development of the existing oil and gas field in Chunxiao in accordance with the relevant laws of China governing cooperation with foreign enterprises" in exploiting offshore resources.[77] Thus, it was a commercial venture like many others China had undertaken. The agreement did identify a block for true joint development in the vicinity of the Longjing field, which straddles Japan's median line, but "whether the project would ever materialize was subject to further negotiation."[78]

The agreement was subject to domestic criticism as soon as it was released. Demonstrations broke out in Chinese cities and "netizens" charged that Beijing had made damaging concessions. Vice-Minister of Foreign Affairs Wu Dawei felt compelled to publicly defend the agreement, and mainline commentators responded to Internet criticism by arguing that China had in no way made any sacrifices.[79] The Japanese media and conservative elements worried about a sell-out. As one put it, "Such a consensus fully embodies China's sovereignty over Chunxiao oil and gas field, as well as Japan's recognition of such an objective fact."[80] In contrast, a Japanese conservative think tank claimed that "nothing has been settled and nothing has been resolved" through the agreement.[81]

The fears of the skeptical Japanese were justified. After a few months, there had been no progress on the follow-up agreements. Chinese officials told their Japanese counterparts that "the implementation of the agreement requires public understanding and support."[82] There was initial public criticism of the deal as "the public reacted fiercely to the announcement . . . and many commentators criticized Beijing for selling out on the issue of sovereignty."[83] But the more enduring opposition was commercial. The Chinese wished to limit the Japanese share of benefits from the Chunxiao field to less than one-third, and they were retreating from the 50-50 split originally envisaged for Longjing. In January 2009, there were reports that Chinese companies had begun drilling in the Tianwai field, which Japan had originally tried to include in the scope of the June 2008 agreement. China asserted that it had every right to exploit those resources independently.

Once the DPJ government of Hatoyama Yukio took office in September 2009, the outlook for Japan-China relations was generally positive, and Japanese officials encouraged China's leaders to accelerate negotiations on implementation. But Beijing replied that Japan should "create an environment to realize last year's agreement" and that discussions should take place at the working level.[84] Three months later, there were reports based on observations by MSDF patrol craft that construction of the natural gas facility in the Chunxiao area had been completed. No progress had occurred on the issue of the "the participation of Japanese legal persons" in the development of the field, as promised in the June 2008 agreement. Foreign Minister Okada Katsuya of Japan had what was termed a "heated exchange" with his Chinese counterpart, Yang Jiechi, in mid-January 2010. Okada reportedly told Yang that "if there is something that would go against the agreement, the Japanese side is ready to take certain action." Yang rejected Okada's warning and reiterated his "create an environment" remark. In response, both the opposition and ruling parties in Japan favored a tough response.[85]

The result is that the dispute is likely to fester at some level. Prospects for a general agreement on the delineation of the continental shelf and the countries' respective EEZs seem remote, in part because the PLA probably wishes to retain the largest freedom of action for the navy. Both countries are concerned about their energy security. Japan also has an abiding interest in freedom of navigation through the sea lanes of East Asia. Strategically, Chinese see the East China Sea as an arena where "the two countries' maritime strategic interests intertwine and clash"; as China's "natural protective screen"; and as the road by which it "realizes its 'going out' economic strategy" and by which it "becomes a maritime great power." Tactically, China may have an interest in *not* solving the East China Sea or Senkaku issues because they provide leverage for other purposes. So there remains some possibility of some sort of clash between the forces of the two sides.[86]

Straits

In the geography of East Asia, straits are strategically important. During the cold war, the easiest way for the Soviet navy to reach the open Pacific was to go through sea passages between the Japanese home islands. And in the 1980s, the MSDF was tasked with closing these gateways in case of a crisis and bottling up the Soviets in its inland sea. Similarly, Japanese straits today are the maritime defiles through which PLAN ships are most likely to move if they seek to go to the open waters of the Pacific. They also represent other points at which the navies of the two countries could come in close proximity and clash.

All coastal states have the right to establish territorial seas with a boundary no more than twelve miles from the coastal baseline. Within a territorial sea, the vessels of seagoing states are allowed only "innocent passage." For example, the ships of another state may not collect intelligence or conduct research or surveys without the coastal state's permission, and submarines must navigate on the surface and show their flag. Straits that are more than twenty-four miles wide include a median strip that is defined as part of the high seas and that is not subject to any restrictions.

Special rules apply for a multi-island state like Japan. It has straits between its islands, and those straits connect either the high seas or exclusive economic zones. When straits are less than twenty-four miles wide, the twelve-mile territorial limit from each side eliminates any space left for the high seas. In such cases, the coastal state has two options:

—It may choose to reduce the breadth of the twelve-mile limit in order to preserve a "high-seas corridor." In fact, Japan chose to reduce the extent of its territorial waters in five straits: the Tsugaru Strait, between the islands of Hokkaido and Honshu; the Tsushima Strait, between Kyushu and the Korean peninsula; the Osumi Strait, between Kyushu and smaller off-shore islands; and the Soya Strait, between Hokkaido and Russia's Sakhalin Island.[87] The reason for its decision was unknown until late 2009, after the Democratic

Party of Japan won the lower house election over the Liberal Democratic Party, which had ruled Japan for more than fifty years. DPJ officials revealed that Japan had taken this unusual step for the convenience of U.S. Navy vessels carrying nuclear weapons that used those straits.[88]

—The coastal state or states may deem the area an international strait. In that case, transiting vessels must conduct continuous and expeditious passage in the normal mode of operation. Submarines do not have to surface ("transit passage").

Concerning transit passage, Japan went one step further and imposed greater limitations. Specifically, it restricted the right of transit passage to those straits that are used for international navigation as a matter of routine or out of necessity. Consequently, they are subject to the stricter, innocent-passage rules.[89] China takes exactly the same position; the United States does not.

The international law concerning straits has come into play in several ways between China and Japan. The previous chapter noted the intense Japanese media attention provoked by a small flotilla of PLAN ships that passed through the Tsugaru Strait. Yet that transit was entirely legal, because the ships threaded the needle of the high-seas corridor that Tokyo had designated.[90]

More serious was the passage of a PLAN Han class submarine through the Ishigaki Strait on November 10, 2004. The Ishigaki Strait is between Ishigaki and Miyako islands, which are at the end of the Sakishima island chain. The MSDF had known about the sub and was passively monitoring it. Then the PLAN sub moved into Japan's territorial waters, and the MSDF elements moved to active sonar, which is usually regarded as a warning among submarine crews. But the Chinese vessel ignored the warning and moved through the Ishigaki Strait. The MSDF was put on a much higher alert and over the two-day period conducted even more intensive monitoring using P-3C patrol planes, airborne early warning planes, and antisubmarine warfare destroyers equipped with helicopters.[91]

Peter Dutton has explored the motives of the Chinese submarine in going through the Ishigaki Strait. Was it to map the ocean floor for future use—for example, in an operation against Taiwan and any U.S. forces that came to its defense? Was it to test Japan's antisubmarine warfare capabilities? Was it to demonstrate its sea power in an area that China had determined that it had a strategic interest? Or was it simply a mistake?

Dutton argues that the first three explanations are implausible because they undercut China's own legal position. To map the ocean floor in Japan's territorial waters was inconsistent with Beijing's opposition to U.S. naval mapping outside of China's territorial sea but within its exclusive economic zone. To transit a strait that Japan claimed was barred from international navigation because it was not usually or necessarily used weakened China's advocacy of using the same criteria in deciding navigation rights. Any knowledge gained about the MSDF's antisubmarine warfare skills did not outweigh the harm done to China's legal position. Dutton also rejects the "mistake" hypothesis because the configuration of the sea floor underneath the strait makes it very unlikely that the PLAN submarine captain would be confused about his location.[92]

In the end, China chose to shelve the incident and its implications for Beijing's legal position. After a few days, the Foreign Ministry issued an apology. As far as is publicly known, there have been no similar incidents involving transit of the Ishigaki Strait. In this case, the Chinese submarine went through the strait beneath the surface of the water when Japan had defined that body of water as one where innocent passage but not transit passage was allowed. Based on that view, the PLAN sub should have made its transit above water. The episode demonstrates the potential that each side has for conducting operations in a way that the other finds challenging.

Taiwan

The Taiwan Strait issue is not like the issues related to the Diaoyu/Senkaku Islands, rights to the continental shelf, and transit of straits, in which the danger is that Chinese and Japanese military units might clash by accident or as the result of mutual testing. The Taiwan point of friction is more complicated—a two-step danger. First, China and Taiwan would descend into conflict because of miscalculation, severely damaging the economic interdependence on which all East Asian countries depend. Second, assuming that Taiwan did not unnecessarily provoke the conflict, it is likely that the United States would come to Taiwan's defense and expect Tokyo to provide assistance and staging areas.

There is no question that Japan and China regard Taiwan as a strategic piece of territory. For China it is also symbolically important. Two PLA strategists wrote this about Taiwan:

> Taiwan is located in the southeast of our sea area and is in the middle of the islands surrounding our coastline. It is in the key area of sea routes of the Pacific Ocean, and is thus crowned as "the key to the southeast coastal area of China" and "the fence to the seven provinces in the

center of China." The sea routes from the East China Sea to the South China Sea, from Northeast Asia to Southeast Asia, as well as the route from the West Pacific to the Middle East, Europe, and Asia pass here. It is where we can breach the chain of islands surrounding us in the West Pacific to the vast area of the Pacific, as well as a strategic key area and sea barrier for defense and offense. If Taiwan should be alienated from the mainland, not only our natural maritime defense system would lose its depth, opening a sea gateway to outside forces, but also a large area of water territory would fall into the hands of others. What's more, our line of foreign trade and transportation which is vital to China's opening up and economic development will be exposed to the surveillance and threats of separatists and enemy forces, and China will forever be locked to the west side of the first chain of islands in the West Pacific.[93]

Military analyst Shigeo Hiramatsu provides a Japanese view of Taiwan's strategic importance:

Taiwan serves as a critical component of Japan's sea-lane. If Taiwan were integrated into China, the South China Sea would become China's sea, bringing the sea lane to the Middle East and Southeast Asian countries under strong Chinese influence. China would have more say over Japan's Nansei Islands and the East China Sea. If the East China Sea were brought under Chinese influence, the Yellow Sea would lose access to high seas and become China's inland sea, while the Korean Peninsula will fall under the sphere of Chinese influence. Moreover, China will probably use Taiwan as a stepping-stone and make its way into the Pacific. . . . Taiwan is Japan's "lifeline."[94]

Although the Taiwan Strait issue became the basis for Japan's and China's mutual mistrust (see chapter 4), the issue nevertheless receded in importance after Ma Ying-jeou won the presidency of Taiwan in March 2008 and his party, the Kuomintang (KMT), expanded its control of the legislature. Ma believed that the best way to guarantee Taiwan's prosperity, security, and dignity was to reassure, not provoke, China. As he has put that approach into practice, the mutual fear that marked cross-Strait relations since the mid-1990s diminished. The danger that the two sides might slip into conflict through accident or miscalculation, which had led the United States to intervene more in the dispute, receded. Japan's concern that a Taiwan-China war might require it to provide rear-area support to U.S. armed forces, making

U.S. bases on the home islands and Okinawa targets for Chinese missiles, also declined.

The results of the interaction between the two sides since Ma's inauguration have been generally positive, yet it remains to be seen how long progress can be sustained. Broadened economic cooperation was intended to benefit the Taiwan economy, but the steps were taken in the context of global economic crisis. China may be unwilling to permit the broader international participation that the public in Taiwan desires. Also at question is China's military buildup, which has continued unabated, despite the fact that the political rationale for the buildup currently does not pertain. More generally, Beijing also appears to suffer from a hangover of mistrust. On international space, it fears that if it makes concessions to a KMT administration (allowing Taiwan observership in the WHO, for example), a Democratic Progressive Party administration will later come to power and use that status as a stepping stone to WHO membership. Similarly, on security, the PLA seems to think that Taiwan independence remains a serious threat and that, as a senior officer put it, "the mission of opposing and curbing secessionist activities remains strenuous."[95]

Japan has had an ambivalent reaction to the relaxation of tensions that has occurred since Ma Ying-jeou took power. As noted, the danger of accidental conflict and all that might follow is much lower. On the other hand, there is a concern that if progress accelerates, Beijing and Taipei will go beyond a mere stabilization of cross-Strait relations and solve the fundamental dispute between them. If either conflict or negotiations lead to Taiwan's incorporation into China, it is believed, Japan's interests would be harmed. Recall the warning by Furusho Koichi, former chief of the Japan Maritime Self-Defense Force, first cited in chapter 4: "If you assume that conditions are balanced now, they would collapse as soon as Taiwan unifies with China. The sea lanes would turn all red."[96]

So far, three significant realities have been identified. The first, discussed in chapters 3 and 4, is the strategic environment. China and Japan cooperate extensively in the economic arena and benefit from that relationship. But the two have been party to specific disputes—such as those over Taiwan and the East China Sea—giving each reasons to mistrust the other's future intentions.

Second, as described in chapter 5, Japan has significant military power, and China's is growing steadily. Both the Self-Defense Forces and the People's Liberation Army have developed their air and naval capabilities. Chinese and

Japanese naval vessels and aircraft are operating closer and closer to each other in geographic space that each regards as strategically significant.

Third, as explained in this chapter, several points of friction serve as a magnet for those military forces: a territorial dispute, disagreement over access to oil and gas resources in the East China Sea, the rules governing maritime transit, and the Taiwan Strait issue. In the first three of these matters, experts in international law play as important a role as sailors and airmen. China especially understands the value of "legal warfare" and seeks through its operations to assert its maritime claims and change the underlying legal framework.[97]

So there is some finite danger that strategic mistrust, military operations, and points of friction might lead to a clash. Any clash is unlikely to be intentional; some degree of accident or miscalculation would be at play. The obvious question is whether the chance of a clash is really high enough to warrant attention. Even if it occurred, one might assume that the two governments would find ways to manage and mitigate any hostile encounter, particularly at a time that the two countries have improved their political relations and share the benefits of economic interdependence. To answer that question, other factors that would come into play must be examined. Broadly speaking, those factors relate to institutions, both military and civilian. They may operate together to mitigate and negate the consequences of a clash, reducing the chances of serious escalation—or they could magnify the effects of a clash. To telegraph my conclusion: the exacerbating elements, taken together, would make it difficult if not impossible to keep a clash from becoming a serious conflict. And as I have noted before, even if the chances of a clash are modest, the consequences would be significant.

7

Features of China's and
Japan's Military Institutions

The armed forces of both Japan and China are significant in their own way, and they have strategic reasons for increasingly operating in the same geographic space. How they interact in that space is shaped by several features of the two countries' defense institutions, including civil-military relations, command and control, and strategic culture. On balance, those institutional factors make a clash more likely to occur than not and they are likely to exacerbate any clash that does occur.

Civil-Military Relations

Civil-military relations concern the extent to which civilian leaders restrict the actions of their armed forces, for whatever reason. Scholars have differentiated several types. The first is the liberal–Whig type, with its bias toward a small military establishment, strong civilian control, and the inculcation of civilian values in the officer corps.[1] Second is the professional type, associated with the late Harvard political scientist Samuel Huntington, wherein there is a division of labor and authority. Civilians make the decisions on the use of force while officers have the autonomy to execute those decisions to the best of their ability. Schooled in professional values, officers stay out of politics.[2] The third type is praetorianism, wherein a relatively developed military often intervenes and rules because civilian institutions are incapable of providing order, stability, sound governance, and development.[3] The fourth is the Leninist type, in which the military is institutionally subordinate to a hegemonic party. The party uses a variety of mechanisms to co-opt the army to ensure that it does not challenge the political leadership or act independently of it. For example, senior officers are given positions in civilian bodies and vice versa, and a political commissariat inculcates values of loyalty to the party. Still, the Leninist military may legitimately assert itself with respect to its functional responsibilities, because modern warfare requires special skills and fosters particular perspectives on strategy and operations.[4]

China

Civil-military relations in China follow the Leninist model. The General Political Department of the People's Liberation Army works to promote officers' loyalty to the leadership of the party. Senior figures in the military hierarchy have positions in the two civilian hierarchies—the Chinese Communist Party and the government. For example, the top two generals of the PLA are members of the party's Political Bureau (Politburo), the regime's most authoritative decisionmaking body; another serves as minister of national defense in the government. The reverse also is true. The CCP general secretary, a civilian, serves as chairman of the party's Central Military Commission (CMC), which is made up of the PLA's senior commanders and acts as its command headquarters; a civilian sometimes serves as a vice chairman of the CMC.[5]

Over the last three decades and particularly since the mid-1990s, several interrelated trends have fostered an evolution in China's civil-military relations.[6] First, although the military and civilian hierarchies continue to be integrated at the top of the system, there is increasing separation further down. The military no longer is involved in governance at the provincial and lower levels, as it once was. Even at the top, the integration is not as complete as it might appear, a point to which I will return.

Second, the PLA has steadily modernized, in terms of both its hardware (equipment) and software (personnel, training, logistics, command and control, and so on). The discussion of China's naval and air forces in chapter 5 illustrates how the PLA has improved its capabilities.

Third, with modernization and depoliticization has come a second wave of military professionalism (the first wave came in the 1950s), one that emphasizes technical expertise and specialized military knowledge and the inculcation in the PLA of a sense of special responsibility for China's security.[7] The political commissar system, through which the party traditionally sought to ensure loyalty by promoting political ideology, has declined in influence.

Fourth, as a result, the PLA's current role in domestic politics is probably at its lowest level since the founding of the People's Republic of China in 1949. The PLA probably has an indirect impact on the selection of senior leaders, but it certainly is not a kingmaker.[8] Although the PLA serves as the second line of defense in the event of civil unrest, backing up the regular police and the armed police, the Tiananmen Square incident was the last time that it took the lead in quelling an uprising and restoring order, and it did so reluctantly. That reluctance led to an emphasis in military propaganda on the need for the PLA to show "absolute loyalty" to the party. That this drumbeat has continued two decades after Tiananmen has surprised some observers.[9]

Fifth, when it comes to policy issues (as opposed to domestic political competition), the PLA has the right to express its views on matters that concern its institutional interests: military budgets and how best to preserve and promote China's national security.

China scholars have debated how much these trends have changed civil-military relations. David Shambaugh goes furthest, arguing that professionalization of the armed forces has fostered a transition away from party-military relations toward civil-military relations.[10] Others would concur that the PLA is more professional and has become an interest group within the PRC system, yet they emphasize that it is the party to which the military remains loyal. Andrew Scobell argues that the PLA has become a party-state military but that civilian control of the military is weak.[11] James Mulvenon argues that the PLA is still a party army, and he endorses Ellis Joffe's concept of "conditional compliance." That is, the PLA supports the paramount leader and the Chinese Communist Party with all the power at its disposal and it stays out of nonmilitary policy areas, focusing on professional development. In return, it has "virtual autonomy" on issues of military modernization and defense planning, and it seeks to influence policymaking on issues of foreign and security policy, such as PRC relations with the United States, Russia, Japan, and South Asia and the Taiwan Strait issue.[12] More recently, Mulvenon has argued that the PLA is "straining against the yoke" of traditional party control because officers require greater autonomy to exercise their expanding capabilities.

I tend to side more with Mulvenon: the PLA protects the regime, it is increasingly professionalized, it offers selective policy input, and it has significant operational autonomy. By all accounts, the PLA remains highly loyal to the communist system and its leaders. Fostering that loyalty is one way to resolve the dilemma of civil-military relations and ensure military compliance.[13] Yet as Mulvenon suggests, compliance is only contingent. The other ways of ensuring civilian control are less than meets the eye, leaving the PLA with significant authority and autonomy when it comes to the best way to protect the system that it has sworn to defend.

ASSESSING CIVILIAN CONTROL.   The degree of civilian control in China's conditional-compliance system may be evaluated on four dimensions.

First is how much actual integration of civilians and officers occurs in the PRC's senior decisionmaking bodies. What is striking, in fact, is the degree of institutional segmentation of the two hierarchies, even at the center. Military and civilian leaders may have posts in each other's hierarchies, but the overlap is limited and asymmetric. Thus there is at least one civilian member of the CMC (the chairman), but he is surrounded by ten generals.[14] The PLA's two most senior generals are on the Politburo, but they are outnumbered by twenty-plus civilians. Moreover, the Politburo does not meet frequently (once a month, reportedly), and with respect to foreign policy and national defense, it tends to ratify the decisions of its Standing Committee, which is composed of its nine highest-ranking members, who are all civilians.

Moreover, the number of other points at which the military participates in civilian decisionmaking institutions is declining. For some years before the CCP's Fifteenth Party Congress, in November 1997, there had been one senior PLA leader on the Politburo Standing Committee (PBSC); since then, there have been none. From 1997 to 2007, a senior military officer was a member of the CCP Secretariat, but none was appointed at the Seventeenth Party Congress in October 2007.[15] Conversely, China lacks a civilian "cell" within its defense establishment analogous to the Office of the Secretary of Defense in the United States or the Internal Bureau in Japan's Ministry of Defense.

Leading groups are important mechanisms for coordinating policy. It is true that the minister of national defense is a member of the Foreign Affairs Leading Group (FALG) and National Security Leading Group (NSLG) and that a deputy chief of staff of the PLA serves on the FALG, NSLG, and Taiwan Work Leading Group (TWLG). But the minister is not the most significant figure in the senior military leadership, and the level of military representation on the TWLG may have been reduced by one level, from a deputy chief of staff to head of the General Staff Department's Second Department. Moreover, by virtue of their membership alone, leading groups appear to be bastions of civilian influence. Michael Swaine may be correct that the military representation on the FALG is to "ensure information sharing and coordination on routine policy issues, rather than critical foreign policy decisions."[16]

Nan Li of the U.S. Naval War College concludes that "while clearer institutional boundaries [between the two hierarchies] may have contributed significantly to cohesion and professionalization of the PLA, increased civil-military bifurcation has also led to pronounced tensions in interagency coordination for crisis management."[17] As a result, the PLA will be tempted to—or believe that it has no choice but to—argue its case directly to the paramount leader in his capacity as CMC chairman. Qi Zhou observes that although the military is represented on the Politburo and leading groups, "when the military reports on intelligence analysis or provides policy recommendations, there is only one channel through which the military can reach the Standing Committee of the Politburo, that is, the CMC. The CMC unifies the voice of the military before it reports to the Politburo."[18]

At a more operational level, it appears that some communications mechanisms tie the two hierarchies together. Reportedly, the general office of the CCP Central Committee has "strong links" to the command-and-control structure of the military. Links also exist between the Foreign Affairs Office, which staffs the FALG, and the military.[19] Still, civilian dominance through top-level integration seems less impressive than at first glance. It is legitimate to ask, as Scobell does, what exactly civilian control of the military means in such a segmented system.[20]

There also is the problem that by the very nature of their tasks, segmented institutions overlap. Foreign affairs has a security dimension and sometimes has a Taiwan dimension. Taiwan has a foreign affairs dimension and a security dimension. National security is inextricably linked to at least some aspects of the conduct of foreign policy and Taiwan policy. To be sure, some of the same agencies are represented on the FALG and TWLG: the Ministry of Foreign Affairs, the Ministry of State Security, and the PLA. But the staffing is done by different organizations, and the key policy gatekeepers are different individuals. It is only in the role of paramount leader as currently defined that the system achieves integration between civilian and military hierarchies.[21]

The second dimension on which the degree of civilian control can be evaluated is the extent to which civilians actually participate in the formulation of defense policy. For example, the civilian leadership might try to control the military through the drafting of the guiding documents that amount to China's national security strategy. China does not have a document by that name, but it does have the functional equivalent. Each time there is a major shift in national military strategy (and there have been only five in the history of the PRC), the "military strategic guidelines" will be revised to address several key "strategic issues": strategic assessment and adjustment of the active defense strategy; articulation of the PLA's strategic missions and strategic objectives; issuance of instructions for military combat preparations; identification of the main strategic direction; and determination of the focus of army building.[22]

The last time that a shift in the military strategic guidelines occurred was in 1993, in response to the fall of the Soviet Union and the stunning, high-tech U.S. victory in the Persian Gulf War. Jiang Zemin, then chairman of the CMC, announced the policy and programmatic change at an enlarged meeting of the CMC in January 1993. The PLA was directed to undertake a change in force structure, institutions, and doctrine to give it the ability to fight and win "local wars under modern high-tech conditions." Thereafter policy documents were drafted that elaborated on the implementation of that objective. The progress that has occurred in force structure, institutions, and doctrine since 1993 is probably due in no small measure to the supervision of the PLA by the CMC.

The Central Military Commission has primary authority to shape defense policy. It assumes the primary responsibility for drafting new strategy statements to respond to any change in China's security situation. The members of the CMC, including the civilian chairman and vice chairman (if there is one), no doubt approve those documents. Civilian leaders may offer guidance on the general approach, and they certainly assert themselves on high policy (see the discussion of Hu Jintao's "new historical missions" for the PLA, for example). But the military still dominates the formulation of national security policy.

A third dimension is how the military participates in decisionmaking on specific issues that bear on China's national security, in which it believes that it has a role. Here the interaction between senior officers and top civilians is complex and sometimes delicate. One example is the response in the mid-1990s to the challenge that the PRC saw in the actions of Taiwan's president, Lee Teng-hui. All parts of the regime believed that Lee posed a problem, but the PLA's assessment was more dire than most,[23] and a debate ensued over how to respond. The high command first took a hard-line approach, advocating increasing the pressure on Taiwan, but at the beginning of 1995 it accepted President Jiang Zemin's preference for a more moderate approach.[24] When Lee did not reciprocate sufficiently and instead forged ahead with a visit to the United States, the PLA again urged a tough, even military response. China's response was mixed, but it did include displays of force in the summer and fall of 1995 and the spring of 1996.

Western scholars disagree on the precise impact of the military on China's response to the Lee visit. Swaine concludes that the steps taken reflected a set of compromises and that "by and large [the response was] the consequence of a collaborative policy-making process led by Jiang Zemin and not the outcome of a factional struggle."[25] Others find that military leaders and some civilians used the Lee visit to impose their views on Jiang, constraining his options and forcing a tougher policy that employed military training exercises as tools of intimidation. Andrew Scobell splits the difference. He confirms that the PLA led the charge, advocating a hard-line response to the Lee visit, but he also finds that by October 1995, civilian and military leaders had reached a consensus on a tougher approach.[26] The bulk of the evidence suggests that the military was able to use the consensus-building process to bias the result, which favored coercion more than diplomacy.

Another example of civilian influence on military proposals was seen in early 2005, when Japan-China relations deteriorated sharply. Koizumi Junichiro continued to visit Yasukuni Shrine. In November, a PLAN submarine had been caught going through a strait that Japan had declared off limits. Tensions were increasing in the East China Sea. Japan was lobbying European countries to maintain their embargo on selling arms to the PRC. Tokyo mounted a new effort to secure a permanent seat on the UN Security Council, provoking demonstrations in several Chinese cities in early April. In response, senior PLA officials decided to form a study group on China-Japan relations, to be composed of both civilian and military experts. Reportedly, the organizers already had an idea of the conclusions that the study group would reach. Among them were the recommendations to "not hesitate to take military action to protect the interests of the gas field in the East China Sea" and to cancel China's 1972 renunciation of war reparations. When Hu Jintao learned about the plan, he decided that "it is better for it to be suspended."[27]

With respect to setting defense policy and intervening on specific security issues, military leaders have a special advantage. That is, recent paramount leaders (the civilians who head the party, state, and military hierarchies) have had little or no military experience. Having led the revolution that brought the CCP to power, Mao Zedong and Deng Xiaoping, the first two paramount leaders of the PRC, were military leaders before they became civilian leaders. They possessed charisma and boldness, and those attributes, plus their personal histories, translated into political authority in the eyes of generations of military officers, among others.

In contrast, Jiang Zemin and Hu Jintao—the more recent paramount leaders—have no military background. In the post-revolutionary era, they climbed the ladder of success in the civilian hierarchy, where charisma and independence of mind and action were not career-enhancing.[28] As a result, both Jiang and Hu landed at the top of the military hierarchy without having established their authority in the eyes of the officer corps, and they were likely to defer to the uniformed military on the details of security policy, particularly in the early years of their tenure. (Contrast this with the pattern in the United States, where civilian and military leaders work together intensively to draft documents like the *National Security Strategy* and the *Quadrennial Defense Review.*)

To foster PLA support, leaders like Jiang and Hu have had to use the tools of their CMC chairmanship: the power to recommend senior promotions; the ability to shape the pace and scope of military modernization by manipulating the budget; and the discretion to bring the military into discussions of foreign policy issues with a national security dimension. Jiang Zemin used all those tools to increase his base of support in the PLA.[29]

The fourth dimension on which to evaluate the extent of civilian control of the military is how aware civilian leaders are of PLA operations. Two cases are revealing.

The first is the PLAN submarine transit of the Ishigaki Strait in November 2004. As noted in chapter 6, that action was at odds with China's position regarding transit through its own straits as well as in violation, in Japan's view, of China's right of transit passage.[30] But that was not the only reason that the incident was an embarrassment to Beijing. Once the Japanese public learned that the transit had occurred and that Japanese air and marine forces were conducting intensive monitoring, the incident became item number one in the Japanese media. Because the operation occurred right before a major meeting of Asia-Pacific leaders, its revelation placed President Hu Jintao at a diplomatic disadvantage in his meeting with Japan's prime minister, Koizumi Junichiro.

Who ordered the transit, which affected both the PRC's legal position and its relations with Japan? It certainly was not a decision that reflected a considered policy of the entire Chinese government. Indeed, the Chinese Foreign Ministry took five days to respond to Japan's demands for an explanation. Presumably it spent that time in difficult negotiations with the PLAN and other concerned parties to come up with a mutually acceptable stance. In the end, in order to preserve China's legal position, Beijing issued an apology that fell back on the excuse that the submarine had entered Japan's territorial waters inadvertently.

It is reasonable to infer that first Jiang Zemin and then Hu Jintao, as chairmen of the CMC, endorsed the broad policy defining the PLAN's mission: to "defend the state's sovereignty over its territorial waters, and safeguard the state's maritime rights and interests."[31] Yet Peter Dutton concludes that it was some node in the military hierarchy that ordered the operation— either the submarine captain himself, which would constitute a high degree of operational independence, or someone at a higher level. In either case, the case suggests a military that on its own chooses how to best implement

China's broad security goals and sometimes disregards Beijing's broader foreign policy interests in the process.[32] (It may be no coincidence that the transit occurred only a few months after Hu succeeded Jiang as CMC chairman.)

The second case is China's test of anti-satellite capability on January 11, 2007, when a mobile, two-stage ballistic missile based on the DF-21 launched a kinetic-kill vehicle that struck a Chinese weather satellite in low-earth orbit. That exercise, part of a program that stemmed from China's defense policy, was clearly within the military's domain. The test was conducted by elements of the General Armaments Department, one of the four principal headquarters under the Central Military Commission. At the time it was headed by General Chen Bingde.[33]

A key subject of analysis of the test was the obvious lack of coordination within the PRC system. For it was not until January 23 that the Ministry of Foreign Affairs—China's face to the outside world—even acknowledged that a test had taken place. That the regime lacked a public relations strategy indicated that those in the system who knew about the test either had no clue about the possibility of international consequences or that they had some idea but chose to do nothing about it. They chose to leave in the dark both the spokespersons of the Ministry of Foreign Affairs and scientists who could have offered advice about the consequences of adding to the already large amount of space debris.[34]

James Mulvenon has evaluated three "analytic hypotheses" to explain the lack of information sharing. The first is that the entire civilian leadership was unaware of both the testing program and the January 2007 test itself. The second is that Hu Jintao, in his capacity as CMC chairman, knew about the testing program but was unaware of when that particular test would occur. The third hypothesis is that Hu Jintao and his senior civilian colleagues were aware of the test but failed to predict the intense international reaction to its success; did not expect that information about it would become public; or planned to use the test as leverage for negotiations on the demilitarization of space.[35]

Mulvenon rejects the first hypothesis in light of Chen Bingde's subsequent promotion to chief of the general staff. He disputes the third hypothesis, believing that a civilian leadership that was aware of the test would have expected a negative foreign reaction and taken steps to prepare for it. Similarly, if the goal had been to press for negotiations on weapons in space, a public relations campaign would have been rolled out immediately. Mulvenon is inclined to accept the second hypothesis, finding that the twelve days of silence during which the system worked to get its public act together "strongly suggests genuine breakdowns in internal coordination or even leadership paralysis."[36]

Japan

If any country has followed a liberal–Whig model of civil-military relations, it is Japan. Until the 1970s, Japan's reliance on the United States for security and the public's anti-militarism combined to produce tight control of the Self-Defense Forces (SDF), exercised by officials of the Ministry of Foreign Affairs (MOFA) and civilian bureaucrats in the Japan Defense Agency (JDA). The goal, it seemed, was to protect the Japanese people from the military, not to use the military to protect the people. That approach began to evolve during the end phase of the cold war, as the United States pushed Japan to take more responsibility for its own defense. Civilian bureaucrats in the JDA lost power to politicians and uniformed officers, reducing their ability to impose control . Mechanisms were developed both to define a national security strategy and force structure and to better coordinate with the U.S. defense establishment. All along, the public was reassured that a return to militarism was not in the offing.

The end of the cold war created new realities. The previous legal and policy infrastructure impeded the SDF's ability to engage in UN peacekeeping, to assist the U.S. military in addressing a North Korea or Taiwan military contingency, and to contribute to global efforts against threats such as terrorism. Gradually, therefore, the limits were removed or reduced to permit greater flexibility (a process facilitated by the virtual disappearance of the Japan Socialist Party, the country's most robust pacificist force). In 1992 the Diet authorized the SDF to participate in UN peacekeeping operations and gradually thereafter reduced the restrictions under which it functioned. The North Korean nuclear and missile episodes during the 1990s led to decisions on how the SDF might support the United States in a regional military contingency and on missile defense. The latter issue in turn required relaxation of the restrictions on the export of arms produced by Japanese defense firms to foreign countries.[37]

Those incremental changes bothered observers in China. They believed that legal and policy restrictions were the most effective way to block a revival of Japanese militarism and worried that their disappearance represented something ominous about Japan's future intentions. (China also believed that the United States had restrained Japan's military revival in the past but might now be facilitating it.) Yet the SDF was far from becoming an independent actor, and the barriers to its action still are considerable. First and foremost is a still robust, multilayered legal infrastructure that defines the birdcage in which the SDF can fly.

THE CONSTITUTION.   The first layer of that infrastructure is the constitution, specifically article 9: "The Japanese people forever renounce war as a sovereign right of the nation and the threat or use of force as means of settling international disputes. In order to accomplish the aim of the preceding paragraph, land, sea, and air forces, as well as other war potential, will never be maintained." A key actor here is the Cabinet Legislation Office (CLB), which reviews all draft bills before they go to the Cabinet and which has had the power to interpret what the article means for defense policy.[38] In support of Yoshida Shigeru's cold war grand strategy, the CLB enunciated a set of principles that became the basis for deductively restricting what the SDF could do:

—The SDF is not a normal military force.

—The SDF may not use force that is greater than minimally necessary.

—Abroad, the SDF cannot act in ways that could be considered use of force.

—The SDF may use force to protect itself and those under its care.

—The SDF cannot engage in activities that are an integral part of any use of force, broadly defined.[39]

On the basis of the second principle, the CLB dictated in 1981 that Japan could not engage in collective self-defense (for example, by coming to the defense or security aid of its U.S. ally). Japan did have the theoretical right to do so under the United Nations charter, but the minimum-force doctrine blocked its exercise of that right.

LAW.   The second layer is legislation of several types that governs how the SDF may be used. This legal framework has changed as the SDF has taken on new roles. From 1954 to 1989, there was only one change in the laws concerning the defense establishment; from 1989 to 2007, there were forty-one.

The first type of law has a programmatic scope; key examples are the law governing the dispatch of the SDF for peacekeeping operations and the law for "supporting U.S. military operations in the case of regional contingencies."[40] Each specifies what the SDF may or may not do. For example, the law on regional contingencies allows it only to offer rear area logistical support, conduct rear area search and rescue operations, and conduct ship inspections. The SDF is prohibited from providing logistical support regarding weapons and materials and services for U.S. forces going to combat.[41]

The second type of law concerns missions for which the United Nations is deemed to have provided insufficient authorization or that are not already covered by programmatic legislation. In such cases, the Diet must pass a special measures law (SML) to create a legal basis for the operation. Examples include the antiterrorism law of November 2001, under which Maritime Self-Defense Force (MSDF) vessels transferred fuel in the Indian Ocean to entities involved in the war on terror; an SML for Iraqi humanitarian and reconstruction assistance, enacted in July 2003, under which Air Self-Defense Force (ASDF) and Ground Self-Defense Force (GSDF) units supported the United States in Iraq; and legislation passed in January 2008 to reauthorize the Indian Ocean fuel replenishment law after it expired. Each contained mission-specific restrictions. The antiterrorism SML prohibited the SDF from operating in combat zones, using force, or operating on land without the host country's permission. The reauthorization for the law tightened the restrictions by ordering refueling operations to stop if combat was imminent nearby, strictly limiting the use of weapons, and cancelling the authorization for search and rescue activities, which were permitted in the original legislation. The Iraq law defines precisely the humanitarian and reconstruction activities allowed (no transporting weapons or fueling combat aircraft), restricts the SDF to noncombatant areas, orders all operations suspended if fighting occurs nearby, and restricts the use of weapons to defense of SDF personnel, other people involved in reconstruction, and the Iraqis under their protection. Because of the latter provision, the soldiers of other countries had to provide security to the GSDF personnel.[42]

Finally, there is the SDF law itself and other domestic legislation that provides the basic legal framework for the institution, including organization, personnel, the procedures that must be followed to use uniformed personnel in either a domestic or an external contingency, and guidelines regarding the use of force. On the last issue, in some cases the SDF follows the law governing the police. Whenever a programmatic or special measures law is passed, necessary conforming changes are made in the SDF law.[43]

POLICY.   Supplementing the legal infrastructure is an elaborate set of policies that spell out the SDF's missions and force structure. Three major missions have been enunciated: operations to defend Japan and to respond to "new threats and diverse contingencies"; to strengthen U.S.-Japan security arrangements; and to improve the international security environment, including UN peacekeeping and disaster relief operations and so on. Those missions and the force structure that stems from them are the result of an elaborate policymaking process that begins with a study by private sector security specialists. The results are then translated into the National Defense Program Outline and the National Defense Program Guidelines (NDPG), which are followed by the mid-term defense program, which is a five-year schedule for the procurement of equipment. Often, a parallel policymaking process is conducted by Japan and the United States to integrate Tokyo's defense policy with alliance priorities. Thus, the nongovernment Council on Security and Defense Capabilities issued a report, "Japan's Visions for Future Security and Defense Capabilities," in November 2004; the government issued new National Defense Program Guidelines and the mid-term defense program in December; and senior U.S. and Japanese officials issued a document on "common strategic objectives" in February 2005 and another on "realignment of the alliance" in October 2005.[44]

BUREAUCRATS AND POLITICIANS.   The close involvement of the government in developing defense policy also contributes to making Japan's armed forces a highly regulated institution. Although the cage within which they operate is less restrictive than it was at the end of the cold war, it is still restrictive. Maintaining the regulatory regime are an army of bureaucrats and, increasingly, legions of politicians. During the cold war, it was mainly bureaucrats. MOFA was responsible for the alliance relationship with Washington. Because the United States was committed to protecting Japan, alliance policy *was* defense policy. The Japan Defense Agency merely administered the Self-Defense Forces, whose only mission was to supplement U.S. efforts in the event of an external invasion. Some of the JDA's senior officials came from other ministries, and the Internal Bureau with its cadre of "civilian counselors" reigned supreme. For example, uniformed officers could not meet with officials from other agencies or members of the Diet without a civilian JDA official present. Animating this system was the "notion that the purpose of civilian control was only to restrict the military," not to allow the SDF the autonomy to conduct its missions in a professional way under the aegis of policies formulated by civilians. During the cold war, politicians were willing to cede responsibility for supervision to bureaucrats because the electoral system and the sensitivity of defense issues gave them little incentive to take it upon themselves.[45]

Politicians began to assert themselves in the 1990s as Japan increasingly was called on to play a greater role in ensuring international security, not just to assist the United States in the defense of Japan. Peacekeeping, aiding the United States in regional contingencies (North Korea and Taiwan), and lending support to efforts outside East Asia loomed as new missions. Politicians concluded that it was no longer politically wise to delegate power to JDA bureaucrats. Prime ministers Koizumi and Abe both believed strongly in normalizing the defense establishment and using the SDF as a tool of Japanese security policy. Changes in the electoral system, party relations, operations of the Diet, and bureaucratic organization created incentives for politicians to assert themselves on defense issues. Whereas the previous multi-member system had encouraged narrow specialization on policy issues, the shift to single-member districts required that politicians not ignore defense. The Liberal Democratic Party (LDP) used a coalition with the more pacifist New Komei Party to strengthen its Diet position, which meant that security initiatives entailed time-consuming negotiations with New Komei.[46] Politically appointed ministers and vice-ministers were now the only officials who could speak for their agencies in the Diet, whereas before bureaucrats could do so. There was an increase in the number of senior ministry positions to which politicians in the Diet could be appointed. As a result, senior government leaders, themselves politicians, could rely on the appointed officials in those positions instead of on bureaucrats. The SDF gained greater access to those officials, to lower-ranking politicians, and to U.S. defense officials. Within that general rezoning of power between career bureaucrats and Diet politicians, the JDA (and after 2006, the MOD) became more influential in defense policy, thereby displacing MOFA on alliance issues.[47]

A case in point is the evolution of SDF officers' access to the most prominent civilian official. Prior to 1985, they did not visit the Prime Minister's Office (*kantei*) for fear of prompting accusations from the opposition that civilian control was not strong enough. Prime Minister Nakasone Yasuhiro broke that taboo by inviting uniformed officers to report to him on security issues. Still, the rules required that civilian defense officials accompany them and prevented them from having contact with other ministries. Prime Minister Hashimoto Ryutaro abolished those rules. Uniformed officers now work in various offices in the *kantei* (mainly in intelligence), and they can visit the prime minister alone.[48] Yet restrictions remain. For example, SDF officers still do not participate in formal meetings in the Diet on security policy (for example, in meetings of Diet committees).[49]

Such constraints gave the SDF some incentive to develop strategies to circumvent the rules in order to get what they wanted. For example, in the fall of 2001, after the September 11 attack, Prime Minister Koizumi was considering ways in which to assist the United States. The staff office of the Maritime Self-Defense Force circulated documents to U.S. defense officials and the defense *zoku* ("tribe") of the LDP detailing ways in which the MSDF could assist the United States in the Indian Ocean, including possible legal rationalizations. It did so to create pressure on civilian Japanese bureaucrats. The maritime staff office came in for criticism for "overstepping" the line, but "hawkish" naval officers were pleased that it was "working very hard."[50]

The issue of civilian control was brought into sharper relief after Koizumi left office by a series of scandals that involved violations of rules governing the handling of classified information, misreporting from the Indian Ocean refueling mission, and the ramming of a fishing vessel by an MSDF ship. Most serious was the revelation in October 2007 that Moriya Takemasa, the administrative vice minister of defense, a career official, had benefited financially from his decisions regarding procurement of military equipment and supplies. Moriya was later arrested and charged.

Observers pointed to structural reasons for the scandal. Ogawa Kazuhisa, a military affairs analyst, argued that the difficulty lay in the relationship between politicians and defense bureaucrats. Although bureaucrats were capable of solving simple problems, they were not good at "forming strategy from a broad point of view, one transcending vertical organizational divisions." According to Ogawa, only politicians were in a position to formulate a "grand design" that would give direction to defense officials, but they did not do so. Only an organization in the prime minister's office, akin to the U.S. National Security Council, could strengthen the weak link between policy and implementation.[51]

Ishiba Shigeru, the serving defense minister when most of the scandals broke, pointed to another structural flaw. He attributed the problems to the overlapping of the responsibilities of the Internal Bureau of the MOD, staffed by civilian counselors, and those of the SDF staff offices, staffed by uniformed SDF officers. It was "a system in which it was easy to evade responsibility." Moreover, "elites in suits" monopolized access to the defense chief and "those in uniform" had little chance to meet with him. Ishiba believed that the only way to fix the problem was to create a more integrated structure in which the civilians and officers functioned as a single unit and where "uniforms" could serve as defense counselors, thus "creating an organization in which it was impossible to evade responsibility."[52]

Ishiba established a council for reforming the Ministry of Defense that proposed a series of reforms in July 2008, including better adherence to rules and regulations and enhanced professional education within the SDF. The council also sought to strengthen the "command functions" of the Prime Minister's Official Residence by using the "three ministers" meeting (involving the chief cabinet secretary, foreign minister, and defense minister) to enhance high-level discussion of security issues and to reinforce the staff support system for the prime minister. Other proposals clearly bore Minister Ishiba's imprint:

—Abolish the system of civilian defense counselors (the key MOD bureaucrats) and appoint aides to the defense minister.

—Establish a defense council made up of senior vice ministers (both bureaucrats and political appointees), civilian officials, and uniformed officers responsible for advising the defense minister in emergencies.

—Improve the system for formulating defense policy by strengthening the Defense Policy Bureau within the MOD and appointing uniformed officers to "take the actual situation into account in terms of operations."

—Dissolve the Operational Policy Bureau within the MOD (staffed by civilians) and make the uniformed chief of staff and joint staff responsible for the execution of operations.

—Consolidate elements of the MOD Internal Bureau and the service staff offices responsible for procurement to ensure optimal performance.

—Appoint uniformed personnel "familiar with actual conditions" to management sections.[53]

It remains to be seen whether the reforms will create a more integrated management structure that will foster effective civilian oversight while encouraging appropriate professional autonomy on the part of the SDF. The accession to power of the Democratic Party of Japan (DPJ) in September 2009 at least stalled Ishiba's reform program. The DPJ decided not to disturb the already legislated action to abolish defense counselors; on the other hand, it terminated the proposal to merge the MOD's Operational Policy Bureau with the staff offices of the branches of the SDF, on which the Diet was to act during the first half of 2010.[54] In March 2010, the DPJ defense minister, Kitazawa Toshimi, launched a study that would be the basis for the DPJ's own reform plan to ensure stronger civilian control.[55] And there is the more fundamental belief of officials and politicians, which is probably stronger in the new DPJ government than in the LDP, that uniformed officers should not participate in the policy process. As a prominent journalist has argued, "it should be the civilians making final policy decisions based upon better knowledge of security issues, including the opinions and expertise given by military personnel."[56] Defense Minister Kitazawa himself "attributed the [1941–45] Pacific War to the emergence of soldiers who did not follow the government's policy, and to the weakened government and parliament."[57]

VALUES WITHIN THE SDF.   The liberal–Whig approach to civil-military relations seen in Japan rests not only on strong institutional controls but also on the inculcation of civilian values in members of the armed forces.

There is clear recognition that values are important. Iokibe Makoto, a former president of the National Defense Academy, has written that the education of SDF officers should "respond boldly" to a changing environment while also identifying and inheriting "strong traditions." The question is what the idea of "strong traditions" embodies. One element of that tradition is that soldiers "never give up [their] post." Moreover, officers should possess both the technical skills required for military missions and "the knowledge and education expected of elite figures of society as a whole."[58]

The reality does not always meet that ideal. One scholarly study found that SDF officers felt anger, frustration, or resignation about the "half-baked" character of their institution and the strong desire that it be "normal" or "real." They resented the elaborate array of euphemisms employed in discussing military matters. They were pleased to make international contributions but would prefer not to be confined to situations that are out of harm's way, and they felt that other countries appreciate their contributions more than the Japanese public does. Regarding the past, some officers are ignorant of the record of the Imperial Army, while others blame their predecessors for pursuing independent and extremist policies and for lack of professionalism.[59]

Another survey, conducted in 2003 of 900 SDF officers ranging from officer candidates to colonels and 100 individuals who were considered civilian elites, found similar attitudes:

—SDF officers are confident and somewhat conservative.

—They support the U.S.-Japan alliance but not necessarily unconditionally. Still, SDF officers are more positive regarding the alliance than the civilian elite are, and both groups are more positive than the general public.

—They are sensitive to combat casualties, with more than 50 percent responding that no more than 100 deaths were acceptable in situations in areas surrounding Japan (U.S. officers have a much higher tolerance for casualties in East Asian contingencies).

—With respect to civilian control, although more than 70 percent of the officers surveyed believed that "officers should not criticize government or society at large," 74 percent believed that "officers have insufficient influence in foreign policy decisionmaking" (76 percent of the civilian elite agreed with the latter statement).

—Some 75 percent of officers believed that the general public has a positive image of the SDF, but many thought that a culture gap existed between civilians and the military. To close the gap, 58 percent believed that the SDF could be a role model for society, but 64 percent (especially younger officers) thought that the SDF should interact more with civilians and introduce the values and customs of society at large into the military.[60]

Some of that ambivalence was on full display in 2008, in the case of General Tamogami Toshio. While serving as chief of staff of the Air Self-Defense Force, Tamogami entered an essay contest sponsored by the APA Group, a hotel and apartment developer and publisher of a conservative magazine. In his essay, he asserted that in the first half of the twentieth century, Japan was not the aggressor in China; he argued instead that Japan's military acted according to rights established by treaty and in response to Chinese provocations of communist origin. He also wrote that today's Self-Defense Forces are "bound hand and foot and immobilized."[61]

The news that Tamogami's essay had won first prize provoked swift calls for action from opposition parties and pacificist groups. Political leaders, uniformed officers, and civilian MOD officials were critical of this deviation from government policy. The media also were generally critical of the essay, and leading outlets asked whether the incident represented a crisis in civilian control. The *Daily Yomiuri*, for example, said that "senior officers of the SDF need to have not only military knowledge and leadership skills but also deep insight, broad perspectives, and a good sense of balance."[62] So Defense Minister Hamada quickly dismissed Tamogami and reduced his own salary to show that the government took the problem seriously.

It then came out that Tamogami was not the only member of the ASDF to enter the essay contest; more than ninety others had done so. Moreover, senior officers in charge of training had urged lower-level units to encourage students to enter the contest and followed up to see whether that was being done. A former president of the National Defense Academy asserted that the expansion of SDF activities during the 1990s had led some officers to become "excessively self-confident" and "arrogant." MOD bureaucrats were concerned that Tamogami's views had "spread widely" among SDF personnel.[63]

The fallout from the Tamogami incident did not end there. One of the general's critics was Iokibe Makoto, the former president of the National Defense Academy. In early March 2009, he was scheduled to address an association of academy graduates in Osaka, but an activist group that included graduates mounted a protest campaign against his appearance. Under siege, the association chairman capitulated and canceled the event.[64]

Tamogami's assertions may have been outrageous, but his dissent was not unprecedented. In July 2009, a former chief of staff of the MSDF publicly offered his views on the constraints that the constitution, laws, and policy interpretations imposed on the SDF.

These constitutional interpretations, which are contrary to military rationality, and the idealistic three reform principles [the Ishiba reforms; see above], which lack specifics, are too far removed from the essence of the security and independence . . . which can only be secured by working out one's own defense capabilities along with diplomatic capabilities and cooperation with allies, etc., in a comprehensive fashion. . . . It is necessary for security policies to reflect the situation at the time, along with changes in the international environment."[65]

The ascension to power of the Democratic Party of Japan in September 2009 caused even more anxiety in the Self-Defense Forces. The DPJ sought to alter the alliance with the United States in ways that reduced Japan's dependence and deference; the SDF, on the other hand, benefited the most institutionally from a close alliance. Specifically, the DPJ wished to overturn a bilateral agreement on the number and location of U.S. military personnel on the island of Okinawa. At one point, as the two countries sought to work out a mutually acceptable arrangement, Hatoyama Yukio, the DPJ prime minister, urged President Obama to "trust me" on the Okinawa issue. That was too much for a colonel of the Ground Self-Defense Force. In February 2010, he said publicly that the alliance "cannot be maintained by diplomacy or political rhetoric. . . . Least of all, it cannot be maintained by the words 'Trust me.'" The officer was quickly reprimanded and later transferred from his command position to a research assignment.[66]

To sum up, there is an intriguing contrast between civil-military relations in China and those in Japan. The members of China's armed forces have a strong commitment to the values of the communist regime and to its preservation, but the PLA as an institution preserves substantial autonomy vis-à-vis civilian leaders in the areas of policy and operations. To be sure, the high command would obey direct orders from the civilian leadership, but it is able to shape the way in which that leadership views national security issues and thereby the orders that it gives. The compliance of commanders is conditional, and their principal condition is civilian respect of their professional ability and therefore their autonomy to do their job as they deem proper. Autonomy and light supervision are most commonly accorded in matters involving military operations. When the PLA asserts itself concerning perceived challenges to national security, it tends to state more extreme positions that shift the spectrum of options considered and so ensures that the policy that is ultimately adopted will be more to the military's liking. Neither autonomy nor a tendency to toughness portends a moderate outcome in a crisis. Moreover, the strong commitment of PLA officers to the PRC regime is more relevant to the military's noninterventionist approach to domestic politics than it is to national defense policy and operations, where professional autonomy is the norm.

In Japan, on the other hand, various civilian policymakers—party leaders, politicians, and bureaucrats—constrain officers of the Self-Defense Forces through legislation and policy. Given the changes in Japan's external environment and Washington's shifting view of the alliance, the constraints are less than they were at the end of the cold war, but they still exist. The complex process of applying existing law and policy to proposed initiatives for using the SDF as an instrument of national policy can delay both the speed and substance of Japan's response. At the same time, uniformed officers appear to be somewhat ambivalent about civilian authority.

Japan is thus the opposite of China. For the most part, civilians (both bureaucrats and politicians) dominate the formulation of defense policy and micromanage operations. When it comes to values, uniformed officers are somewhat ambivalent, and it is difficult to know how that ambivalence could affect military operations.

Yet there is an irony at work in any discussion of civilian control in Japan, whether it is control by bureaucrats or politicians. Not all of the SDF's activities are regulated equally. Peacekeeping and other high-profile overseas missions receive the most intense scrutiny from politicians, not operations that focus on the defense of Japan, particularly surveillance of sea lanes and of Japan's large air defense identification zone. However, because the latter activities occur in proximity to PLA operations, they are more likely to involve some sort of conflict. That is not to say that surveillance activities are not regulated through rules of engagement and command-and-control procedures, but MOD bureaucrats and SDF officers impose those limits, not politicians. In short, there is not a single birdcage in which the SDF "flies": the birdcage varies according to the mission, and the one of most concern is the least restrictive.

Command and Control

Command and control refers to how a headquarters regulates the operations of units in the field. Military establishments vary with respect to how they design systems of command, control, and communications (C3). Is the power of command concentrated or not? How well are actions of different branches and services coordinated? What are the criteria for differentiation of institutions—the branches of the military service, institutional function, or geography? Is control of field units centralized or decentralized? In a decentralized system, headquarters will allow lower-level commanders to make tactical decisions without central direction. Such a system relies on established rules of engagement (ROEs) and frequent training of local commanders to ensure that they respond well in novel situations. This approach uses communications when possible but ensures that local units can continue to operate if they are cut off from headquarters. In a centralized system, in contrast, central commanders issue orders on tactical operations in real time, based on the information available. Under this approach, maintaining communications between high and low levels is essential. Training also is important, but its focus is on ensuring that officers at the tactical level follow orders, not that they are able to respond on their own—and effectively—to unexpected events.[67]

China

The Central Military Commission serves as China's military command headquarters and thus the PRC's national command authority. Beneath the CMC is a three-tier institutional structure: the four general departments (for operations, equipment, logistics, and politics); the branches and services other than the ground forces (navy, air force, the missile force, and the paramilitary People's Armed Police); and seven geographic military regions and their subordinate units, in which ground forces predominate.[68] Command authority runs from the CMC through the general departments to subordinate line units.[69] The headquarters of the People's Liberation Army Navy and the People's Liberation Army Air Force are divided internally into four major units that replicate the functional template of the first tier. Subordinate units are associated with military regions (MR). PLAN and PLAAF commanders at the regional level are deputy commanders for their MRs, and the commander always comes from the ground forces.

For a variety of reasons, this structure and chain of command create confusion. At the very top, there are cases in which the individual who occupies the posts of general secretary of the party and president is not simultaneously the chairman of the Central Military Commission. That was the case with Jiang Zemin in the early 1990s (Deng Xiaoping remained as CMC chairman) and Hu Jintao in the early part of the 2000s (Jiang Zemin stayed on as CMC chairman for two years). That creates a division in the leadership of the civilian and military hierarchies, what the Chinese call the problem of "two centers." Indeed, Jiang Zemin came under open criticism from the PLA for selfishly retaining the position of CMC chairman and thereby dividing authority. Employing a subtle play on words, the critics said that having one center inspired loyalty but that having two just created trouble.[70]

A similar problem faces local commanders, in part because the PLAN and PLAAF are not on the same level as the ground forces. The latter have always had pride of place in the military hierarchy, and they have no separate command, as do the PLAN and PLAAF. The General Staff Department (GSD) is both a joint headquarters for all services and branches and the headquarters of the ground forces. Consequently, the commanders of the PLAN and PLAAF, who are in Beijing, have the same grade as the commander of a military region, who is from the ground forces.[71] Because historically the task of the relevant PLAN and PLAAF units was to support the ground forces, the commander is superior to the top-ranked navy or air force officer assigned to the same military region. Indeed, only in recent years were the commanders of the PLAN, PLAAF, and the Second Artillery (the missile force) given seats on the CMC, reflecting the growing importance of those branches to China's security strategy. Representatives of these services also have a growing presence in the GSD and central command centers. Yet organizationally there is a lingering bias in favor of the ground forces.

On the other hand, the existence of twin axes of command, one vertical and the other horizontal, creates complexities for which there are shifting but never final solutions.[72] During most of the 1990s, according to John Lewis and Xue Litai, MR commanders did not control the units of the navy, air force, and rocket forces assigned to their area of operations and were frustrated by those forces' relative independence.[73]

Then, in the late 1990s, after the Taiwan Strait crisis of 1995–96, the PLA instituted changes in the existing arrangements. For the purpose of conducting exercises, the CMC created theater-based joint commands that included flag officers from the GSD and the headquarters of the three services and staff officers from the local navy, air force, and missile units. Thereafter, the CMC issued regulations that enhanced the powers of unit commanders at all levels. Reportedly, they now had full authority over the departments and forces assigned to their area of operations. Finally, it decided to enhance the authority of theater-based joint commands by allowing them to cope with crisis situations as well as to conduct exercises.[74] The result, however, was that PLAN and PLAAF commanders were more likely to get orders from two directions. Hekler, Francis, and Mulvenon report that fleet commanders can get orders from PLAN headquarters, from the leaders of the military region to which their unit is attached, and from offices in the GSD on operational matters. PLA commentators have increasingly asserted that having several superiors directing the actions of a single commander is inappropriate for modern warfare, because they "simply cannot respond to multiple, often conflicting orders."[75]

With respect to control, the tradition within the PLA has been tight centralization. Swaine reports that "the PLA command and control apparatus is highly centralized, vertically structured, and very personalized."[76] For example, the Political Bureau of the Standing Committee and the Central Military Commission together have the authority to use nuclear weapons.[77] Local commanders may move only small numbers of troops on their own authority and not very far. Moreover, within any particular unit, only a restricted number of senior officers may receive and send operational orders. In wartime, the supreme command would create a coherent, joint command structure.[78]

A historical reason for the generally high degree of centralization of control is the PRC's relative backwardness in communications. The weaker the communications architecture—and the greater the possibility of a breakdown—the more likely that headquarters will deny discretion to field commanders. Therefore, even in the early 1990s, the PLA used wireless radio transmitters or secure underground telephones and telexes to convey operational information.[79] Two decades later, reportedly, "the PLA has only a limited capacity to communicate with submarines at sea and the PLA Navy has no experience in managing a SSBN fleet that performs strategic patrols."[80]

The PLA leadership has long understood its weaknesses in the field of command, control, communications, computers, intelligence, surveillance, and reconnaissance (C4ISR) and recognizes the advantage that U.S. superiority in those areas provides U.S. combat forces. If the PLA is to be able to fight and win "local wars under informatized conditions"—its central objective—then it must have advanced C4ISR systems that are reliable, survivable, interoperable, and integrated, on land and sea and in the air and space. According to the U.S. Department of Defense, the apparent objective is to secure the integration of campaign and tactical command networks at the theater level and, through enhanced training, to increase the ability of battlefield commanders to employ automated systems in a combat environment.[81]

China's efforts to modernize its military communications have had results. Some experts believe that communications systems are improving faster than operations are expanding; as a result, relatively centralized control of operations can be maintained. In general, it is only when operational missions expand faster than communications capacity that control may diminish. Yet even as "informatization" is occurring in the PLA, there are other factors at play. Better communications systems permit more actors in the chain of command to know what is happening and to seek to participate in decisionmaking based on the available information.

Second, as already noted, in some areas operational requirements tend to conflict with the PLA's preference for centralized control, giving commanders in the field more autonomy. The PLAN's quieter diesel submarines are better able to put U.S. carrier strike groups at risk, but if they must surface to get new instructions from headquarters, they put themselves at risk. In addition, in the abstract, the PLA appreciates the "new-type military talent" and "innovative" abilities that enable field commanders, as Nan Li indicates, "to resolve practical problems and to exploit fast-changing circumstances to maximize gains and minimize losses." To what extent practice follows theory in fostering officers' independence is another question, but the issue demonstrates the tension involved in China's approach to command and control.[82]

Then there is the other Chinese actor in the East China Sea: the Marine Surveillance Force (MSF). As noted in chapter 5, it is under the jurisdiction of the State Oceanic Administration and the Ministry of Land and Resources, which is part of the Cabinet. Thus, the top person in the MSF's hierarchy is the premier, but the senior person in the military hierarchy is the chairman of the CMC. The only place where those hierarchies formally intersect is in the Politburo Standing Committee, of which the CMC chairman and the premier are members. A Chinese commentator observed that coordination between the MSF and the PLAN was lacking and that "China's maritime security forces are subordinate to various departments. . . . Accordingly, although in recent years China's maritime security forces have been developing very rapidly, they are urgently in need of centralized reconfiguring in order to see that there is unified leadership." Sun Zhihui, head of the State Oceanic Administration, candidly admitted that because incidents occurred suddenly, there could be only "ad hoc discussions [and] reactions were hasty. It was difficult to make thorough considerations, and results were less than ideal."[83] Perhaps to address that problem, there was talk in late 2008 of incorporating the MSF into the reserve force of the PLAN. Yet there has been no subsequent confirmation of movement toward that end.[84]

Other efforts have been under way to achieve integration at the operational level. In July 2008, the main military newspaper reported on the efforts of an unspecified naval base to foster "centralized control of ocean regions based on the requirements of the mission" and a "new mechanism for military area unification, regional coordination, and naval/air force integration."

A central command-and-control system was established for a specific ocean region and PLA assets (both air and naval), police, and the civilian population were brought under it. Relying on sophisticated surveillance technologies, the command then created a division of labor: large naval vessels were to intercept commercial shipping, smaller vessels were to intercept smaller ships engaged in fishing, and helicopters were to carry out surveillance.[85]

Japan

In the Japanese system, the prime minister, as the representative of the Cabinet, is the "supreme" authority over the Self-Defense Forces. The minister of defense is responsible for integrating the missions of the SDF and works through both civilian organizations and the SDF high command. In the Ministry of Defense, the civilian Operational Policy Bureau "manages all the issues that involve JSDF domestic and international operations."[86] The chief of staff of the Joint Staff Office (JSO) and the military service chiefs of staff are the senior leading uniformed officers. Each is supported by the relevant staff office, with directorates for personnel, operations, and so on.[87]

Historically, the staff structure did not foster much coordination among the services. The Joint Staff Office was enlarged in the early 1980s to establish better lines of communication between the internal bureaus and the three staff offices and to increase the SDF's policy role. Yet the fundamental problem did not go away. As mandated by the SDF law, the chief of staff of each service reports directly to the minister when it involves activities solely under the jurisdiction of that service; the chief of staff of the JSO comes into play only in affairs under that unit's jurisdiction, in which case he is to "plan the synchronization of deployment of forces."[88]

Several changes to the traditional structure are in train. First, in spite of the letter of the SDF law, there is a transition to more joint operations that places all the SDF operations under the jurisdiction of the Joint Staff Office.[89] Second, the Operational Policy Bureau of the Internal Bureau was to have been abolished by 2010 and consolidated into the Operations Directorate, but, as noted above, the new DPJ government that took office in September 2009 canceled the reorganization. Third, in March 2008, the power of the SDF fleet was increased vis-à-vis that of the regional district commanders. Whereas before surface ships, submarines, and airplanes were allocated to each district and placed under the control of its commander, now the SDF fleet has the authority to determine which assets will be used for each deployment, depending on the circumstances. The SDF fleet is the "force provider"; district commanders are "force users."[90]

Not to be ignored is the Japan Coast Guard (JCG). Recall that it falls under the jurisdiction of the Ministry of Land, Infrastructure, and Transport, not the Ministry of Defense.[91] Headed by the JCG commandant, it is centrally organized, with an internal bureau that in turn has four departments: administration, equipment and technology, hydrography and oceanography, and maritime traffic. The JCG has an extensive field network of offices, stations, air stations, and other units.[92] It has a strong sense of mission but, as with China's Marine Surveillance Force, there is frustration that the need to coordinate the actions of multiple agencies reduces response time in an emergency.

Because the JCG and the MSDF are in different institutional hierarchies that intersect only at fairly high levels, the issue of coordination between the two becomes important when they support the same mission, such as to protect the Senkaku/Diaoyu Islands. There has been a history of bureaucratic rivalry between the two. The "grudge" between them began when many officers of the subordinate unit of the JCG that was the organizational predecessor of the MSDF left the JCG when the MSDF was founded in 1954, thereby creating "ill will." That the MSDF was placed under the jurisdiction of the director of the Japan Defense Agency before 2007 and under that of the minister of defense thereafter only caused the "internal strife" to fester. The tension between the two services had lessened somewhat by the mid-2000s, but it was not until 2009, when both were dispatched to the Gulf of Aden on an anti-piracy mission, that one observer was willing to predict that a "historic reconciliation" was likely.[93] Clearly, cooperation did not come naturally.

It should be no surprise that control of SDF operations is tight, given the degree of civilian oversight of the SDF when it comes to policy. As discussed, an elaborate legal framework regulates what the SDF may and may not do in various situations. If the SDF is mobilized when Japan is under attack or in imminent danger, the forces may by law use their weapons but only as long as they do not "go beyond what is considered reasonable and [do] not violate the generally accepted principles in international law and custom" and do only what is "minimally necessary" to address the threat.[94]

Moreover, in a number of contingencies other than defense of the homeland, the rules created for law enforcement agencies dictate what the SDF may do regarding the use of force. The relevant article of the police law permits policemen to use their weapons only when it is reasonable and necessary in order to arrest suspects or prevent them from fleeing; to protect themselves and others; and to deter resistance.[95] That concept is applied, for example, to MSDF operations for maritime security, which usually take place to support the coast guard and which may entail boarding suspicious ships or restricting their movement. But the JCG law has been strengthened to explicitly allow the MSDF to use weapons when the suspect ship takes flight (as it did in the case of a North Korean vessel in 2001).

Generally, the ROEs applied to the air defense mission of the Air Self-Defense Force are strict, requiring that there be an "imminent danger" before a shoot-down can occur. Apparently, there are special rules for sensitive places.[96] On the other hand, the SDF law does allow pilots to take "necessary measures," and Yuki Tatsumi concludes that "much ambiguity remains on what the appropriate rules of engagement should be."[97]

On the positive side, the SDF possesses a sophisticated command-and-control infrastructure, which Bernard Cole asserts is one of its most significant capabilities. The combination of on-shore and field systems permits the MSDF and ASDF to operate in a "linked" fashion with each other and with the United States. "This allows JMSDF units operated at sea to gain synergistic increases in effectiveness through their real-time ability to conduct coordinated and integrated operations. Only the United States is similarly capable in East Asia."[98] But ambiguities remain, particularly regarding the independence of the JCG and the vagueness of some MSDF and ASDF principles of operation.

Nonetheless, the prevailing impression is one of multiple chains of peacetime command and a struggle to ensure coordination among them. That can create confusion for the commanders of field units, and it can create chaos should those units get into trouble. Control has been centralized, but the expansion of operations creates pressure for allowing greater flexibility in conducting operations.

Summing up, both Japan and China take a generally centralized approach to command and control. Each government has its own reason for doing so, but the goal is to ensure that those in the field—ship captains, pilots, and so on—conduct their operations in a manner that is consistent with the objectives of headquarters. That no serious clash has occurred so far is no doubt due in part to those centralized procedures. However, factors can still intervene to frustrate control. PLA field units are subject to multiple lines of authority in peacetime, which can slow response times or lead local commanders to fall back on their intuition, which is shaped in part by strategic culture. SDF operators are subject to ambiguous rules of engagement, which, despite the bias against the use of force, can produce instinctive responses, especially when shots are fired in anger. And any rule-based systems tend to encourage stratagems to skirt the rules. Finally, and most important, the units on the front line are not in the military chains of command at all. The Japan Coast Guard and China's Marine Surveillance Force are increasingly important players in the East China Sea game, and the lack of coordination between them and their defense establishments becomes a wild card in the two countries' interactions.

Strategic Culture

Strategic culture refers to a military establishment's views on the nature of war, the character of the adversary, the problem of risk, and the use of force. Those views shape the interactions with an adversary of commanders in the field and at headquarters. Is war the exception in human affairs or the rule? Under what circumstances is the use of force an efficacious tool of national policy? Does the adversary pose a zero-sum threat or not? How should that threat be met? With accommodation? With a defensive posture? Or with a more offensive, coercive approach?[99] In the early twentieth century, European military establishments all adopted a "cult of the offensive" despite clear evidence that defenders would have a combat advantage. An inclination toward diplomatic brinksmanship and preventive war, the fear that "windows of vulnerability" were opening, and the belief that victory would be quick all made the outbreak of World War I more likely and dictated the costly operations that marked what became an extended war of attrition.[100]

China

Andrew Scobell succinctly summarizes the conventional wisdom about Chinese strategic culture: "Beijing preferred to avoid war and was cautious and deliberate in its deterrence signaling. And when conflict did occur, China's leaders made their utmost efforts to limit its scope and duration."[101] That is to say, Chinese security rhetoric emphasizes a "cult of defense." More recently, scholars have challenged that view. Scobell, for example, observes that such principles of Chinese security rhetoric are in tension with several other ideas that have important operational consequences. One is the "siege mentality"—the perception of multiple external and domestic threats—that dominates Chinese political and military leaders' perceptions. Another is the concept of "active defense" (offensive operations and tactics within a broader defensive strategy), which blurs the distinction between offense and defense and permits, among other things, preemptive attacks.[102]

Thomas Christensen finds that China has used force most frequently when it perceived an opening window of vulnerability or a closing window of opportunity. When Beijing assesses a tactical military situation, it may choose to fight even if the adversary has the advantage if it is clear that the advantage is only going to grow. Similarly, it might accept conflict even if a traditional military victory is not possible if doing so might yield political benefits. That is not to say that China is "particularly prone to conflict." Rather, "the reasons that the PRC has used force in the past would not always appear obvious to the casual observer, who might not expect a weaker actor to lash out at much stronger states or those stronger states' allies."[103]

Christensen also mines useful findings from the PLA doctrinal textbook, *Zhanyixue* [On the Study of Campaigns]. First, he finds that Chinese strategists are realistic about the size of the gap between the PLA's capabilities and those of more advanced militaries and about the difficulties of conducting most types of military campaigns. But they also emphasize the possibility of "the weak overcoming the strong" by exploiting the enemy's points of vulnerability (for example, through accurate ballistic missiles and information and electronic warfare). Second, he stresses that *Zhanyixue* identifies the adversary's will to fight as its key point of vulnerability. The PLA need not destroy its adversary's ability to fight; it need only destroy its desire to fight. Finally, he notes the temptation that China would feel to act preemptively, with "surprise, robust, offensive attacks" to increase the chances of victory in the face of an adversary's superior power.[104]

Lonnie Henley focuses on escalation control, a subject that Chinese military strategists have only recently begun to investigate.[105] He finds that Chinese scholars who study the issue (which they call "war control") cover the right topics but that the concept of initiative remains prominent in Chinese military writings, with important implications for escalation control. Seizing the initiative means

> rapid reaction to an incipient crisis, including immediate deployment of sizeable forces as early as possible. It requires clear, quick, and correct decisionmaking. It requires strong standing forces. . . . It requires a resolute and principled political stance, firmly asserted at the outset and throughout the confrontation. It requires a rapid transition to war when events reach that level, and employment of formidable military power at every stage.[106]

Yet gaining the initiative, particularly in the eyes of a fearful adversary, may be the same as overreaction and escalation.

With respect to the air force, in 2004 the CMC approved a strategy for the PLAAF that called for "integrated air and space operations" and "simultaneous offensive and defensive operations."[107] Mark Stokes identifies some of the guiding principles that translate that broad strategy into the use of airpower, including "surprise and first strikes, concentration of force, offensive action as an important element of defense and close coordination." The first of these includes seizing the initiative to frustrate the adversary's air operations, crippling its air defenses, neutralizing its early-warning radar systems, preparing future strike operations. Surprise does not occur without deliberate planning and training. The hope is that the first strike will be decisive.[108]

On the maritime side, the PLAN has adapted the broad national military strategy of "active defense" to its own operations. "Offshore defense," which the Central Military Commission formally approved for the navy in 1985, includes several elements: defensive strategy but offensive operations; no spatial or temporal limits on operations; no constraints on offensive operations; launching of operations under favorable conditions; exploiting the enemy's weaknesses; and so on.[109] It is a strategy, it seems, biased in the direction of action rather than restraint, at least on the tactical level.

Although not part of the PLA, the Marine Surveillance Force (MSF) is an important actor in the East China Sea. Its leadership believes that its operations have been too passive and has called for a more proactive approach by strengthening the understanding of maritime rights, tracking "hot-spots," and strengthening both routine patrols and preparations for emergencies: "We must establish a law-enforcement system that covers all of China's subordinate sea areas with regular patrols to safeguard rights and discover and legally prosecute any incidents of a violation of rights related to foreign countries in a timely manner."[110] With specific reference to Japan, Sun Zhihui, the head of China's State Oceanic Administration, displays a preference for showing strong resolve: "China does not wish to have a sharp conflict with Japan and *the reason for taking a hard-line attitude is to enable Japan to see China's determination* to safeguard its sovereignty *so that it will beat a retreat* in the face of difficulties and properly handle the issue" (emphasis added).[111]

Woven together, these various strands suggest a strategic culture that is prepared to read the worst in an adversary's actions; that emphasizes both seizing and holding the initiative before any conflict, which only makes conflict more likely because of the alarm that doing so would likely provoke on the part of an opponent; and that is highly opportunistic with respect to both emergent vulnerabilities and opportunities. It is a strategic culture that is consistent with the shift in the location of China's security challenges from inland borders to the Western Pacific littoral and with the increasingly dynamic nature of air and naval warfare. It fits well with the proposal of a researcher at the Sanlue Institute of Strategic Management Science in Beijing concerning China's maritime interests:

> Maritime rights and interests are a very complicated issue. It is obvious that "fighting" is inappropriate and instant resolution is impossible. However, we should not lopsidedly make concessions on all issues. We should take various active measures—including military measures— to "struggle" for these rights and interests.[112]

Japan

The study of Japan's strategic culture is not as developed as that of China's. Indeed, some might even question whether postwar Japan and the Self-Defense Forces even had a strategic culture.

That skepticism certainly is understandable. One stream of scholarship concludes that pacifist and anti-militarist norms have severely constrained Japanese security policy in spite of pressures to mount a robust response to the threats that have emerged since the end of the cold war. Those norms reflect deep public resentment toward the Imperial Army, its usurpation of power in the 1930s, and the disasters that its aggression in Asia eventually brought down on Japan and its people. "In Japan . . . it was the military institution itself which became the primary target of criticism after the war." Japan's culture of anti-militarism is manifest in support for article 9 of the constitution and the other institutional restrictions on the SDF and, in the 1970s, in a broad vision of national security that emphasized diplomacy, foreign aid, and economic development. If the international environment dictated a greater role for the SDF, any changes occurred incrementally.[113]

Pacifism and anti-militarism certainly had their impact in placing constitutional, legal, and policy constraints on the SDF. Taken together, they suggest uniquely Japanese answers to the questions regarding strategic culture posed at the beginning of this discussion. First, war may be the rule in human affairs, but it is the exception for Japan. Second, in shaping the government's actions, Japan's pacifist character is more consequential than the nature of any adversary. Third, force is an improper exercise of Japanese state power, except in the most exigent circumstances, as when the existence of the Japanese state is threatened. Fourth, therefore, the best way to cope with the threat that an adversary poses is to adopt an accommodating, defensive posture. The second of the above principles—no use of force greater than is minimally necessary—would seem to foreclose any thought of an offensive and coercive approach.

Still, the effect of anti-militarist norms should not be exaggerated. They are perhaps strongest among some parts of the public. Once translated into institutional arrangements, those norms arguably had a greater impact within government on the attitudes of civilians than of uniformed officers. Moreover, there is some question as to how much norms and culture have shaped policy, even during the cold war. Richard Samuels argues that although pacifists had their role in the security debate, they did not dominate it. Instead, they were "indulged" by more centrist leaders who used their views as an excuse to pursue a more calculated policy. And of course, the cold war ended almost two decades ago.[114]

Besides norms, a second way to clarify Japan's strategic culture is to take seriously the evolution of its grand strategy. Samuels believes that Japan has long possessed a grand strategy animated by a sense of existential vulnerability born of its location in a dangerous neighborhood and its lack of natural resources. There emerged a set of stable, enduring, yet competing responses to that vulnerability, depending on how Japanese strategists balanced different goals (for example, prestige and autonomy). The different approaches were more or less appropriate for an evolving external environment: Western imperialism in the late nineteenth century, the weakening of the Chinese state in the early twentieth, the rise of the Soviet Union and the United States thereafter, the cold war, and the post–cold war era.[115]

After the fall of the Soviet Union, Japan saw threats from rogue states and their weapons of mass destruction (North Korea); the rapid rise of a regional neighbor (China); terrorism (al Qaeda and, again, North Korea); and the destabilizing effects of failed states. The United States remained a willing ally, but beginning with the Persian Gulf War, it began calling on Japan to play a role in international security that included the dispatch of the Self-Defense Forces overseas. North Korea and China not only posed looming, direct threats to Japan for the first time but also foreshadowed the possibility that Japan could get drawn into conflicts between them and the United States (in the case of China, over Taiwan). If the alliance with the United States was still valuable to Japan (and it was), the days of "free riding" or "cheap riding" were over.

Japan's leaders struggled to come up with a new strategy to address the new challenges. Watching the debates, some scholars argued that the Japanese were becoming, in Michael Green's phrase, "reluctant realists." Samuels explores systematically how the different viewpoints produced different answers to the question of ends and means in the post–cold war era. Four analytic categories emerge:

—*Pacifists:* They seek autonomy through prosperity, reliance on soft power, reduction of military forces and constraints on those that remain, and rejection of the alliance.[116]

—*Middle-power internationalists:* They propose to achieve prestige by increasing prosperity and reducing Japan's growing global security footprint. This is essentially a return to the Yoshida Doctrine: increasing economic interdependence and hopefully political harmony with Asia (including China) and continued reliance on the U.S. alliance but resistance to U.S. demands for a greater international role.

—*"Normal nation–alists":* They wish to achieve prestige by building national strength. They would strengthen Japan's military power with even more robust capabilities and equalize what heretofore has been an unequal alliance. Tokyo would take on the burden of collective self-defense. The SDF and the U.S. armed forces would operate together overseas in support of a variety of missions.

—*Neoautonomists:* They seek autonomy by building national strength. They desire a stronger SDF, but one in service of an independent security policy based on acquiring a fuller spectrum of military capabilities, including nuclear weapons. They "would shift Japanese doctrine from a tethered, defensive realism to an untethered, offensive realism."[117]

Samuels believes that the "normal nation–alists" constitute the mainstream among Japanese security thinkers and policymakers. Yet a variety of domestic and external reasons restrain their temptation to emphasize prestige over autonomy and military power over prosperity. There will emerge instead a "Goldilocks consensus," an approach that "positions Japan not too close and not too far from the hegemon-protector, that makes it stronger but not threatening, and that provides new and comprehensive security options."[118]

The discussion of grand strategy and the strategic culture that underlies it is interesting, but it goes only so far. The strategic culture at this level is a national strategic culture that is relatively general. It does not tell us much about the defense establishment's strategic culture, particularly that of the SDF. What are its views of the role of war in human affairs, of the character of adversaries and the threat that they pose, of the efficacy of the use of force, of how best to cope with threats?[119]

A third cut at clarifying Japan's strategic culture, then, is to mine the Japanese defense establishment's approach to its tasks for clues about its strategic culture. With respect to dispatching the SDF to participate in operations under the rubric of "international cooperation," anti-militarist norms and the policy of exclusive defense are clearly at play. It is here that politicians and civilian bureaucrats work together to formulate detailed legislative frameworks. For example, there are five principles that guide the SDF's participation in UN peacekeeping operations (PKO):

—The warring parties must reach a ceasefire agreement.

—The warring parties must consent to a UN force and Japan's participation therein.

—The UN force must not side with any of the warring parties.

—Japan must ensure that if any of the three principles above are not met, its peacekeepers can be withdrawn.

—The use of weapons by SDF personnel should be limited as much as possible to contingencies "that are conceivably necessary to protect [their] lives."[120]

The intent of the PKO law, therefore, was to reduce to a minimum the chances that SDF personnel might have to use deadly force at a purely tactical level, to say nothing of its use in a more strategic way. Similarly, when the GSDF was deployed to Iraq to carry out reconstruction work, there was concern in Tokyo that local insurgents might attack the Japanese troops, so the Koizumi administration insisted that other foreign contingents defend them.

More revealing are the guidelines developed for aggression against the home islands. Closer to home, the guidelines under which the SDF operates suggest a more robust culture. First of all, the strategy for countering a coastal landing is to destroy the enemy invasion force before it gets ashore. The operations "must [aim] to destroy enemy forces as early as possible by countering them between the sea and coastal areas, as well as at landing sites." The three services are to jointly strike the aggressor's transport assets, both at sea and in the air, at least to degrade their capability if not to force them to retreat altogether. They are to lay mines and concentrate forces at potential landing sites to make any invasion as costly as possible. In the event of a naval attack on coastal areas, the MSDF must rely first on detection and then on mobilizing a full-scale counterattack, supported by the ASDF and GSDF as required.[121]

Second, the MOD recognizes that special operations forces and guerrillas "pose a serious threat" to Japan's security. The SDF is responsible for defending against armed attacks on people, destruction of facilities, assassination of leaders, and other types of raids; the police are responsible for violations of law by enemy agents. To meet the threat of guerrillas and special operations forces, the principal objective is to "quickly gain control of the situation to minimize damage from assault." In that effort, good intelligence is the first line of defense; the second is to interdict the problem units offshore with submarines, destroyers, and ASDF aircraft and to use the GSDF to patrol the coasts and guard key facilities. If infiltrators actually get ashore, ground and air assets are to be used to locate them, after which "combat forces will be promptly assembled . . . to besiege them, upon which they will be captured or destroyed."[122]

The Ministry of Defense has given specific attention to how to respond to "aggression" on offshore islands such as the Senkaku, which is one of the specific points of friction with China. Here, the guidance is similar to that for an invasion of the home islands. Routine patrols and intelligence collection seek to detect evidence of hostile intent. If a landing seems imminent, "operations will be conducted to prevent invasion of the enemy forces." If, in the absence of advance intelligence, adversary forces should get ashore, Japan will undertake joint operations to "defeat" and "destroy" the enemy.[123]

In sum, although there is no way to predict how Japan's armed forces would react—or be allowed to react—in the event of an actual clash, the SDF's own guidance suggests an inclination toward a robust and even preemptive response.

Third, there is past practice with regard to operations in the East China Sea. In the case of the passage of a PLAN Han class submarine through the Ishigaki Strait in November 2004, it was the Maritime Self-Defense Force that was on the front line. Dutton concludes that the MSDF chose to "actively pursue the submarine, rather than relying only on the de-escalatory measures contemplated by UNCLOS." Japan in effect "signaled to China that it is willing to flex military muscles of its own."[124] Presumably, the MSDF employed its various assets under the direction of its headquarters in Tokyo. But the response was relatively robust all the same.

Fourth, a distinct discomfort can be detected among Japanese politicians about willingly absorbing a first-strike attack. Admittedly, few cases speak to that concern. The only recent one concerns North Korea's April 2009 long-range missile test and its May 2009 nuclear test, when Prime Minister Aso Taro repeatedly stated his view that it would be constitutional for Japan to possess the capability to hit enemy bases and that "under certain conditions" it would be legal to strike those bases. Conservative leaders in the LDP also promoted the idea, and Japan Defense Agency head Nakatani Gen declared, "Japan cannot 'sit back and wait for death.'"[125] Thus, at least some of Japan's political leaders have rejected a purely defensive posture and expressed a willingness to attack the enemy before it hits Japan.[126]

Chapter 6 describes two incidents in which the Japan Coast Guard acted rather aggressively. In one, its ships rammed a Taiwan fishing vessel. In another, a JCG patrol boat repeatedly ordered ships of the Chinese Marine Surveillance Force to leave the Diaoyu/Senkaku Islands area. After the Chinese captains ignored the orders, the Japanese ship threatened to "squeeze out" and "crash" the intruders and to block their route.[127] Another incident involving the JCG and a Taiwan fishing boat occurred in September 2009. When two officers of Taiwan's coast guard boarded the vessel in order to try to help resolve the dispute, JCG officers reportedly pinned them to the deck. Indeed, to the extent that such aggressive responses reflect something more fundamental about Japanese strategic thought, the JCG is probably a greater problem than the MSDF. Its rules for the use of force are more flexible because it has a law enforcement function. It also has more flexibility because it is not clear whether an intruding maritime craft poses a law enforcement or national security challenge. Although the JCG does not have the capabilities needed to engage in naval warfare, it can "perform missions that, if executed by the MSDF, might be considered provocative or acts of war." And several Chinese commentaries have drawn negative conclusions from its actions. In January 2005, an article in a PLAN journal said that the JCG was "an emerging threat to Chinese maritime security."[128]

In short, neither China nor Japan is as pacific in its conduct of military operations as each would like outsiders to believe or as outsiders might expect. China has the more explicit strategic culture, one with a preemptive character. Moreover, the PLA has more autonomy than the SDF to develop its strategic culture independently of civilian authority. As seen, however, the defensive and accommodationist side of Japanese strategic culture becomes less pronounced as missions get closer to home, where a more aggressive, even preemptive, posture is in evidence. In those theaters there is less civilian monitoring and a clash with PLA units could actually occur. Finally, in the East China Sea, it is China—the party with the more aggressive culture—that is acting in a revisionist fashion. It dislikes the current status quo and seeks through its operations to create a wider strategic space for itself, to the disadvantage of Japan and the United States.

Chinese strategic culture has a distinct emphasis on preemption when it comes to tactical behavior, although more caution is evident at the level of broad strategy. With regard to Japan, it is not immediately clear that the Self-Defense Forces have their own strategic culture because they operate within a rather restrictive birdcage constructed for them by civilians. If they do, the posture is defensive. Still, there are hints of a modest temptation to aggressiveness on the part of the MSDF and the JCG. The limits on the SDF are a reminder that strategic culture can correlate with and reinforce civil-military relations. The People's Liberation Army has both substantial autonomy from civilian leaders and a bias toward preemptive action. The SDF, on the other hand, is both more restricted by civilian leaders and less offensive in terms of its strategic bias. Strategic culture can also correlate with strategic goals. Japan is relatively content with the status quo in maritime East Asia, as is the United States. It is China that seeks to alter that status quo in order to establish a larger strategic buffer between it and perceived potential threats to its security.

8

Decisionmaking in China

As discussed, China and Japan have significant military capabilities that they exercise in the same geographic space, a space that each regards as important to its national security. There are specific points of friction in that space that draw the two powers together and create the risk of clashes. Some institutional features of the People's Liberation Army and the Japan Self-Defense Forces would exacerbate the clash rather than contain it.

Accidental clashes between military forces occur occasionally but generally do not become foreign policy crises. Governments find ways to manage the dispute and avoid escalation. But sometimes they don't. Witness the beginning of World War I in Europe. Recall the game of chicken that China and Japan found themselves playing during the summer of 1937. So institutions matter, as some scholars in China and Japan understand. Peking University's Ye Zicheng writes: "If China truly wants to become a power with world influence, apart from developing its own military and economic strength, it should make big efforts in system building." That is, China should get its institutional house in order.[1] Shinoda Tomohito of the International University of Japan argues, "Centralized policy making is essential to foreign-policy issues that require interagency coordination" (as most important issues do).[2]

Even though the chance of a China-Japan clash may be modest, the prospects that the two governments will be able to contain it and prevent a foreign policy crisis are low—for two reasons. First, neither government is organized well for crisis management. Second, in each country the politics of Japan-China relations easily acquires a hostile tone and limits policymakers' ability to contain a crisis. This chapter and the next describe the structure of decision-making in China and Japan and the routine operations of their institutions.

Structure of Decisionmaking

In sharp contrast to the more centralized arrangements under Mao Zedong and Deng Xiaoping, the Chinese system today is more open to diverse sources of information, more pluralistic in terms of competing bureaucratic interests, and more inclusive in terms of actors.[3] Yet it remains both quite centralized and personalistic at key points, and it lacks effective mechanisms to reconcile competing views. Moreover, it is a system that remains segmented institutionally into civilian and military wings.

The Core Executive

China's senior leadership is composed of the two to three dozen individuals who are in charge of the three hierarchies of the Chinese Communist system: the party, the government administration, and the military.[4] Those individuals are members of the Political Bureau (Politburo) of the Chinese Communist Party (CCP); vice premiers and state councilors of the State Council (the government cabinet); and members of the Central Military Commission (CMC). There is some overlap in membership among the bodies, particularly between the Politburo and the State Council. For the list of members as of the summer of 2009, see appendix 8A.

The Politburo Standing Committee (PBSC) of the CCP is the regime's most authoritative decisionmaking body. It meets at least once a week. In early 2010, six of its nine members were leaders of key formal institutions: the legislature, the State Council, the Chinese People's Political Consultative Conference (the united front assembly), the CCP Propaganda Department, and the CCP Discipline Inspection Commission. Two more members were being groomed for succession to top positions. The ninth member was Hu Jintao, who is known as the "paramount leader" by virtue of the fact that he serves as general secretary of the CCP, president of the People's Republic of China, and chairman of the CMC—that is, he heads the three hierarchies. It is worth noting that none of the PBSC members, including Hu Jintao, has had a career specializing in foreign or defense policy. In many respects, it is a collective leadership made up of domestic generalists.

The Politburo has twenty-five members, including the standing committee members plus sixteen others. Like that of the PBSC, membership of the Politburo is on an ex officio basis and bridges the tops of the three hierarchies. The only members of the Politburo who have a foreign or defense policy background are two vice chairmen of the Central Military Commission. It meets routinely only once a month because some members have jobs outside of Beijing, and it deliberates only the more important external policy decisions.[5]

It is the PBSC that makes the decisions on critical matters, particularly those that concern the survival of the party and national security; for that purpose, it may meet on an "enlarged" basis in order to foster consensus. When the Politburo meets on national security matters, it does so more to build consensus for and confer legitimacy on the decisions of the paramount leader and the PBSC. For the most part, the PBSC seeks Politburo endorsement on domestic matters and ideological direction, but it would also do so before going to war or addressing an existential crisis.[6] In principle and often in practice, the PBSC and the Politburo make decisions on a collective basis. At this level, Lieberthal notes, the Chinese system "has been intensely personal, with individual relationships extremely important in determining . . . political decisions."[7]

Like all leadership organizations in China, the Politburo and its standing committee have subordinate organizations that provide staff support. For the central party leadership, that body is the 3,800-person General Office of the Central Committee, which provides day-to-day support for members of the PBSC. It also is a key mechanism in the flow of information and documents from all parts of the regime, and as such, it has the power to screen what senior leaders see and to comment on what gets through the screening process. Moreover, the PBSC relies on the General Office to "communicate, coordinate, and oversee the implementation of critical party-state decisions." Reportedly, it has established "strong links" with the military's command-and-control structure.[8] (See figure 8-1.)

Organizing for Foreign and Defense Policy

Since the founding of the People's Republic, the Chinese Communist leadership has organized the formulation and implementation of policy by differentiating issue areas.[9] Each designated issue area is placed under the responsibility of a member of the Politburo, who supervises all the agencies that do work related to that issue; those agencies make up the "system" (*xitong*) for that issue. In most cases, the *xitong* cut across the three key institutional hierarchies of party, government, and military, so that agencies from each hierarchy might be part of the same *xitong*. But the system is not rigid. Issue areas and their *xitong* vary over time, depending on the salience of issues and the relative power of leaders.[10]

The issue areas that are relevant to the subject of this volume are military affairs, foreign affairs, national security affairs, Taiwan, and energy. As

Figure 8-1.

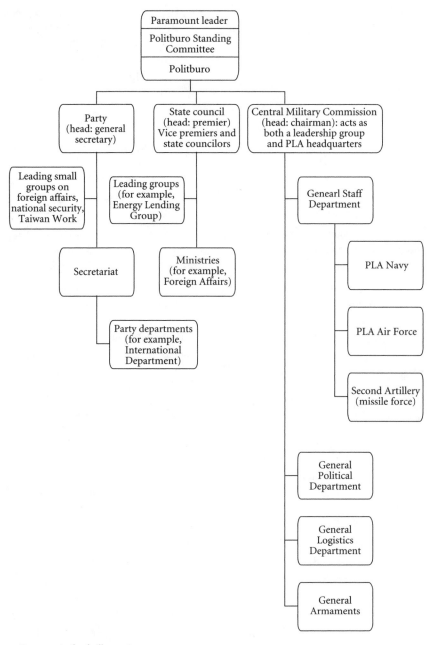

Sources: Author's illustration.

it happens, Hu Jintao is the leader responsible for the first four, as was Jiang Zemin, his predecessor as president, general secretary, and CMC chairman.[11] That reflects both the policy and political importance of those issues. Premier Wen Jiabao is the leader responsible for the energy issue area.[12]

Hu and Wen delegate some of their authority in each issue area to one or two subordinate officials. Senior CMC leaders do the work on military issues; deputy premiers assist on energy. As of mid-2008, the person assisting Hu Jintao on foreign affairs, national security affairs, and Taiwan was state councilor Dai Bingguo, who has been associated with Hu since the mid-1990s, when Hu was vice chairman of the party and Dai was the head of its International Department.[13]

Policy Coordination Bodies: Leading Groups and the Central Military Commission

Having chosen to organize the regime's work by issue area, each with its system of related agencies, the leadership then creates an institutional mechanism to *try* to get each system to act according to its preferences and to foster better coordination. Many of the bodies are known as leading groups (*lingdao xiaozu*, literally "leading/leader small group"); others have the title of "commission."[14]

One or more members of the Politburo lead each leading group, serving as head and deputy head. Securing these roles is a significant focus of political struggle among senior leaders. The other members are the senior officials from the government, party, and military agencies of the *xitong* for that issue. Throughout the PRC system, there is a "dynamic tension" between the personal interaction within leadership groups and the "very large, complex system of bureaucratic organization."[15] The leading groups are the point where that tension is most at play; roughly speaking, they form the zone where policy formulators meet policy implementers.[16]

CENTRAL MILITARY COMMISSION.   In terms of function, the leading group for military issues is the Central Military Commission. Its institutional rank is at the level of the Politburo in the party structure and the State Council in the government structure, whereas civilian leading groups are subordinate to the two latter bodies.[17] Moreover, the CMC is both a leadership group and a command authority, as befits a military organization,[18] but in the first role the CMC bears a strong similarity to other leading groups. The paramount leader is chairman. The two PLA members of the Politburo are CMC vice chairmen, analogous to the deputy heads of leading groups. Sometimes the minister of defense and the state vice president also are vice chairmen.[19] The regular members of the CMC are the heads of the key line agencies within PLA headquarters: the four general headquarters (general staff, political department, logistics department, and armaments departments) and the commanders of the three other services: the Second Artillery (the missile force), the People's Liberation Army Navy (PLAN), and the People's Liberation Army Air Force (PLAAF). For the CMC membership in mid-2009, see appendix 8A.[20] Note, however, that the CMC as leading group does not include officials from civilian agencies, whereas civilian leading groups that address external policy issues include military officers as members.

CIVILIAN LEADING GROUPS FOR EXTERNAL POLICY ISSUES. Civilian leading groups that are responsible for external affairs are party organizations. According to a Politburo decision of December 1987, they became "decisionmaking consultation bodies" (*juece zixun jigou*) as opposed to executive bodies and service institutions. Their function also expanded from policy coordination to policy formulation.[21] They can make decisions on major policy issues, subject to concurrence by the Politburo or the PBSC; make judgments on major events or long-term trends, based on commissioned studies and reports; coordinate among different functional departments in the government and between the civilian and military hierarchies; and conduct crisis management in emergencies.[22]

Appendix 8B presents the membership of the Foreign Affairs Leading Group (FALG) and the Taiwan Work Leading Group (TWLG).[23] As noted, Dai Bingguo became the state councilor responsible for foreign affairs, national security, and Taiwan in 2007. A PLA deputy chief of staff has served on each for a number of years, and apparently was joined in 2008 by the head of the Second Department of the General Staff Department, which is responsible for human intelligence gathering.[24]

The National Security Leading Group (NSLG) was established in 1999, after extended debate about setting up some kind of crisis management mechanism.[25] Jiang Zemin had pushed for a U.S.-style National Security Council, but existing institutions apparently resisted the proposal, particularly because the new body would be a decisionmaking entity separate from the PBSC. The ultimate compromise was to create the NSLG whose membership was exactly the same as that of the FALG.[26]

Another leading group, relevant to China-Japan relations, is the National Energy Leading Group, staffed by the State Energy Office, which is connected to the National Development and Reform Commission (NDRC). It was established in 2005 under the leadership of the State Council, reflecting its economic mission. Headed by the premier, the executive vice premier, and the vice premier in charge of industry and energy, its members include the ministerial-level heads of various economic agencies, the minister of foreign affairs, and a PLA deputy chief of the general staff.

It is sometimes assumed that interagency coordination occurs only at the level of the leading group, but it turns out that at least for the FALG, there has emerged a practice of holding meetings at subordinate levels in addition to the level of the leading group itself. At subordinate levels, ministers are the principal participants, by and large; reportedly, however, deputy ministers attend some meetings and director-generals (*sizhang*) are the key actors in still others. That in fact replicates the three-level structure of decisionmaking meetings in the U.S. foreign policy establishment: the principals' committee, made up of cabinet secretaries; the deputies' committee, made up of deputy secretaries; and interagency working groups, made up of lower-level policy officials.[27] In China, the need to consider issues at several levels may impede action.

STAFF SUPPORT.   Because leading groups lack their own staff, an office elsewhere in the system is tasked with supporting the operations of each leading group. The Foreign Affairs Office does so for both the FALG and the NSLG, and the Taiwan Affairs Office does so for the TWLG; each is a ministerial-level unit. The Foreign Affairs Office is led by a director and two deputy directors and has a staff of only about two dozen people, mainly career diplomats and officers from the party's international department. It has three departments, one for administration and secretariat functions (that is, a general office), one for the management of foreign affairs, and one for long-term policy research.[28]

On the military side, staff support for the CMC comes from its general office, which is the central communications mechanism through which information flows and is interpreted for the high command. It also smoothes interactions among the senior PLA leaders and various PLA organizations.[29]

Line Agencies: Military

Several key line agencies are linked to the CCP leadership by the CMC, FALG, and NSLG, including military and civilian organizations.

CENTRAL MILITARY COMMISSION AS COMMAND AUTHORITY.   In its role as a command authority, the CMC has administrative control and oversight of the PLA's four general headquarters, which are responsible for general staff functions, procurement, logistics, and the political loyalty and welfare of the troops. The CMC also has command authority regarding the branches of the armed services (PLAN, PLAAF, and the Second Artillery) and over military regions. It exercises that command through the General Staff

Department (GSD). In conjunction with the State Council, the CMC establishes and manages the military budget and national defense investment.[30]

In addition to its general office, discussed above, the CMC is also served by one or more permanent-alert command centers, through which flows operational and intelligence information from the field and from which orders are conveyed to subordinate units. One such center is said to be in the city of Beijing at the Ministry of National Defense Building, headed by the CMC vice chairman in charge of daily affairs, who is assisted by the deputy chiefs of staff for operations and intelligence and supported by "task teams" from the General Staff Department. Another, a GSD unit, is reportedly located in the Western Hills outside of Beijing, acting as the "nerve center" of the PLA's various services.[31]

GENERAL STAFF DEPARTMENT.   The General Staff Department plays a pivotal role in the military hierarchy. As the operational headquarters of China's armed forces, it is functionally more important than the other general departments, to which it is nominally equivalent. One Chinese description of its tasks lists the following:

—planning, organizing, and directing military operations

—conducting staff work for the top leadership of the PLA to assist in decisionmaking

—serving as the lead organization in the PLA for military modernization program decisions

—coordinating the work of the four general departments

—administering military legislation and the military legal system

—providing guidance for logistical support

—providing guidance for military science research and defense science and technology studies

—providing information studies.[32]

The GSD is a large organization, with as many as 100,000 total staff.[33] It is headed by the chief of the General Staff (CGS) and a few deputy chiefs of the General Staff (DCGS), each with a separate portfolio.

The most important GSD units for the purposes of this discussion are units that link senior leadership and units in the field by transmitting incoming data from subordinate PLA units and intelligence and issuing orders to those organizations. They provide advice to those higher up in the hierarchy on how to respond to the situation of the moment. Those units include the General Office and the First, Second, and Third Departments:

The General Office, the GSD's key administrative unit, serves as the communications link between the CGS and DCGSs and the rest of the organization. It controls the schedules of and the paper flow to these senior officials, drafts speeches for them, and convenes meetings. Within the General Office is the military research section, which conducts research on domestic and international issues of concern to the GSD leadership.[34]

The First Department is responsible in peacetime for monitoring the current activity of the PLA and of foreign armed forces and for preparing the PLA's war plans. In wartime, it would undertake national-level command and control for the CMC over PLA operations.

The Second Department is responsible for collecting and analyzing political and military intelligence at strategic level, relying significantly on human intelligence.[35]

The Third Department does signals intelligence (sigint).[36] Almost nothing is known about its operations. Presumably it has the same sorts of objectives, targets, collection and processing technologies, and organizational pathologies that sigint agencies of other countries do. And presumably the product of its operations is fed to the same sort of "customers" to whom information from the Second Department is delivered.

The People's Liberation Army Navy.   The PLAN is under the jurisdiction and command of the CMC, exercised either through the GSD or directly through its own headquarters. The commander and commissar are grade 3 officers, which is equivalent to a military region commander.[37] The headquarters has four first-level departments that replicate those of the GSD and the political, logistics, and equipment departments. Within headquarters are organizations that conduct daily operations and collect and process information on foreign countries.[38]

The People's Liberation Army Air Force.   Organizationally, the PLAAF is similar to the PLAN, with an administrative chain of command centered at its headquarters and with several subordinate levels: military region air forces; air corps, command posts, and bases; and operational units.[39] The PLAAF headquarters is under the jurisdiction of the CMC, which exercises command and control either through the GSD or directly. It has four first-level departments: staff, political, logistics, and equipment departments. The headquarters has eighteen second-level units, of which the most important are the general office, the operations department, and the intelligence department.[40] Regional air forces are aligned with the ground force military regions: Beijing, Shenyang, Lanzhou, Jinan, Nanjing, Guangzhou, and Chengtu. The regional air force commander is the deputy military region commander. The military region commander has operational command over the air units and responsibility for combined operations. The air force commander has responsibility for flight operations.[41] The military regions most relevant for Japan are likely Beijing, Shenyang, Jinan, because of their greater geographic proximity, and Nanjing, because it would be the core of the combat front organization in any conflict with Taiwan.

Line Agencies: Civilian

On the civilian side of the PRC system, several organizations are involved in the conduct of external affairs, broadly defined. The National Development and Reform Commission coordinates economic and social strategies and has oversight over energy policy and projects.[42] The Ministry of Commerce is in charge of much of China's external economic relations, including its foreign aid. Through its case officers overseas, the Ministry of State Security (MSS) collects foreign intelligence. The Xinhua News Agency collects information (and intelligence) about the countries in which it has bureaus, while the international communications office of the State Council is responsible for making China's public case to the world.[43] All of these entities are important for the conduct and impact of China's external policy. For the purposes of this discussion, the more significant agencies are the Ministry of Foreign Affairs, which is most relevant to the conduct of relations with Japan; the Communist Party's International Department; and the MSS and Xinhua, which provide some of the information that Beijing policymakers use to make decisions.

MINISTRY OF FOREIGN AFFAIRS.   The Ministry of Foreign Affairs (MFA) translates the general directions of the senior leadership into more specific and operational policy steps and then carries them out. It seeks to coordinate and control the external actions of other bureaucratic actors, and it also provides a substantial amount of information regarding foreign developments to the leadership.[44]

The ministry's headquarters has the inevitable general office, plus departments responsible for eight geographic regions; seven functional areas (policy planning, international organizations, arms control, treaty and law, information, protocol, and consular affairs); and eleven more administrative tasks.[45] Then there are foreign affairs offices within China itself, at the provincial and subprovincial level.[46]

There are inherent tensions between the ministry's different departments: between those covering different geographic regions and between geographic departments and functional ones.[47] Exacerbating the tensions is the tendency of diplomats to cluster in factions or "schools." "Once a bureaucrat becomes a member of one faction or school, he or she cannot break free; in addition, each school treats all nonmembers as outsiders and offers no support or assistance to any nonmember."[48]

An important division of the MFA is the Department of Policy Planning. According to the ministry's website, it has three main functions. The first is to conduct analysis on "issues of overall and strategic importance in global situation and international relations." The second is to coordinate the policy analysis and "situation assessment" done by all MFA units, whether in Beijing or in the field. The third is to "draft speeches and documents on foreign affairs for Party and state leaders and ministry leaders."[49]

THE INTERNATIONAL DEPARTMENT OF THE COMMUNIST PARTY.   The International Department (ID) is responsible for ties with parties (particularly communist parties) of other countries. It had a more prominent bureaucratic role during the early period of the People's Republic, when the bulk of China's diplomatic relations was with communist countries, yet for some countries it remains a parallel diplomatic modality that they can use. Among its functions relevant to decisionmaking, the ID collects current intelligence on the domestic politics and foreign policies of countries around the world; assists PRC embassies in monitoring other nations' domestic politics; and conducts research on various aspects of the international environment that bear on China's interests.[50] With respect to Japan, the ID has maintained relations with Japanese political parties when bilateral ties between the governments were problematic—for example, with the LDP during the Koizumi period.[51] In 2004, there were thirteen exchange delegations with Japan, the largest for any country in the world.[52] In terms of structure, the ID has eight regional bureaus, of which Bureau II is responsible for Northeast Asia and Indochina. The "research office" is responsible for the intelligence effort. As a party department, the ID reports to the Central Committee's Foreign Affairs Office and to the General Office.

THE MINISTRY OF STATE SECURITY.   Institutionally the Ministry of State Security is analogous to the old Soviet KGB. Its primary function is the clandestine collection of intelligence, both domestic and foreign. Little is known about the structure of MSS headquarters, but it is reasonable to assume that it possesses geographic bureaus like other Chinese foreign affairs agencies.[53]

The China Institutes of Contemporary International Relations (CICIR), established in 1965, is a unit of the MSS.[54] The U.S. agency whose function is closest to that of the CICIR is the CIA's Directorate of Intelligence. Both are civilian analytical organizations that draw on information from all sources, including various types of clandestine intelligence, and prepare short- and longer-term assessments for policymakers.[55] Research institutes exist for the most important topics, including Japan.[56]

THINK TANKS AND SCHOLARS.   China also has an array of research organizations whose job is to prepare analyses of the foreign and security challenges that China faces. There are three basic types: government think tanks, academic specialized think tanks, and university-affiliated think tanks.[57] Government think tanks are research organizations directly associated with agencies of the regime, and each major foreign policy and national security organization has its affiliated think tank. The Foreign Ministry has the China Institute for International Studies. Directly subordinate to the CMC are the Academy of Military Sciences (AMS) and National Defense University (NDU). Each does research-based analysis for the CMC (and sometimes for the General Staff Department) on foreign militaries and strategic issues. The AMS is the more important in shaping thinking at the CMC, and it tends to focus more on the future of warfare. The NDU is primarily a teaching institution, and its studies for the CMC, which examine the present state of the world and the PLA's current challenges, are more academic in character.[58] The General Staff Department itself has the China Foundation for International Strategic Studies. Linked to the PLA's General Political Department is the Center for Peace and Development Studies.[59] Sometimes think tanks are related to more than one policy organization. Thus, the Center for Peace and Development Studies has ties to the Ministry of Foreign Affairs and the Ministry of State Security as well as the General Political Department.[60]

The most obvious "academic specialized think tank" is the Chinese Academy of Social Sciences (CASS), under the jurisdiction of the State Council. It has a number of institutes that do policy-relevant research, which it conveys to government agencies. Among them is the Institute for Japan Studies, founded in 1981, which has divisions that examine Japan's politics, economy, society and culture, and foreign relations. In addition to the research and writing of its scholars, it also holds conferences and symposiums on issues bearing on China-Japan relations and disseminates a public journal— *Riben Xuekan* [*Japanese Studies*]—and a restricted one, *Riben Wenti Ziliao Tekan* [*Special Publication on Materials Concerning Japan Issues*]. There are similar research institutes on Japanese studies at provincial-level specialized institutes and within Chinese universities.

Institutes convey their views through channels to the leadership. In addition, specific scholars have access to the policy process because of the personal regard in which they are held. If university-based specialists have links with the policy world, it is likely for that reason rather than because of their institutional affiliation.[61]

Concluding Observations

Several points are worth noting about China's decisionmaking structure. First of all, it is a segmented system, in which civilian and military hierarchies intersect and coordinate at very few points; the most important point of intersection is the CMC itself. And there is an asymmetry between civilian leading groups that address external policy issues, which have senior military officers, and the CMC as leading group, which does not include officials from civilian agencies besides its chairman and, sometimes, the vice president.

Second, it was only gradually that the paramount leader took over the key bodies responsible for policy coordination. Jiang Zemin became chairman of the Central Military Commission in 1992 and head of the Taiwan Work Leading Group in 1993. It was not until 1998 that he became head of the Foreign Affairs Leading Group. He became the first head of the National Security Leading Group when it was formed in 1999. Other members of the Politburo Standing Committee had held some of those responsibilities before Jiang acquired all three posts. Perhaps it was a measure of his ambition, but it likely also reflected his and his colleagues' view that the issues involved were too important to be left to someone else. Hu Jintao followed Jiang's pattern. He became head of the FALG, TWLG, and NSLG in late 2002, after becoming CCP general secretary. It was not until two years later that he became chairman of the CMC.

Third, it was not until 1987 that a representative of the military was given a seat on the FALG (in that case, the minister of defense, Qin Jiwei).[62] Thereafter, the PLA gained a representative on the TWLG and two on the NSLG, one of whom is the minister of defense. At the same time, PLA representation on the PBSC and the Party Secretariat ended.

Fourth, the influence of the offices that support the various leading groups can wax and wane. The Foreign Affairs Office (FAO), for example, had significantly more power prior to September 1998, when, Lu Ning reports, it was the "central processing unit" of China's foreign affairs establishment and the key communications link between senior leaders and implementing bureaucracies within the party, government, and military hierarchies. All decisions that were not within the immediate province of a single agency had to go through the FAO, and it was responsible for interagency coordination. Staffed by MFA personnel, it was "regarded as a bastion of MFA influence." Yet when its director, Liu Huaqiu, tried to expand the office's influence even further, its power was reduced from policy coordination to policy consultation.[63] In recent years, however, the FAO has made a comeback under the leadership of Dai Bingguo.

Finally, the PRC system does have a competitive feature, in that it has a large number of leading groups, several of which are for external affairs. That arrangement fosters the very coordination problems that the leading-group system was designed to overcome. The United States system has a number of issue-specific working groups. but they are at a relatively low level. There is only one deputies' committee, one principals' committee, and one National Security Council.[64]

Process: Routine

Routine policymaking in China occurs from both the bottom up and the top down. When it comes to policy toward Japan, power in China tends to flow downhill. Moreover, there is some tension between more action-oriented, top-down parts of the system and those where procedural routine is the norm. That distinction is not exclusive to China; it is found in all well-established organizations, including states. Standard operating procedures can provide standardization, predictability, and accountability—which are not insignificant outcomes—yet they can be a drag on innovation and effective response in a crisis.

Information: Process and Quality

A certain amount is known about how information is processed within the PRC system. What is most striking is the number of filters between the raw information itself and the decisionmaker and thus the number of chances for distortion of the information to occur. Second is the tendency to trust some (or one) source of information and not others.

The PRC leadership is inundated with an avalanche of items on a daily or near-daily basis. Each significant line agency provides a regular document that reflects its sphere of work and concerns. The GSD watch center daily sends the Politburo and the CMC both an intelligence summary and a report on the threat environment (the latter regularly covers Japanese military activity). The CCP General Office prepares a daily report for the leaders on major issues and intelligence. CICIR sends a summary of finished foreign intelligence, and the Xinhua News Agency prepares *Cankao Ziliao* [*Reference Materials*]. Each line agency produces its own internal reports, some of which are shared with other agencies on a limited basis.[65]

Daily briefing reports and emergency bulletins are only a small part of the flow of information that works its way to the senior leadership and shapes its thinking. Reports come from various government agencies and think tanks of various sorts through both formal and informal (personal) channels. As Chinese foreign policy specialists inside and outside the regime have grown in number and gained wider access to information, the flow of information toward the top has increased. Bonnie Glaser and Phillip Saunders conclude that as the number of think tanks has grown, their competition to shape leadership thinking has mushroomed, which has "increased the volume of reports written for Chinese leaders, but has not always translated into higher quality."[66]

Indeed, one Chinese scholar concludes: "As a consequence of the competition among governmental or semigovernmental think tanks, the number of reports prepared for Chinese policymakers is excessive. *Basically, there are just too many reports written for Chinese policymakers.*"[67]

Given the surge in volume, efforts have been made to channel it. Agencies with a variety of offices preparing reports must route all of them through a single internal reports section before sending them forward. At the top of the system, the key gateways are the general offices of the Central Committee of the party, of the State Council of the government, and of the Central Military Commission. That is, agencies must send products intended for the leadership through the choke points of their relevant hierarchy. Thus, the Japanese Studies Institute at the Chinese Academy of Social Sciences (CASS), which probably distributed reports on its own before, now must send them to the CASS reports section, where they are reviewed before being sent to one of the general offices. The gatekeepers at the top then distribute the reports to the leadership and to agencies with a need to know. Yet a Chinese scholar told me that the individuals filtering reports at the top do not necessarily have the specialized knowledge needed to evaluate the reports.[68]

The general office of the party Central Committee also has the power to task agencies to provide information on breaking developments, both internal and external. With a twenty-four-hour watch center, "the Central [Committee] GO [General Office] is said to be able to obtain the urgent information about a major incident anywhere in the country and pass it on to the Central leaders within fifteen minutes."[69] But an emphasis on speed often sacrifices accuracy, which is at a premium in the initial stages of a crisis or a disaster. Indeed, first reports often are wrong.

In reality, the delivery of reports to a senior leader means delivery to that leader's personal office. And here, the leader's personal secretary (*mishu*) or group of secretaries comes into play. These individuals, who exist throughout the Chinese system, serve as the official's interface with other leaders and agencies. The English word "secretary" does not do them justice (the Chinese is literally "secret books" or "secret writing"). They can become an extension of their bosses themselves, but they can also provide them with a reality check. Kenneth Lieberthal writes: "The *mishu* system provides key assistance to top leaders who are not well versed in some of the matters they must deal with."[70] In a collective leadership in which most members of the PBSC know little about foreign and national security policy, the secretaries who specialize in those areas serve a special educative—and filtering—function for their principals. (To the extent that decisions are considered on a collective basis, those secretaries also play an important role in coordinating the views of standing committee members.) How well they do their job in sifting and interpreting, particularly for leaders with little knowledge of or experience in foreign matters, can have a critical impact on the decisionmaking process.

A similar phenomenon occurs in line agencies. In the Ministry of Foreign Affairs, for example, the secretaries of senior MFA officials screen the large number of items that arrive in their offices on a daily basis. "By controlling the information that reaches the desks of ministerial policy decisionmakers, their secretaries play a crucial role in helping shape the perceptions of the ministerial leadership."[71]

In spite of the large number of reports, there apparently is no institutionalized mechanism to reconcile differences between reports. Whether the General Office or the principal senior leader for the relevant policy area (for example, Dai Bingguo, the state councilor responsible for foreign affairs and Taiwan in 2008) will offer an interpretation of the intelligence is unclear. There are pros and cons for reconciling differences and offering interpretations. If senior leaders receive several conflicting reports, they could end up confused. But if there is an effort to reconcile them when doing so is not justified, then leaders are denied the knowledge that there was disagreement among the agencies that submit the reports. Further, they are subject to manipulation by whoever is homogenizing the information.

What appears to happen is that leaders tend to rely on sources of interpretation in which they have gained confidence. Thus, Lu Ning, writing around 2001, reported that the leadership tended to place a higher value on the information that it received from the MFA than that from other agencies.[72] With the transition from Jiang Zemin to Hu Jintao and Dai Bingguo's emergence as Hu's most trusted foreign affairs aide, the Foreign Affairs Office (FAO), which Dai headed from 2002 to 2007, became the most trusted source of information for the leadership. Bureaucratic agencies and think tanks send reports to the FAO's policy research department, whose staff then summarize them for Foreign Affairs Leading Group members.[73]

There is evidence that in the 1990s, General Xiong Guangkai, during his tenure as deputy chief of staff for foreign affairs and intelligence, had a significant impact on the thinking of the senior leadership, particularly Jiang Zemin. Reportedly, he made himself very useful to the various leading groups of which he was a member by helping other members make sense of conflicting intelligence reports.[74] James Mulvenon's judgment at the time of Xiong's retirement was as follows: "For more than a decade, General Xiong Guangkai used his position as the head of military intelligence to shape and influence Chinese leadership assessments of foreign and security policy, especially Sino-U.S. relations."[75]

A different issue is the quality of the interpretations of Chinese analysts. If they are wrong, then the decisions on which they are based will be flawed. One can point to a number of cases in which the Chinese regime came to an incorrect conclusion about why a crisis occurred and then adopted a policy response accordingly: for example, the U.S. bombing of the PRC embassy in Belgrade in May 1999; the clash between a U.S. reconnaissance plane and a PLAN interceptor in the South China Sea in April 2001; the belief that the Dalai Lama is primarily responsible for recurring unrest in Tibet; why Taiwan president Lee Teng-hui objected to Beijing's approach to solving the dispute between Taiwan and China.[76]

For an example of how an important segment of the PLA establishment viewed China's security environment, consider the presentation that Major General Luo Yuan of China's Academy of Military Sciences gave at various academic institutions in the United States in October 2008.[77] General Luo placed his security analysis within the general frame of the PRC's twin goals on peace and economic development, making the point that neither goal is close to achievement. (Implicit in that framing is the questionable idea that the absence of development is the cause of war.) He noted the contradictions between development and lack of development and between unipolarity (read U.S. hegemony) and multipolarization. He then proceeded to identify the "four security concerns confronting China." The first was that Western countries—particularly the United States—were plotting to "Westernize" and "divide" China.[78] Second was "Taiwan independence," described as the "most important and most pressing" threat. Luo identified the reasons why, in his mind, the election of Ma Ying-jeou in Taiwan had not improved

China's security position: the Democratic Progressive Party (DPP), which had suffered a setback in the elections of 2008, still enjoyed the support of 40 percent of the voters; the Taiwan military was increasing its capability to "resist unification by force"; and Ma himself intended to maintain Taiwan's distance from mainland China and to "preserve a separatist regime."

Peripheral "hot spots" made up the third threat. First among these was the North Korea nuclear issue. The second was Japan, with which "disputes were intensifying" and there existed "the danger of military conflict erupting." Politically, relations had been "cold" because there had been no leaders' summits for five years; economically, relations were "warm" because trade continued to increase; militarily, there were "disputes" because "Japan sees us as an important military threat." Cited as a specific dispute was the East China Sea and Japan's claim to share in development on the continental shelf. Other peripheral issues included "color revolutions," terrorism, regional conflicts such as Iraq and Iran, sovereignty over the South China Sea, sea lanes of communication, and territorial disputes. Even though these presentations were tailored for a foreign audience, they still reveal an overly suspicious assessment of the actions and intentions of others. The description of U.S. intentions is flawed, and the analysis of Japan ignores how much relations improved after the end of the Koizumi era.

The China Foundation for International Strategic Studies (CFISS), which is backed by the Second Department of the PLA General Staff Department, China's human intelligence organization, publishes a journal that may well reflect PLA views. It has regular articles on Japan's movement toward becoming a "normal country." They describe in some detail the measures taken to dismantle the purported measures that had dictated Japan's postwar security strategy of "exclusive defense" and imposed restrictions on the Self-Defense Forces; the buildup of military capabilities; and the increasingly close policy and operational alignment with the United States. But the approach is fairly legalistic and does not fully take into account the changes in Japan's security environment that stimulated those changes. Nor does it identify the significant constraints that still exist or recognize that many past restrictions were less binding than they seemed. And sometimes it reads the worst into Japanese actions, for example, by concluding that Japan's acquisition of early warning aircraft, Aegis missile defenses, reconnaissance satellites, helicopter-equipped destroyers gives it capabilities that are both offensive and defensive in character—a claim that most objective experts would contest and does not speak to the questions of intentions at all.[79]

Bottom-Up Policymaking

In China, a lot of policy *activity*—though not necessarily policymaking—occurs within line agencies according to standard operating procedures, moving from lower levels to higher levels and, when necessary, reconciling the conflicting views of elements within the agency. In the People's Liberation Army Navy, for example, there is an established, seven-step process for developing new tactics and training concepts in preparation for the adoption of new equipment, a process that can take several years to complete.[80] In the Ministry of Foreign Affairs, responses are crafted for issues on which precedents do not suffice through a process of consensus building. Based on consultations with the superiors in the division (and the department if necessary), the relevant desk will draft a "request for instructions" (RFI). Once approved, the RFI will go up the bureaucratic chain for ministerial approval. If more than one department is involved, the RFI is coordinated between or among them.[81]

Obviously, most issues of external policy involve more than one agency, each with its own domain. Here, there are mechanisms for interagency coordination. On the most routine questions, one of the agencies involved will be given the lead in drawing up the RFI. Differences between other relevant agencies will be reconciled if possible, by the agency heads if necessary.[82] Here, an interesting feature of the communist system comes into play. Different ministers have a party rank as well as their institutional position. Thus, not all ministers are created equal. A minister with a high party rank can ignore the policy of a ministry whose chief has a lower rank.[83]

THE EAST CHINA SEA.   One apparent example of this bottom-up interagency coordination concerns the formulation of China's negotiating position on development of the East China Sea oil fields (described in chapter 6 of this volume). Although there are leading groups for foreign affairs and energy, the issue apparently falls between the two and the agencies concerned come together on an issue-specific basis. The National Development and Reform Commission (NDRC), which is the successor of the old State Planning Commission, reportedly is the convener. Also participating are representatives from China's state-owned oil companies, the People's Liberation Army, and the Ministry of Foreign Affairs.[84]

Although the issue concerns negotiations with a foreign country and a successful resolution of the matter would remove a flashpoint in bilateral relations, the MFA is not able to call the tune in interagency discussions. The oil companies have their commercial interests, which are linked to China's broader energy security. As a lead economic agency, the NDRC supports the oil companies. Moreover, the military regards the East China Sea as its strategic buffer and opposes concessions to Japan that would restrict the PLAN's freedom of movement. These institutional rivalries have created a rigidity in China's position ever since the East China Sea issue was moved to the diplomatic channel in 2004, in spite of the pressure to produce an agreement before Prime Minister Fukuda's visit to Beijing in December 2007 and President Hu Jintao's visit to Japan in May 2008. In the end, the PLA may have been excluded from the negotiations that reached a "consensus in principle" in June 2008.[85]

TAINTED DUMPLINGS. Another instance of failed ad hoc interagency coordination was the case of the tainted dumplings (*jiaozi* in Chinese, *gyoza* in Japanese). In late 2007 and early 2008, a small number of Japanese citizens became ill after eating frozen dumplings produced in China. Chemical analysis revealed that the dumplings contained high concentrations of a poisonous pesticide. Early on, China's assistant foreign minister, He Yafei, extended an apology to Japan's foreign minister, Komura Masahiko.[86]

There was an effort on the part of the food safety and public safety authorities of the two countries to collaborate in determining the source of the contamination but to no avail. Soon the spirit of cooperation waned. To make matters worse, a senior official of China's General Administration of Quality Supervision, Inspection, and Quarantine (AQSIQ) held a press conference on February 13, 2008, to announce that the agency had inspected the factory that produced the offending dumplings and found no evidence of the pesticide and therefore had concluded that it must have come from a Japanese source. The AQSIQ did so even after having been advised by two former ambassadors to Japan (Wang Yi and Wu Dawei) that it was highly unlikely that the pesticide had been introduced into the dumpling packages in Japan. The AQSIQ announcement only inflamed Japanese opinion even more, and a consensus began to grow in early March that Hu Jintao should delay his state visit to Japan until the clamor subsided. There was concern in Japan that if the summit went ahead as scheduled, Fukuda's sinking popularity would decline even further. In China there were concerns that demonstrators would throw dumplings at Hu Jintao.[87]

Apparently, Hu had been unaware of the negative trend in Japanese public opinion. A Chinese diplomat told a Japanese journalist in late February that "the situation in Japan has not been communicated well to the President." That was not too surprising since the leadership had been coping with the consequences of an unusually heavy January snowfall in South China and preparing for the Eleventh National People's Congress in early March. The Foreign Ministry, however, was sympathetic toward Japan over the episode and angry at the effect of the news conference on the summit. It therefore decided to violate the consensus norms of the interagency process and send a report directly to Hu describing the situation. Aware of the problem for the first time, he was reportedly "furious." He summoned the AQSIQ minister, Li Changjiang, and the minister of public security, Meng Jianzhu, to express his displeasure, demanding to know whether "you thought about international public opinion?"[88]

TAIWAN.   Another case occurred in the spring of 2008, after Ma Ying-jeou won the Taiwan presidential election. A strategic opportunity was emerging to transform cross-Strait relations through a process of reassurance and engagement and thereby to reduce the mutual fear and risk of conflict that had existed for at least a decade and to foster broad political support on Taiwan for that positive outcome. But that would occur only if Beijing were to take steps sooner or later to accommodate Taiwan's desires for greater international space and for a deeper sense of security. At the time, PRC analysts who were connected with government ministries conveyed to American scholars a profound sense of caution, offering all the reasons why Beijing would not take even initial steps. In the event, Hu Jintao took quick action; he, at least, understood that there was a strategic opportunity for China to seize. One American scholar concluded: "[This] confirms the critical role played by top-level decisionmakers—especially Hu Jintao—to promote progress in cross-strait relations. Absent new guidelines from the top, lower-level players are risk averse and therefore unwilling to propose creative solutions that depart from current policy."[89]

Top-Down Policymaking

Hu Jintao's intervention in the dumpling case and his response to the election of Ma Ying-jeou demonstrate the constraints on bottom-up policymaking and why leaders must dominate the process if policymakers are to act cohesively and reflect their will. Indeed, there are a number of matters on which the senior leadership is understood to take a special interest and reserve the right to make the decisions. According to Lu Ning, they include:

—issues that determine the basic orientation of Chinese foreign policy

—military operations that involve actual or potential external conflict

—regional policy and policy toward great powers like the United States, Russia, and Japan

—significant questions concerning implementation of policies

—policy toward "sensitive" regions or countries like Taiwan and North Korea

—policy concerning "sensitive" issues that have "strategic significance," such as China's entry into the World Trade Organization, the Shanghai Cooperation Organization, energy security, and so on

—any external policy issue that can disturb domestic order and stability.[90]

Obviously, there may be definitional questions over whether a specific problem falls within these general categories, but the general principle is clear. Hence, on those issues where the senior leadership takes initiative and sets a policy line, it is not challenged from below. Ironically, the top leaders are said to be less engaged on Japan than they are on the United States, even though Japan is a "major country."[91]

POWER OF THE PARAMOUNT LEADER.   Top-down policymaking raises the question of who makes it: a collective or the paramount leader himself. In theory—and often in fact—the Politburo Standing Committee is the locus of decisionmaking. Yet there is convergent evidence that on external policy the paramount leader often receives the deference of his colleagues. The other members of the PBSC are concerned mostly about domestic issues. Even on military issues, it is only on the defense budget that the paramount leader cannot go his own way.[92] Apparently, final decisions in the PBSC are made not on the basis of votes but by consensus; if consensus is not possible, even after informal consultations, the members usually defer to the paramount leader, who makes the final decision because external policy is his domain.[93]

Yet there are exceptions to that general rule. First of all, the paramount leader appears to be most constrained at the beginning of his tenure. His offices do not automatically confer power and authority; he must acquire them over time. Thus, Jiang Zemin was more deferential to his PBSC colleagues in the early 1990s, consulting them on speeches and meetings with foreign leaders and taking their opinions into account in resolving contentious issues. Gradually, however, his preferences prevailed.[94] Hu Jintao appears to have followed the same pattern of early deference and increasing assertiveness.[95] And, as noted previously, he did not become chairman of the Central Military Commission until two years after he became CCP general secretary.

Second, issues cannot be neatly categorized as external and domestic. There are some nominally external issues that if mishandled could evoke a harsh popular reaction that rebounds on the leadership, undermining both its standing and the social stability on which CCP rule rests.[96] Japan and Taiwan certainly belong in that category. All members of the Politburo and its Standing Committee might worry, for example, that a demonstration against Japan might turn against the regime.

Third, there are cases in which PBSC members have sought to blame the paramount leader for a policy setback as a way of reducing his power or increasing their own. Qiao Shi, for example, attacked Jiang Zemin in 1995 after Lee Teng-hui's visit to the United States.[97]

It may be too much to say that with respect to external policy China approaches a presidential system, as one Chinese scholar claimed to me. Whether and how the paramount leader tries to dominate decisionmaking within the PBSC depends on the issue, including its implications for domestic stability, and how he assesses his power relative to that of his colleagues. Hu Jintao has not wished to shoulder the entire responsibility and sought the support of his colleagues, particularly in his early years. The more sensitive the subject and the higher the stakes, the more extensive his consultation; the more routine the issue, the more likely he is to act independently.[98] Still, he reportedly intervened to end interdepartmental debates on issues of sensitive cooperation between China and the United States not too long after he became the paramount leader.[99] And by mid-2008, as one Chinese insider put it, Hu was "in complete, absolute control of Taiwan policy."[100]

There are several implications of this power configuration. First, the personality and outlook of the paramount leader can have a substantial impact on how policy is framed. As one observer said of Jiang Zemin, he "has a big ego and that makes him different from Hu Jintao. It was his ego that made issues out of [the] EP-3, Falun Gong, and Taiwan. But it is also true that U.S.-China relations became easier to manage because of his ego."[101] Regarding Japan, it was Jiang's memory of the Japanese occupation in East China (he was a native of Yangzhou in Jiangsu province) that led him to place greater emphasis on history issues than many observers thought was productive and made it hard for him to appreciate Japan's apology fatigue. There was, in effect, a generational mismatch between him and Japanese leaders like Koizumi Junichiro.[102]

Second, when it comes to tough calls, which ultimately the paramount leader has to make, the bureaucrats become very cautious and reluctant to offer creative advice. Instead, they just provide information and the leader is forced to make the decision on his own. For example, when Abe Shinzo succeeded Koizumi Junichiro as prime minister of Japan, he sought to improve relations with China and South Korea. In a secret approach to Beijing, he offered to visit China soon and included the message, subtly conveyed, that he would not visit Yasukuni Shrine while he was prime minister. However,

China's stated condition for a resumption of high-level summits was that the Japanese prime minister make an *explicit* pledge not to visit the shrine. China's interagency process deadlocked over whether to abandon the explicit condition and accept Abe's offer of a visit, risking the fallout from a nationalistic public. In the end, Hu Jintao had to make the decision, and he chose to accept Abe's offer—a choice that turned out to be successful.[103]

Third, it takes the actions of the paramount leader to change a policy decreed by his predecessor. "Bad or absurd policies can last a long time because leaders are unwilling to make an unpopular decision."[104] Fourth, the quality of the personal relationships between the paramount leader and key aides can have a major impact on the conduct of foreign policy. Thus the confidence that Jiang Zemin placed in Xiong Guangkai's ability to interpret situations affected how China responded to those situations. The same goes for Hu Jintao's relationship to Dai Bingguo.

And fifth, when PBSC members decide to participate in decisionmaking or when the paramount leader decides for whatever reason to be guided by their judgment, it can take longer to arrive at a decision. For example, the response to the April 2005 demonstrations over Japan's desire to become a permanent member of the UN Security Council and the revision of some Japanese history textbooks was delayed because some PBSC members, including Hu Jintao, were initially out of town.[105]

INTERVENTION BY SENIOR LEADERS.   In their capacity as chairmen of leading groups, Hu Jintao and Wen Jiabao seek to put issues on the policymaking agenda and forge greater coherence among agencies in the relevant *xitong*. Leaders use leading groups as task forces to initiate action (indeed, policy leading groups often are termed *bangzi*, meaning "team," with the connotation of a task force). At their best, leading groups can override bureaucratic recalcitrance and passivity if they have the support of the PBSC and the offices that support them. In that role, the General Office of the Central Committee can support leading groups. Its purpose, write John Lewis and Xue Litai, "is to guarantee the bureaucracy's focused and uninterrupted performance in times of crisis and the conduct of high-profile national tasks."[106]

Leaders set the agenda for leading groups by issuing written instructions or by making notations on documents that they have read. Rather than making major proposals, the agency heads who sit on a leading group generally wait for leaders' directions. Once they receive them, they or their agencies develop proposals accordingly, which are then submitted for top-level approval. Ideas sometimes rise from below, but only if the author of the idea has special access to the top. Once the leadership adopts a new policy direction, implementation is facilitated by the prior coordination within the leading group. When a line agency has a policy recommendation or a proposal for how to flesh out policy guidance that it received previously, it likely sends it to the leading group. As seen, moreover, the leading groups are only the top level of a three-level consultation system. Deputy ministers attend second-level meetings and department heads go to the third-level ones.[107]

The leading groups meet regularly (once a week according to one estimate) to review developments in their policy area and work on policy proposals. The staff office for the relevant leading group convenes the various meetings, often on instruction from the official at the vice-premier level who is in charge of the issue area. Thus, prior to 2008, state councilor Tang Jiaxuan would likely call Dai Bingguo, the director of the Foreign Affairs Office, to convene meetings of the Foreign Affairs Leading Group or lower-level groups. Now Dai Bingguo is the person who orders the heads of relevant offices to convene meetings of the Foreign Affairs Leading Group, National Security Leading Group, and the Taiwan Work Leading Group.

Regarding the Central Military Commission, which is the functional equivalent of a leading group for the military *xitong*, its vice chairman and members meet weekly in a work conference to address both major policy issues and important operational matters; it appears that the chairman, the paramount leader, does not always attend. The CMC also holds enlarged conferences at the end of the year or on extraordinary occasions to ratify major policy changes and unveil new initiatives. It may also task ad hoc working groups and committees to study specific issues and make policy recommendations.

Sometimes, leading groups—for example, the FALG and the NSLG— meet on a joint basis; that confirms the existence of overlap between the two. Apparently, the criterion by which specific cases warrant NSLG consideration is related to the use or possibility of the use of force. For example, since its founding, the NSLG has never discussed a matter concerning Japan.[108]

Participation at meetings is sometimes quite flexible, as was apparent from the report of a meeting of the FALG concerning North Korea, held in a secret building in the Wangfujing area not far from Tiananmen on October 19, 2006, ten days after Pyongyang went ahead and conducted a nuclear test after China urged it not to. The meeting "was attended by about 50 party, government, and military experts," from the Ministry of Foreign Affairs, the People's Liberation Army, the Chinese Communist Party's International Department, and "Korean Peninsula experts," presumably from think tanks. The meeting took four actions to both analyze the new situation and prepare for any negative consequences. The TALG reportedly brings in representatives from a number of bureaucratic actors as it formulates and implements policy regarding Taiwan, because that issue by nature cuts across institutional boundaries.[109]

When senior leaders intersect with line agencies in any decisionmaking structure, a balance must be struck between the flow of information and recommendations from line agencies on one hand and the need for coherence, order, and, sometimes, speed in coming to a decision on the other.[110] Too much participation and competition among advisers may create confusion and delay; too much order may deny leaders an understanding of all the options available. Either type of excess can produce mistakes.

In that regard, the PRC system is fairly formalized. The paramount leader preserves a certain distance from line agencies, a practice that no doubt has deep roots in traditional Chinese statecraft and broader cultural norms. Moreover, his interaction with them is mediated through individuals who serve a "chief of staff" function (for example, Dai Bingguo as of 2009). Yet such a system can cut the paramount leader off from information, conflicting assessments, and policy options.

SENIOR LEADERS' PROMOTION OF THEIR POLICY PREFERENCES. We have already noted several ways in which senior leaders promote their preferences. They make clear the issues on which they insist on taking the lead (including relations with Japan and the United States). They act on information that they receive that reveals problems that undermine their preferences (as in the poisoned dumpling case). They make decisions when the policy process is stalemated. They take charge in near-crises, mini-crises, and full crises (more on that later).

Another way China's paramount leader can assert his priorities is to control the process for drafting and disseminating authoritative statements of policy (*tifa*). Establishing a new orthodoxy is one of several arenas in which policy change occurs in China.[111] Altering a *tifa* is not sufficient for a change in policy—change in other arenas like personnel, institutions, and procedures must also occur—but it is certainly a necessary step, and it is one over which senior leaders have the most control. If the top leader can define the policy categories that his subordinates think and talk about, he is bending the system to his will.[112]

From the operation of leading groups, it may be inferred that they play a critical role in creating consensus on a new *tifa* among various bureaucratic stakeholders on behalf of the paramount leader. In the process, they rely on the support of those elements that are on the side of change and new thinking, but they also must cope with opposition from defenders of the existing policy and its associated concepts while reining in radical ideas that go beyond the expected consensus. During this phase, debates over controversial issues can often be seen in publicly available journals. At some point, the new *tifa* must be put to paper, and each high-level policymaking body has its own document-drafting body.

Once consensus behind the new *tifa* is forged, public and private debate ends and the propaganda system disseminates and justifies the new formulation to those implementing the policy and those affected by it. There are inculcation sessions throughout the relevant *xitong*, which sometimes take the form of a major policy meeting that brings together representatives of the agencies in that *xitong*.[113]

Examples of shorter *tifa* in the external policy area include the sections on foreign affairs, defense, and Taiwan policy of the CCP general secretary's reports to the party congress every five years and to plenary sessions in intervening years. For example, in October 2007, Hu Jintao, speaking to the Seventeenth Party Congress on foreign affairs, first offered a definition of the situation ("Peace and development remain the main themes of our era. . . . At the same time, the world is far from tranquil."). He then offered normative prescriptions for how all countries should act in this environment and the sort of policy that China should pursue both generally ("China will unswervingly take the road of peaceful development") and with respect to different kinds of countries and issue areas.[114] In August 2007, Hu Jintao gave an address of almost 5,000 words on the eightieth anniversary of the founding of the PLA, in which he enunciated the prevailing principles concerning the military's missions, its place in the regime, its relative priority regarding resource allocation, and its relation to society.[115] Then there are longer documents that elaborate on the leadership's view of China's external policy at greater length. For example, in December 2005 the PRC State Council's Information Office issued a long statement on "China's Peaceful Development Road" that was an extended discussion of Hu Jintao's principal policy idea.[116] There have been a series of white papers on Taiwan policy and the biennial defense white papers.[117]

Changing the *tifa* is one way that a new leader may put his stamp on, or at least become associated with, new policies and institutions. For example, Hu Jintao enunciated the PLA's "new historic missions" in a speech in December 2004, soon after he became CMC chairman. The four missions were "providing an important guarantee of strength for the party to consolidate its ruling position; providing a strong security guarantee for safeguarding the period of important strategic opportunity for national development; providing a powerful strategic support for safeguarding national interests; and playing an important role in safeguarding world peace and promoting common development."[118] They were portrayed as both a logical extension of Hu's concept of "scientific development" and a response to the security environment of the early twenty-first century, both internal and external. Within a couple of months after Hu's speech, the PLA propaganda apparatus was in high gear to disseminate and elaborate on the new concept through publications, authoritative media articles, meetings at high and not-so-high levels, changes in training documents, and the identification of "models" whose actions and work style illustrated how to carry out, in concrete terms, the new missions. In August 2007, a new term—"diverse military tasks"— was introduced as at least a supplement to that of "new historic missions." The idea was that the PLA faced both combat and noncombat tasks and both traditional and nontraditional security threats, but that idea certainly was not inconsistent with Hu's original formulation.

Creating a new *tifa* can trigger a broader process of institutional change. David Finkelstein has described the process by which the PLA reengineered itself in response to the Persian Gulf War. It began when Jiang Zemin, who had become CMC chairman only months before, gave a speech on the "military strategic guidelines for the new period" in January 1993.[119] Yet the PLA's "strategic guidelines" are only the highest level of a hierarchy of guidelines that define, ultimately, the hardware that it needs, the design of its institutions, and its doctrine for fighting wars. The other elements include the strategic assessment, the content of the "active defense" strategy, the strategic missions and strategic objectives, guidance for military combat preparations, the main strategic direction, and the focus for army building.[120]

A new set of military strategic guidelines triggers a highly institutionalized and lengthy process of revising all the other elements, with lower elements derived from higher ones and each one integrated with the others. As each element is approved by the CMC, it is disseminated within the military establishment. Conceptual change is the driver of institutional change. Finkelstein concludes that because of this process of re-conceptualization and its impact on procurement, institutions, and doctrine, "the decade of the 1990s should be viewed as a period during which the PLA made tremendous strides as a professional military force."[121]

China's policy formulation concerning relations with Japan evolved in late 2004 and early 2005 in an effort to staunch the deterioration of China-Japan relations over issues related to the East China Sea, Taiwan, Yasukuni

Shrine, and Japanese textbooks, as well as to contain domestic anti-Japanese sentiment.

The process began in November 2004, when President Hu Jintao met with Prime Minister Koizumi in Santiago, Chile, on the edges of the annual meeting of the Asia-Pacific Economic Cooperation forum. Based on a Chinese press report, Hu began his remarks to Koizumi by stressing that China and Japan were increasingly complementary and that they had a joint responsibility to work for peace and development in Asia and the world. He then laid out a series of "guiding principles" on developing the relationship:

—Adhere to the principles of the "three documents" (the 1972 normalization communiqué, the 1978 peace treaty, and the 1998 joint declaration).

—Persist in "taking history as a lesson and facing the future"—a stock Chinese phrase deployed when problems exist on the history front.

—Undertake overall planning, strengthen exchanges, and deepen cooperation.

—Strengthen coordination and cooperation on regional and international affairs.

—Intensify cultural, educational, and youth exchanges.

—Deepen economic and trade cooperation and give greater attention to joint efforts on energy and environmental protection.

On the history issue, Hu pinpointed Yasukuni Shrine as the crux of difficulties and called on Japan to "properly handle" it by taking into account the views of other countries. He placed special emphasis on the role of leaders in this regard. Hu later revealed that he had urged Koizumi to seize the opportunity of the sixtieth anniversary of the end of World War II to handle "a number of sensitive issues" properly and so put China-Japan relations on a healthy course. Finally, Hu specifically raised the Taiwan Strait issue, likely because Taiwan president Chen Shui-bian, leading his party in a legislative election campaign, was advocating proposals that China found disturbing. He expressed appreciation for Japan's past stand on Taiwan and noted that how the issue was handled affected the broader bilateral relationship.[122]

By and large, Hu's statements replayed old themes and emphasized process over substance. The key message was that Koizumi had to change his tack on Yasukuni Shrine if relations were going to improve.

With Hu's November meeting as a baseline, the next major opportunity for an authoritative statement was the annual meeting of the PRC's legislature, the National People's Congress, in March 2005. After the annual meetings, China's premier always conducted a press conference at which he made statements on a variety of policy issues. In anticipation of the opportunity,

Hu Jintao reportedly summoned officials involved in policy toward Japan, including the PRC ambassador to Japan, Wang Yi, and ordered them to draft a new policy framework.[123] In the interim, relations had continued to deteriorate, particularly over the East China Sea and Taiwan. On the latter, Japan had lobbied the European Union not to terminate its arms embargo against the PRC and had agreed with the United States that peaceful resolution of the Taiwan Strait issue through dialogue was a "common strategic objective"—a view that China interpreted as a Japanese commitment to the defense of Taiwan.[124]

On March 14, Premier Wen Jiabao presented the new rhetorical approach, which became known as the "three principles and three proposals." Wen began by saying that "the Sino-Japanese relationship is China's most important bilateral relationship," an arguably untrue statement. He agreed with the view that the countries' economic ties were much better than their political ones and said that the "fundamental problem" was whether "the Japanese side will correctly handle the history issue." He reiterated the standard requirement that both sides adhere to the "three documents" concerning their relationship. He then proceeded with three additional principles:

—"Taking history as a mirror [using history as a point of reference or a basis for judgment] and looking forward to the future": Wen acknowledged that the war brought suffering to Japanese as well as Chinese and other Asians and urged Japan to seize the opportunity of the sixtieth anniversary to promote friendship.

—"Persistence in the one-China principle": Taiwan was an internal Chinese affair, so it was inappropriate for it to be a focus of the U.S.-Japan alliance.

—"Strengthening cooperation for common development."

Wen also made the following three proposals:

First, conditions should be vigorously created to promote a high-level exchange of visits between China and Japan. Second, the foreign ministries of the two countries should work together to launch strategic studies on ways and means to promote friendship between the two countries. And third, problems left by history should be properly addressed.[125]

In essence, Wen repackaged Hu's November guiding principles into three key points, elevating the Taiwan Strait issue in the process. The three principles and three proposals became the mantra for Chinese discussions of Japan policy. State councilor Tang Jiaxuan—then the lead official for coordination of foreign affairs—cited them as late as April 12, 2005, in a meeting with the president of Kyodo News Agency.[126]

The next occasion on which China might deploy a new *tifa* was the meeting of Hu Jintao and Koizumi Junichiro in Jakarta, Indonesia, where both would be attending an event commemorating the fiftieth anniversary of the Bandung Conference, a meeting of Asian and African states in 1955. There was no compelling reason to do so, because Wen's formulation probably would have sufficed as a matter of substantive policy. Yet the relationship had deteriorated further. Tokyo's pursuit of a permanent seat on the UN Security Council and revisions to a few Japanese textbooks had sparked violent anti-Japan demonstrations in many Chinese cities. Although Koizumi tried to create a good atmosphere for the meeting by reiterating a previous official statement of "deep remorse" and "heartfelt apology" about the war, Hu apparently saw the need to toughen China's stance.[127]

He therefore transformed Wen's three principles into five points: strictly adhere to the three documents; persist in taking history as a mirror and looking to the future; correctly handle the Taiwan issue; properly handle bilateral differences through dialogue and negotiations on an equal footing; and strengthen people-to-people contacts and multifaceted exchanges and cooperation.

There was nothing new in the five points; what was different was the context, tone, and specificity of Hu's statements. In terms of context, he cited his November meeting with Koizumi in Chile and the hope that he had expressed for proper handling of sensitive issues. "Recently, however, the Japanese side's actions on the history and Taiwan issues have *betrayed its own promise* and hurt the feelings of the Chinese people." In terms of tone, Hu noted that the development of the relationship "proves that peace between China and Japan benefits both" but warned that "*war between the two harms both.*" The warning was striking because no one had been talking about the possibility of war. Hu insisted that Japan take "concrete action" to bring about improvement with respect to its commitment to the relationship as a whole, the history issue, and Taiwan. He further insisted that "things that hurt the feelings of the Chinese people . . . should *absolutely* not be committed any more." Remorse, he said in reference to Koizumi's recent apology, was not enough.[128]

Hu's pronouncement became the latest mantra. The official media and think tank scholars quickly jumped to endorse it.[129] His apparent intervention—and the way he did it—exemplifies one way in which Chinese senior leaders seek to influence policy.

When the system works well to bring about a change in authoritative formulations, it represents an impressive institutional feat.[130] It is one lever leaders can pull to change policy. Yet several points stand out about the use of *tifa* and about routine policymaking in China more generally.

First, although *tifa* clearly enunciate the principles and goals that supposedly animate the policies preferred by the leadership, they may lack strategies that relate goals to observable actions.[131] There is a sense that Chinese leaders believe that if they can only get the formulation right—in response to Koizumi's Yasukuni visits, for example—that it will be sufficient to ensure that the other party makes the changes desired. Second, the policies that leaders adopt are only as good as the analyses on which they are based. But leaders are overwhelmed with information that is subject to filtering at a number of levels and that, it seems, sometimes paints an inaccurate picture.[132] Third, as leaders debate principles, they may also bargain over more practical things. It appears that the PLA may be willing to accept moderate policy formulations in return for a commitment to improve its capabilities.[133] And finally, the consensus-building process can take an extremely long time (two years in the case of a Taiwan policy review in the mid-1990s). If there is no pressure to make a decision, the bureaucratic inertia that marks decisionmaking from the bottom up can be present from the top down as well.

Concluding Observations

So both bottom-up and top-down approaches to decisionmaking can have negative consequences. Attempts to move policy decisions upward may create stalemates because line agencies cannot agree. A top-down approach can restore dynamism, but it requires that any particular initiative compete for the attention of leaders who are overwhelmed by a flood of issues—for the most senior, there is always a crisis somewhere. A focus on crafting authoritative formal, or formalistic, policy statements does not necessarily lead to state action. Finally, the weaknesses of both bottom-up and top-down policymaking become most obvious when the Chinese system faces situations of stress, a subject discussed in chapter 12.

Appendix 8A
China's Senior Leadership as of 2010

Chinese Communist Party Politboro

Standing Committee members (nine members, rank order)

HU JINTAO	PRC president; chairman, CCP and PRC CMC
WU BANGGUO	Chairman, National People's Congress
WEN JIABAO	State Council premier
JIA QINGLIN	Chairman, Chinese People's Political Consultative Conference
LI CHANGCHUN	Supervisor of ideology/propaganda system
XI JINPING	CCP vice chairman; PRC vice president; executive secretary of the CCP Secretariat
LI KEQIANG	Vice premier; likely future premier
HE GUOQIANG	Chairman, Central Discipline Inspection Committee
ZHOU YONGKANG	Secretary, CCP Politics and Law Commission

Regular members (sixteen members, stroke order)

WANG GANG	Vice chair, Chinese People's Political Consultative Conference
WANG LEQUAN	Deputy head, Central Committee Political-Legal Committee
WANG ZHAOGUO	Executive vice chairman, National People's Congress Standing Committee; president, All-China Federation of Trade Unions
WANG QISHAN	Vice Premier
HUI LIANGYU	Vice premier
LING JIHUA	Director, CCP General Office
LIU QI	Secretary, Beijing Party Committee
LIU YUNSHAN	Member of Secretariat; director, CCP Propaganda Department
LIU YANDONG	State councilor
LI YUANCHAO	Director, CCP Organization Department
WANG YANG	Secretary, Guangdong Party Committee
ZHANG GAOLI	Secretary, Tianjin Party Committee
ZHANG DEJIANG	Vice premier
YU ZHENGSHENG	Secretary, Shanghai Party Committee
XU CAIHOU	Vice chairman, CMC
GUO BOXIONG	Vice chairman, CMC
BO XILAI	Secretary, Chongqing Party Committee

State Council

Premier
WEN JIABAO

Vice premiers
LI KEQUIANG
HUI LIANGYU
ZHANG DEJIANG
WANG QISHAN

State councilors
LIU YANDONG
LIANG GUANGLIE
MA KAI
MENG JIANZHU
DAI BINGGUO

CCP and PRC Central Military Commissions

Chairman
HU JINTAO

Vice chairmen
GUO BOXIONG
XU CAIHOU

Members

LIANG GUANGLIE	Minister of national defense
CHEN BINGDE	Chief of general staff, PLA General Staff Department
LI JINAI	Director, General Political Department
LIAO XILONG	Director, PLA General Logistics Department
CHANG WANQUAN	Director, General Armament Department
JING ZHIYUAN	Commander, Second Artillery Corps
WU SHENGLI	Commander, PLA Navy
XU QILIANG	Commander, PLA Air Force

Source: For the Politburo members of the Seventeenth Central Committee: ChinaVitae (http://chinavitae.org/library/cpc_politburo%7C17); for the members of the State Council (2008–13): ChinaVitae (http://chinavitae.org/library/state-council); for the CMC: James Mulvenon, "Chinese Military Leadership Monitor after the 17th Party Congress: Hu's Guys or Whose Guys?" *China Leadership Monitor* 23 (Winter 2008) (http://media.hoover.org/documents/CLM23JM.pdf), pp. 3–4.

Appendix 8B
Foreign Affairs and Taiwan Work Leading Groups, Fifteenth Central Committee (1997–2002) and Sixteenth Central Committee (2002–07)[a]

Foreign Affairs Leading Group	Taiwan Work Leading Group
Party general secretary, head	*Party general secretary, head*
Vice president, deputy head	Chairman, Chinese People's Political Consultative Conference
Premier	*Relevant vice premier/state councilor*
Relevant vice premier/state councilor[b]	*Executive secretary, Party Secretariat*
Vice premier/state councilor for foreign trade	*Head, Party United Front Work Department*
Minister of foreign affairs	*Minister of state security*
Head, Party International Department	*Chair, Association for Relations across the Taiwan Strait*
Minister of state security	*Deputy chief of general staff for intelligence*
Minister of defense	*Director, Taiwan Affairs Office*
Deputy chief of general staff for foreign affairs and intelligence	
Director, Foreign Affairs Office	Head, Party Publicity Department
Head, Party Publicity Department	Vice premier/state councilor for foreign trade
Minister of public security	
Director, State Council Hong Kong–Macao Office	Vice chairman, Chinese People's Political Consultative Conference
Head, Party-State Information Office	Vice chairman, Central Military Commission
Minister of commerce	
Director, Overseas Chinese Affairs Office	

Sources: Lu Ning, "The Central Leadership, Supraministry Coordinating Bodies, State Council Ministries, and Party Departments," in *The Making of Chinese Foreign and Security Policy in the Era of Reform,* edited by David Michael Lampton (Stanford University Press, 2001), p. 45; Taeho Kim, "Leading Small Groups: Managing All under Heaven," in *China's Leadership in the 21st Century: The Rise of the Fourth Generation,* edited by David M. Finkelstein and Maryanne Kivlehan (Armonk, N.Y.: M.E. Sharpe, 2003), pp. 126–27; Qi Zhou, "Organization, Structure, and Image in the Making of Chinese Foreign Policy since the Early 1990s," Ph.D. dissertation, Johns Hopkins University, 2008, pp. 151–52, 158–59; "The National Security Council That Jiang Zemin Did Not Create—Part 3," *Duowei Yuekan,* August 31, 2009 (www.dwnews.com/gb/MainNews/Forums/BackStage/2009_8_31_9_24_30_579.html).

a. Positions in italics were members in the period of both the Fifteenth and the Sixteenth Central Committee; those in regular type were apparently added after the Sixteenth Party Congress in November 2002.

b. The individual occupying this position is also the secretary general of the leading group.

During the 1997–2002 period, the deputy heads of the FALG were Premier Zhu Rongji and Tang Jiaxuan, the state councilor given day-to-day responsibility for foreign affairs. After 2002, the deputy head was the vice president. During the 1997–2002 period, the deputy head of the TWLG was Qian Qichen, the vice premier given day-to-day responsibility for the Taiwan issue. After 2002, it was Jia Qinglin, chairman of the Chinese People's Political Consultative Conference (CPPCC), a body of non-CCP individuals who represent the constituents of the party's United Front Work Department.

Also during the 1997–2002 period, Wang Huning, the director of the policy research office of the Central Committee's General Office and a close associate of Jiang Zemin, attended FALG meetings. It is not clear whether he did so because he was an FALG member or because he was acting as Jiang's representative (see Kim, "Leading Small Groups," p. 137).

Sources are in conflict on whether Xiong Guangkai was a member of the FALG before 2002. Clearly, he attended meetings, and Michael Swaine, writing in 1996, indicated that he was the PLA's "representative" on the body and by implication a member; see Michael D. Swaine, *The Role of the Chinese Military in National Security Policymaking* (Santa Monica, Calif.: RAND Corporation, 1996), pp. 24, 32. Taeho Kim was not so sure, surmising that he may have been present on behalf of the minister of defense (see Kim, "Leading Small Groups," p. 137).

On the TWLG, Liu Yandong was head of the party's United Front Work Department before 2007 and vice chairman of the CPPCC thereafter. She remained on the leading group, but her replacement did not become a member of the leading group (see Zhou, "Organization, Structure and Image," pp. 158–59).

9

Decisionmaking in Japan

Power among Japan's institutions has shifted over time. Prior to 1990, for the most part, civilian agencies and the LDP constrained both the prime minister and the Self-Defense Forces (SDF). From late in that decade, the core executive gained power vis-à-vis line agencies and the Liberal Democratic Party to enhance the government's capacity to respond to crises. The SDF gained autonomy vis-à-vis civilian agencies. Today the balance of power is changing again, the result of the victory of the Democratic Party of Japan in elections for the lower house of the Diet in August 2009. The DPJ, which already had a dominant position in the upper house, had campaigned on a platform of reducing the power of bureaucrats. It and its minor coalition partners have a more skeptical attitude toward the views of the LDP on external policy. It is an open question how the DPJ's reforms will affect the responsiveness of the Japanese decisionmaking process with respect to foreign affairs and national defense and the military's role in its responses.

Structure

In order to provide some context for understanding the DPJ reforms, this section focuses on the structure of the Japanese system under Liberal Democratic Party rule. (See figure 9-1.)

The Core Executive

Japan's core executive consists of the prime minister (PM) and the Cabinet. In the Prime Minister's Official Residence (PMOR), the Cabinet Secretariat and the Cabinet Office provide staff support to the PM. For the most part, officers from various ministries staff these organizations, and they

160

Figure 9-1.

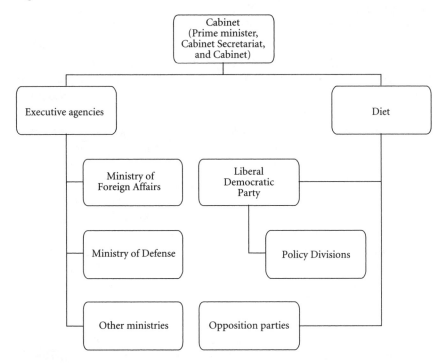

Sources: Author's illustration.

traditionally have acted to protect the interests of their organizations vis-à-vis the PM rather than the other way round. Four positions in the core executive were pivotal during the LDP era: the chief cabinet secretary, two parliamentary deputy chief cabinet secretaries, and the deputy chief cabinet secretary for administration (the DPJ eliminated the latter position).

The chief cabinet secretary (CCS) is the head of the Cabinet Secretariat. He is a member of the Diet, the Cabinet, and (usually) the PM's political faction. His chief responsibility has been to mediate disputes among senior officials and leaders of the ruling party, which requires "political skill, experience, and connections as well as knowledge of the content and implications of specific policies."[1] The two parliamentary deputy chief cabinet secretaries (DCCSs), one a member of the lower house of the Diet and the other of the upper house, have assisted the CCS in his mediation task, particularly vis-à-vis the ruling party. The CCS also serves as the chief spokesman. As such, he is the daily face of the Japanese government.

Before the arrival of the DPJ government, the deputy chief cabinet secretary for administration (DCCS-A) was the senior bureaucratic officer in the government and the principal liaison with the bureaucracy for purposes of policy coordination. This post demonstrated the bureaucracy's dominance of the LDP core executive. The DCCS-A presided over the weekly subcabinet meeting of administrative vice ministers (the highest career officials in each agency), who approved all proposals to be submitted to the Cabinet. As Michael Green points out, this coordination meeting was a device to exclude ministers from decisionmaking and to allow each ministry to protect its interests, even if policy problems called for more integrated action.[2] Based on the results of the meeting, the DCCS-A then prepared the agenda for Tuesday cabinet meetings and presided over them. He also had great influence over senior bureaucratic appointments.[3] Whether under LDP or DPJ rule, neither the CCS nor the DCCS-A has commonly been an expert in foreign and security policy.[4]

Assisting the CCS are several assistant chief cabinet secretaries, who are responsible for internal and external affairs. They play an important role in interagency coordination.

Key Civilian Agencies

The Ministry of Foreign Affairs (MOFA)—*Gaimusho* in Japanese—is the lead agency for the conduct of external affairs. In addition to its Tokyo headquarters, it has 268 missions overseas (embassies, consulates-general, and permanent missions) and more than 5,000 personnel, about 60 percent of whom are overseas.

The ministry's senior leadership includes the minister, who is a member of the Diet; two state secretaries and three parliamentary vice ministers; the vice minister, who is the senior career official; and two deputy ministers, also senior career officers. Beneath the leadership are eleven bureau-level organizations (*kyoku*). Most are geographical, covering affairs for Asia and Oceania, North America, Latin America and the Caribbean, Europe, and the Middle East; functional bureaus address economic affairs, international cooperation (foreign aid), international legal affairs (including the United Nations), consular affairs, and the Intelligence and Analysis Service. Last but not least is the Foreign Policy Bureau, a recent creation.

The Ministry of Defense

Since January 2007, the Ministry of Defense (MOD) has been the primary organization of Japan's defense establishment. Staffed by civilians, it supervises the Self-Defense Forces.

The key civilian organization within the MOD is the Internal Bureau (*naibu bukyoku*), which is a kind of "super-bureau," with about 22,000 civilian personnel. It supervises the principal functions of the SDF (personnel, acquisitions, planning, and operations) and handles relations with U.S. forces in Japan. One analyst suggests that historically the job of the Internal Bureau was "keeping the SDF down."[5]

In addition to the minister's secretariat, the Internal Bureau has five subordinate bureaus (*kyoku*), for defense policy, operational policy, finance and equipment, personnel and education, and regional cooperation.[6] The first two are the most important. The Defense Policy Bureau's main job is to develop Japan's defense strategy. It shapes defense policy, manages defense exchanges, does organizational planning, and controls intelligence collection and analysis for the ministry.[7] The Operational Policy Bureau is responsible for employment of the SDF's capabilities for both domestic and international missions.[8]

Prior to 2007, the civilian master of the SDF was the Japan Defense Agency (JDA). A unit of the Cabinet Office and nominally under the direction of the prime minister, it was staffed by a cadre of civilian officials ("suits") seconded from other agencies who supervised the JDA's key functions and the activities of SDF officers ("uniforms"). A bureaucrat from the Ministry of Finance (MOF) was responsible for the defense budget; one from MOFA was responsible for security policy; and another from the Ministry of International Trade and Industry took charge of equipment procurement. The members of the Diet who served as JDA director did not regard the position as career enhancing.[9] In the transition from JDA to MOD, the organizational structure remained the same, but the minister gained the same autonomy over budget matters as other ministers.

The Cabinet Legislation Bureau

The Cabinet Legislation Bureau (CLB), which is nominally a unit of the Cabinet Office, is really an arm of the bureaucracy and has acted independently of the prime minister. It traditionally has reviewed all draft bills before they go to the Cabinet. It has played a special role in security policy, judging whether initiatives are consistent with article 9 of the constitution ("The Japanese people forever renounce war as a sovereign right of the nation and the threat or use of force as means of settling international disputes. In order to accomplish the aim of the preceding paragraph, land, sea, and air forces, as well as other war potential, will never be maintained."). The CLB early on enunciated two core principles that became the basis for deductively restricting what the SDF could do. One was that it could employ only the minimum amount of force necessary to defend Japan; the other was that its activities could not be integrated in any way with the use of force by other countries.[10] The result was a cramped "birdcage" that constrained the SDF's ability to "fly." But as Japan's external environment changed, some PMs saw the need to relax the restrictions on SDF missions (as did MOFA, which worried most about Japan's reputation and its U.S. relationship). The SDF was not power-less in the face of CLB legalisms, but the agency was more an obstacle than a facilitator.

Intelligence Agencies

Japan has a balkanized intelligence community. Each major national security agency has its own intelligence organization, as does the Cabinet Office.

Within the defense establishment, there is the Defense Intelligence Head-quarters (DIH). Created in 1997, it consolidated a number of different military intelligence organizations: those in the three branches of the armed services, units of what was then the Joint Staff Council and the Japan Defense Agen-cy's Internal Bureau, and the signals intelligence apparatus, previously in the Ground Self-Defense Force (GSDF). It is Japan's largest intelligence organiza-tion, and it has directorates for management and coordination, planning, anal-ysis, joint intelligence, imagery and geography, signals, and communication.[11]

MOFA's Intelligence and Analysis Service (IAS) is a relatively small unit, with only around 100 staff. It has four divisions: the first is responsible for coordination within the IAS; the second is charged with intelligence collec-tion and functional issues; the third covers Asia and Oceania; and the fourth watches the rest of the world. Recent reforms, which have emphasized organizational expertise, agility, efficiency, and comprehensiveness and the capacity to arrange work in a flexible way, have increased the capacity of the IAS to coordinate on internal analysis.[12]

The National Police Agency (NPA) also has an external intelligence func-tion, even though its principal mission is domestic security. It focuses mainly on threats that occupy the grey area between public order and foreign policy, such as terrorism, cyber warfare, and organized crime.[13]

Finally, the Cabinet Office has an intelligence arm: the Cabinet Intelli-gence and Research Office (CIRO). The director of CIRO, who serves con-currently as the director of central intelligence, is usually a senior NPA offi-cial because internal security was the bigger challenge when the office was founded in the 1950s.[14]

This description understates the degree of pluralization. Each of the ser-vice staff offices maintained a research unit even after the creation of the

Defense Intelligence Headquarters. Moreover, the MOD's Defense Policy Bureau has its own research division, although it is hampered because of its small staff.[15]

The Liberal Democratic Party

During the decades of Liberal Democratic Party rule, the LDP and the bureaucracy (the ministries and other agencies of the executive branch) formed a dual structure that dominated policymaking in Japan until the LDP lost its majority in the lower house of the Diet in the August 2009 elections. The divisions of the LDP's Policy Affairs Research Council, which was analogous to the Cabinet, paralleled civilian agencies like the Ministry of Foreign Affairs and the Ministry of Finance, and the council's operations were "extensive, formalized, and institutionalized." The members of each division come from the relevant "tribe" (*zoku*) of legislators (*zoku giin*), who see a political value in specializing in a particular issue area. Thus legislators in the defense tribe (*boei zoku* or *kokubo zoku*) dominated the LDP's National Defense Division, while the foreign affairs tribe, the *gaiko zoku*, did so in the Foreign Affairs Division.[16] A division's members also served on the relevant standing committee of the Diet. *Zoku* support for a PM's initiatives could contribute significantly to their enactment; opposition was a serious obstacle.[17]

Historically, the defense tribe focused on the interests of defense industries and of communities close to military bases.[18] Indeed, one commentator alleged that it served "purely as windows for handling petitions" from those interests.[19] More recently, however, the members of the defense *zoku* became more focused on defense policy and more knowledgeable about the activities of the SDF; one of their leaders called them a "new breed."[20] They were, as one of their number put it, "the generation who are able to think about Japan's security without sentimental attachment and romantic illusion."[21] They believed that Japan was "*heiwa boke*": out of touch with reality after many years of peace.[22] They favored expanding the SDF's authority; establishing the right of collective self-defense; increasing defense spending; acquiring missiles that can take out North Korean missile-launch sites; relaxing restrictions on arms exports (which would be good for the defense industry); enacting a law to permanently authorize the government to dispatch SDF on international cooperation missions; and transforming the JDA into a ministry.[23] They favored Koizumi Junichiro's liberalization of security policy—for example, the legislation that he sponsored on responses to emergency situations in Japan.[24]

Another feature of the recent Japanese system for more than a decade before 2009 was the LDP's coalition with the New Komei Party, with which the LDP had to coordinate its policy proposals at some point in the process. Coordination could be done through policy teams composed of Diet members from the two parties.[25]

Before 2000: Limits on the Core Executive Imposed by the Bureaucracy and the LDP

On the surface, the Japanese system looks like a British parliamentary system.[26] A bicameral legislature, the Diet, is "the highest organ of the state power" (article 66 of the constitution). The head of the party that wins a majority of seats in the lower house of the Diet becomes prime minister (PM); other senior figures of the ruling party become ministers of executive branch agencies. Conventionally, the PM is understood to be Japan's head of government (the emperor is the head of state).

But the reality of power was more complex under the LDP, which had a bias toward dispersing power rather than concentrating it in the PM. The constitution specifies that "executive power shall be vested *in the Cabinet,*" and the PM is only the head of the Cabinet (articles 65 and 66). Formally, he has the power to appoint ministers (article 68) and submit bills and reports to the Diet, but he does so on behalf of the Cabinet (article 73). The PM also is commander-in-chief of the Self-Defense Forces, but again, he acts on behalf of the Cabinet. The only partial exception is foreign affairs: constitutionally, it is again the Cabinet that shall "manage foreign affairs" and "conclude treaties" (article 73), but in practice the PM has been Japan's chief diplomat, working with the Ministry of Foreign Affairs.

Another manifestation of cabinet government was the Security Council of Japan (SCJ). Formed in 1986, it has always had a large membership based on a broad definition of security and, because MOFA and the JDA feared that the council would undercut their power, rather limited jurisdiction.[27] It did not meet on a regular basis. For example, it was not convened between North Korea's launch of a ballistic missile in August 1998 and the September 11 attacks in 2001.[28] One informed observer concluded that "the council's deliberations have turned into a mere formality."[29]

Under the LDP system, the PM had only limited authority over the ministries of the executive branch. He could not order an agency to do anything. To do so required a cabinet consensus, but the ministers who composed the Cabinet usually took positions that reflected the interests of their institutions.[30] Meanwhile, the Cabinet Secretariat and the Cabinet Office traditionally were weak instruments of the PM's will because they were staffed by officials from ministries whose primary loyalty was to their home ministry. The only agencies over which the PM had direct authority were those attached to the PMOR. As noted, the leading example was the Japan Defense Agency before it became the Ministry of Defense in January 2007. But its civilian leadership was dominated by officers from relevant ministries and the Cabinet Legislation Bureau issued constitutional and other limits on what the SDF could do.

Similarly, senior figures within the LDP limited the PM, especially before the 1990s, when the system of multimember districts for Diet elections required LDP candidates to run against each other in the same district and so fostered factional groupings with powerful leaders. They had the power to withdraw support from the PM when he lost public approval.

Post-2000 Reforms

In the late 1990s, Prime Minister Hashimoto Ryutaro engineered a series of institutional reforms designed to strengthen the power of the core executive relative to that of the LDP-bureaucracy duopoly. The stimulus for change was a series of incidents during the 1990s that exposed the inability of the Japanese system to respond quickly to fast-moving challenges, including the Persian Gulf War and the attendant U.S. demands for concrete assistance; U.S. preparation for war on the Korean peninsula in the spring of 1994; the Kobe/Hanshin earthquake in January 1995; sarin gas attacks by the Aum Shinrikyo terrorist group; and the North Korean missile launch in August 1998.[31]

STRENGTHENING THE CORE EXECUTIVE.   The Hashimoto administrative reforms, which passed the Diet in July 1999, gave the PM and the Cabinet Secretariat more explicit authority.[32] Among other things, the revised cabinet law passed in 2001 made explicit the PM's authority to take important policy initiatives at cabinet meetings, a power that had been only weak and implicit before. Generally, it strengthened the power of the Prime Minister's Official Residence, the *kantei*. The PMOR gained the authority to "plan and draft concrete proposals under the direction of the cabinet and the prime minister," a power that it had previously lacked.[33] At some point, a "three ministers meeting" was instituted, bringing together the chief cabinet secretary, the foreign minister, and the defense minister for high-level discussions of security issues.[34]

The revisions also sought to strengthen the *kantei*'s coordination role and thus the prime minister's ability to guide the actions of various agencies.

They strengthened the Cabinet Secretariat, giving the PM a hierarchy of advisers and aides responsible for various issue areas, increasing his capacity to try to bend the system to his preferences.[35] The guidelines stressed that the secretariat was the final point of coordination and defined its role: "to present policy direction for the government as a whole, and coordinate policy strategically and proactively."[36]

The chief cabinet secretary remained the leader of new PMOR system. Assisted by his staff, he mediated disputes among senior officials and leaders of the ruling party. To better cope with sudden problems, the post of deputy chief cabinet secretary for crisis management (DCCS-CM) was created. When a crisis occurs, the DCCS-CM, who traditionally was seconded from the National Police Agency, takes charge in a crisis management center, reporting to the PM and the CCS. In routine times, he heads a situation room that collects information and distributes it to relevant agencies. Both centers are in the basement of the *kantei*. The DCCS-CM has a staff that includes military officers and enlisted men, up to the field-grade level.[37] The cabinet crisis management center now also has an intelligence satellite center and information collection center, under the authority of the director of CIRO.[38]

Another set of reforms concerning emergency response, passed in 2003, altered the composition of the Security Council of Japan and broadened its jurisdiction to include not only security policy but also response to crisis situations. In effect, it is now a subcabinet, but the prime minister has a great deal of discretion in whether to call meetings.[39] He has also met with a "war cabinet" that is limited to the prime minister; the chief cabinet secretary; the foreign minister; the minister of land, infrastructure, and transport (which has jurisdiction over the coast guard); the minister of defense; and the chairman of the National Safety Commission. This smaller group decides on countermeasures—for example, an order to put the SDF on alert, followed by a mobilization order.[40]

In whatever guise the Security Council meets, it has not lacked the guidance of bureaucrats. The 2003 legislation set up an "expert committee for coping with situations" to serve as a support structure for the Security Council. The chief cabinet secretary is the chairman, and the members include officials from the Cabinet Office and agencies that make up the "war cabinet." There is even the suggestion that uniformed SDF officers might be included.[41] Yet as noted, the Security Council meets infrequently—usually when the prime minister decides that one of the situations specified by the law prevails. Consequently, the expert committee likely duplicated the work of the relevant personnel of the Cabinet Secretariat.

CHANGES IN LINE AGENCIES.   At the same time that the powers of the *kantei* were growing, changes occurred in line agencies. The Foreign Policy Bureau was created within MOFA in 1993 and strengthened in 2004 to improve coordination among the geographic and functional bureaus, which had operated as separate fiefdoms, and to shape diplomatic strategy, conduct crisis management, improve intelligence collection and analysis, and so on. Its policy coordination division seeks to foster better consensus within MOFA and between it and other agencies, in particular through several foreign policy coordinators. The National Security Division focuses on policy relevant to security affairs.[42] Overshadowing these sensible reforms were a series of scandals that were exposed after the turn of the century. They damaged MOFA's reputation, gave politicians more of an advantage, and undermined its clout vis-à-vis the prime minister's office.

Similarly, there was growing demand for the SDF to participate in international peacekeeping and Washington looked to Tokyo to be a more reliable partner in meeting security challenges like North Korea and global terrorism. Consequently, policy constraints on the SDF's activities were gradually relaxed to try to meet changing circumstances, making the SDF's birdcage somewhat larger. MOFA lost some of its control of defense policy. The Japan Defense Agency became the Ministry of Defense on January 7, 2007. Whereas the JDA had to submit budget proposals before they went to the Ministry of Finance and send requests to the PM for cabinet meetings through the Cabinet Office, MOD does not. The minister of defense has more exclusive authority for national defense than did the director of JDA.[43]

Within the SDF, the Joint Staff Office (JSO) was created to strengthen coordination among uniformed services. The JSO, which is headed by the chief of staff, has about 500 personnel. The chief of staff's responsibilities include supporting the minister of defense and executing his orders, plus supervising the three branches of the Self-Defense Forces and administering the Joint Staff.[44] The Joint Staff, which supports the chief of staff, has five principal departments: general affairs, including accounting, personnel, and education (J-1); operations (J-3); logistics (J-4); defense plans and policies (J-5); and systems, which addresses issues of command and communications (J-6).[45]

In addition, scandals in defense establishment, which were blamed on excessive segmentation between civilian officials and uniformed officers, provided an opportunity to re-gear that relationship to the advantage of the SDF. To improve the system for defense policy formulation, the defense policy bureau was strengthened and uniformed officers were to "take the actual situation into account in terms of operations." The operations policy bureau (staffed by civilians) was to be dissolved and the uniformed chief of staff and joint staff made responsible for the execution of operations. Uniformed personnel "familiar with actual conditions" would be appointed to management sections.[46]

Thus the traditional LDP system and the power that it gave to ministries, the ruling party, and coalition partners significantly constrained the PM and his exercise of leadership. The Hashimoto reforms created institutional opportunities that an activist PM could exploit if he chose to do so (as Koizumi Junichiro did). When the government as a whole acted according to the PM's will, it was usually because he sought to dominate policy and used the Cabinet Secretariat effectively to do so. When it did not, it reflected both his lack of dynamic leadership and the secretariat's failure to harness the horses of the permanent government and the ruling party. More generally, that configuration of power limited the Japanese system's ability to respond to crises.[47]

The constraints on the PM have been most obvious in the area of national defense. Even Koizumi Junichiro's energetic top-down leadership, deployed to expand the powers of the core executive in the security field, created only a patchwork of contingency-specific rules that reflect the cumulative impact of the constitution, constitutional interpretation, and laws passed by the Diet.[48] The PM, as commander of the Self-Defense Forces, may mobilize defense forces in case of an external attack or when the public peace is disturbed, but he may do so only on behalf of the Cabinet. For example:

—When Japan faces an armed attack or the threat thereof and the PM decides to order the SDF to mobilize, he must get the approval of the Diet for the defense response plan, both in concept and in detail.

—In the case of incoming objects like missiles, the PM merely approves a request from the defense minister but must make a post hoc report to the Diet on the SDF's response to the attack.

—When the police fail to maintain public order and it is necessary to use the SDF, the PM on his own may order a "security mobilization," but he must secure the Diet's approval within thirty days.

—The PM is authorized to mobilize the SDF to defend Japanese and U.S. military installations in Japan, but he also must consult with prefectural governors and ensure that there is a proper division of labor between soldiers and policemen, depending on the specific circumstances.

Laws of a more generic sort authorize the dispatch of SDF forces to take part in UN-sanctioned operations (particularly peacekeeping) and to assist

U.S. forces during regional contingencies. But specific legislation is required for all other deployments outside Japan (for example, of ground units to Iraq to help in reconstruction).[49] Given the constraints, it is not surprising that Japan's prime ministers "have been cautious about mobilizing the Self-Defense Force."[50]

Yet a pressing requirement for a government in a crisis is to be able to act quickly and with unity and coherence. By tying down the prime minister through legal and political limits, Japan's decisionmaking system makes that kind of response unlikely.

Process

The structure of Japan's decisionmaking system under the LDP, in which the bureaucracy and the ruling party limited the power of the core executive, was biased toward a bottom-up process. The point of departure was the relevant division (*ka*) within a ministry. The deputy director of the division would make proposals based on its specific area of responsibility that were discussed within the division, then with bureaus within the ministry, then with the ministry secretariat for legal and budgetary clearance. Coordination with members of the relevant *zoku* in the ruling party and the affected group interests outside the government usually occurred in parallel. Once the process of consensus-building was complete, the proposal went to the director general of the bureau for approval. Once the director general decided, the process was complete, except for ratification at higher levels.

When the issue cut across more than one agency, another complex phase of consensus-building occurred, since ministries might have very different views of the policy in question. Only when agencies agreed on a measure did the high-level policy bodies of the LDP approve it. After that came review by the administrative vice ministers (the senior agency bureaucrats) in their subcabinet meeting; endorsement by the Cabinet; and finally, as appropriate, submission to the Diet.

If this bottom-up, consensus-building (*nemawashi*) process is the most common one, it is not the only one. Once Japan's postwar economic growth slowed and budget deficits grew (long before Koizumi), there was a general shift away from a bottom-up process. Strong prime ministers, leading ministries (particularly the deficit-conscious MOF), LDP heavyweights, the business elite, and external pressure from the United States sometimes combined to act on a top-down basis. Thus, Nakasone Yasuhiro initiated a number of changes in defense policies during the mid-1980s, just as Koizumi Junichiro did after 2000. The role of the bureaucracy and the LDP then shifted from pushing new policies to re-shaping—or subverting—the initiatives of the "central structure." There was more of a mix of bottom-up and top-down activities.[51] The late 1990s reforms, which gave the prime minister and the *kantei* more scope for initiating policy and using the coordination mechanisms of the Cabinet Office, reflected a new effort to constrain the choices of bureaucrats and politicians.

One way in which prime ministers sought to break out of the strait-jacket that bottom-up, bureaucratic policymaking forced on them was to have a skillful Cabinet Secretariat that would identify and bring to the prime minister's attention important issues that segments of the bureaucracy and ruling party sought to monopolize. It would not wait to react to initiatives from agencies; instead it would seed the PM's ideas within the bureaucracy and ruling party, cultivate their growth, and use its coordination authority to weed out efforts to distort policy formation. Consequently, the decisions presented to the Cabinet sometimes reflected what the PM wanted. But he used his staff in a consensus-building process that increased the probability that he would prevail.[52]

Another method that some PMs used was to create advisory councils that studied a particular issue and then presented recommendations to the prime minister. The councils have been composed of scholars, businessmen, senior bureaucrats, and former officials. For example, every five years, the defense establishment formulates the National Defense Program Guidelines, which assesses Japan's security environment, sets defense objectives, and provides guidance for procurement of equipment. But in tandem with that process, a panel composed mainly of outsiders conducts its own inquiry and reports its assessment and recommendations. For example, in 2004, the Council on Security and Defense Capabilities, headed by Araki Hiroshi, a senior adviser to the Tokyo Electric Power, issued a report that informed the defense outline that was published not long after.[53]

Those changes neither transformed the Japanese system into a Westminster model nor made the prime minister into a Japanese version of his British counterpart. As Ellis Krauss and Robert Pekkanen wrote during the middle of Koizumi's tenure: "Much of the drama of contemporary Japanese and LDP politics is now found in the current dynamic of an active and popular prime minister trying to lead on certain issues according to a Westminster (or even 'presidential' model) . . . in conjunction with his coalition party partners, but coming into conflict with the entrenched interests and continued prior policymaking power of the *zoku giin* in these PARC divisions."[54]

How much the PM called the tune was a function of the power of his personality and the issue under consideration. Tomohito Shinoda makes the case that Koizumi Junichiro successfully secured changes in national security policy in part because of his strong will and opportunistic style, which produced a top-down process.[55] But Aurelia George Mulgan documents how even Koizumi confronted difficulties in pulling off financial and economic reform in the face of resistance from his own party and the bureaucracy.[56]

Christopher Hughes and Ellis Krauss end up in the middle. They acknowledge that the Japanese system was closer to the Westminster model at the end of the Koizumi administration than at any time since the end of World War II, with a strong prime minister and a relatively centralized LDP. But they caution that "the unity is grounded in the prime minister's popularity"—an idiosyncratic factor.[57] When the PM's standing in public opinion declined, ministers, LDP executives, and Komei leaders were more likely to oppose his initiatives. Koizumi was successful in promoting his ideas in part because he remained popular with a public that sought a change in the status quo.[58] His successors (Abe Shinzo, Fukuda Yasuo, and Aso Taro) were less popular and so vulnerable to opposition.[59]

In short, the capacity for decisive action was not institutionalized in the Japanese system. It depended more on idiosyncratic factors such as the prime minister's personality and evanescent power and the skill of his Cabinet Secretariat in harnessing the energies of line agencies to support the prime minister's priorities. Such skill—or the lack of it—has a significant effect on both the general effectiveness of the Japanese system and how well it responds in a crisis.

Policy Coordination by the Kantei at the End of LDP Rule

During the late LDP period, coordination by the *kantei* fell on a day-to-day basis to three assistant chief cabinet secretaries (ACCS): one for internal affairs (ACCS-I), one for external affairs (ACCS-E), and one for national security and crisis management (ACCS-NSCM). Customarily, the first two were detailed from the Ministry of Finance and the Ministry of Foreign Affairs, respectively. The ACCS-NSCM came from either the National Police Agency or Ministry of Defense. He assisted the DCCS-CM in times of crisis and plays a primary role in the Cabinet for shaping national security and defense policy on a day-to-day basis. For example, during the Koizumi period the ACCS-NSCM was a key actor in drafting the legislation and policy that authorized deployment of the SDF and liberalized its freedom of operations during national emergencies.[60]

For staff support, the three ACCSs have relied on personnel from the office of the assistant chief cabinet secretaries, which is part of the Cabinet Office. Among them has been a group of chief counselors, who were officials at the bureau-chief level from various agencies and who supervised the work of a number of policy groups. These groups in turn were headed by counselors, who were officials at the director level. Both chief counselors and counselors have been seconded from line agencies. Staffing the policy groups were lower-level officials from agencies relevant to the work of the unit. There were six groups under the ACCS-I and ACCS-E, one of which was clearly dedicated to foreign affairs; the others focused mostly on domestic affairs. The ACCS-NSCM was in charge of five other policy groups, which were responsible for domestic and external security issues.[61]

There is one other piece of the *kantei* structure. The PM had five personal assistants, and one of them was with him all the time, providing a link from him to the *kantei*. One of the assistants was a political aide; the rest were seconded from the Ministry of Finance; the Ministry of Foreign Affairs; the Ministry of Land, Infrastructure, and Transportation; and the National Police Agency.

The result was a network designed to encourage communication among various elements of the Japanese senior executive and respond effectively to various policy issues. The PM's private secretary, who accompanied him during his daily activities, was his link with the DCCSs and ACCSs as appropriate. The DCCSs were high-level links between the *kantei* on the one hand and the bureaucracy and the Diet on the other. The ACCSs and the various counselors and staff under them provided operational links to the executive agencies of the bureaucracy.

When a problem arose, the ACCSs decided how to deploy counselors and lower staff to address them. Sometimes more than one ACCS would work on a specific issue; collaboration among two or more counselors was not uncommon. The ACCSs could set up ad hoc policy rooms to address specific issues that may not have a long duration.[62] Issues that the ACCSs could not resolve were kicked up to higher levels. On sensitive issues on which legislation was required, the relevant ACCS would draft the bill; previously agency bureaucrats did the drafting.

Also within the Cabinet Office are two organizations designed to provide coordination within the intelligence community. More important was the lower-ranking unit, the Joint Intelligence Council, which was chaired by the DCCS-A and met twice a week. Its members were the DCCS-CM, the ACCS-NSCM, the director of cabinet intelligence, and the director generals of appropriate agencies in Japan's four other intelligence organizations: the NPA, the defense intelligence headquarters of MOD, the intelligence and analysis service of MOFA, and the public security investigation agency of the Ministry of Justice. Higher in rank but less important from an operational perspective was the Cabinet Intelligence Council. Chaired by the CCS, it brought together all the DCCSs, the ACCS-NSCM, the director of cabinet intelligence, and senior officials from the other four agencies. But it met only twice a year.[63]

This network approach had several limitations. First, personal relationships affected how well the flexible staff structure worked. One institutional triangle—the one among the relevant ACCS, the relevant administrative vice minister, and the appropriate personal secretary of the PM—could be crucial. Ideally, for example, the ACCS-E would have good personal relations with the PM's personal secretary, assigned from MOFA, and with the administrative vice minister for foreign affairs. Another consideration is how the different ACCSs work with each other on issues that bridge their jurisdictions. Here, apparently, if the ACCSs have not served the same number of years, the discrepancy becomes an obstacle to easy cooperation.[64] Lacking the right personal chemistry could slow down the process. A prime minister who ignores personal relationships, as did Aso Taro, the last LDP PM, can get into trouble.

Second, the practice of staffing the *kantei* coordination mechanism with officials of various ministries has had advantages and disadvantages. On one hand, it has given senior officials like the ACCSs the channels that they need to connect with those within agencies that are key to solving problems. On the other, officials seconded from agencies are not necessarily committed to promoting the priorities of the *kantei*. A defense expert observed that "the cabinet secretariat is composed of a 'hodge-podge' of personnel from various ministries and agencies that are strongly criticized for being 'inclined to be loyal to their former ministries and agencies.'"[65]

Seconding personnel to work in the cabinet office is not, of course, necessarily bad. The staff of the U.S. National Security Council is composed predominantly of detailees. The issue is the norms under which seconded personnel work and whether those norms are enforced. There was some evidence that Japanese officials who worked in the *kantei* were beginning to show greater commitment to it and its work, as opposed to the parochial interests of their agencies. The more fluid nature of task assignments since the administrative reforms were implemented encouraged greater loyalty to the core executive.

Third, the defense establishment has been underrepresented in the *kantei* coordination system. MOD was not one of the ministries that provided an official to serve as the PM's personal secretary. MOFA was so blessed, which may have affected how national security issues were presented to the PM. As a result, the ACCS-NSCM and the MOD administrative vice minister had to work through another personal secretary to secure or convey information from the Self-Defense Forces. Similarly, uniformed officers were not assigned to the *kantei*. The ACCS-NSCM often came from MOD, but that person was a civilian. Again, that can have implications for how senior policymakers understand the operational dimensions of defense matters. There were active duty and retired officers working in the intelligence organizations within the *kantei* and field-grade officers working under the DCCS-CM, but such officers were not senior enough to participate in policy discussions.[66] Morimoto Satoshi has observed, in commenting on the November 2004 Chinese submarine intrusion, that

> because the people who do not have knowledge of military affairs are around the prime minister, and they tend to think of diplomatic consequences first, like saying, "We do not want to agitate China," the issuance of the order was delayed. . . . Without a system to send a member of the Joint Staff Council immediately upon the occurrence of such an event to the Prime Minister's Official Residence to assist the prime minister, judgments that are militarily nonsensical will be made repeatedly.[67]

The Information Issue

Several factors limit the ability of Japan's intelligence community to provide good information to policymakers. First is its small size. The Defense Intelligence Headquarters is the largest component, with 2,400 people. The U.S. Defense Intelligence Agency, in contrast, has about 16,500 uniformed and civilian personnel worldwide.[68] The State Department's Bureau of Intelligence and Research has 165 analysts, which is more than MOFA's IAS, yet Japan has no organization equivalent to the analytical arm of the Central Intelligence Agency, which has ten times the number of analysts that its State Department counterpart has.[69] Although Japan does not face the intelligence challenges of the United States, modest numbers limit the work that it can do.

Second, those numbers give an exaggerated sense of the extent of work on external matters. Japan's postwar intelligence community began with a domestic mission and to a great extent its mission still is domestic. And although the threats to Japan's security are now more external than internal, the National Police Agency remains the dominant intelligence institution, and it is a significant presence in the Cabinet Intelligence Research Office and its leadership.

Third, the system remains fairly balkanized; one Japanese analyst characterized it as exhibiting "rampant sectionalism."[70] In CIRO, the majority of the personnel are seconded from other agencies—and a majority of them are from those that focus on internal security—and they are likely to guard the interests of their home organizations.[71]

Fourth, there is the issue of coordination of the analytic views of various agencies that "approach their respective intelligence activities from different perspectives."[72] To be sure, there is a happy medium to be struck between making no effort at all to foster a substantive consensus and producing an outcome that hides differences of opinion. In recognition of that problem, the Joint Intelligence Council was created to foster coordination within the intelligence community on a regular basis. But the intelligence components of MOFA and MOD (and formerly JDA) have resisted efforts to strengthen the *kantei*'s coordination capability powers because they fear a loss of jurisdiction.[73] So balkanization persists, aggravated by the reluctance of agencies to share information.[74] In times of crisis or near-crisis, when horizontal interaction is most necessary, information reportedly still flows vertically through the respective agencies to the top.[75]

Fifth, with respect to intelligence from the military itself, civilian dominance continues to some extent. The uniformed director of DIH does brief the prime minister on a regular basis, but he is always accompanied by the civilian director of MOD's Defense Policy Bureau and a cabinet intelligence officer, an arrangement that may limit the frank transmission of the SDF's analytic views. Moreover, it is the director of MOD's defense policy bureau, not a uniformed officer, who represents the DIH at meetings of the Joint Intelligence Council, which is therefore composed entirely of civilians. Reportedly, senior SDF officers may now go to the prime minister's office alone, whereas before an Internal Bureau civilian always had to accompany them. For the most part, however, the military's viewpoint may not be fairly represented. There is no interaction between military officers and members of the Diet.[76]

Sixth, Japan's intelligence agencies have a reputation for poor information security. Because Japan has lacked a law against unauthorized disclosure of information, procedures have been ineffective and penalties for unauthorized disclosure of intelligence are modest.[77] Thus, there is always a chance that sensitive information may be leaked to the media, thus transforming how the government handles the issue and making policymaking more difficult.

Finally, the limits of Japan's own intelligence capabilities—balkanization and relatively small staff—force the government to rely on information from the United States, which is constrained by concerns about lax information security in Japan.[78]

In part because of these limitations, Japan's understanding of China suffers. For example, its analysis of Chinese elite politics and policy after 2002 placed much emphasis on a struggle between Jiang Zemin, the previous paramount leader, and his successor, Hu Jintao. That view is common not only in the media and academia but also in government circles.[79] Thus, the National Institute of Defense Studies, a Ministry of Defense think tank, observed in the spring of 2005:

> Two years have elapsed since President Hu Jintao assumed power, but a new era is yet to arrive. . . . Even after Jiang Zemin's retirement [in September 2004 from his position as chairman of the Central Military Commission, his only remaining post], it is not clear whether a Hu Jintao line that would mark an epoch distinct from the Jiang era is in existence.[80]

U.S. analysts, on the other hand, saw the Jiang-to-Hu transition as evidence of the institutionalization of Chinese leadership politics and a decline in the kind of factionalism that existed in the past and that Japanese observers seem to believe still exists.[81]

Different Japanese ministries have different views on developments in China and how they affect Japan's national interest. The Ministry of Finance places the highest priority on balancing the government budget; the Ministry of Economy, Trade, and Industry (METI) has a very positive view of China's current and future economic growth and advocates economic complementarity; the Ministry of Foreign Affairs has supported the PRC's reform and opening up process and opposed provocative stances on issues like history. The policy approaches of these ministries have different analytic points of departure and produce different attitudes toward the "rise of China." MOF officials fear that with continued Chinese growth will come greater risk, new problems in governance and macroeconomic management, and deeper social inequality and polarization. METI bureaucrats worry that the continued success of China's economic reforms will lead to greater eclipse of Japan, the PRC's emergence as the dominant economic power in Asia, and the emergence of a new industrial state. MOFA officials have a similar anxiety.

China's growing power will strengthen its clout in Asia and the rest of the world and with other major powers, giving it the ability to block Japan's diplomatic initiatives.[82]

The assessments of the defense establishment are more in accord with reality. In its annual assessments of China's defense posture, the Ministry of Defense has expressed incrementally more concern about China's growing military power and its implications for Japan's security. Early in the first decade of the 2000s, the ministry focused on the facts, with very little interpretation, but it did call for more transparency in China's defense policy. In the discussion of deployments and exercises, the report took special note of missile units near Taiwan, construction of facilities in the South China Sea, and maritime activities near Japan.[83] Thereafter, the assessments speculated on the motivation behind China's security policy and military modernization, dwelling in particular on PRC actions that were likely taken to prepare for a war against Taiwan.[84]

Japan's evaluations of China's growing maritime strength and widening scope of operations manifest a similar and growing anxiety. The Japan Defense Agency's 2000 white paper took note of maritime activities near Japan for oceanographic research, training, and information gathering.[85] Two years later, the document added the need to study Chinese maritime moves "because China may aim at building the so-called 'blue water' Navy in the future."[86] The 2006 white paper went further, offering an interpretation of China's objectives: to defend PRC territory and territorial waters, deter Taiwan independence, protect maritime rights and interests in oil and gas fields, and protect sea lanes—all of which had a significant bearing on Japan's security.[87]

If anything, the MOD was too guarded, at least in its public assessments. The views of Japanese retired officers, military commentators, and instructors at military educational institutions may reflect better what the defense establishment really thinks. They cite the growth of Chinese military power as reason for Japan to enhance its capacity both to deter and engage in robust defense. They assert that the Senkaku Islands basically are defenseless and open to the threat of PLA landings. They analyze in some detail the vulnerabilities of the Self-Defense Forces vis-à-vis the PLA. And they questioned the degree of civilian control of the military in the PRC system.[88] One former director of the Japan Defense Agency warned of China's designs vis-à-vis Taiwan, the Senkakus, and restricting U.S. military access and concluded that China wished to "replace the United States as the dominant power in the East Asian region."[89] Those judgments, however, may go too far in the other direction.

Cases

Battles among agencies of the Japanese government occur on a regular basis, as each brings to the issue at hand a different perspective on the legal imperatives and the national interest. For example, after North Korea tested a nuclear device and the UN Security Council authorized economic sanctions against North Korea, the question was whether Japan could join the United States in intercepting North Korean shipping. MOFA favored invoking the law governing Japanese cooperation with the U.S. armed forces, in order to be a good ally. The JDA—that is, the civilians in the defense establishment—opposed it, reportedly because MOFA did not consider the safety of SDF units in the field. In the end, through some process of adjudication, the JDA position prevailed.[90] When it came to blocking Chinese intrusions into the Senkaku/Diaoyu Islands, MOFA took a dovish position. It argued that the Japan Coast Guard should not be too aggressive because it might create tensions with China. The JCG complained that MOFA officials "disregard maritime safety officials' hardships in patrolling Japan's territorial waters but show concerns for China. This makes us wonder which country's foreign minister they are."[91]

The most complicated issues probably are those that display a combination of high-level initiative and self-assertion by relevant agencies and the ruling party. The decision to dispatch troops to Iraq and naval ships to the Gulf of Aden displayed that dynamic.

Dispatching Troops to Iraq

Shinoda Tomohito provides a useful case of top-down leadership: Koizumi's successful effort in mid-2003 to get authorization for the deployment of GSDF personnel to Iraq after the United States invaded in March.[92] In this case, the prime minister had the political resources to bend both the bureaucracy and politicians to his will.

The odds were not good for Koizumi. Public opinion was deeply divided on the unilateral U.S. action. Koizumi had neither a power base in the LDP nor diplomatic experience. Nor did he reflexively support George W. Bush's decision. Once he did, however, he backed the U.S. effort wholeheartedly, despite some decline in the polls. And as an indication of his approach, he chose to use his own words in announcing his support, rejecting language prepared by MOFA.[93]

Even before the invasion, Koizumi realized the need to bolster political support for his general inclination to assist the United States as needed, particularly from the LDP's coalition partners, the New Komei Party and another smaller party. He accepted the suggestion of Aso Taro, the head of the LDP Policy Affairs Research Council, that because weapons of mass destruction were at the core of the Iraq and North Korea problems, Japan could secure the U.S. support that it needed on North Korea by backing Washington on Iraq. LDP secretary general Yamazaki Taku, like Aso a Koizumi ally, agreed and formed a ruling parties' council for Iraq and North Korea. The council agreed to a preliminary proposal to support the Bush administration on March 12, a week before the U.S. invasion.[94]

Two days after the invasion, Koizumi convened an unusual meeting of the Japan Security Council, which decided, among other things, to provide emergency humanitarian assistance to the Persian Gulf region. He then convened an emergency cabinet meeting at which the following proposals were approved: to aid Iraq's neighbors; strengthen support for the counterterrorism fight in Afghanistan; and prepare new legislation so that Japan could contribute to the reconstruction of Iraq.[95]

The next step was to form a project team within the *kantei*. Fukuda Yasuo, the chief cabinet secretary, ordered Ohmori Keiji, assistant chief cabinet secretary for national security and crisis management, to form such a team to prepare legislation. The team, which was composed of twelve officials from MOFA, JDA, and other agencies, worked in a temporary building next to the Cabinet Office, across the street from the Prime Minister's Official Residence. In MOFA, the most active components were the National Security Division and UN Policy Division of the Foreign Policy Bureau and the International Legal Affairs Division of the Treaty Bureau. JDA formed its own internal task force for operational matters and tasked the Defense Policy Bureau and the Plans and Program Division of the SDF's Staff Office to support the Iraq team's legislative drafting. Actually, elements of the bureaucracy were ahead of the game in preparing a bill: MOFA and JDA had been planning Iraq reconstruction for six months already.[96]

The Iraq team announced its action plan in early April 2003. It included various kinds of assistance in the civilian sector, plus mine sweeping and dismantling weapons of mass destruction (WMD). The latter items would require SDF personnel, and because the chances of a UN-authorized peacekeeping force seemed slim, the Cabinet Secretariat began drafting special legislation.

Not only did the Cabinet need a draft bill, Prime Minister Koizumi needed a strategy to get it passed, in light of some opposition to the U.S. invasion. He repeated a tactic he had used for the antiterrorism legislation in 2001—to gain consensus with the LDP's coalition partners before he got approval from within the LDP. Because the Diet was considering other important security legislation in the spring of 2003, he did not publicly reveal that Iraq legislation was in the works until May 21. By then, the UN Security Council had passed a resolution authorizing reconstruction in Iraq, which legitimized his initiative.[97]

Once the Cabinet Office went forward with the draft legislation on Koizumi's behalf, the effort ran into opposition, principally from within the LDP. Koizumi and Fukuda met with the secretaries general of the three coalition parties on June 7 and announced their intention to go forward. On June 9, ACCS-NSCM Ohmori Keiji presented the main principles of the bill to the Ruling Parties Council, which agreed with the outline and with fast-track consideration. The next day, Ohmori gave the same briefing to three policy subcommittees of the LDP (cabinet, defense, and foreign policy). The joint committee raised questions about the legislation, particularly whether the principle that the SDF would conduct activities only in noncombat areas was realistic given conditions in Iraq. An approval decision was postponed and the LDP General Council met the same day. Led by anti-Koizumi members, it had objected to the "hasty and autocratic" way in which decisions were made as well as some substantive points. The joint subcommittee met again on June 11 and 12 and finally approved the measure after getting assurance that deployments would be based on on-the-ground research and that the government would consult with the LDP beforehand. On June12, by which time the LDP's coalition partners had approved the legislation, the LDP General Council met. Members objected to using the SDF at all and to including destruction of weapons of mass destruction as a mission. Within a day, that latter provision was removed in order to get the LDP's grudging approval.[98]

Securing passage in the Diet was the next challenge. The Democratic Party of Japan took issue with Koizumi's approach and submitted its own bill, which excluded a role for the Self-Defense Forces, on the grounds that putting forces into circumstances that could become violent would be a violation of article 9. DPJ opposition did not stop passage of the government bill in the lower house on July 4. Upper house passage came three weeks later.[99]

About four months elapsed from the time that the United States invaded Iraq to the time that the Diet passed Koizumi's legislation. Thereafter, opponents of the deployment both inside and outside the LDP were able to use deteriorating security in Iraq and the killing of two Japanese diplomats there in November to limit implementation of Koizumi's policy. In December, the

Cabinet restricted the deployment to one year, to 600 Ground Self-Defense Force troops, to humanitarian and reconstruction activities, and to a relatively safe area in the southeastern part of the country. After further consultation with the parties in the coalition, the troops left Japan for Iraq on January 16, 2004.[100]

Dispatching the MSDF to the Gulf of Aden

Over the course of 2008, Somali pirates posed an increasing threat to international shipping.[101] In June, the UN Security Council passed a resolution that urged member-states to send vessels and planes to help protect commercial shipping. Those calls to action posed a policy challenge to Japan, a maritime nation. Would it join the international campaign or free-ride on the efforts of others? Even if it did, would it send enough MSDF ships to do the job? Would they have the necessary freedom of action?

As early as mid-August 2008, LDP executives and some media organizations were calling for dispatch of the MSDF.[102] The main obstacle was the lack of legal authority for a robust MSDF mission. The available legal option was the provision for "marine policing" in the existing SDF law, but the provision had been written with the protection of Japan's territorial waters in mind, not distant waterways. The prevailing legal interpretation was that for a policing action on the open seas, the MSDF could provide protection only for Japanese ships and ships with Japanese crews, and it could use force only in self-defense or in an emergency evacuation. In other scenarios, such as a nearby attack on a foreign commercial vessel, the MSDF could not act.[103] The alternative was to pass a new law that expanded the SDF's authority, and the Maritime Staff Office in MOD was reportedly assessing two approaches to a new law.[104] But little progress was made, and Prime Minister Fukuda's resignation on September 1 and Aso Taro's campaign to replace him intervened.

The issue came back in October. Piracy was continuing. The Japan Shippers' Association raised concerns about safety with the Ministry of Construction and Transportation, citing twenty-six attacks in September alone. Word leaked out that in April the Ministry of Defense had been refused authority to divert a destroyer from the Indian Ocean to protect two Japanese tour liners with a total of 1,600 people on board.[105] On October 17, during a Diet committee session, a DPJ member asked Prime Minister Aso about sending MSDF ships to the Gulf of Aden. Aso responded that the idea was worth studying, but a senior MOD official soon observed that there were too many legal hurdles and Kawamura Takeo, the chief cabinet secretary, noted that new legislation might be needed.[106] MOFA was reportedly "particularly enthusiastic" about dispatching the MSDF, noting that free-riding on the protection of others hurt Japan's image.[107]

Work began on a revision to the SDF law to give the MSDF the authority to operate in the piracy-plagued Gulf of Aden. Two options were at play: one was permanent legislation that would liberalize restrictions in all anti-piracy operations, and the other was language that applied to the Somalia situation. The latter apparently was the preferred option in November, and reportedly a nonpartisan group of midcareer and junior Diet members from the LDP, DPJ, and New Komei Party were working on a bill.[108] But enacting legislation would take time, and time was not plentiful as the rest of the world waited to see what Japan would do. Defense Minister Hamada Yasukazu then raised an important operational issue on November 21: whenever the MSDF was sent, "it is necessary to secure proper authorization on the use of weapons to deal with the matters of safety of the personnel and their mission." Restrictive rules on the use of force were unacceptable.[109]

Japan's sense of urgency grew in December. On December 16, the United Nations passed a new resolution. More alarming to Tokyo was China's announcement on December 18 that it would send a flotilla—Japan's competitor for influence was stealing a march.[110] So on Christmas Day, Prime Minister Aso signaled that Japan would indeed send destroyers to the Gulf of Aden. To address the legal issue, he proposed sending ships under the existing maritime policing authority immediately and passing legislation to relax operational constraints later. The next day, Aso ordered Minister Hamada Yasukazu to accelerate consideration of his proposal, stressing the need for quick action. Hamada indicated that maritime policing would be only one option to consider, given the restrictions on whom the MSDF could protect and its use of weapons. Some observers predicted that Aso would decide the issue himself, and the media speculated that a new law would be introduced in the Diet in January and ships would be on station by February.[111]

Thus the lines were drawn by the end of 2008. On one side were the prime minister, an array of politicians, MOFA, and the shipping industry. On the other side was the Ministry of Defense, which balked at the restrictions under which it would have to operate and that would impede its performance. In discussing the risks, a senior MOD official cited a scenario in which pirates take a foreign ship, which the MSDF is not authorized to protect, and kill the passengers or crew. "What we are all worried about the most is letting someone die without taking action. We will be blasted if we let that happen. . . . We must avoid both killing and letting anybody be killed."[112]

The LDP and the New Komei Party formed a project team on January 9, 2009, and only after some discussion did the representatives of the more pacifist New Komei agree to a dispatch under a maritime-security aegis. Although Minister Hamada continued to argue for new legislation, the team was ready by January 20, presenting a stopgap approach to the two parties. Each party approved the proposal two days later. To expand the scope of the operation, the legislation reinterpreted existing rules to mean that MSDF vessels could escort foreign ships carrying Japanese cargo. To support the MSDF in encounters with pirates, a specialized ship-boarding unit would be assigned to assist. To facilitate legal action against any captured pirates, personnel of the Japan Coast Guard, which had law-enforcement powers, would be present. And to assuage Minister Hamada, the team pledged to finish the draft bill by mid-March. If it was passed quickly, Hamada might get his new authority in time, since it would take sixty to ninety days to develop rules of engagement and other guidelines, fit out the ships, get proper communications equipment, and complete the required training. It would take another twenty days to get to Somalia.[113]

The project team began working on the draft bill on January 28, the same day that Minister Hamada issued his order to the MSDF to begin preparations and five weeks after Aso's December 26 instructions to MOD.[114] Weapons use was still a key issue, and the initial signs were that the team would adopt the template used for Japan's police personnel, yet there was no guarantee that it would be flexible enough for an antipiracy mission. As Akahoshi Keiji, the MSDF chief of staff, remarked, "Ever since the MSDF was created, we have never discussed, examined, or provided education on piracy. So I have almost no idea what the situation would be like." His goal was to ensure that "commanders at sea will not waver over their judgments or their units will not be confused."[115]

Still, passage of a new law was not certain, although polls showed that the public generally supported rapid deployment. Kitagawa Kazuo, the secretary general of the New Komei Party, the LDP's coalition partner in the Diet, offered reasons why liberalization might be unnecessary; the DPJ had yet to take a formal position on the legislation.[116]

The ruling coalition's project team approved the legislation on March 4, but it was not until March 10 that the LDP did so. The flotilla left Japan on March 14 and arrived in the Gulf of Aden on March 30.[117] In the meantime, the defense establishment incrementally expanded the MSDF's role. In April, MSDF headquarters authorized its ships to use force against pirates who attacked ships that had nothing to do with Japan, arguing that although the domestic maritime policing law did not authorize such actions, a provision of the mariners' law to assist vessels in distress did.[118] Also in April, there was a decision to send P-3C surveillance aircraft to assist the surface ships, which led in turn to the dispatch of GSDF personnel to Djibouti to provide on-shore support. Those actions took place in late May.[119]

The legislation to liberalize the MSDF's operating procedures was not passed until mid-June 2009. It allowed the MSDF to protect any ship from piracy, fire on aggressive pirate vessels that ignored warning shots (dropping the prior self-defense limitation), and "punish acts of piracy as Japanese criminal acts." It granted the use of weapons but ensured that the permission conformed to the relevant sections of the law on the execution of police officials' duties. The opposition parties, led by the Democratic Party of Japan, opposed the bill unless it required the Diet to approve each new anti-piracy mission. The opposition used its majority in the upper house to reject the version passed by the lower house. Fortunately for the government, the LDP and its coalition partners still had more than a two-thirds majority in the lower house, and so pursuant to the constitution it could override the upper body's veto.[120]

It took ten months from the time Aso Taro first called for the MSDF deployment for the legal framework to catch up with operational requirements. It took seventy-nine days from Prime Minister Aso's December 26 deployment order to MOD to the time that the ships began their escort duty. Commenting on Japan's slow response, Richard Lawless, who was a key policymaker on U.S.-Japan security relations in the Department of Defense during the Bush administration, drew a contrast with China. It took Beijing "about ten seconds" to decide to join the anti-piracy effort, he said, with some hyperbole. That Japan took months was "not bad, but sad."[121]

Regime Change

The LDP's dominance of the Japanese government came to an end in the summer of 2009. The party had suffered from declining public confidence and the low popularity of the prime ministers who followed Koizumi. That the LDP lost the dominant position in the upper house of the Diet in 2007 was only a prelude to its stunning defeat in the lower house elections on August 30, 2009, at the hands of the Democratic Party of Japan (DPJ) and its minor coalition partners (the Social Democratic Party of Japan and the People's New Party). The DPJ won 308 seats, while the LDP fell from 296 seats to 119.

The DPJ came into office with some clear ideas about how to reform the political system and put politicians more in charge. As Prime Minister Hatoyama Yukio articulated in an early policy address:

The Hatoyama Cabinet has done away with the structure of government within which politicians depend on the bureaucracy. We are instead working to turn this structure around 180 degrees to a new type of politics, politics of political leadership and popular sovereignty. Decision-making at government ministries and agencies will not involve bureaucrats but will rather be done by the "council of the three political-level appointees" consisting of the minister, senior vice minister, and parliamentary secretary.[122]

Soon after taking office, the DPJ not only ended the weekly subcabinet meetings at which administrative vice ministers, the senior civil servants in each ministry, met to approve initiatives that the Cabinet would later ratify. It also proposed to abolish the posts of administrative vice minister in each agency, thus giving more power to political appointees. It terminated the right of the head of the Cabinet Legislation Bureau to appear before the Diet and, in effect, make policy; it was the Cabinet, not that official, that should interpret the constitution.[123] In January 2010, Prime Minister Hatoyama abandoned the practice of using text provided by line agencies to compose the policy speech given at the beginning of each Diet session, choosing instead to write the address himself with the help of personal aides.[124] And in February, he unveiled legislation that would end the monopoly that line agencies had possessed over their own personnel appointments and give the prime minister some say in appointing senior officials.[125] The goal for policymaking was to "create streamlined, top-down cabinet government that shifts the balance of power in policymaking in the Cabinet's favor at the expense of the bureaucracy and the ruling parties." Specifically, a new national strategy bureau was to have power over the budget process. Small, minister-level cabinet committees would shape policies on their issue areas. Instead of the deputy chief cabinet secretary for administration (the senior bureaucrat), it would be the DCCSs from the lower and upper houses who would play the key role of interagency coordination with the *kantei*.[126] And a committee with representatives of the parties forming the coalition (DPJ, the Social Democratic Party of Japan, and the People's New Party) would jointly review the government's policy proposals. The senior and most prestigious ministers would constitute an inner cabinet.[127]

Motivating the shift was a belief that bureaucrats used their control over information to shape policy to their liking, an unwelcome pathology if taken to the extreme. Yet bureaucrats also have expertise that can be important in shaping policy. For politicians to ignore information and expertise when it is available and act on their instincts can produce other pathologies. [128]

At the same time, the decision of the DPJ to abolish its Policy Affairs Research Council may have unintended consequences. The LDP's council did frustrate the power of the Cabinet, to be sure, but it also was a training ground for younger members and a mechanism to ensure Diet support for policy initiatives. DPJ leaders had their reasons for creating a new approach to the relationship between authority and expertise, different from that of the LDP. But it may not foster better policymaking. And there was the widespread suspicion that it is not senior government officials that make the key decisions but the secretary general of the party, Ozawa Ichiro.

The initial reviews of DPJ performance were not favorable. Tokyo University professor Kitaoka Shinichi, himself an adviser to the new government, made caustic comments about the new leadership in a January 2009 talk in Washington, D.C.: "The defense minister, the foreign minister, and the prime minister were all ignorant of the policy environment when the Hatoyama administration was launched. The defense minister and the foreign minister have gained knowledge little by little, but the prime minister has made little progress." Kitaoka's reason for the two ministers' improvement was that they are "surrounded by superior diplomats."[129] There was particular criticism for the handling of the U.S. military presence on Okinawa, a signature campaign issue for the DPJ. Prime Minister Hatoyama's position on the Okinawa issue vacillated, while Foreign Minister Okada and Defense Minister Kitazawa were marginalized regarding the matter, Chief Cabinet Secretary Hirano made a succession of errors, and the shadowy figure of Ozawa lurked in the background.[130]

With respect to the relationship between the Self-Defense Forces and civilians in the Ministry of Defense, there has been a reversal of sorts. On one hand, no change was made in the already legislated action to abolish defense counselors (key positions for supervising the SDF). On the other hand, the proposal to merge the Operational Policy Bureau with the staff offices of the branches of the Self-Defense Forces, on which the Diet was to act during the first half of 2010, was terminated.[131] Then in March 2010, Hatoyama rejected a proposal from his foreign minister to relax the restrictions on SDF peacekeepers, which, if adopted, would have allowed them to engage in a wider range of activities.[132] As of the spring of 2010, it was impossible to know what other changes would occur in a policymaking structure that was appropriate for the previous LDP-bureaucracy duopoly. Changes concerning the SDF were likely to affect its role in regional hotspots such as South Asia rather than its routine operations in the East China Sea. Finally, it was too early to tell whether the cumulative effect of those changes would leave Japan better or worse off in coping with policy challenges.

Prime Minister Hatoyama stepped down on June 1, 2010, and was soon replaced by his deputy, Kan Naoto. Kan quickly sought to sooth the bureaucrats' feelings and promised that politicians would pursue a more cooperative relationship. "By no means did we mean you bureaucrats are unnecessary or incompetent," he said. "It can't be denied that over the past nine months, the relationship between politicians and bureaucrats has become awkward, partly because we politicians had our shortcomings and both sides were unaccustomed to the new relationship."[133] How Kan's readjustment will affect day-to-day decisionmaking and whether the new system will foster better responses to policy challenges remains to be seen. Will DPJ ministers resemble their LDP predecessors, or will they still have a more prominent role after Kan's retreat? If the latter, how can they ensure that they have both the information to make good decisions and the power to get bureaucrats to implement those decisions in a way that reflects their intent? How will they avoid becoming overwhelmed? What balance will be struck between a bottom-up and a top-down approach?[134] When ministry priorities conflict, how will they ensure effective coordination now that the administrative vice ministers are not there to do it for them? Will the Cabinet Secretariat regain some of its former power in that regard?[135] Whatever the new arrangements and balance of power, will Japan's ability to respond well in a crisis be better or worse?

Concluding Observations

There are interesting parallels between the policymaking systems in China and Japan, even though one is an authoritarian system led by a Leninist party and the other is a parliamentary democracy.

—In each, the senior decisionmaking body—the Politburo Standing Committee in China and the Cabinet in Japan—is in a real sense a collective. Although senior leaders may defer to the CCP general secretary in the former and to the prime minister in the latter, they do not defer on the most pressing issues.

—Within the core executive, personalities and personal relations among officials are very important for effective decisionmaking. Most important is the personality of the top leader.[136]

—In each, the ruling party has mattered, but in different ways. China is a party-led state. In Japan before August 2009, the policy divisions of the LDP worked hand in glove with their ministerial counterparts to fashion policy.

—In both Japan and China, line agencies have a lot of jurisdiction and are highly conscious of their turf. Japan's Ministry of Foreign Affairs has generally had more power and independence than its Chinese counterpart, but each has sought to preserve its clout.

—In each system, the intelligence communities are balkanized; information flows up though parallel stovepipes and then overwhelms leaders at top levels. The interpretation of information is subject to misperception. The usual pathologies in the relationship between intelligence and policy are probably common: a high ratio of "noise" to signals; preexisting beliefs and policy preferences on the part of information handlers; "group think"; assuming that one's own government has the best of intentions and imputing the worst to the adversary; hoarding information instead of sharing it with other agencies; and signals from decisionmakers that assessments should support—or at least not undermine—policy; providing information that supports the analysts' policy view.[137]

—Coordination among agencies is a problem in each government, even though they have different approaches. China has leading groups that link senior leaders with the agencies whose job it is to implement policy. In Japan, ministries dispatched officials to the Prime Minister's Official Residence. Each system has a rather formal model for integrating leaders and other actors for policymaking, with an orderly structure, clear hierarchy, fixed procedures, and a structured staff headed by a chief of staff.[138]

—Both systems find it difficult to address policy issues through coordination by line agencies alone. Each requires top-down initiative to craft responses, which line agencies implement. But top-down leadership is constrained by heavy workloads and limits on the amount of information that leaders can absorb. And even leaders' initiatives do not necessarily end the conflict between agencies.

Whether the above similarities between the Chinese and Japanese systems will continue is an open question. Whatever the outcome, the record so far suggests that neither functions well or quickly in routine mode. Compounding that weakness is the way that information flows in the two systems. The difficulties are intensified when each government seeks to handle stressful situations, when the implications for national interests are high and the time to decide is short.

10 | *The Chinese Politics of*
PRC-Japan Relations

While institutional phenomena in both the defense establishments and civilian hierarchies of Japan and China do more than enough to complicate the challenges that leaders face, politics makes them worse. Strong public reactions to incidents in bilateral relations limit options, strengthen hard-liners in each country, and create incentives for the governments to take a tough approach to their mutual problems. Domestic politics is the focus of this chapter, on China, and the next one, on Japan.

Clearly, the PRC lacks the more open, competitive character of Japan's democratic system. Through the mid-1980s, the central leaders and executive agencies pretty much had their own way on all aspects of policy. But since then, mass politics has become a part of Chinese political life. In uprisings in western minority areas like Tibet and Xinjiang, dissidents play on the theme of oppression by the majority Han population and the PRC state. As urbanization and industrialization spread across the landscape of Han areas, people in rural areas draw on narratives of corruption and injustice to protest the seizure of their land, destruction of the environment, and ruin of their way of life. And nationalistic urban citizens who worry about China's place in the world no longer defer to the government's monopoly on policy.

Thus the emergence since the 1980s of Chinese public opinion has had a significant impact on the making of China's Japan policy. It is a reality that officials believe that they ignore at their peril and, Chinese scholars argue, that Japanese officials have been slow to appreciate.[1] Three significant political developments are relevant for Japan. The first is the appearance of actors who may be at least formally connected to the state but whose independent interests lead them to favor policies that differ from those of the central government. They include subnational governments, companies, and public intellectuals. The second development has been the gradual emergence of public opinion. Individuals and groups outside the communist regime have some degree of freedom to voice their views on a variety of policy issues, and Japan is one of those issues. And the third development is the increasing reality that public opinion regarding China's relations with other countries— Japan included—can sometimes burst forth in the form of mass action that is both a genuine reflection of popular feeling and a challenge to the regime's sense of its own security. Those trends are so powerful, concludes political scientist Susan Shirk, that domestic politics has become a significant factor in shaping foreign policy even though the public's definition of the national interest may differ significantly from that of government officials.[2] For example, when agencies develop contingency plans or countermeasures for a crisis or near-crisis, "acceptability by ordinary people" is one of the criteria to be used, along with conforming to the national interest and upholding justice.[3]

This chapter explores the implications of those trends for relations between China and Japan. Specifically, I argue that because the animus of some parts of the Chinese public toward Japan is so strong and because it can be transformed into political action, the leadership would find it difficult to respond in a measured way to any clash between Japanese and Chinese military units. Under pressure from the public, it would conclude that it had to react in a vigorous fashion. Moreover, some elements of the nationalistic public have a capability—cyber warfare—that the regime cannot control. The two sections that follow concern two sets of actors: public intellectuals and the vocal, nationalistic segment of the general public.[4]

Public Intellectuals: The "Commentariat"

In the years after Deng Xiaoping returned to power in 1977, intellectuals gradually gained freedom to express themselves on issues of public policy as well as greater confidence that they would not suffer for speaking their minds. The Tiananmen Square crackdown reversed that trend, but only temporarily. Intellectuals still must be aware of where the boundaries of tolerated commentary are drawn at any point in time, and they are. Some have assumed a very public role for themselves. Others are happy to do their scholarly work. But there is no question that the boundaries have broadened over time.[5]

Public intellectuals are not the policy elite, and their role differs from that of high-level officials in the government, the Communist Party, and the military. That is, they "take part in public discourse and try to influence informed public opinion and government policy on a range of issues." Some work for government think tanks and others do not. They may write for the government, for each other, or for the broader public.[6]

As China's media outlets have proliferated and begun to operate more and more according to commercial criteria, foreign policy specialists and their expertise have become commodities. They voice their general and conflicting policy viewpoints, whatever the specific issue of the day happens to be, seeking to gain the intellectual advantage. Their media activities (TV and radio appearances, op-ed essays) can generate a significant income stream, although it may reduce their access to policymakers. But their opinions can have an impact on the broader viewing, listening, and reading public and thereby affect policy indirectly.

During the 1980s, mainstream public intellectuals were anti-tradition and anti-establishment. They were nationalistic or patriotic in their dream of a strong China (*qiangguomeng*), but they blamed China's backwardness and failures on its traditional culture and modern nationalistic culture.[7]

Attitudes changed after Tiananmen Square. The response of the West, particularly the United States, to the tragedy (economic sanctions, opposition to Beijing hosting the 2000 Olympics) fed a reversal of Chinese intellectuals' attitudes. In particular, a significant body of Chinese opinion concluded that the United States had adopted a policy of trying to block China's emergence as a great power or worse, to undermine the Chinese nation-state. Chinese analysts assembled an array of evidence to justify that perception of a U.S. policy of contemporary containment.[8] After 1989, therefore, the trend was toward a nationalism that both supported a strong state and sought strength and inspiration from indigenous culture and tradition. Initially, the shift was a reaction to the immediate post-Tiananmen environment, but it was fed by China's growing power.[9]

Intellectuals' new argument for a strong state seemed compelling when, as they saw it, Western countries were exerting pressure in various ways at the very time that the Soviet bloc had collapsed and China's survival seemed open to question. Top-down, state-led modernization of the economy became the only option.[10] Those who focused on traditional culture called for a rejection of Western intellectual hegemony and a return to China's roots. Post-colonialism, neo-leftism, and a rejection of Western competitiveness were all in vogue.[11] Complementing the eclipsed anti-traditionalists and the currently dominant statists and nativists is a more pragmatic nationalism that sees both internal and external causes for problems and argues for selective borrowing from abroad in order to make China strong again, plus an assertive foreign policy.[12]

That is the general lens through which Chinese public intellectuals view the world. For them, Japan, although an Asian country, falls within the category of "the West" for purposes of the Chinese debate over the best models of development and sources of values. After the Meiji Restoration and World War II, Japan was the most successful nation when it came to adapting to the Western international system. But it has a unique place in the Chinese consciousness because of the way in which Imperial Japan took advantage of China's weakness for several decades beginning in 1895, and Chinese public intellectuals therefore view Japan's actions and its implications for Beijing's interests through a special lens.

Careful analysis of the writings of China's Japan specialists reveals the framework by which they assess Japan. It includes the following elements:

—What kind of power is Japan and what kind of power does it wish to be? The consensus is that Japan has been a global economic power (one of the world's largest, in fact). There is division on whether it wishes also to become a political power and/or military power. Most analysts believe that it wishes to be at least a global political power, through, for example, becoming a permanent member of the UN Security Council. A number also think that it wishes to be a global military power.

—What is the strategic structure (*zhanlue geju*) between China and Japan? The broad consensus is that a strategic rivalry exists between two rising powers in the same East Asian region. Chinese scholars would prefer that Japan accommodate China's rising power and that economic interdependence and contacts and exchanges at various levels be used to mitigate mistrust and competition. But there is disagreement over how likely that will be.

—How does Japanese politics affect the bilateral relationship? There is a general consensus that China's rising power combined with a Japanese tendency to view power relationships in very hierarchical terms has created a strong psychological anxiety in Japan. Compounding the problem has been the perceived growing strength of right-wing sentiment in Japan since the end of the cold war. Those two trends—at the public and the elite levels—undermined support for positive China-Japan relations. A minority of scholars believe that the right-wing shift was either exaggerated or has abated.

—What are the indicators of Japan's strategic intentions? Most Chinese scholars point to five. The first is the political strength of right-wing political forces vis-à-vis politicians who are pro-business or pacificist in their inclinations. Second is whether the postwar constitutional and legal restrictions on the use of Japan's armed forces are maintained or relaxed, and this trend appears more important than changes in capabilities. Third is whether the U.S.-Japan alliance is becoming more integrated or not. Fourth is whether it appears that Japan is intent on supporting the separatist trend on Taiwan. And fifth is whether Japan is serious about accounting for its aggression in and occupation of China during the 1930s and 1940s. These indicators together define the "shadow of the future," and scholars vary on how dark that shadow is.[13]

Within this general framework, China's Japan scholars may differ on key points, and they can engage in strenuous debates. One example of such a debate is the series of exchanges that began in late 2002 concerning "new thinking" on Japan policy.[14] Ma Licheng, a member of the commentary department of *Renmin Ribao (People's Daily)* called for just such new thinking after an extended visit to Japan. He warned that people in both nations were viewing the other with fear and misunderstanding but argued that mutual hostility fueled by narrow-minded nationalism on China's part was not in Beijing's interests. Instead, China should act magnanimously, resolve the matter of Japan's apology concerning past aggression, and minimize concerns about its expanding military role. "What is more important is that we must look forward."[15] Shi Yinhong, a professor at People's University, weighed in a couple of months later. He agreed with Ma that the deterioration in relations with Japan was not in China's interests. At a time when China's position vis-à-vis the United States was uncertain and Tokyo was moving into a tighter alliance with Washington and tenser ties with Beijing, Shi saw the opportunity for a "diplomatic revolution." China should induce Japan to move in its direction and away from the United States. Shi acknowledged such a strategy would entail costs. Japan would have to be accommodated on a number of issues—he said, for example, that history should be set aside—but the strategic gains would be substantial.[16]

Ma's and Shi's articles prompted a vigorous debate during 2003. A number of scholars criticized them, sometimes sharply. Feng Zhaokui, a senior Japan scholar at the Institute of Japan Studies of the Chinese Academy of Sciences (CASS), did not completely agree with the views of Ma and Shi, who were not Japan experts, particularly on the matter of the past, but he concurred on the need for a moderate policy approach. China should be relaxed about Japan's emergence as a political power and even about its military buildup. Shared economic interests remained the foundation of the relationship and nontraditional security issues such as counterterrorism provided a strategic basis. The history issue should and could be resolved by developing the overall relationship.[17]

Jin Xide, also a Japan scholar at CASS, argued that their proposals were too conciliatory and betrayed a lack of understanding of China-Japan relations:

> If we [China] unconditionally cater to all Japanese demands without the necessity for any reciprocity from Japan, the result will only be to cause strategic passivity, and it is extremely doubtful whether a situation of "Sino-Japanese rapprochement" will come about in the end.[18]

In the summer of 2003, the journal *War of Resistance against Japan* published a number of essays on the history issue; unsurprisingly, most disagreed with Ma. One author, Bai Jingfan, charged him with reversing cause and effect. China, he said, was not in the wrong, or too harsh, or too nationalistic; the fault lay in Japan.[19] Feng Zhaokui weighed in again in the autumn, this time specifically on the history issue. He explained why it was "difficult, complex, and emotional." Because it was all of those things, it would be resolved only over the long term.[20]

Yet the "new thinking" debate did not remain within the confines of academic and policy journals. Members of the broader public attacked Ma and Shi on the Internet, going so far as to question their patriotism. Ma's address and phone number were posted, and he received a number of death threats. Eventually, he resigned from *Renmin Ribao* and moved to Hong Kong.[21]

The Public

Beyond elite policymakers and the sub-elite intellectuals is the general public, or at least the members of the public that pay some attention to foreign affairs. They have relatively modest knowledge of the world at large and no direct impact on external policy, but they still have views on China's foreign relations. These individuals articulate their views in Internet chat rooms and bulletin boards, sometimes in a vociferous and xenophobic fashion. When elements of the populace are angry enough—as in the spring of 2005, when Japan sought a seat on the UN Security Council and the Japanese Ministry of Education approved new textbooks—they come out to demonstrate, which sometimes results in violence. Because the leadership worries about political stability, public attitudes are relevant to government decisionmaking. So it keeps an eye on mass opinion through polling and other means.

The Narrative of Nationalism

Without a doubt, it is nationalism that animates the Chinese public when it chooses to speak and act—and is allowed to act—on foreign policy issues.

Following Michael Brittingham, nationalism is an "ideology that holds the nation should be the highest object of political loyalty, should be politically independent . . . , and [its] interests must therefore be defended."[22] In the Chinese context, that means placing the highest priority on restoring the strength of the Chinese nation-state and mobilizing the Chinese population toward that end above all others. It also means advocating a firm response whenever other nations are perceived to challenge that goal (as the United States is often perceived to do). When Japan is the target of nationalistic sentiment, special and bitter memories come into play because Chinese believe Japanese aggression was the primary reason for the weakness of their state in the first place.

Chinese nationalism has several layers. The first is racial and ethnic, the belief that the Chinese nation is best equated with the Han Chinese people, who make up around 94 percent of the population, and the conviction that they are superior to any other racial or ethnic group. This layer has taken two forms. There is the long-time Confucian claim that traditional China was the acme of civilization, to which other, barbarian people should show deference and which they should emulate. Less benign was the strong ethnic and even xenophobic strain that spread during the late nineteenth and early twentieth centuries, as the Chinese mounted a political challenge to the Manchu Qing dynasty and to foreign "imperialism."[23] Ethnocentrism remains strong today.

A second layer of contemporary Chinese nationalism derives from the history of China's encounter with the West and Japan, at least until the victory of the Chinese Communist Party in 1949. In this narrative, a great and virtuous civilization experienced "one hundred and fifty years of humiliation" at the hands of barbaric and rapacious foreigners. Those imperialists, relying on their superior power and taking advantage of the weakness and stupidity of China's prior leaders, were able to impose their unjust, exploitive dominance, bringing shame to the Chinese people. Worse yet, foreign armed forces took advantage of China's weakness to defeat it in wars and lesser military actions, commit horrible abuses against a defenseless people, and acquire some of the country's sacred territory. This history of victimization represents, in the Chinese nationalist consciousness, a stain that must be washed clean, a blood debt that must be repaid.[24] At the worst, events— the bombing of the Chinese embassy in Belgrade by U.S. aircraft in May 1999 is an example—have shaped this mentality in Manichean, black-and-white terms. According to Peter Gries, "these developments threaten to lock Chinese and American national identities into a dangerous state of negative interdependence, where every American gain is perceived as China's loss, and vice versa."[25]

Imperial Japan is remembered as the cruelest of China's victimizers, and, as seen in chapter 2, those memories have been institutionalized. Ironically, the current focus on victimization is of recent vintage. In the Mao period, Marxism-Leninism transmuted nationalism into anti-imperialism, and accounts of China's past emphasized the Chinese people's victory over foreign aggression and exploitation. Victimization became the dominant narrative in the 1990s, as China was growing stronger, with Japan's past crimes as the primary focus.[26] Nationalistic memories help shape at least the current Chinese view of Japan. As discussed in chapter 4, the recurring themes are the following:

—China as victim of an evil Japan. This is the predominant theme of Chinese thinking about Japan's aggression.

—China as judge of the sincerity of Japan's atonement. The way that China has exercised that role creates doubts in Japanese minds about whether reconciliation is even possible.

—China as the frustrated surging power. Japan and the United States, of course, are the source of China's frustration.

Those basic tropes get applied to concrete circumstances.[27] Thus, in early 2006 the CCP propaganda department criticized the weekly supplement *China Youth Daily* for an article that asserted that when it came to Japan's aggression in the twentieth century, China's textbooks were as ideological as Japan's were ahistorical.[28] In July 2007 there was an "outbreak of cheers" on China's Internet about the news of an earthquake in Japan.[29] After the Sichuan earthquake of May 2008, some Chinese were deeply grateful for the efforts of a civilian Japanese rescue team. But when news leaked in Japan that the government was planning to use planes of the Air Self-Defense Force to transport relief goods, which would be the first Japanese military aircraft to fly over Chinese territory since 1945, netizens in China erupted and the plan was dropped.[30]

One feature of Chinese nationalism regarding Japan is a paranoid vigilance regarding "traitors in our midst." One likely belief underlying this attitude is that real patriotism does not include giving the hated country the benefit of the doubt or accommodating its power; there also may be a suspicion that Japan and the United States could not carry out their anti-China agendas without the naïve or unwitting help of individual Chinese. An example of this mentality is an article that appeared on the Sino-Japanese Forum of the Internet bulletin board of the Communist Party's newspaper, *People's Daily*.

It was entitled, unsubtly, "An Updated Ranking List of Contemporary Chinese Traitors" and included some of the most prominent Chinese scholars of international relations. Shi Yinhong of People's University was criticized for favoring Japan's inclusion as a permanent member of the UN Security Council. Wu Jinan of the Shanghai Institute of International Studies made the list for saying that Japan "cannot be forever labeled as a 'defeated country' and China should accommodate its desire to play a broader international role." Ma Licheng, senior editor of *People's Daily*, was blamed, among other things, for saying that "patriots are actually thieves acting under the guise of patriotism."[31]

A nationalism that views the United States and Japan as the source of China's past humiliation and victimization and an obstacle to future development is not the only attitude common among the public. It competes to some degree with a cosmopolitanism that finds global popular culture very attractive, whatever its origin. And there are cases in which Chinese actually express gratitude for Japan's positive actions or moderate members of the public rebuke others for excessive expressions of anti-Japanese sentiment.[32] But when it comes to managing public pressures that bear on the formulation of foreign policy, the most relevant "ism" is popular nationalism of a nativist sort.[33] Ironically, the PRC government, which promoted nationalism to bolster its legitimacy after Tiananmen, must sometimes restrain "patriotic" pressures that threaten the regime's control or that conflict with the country's interests as the CCP defines them. Although the regime certainly fosters nationalism through the educational and propaganda systems, popular sentiments have a reality that is independent of and sometimes poses a challenge to the government.[34]

Channeling Nationalist Sentiment and the Role of the Internet

The transformation of China's information system since the early 1990s has facilitated the emergence of the nationalistic public as a political actor. The print and broadcast media used to be an arm of the regime, and they still must stay away from the "forbidden zones" delimited by the party's publicity (aka propaganda) department. But newspapers and television have also become commercial enterprises, so they must compete for audience share and tailor content to their clientele. As Susan Shirk reports, "That means [this publication of] a lot of reports about China, Taiwan, and the United States, the international relationships that are the object of intense interest and emotion." By playing up nationalist themes on these issues, the media both satisfy their audience but also stay on the politically correct side of their minders in the publicity department. But such coverage also "constrains the way China's leaders and diplomats deal with them."[35]

Yet the key driver of public participation in foreign policy is the Internet. In a system in which control of information was the key lever of the regime's power, technology now allows citizens both to circulate information that contradicts and may undermine government policy and to mobilize political action—all while preserving a measure of anonymity. As a result, the institutions that formerly channeled public demands or simply suppressed them are no longer as effective.

The Internet expanded from no users in 1994 to almost 300 million users at the end of 2008 (about one-quarter of the population and a substantial share of the urban population).[36] By one estimate, more than 70 percent of users are the age of thirty or younger.[37] Three factors fuel online activism: the emergence of a civil society, controversy over issues of domestic and external policy, and the creativity of Internet users. One part of that creativity is the ability to circumvent the controls that the authorities try to place on the Internet; another is knowing which issues to emphasize and which to avoid. That creates a bias in favor of nationalistic content for the precise reason that it is politically legitimate.

Japan is one of the issues on which the information and mobilization functions of the Internet combine, as evidenced by a series of incidents in 2003:

—In June, two websites organized the "Defend Diaoyu Operation," an effort to land Chinese activists on the Diaoyu Islands. When the Japan Coast Guard (JCG) sent ships and helicopters in response, the websites became the vehicle for a mass appeal to the government to defend the activists.

—In July, "Patriot Alliance Net" mounted an online petition against a proposal for Japan to provide high-speed train service between Beijing and Shanghai. More than 90,000 users signed the petition.

—In August, a similar petition drive was mounted after a Chinese worker died and dozens were injured from contact with an old Japanese chemical weapon that was buried in northeast China. The petition demanded that Tokyo apologize, provide compensation, and clean up the weapons. Over 1 million netizens signed.

—In the fall, there was a virulent public response to an orgy involving Japanese tourists and Chinese prostitutes in south China and to an offensive skit performed by Japanese students in the northwestern city of Xian.

Virtual activity and the real-world actions that it inspires create a dilemma for the government. If it does not support Internet protests, it is open to charges of weakness, but too much support for anti-Japanese sentiment may undermine policy and bilateral relations. And there is the danger that public anger over Japan policy might evolve into opposition to the regime.[38]

In striking a balance, the regime permits Internet users to vent in ways that were not possible twenty years ago. For example, during Hu Jintao's May 2008 trip to Japan, netizens could post comments on the Strong Nation Forum, a bulletin board of the *People's Daily* website, Renmin Wang. In response to a press summary whose headline spoke of a "breakthrough" in China-Japan relations, one person commented, "It won't break through with most ordinary people in our country." Although some postings spoke of the need to maintain good neighborly relations and to learn from advanced countries, many comments were negative, even nasty:

—"Should not go. . . . This is a matter of principle. It's not a matter of friendship. This time it has ignited flames of anger in our citizens."

—"To be backward means having to take a beating. Only if we're wealthy can we . . . face squarely up to the Japanese [and] make China strong."

—"It's not enough just to be warm to Japan; we must be tough, with both hands."

—"There's a blood feud between China and Japan. I am resolutely opposed to Chinese leaders visiting Japan"[39]

Government officials pay more attention to what is being said online and officials make a show of engaging Internet users.[40] For example, in June 2008, at the time of the sixtieth anniversary of *People's Daily*, Hu Jintao himself logged on to Strong Nation Forum and revealed how he keeps in touch with public attitudes: "Although I am rather busy at work all the time and cannot go online every day, I try to get some spare time to get online. I would like to stress that Qiangguo Luntan [Strong Nation Forum] of Renmin Wang is one of the websites I frequently visit."[41]

Most exchanges on the Internet are not so civilized. Consider what happened to Ge Hongbing (literally, "Red Soldier Ge"), a literary critic. He posted a statement on his personal blog that criticized what he called China's "revenge-centered education" concerning Japan. He argued that the Japanese people also were victims during the war and that true reconciliation would come only when China assumed some responsibility for resolving the history problem by displaying tolerance and understanding and, in the end, forgiving Japan. Ge was soon the object of scorn from countless people expressing the "will of the netizens" (*wangluo minyi*). Some published his address and phone number and called for a campaign of calls and letters to his workplace, branding him a traitor. In the end, he withdrew his article and expressed an apology. Few people came to his defense. One was a dissident Christian writer who criticized the majority for using patriotism as "an excuse to persecute others" and take away their freedom of speech. He also observed that the regime had a double standard when it came to demonstrations, allowing them against Japan when it suited its political purposes but preventing them in most other cases.[42]

Popular Attitudes about Japan: What Polling Suggests

Although it is devilishly difficult to get an accurate handle on the Chinese public's views of Japan, one recent set of surveys conducted by Genron NPO of Japan, *China Daily*, and Peking University provides something of a baseline. The three organizations have conducted opinion polls in several Chinese cities in the spring of every year since 2005. The first one was done right after the protest demonstrations in Chinese cities concerning Japanese textbooks and Tokyo's proposal for a UN Security Council seat, and subsequent polls punctuated the gradual improvement in relations during the latter part of the decade.[43]

The 2007 poll—the middle one in the series—found that among the adults, only 1.1 percent had visited Japan; 92.4 percent had never had a Japanese acquaintance; and only 1.27 percent had had a close acquaintance. Around 90 percent of Chinese respondents cited the Chinese media as their main source of information about Japan, and 60 percent believed that the Chinese media reported objectively. More than 70 percent had heard of Koizumi Junichiro and 33 percent knew of Abe Shinzo.[44]

When presented with a set of terms and asked which "applied to current Japanese political trends," in 2007, 59 percent of adult respondents picked "militarism," 38.5 percent picked "capitalism," 36 percent chose "nationalism," 30 percent picked "great-power ambition," and 19.6 percent said "statism." When asked about their "impressions of Japan," the trend of responses from the adult sample improved markedly from 2005 to 2009 (see table 10-1). There was a similar improvement over the five years in views concerning the state of China-Japan relations, as shown in table 10-2.

When asked to predict whether Japan's influence would persist or decline, 29.2 percent of respondents in 2007 thought that it was likely to continue, 28.4 percent thought that it would decline, and 38.1 percent were unsure.[45] But when asked which countries would pose a military threat to China in the future, 41.2 percent of the 2007 respondents picked Japan, which came in second only to the United States (55.6 percent). When asked why Japan was a threat, 61.8 percent replied that "Japan had wars of aggression in the past, and some people want to revive militarism"; 40.3 percent said that "Japan's

Table 10-1. *Responses to Survey Question "What are your impressions of Japan?"*
Percent

Survey	Very good/ relatively good	Average/ can't say	Not very good/ very bad	No answer/ hard to say
May-June 2005	11.6	23.0	62.9	2.5
May-June 2006	14.5	28.2	56.9	0.4
May 2007	24.4	36.9	36.5	2.4
June-July 2008	27.3	30.8	40.6	1.3
May-June 2009	32.6	. . .	62.2	2.2

Source: Genron NPO, "Japan-China Joint Opinion Polls." In the 2009 poll, respondents were not given the option of "average" or "Can't say either way." Apparently, on the basis of the previous year's responses, most of the people whose views were actually in the middle offered a negative evaluation when forced to make a choice between some degree of "good" and "bad."

military capabilities are already powerful"; 39.4 percent said that "Japan follows the U.S. strategy"; and 32.1 percent cited Japan's involvement in international security operations such as peacekeeping and its growing military capabilities, surmising that it was "trying to become a military superpower."[46]

Two things are significant about this poll. The first is the extent to which, more than six decades after the end of World War II, Japan is still viewed through the frame of militarism and aggression. The second is the volatility of attitudes. They improved fairly significantly from a low base after 2005 because of the efforts of Hu Jintao on the Chinese side and Abe Shinzo and Fukuda Yasuo on the Japanese side. But that positive trend is fragile and remains susceptible to effects of events that well-meaning leaders cannot control.

Another survey sought to probe the attitudes of Chinese university students relating to history, current threats, and appropriate responses. The survey found that Chinese young people had generally negative attitudes about Japan's colonial rule in China's northeast (Manchuria) from 1931 to 1945. Further, the more negative students' attitudes about the past were, the stronger their perception of a current threat from Japan and the stronger the government response that they advocated.[47]

Cases

Just as patterns can be detected in the way that the regime seeks to address routine external policy issues, patterns also can be found in the way that public intellectuals and the vocal public assert themselves. In normal periods,

Table 10-2. *Responses to Survey Question "What do you think about current Japan-China relations?"*

Percent

Survey	Very good/ relatively good	Average/ can't say	Not very good/ very bad	No answer/ hard to say
May-June 2005	10.5	30.7	54.9	4.0
May-June 2006	10.4	45.8	41.2	2.6
May 2007	24.9	44.6	24.7	5.8
June-July 2008	54.3	31.7	13.1	0.9
May-June 2009	71.0	...	20.5	8.4

Source: Genron NPO, "Japan-China Joint Opinion Polls." In the 2009 poll, respondents were not given the option of "average" or "Can't say either way," but the results are roughly consistent with those of the previous year.

when there are no major problems in China's foreign affairs, both public intellectuals and the public at large seem to act rather like a Greek chorus, commenting on the action of the play and raising issues that the key actors would not. Although intellectuals and the public may not have a direct outcome on policy in routine periods, the fact that officialdom is conscious of their presence means that their role is not trivial.

When there is a major incident, however, public intellectuals or the public or both become actors in the policy process. I cite two cases by way of illustration. The first, which concerns the United States, not Japan, occurred during the U.S.-led war over Kosovo in 1999. Although the public was very much involved in the Chinese response to this crisis, it is the role of public intellectuals that is of more interest here. In the second case, which concerns Japan directly, the public was the main actor: the demonstrations in April 2005.

The "Peace and Development" Debate of 1999

In the middle months of 1999, China conducted a public debate on the fundamental assumptions of the country's foreign policy since Deng Xiaoping determined in 1979 that accommodation with former adversaries like the United States was the only way to create the "peaceful international environment" essential for rapid economic growth—which was in turn the only way to ensure the Chinese Communist Party's hold on power. There had, of course, been debates during the previous two decades, but they had occurred within the regime. This one was conducted in public as part of a calculated strategy by President Jiang Zemin to defuse criticism of his policies.

The occasion for the debate was whether NATO's intervention in Kosovo in March 1999 reflected a more unilateral and aggressive posture by the United States that would have dangerous implications for China. The trigger was the accidental U.S. bombing of the Chinese embassy in Belgrade on May 9, 1999, which provoked violent public demonstrations. The bombing, in which three people died, magnified the themes of victimization and U.S. containment of China, raising the public's sense of righteous indignation and moral grievance to a peak of intensity and fueling the most serious demonstrations in China since Tiananmen.[48] But, as David Finkelstein observes in his sophisticated analysis, "much of the debate was driven by long-simmering Chinese concerns about U.S. strategic intentions and policies in the post-Cold War world order in general and towards China in particular."[49]

At the outset of the crisis, Jiang Zemin and his colleagues reacted on two levels. On one hand, they did not try right away to suppress the uproar that the incident had provoked; instead they permitted somewhat violent demonstrations at the U.S. embassy in Beijing and did not restrict discussion on call-in shows, thus allowing the public to vent its anger for a while. However, although the general yet vocal public did not have a trivial impact on the final outcome of the debate, it did not determine it.

On the other hand, the leadership fostered a debate on foreign and security policy among intellectuals to determine whether "peace and development" remained the key trend of the times. If it was, then policy continuity was possible. If "hegemonism" was the key trend, then policy should be changed. Two types of intellectuals participated, university professors and analysts at government think tanks. The university professors and some think tank scholars (the "public intellectuals") offered their views in public and to the mass media. Government intellectuals tended to speak at closed-door conferences.

There was something of a synergistic interaction between the media and public intellectuals. The intellectuals offered their views to the media, feeding media coverage, and the coverage enhanced their prestige. Generally, this was an unusual opportunity, for the normal constraints on free thought had been purposefully relaxed.

The "official debate"—the one that occurred among government intellectuals as opposed to academics and the public—unfolded over time. The opening came when Jiang Zemin gave a speech in which he offered some of his own views on the crisis and posed some questions about the world situation. The Foreign Affairs Office of the Central Committee of the Chinese Communist Party then asked analysts to address what Jiang had said, offering their views on whether "peace and development" was still the major global trend; whether the United States was becoming more interventionist; and whether China's security environment had deteriorated.[50]

Discussion of those issues among members of the leadership and government intellectuals occurred from May to August 1999. There were, of course, those who took the hitherto orthodox viewpoint, arguing that Kosovo did not represent a significant change in the geopolitical equation, the intentions of the United States, or China's security. They argued that for a relatively weak China to confront the United States would be too dangerous. Others had a darker interpretation. They asserted that the United States was "bent on maintaining its global hegemony by military means," including through intervention in the civil wars of sovereign states. Kosovo was only the latest in a series of U.S. interventions that indicated a new trend and also raised the possibility of intervention in Taiwan, the South China Sea, the Korean peninsula, and even Tibet, Xinjiang, and Inner Mongolia. Hence, China's security was in greater jeopardy. This camp argued that China should therefore take the lead in organizing a coalition against U.S. hegemonism.[51]

In the middle of the official debate, beginning in late July, the media began asking government analysts and academics to express their views on the Kosovo conflict, again energizing the broader public's engagement. Then in August, the leadership met for its annual retreat at Beidaihe, where it arrived at a new consensus that emphasized continuity ("peace and development" was still the dominant trend) but that bowed toward the more negative view in admitting that "hegemonism and power politics" were on the rise. Thereafter, public intellectuals no longer offered their opinions to the media, and academics did so only until the end of the year.[52]

How Jiang Zemin managed the politics of foreign policy in the face of public unrest was rather skillful. He permitted the controlled expression of conflicting views, some of them implicitly critical of his leadership. Through the debate process, he was able to cool passions and steer thinking within the regime toward an outcome of policy continuity. Allowing the public to vent made it feel that it was participating in the process—without accommodating its views in any significant way when it came to adjusting policy.[53]

Yet Jiang had certain advantages in this mini-crisis. The anti-American demonstrations were a threat to social order, but they could be channeled (and were) toward U.S. diplomatic facilities. Criticism of the Belgrade bombing also had an anti-government dimension, but it was not significant. And in addressing the larger policy implications, Jiang had the luxury of prolonging the debate over a series of months. There is no guarantee that those advantages will exist in future crises.

The April 2005 Anti-Japan Demonstrations

Anti-Japanese public sentiment had been building through the late winter and early spring of 2005. In November 2004, the Chinese government issued an apology regarding the transit of the Han class submarine through a strait in the East China Sea, for reasons that the public either did not know or did not understand. Prime Minister Koizumi gave no signal that his visits to Yasukuni would end, and in fact the Liberal Democratic Party (LDP) endorsed the practice in mid-January. In February 2005, the United States and Japan announced that the peaceful resolution of the Taiwan Strait issue was a "common strategic objective." Chinese tended to focus on the "common strategic objective" part of the formulation and thus concluded Japan would help the United States if it went to the defense of Taiwan. Because they also regarded Taiwan's president as a separatist, the declaration was read as a new challenge to China's fundamental interests. Around the same time, Japan, along with the United States, began to lobby European countries not to drop the embargo on arms sales to China, which they had adopted after the Tiananmen Square incident.

In that deteriorating context, UN Secretary-General Kofi Annan's remark that Japan deserved to become a permanent member of the UN Security Council lit a fuse. A Chinese nationalistic website took up a petition campaign in opposition. It had 1 million signatures within twenty-four hours and 10 million in a week. The animating idea was that a country that, opponents alleged, had not yet addressed its responsibility for aggression had no right to be on the UN Security Council. Then on April 1, the Japanese government announced that it would grant Japanese companies the right to explore for oil and gas in the East China Sea. (That was in response to the China National Offshore Oil Company's announcement that it would start producing gas in one of those fields in about six months.) It was perhaps the worst of times in postwar Japan-China relations.

Chinese public unhappiness moved quickly from the Internet to the streets.[54] On the weekend of April 2–3, there were demonstrations in twenty cities around China. The most serious activity was in Shenzhen (near Hong Kong) and Chengdu and Chongqing in west China. Japan's diplomats quickly called on the Chinese government to ensure the safety of Japanese citizens in China. On April 5, the Chinese Communist Party's publicity department issued a circular that prohibited media coverage of the demonstrations and warned against opposition elements who would use anti-Japanese sentiment to pressure the regime.[55]

On the same day that the Chinese government sought to damp down the protests, the Japanese government gave it a new source of life and lost its moral high ground in the process. The Ministry of Education approved new middle-school history textbooks, some of which were criticized for downplaying Japan's aggression during the first part of the twentieth century. The public reaction in China was strong. One contributor to the Strong Nation Forum argued that soft diplomacy was pointless. "The root cause of the deterioration in China-Japan relations is that Japan considers China an enemy, so the focus of our diplomacy should be on how to make the Japanese Government change its hostile policy toward China. . . . The Chinese Government and people have the power and the resolve to stop the Japanese Government from harming world peace and development. The right-wing forces in Japan will certainly be defeated."[56] The regime banned media coverage of the demonstrations in order to reduce the size of future ones, but to no avail.[57]

On the weekend of April 9 and 10, there were large demonstrations in Beijing, Shanghai, Guangzhou, and Shenzhen, mobilized through the Internet. The demonstration in Beijing on April 9 was organized by college students who announced the protest route, slogans, and what to avoid on Internet chat rooms and bulletin boards. The more than 10,000 protesters, who ranged in age from late teens to early thirties, broke windows and did other damage at the Japanese embassy and ambassador's residence. Reportedly, "dozens" of uniformed police officers were present and did nothing to stop the rally and even ushered the protesters forward. Japanese shops and offices in various parts of China were vandalized. The Japanese government formally protested the PRC's failure to protect its diplomatic property and demanded both an apology and compensation. On one occasion, a Chinese Foreign Ministry official expressed "regret" for the disturbances, but the main response was that the Japanese actions that sparked the demonstrations negated any need for an apology or compensation.[58]

One reason for the apparent confused government reaction to the public outcry was the fact that both President Hu Jintao and Premier Wen Jiabao were not in Beijing at the time of the later demonstrations (Hu was in Shandong province, and Wen was in Southeast Asia). It was not possible to formulate a response right away through the preferred mechanism, which was to call a meeting of the Politburo Standing Committee. Another factor, no doubt, was that the Chinese government found itself between rock and a hard place.[59] As the Japanese media opined, "While the Chinese government is trying to prevent anti-Japan demonstrations from escalating into violent rioting, Beijing appears to be allowing large-scale protests against Japan for fear of being criticized as taking a weak-kneed approach to diplomacy."[60] Reportedly it was not until Hu returned that senior officials met to formulate a response.[61]

That response was to try again to damp down the uproar. The regime closed some anti-Japanese websites, ordered that words relevant to demonstrations be blocked from instant messaging, warned against demonstrations without a permit, provided no coverage of the protests in the official media, and trotted out senior officials to speak on China-Japan relations.[62] The most senior of those officials, Tang Jiaxuan, acknowledged that some "excessive actions" had occurred but claimed that the government had acted properly and stressed that the "grim and complex situation in Sino-Japanese relations" could be resolved only by "identifying deep-seated causes from the origin." He then dwelt on Japan's handling of the history issue and blamed the media in the two countries for exacerbating the situation.[63]

None of those steps stopped another round of demonstrations on the weekend of April 16 and 17 in more than ten cities. Only in Beijing, where the authorities learned of a demonstration at Tiananmen Square, did an overwhelming police presence prevent protests. In Shanghai, probably 20,000 people moved through the center of the city and hurled bottles and rocks at the Japanese consulate. At the same time, antigovernment entries on Chinese websites were increasing.[64] But through a propaganda offensive and tighter control, the government brought the demonstrations to an end. One reason, no doubt, was that Chinese president Hu was to meet Japanese prime minister Koizumi at an international meeting on April 23.[65]

There was another dimension to the anti-Japan fervor of April 2005. Chapter 5 notes that Chinese cyber warfare is a weapon with two special characteristics. On one hand, it can be used to attack one of an adversary's weak points: the general reliance on information technology to run everything in modern societies. On the other hand, ordinary citizens and groups as well as the PRC government have cyberwar capability. That Chinese have conducted such asymmetric attacks is an established fact. In 2003, 60 percent of Japanese companies were victims and spent more than $8 million to repair the damage.

During the events of April 2005, angry Chinese did not rely solely on their ability to amass large numbers of people through the Internet or to throw rocks and bottles at the Japanese embassy and other Japanese installations. Some Chinese also engaged in low-level cyberwar. They mounted attacks on the websites of the Prime Minister's Official Residence, the Foreign Ministry, the Self-Defense Forces, the National Police Agency, Sony, and Kumamoto University.[66] The National Police Agency reported that cyber attacks from China fluctuated around 4,000 attacks a day during March 2005, dropped to less than 3,000 attacks a day during the first ten days of April, rose to between 4,000 and 5,000 attacks a day for most of the rest of the month, and exceeded 6,000 attacks a day a couple of times during May.[67]

During the anti-Japanese demonstrations in Beijing on April 9, 2005, there were two telling moments. The first incident occurred in the Haidian district, where most major universities are located. The plan was that demonstrators would march to Zhongguancun Park and hold a rally there. Someone in the crowd yelled, "There is no meaning in taking an empty office street like this. Let us head for the Japanese embassy." The leaders of the demonstration sought to dissuade them, but when the marchers arrived at the intersection where a right turn would take them to the park and a left turn would take them in the direction of the Japanese embassy, there were clashes with a police line. In the end, most of the crowd turned left and walked more than twelve miles to the embassy, where they threw stones. The police were unhappy with the leaders of the demonstration for failing to control the crowd.[68]

The second incident occurred in the eastern part of the city, in the area outside Jianguo Gate. Thousands of demonstrators streamed westward on the main east-west artery, Changan Boulevard, in the middle of the city. Intersecting with Changan is Ritan Road, the northbound street that would take the protesters toward their supposed objective, the Japanese embassy. Helpfully, a police cordon had been established on the west side of the intersection to steer the crowds in that direction. And indeed, many of the demonstrators did turn right. But another portion of the crowd pushed against the police line and shouted, "Let's go to Tiananmen!" Their likely target? The Chinese leadership compound at Zhongnanhai, just west of Tiananmen Square. The police line strained to block the westerly route before all the protestors marched to the Japanese embassy.[69]

The lessons: first, the leaders of nationalistic demonstrations cannot necessarily control their followers; and second, protests in China can have two targets: the country that is "offending" China and the Chinese government because its policies are too soft. Like the police cordon near Zhongguancun Park and at Ritan Road, the regime's capacity to contain anti-Japanese outrage is not guaranteed.

11

The Japanese Politics of
PRC-Japan Relations

Japan has a democratic political system, but it is one that has unique characteristics. Some regard Japan's democracy as an enigma.[1] Chapter 9 notes the "un-Westminster" character of its parliamentary system.[2] Gerald Curtis looks behind the labels and finds an activist state that interacts with strong social institutions. It is not necessarily a strong state, and it does not speak with one voice, but its managers seek to reconcile the multiple and conflicting demands and policy preferences of those institutions.[3] Not all social forces have effective access to the political process (for example, labor), but many of those who are dissatisfied on specific issues form social movements or enlist groups of politicians to their cause. Then, there are episodes of popular revolt, when voters have used elections to display their dissatisfaction with the political system's performance and responsiveness when the "regular" interaction between state and society has worked badly. The key milestones were the upper house elections in 1998 and 2007, which reduced and then eliminated the plurality of the Liberal Democratic Party (LDP), and the lower house election in 2009, which decisively brought an opposition party, the Democratic Party of Japan (DPJ), to power for the first time.

So just as China, with its strong, authoritarian state, cannot routinely ignore public opinion and occasionally faces populist outbursts, so Japan's activist state does not satisfy all the people all the time, and the LDP has paid the price for that shortcoming.[4] This chapter looks at the role, if any, of the broader public when it comes to Japan's relations with China. On one hand, popular sentiment toward China has been fairly negative. On the other, China is not an especially salient issue in Japanese politics. The media play the key role in shaping popular sentiment, and they do so in ways that play on Japanese fears. That dynamic would likely be at play in any clash between the two countries' armed forces.

Negative Public Sentiment toward China

There is no question that Japanese opinion regarding China, which was favorable twenty-five years ago, is now quite negative. Genron NPO's surveys in Japan asked respondents which countries they thought were a military threat to Japan. In 2007, 72 percent said North Korea and 43 percent said China. In 2008, the North Korea figure stayed about the same but the China figure had risen to 55 percent. In 2009, when North Korea launched a missile and tested a nuclear device, 79 percent of Japanese respondents thought it was a threat; the figure for China declined to 45 percent. The 2007 poll asked those who believed China was a threat why they believed that it was, and the most common responses concerned the PRC's growing military power; the fact that China had nuclear weapons; and the frequency with which China "infringed on Japan's territorial waters."[5] What has caused this strong negative sentiment? Three factors come to mind: nationalism, politicians and political parties, and China's actions.

Nationalism

A possible explanation for negative Japanese sentiment toward China is growing Japanese nationalism, which sees countries like China as the "other." The *International Herald Tribune* reported in September 2006: "When Junichiro Koizumi steps down next week, there will be no mistaking the restively nationalistic society Japan's next prime minister will inherit."[6] Less alarmist but no less concerned was former diplomat Tanaka Hitoshi, who warned a few months later that the growth of "nationalistic sentiments" during the Koizumi years "may turn into a strain of exclusive, confrontational nationalism." He attributed the trend to public frustration that Japan's relatively benign security policy was not congruent with an increasingly worrisome regional environment.[7]

There is no question that a hard-edged nationalism of a right-wing variety has existed in Japan for a long time.[8] The National Police Agency reported in 2008, for example, that approximately 1,500 organizations were mobilized to conduct criticism of China and around two-thirds of them employed loudspeaker trucks (most of the groups must have been small because the number of persons mobilized was only 4,260).[9] This political tendency also manifests itself in figures like Air Self-Defense Force (ASDF) chief of staff Tamogami

Toshio who deny that Japan acted immorally in China and Asia before 1945; in pressure to adopt textbooks that tend toward denial of Japan's pre-1945 actions; and in visits by political leaders to Yasukuni Shrine, where Class A war criminals are among those honored.[10] As discussed in chapter 8, Chinese observers focused on right-wing nationalists as a key driver of Japanese foreign policy.

Yet there is no compelling evidence that "right-wing nationalists" constitute a broad segment of the Japanese public or are the wave of the future. Surveys by the Cabinet Office indicate that over time the level of "patriotic feeling" is only in the 50 percent range, lower than that in other Asian countries.[11] A significant majority of the public (around 85 percent) take the view that "militarist Japan brought suffering and hardship to Asia."[12] Only a bare majority (54 percent) supported Koizumi Junichiro's visits to the Yasukuni Shrine (in polls taken around 2005), and almost the same share believed that he should not do so in the future (around 37 percent said the visits should continue).[13] Finally, such indicators as high school textbooks, often cited as evidence of a rightward shift, are part of a more complex picture. Thus the few textbooks that exhibit historical amnesia are published by firms that do badly commercially.[14] "Public and elite opinion," Matthew Penney and Bryce Wakefield conclude, "do not, on close inspection, sit well with a narrative claiming that Japan is beset by right-wing nationalists."[15]

Moreover, Japan possesses a variety of nationalisms. Some focus on primordial sentiments like race, ethnicity, and nationality, while others, such as economic nationalism, have a more contemporary, concrete basis. These different tendencies do not reinforce each other or point in one single direction, and they can be mutually contradictory. Nor is populist nationalism necessarily directed against other nations. Indeed, it took an anti-state form after World War II, blaming "militarists" for the disaster that resulted from aggression.[16]

Manifesting a similar ambivalence are different and competing definitions of Japanese identity that are relevant to politics and foreign policy. Three were presented in chapter 4: Japan as the World War II aggressor; as the falsely accused defendant or World War II victim; and as a civilian or middle power. That ambivalence is present with respect to China. Those Japanese who acknowledge that Japan did commit aggression in China may also believe that Beijing's "playing the history card" is inappropriate because it deflects the public's dissatisfaction with the regime toward an external "adversary" (Japan). Those who advocate a civilian, middle-power approach want the Chinese to recognize Japan's contributions to the PRC's development, something that China's leaders started to do only after Koizumi's departure.[17]

Politicians and Political Parties

Another possible explanation for anti-Chinese sentiment might be the efforts of politicians and political parties to mobilize it. If so, China might be expected to be an issue in Japanese elections, and changes in the postwar electoral system after 1994 would make that even more likely. Until then, the electoral system was unsuited to rendering a popular judgment on policies. In its multimember system, competition was mainly among LDP candidates in each district, so personalities and organizational capacity, not policy issues, determined outcomes. With the 1994 reforms, five-eighths of the seats contested for the lower house are filled from single-member geographic districts (the rest are selected through proportional representation in eleven regional districts). This type of system produces more of a policy focus and reduces the number of parties. So, as Ellis Krauss observes, "elections under the new system are much more about policy and issues than under the old system."[18]

Yet even under the new system, foreign policy has never been a significant election issue and China policy much less. Local issues often are most important, and even when Diet elections become a referendum on national policy and an occasion for voters to vent frustration, their frustration is with domestic matters. The 2007 upper house elections and the 2009 lower house elections, in which the LDP did badly, are cases in point.

Moreover, elected representatives apparently do not adopt positions that reflect the public's broad antipathy toward China. In a survey of mid-career members of the lower house of the Diet, only twenty-three wished to build Japan's military strength and strengthen the alliance with the United States (a mindset consistent with and perhaps formed by suspicion of China's intentions). Almost as many Diet members took a pacifist stance or thought that Japan should be a middle power. Only 2 percent wanted Japan to pursue an independent security stance with the military power to match—the most nationalistic option. The rest took a more ambiguous position on these issues, which does not suggest hostility toward China.[19]

This portrait of politicians suggests that the prevailing attitude toward China is one of ambivalence, an ambivalence that is shared by political parties as a whole. The mainstream view, apparently, is that China presents both an economic opportunity and a potential threat. Koizumi Junichiro sought good relations with China even though he would not bow to Beijing on his visits to Yasukuni. He engineered the liberalization of security policy for reasons other than China, particularly North Korea. Public opinion was not a factor in his decision, and in the case of deployment of SDF troops to Iraq, it was opposed. Koizumi's successors as LDP prime minister sought to improve relations with China by declining to visit the Yasukuni shrine.

The foreign policy of the Democratic Party of Japan, which took power in September 2009, displays that same ambivalence. On one hand, the DPJ has talked of reinserting Japan as a "member of Asia" and putting its alliance with the United States on a more equal footing.[20] The chair of the DPJ's Diet Affairs Committee reportedly stated that "relations between Japan, China, and the United States should be equally balanced, like an equilateral triangle."[21] Its leaders have cultivated good ties between the DPJ and China.[22] On the other hand, the DPJ's formal position sounds like that of the former LDP government, and it is not silent on outstanding issues. In his speech to the Diet, Foreign Minister Okada Katsuya said:

> With regard to Japan-China relationship, we will enrich and give shape to the "mutually beneficial relationship based on common strategic interest." We will also engage in resolving pending issues between the two countries, such as resource development in the East China Sea and food safety issues. We expect China, with its growing international status, to play a responsible role in the region and in the international community with improved transparency.[23]

And the DPJ shares past concerns about China's military capacity. In a December 2009 visit to Beijing, Ozawa Ichiro, the party's secretary general and eminence grise, warned China's defense minister that Japanese see China's military modernization as a threat and that Japan-China relations would suffer if Tokyo felt compelled to "strengthen armaments."[24] (In 2002, Ozawa, then in the opposition, warned the Chinese that Japanese would get "hysterical" if China's power grew too much. One response would be to produce nuclear weapons, and Japan had enough plutonium for several thousand warheads.)[25] Defense Minister Kitazawa, responding to proposals that all of the U.S. Marines on Okinawa be withdrawn, specifically cited their deterrent role vis-à-vis China.[26]

China's Actions

If the presence of strong, uniform nationalistic sentiment per se does not explain attitudes toward China, what does? A plausible explanation is that just as Chinese nationalism is often reactive in character, anti-China

Figure 11-1. *Japanese Public Opinion on Affinity toward China, 1978–2009*

Percent

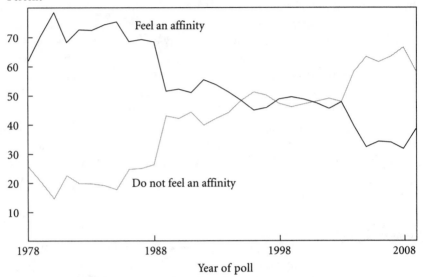

Year of poll

Sources: "Zu 10: Chugoku ni taisuru shinkinkan [Figure 10: Affinity toward China]," "Gaiko ni kansuru yoronchosa (Heisei 21 nen 10 gatsu) [Public Opinion Poll Regarding Foreign Policy (October 2009)]," Government of Japan Cabinet Office (www8.cao.go.jp/survey/h21/h21-gaiko/images/z10.gif).

sentiment is more a response to Chinese actions than the cause of Japanese actions. In other words, Japanese opinion about China has become more negative as Beijing's behavior has led the Japanese to question their previously positive views.

Prior to the Tiananmen Square incident in 1989, the percentage of those polled who felt an "affinity" toward China was usually in the high sixties or low seventies; afterward it dropped sharply into the low fifties or high forties. Then in 2004, as Japan-China relations deteriorated over a number of issues, the feeling of affinity dropped again, first to 38 percent and then into the low thirties (see figure 11-1).[27] A similar trend is evident when it comes to evaluations of the bilateral relationship (see figure 11-2): the percentage of those who believed that ties were favorable or satisfactory dropped from 76 percent in 1986 to 50 percent in the year of Tiananmen, hovered around that point for another fourteen years, and then dropped again. The low point was 2005 (20 percent); the percentage then started to climb only gradually

Figure 11-2. *Japanese Public Opinion on Japan-China Relations, 1986–2009*

Percent

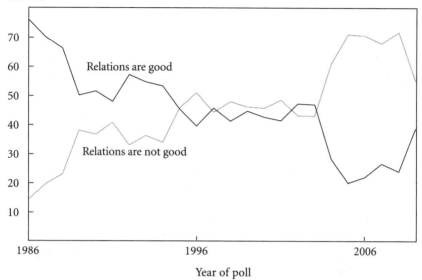

Year of poll

Sources: "Zu 12: Genzai no nihon to chugoku no kankei [Figure 12: Current Japan and China Relations]," "Gaiko ni kansuru yoronchosa (Heisei 21 nen 10 gatsu) [Public Opinion Poll Regarding Foreign Policy (October 2009)]," Government of Japan Cabinet Office (www8.cao.go.jp/survey/h21/h21-gaiko/images/z12.gif).

into the mid-twenties. So even as official relations were improving, public sentiment was not. Opinion did move in a more positive direction in a poll taken soon after the assumption of power by the Democratic Party of Japan government, which promised to tilt more in China's direction. (Percentages rose into the high thirties on both measures.) Whether that improvement continues remains to be seen.[28]

The Role of the Media

If anti-China sentiment in Japan is the cumulative result of responses to Chinese actions, its level of intensity will determine whether it has an impact on government policy. In Japan, that intensification, when it occurs, comes from the mass media. It is the print and electronic news organizations that make incidents with China known in the first place, generating the public attention that forces them toward the top of the political agenda.

Although Japan has many regional and local dailies, the national media companies are most important for national political and foreign policy news. There are five national dailies: *Yomiuri Shimbun, Asahi Shimbun, Mainichi Shimbun, Nihon Keizai Shimbun,* and *Sankei Shimbun.* Each of the "Big Five" has a companion commercial television channel: Nippon TV for *Yomiuri,* Asahi-TV for *Asahi Shimbun,* TBS for *Mainichi,* TV Tokyo for *Nihon Keizai Shimbun,* and Fuji-TV for *Sankei Shimbun.* Those channels supplement the public TV channel, NHK.[29] In addition, there are a variety of weekly and monthly magazines, some with a definite political slant. Among the monthlies, *Bungei Shunju* has a nationalistic perspective on external affairs; *Chuo Koron* has moderate-to-conservative stance; *Ronza,* which is published by Asahi, has been more likely to blame Japan's own policies for its foreign policy problems; *Seiron,* published by Sankei, is quite conservative in its point of view.

As in the United States, most people get their political news from television. A 2008 poll revealed that 36.8 percent of respondents got political news from the commercial channels and another 25.8 percent got it from NHK. The Internet was the source for 15.5 percent of those surveyed while 15.4 relied on newspapers (multiple responses were allowed).[30] Yet newspaper circulation is still very high: 644 copies per 1,000 households in the mid-2000s, which is highest among major countries and second only to Norway. The U.S. figure around the same time was 233 copies per 1,000 households. The public regards newspapers as its most reliable source of news.[31]

Japan's newspapers have probably the highest level of business competition among advanced industrial countries. Competition among television channels is also quite high. A common critique, however, is that there is relatively little diversity when it comes to content. A variety of factors are at play; one may be reluctance to lose market share by being different.[32]

Conformity may be the general rule, but it does not apply to how the five newspapers cover foreign policy and national security. The spectrum ranges from left to right or, to put it crudely, from opposing to favoring greater activism by Japan in the international security realm. *Asahi Shimbun* is generally the most cautious, with *Mainichi Shimbun* next. *Nihon Keizai Shimbun,* the Japanese analog to the *Wall Street Journal,* is in the middle. *Yomiuri Shimbun* is to the right of center, while *Sankei Shimbun* is most vocal in arguing for a change in the policy of exclusive defense and is most suspicious of China's future intentions. Shinoda Tomohito demonstrates convincingly that on a variety of security issues since 1990, "the five major newspapers demonstrated diverse opinions." Moreover, the debate among them became more "concrete" and "realistic" as the more pacifist papers focused less on matters of principle regarding security issues and more on questions of practicality.[33] Moreover, there was a tendency for *Nihon Keizai Shimbun* to move from a center-left position to center-right. Finally, Shinoda found a correlation between newspaper opinion and public opinion. In short, "these newspapers are very influential to the formation of public opinion, and are the media which is expected to reflect public opinion in order to influence the decision makers in the government."[34]

Nor is conformity the norm regarding weekly and monthly magazines. There also is vibrant debate among foreign policy and national security specialists, who run the gamut in terms of strategic outlook ("normal nationalists," autonomists, and so forth). Chapter 7 surveyed some of those views.

Confirming the importance of the Japanese media as an intensifying factor is a new understanding of the role of the media vis-à-vis the state. Analysts previously saw the media as the servant of the state, its watchdog, or simply a spectator; there were arguments in favor of each point of view. But a number of specialists see a different role that combines elements of all three—the media as "trickster."[35] Okazaki Hisahiko, a retired ambassador, asserts that the Japanese media are prone to creating "pseudo-events" that end up changing reality. He cites the case of one of Koizumi's visits to Yasukuni Shrine. China sought to treat the matter in a low-key way but the Japanese media gave it extensive coverage, "pestering" Chinese officials for comments. In the end they were backed into a position from which they could not retreat.[36] As John Creighton Campbell writes, "the media are tricksters, supporting one moment but mocking the next, essentially unreliable. When the media are drawn to an issue, they bring unpredictability and danger. . . . What policy changes will be favored by media involvement cannot always be controlled."[37]

Contributing to the media's trickster role is the state's lack of discipline when it comes to the security of information. More likely than not, someone in the government or ruling party finds the temptation to leak information about sensitive matters irresistible, even when it is arguably in the national interest to keep it secret. In many cases, that is because on any issue, there is someone in the Japanese system who has an interest in ensuring that there is public scrutiny. In the spring of 2007, U.S. secretary of defense Robert Gates reportedly termed this a government-wide problem.[38] Thus there is a high probability that no foreign policy crisis will remain under wraps in Japan and that by making it public, the media will make it more difficult for the government to handle.

Cases

The November 2004 Han Submarine Intrusion

At 9:17 a.m. on November 10, 2004, a banner headline moved across the screen during regular programming on NHK, the public television channel: "An unidentified submarine in Japan's territorial water; order of maritime security operations issued to Maritime Self-Defense Force."[39] Thirteen minutes later, a special bulletin interrupted the program to say that the submarine had traveled near Okinawa, through the Ishigaki Strait (see chapter 6) and that MSDF destroyers and P-3C aircraft were tracking it. The report included a clip of Chief Cabinet Secretary Hosada Hiroyuki announcing the development. Hosoda mentioned that the order had been issued once Prime Minister Koizumi had approved it and only after the submarine had left Japanese waters. In addition, an Air Self-Defense Force AWACS aircraft joined the search and watched for jets from China.[40]

There ensued a flurry of press coverage and commentary. In spite of early claims of ignorance from the PRC Foreign Ministry, suspicion centered immediately on the People's Liberation Army Navy (PLAN), which had been conducting research of the ocean floor in or near Japanese territorial waters. NHK made the suspicion graphic by running pictures of PLAN surface vessels recently spotted near Japan. And within two days, there was confirmation that the sub was Chinese.[41]

Speculation swirled on what Beijing intended by the intrusion. Was it to demonstrate to Japan that it had a nearby "military presence" that could be displayed at will? Was it a signal of antagonism related to the dispute over oil and gas fields in the East China Sea? Was it to rescue a stranded PLAN submarine? Was it to test Japan's antisubmarine warfare capabilities? Expert consensus quickly converged on a Taiwan explanation: the PLAN was preparing for the possibility of war with Taiwan and the United States to respond to a move toward de jure independence by the island's president, Chen Shui-bian. And a central element of Chinese strategy was to block or impede U.S. carrier battle-groups from entering the conflict, an operation in which submarines and knowledge of the ocean floor would be key.[42]

The Japanese government came in for quick criticism. LDP and New Komei Party politicians and the defense policy unit of the LDP complained that they had not been informed of the maritime security order. One LDP official alleged that the action was delayed until after the submarine had left Japanese territorial waters in order to protect the possibility of a bilateral summit between Prime Minister Koizumi and China's president, Hu Jintao, at the upcoming meeting of the Asia-Pacific Economic Cooperation forum in Chile. The right-wing *Sankei Shimbun* echoed that speculation: "Whether the government can continue to take a firm stance on this will be a test of Japan's diplomacy towards China." In confirmation of the allegations, it was revealed that the government had originally planned to keep the submarine's nationality quiet and forgo a protest. When it became obvious that, as Chief Cabinet Secretary Hosada acknowledged, "everybody was furious," the Koizumi administration reversed itself.[43]

The editorial comment reflected each newspaper's ideological orientation. Thus on the day after the government's announcement, before the sub's identity became known, *Yomiuri Shimbun* argued that if China was responsible that would reveal that it was a real threat and Japan's government should lodge a strong protest and generally be on guard. *Sankei Shimbun* asserted that the action was intentional, designed to test Japan's capabilities; although Japan was correct to respond, it should have done so more aggressively. Each paper questioned whether the government's defense and crisis management capabilities were sufficient. On the other hand, neither *Asahi Shimbun* nor *Mainichi Shimbun* rushed to judgment on whether China was responsible but acknowledged that the government had to act if it was China. Both said Tokyo should ask for an "explanation"; *Mainichi* said a protest was in order. Both noted the poor climate of bilateral relations in which the incident took place. Similarly, *Nihon Keizai Shimbun* said that a protest was required but counseled against rash action.[44] A similar difference of opinion was evident in the titles of the newspapers' editorials once the submarine was identified as Chinese and China issued a statement of "regret" on November 16: *Nihon Keizai*'s op-ed title was "China's Apology for Intrusion into Territorial Sea Commendable"; *Sankei*'s was "We Demand the Punishment of Officials Concerned."[45]

April 2005 Anti-Japanese Demonstrations in China

For three weekends in April, Chinese angry with Japan's bid for a permanent seat on the UN Security Council and the approval of textbooks that downplayed Japan's twentieth-century aggression conducted protests in major Chinese cities. The demonstrations received wide coverage in Japan in both the print and broadcast media, which have bureaus in China.

There was an interesting pattern to the Japanese response, as reflected in editorial opinion. After the first weekend of mainly peaceful demonstrations (April 2–3), the major newspapers were restrained in their commentaries; the few that were published were fairly analytical, while emphasizing different factors. *Asahi* stressed the mutual mistrust between the two countries, placing more blame for that on Koizumi's visits to Yasukuni than on China's "patriotic education." *Mainichi* cited an "anti-establishment mentality" that found an outlet in anti-Japanese protests, but it also said that Japan had to address the consequences of factors like the Yasukuni visits. *Sankei* dwelt on how the Beijing regime uses its patriotic education campaign to maintain its rule, even as it tries to prevent anti-Japanese feeling from affecting day-to-day relations.[46]

The tone changed after protests in Beijing became violent, resulting in extensive damage at the Japanese embassy while the authorities looked on. To make matters worse, there were mixed messages from the Chinese government: a Foreign Ministry official expressed regret over the attack and the PRC ambassador to Japan stated that his government did not endorse the violence, but the Foreign Ministry spokesman said that responsibility for current China-Japan relations did not lie with China. *Sankei*, blaming the government's lax security and demanding "strict action regarding anti-Japan activities," called the violence "unforgivable." *Yomiuri*, noting the contrast between the regime's repression of any activity that it finds "inconvenient" and its toleration of the protests, blamed the patriotic education campaign. Those perspectives were to be expected. *Nihon Keizai Shimbuni* agreed with *Yomiuri*, saying that the vandalism against the embassy "went against common sense." *Mainichi* criticized the weak security and warned that the whipping up of anti-Japanese sentiment in China was a new threat to Japan and counterproductive for China. *Asahi* was something of an exception, expressing puzzlement over the PRC's weak response to the demonstrations but also worrying about the danger of allowing mutually hostile sentiment to become deeply entrenched.[47]

The two episodes themselves plus the intense media coverage were associated with a deterioration in Japanese public opinion concerning China. In December 2003, eleven months before the submarine incident, the share of respondents in the annual Yomiuri-Gallup Poll who regarded the bilateral relationship as "bad" or "very bad" was 31.5 percent. In December 2004, one month after the episode, the share was 59.1 percent. One year later, eight months after the demonstrations, the share was 72.5 percent.[48]

The submarine intrusion and the protests were not, of course, the only reasons for the sharp shift in opinion. Yet the shift does indicate that public views, intensified by the media, will be a factor in any future incident, constraining attempts by officials to manage it. Japanese public antipathy toward China may not make a big difference in government policy under normal circumstances, but it could well be a different story in times of crisis or near crisis, putting the government and ruling party on the defensive and calling for a robust policy response.

12

The Chinese and Japanese
Systems under Stress

Previous chapters examine a variety of factors that bear on the interaction between Japan and China. Combining those perspectives can produce
a variety of security scenarios, some benign and some not so benign. Among
the negative scenarios is a clash of some kind between the law enforcement
units or armed forces of the two countries. Indeed, a group of American
specialists who reviewed Japan-China security relations in 2005 and 2006
concluded that

> the prospect of incidents between Chinese and Japanese commercial
> and military vessels in the East China Sea has risen for the first time
> since World War II. If an incident occurs, it could result in the use of
> force—with consequences that could lead to conflict. This is more a
> sovereignty issue than an energy resource issue, which makes it espe-
> cially dangerous.[1]

They predicted that such a conflict was "not unlikely."[2] They were not
alone. In November 2009, a senior People's Liberation Army officer at China's National Defense University warned that disagreements over oil and gas
fields in the East China Sea increased the danger of incidents. "Small-scale
conflicts could arise if [the issue] was not resolved." He failed to note that
Japan had sought a resolution more than China had.[3]

The probability of such a contingency may be modest, but its consequences for the broader bilateral relationship would be serious. The outcome would shape the perceptions of each about the long-term intentions of
the other. It could aggravate the security dilemma that already exists. Under
the stress of such a scenario, how capable are the two systems of containing
and minimizing those consequences? That is the subject of this chapter. But

first a recapitulation of the argument so far and the factors that would work together to increase the prospects for a clash.

Surface and subsurface vessels of the Japan Maritime Self-Defense Force (MSDF) regularly patrol the East Asian littoral in order to protect vital sea lanes of communication and to assert the country's maritime rights. Planes of the Air Self-Defense Force (ASDF) monitor Japan's large air-defense identification zone and scramble to challenge intrusions by foreign military aircraft. Both the MSDF and the Japan Coast Guard (JCG) are responsible for protecting the Senkaku/Diaoyu Islands, which Japan regards as its sovereign territory. The JCG is the first line of defense and the MSDF the second.

China views the East China Sea differently. It claims the Diaoyu/Senkaku Islands as Chinese territory. It has undertaken oil and gas drilling in the continental shelf east of Shanghai, partly in an area that Japan claims as its exclusive economic zone (EEZ) and an appropriate site for its own drilling. China's defines its EEZ to encompass the entire shelf, thus contradicting Japan's claim, and it believes that the UN Convention on the Law of the Sea (UNCLOS) forbids another power to conduct military surveillance anywhere in its exclusive economic zone. In 2004 and 2005, the contest for resources fostered concerns in each country about the security of its drilling platforms and there was a danger that the dispute might become militarized. Tokyo and Beijing, seeking a diplomatic solution, reached a "political agreement" in June 2008, but efforts to implement the agreement have made little progress. More broadly, China seeks to establish a strategic buffer in the waters east of its coasts. So the People's Liberation Army Navy (PLAN) and Air Force (PLAAF) are expanding their area of operation eastward, and China's Marine Surveillance Force (MSF) makes its own contribution to "defend the state's sovereignty over its territorial waters, and safeguard the state's maritime rights and interests." By challenging Japan in the Diaoyu/Senkaku Islands, expanding naval operations, sailing through maritime straits near Japan, surveying the seabed, and so on, China creates "facts on—and under—the sea." Stretching PLAAF patrols can create "facts in the air." Lurking in the background is the Taiwan Strait dispute, and the concern that Japan, as a U.S. ally, would be drawn into any conflict between the United States and China over the island.

So a clash between East Asia's most robust navy and air force (Japan's) and those of a China in revival is not impossible. As the American experts cited above concluded, the most likely site is the Senkaku/Diaoyu Islands, which each country believes strongly to be its sacred, sovereign territory.

In this scenario, China's MSF would challenge the perimeters that the JCG maintains around the Diaoyu/Senkaku Islands—even more aggressively than it did in December 2008. Because the JCG's rules of engagement are ambiguous, a JCG ship would then ram an MSF vessel, as one did in response to an intruding Taiwan fishing vessel in June 2008. Surface ships of the PLAN and the MSDF would then hurry to the area and take up positions. Planes of Japan's ASDF and the PLAAF would soon hover overhead. Submarines would lurk below. Ships of the two navies would maneuver for position. And although fairly tight rules of engagement regulate the units of each military, they may not be exactly appropriate for this situation, leaving local commanders a modest opportunity for independent action in the heat of the moment.

Chinese strategic culture, with its emphasis on preemption and preserving initiative, could come into play. Perhaps the captain of a PLAN ship sees fit to fire at an MSDF vessel. The MSDF vessel returns fire, because its commander believes that doing so is the proper response and does not wish to be overruled by cautious civilian bureaucrats in Tokyo. Planes of two air forces get involved. The longer the encounter goes on, predicts Bernard Cole, the more likely it is that the MSDF's "significantly more advanced naval capabilities would, if employed, almost certainly cause the destruction of PLAN units, with significant loss of life."[4]

At some point, commanders in the field would have to inform their headquarters in each capital about the incident. Would they convey a totally accurate picture, or would they shade reality to put themselves in the best possible light? Would they necessarily know exactly what happened? When a PLAN fighter jet collided with a U.S. reconnaissance aircraft off the island of Hainan in April 2001, the local command probably lied to those higher up about which side was responsible. By the time the Central Military Commission (CMC) in Beijing reported to civilian leaders, the story of the encounter between the two planes was very different from the truth. But the failure to tell "the whole truth" is certainly not unique to the PLA.

In the Diaoyu/Senkaku scenario, the odds are that civilian and military decisionmakers in Tokyo and Beijing would not receive a completely accurate picture. They would have to respond in a fog of uncertainty, giving free rein to a variety of psychological and organizational factors that would affect the handling of information. The military services would have a monopoly on information, impeding the voicing of contrarian views. The preexisting beliefs of each side about the other would distort their views of the reports from the field. Each side also would likely be subject to "attribution error"— the tendency to judge one's own actions in the best possible light and those of the adversary in the worst. Groupthink, the temptation to shade reports so that they are consistent with what are assumed to be the leaders' views, and a tendency to withhold contrarian views in a tense situation would be at play.

So there is a real chance that decisionmakers in each capital would receive a picture of the incident that was at variance with the "facts," a picture that downplayed the responsibility of its units and played up that of the other side. Working with distorted information, they then must try to prevent the clash from escalating into a full-blown crisis without appearing to back down. At that point, the imperfect ways in which civilian and military agencies in each capital interact with each other and in which senior leaders attempt to fashion a response that is appropriate to the situation would make it difficult to avoid misperception and miscalculation. The annual report on China of the U.S. Department of Defense warns that China's neighbors could underestimate how much the PLA has improved; China's leaders could overestimate the PLA's capabilities; and both might ignore the effect of their decisions on the calculations of others.[5]

To be clear, civilian leaders in neither China nor Japan would desire a wider conflict. Neither would want to see a serious deterioration in bilateral relations. Each country gains much from economic cooperation with the other. If the two leading countries of East Asia could not coexist—if indeed "two tigers cannot lie on the same mountain"—the leaders of each would conclude that they had failed. Yet even if objective interests would dictate a mutual retreat from the brink, leaders may see some outcomes, especially the appearance of capitulation, as worse than a growing conflict. And engineering a retreat from the brink would require great skill. It is here that institutional capacity and political dynamics come into play.[6]

First is the interface between senior military officers and civilian officials. As discussed previously, in China the interface between the military, party, and government hierarchies occurs at only a few points. The most significant point of contact is at the top, in the CMC, where the party general secretary and PRC president (currently Hu Jintao) is usually chairman. But that person may be the only civilian among about ten senior military officers. Moreover, the PLA guards its right to speak on matters of national security and its autonomy in conducting operations, so the institutional bias in this instance is likely to be against restraint. On the Japanese side, civilian control has been the rule, but the autonomy of the SDF has increased since the late 1990s; moreover, senior officers have resented their exclusion from policymaking circles. Therefore, in the event of a clash there would likely be tension and disagreement between "suits" and "uniforms" over how to respond.

Next is the issue of the structure of decisionmaking in Japan and China. In both, bottom-up coordination between line agencies is difficult at best, so if initiatives are to occur, they have to come from the top down. Yet in theory and often in practice, the "top" in each system is a collective: the Cabinet and the ruling parties coalition in Japan and the Politburo Standing Committee (PBSC) in China. There are exceptions, of course. Koizumi Junichiro demonstrated the ability to create a cabinet consensus that accorded with his policy preferences, and the members of the PBSC, who are not national security specialists, often defer to the paramount leader. On matters of war and peace, however, the need for consensus within Japan's Cabinet and China's PBSC grows. That creates a practical problem: the need for all members of each body to be present to discuss a course of action.

There also are problems associated with the decisionmaking process. Neither the Japanese nor the Chinese system is flawless when it comes to handling fairly routine matters. Coordination among line agencies is often contentious, which slows down any policy response. The Chinese system is segmented between the civilian and military wings of the hierarchy. Policy coordination mechanisms exist that facilitate top-down leadership, with Chinese leaders probably more dominant than their Japanese counterparts. But tensions still exist between the priorities of the core executive and those of the bureaucracies.

In more stressful situations, it is likely that, first, leaders receive information from below that is biased and self-serving. Ineluctably, they view that information through a lens that distorts the images of both their own country and the other. Second, they act in the context of a security dilemma, in which military capabilities, recent experiences on specific issues, and sentiments about past history shape the perception of each of the intentions of the other. Third, each decisionmaking collective relies for staff support on bodies that themselves are a collection of agency representatives: in Japan the group working under the deputy chief cabinet secretary for crisis management and in China both the appropriate civilian leading group and the CMC. Each agency represented has its own perspective. Neither system has shown itself adept at responding to situations of stress that do not rise to the level of seriousness of a military clash. Neither, therefore, is likely to do well in the conflict scenario envisioned here.

Fourth is the matter of domestic politics. Although each government would have reason to keep such a clash secret, the Japanese side would probably be unable to do so because the government is rather porous and the media would see little advantage—commercial or otherwise—in suppressing a "hot" story. A leak from the SDF, the Ministry of Foreign Affairs, or the Ministry of Defense is all but certain. Not only would that energize the Japanese press, with its predilection for viewing security issues in zero-sum terms, but it would also doubtlessly inflame the Chinese public. Demonstrations of greater magnitude than those in April 2005 could be expected. The regime, worried about domestic stability and defensive about inevitable charges of softness, would be more inclined to a tough response—that is, the PLA's preference for firmness and tendency toward nationalistic outrage would combine to squeeze civilian leaders.

To make matters worse, at least some of China's nationalistic citizens have tools with which to mount their own tough response: cyber warfare. They would mount an array of attacks on Japanese institutions—attacks that the Chinese government would be incapable of stopping even if it chose to do so. The cyber offensive would in turn anger the Japanese public and incline the government to taking a stronger stance. Inexorably, the spiral would descend. In earlier decades, the governments were more capable of containing incidents through the use of special channels ("pipes"). But those days are gone. In both countries the public is now a significant actor, constraining the choices of the government.

None of the steps in this scenario is certain. That a clash between China and Japan occurred would not necessarily mean that the two governments could not contain it and prevent it from escalating. Yet each loop in the downward spiral would increase the probability that subsequent, reinforcing loops would occur, and their cumulative effect would be to reduce Tokyo's and Beijing's chances of succeeding in their efforts to manage the crisis.

At least one group of American security experts is skeptical—the team mentioned previously that stated that a naval collision in the East China Sea was "not unlikely." It reached these conclusions about the chances that China, Japan, and the United States could contain the clash once it happened:

> All three parties would attempt to exercise restraint and to give others the opportunity to act in similar fashion. Yet there is also good reason to think that the crisis management strategies of either Tokyo or Beijing could back the other into a corner in which restraint would serve its interests poorly and some escalation would seem like a reasonable risk. Successful avoidance of escalation would require a level of clear and consistent signaling between the parties that, in a crisis, cannot be taken for granted.[7]

Crisis Management: General Considerations

The subject of crisis management requires some precision regarding the definition of crisis. Borrowing from Jonathan Wilkenfeld, three factors or conditions must be present to create a foreign policy crisis for a state: "(1) a threat to one or more basic values, (2) an awareness of finite time for response to the value threat, and (3) a heightened probability of involvement in military hostilities."[8] The need to protect fundamental values on one hand and a finite time frame and the prospect of military hostilities on the other are what make the task of crisis management so difficult.[9]

A "near crisis" contains the first two conditions but not the third, regarding military hostilities. A full or near crisis occurs when one actor (or both) makes the critical judgment that it has no choice but to act; that it should oppose the adversary's challenge to its core interests; and that it has an opportunity to act preemptively. If at least one side is willing to back down rather than escalate, there is no crisis.[10]

Even if a near crisis does not develop into a full one, it can still seriously hurt the relations of the parties concerned. And it is important, obviously, that policymakers distinguish correctly between the two types and that both states involved in a crisis have a common understanding of which type of crisis it is. Without that consensus, the chances of escalation increase.[11]

In considering China's and Japan's ability to prevent escalation, I prefer to consider a broader class of cases—"situations of stress."[12] A full or near crisis certainly qualifies as a stressful situation, but other tense situations that might occur may not precisely fit the definitions noted above. The threat posed may be to significant values rather than basic ones, but the pressure for a quick response and the increased probability of violence may remain. Again, a clash that does not thrust two parties into a near or full crisis may still have a profound impact on their relations. Moreover, there may be disagreements in each country on the stakes involved. If the public in either country believed that basic values were threatened and it acted on that perception, it might not matter that decisionmakers did not consider the challenge so great. So the insights of the crisis management literature are still useful for understanding situations of stress. How the Chinese and Japanese governments have responded in situations of stress—and whether they can prevent escalation—can reveal how they would respond in a real crisis.

Even though actors under stress may wish to avoid conflict and war, doing so depends on the capability and skill that they bring to crisis management.[13] A number of variables are germane. First of all, what is the character of the trigger? It may be accidental or not. It may be a complete surprise or not.[14] Second, what are the views of decisionmakers on the character of their own country and the adversary's; on the relative values of coercion, accommodation, and persuasion; on risk taking; on how to control escalation and preserve deterrence; and on how to signal intentions in a crisis?

Michael Swaine offers two ideal types as polar points of analytical reference. On one extreme are actors who view crises mostly in zero-sum terms and assume that an adversary will behave aggressively, while they themselves are "peace-loving" though resolute. Those who take this approach also believe that escalation can be controlled and have a preference for faits accompli or strong coercive actions. On the other pole is the actor who assumes that neither side in a crisis needs to lose and that both are acting from a defensive orientation. In this view, escalation control is difficult, particularly if coercion is employed, and is best avoided through incrementalism and accommodation.[15]

Third, depending on where the actors are on this broad continuum, do they pick an appropriate strategy or not? They have a range of specific options from which to choose. Offensive options include blackmail; a limited probe of the adversary's resolve that can be reversed; controlled pressure; creation of a fait accompli; and attrition. Defensive strategies include

— employing coercive diplomacy (threats of force or gradual escalation of the use of force to get the adversary to abandon its course of force)

—"drawing a line"

—conveying resolve in order to reduce the chance of the adversary's miscalculating one's intentions

—buying time to explore negotiations

—limiting escalation

—taking a tit-for-tat course of action (proportionate responses to the other's actions)

—testing the opponent's capabilities.[16]

The last three types may be accompanied by steps to deter an escalatory response by the other side.

Fourth, if actors pick a good strategy, do they implement it well? In particular, how well do civilian leaders make informed use and maintain control of their military forces? A key part of this issue is an inherent problem in crisis management: the tension between the "military logic" of how to respond to the adversary's challenge and the desire to preserve diplomatic options for resolving the crisis. The latter may well reduce the chances of escalation; the former may increase them.[17]

Fifth, what is the nature of crisis bargaining? This always involves some mix of persuasion, gestures of accommodation, and coercive threats and actions. The mix should be appropriate for the nature of the crisis, but that is not necessarily the case. Too tough a combination may feed escalation. Too soft a mix may lead to one side capitulating and thereby failing to protect fundamental interests.

Sixth, what is the quality of information? Poor or late intelligence can lead policymakers to respond to a situation that does not exist. More generally, misperception and miscalculation can exacerbate a crisis.

China and Crisis Management

Stanford scholars John Wilson Lewis and Xue Litai offer a description of how China's institutions are supposed to operate in a crisis or near crisis:

—The Politburo Standing Committee takes the lead, reviewing intelligence and reports that the General Office of the Central Committee has filtered. It seeks counsel from the relevant ministers, intelligence agencies, and, sometimes, trusted scholars. Members offer their views on issues in their areas of expertise (but recall that most PBSC members specialize in domestic matters).

—The PBSC seeks consensus on an appropriate approach. If it cannot achieve consensus, the issue is turned over to the Politburo, where PBSC members usually receive deference. If possible, a PBSC member is designated as crisis manager to convene other meetings to formulate specific policies and plans. He will summon those officials who are relevant to the problem, who in turn are supported by crisis cells that have been activated in their respective organizations. They engage in open discussion, with each "offering their professional expertise and personal judgment." Participants also keep in touch between meetings, and the crisis manager reports regularly to the PBSC. When he is satisfied with the course of action proposed, he submits a decision document to the PBSC.

—Once a high-level decision is reached, it is passed to the relevant leading group for implementation. There is some jockeying among leading groups for this role.[18]

Note several aspects of this process. First of all, adoption of an initial approach requires the PBSC to assemble; if not all members are in Beijing, then there is a delay. Convening the Politburo requires an even greater delay, since some of its members do not work in the capital. Second, military views are usually conveyed to the PBSC by the paramount leader in his capacity as CMC chair, which assumes some prior interaction between him and the high command. In the Politburo, in contrast, the two most senior uniformed officers are present. Third, although Lewis and Xue say that leading groups are not involved until the implementation phase, the meetings convened by the crisis manager actually sound like meetings of the relevant leading group.

Lewis and Xue acknowledge that this process is "best suited for slowly evolving but somewhat predictable crises." But they regard it as more of an ideal model, pinpointing a number of institutional problems. First, the process described still lacks the capacity to predict and prevent crises. Second, the volume of information that enters the key node of the General Office is immense. "Prior to high-level meetings, not to speak of emergencies, the communications can become overloaded and vulnerable to false or misleading signals." Third, senior bodies are not efficient when there is a need for rapid and decisive decisions, in part because of a risk-averse culture. In particular, the important role of secretaries and relationships (*guanxi*) may complicate crisis management even as they facilitate routine operations. Fourth, at a certain point in the emergence of a crisis, the PLA will activate the command center in the Western Hills, which is physically and institutionally remote from decisionmakers in downtown Beijing. Finally, the PLA's command-and-control mechanisms have not been tested in war. Lewis and Xue sense that even routine policymaking is undermined by "communication breakdowns, personal rivalries, and incompetent or indifferent leaders."[19] One can only infer that such problems would be more extreme in situations of stress.

Michael Swaine makes a different cut at the problem, focusing on the attitudes of decisionmakers involved in the process. Swaine argues that how Chinese leaders have handled crises has improved since the beginning of the reform period in 1979. Before then, their belief system was grounded in their sense of past victimization and a desire to avoid the appearance of weakness. They regarded perceived challenges to China's sovereignty and territorial integrity in zero-sum terms and as a test of its resolve and regime stability that had to be firmly repulsed. Chinese scholars report that today the leaders no longer regard crises or mini-crises in absolute terms and are more inclined to avoid them or resolve them early on.[20] But the shift is probably relative.

Second, before 1979 Chinese crisis behavior followed the guideline of "on just grounds, to our advantage, and with restraint" (*youli, youli, youjie*). That approach combined, on one hand, the Maoist principles of using force only defensively, fighting only when certain of victory, exploiting enemy weakness, and matching capabilities and objectives and, on the other, the use of coercive threats and force to achieve a political and psychological impact plus an emphasis on retaining the tactical initiative. Chinese scholars assert that after 1979 their leaders have been less willing to use coercive diplomacy;

the Taiwan Strait issue is the main exception. Or, as Swaine summarizes the Chinese scholarly view,

> the Chinese leadership today regards the use of force in a foreign policy crisis as a last resort, to be considered only if core national interests are at stake, other . . . alternative approaches are exhausted, or China is faced with extreme provocation. . . . The challenge, of course, is to determine when such conditions prevail.[21]

Third, the Chinese apply the *youli, youli, youjie* principle to issues of risk and escalation control. When China succeeded in past crises in using force or threats of force to achieve its political ends, it did so when it had gained local superiority; when the senior leadership had strong control over the armed forces; when military moves were coordinated with political and diplomatic moves; when China had seized the initiative; when it had a good sense of the limits of action; when it gave clear and effective signals of its intentions; and when it gave the adversary a way out. Yet Beijing did not secure those conditions in every crisis.[22] With respect to signaling in particular, effective channels often do not exist, and when they do the messages are sometimes misinterpreted for cultural or other reasons.[23]

In short, although some of the negative features of U.S.-China cold war crisis behavior no longer exist, some still do. "A strong sense of mutual distrust, continued signaling problems, the tendency to display resolve through decisive action, and a proclivity to fall into the commitment trap all raise alarm. Other complicating features, such as growing popular nationalistic pressures and a more complex decision-making process in China, have emerged."[24]

Japan and Crisis Management

Until the 1990s, the Japanese system was insufficiently prepared for situations of stress.[25] Tokyo assumed that the United States would handle international crises, and although a variety of agencies planned for internal disasters like earthquakes, the capacity for centralized coordination of their various activities was weak. A series of episodes in the 1990s exposed that reality.

First was the Persian Gulf War (1990–91), when, for the first time, the United States called on its Japanese ally to contribute materially to the international response to Saddam Hussein's invasion of Kuwait. Tokyo was paralyzed, and in the end contributed only financial assistance plus some post-conflict mine sweeping. The slow response was what Japanese officialdom and the public remembered (to say nothing of Washington).

The second was the North Korea crisis of 1993–94, when the probability of war in East Asia increased to its highest level since the end of the Vietnam War. U.S. policymakers, who assumed initially that Japan would provide various kinds of rear-area support, were taken aback when their counterparts in Tokyo described the legal and policy restrictions on doing so. The lesson for both sides was that the alliance was not ready to cope with regional contingencies. The lesson for a senior Japanese official was "With the poor functioning of the Cabinet, we could not respond to a real crisis."[26]

The real shock for Tokyo came with the Kobe (Hanshin) earthquake of January 1995. After years of planning for such an event, it was clear that "Japan . . . simply did not possess a reliable crisis management system that could respond to major incidents." In particular, the top of the hierarchy lacked the capability to lead because it did not know the roles and skills of various agencies; it could not communicate well with field units; it was short of staff; and training in the established procedures had been insufficient.[27]

There ensued under the leadership of Prime Minister Hashimoto Ryutaro an effort to improve the crisis management capacity of the government in general and the prime minister's office in particular. Most significant was the creation of two posts in the Prime Minister's Official Residence (PMOR; *kantei* in Japanese). The first was the post of deputy chief cabinet secretary for crisis management (DCCS-CM), who normally is seconded from the National Police Agency (NPA). The DCCS-CM has a staff of around thirty individuals.[28] The second position was that of assistant chief cabinet secretary for national security and crisis management (ACCS-NSCM), who assists the DCCS-CM. Customarily, that person comes from either the National Police Agency or Ministry of Defense (MOD) and supervises a group of counselors from other agencies. Koizumi Junichiro pushed for even more reform after September 11, in particular the 2003 legislation to specify roles and authorities in crises.

Under Liberal Democratic Party (LDP) governments after Hashimoto, the plan was that in an emergency the DCCS-CM, situated in a crisis management center, would take charge. Assisted by the ACCS-NSCM, he would work under the supervision of the deputy chief cabinet secretary for administration (DCCS-A), reporting to the PM and the chief cabinet secretary (CCS). They in turn would issue instructions to relevant officials in the Cabinet Secretariat and to those in ministries and agencies that would play roles in the crisis response. Those bodies would provide personnel to the crisis management center. Depending on whether the crisis was minor, major, or severe, bodies of increasing significance would be established under the prime minister.[29] And in 2003, legislation expanded the membership of the ministerial-level Security Council of Japan and clarified the circumstances under which it must and might meet.

Observers conclude that these reforms strengthened Japan's crisis management capacity, by giving more authority to the prime minister's office, particularly to his Cabinet Secretariat. Whether the DPJ government that took power in September 2009 will continue the reforms remains to be seen. Even if it does, a number of issues remain, which likely necessitate further reforms.

The key problem remains one of institutional design. Although the prime minister gained power, it was still insufficient. Koike Yuriko, a former LDP defense minister, wrote:

> At present, [officials] gather in small rooms divided by thick walls of ministries and agencies, and intelligence never reaches the landlord that is the prime minister. . . . We need to consider how everyone can gather in a large room to provide ideas to the prime minister so he can make decisions from a broader standpoint.[30]

Having ministries and agencies send officers to the *kantei* was a step, but they still "retain[ed] a certain amount of loyalty to, or bureaucratic habits from, their former office." Those agencies continued to compete for influence rather than create ways to work in concert. As one official said of the competition among intelligence organizations for direct access to the prime minister, "If this anarchic situation continues, the government could make a serious mistake in judgment."[31] Moreover, given the degree of turf-consciousness, that the prime minister must build a consensus among relevant agencies slows down response time when the need for a response is pressing.[32] Finally, at the staff level within the crisis management mechanism, the Self-Defense Forces are probably underrepresented. Because the focus of that mechanism is on domestic contingencies like earthquakes, the relevant deputy chief cabinet secretary is from the NPA, whose mission is internal security. The assistant chief cabinet secretary subordinate to him is only sometimes from the defense ministry. And with no uniformed SDF officer in the *kantei*, decisions that have a military dimension can be "nonsensical." [33]

Defects in institutional design can slow down response time in a crisis. After passage of the 2003 legislation on emergency situations, the *Daily Yomiuri* offered its readers a speculative analysis of what might happen if a country like North Korea deemed Japan a hostile nation and mobilized its forces.[34] First, the prime minister convenes the Security Council of Japan (a sub-cabinet, ministerial-level body). It receives reports from its staff, deems that an armed attack is possible, and, based on the existing legal framework, decides to draft a policy response. The full Cabinet then meets, confirms those actions, and establishes an emergency headquarters chaired by the prime minister. He then issues a stand-by order to the SDF; the minister of defense would identify likely deployment areas. The prime minister would inform the public, and evacuation of citizens would begin, as appropriate.

By law, nothing more can happen as long as an attack is only "predicted," even if the adversary country takes an action that makes an attack appear more likely—fueling a missile, for example. But unless it is clear that Japan is in fact the target of the attack, the government cannot proceed. When the adversary's intentions become clear—for example, through a hostile action or an announcement—then and only then may the Cabinet meet to declare that an attack is occurring and approve the response policy. The Cabinet must also seek Diet approval for a defensive mission. Once that occurs, the SDF may deploy.

Not every stress situation will qualify as an armed attack. Yet other contingencies are likely to face the same legal constraints, procedural requirements, and checks and balances that would complicate a timely and effective executive response to an armed attack.

Another limitation in the Japanese government's capacity to act in a crisis-like situation has to do with information and its transmission. Intelligence assets are limited, and even where the government has sought to make progress, as in satellites for imagery, constraints remain. Until the passage of the basic space law, which gave stronger direction on the collection of satellite imagery, the resolution of the images was not militarily useful.[35] Japanese officials have resented their dependence on the United States for high-quality intelligence in emergencies—missile launches by North Korea, for example. Connectivity is not comprehensive, impeding the transmission of information. At the time of the North Korean missile test in July 2006, the MSDF's Aegis destroyers, which were watching for the launch, lacked the capability to communicate directly with the Japan Defense Agency (the predecessor of the Ministry of Defense).[36] More generally, the process of sending critical intelligence to MOD or the PMOR can be slow, in part because "flash" reports have gone through the ministry's Internal Bureau. And sometimes the information is simply wrong. At the time of the April 2009 North Korean missile launch, an ASDF missile defense unit sent an alert that a U.S. early-warning satellite had detected the launch, which quickly proved to be inaccurate. Based on that false report, the PMOR quickly notified national and government agencies.

There are other issues. Units at the national level remained understaffed.[37] Insufficient training on new routines impedes the integration of the various actors into a coherent and effective operation. Procedurally, there is a "preoccupation . . . with legal remedies to organizational problems." Challenged by a crisis, Japanese officials still tend to focus on legal restrictions and precedents rather than what is the most appropriate policy. For example, after the North Korean nuclear test of October 2006, the Foreign Ministry and the Japan Defense Agency (JDA) disagreed on whether the test had triggered application of the law to ensure Japan's peace and security in situations in areas surrounding Japan. The final interpretation would in turn dictate whether Japan could join the United States in intercepting North Korean shipping. The Ministry of Foreign Affairs (MOFA) favored invoking the law in order to be a good ally. The JDA, or at least the civilians in the JDA, opposed it, reportedly because MOFA did not consider the safety of SDF units in the field. In the end, the JDA position prevailed.[38] Another example is that crisis management capability is mobilized only when the prime minister declares that a "significant emergency" exists. If he does not, the agency or agencies most directly concerned with the issue area take charge, often losing the opportunity to benefit from the assets of excluded agencies and of coordination with them.[39]

If Japanese officials learned to their dismay in the mid-1990s that the government's crisis-management capacity was weak, it still is not clear, more than a decade later, that the subsequent institutional reforms have enabled Japan to perform better in a real crisis. Moreover, the arrival of the Democratic Party of Japan (whose senior officials lack government experience), a bias against bureaucratic expertise, and the need to fashion new interfaces among the *kantei* and ministries probably means that, for a while, Japan will be even less capable of responding to stress situations than it was under the LDP.

China Cases

Three cases illuminate the workings of the Chinese system under stress. The first is the response to the visit of Taiwan's president, Lee Teng-hui, to the United States in June 1995. Second is the collision of a PLAN fighter with a U.S. reconnaissance aircraft in April 2001. And third is the aftermath of the U.S. bombing of the Chinese embassy in Belgrade, Yugoslavia. A key difference among the three episodes is the degree of public protest: least on Taiwan and most on the Belgrade bombing.

Taiwan

As discussed in a previous chapter, the Chinese leadership's response to what it regarded as a challenge from President Lee Teng-hui was based on gradual consensus building. The issue became more urgent when, despite the relatively mild and conciliatory policy that President Jiang Zemin declared in January 1995, Lee went ahead with a visit to the United States, where he gave a speech at his alma mater, Cornell University, in June 1995. In a misjudgment, Beijing had relied on the Clinton administration to block the visit but had not counted on Lee's ability to mobilize congressional and public opinion to turn Clinton around. China took the reversal as a U.S. betrayal and support for what it saw as Lee's "creeping independence" (a misperception).[40] It was even more upset when Lee's Cornell speech was more political than it had expected, although he said nothing at Cornell that he had not said before in Taiwan.

It was in the Politburo Standing Committee where Chinese leaders debated their response to what they saw as Lee's challenge to China's core interests and U.S. complicity in that challenge. Swaine reports that "a larger number of senior party and military leaders" were involved in this instance than normal and that retired leaders ("elders") probably expressed their views. The various leaders disagreed on the content and timing of the steps to be taken and the balance to be struck between coercive and political measures. Military leaders like Liu Huaqing and Zhang Zhen argued for a military response and downplayed the costs. Diplomats, led by Foreign Minister Qian Qichen, agreed that a tough response was necessary to deter other countries from accepting visits from Lee, but they worried that coercive steps would indeed damage U.S.-China economic and political relations.

The result was a mixed package of measures: suspension of dialog with Taiwan and the United States; propaganda attacks on Lee Teng-hui and the Clinton administration; and military exercises in the Taiwan area in the summer and fall of 1995 and during the March 1996 Taiwan presidential election. Swaine concludes that the package reflected a set of compromises and that is was "by and large the consequence of a collaborative policy-making process led by Jiang Zemin and not the outcome of a factional struggle." Key decisions were made by the PBSC, specifically Jiang, Premier Li Peng, and Admiral Liu Huaqing, vice-chairman of the Central Military Commission.[41]

Some analysts disagree with that view. Robert Suettinger, John Garver, and Tai Ming Cheung find that military leaders, along with some civilians, had opposed civilian policies for some time and used events like the Lee visit to impose their views on Jiang, constraining his options and forcing a tougher policy that employed military training exercises as tools for intimidation. Cheung reports that military leaders argued that the Lee visit confirmed their pessimistic analysis of his intentions. Andrew Scobell splits the difference. He confirms that the PLA led the charge in advocating a hard-line response to the Lee visit but also finds that by October 1995, civilian and military leaders had reached a consensus on a tougher approach.[42]

Whatever the case, the content of Lee's Cornell speech—more political than expected—led Jiang to accept the military's argument for a coercive response, and some of the political and diplomatic steps were taken in the weeks after the speech. In early July 2005 he ordered the PLA to develop plans for an immediate military display against Taiwan, and the Second Artillery carried out missile exercises in the third week of July, followed by other drills in August. By mid-month, the military leadership also presented a proposal for more exercises prior to Taiwan's legislative elections in December and the presidential election in March 1996. Apparently, the proposal was approved in August at the summer conference that the leadership had at that time at the beach resort of Beidaihe. At the same time, the leadership decided to concentrate China's ire on Lee Teng-hui and reduce pressure on Washington. The bifurcated strategy worked, more or less, until March 1996, when, to Beijing's surprise, the Clinton administration responded strongly to the PLA's missile and other exercises.[43]

The PRC's coercive diplomacy was its policy response to its judgment that Lee's actions reflected his separatist intentions, which, combined with U.S. complicity, were a threat to China's vital interests.[44] Yet that judgment rested on China's misperceptions and miscalculations. Although Lee certainly was not the compliant interlocutor that Beijing might have wanted, the case can be made that his actions were in fact his *response* to Beijing's rigid approach to cross-Strait relations (concerning unification formulas, Taiwan's international space, and so forth). Moreover, Beijing apparently ignored the Clinton administration's warnings about the role of Congress, or the Foreign Ministry did not wish to acknowledge that warnings were received.

In summary, the Chinese policymaking system had already been conditioned by the analytical assessments of the early 1990s to regard Lee Teng-hui as a separatist. Consistent with its strategic culture, the PLA had proposed a tough-minded response to that perceived trend but lost the argument in the debates with the civilian leadership that preceded Jiang's eight-point speech. The U.S. decision to allow Lee to visit and the content of his speech led Chinese leaders to conclude that a negative trend was not abating but was in fact accelerating. Whether that was true or not, the PLA got a second chance to argue for coercive diplomacy. The policy response may have reflected a consensus, but the leadership fixed the point of agreement where it did because the military leadership shifted the terms of the debate.

The EP-3 Incident

On the morning of Sunday, April 1, 2001, Beijing time, a U.S. reconnaissance plane was flying along the South China coast near Hainan Island. Two People's Liberation Army Navy F-8 jets flew up to intercept it and monitor its movements as part of an effort to challenge what the PLA saw as increasing surveillance along the Chinese coast.[45] Consistent with a recent pattern, one of the Chinese pilots brought his plane dangerously close to the EP-3. Too close, in fact: the Chinese plane collided with the U.S. jet around 9:15 a.m. The F-8 broke up in flight, and the pilot bailed out. The pilot of the EP-3, who was just barely able to regain control of his aircraft, flew it to Lingshui airfield on Hainan. He tried to notify the tower that he was in distress and sought permission to make an emergency landing. There was no reply, but the pilot landed anyway. The U.S. crew was then taken into custody, and a tense stand-off between the United States and the PRC ensued.

This incident qualifies as a near-crisis since there was little danger of military hostilities. It is interesting in two respects. On one hand, it represents a failure of crisis prevention, because the probability of some sort of collision was not small. Aerial surveillance off the China coast by U.S. military aircraft had gone on for a long time, and nonthreatening intercepts by Chinese military aircraft were increasingly common. During 2000, however, fighters from Hainan flew in a more aggressive manner, moving just ahead of the U.S. reconnaissance planes and creating turbulence (exactly like the pilot in the April 2001 incident, who lost his life). The U.S. defense attaché in Beijing protested this new and dangerous pattern in December 2000 but received no reply, and the intercepts continued.[46]

On the other hand, once the triggering event had occurred, each side had to scramble to find out what had happened. Much more on the Chinese than the U.S. side, policy in a situation of stress was crafted on the basis of bad information.

As of late morning, the U.S. embassy in Beijing knew of the intercept, the collision, and the emergency landing but not how the collision had occurred. In part because of concern over the status of the twenty-four-person crew, U.S. diplomats sought to contact their counterparts in the Chinese government. For the rest of the day, their phone calls produced either no response at all or no useful information.[47] The lack of responsiveness did not affect the outcome of the incident, but it did aggravate the concern and mistrust of the U.S. government.

Most likely the ministries of foreign affairs and national defense were reluctant to return phone calls because the Central Military Commission needed time to get information from the relevant PLAN units on Hainan. Moreover, the military was probably slow in briefing the MFA. James Mulvenon makes a compelling case that military units in Hainan were the only source of information about the collision and the landing of the EP-3 at Lingshui and that reports were kept within military channels until they got to very high levels in the chain of command, probably to the General Staff Department and the CMC:

> Thus the reports passed through multiple layers of the PLA hierarchy before any civilians were involved, increasing the chances that the story was "massaged" or "sanitized" by senior military officials predisposed to tell a PLA-friendly story and place the U.S. actions in the worst possible light. The high rank and seniority of the military officers presenting the reports also likely bolstered the authority of the accounts, or at least raised the costs of questioning the story for the civilian participants in the discussion. As a result, the PLA's version of the collision appears to have quickly become the official position of the government.[48]

Another reason for the slow response was that April 1 was Arbor Day in China, and senior leaders were planting trees outside of central Beijing at the time of the collision. Some segment of the leadership came together late on that Sunday afternoon to review the situation, but it is not clear who was involved. It is known that "the Standing Committee of the Political Bureau approved all major decisions" and that "top leaders played a core leading role." Perhaps the latter is a reference to the Foreign Affairs Leading Group.[49] After hearing emergency reports, the leaders decided to put the MFA in the lead for resolving what was essentially a dispute between the U.S. and Chinese militaries, and they put out a directive on the treatment of the crew. They also decided that because the United States Pacific Command (PACOM) in Hawaii had issued a press release at around 3:00 p.m., Beijing time, that China should issue a public statement as well.[50] Jiang Zemin was to leave China for a South American trip on April 4, and Vice President Hu Jintao was in charge during his absence. Hu presided over meetings of "chief officers of many relevant departments," but Jiang was able to "maintain his leadership over the handling of the event and [provide] important instructions" from a distance.[51]

What is striking is how, early on, the United States and China dealt differently with the causes of the collision. The PACOM press release (issued on the afternoon of March 31, local time in Hawaii) stated the basic facts of the incident and U.S. expectations regarding the treatment of the crew and the aircraft, but it did not assign blame for the "contact." (Nor did it mention the crash of the F-8 and the death of its pilot, probably because those facts had not been established.)[52] The Chinese version addressed causality directly and in a way that was consistent with the PLA's story. Clearly, the leadership had rushed to judgment. Mulvenon notes that no civilian leader could have questioned the PLA's story (and its loyalty to the party) without strong evidence to the contrary, evidence that was unavailable. Challenging the story would be difficult politically, because it would mean setting aside the China-as-victim image.[53]

China rolled out its version of the incident on the evening of April 1, first in an emergency meeting that Assistant Foreign Minister Zhou Wenzhong called with U.S. ambassador Joseph Prueher at around 9:30 p.m., Beijing time, a little more than twelve hours after the episode. He presented the Chinese government's view of the incident, which was identical to an MFA statement that was released about 10:30 p.m., while the meeting was taking place.[54] Zhou told Prueher that the EP-3 and the F-8 had been flying on parallel courses approximately 400 feet apart. The EP-3, Zhou charged, banked sharply to the left and hit the F-8. The United States was to blame and should take full responsibility for the incident.[55]

It happened that Prueher was a retired naval aviator, and he noted a fundamental problem with the Chinese version of events, one that Chinese officials either did not realize or understood but failed to mention. That was, if the lumbering EP-3 had banked hard left and traveled a distance of 400 feet, the faster F-8 would have flown much more than 400 feet forward, thus making a collision impossible. But even if Assistant Minister Zhou now appreciated the problem, it was too late to stop the public statement, too late to stop the media attack on U.S. perfidy, and too late to back out of an embarrassing position.

One factor at play in this situation may have been "attribution bias," a concept drawn from social psychology. That is, if a member of an out-group does something "bad," the action is attributed to the individual's bad character; however, members of the in-group who do something "bad" are given the benefit of the doubt. In this case, the Chinese gave the F-8 pilot the benefit of the doubt while the U.S. plane was assumed to be in the wrong.

Chinese observers have faulted the United States for making the collision public so quickly, arguing that "quiet diplomacy" would have been the best way to investigate and resolve the matter.[56] It is asserted that the Chinese stance was shaped by statements by the U.S. PACOM commander, Admiral Dennis Blair, and by President Bush himself. Yet such assertions ignore that the initial PACOM statement was the only U.S. public statement that had been made by the time the Chinese leadership made its fateful decision on the cause of the collision and that the PACOM statement stated only the facts and the expectation that Beijing would act in accordance with international practice in dealing with the crew and aircraft. Moreover, the statement reflected a U.S. government preference, learned through experience, to take the initiative and shape public discussion by making reliable information available rather than allow "rumors, leaks, and unofficial statements" to dominate public discussion.[57]

In the days between the clash and the release of the crew, there was a striking divergence in Chinese press coverage that reflected differences between the civilian hierarchy and that of the PLA. On the face of it, the military media expressed the military's loyalty to the party and to the four demands that Jiang Zemin announced on April 4, which Foreign Ministry officials conveyed to Ambassador Prueher. Yet while Jiang Zemin and Foreign Ministry officials emphasized the importance of U.S.-China relations and the need to resolve the dispute, the PLA's commentary emphasized instead U.S. hegemonism. Although the difference could reflect the regime's taking a hard and soft line simultaneously to appeal to differences among members of the same audience, it could well reflect differences over policy (the evidence is slim for making any kind of judgment). Reinforcing the latter interpretation is that PLA officers were reportedly unhappy with the final compromises that the MFA reached to resolve the crisis and believed that the civilians had been too weak.[58]

The Chinese public was a significant actor in the EP-3 incident. There was an outpouring of nationalist fervor and intellectual commentary concerning the incident. It was generally unknown that the United States military had been conducting surveillance so close to the Chinese coast—and that China tolerated the flights of reconnaissance aircraft. The regime treated Wang Wei, the Chinese pilot who perished in the crash of his plane, as a national hero, it being convenient to paint him as a new example of China's victimization and inconvenient to admit that he caused the whole incident. Yet the popular reaction was neither as intense nor as enduring as with the Belgrade bombing. The regime understood the danger of letting the responses get out of hand and the imperative of restoring normal ties with the United States at the beginning of an administration whose intentions were unclear. Diplomats on both sides therefore ultimately found a way to resolve the matter so that the crew was released quickly and the plane returned later (in pieces).

Still, the military's control of information concerning the incident and likely misrepresentation of what happened put civilian officials in an untenable position and complicated their task in resolving the matter. They made demands based on faulty information. Certainly, there may have been other factors at play. Civilian officials may have chosen not to challenge the authority of the PLA regarding its operations. Yet because decisionmakers lacked essential facts, resolving the dispute was more difficult than was objectively necessary, and ill will lingered on both sides.

The Belgrade Bombing

Close to midnight Yugoslavia time on Friday, May 7, 1999, U.S. bombers mistakenly bombed the Chinese embassy in Belgrade as part of the NATO campaign against Serbia. There ensued a period of serious strain in U.S.-PRC relations, which already were tense because China opposed NATO's Kosovo intervention in the first place and because Washington had rejected a Chinese offer regarding China's accession to the World Trade Organization and humiliated Premier Zhu Rongji in the process. To make matters worse for the leadership, the bombing occurred in the middle of a regime-initiated debate on China's relationship with the United States, a debate that the public outrage over the Belgrade attack exacerbated. The focus here is on how the Chinese government came up with its initial response and managed the public outcry.[59]

In Beijing it was already 5:45 a.m. on the morning of Saturday, May 8, when the attack took place. Government authorities in China had an understandably hard time getting authoritative information on Yugoslavia since heretofore information had come from the embassy, which was now seriously damaged. Intelligence agencies could only rely on Western news services for information. It was almost two hours after the attack that the PRC ambassador in Belgrade called to confirm the bombing. Again not surprisingly, because of the dearth of data "no intelligence agencies had time to accomplish an all-out analysis before the senior leadership convened" for the first time at 10:00 a.m. on May 8.[60]

An account by Wu Baiyi, a senior Chinese scholar, describes it as an "emergency meeting" attended by "top leaders."[61] Zhou Qi's version, drawing on published accounts that cannot be verified but that seem credible, says that it was an expanded meeting of the PBSC. Also attending were "representatives of the relevant government ministries and party departments, including the Central Military Commission, the Foreign Ministry, and the Information Office of the State Council, as well as some retired senior officials."[62] That suggests that the decision circle may have been, in effect, the PBSC, the FALG, the CMC (the leading group for the military), plus some elders. As Wu says, "almost all key leaders who shared supreme policy-making power took part in the entire decision-making process."[63] Wu makes the general point that these senior leaders conducted their decisionmaking by high-level discussions in an atmosphere of tension fostered less by the attack itself than by the emotional domestic reaction to it.

All participants at the first meeting were reportedly shocked and indignant about the bombing, and none believed that it was not deliberate. On that premise, they sought to figure out the U.S. motivation in the absence of reliable information and in light of improving U.S.-China relations. The explanations tended to impute a rational basis to U.S. actions and focused on a U.S. desire to test China's strength and will or to destabilize the country. When it came to formulating a reaction, the emphasis was on channeling students' patriotic fury to ensure that social stability was not undermined. To that end, the government needed to show firmness and resolve to maintain the public's confidence. There was initial disagreement on how to respond to the United States and whether, more broadly, to change China's general foreign policy of restraint and accommodation. In the end, it was decided to let Jiang "weigh the long-term interests of the country against the short-term emotions of the people."[64]

By noon on April 8, the leadership had formulated an initial policy response that included several elements. There was a stern government statement that condemned the attack as a violation of Chinese sovereignty and international law and demanded that NATO bear all responsibility; a call for an emergency meeting of the UN Security Council; and a series of measures designed to tolerate the protests but keep them organized so that they would not threaten social stability. The Ministry of Foreign Affairs took charge of implementing the steps under its jurisdiction. The CCP propaganda department and the Ministry of Education swung into action to try to shape the domestic reaction to the regime's purposes. Where responsibilities crossed bureaucratic lines, there was interagency coordination.[65]

The leadership mandated one other step on the first day. The Foreign Ministry was to summon the U.S. ambassador, James Sasser, to convey a protest. Yet there was no decision at that point on what to demand of Washington or what would be changed in U.S.-China relations. Nor was there a decision regarding whether Jiang Zemin himself would speak to the nation on the bombing.

Nonetheless, there never seems to have been any Chinese doubt about the U.S. motivation: the Chinese believed that the Belgrade embassy was bombed because it was Chinese. As far as relations with the United States were concerned, the issue of intention was important because of its implications for the policy response. If China decided quickly that the attack was intentional, then it would be more inclined to embark on a tough and irreversible course of action. If on the other hand it reserved judgment until more information was available, then it might have greater flexibility to resolve the conflict with the United States.

By daytime in the United States on May 8, the U.S. government sought to clarify the question of intention. President Clinton, traveling in Oklahoma, said that the attack was a "tragic mistake" and "tragic accident." He also offered regret and condolences to the leaders and people of China. (It would take the U.S. government several days to realize that the NATO command intended to bomb the building that it hit but believed in error that it was a Yugoslav government facility.)[66] That evening, Secretary of State Madeleine Albright delivered an official apology to the Chinese embassy in Washington. But the U.S. government was handicapped by the difficulty of mobilizing a response on a Saturday when the president was out of town and by the twelve-hour time difference between the two countries. By the time Secretary Albright delivered the apology, it was already the morning of May 9 in Beijing. (President Clinton issued an apology the next day.)[67]

How did the Chinese leadership jump to the conclusion that the attack was intentional? One possibility is attribution bias. The history of China's past victimization at the hands of the United States biased the Chinese— whether regime leaders or people in general—against the United States, and so they inferred that the bombing was deliberate without considering the possibility that it might have been accidental.[68] Then there is the possibility that a specific analysis may have prompted (or reinforced) the leadership's refusal to give the U.S. military the benefit of the doubt. An assessment from the Academy of Military Science, which was the first think-tank report on the bombing that senior leaders saw, concluded that the United States had deliberately bombed the PRC embassy. Certainly the authors believed that their analysis helped define how the leadership viewed the incident and shaped its response.[69] One may speculate that General Xiong Guangkai, deputy chief of staff with special responsibility for intelligence—a favorite of Jiang Zemin and a likely participant in the May 8 meeting—called attention to the views of these analysts in the military *xitong.*

There is another explanation for the leadership's interpretation of U.S. intentions—that it concluded that the United States deliberately bombed the Chinese embassy because that was what the outraged Chinese public believed. One could surmise that if the regime chose to challenge that view for the sake of U.S.-China relations, the public would have regarded it as weak and feckless and domestic stability would be in even greater jeopardy. In playing a two-level game of foreign policy and domestic politics in a crisis mode, the Chinese leadership's near-term approach was to put more emphasis on containing and co-opting domestic unrest by demonstrating public resolve than on problem solving with the United States.

That approach was clear in the media commentary on Sunday, which reflected leadership guidance from the meetings on Saturday. A *People's Daily* (*Renmin Ribao*) article charged that "NATO's subsequent chicanery, which claims that it did 'not intentionally target the Chinese embassy,' cannot cover up the bloody fact. The fact that three missiles blasted the embassy from different angles completely exposed the aggressors' evil intentions." Two Xinhua News Agency articles disseminated later that same day assumed an intentional attack.[70] Underlying all of this was the assumption that the attack was directed at the Chinese embassy because it was the Chinese embassy.

"Top policy makers" met again in an expanded PBSC meeting on the afternoon of Sunday, May 9. According to one report, Jiang Zemin spoke and made several points: The attack was intentional, a reflection of U.S. hostility toward a rising China. Although China had justice on its side, it lacked the power to challenge the United States directly, and China must maintain stability in order to build its power. The "patriotic zeal" of the people should be supported and guided to prevent it from getting out of control.

Several new decisions were made during the meeting. First, China should follow the principle of "struggle but don't break" in coping with the United States. Second, Vice President Hu Jintao, not Jiang Zemin, would make a statement on television that evening (preserving Jiang's relationship with the United States?). His statement reiterated the themes of violation of international law and NATO accountability, but it also sought to restrain the spreading and sometimes violent demonstrations. Third, the leadership decided what demands to make to "the U.S.-led NATO." There were four, which Foreign Minister Tang Jiaxuan delivered to U.S. ambassador James Sasser on Monday morning, Beijing time. The four steps were to make an "open and official" apology; carry out a "complete and thorough" investigation of the attack; promptly publicize the details of the investigation; and severely punish those responsible.[71]

That Jiang Zemin took the lead in both meetings is reflected in a later assessment by Wu Baiyi that the leadership reached a consensus "in light of decisive ideas suggested by the highest leader himself."[72] It also confirms my earlier surmise that a paramount leader who has been in office long enough to establish his authority is more likely to be able to shape the policy outcome than one who has recently taken office.

There reportedly was a final decision at the May 9 meeting: to reject any U.S. claim that the bombing was accidental.[73] Whether that was because it would have been impolitic to reopen the issue or that it would damage the reputation of those who had made the initial call is unclear. But the leadership chose to treat this as an issue not of fact but of morality. In that regard, the slowness with which U.S. officials moved from terms like "regret" to "apology" apparently made it difficult for China to ascertain U.S. intentions and cool off the crisis. There was a tendency to read the Clinton administration's failure to apologize as a form of pressure, which increased the incentive to give a tough-minded response, if only to demonstrate resolve to a nationalistic public.[74] That may all be true, but it ignores the reality that the U.S. government had to react on a Saturday when the president was out of town and that early on precious few facts were known about what exactly had happened.

In conclusion, Wu Baiyi is correct that in the days right after the bombing the leadership stressed domestic concerns over external ones. Diplomacy was "subordinated to and serving domestic interests." There was, no doubt, some anxiety that the demonstrators who were protesting so vehemently against hegemonic aggression by the United States against China, the morally pure victim, might turn on the regime for not standing up to U.S. intimidation sufficiently. The popular anger concerning the bombing may have reinforced a tendency within the regime to focus on the consequences of the bombing rather than on clarifying intent. The former preference allowed it to align itself with the nationalism of the crowd; the latter would have exposed it to charges of defending the bullying Americans.

In the end, the leadership's domestic political strategy in the wake of the bombing—allowing some nationalistic venting before reiterating China's fundamental interest in good relations with the United States—would turn out to make good sense.[75]

Yet neither the information available on how the PRC policy process responded to this surprise, even in the critical first forty-eight hours, nor the inferences that may be drawn from it are encouraging. Although Wu Baiyi gives the leadership good marks for its steady management after that initial period, he does admit that "China's decision-making was done without adequate information and in-depth analyses. Intelligence or expertise analyses did not accumulate until time passed and tension decreased."[76] The analysis in this chapter indicates that the leadership rushed to judgment on the threshold question, whether the bombing was intentional, mainly because of its anxieties about social stability. On the basis of its judgment that the attack was deliberately aimed at China, Beijing then made demands on the United States. There was no way of knowing in advance whether one of those demands, that those responsible for the attack be severely punished, could be met. In this case, China did not pay a price for its response to the bombing, in part because it was a political problem from the beginning. In a true military clash, even a minor one, the results of such an overreaction might be much less optimal.

Japan Cases

Three episodes in which the Japanese government acted under some measure of stress are analyzed below: two North Korean missile launches (in 2006 and 2009) and the effort to dispatch SDF units in response to the December 2004 tsunami in Indonesia.

North Korean Missile Tests

There are occasions when Japan responds quickly and well. Its response to North Korea's launch of seven missiles into the Sea of Japan on July 4–5, 2006, is a case in point.

Most of the rockets were relatively short range and did not reach Japan, and the long-range Taepodong-2 did not fly for more than a minute before crashing into the sea. After the launch, senior officials converged on the *kantei* early on the morning of July 5, as did the U.S. ambassador, Thomas Schieffer. And in less than a day, Tokyo had requested an emergency meeting of the UN Security Council, at which it tabled a tough resolution that framed consideration of the international response. It appeared to be an effective exercise of crisis management—particularly by Abe Shinzo, who was then the chief cabinet secretary—and a surprise to the international community.[77]

Yet the appearance of smooth crisis management is deceiving. Because North Korea takes time to prepare a launch—two months in this case—the Japanese government knew that missiles probably would be fired; the only real question was when. It therefore had plenty of time to ready its response. Abe tasked ACCS Ando Hiroyasu with researching which cabinet officers should come to the *kantei*, how citizens should to be informed, when to call a meeting of the Security Council of Japan, and what countermeasures to undertake. He met with Ambassador Schieffer on June 15, and the two agreed to form a U.S.-Japan project team. Around that time, the government also finalized its draft sanctions package. It was agreed that Abe, two of his deputies, and the relevant ministers would remain in Tokyo even on weekends. A press conference to inform the public also was planned.[78]

On July 4, Tokyo time, it became clear that a launch was imminent. The bilateral project team met in the evening to review the sanctions package, and Abe argued to keep it tough. The first information about the launch came around 4:00 a.m. on July 5. Abe immediately went to the PMOR and its crisis management center. By prior arrangement, Foreign Minister Aso Taro and JDA chief Nukaga Fukushiro arrived at 5:00 a.m. They consulted Prime Minister Koizumi and received his approval for their proposed response. Koizumi stressed the need, in reporting to the public, for accurate information and an appropriate combination of firmness and calm. The news conference occurred at around 6:15 p.m.

Ambassador Schieffer arrived before 7:00 p.m., and only then did the Security Council, a sub-cabinet body, meet.[79] It approved steps that were consistent with those that already had been drafted within a small circle of Japanese officials and discussed with U.S. representatives. Some of the constitutionally designated members of the Security Council would be instrumental when it came to implementing the sanctions that Japan imposed unilaterally on North Korea. On this occasion, other senior officials in relevant organizations plus General Massaki Hajime, chairman of the Joint Staff Council, and other senior SDF officers were present, a break from the normal practice of excluding "uniforms" from high-level policy meetings.[80]

In July 2006, therefore, key decisionmakers had scripted their response to an event that they were fairly sure would occur. The time pressure that is usually associated with a crisis was absent. The element of surprise came later, when there erupted a very public debate on the broader policy question of whether Japan, as part of its self-defense posture, could mount a preemptive attack against missile threats.

The response in April 2009 was rather different. As with the July 2006 event, there was plenty of advance warning that a launch was coming, both in terms of timing and flight path. On March 12, the day that the International Maritime Organization disseminated information from North Korea on the time period and closure area for the launch, Prime Minister Aso Taro's office established an information liaison office in the crisis management center, to which were seconded officials from the foreign, defense, and internal affairs ministries and from the National Police Agency. This task force outlined a series of steps to be taken once the launch occurred: CCS Kawamura Takeo, Foreign Minister Nakasone Hirofume, and Defense Minister Hamada Yasu-kazu would arrive at the PMOR within ten minutes and would meet with Aso within an hour. Aso would hold an emergency press conference soon thereafter.[81]

Yet Tokyo was more ambitious in 2009 than in 2006. For the first time, it made preparations to shoot down an incoming missile should it or parts thereof threaten Japan. Reportedly, the head of the Cabinet Information Research Office advised Aso that he could reverse his falling approval numbers by successfully intercepting the North Korean missile. Under the SDF law, the prime minister had to give the defense minister advance authority to order an intercept of a missile because the time from launch to a strike on Japan could be only a matter of minutes.[82]

Yet there were procedural issues to sort out. One was whether to give the unpopular Aso political cover by having some senior body authorize the order.[83] Defense Minister Hamada proposed a meeting of the Cabinet in order to show its full backing of the prime minister, but the Cabinet Secretariat and the Foreign Ministry worried that a cabinet authorization would anger North Korea. In a compromise, the Security Council of Japan met on March 27. Second was which provision of the SDF law should be the basis of the order. In one provision, the missile threat to Japan was treated as a near certainty; in the other, it was considered only a possibility. In the end, Minister Hamada's order to the SDF, issued also on March 27, relied on the latter authority because it was "seen to be less likely to upset North Korea and also less prone to ramp up public fears." But his orders included rules of engagement that permitted the commanding officer of the joint command created for this contingency to respond to a North Korean missile immediately rather than seek new authority.[84]

On the basis of the order, Patriot missile batteries under the control of the ASDF moved into position in northeastern Japan and MSDF Aegis destroyers deployed to the Sea of Japan.[85] It was expected that the United States, which had sensors that could detect a launch in real time, would convey that information to the SDF's central command post, which in turn would transmit it to Japan's civilian leadership and missile defense units in the field. Within five to ten minutes after launch, the central government would notify local governments.[86]

Despite all the planning, the response was flawed. Apparently, the Aegis units performed well in acquiring the launch data and concluding that the missile's first stage would not hit Japan after it separated. But Japanese units on land jumped the gun. Without foundation, SDF personnel in Akita prefecture notified the local government that the launch had occurred at 10:48 a.m. At a little after noon, a radar unit in Chiba prefecture mistakenly interpreted a benign flying object as a missile and notified the central government, which in turn notified the population. There were other problems with the transmission of information from the field and its interpretation at the SDF command center.[87]

So despite elaborate preparations, some parts of the Japanese government mishandled critical information in the case of the April 2009 launch, thus reducing confidence in its ability to act appropriately in a crisis. By inference, the response to a true surprise could be even more deficient.

2004 Southeast Asian Tsunami

On December 26, 2004, a massive tsunami smashed onto the beaches of Thailand, Malaysia, the Indonesian island of Sumatra, the Maldives Islands, and Sri Lanka. Countries around the world, including Japan, moved to provide assistance in the relief and reconstruction effort and in many cases used military personnel to carry out the tasks involved. But some nations moved faster than others.

—U.S. units were in the area a few days after the disaster.

—Australia landed an engineering corps complete with bulldozers and helicopters on December 31 and soldiers were fully active by January 3.

—Singapore sent 500 ground troops on landing ships on New Year's Eve day.

—South Korea and Greece sent C-130 transport planes, which were on station around January 1.

—Germany, the Netherlands, Spain, France, and Russia each had deployed ground troops by mid-January.[88]

Tokyo understood the opportunities that participation in the relief effort presented. Japan could gain political capital in Southeast Asia at a time when it was competing with China for influence. That was political capital that could be used in mounting a bid for a permanent seat on the UN Security Council. It could demonstrate again to the United States its willingness to act as an ally on a global platform. Using the SDF as one tool in the relief effort might lead Japan's neighbors to view its overseas military deployments as a normal phenomenon, and the Japanese defense establishment saw the chance to argue for better equipment to engage in such missions.[89]

The Koizumi government took a number of steps quickly to contribute to the relief operation:

—On the same day as the tsunami, the Ministry of Foreign Affairs set up a crisis center in the ministry and directed its missions in the affected countries to help in any way that they could.[90] MOFA was focused on the safety of Japanese citizens who were victims of the tsunami.

—Also on December 26, the ministry ordered disaster relief teams from the Japan International Cooperation Agency (the foreign aid agency) to go to Sri Lanka. The teams, which included personnel from the National Police Agency, the Japan Coast Guard, and the Tokyo Metropolitan Fire Department, left the next day.[91]

—On Monday, December 27, Prime Minister Koizumi pledged that Japan would assist in reconstruction after studying what kind of help was most appropriate.[92]

—On December 28, MOFA announced that Japan would grant US$30 million in aid to the affected countries and would emphasize development of a tsunami early warning system at a UN conference on disaster reduction to be held in Kobe on January 18. It subsequently increased the $30 million to $500 million when it heard that China would donate $60 million and the United States $350 million.[93]

—In response to requests from Indonesia, the Maldives, and Thailand, MOFA dispatched medical teams, which probably arrived on December 29.[94]

—Finally, the government of Thailand requested that Japan send helicopters to assist in search and rescue. Civilian helicopters would take too long to arrive, so MOFA sought the help of the Japan Defense Agency. It happened that the three-ship flotilla equipped with helicopters that was used for refueling Allied ships was returning from the Indian Ocean. It was near Singapore, so on December 28, Yoshinori Ono, director general of the JDA, ordered the flotilla to sail to the Thai coast near the vacation town of Phuket. The helicopters operated there until January 1, when the Thais ended that mission.[95]

During the six-day end-of-year holiday, the civilian government seemed to ignore further use of the SDF.[96] The JDA, on the other hand, was not idle.

During that time, it sent officials responsible for disaster relief to Southeast Asia. By Saturday, January 1, the agency had developed a plan to send as many as 1,000 SDF personnel to provide assistance. By mid-January, small elements of the Air Self-Defense Force and the Ground Self-Defense Force (GSDF) would arrive in the area, but the bulk of the expedition did not start its work until January 26, a full month after the crisis hit.

Why did Japan take so long to seize the opportunity presented by the tsunami? It is significant that there was no legal bar to the expedition and no need for special legislation; the SDF law permitted deployments for emergency international assistance. Moreover, this would not be the first such deployment. Tokyo had sent SDF units to Honduras in 1998, Turkey in 1999, and India in 2001 to help cope with the aftermath of floods and earthquakes.[97] The primary reason for the slow response was the difficulty of coordination among different elements of Japan's decisionmaking structure; in addition, the SDF lacked important capabilities to carry out this sort of mission.

It was not until the government came back to work on January 4, nine days after the disaster, that it addressed the question of whether to use the military as a tool of disaster diplomacy. On that day, representatives of twelve different agencies gathered at the Prime Minister's Official Residence to discuss Japan's general response to the disaster and to the SDF deployment in particular (word of that idea had leaked on January 2).[98] The JDA presented its plan, which called for at least 800 personnel from the ASDF, MSDF, and GSDF to provide medical aid, epidemic prevention, and transportation of goods. The officials approved the deployment, and JDA director general Ono ordered the SDF to prepare for the mission and for advance teams of JDA and SDF personnel to go immediately to Thailand, Indonesia, and Malaysia. Chief Cabinet Secretary Hosoda Hiroyuki, who likely chaired the meeting and who understood the impact of delay, stressed the need for Japan to "urgently implement" its assistance program. The advance teams left Tuesday evening.[99] In the end, the principal area of GSDF activity would be Sumatra, supported by MSDF ships on the water and transport planes flying out of Utapao Air Force Base (AFB) in Thailand.

Despite Hosada's injunction, implementation of the plan occurred at a pace similar to the pace of the decisionmaking itself. The first ASDF C-130 transport plane, with first-aid equipment aboard, left Okami AFB on Thursday, January 6, but because of its short range it had to refuel on Okinawa; bad weather over the island forced it to delay its departure, and it did not arrive at Utapao AFB in Thailand until January 7.[100] On the same day, the

MSDF transport ship *Kunisaki* left the port of Kure for the Yokosuka naval base, where it was to pick up forty GSDF troops, three Chinook helicopters, and two Blackhawk helicopters, plus water tankers, medical equipment, and disinfecting sprays. It would be joined by the *Kurama*, a helicopter destroyer, and the *Tokiwa*, a refueling ship. But the *Kunisaki* and the *Tokiwa* did not leave Yokosuka until January 12, and the *Kurama* did not leave the Sasebo naval base to meet up with the other two vessels at the island of Kyushu until January 14. The projected time of arrival off Indonesia was the end of the month. Because of the time lag, there was public criticism that Japanese soldiers would arrive on the scene long after the units of other foreign militaries, so the JDA sent a twenty-person GSDF team ahead of the others, which arrived on January 16 in Aceh.[101] It is worth noting that on January 4, ten Japanese nongovernmental organizations already were providing relief assistance.[102]

One reason for delay was a host of problems in getting the ships under way. Slow loading of various materials was a problem. The helicopters presented a particular problem because their rotors did not bend and so had to be removed and stored. Moreover, the GSDF choppers were not waterproof, so it took four days to apply a protective coating. In order to ensure that the GSDF helicopters were not damaged by salt spray, the ships traveled at a lower speed. Once the ships arrived, the rotors had to be reinstalled, which took several days. So regular operation of the aircraft did not begin until after January 29, around two weeks after the flotilla left Japan (the other 160 GSDF personnel flew by Japan Airlines to Singapore, where they boarded the MSDF vessels).[103]

There also was a political reason for some delay: the government wanted to "prevent the SDF dispatch from standing out, in consideration of a country where the Japanese Imperial Army was once deployed, and to observe moves that might be made by militaries of other countries." But, as one commentator noted, "this caused Japan to end up being a step behind."[104] And a Japanese government source offered this post mortem on the episode:

> It might have been possible for the government to issue dispatch orders at the end of last year [2004], if politicians and bureaucrats had better known the basics of military affairs, such as a military's organization structure and deployment capability, as well as the limit of the SDF.

As it was, slow decisionmaking caused Japan to place badly in the international "relief activity race."[105]

Summing Up

Both the general discussion of how the Chinese and Japanese systems respond in situations of stress and the case studies suggest the problems that they would have in coping with a bilateral clash between their two militaries. Drawing on the questions posed at the beginning of the chapter:

Such an incident would certainly be a surprise for decisionmakers in Beijing and Tokyo, because it would stem from interactions in the field over which they did not have absolute control. On the other hand, it would not be totally accidental. The clash envisaged would be the result of a test of wills between units that believe that they are carrying out the policy of their respective countries. While neither the Japanese nor the Chinese government has a lot of experience in handling surprises, the Japanese government has less (unless one includes North Korean missile launches that have a long lead time).

A key variable in a clash at sea would be the degree of involvement of the Chinese and Japanese navies. It is assumed that the first encounter would be between law enforcement agencies: the Japan Coast Guard (JSG) and the Chinese Marine Surveillance Force (MSF). If the vessels of the two navies, which provide backup for the JCG and the MSF, intervene, the chances grow that local commanders will exercise their own discretion and the clash will escalate on the spot. At least one expert believes that the longer a clash continues, the chances of a Japanese tactical victory increase.[106] That outcome, in and of itself, would make crisis management very difficult.

The stress of the situation would then be exacerbated because it is likely that the information flowing to decisionmakers would not be totally accurate. In any conflict, people at headquarters have difficulty getting accurate information and, at the same time, the volume of "noise" increases exponentially. Field units may shade their reports to create a more positive picture of their actions, and sometimes they may lie. The military hierarchy can try to manipulate how civilian officials understand the situation. How key officials in the civilian decisionmaking structure interpret—or misinterpret—the available information can lead to a rush to judgment. Both the Chinese and Japanese intelligence communities are stove-piped, the Japanese especially so. Skewed information leads to skewed responses.

As leaders in both capitals sought to respond, what they did would be shaped by how they view the other country and their own. Here, Japan's past and China's future come into play. Chinese leaders, particularly military leaders, would tend to view the current clash through the history of Japan's aggression toward and occupation of China before 1945. Japanese leaders would see the incident in light of their fears of a China whose military power is increasing as Japan's stagnates. Each group would believe, of course, that its country is unaggressive and peace loving.

But it is not just leaders who would affect any effort to limit escalation. The public in each country would have its own view of the clash. Leaks on the Japanese side and media that see danger around every corner would ensure that it became a public matter. The Japanese would likely see China through the same lens as their leaders: that of China's growing and prospective military power. The Chinese public, particularly the more nationalistic elements, would likely head for the streets, mounting demonstrations that would raise government concerns about internal stability. Some members of the public would head for their computer terminals to mount cyber attacks against Japanese government agencies and key actors in the Japanese economy. Protests and cyber attacks both would aggravate the Japanese public's negative attitudes.

The combination of an initial escalation in the field, flawed information, and public furor would put leaders in both countries in the hot seat, and the norms in each system that favor collective decisionmaking and consensus would slow the decision process and complicate formulation of a coherent policy response. The Japan SDF arguably would play too small a role in advising civilian policymakers, even though it would be involved in the outbreak of the episode and perhaps be the central actor in implementing the response. In China, the PLA might assert its authority to frame the discussions because national security interests would be involved. And it might have preferential access to the key civilian decisionmaker, the party general secretary, who is also chairman of the Central Military Commission.

The crisis context would no doubt bias the reactions of both governments, but particularly China's. Having won the initial engagement, Japan might adopt a more accommodating posture, but in Beijing the PLA would likely argue for a strong, coercive response in order to get Japan to back down and to restore national and institutional honor. What actions it might propose are hard to predict, but missiles over Okinawa or mobilization to seize the Senkaku Islands are possibilities. The broader the response, the more difficult it would be for civilian leaders to control implementation. Japan would no doubt read China's coercive stance as a threat to its security and would be more likely to seek a diplomatic solution. Yet the channels to accomplish that may not exist (or may not work if they do). Tokyo would also fear that too accommodating a response would amount to humiliating capitulation.

So the prospect of limiting the possibility of escalation in such a situation of stress is not good. Each system would respond with a mix of panic and gridlock. Those who argue aggressively for a strong stance would get a serious hearing. In such a difficult situation, Japan would have one more card to play. That is the United States, whose role is the subject of the next chapter.

13

Implications for the United States

Article 5 of the U.S.-Japan mutual security treaty states the following:

> Each Party recognizes that an armed attack against either Party in the territories under the administration of Japan would be dangerous to its own peace and safety and declares that it would act to meet the common danger in accordance with its constitutional provisions and processes.[1]

Note that the geographic scope of the treaty is "territories under the administration of Japan." The Senkaku/Diaoyu Islands are under Japan's administrative control, even though Washington takes no position on whether China or Japan has sovereignty over them under international law. In February 2004, a senior Bush administration official publicly and explicitly reaffirmed that the treaty applied to "territories under administration," thus suggesting that the United States would be obligated to assist Japan if the People's Liberation Army attacked or seized the islands.[2]

The previous chapter began with the judgment that a clash between China and Japan over the Senkaku Islands (or some other part of the East China Sea) was "not unlikely" and closed with the prediction that in any clash that could not be immediately contained, Tokyo would look to Washington for help in standing up to China's probable reliance on coercive diplomacy. This chapter examines the dilemmas that the United States would face in addressing a Senkaku Island or other scenario. Washington seeks good relations with both China and Japan. It does not want to get drawn into a conflict between the two, especially if it believed that the conflict was not necessary to protect the vital interests of either. Even in more ambiguous contingencies, such as a fight over oil and gas fields in the East China Sea, Washington would not be legally obligated to render assistance to Japan, but Tokyo would likely pressure it to do so. The United States would understand that *not* responding would impose serious political costs on its relations with Tokyo and would raise questions about U.S. credibility not just in Japan but also among other states that depend on the United States for their security.

The Taiwan Precedent

A clash between China and Japan would not be the first time that Washington has been in such a conundrum, one in which two countries have better relations with the United States than they do with each other. And as much as the United States hopes that the two actors have positive and mutually beneficial relations themselves, they tend to view their own interaction in zero-sum terms. Moreover, each is tempted to view the U.S. role in similar terms. Indeed, for Washington, coping with conflict or potential conflict between its friends has been a daunting challenge, particularly since the end of the cold war.

The Taiwan Strait issue is the clearest example in East Asia. The United States has strong incentives to foster good relations with both Taiwan and the PRC. It is an economic partner of both and seeks China's contributions to managing a variety of global and regional issues. Taiwan and China developed complementary economic relations after 1985, as Taiwan companies moved production and assembly operations to mainland China, employing large numbers of Chinese in the process. There was some hope of a political reconciliation after decades of hostility. Yet a corrosive political dynamic took over in the early 1990s that created the risk of a conflict that could foreshadow the possibility of a wider war, a war in which the United States might well choose to intervene.[3]

The process was complex, but its outcome, the result of deepening mutual suspicion, was that Taiwan and China each feared that the other was preparing to challenge its fundamental interests. China, whose goal is to convince Taiwan to unify on the same terms as Hong Kong, feared that Taiwan's leaders were going to take some action that would have the effect of frustrating that goal and permanently separate Taiwan from China—the functional equivalent of a declaration of independence. Beijing increased its military power to deter such an eventuality. Taiwan feared that China wished to use its military power and other means to intimidate it into submission to the point that it would give up what it claims to be its sovereign character. Taiwan's deepening fears—and this is important—lead it to strengthen and assert its sense of sovereignty.

There was misunderstanding at work here. For a Taiwan leader like Lee Teng-hui to stress Taiwan's sovereignty did not necessarily mean de jure independence, and it did not rule out certain kinds of unification in the future. But China, in a misreading of what was happening, saw Taiwan's assertions of sovereignty as a plot to promote de jure independence and permanent separation. So the vicious circle of mutual fear and mutual defense mechanisms—military on the Chinese side and political on the Taiwan side—continued and worsened.

To complicate matters further, some Taiwan leaders saw a political advantage in waving the sovereignty flag: it was a useful tool for mobilizing their political base at election time and putting the competition at a disadvantage. And if such tactics provoked China in the process—but not too much—that was fine, too. China, on the other hand, could never tell whether the flag waving was simply a political ploy or a way to undermine its interests, but it chose to interpret it as a major threat.

For example, in the Taiwan legislative and presidential elections of 2008, former president Chen Shui-bian sought to mobilize support for his Democratic Progressive Party by proposing that a referendum be held on election day to decide whether Taiwan should apply for membership in the United Nations and do so under the name of Taiwan, rather than its official name, the Republic of China. China regarded that as highly provocative, a way to creep toward legal independence, and it declared that there was a "period of high danger."

The United States came to play a special role in this deteriorating situation. China's first line of defense when facing such "dangers" was to mobilize Washington, on the assumption that it had sufficient control over Taiwan to end the problem. Taiwan, on the other hand, assumed that the United States would take its side as China's rhetoric became more threatening. Each was unhappy when Washington appeared to take the side of the other.

Actually, the U.S. role was rather different from what observers in China and Taiwan believed. Washington's main goal has always been the preservation of peace and security in the Taiwan Strait. While it did not oppose an outcome that the two sides worked out on a mutually acceptable basis, it did oppose the use of force and intimidation or what it called "a unilateral change in the status quo by either side." It also worried that the two sides might inadvertently slip into a conflict through accident or miscalculation. The United States would then, unhappily, have to choose sides in that conflict.

So, first the Clinton administration and then the George W. Bush administration employed an approach of "dual deterrence." They warned Beijing not to use force against Taiwan, even as they offered reassurance that they did not support Taiwan independence. They warned Taipei not to take political actions that might provoke China to use force, even as they conveyed reassurance that they would not sell out its interests for the sake of the China relationship. Effective deterrence requires both warning and reassurance, and in that way, Washington sought to lower the probability of any conflict.

The United States and China-Japan Security Relations

The interaction between Japan and China in the East Asian littoral has the potential to create a challenge to U.S. interests similar to that posed by cross-Strait relations between China and Taiwan. Nonetheless, there is no evidence that Washington views it in those terms. So far it has eschewed taking a dual deterrence approach concerning Beijing-Tokyo tensions over the East China Sea. It is true that the George W. Bush administration was concerned enough about the unraveling of Tokyo-Beijing ties for the president to use the APEC summit of 2005 to express a more general interest in their improvement, urging leaders on both sides to get beyond their mutual mistrust.[4] Similarly, there was a hint of U.S. involvement on the issue of the Chinese and Korean women whom the Imperial Japanese Army forced to work in military brothels ("comfort women"). That had been a long-festering sore among China, Korea, and Japan, but it became more salient in 2007 because of an effort in the U.S. Congress to pass a resolution criticizing Japan. During Prime Minister Abe's visit to Washington in April of that year, Abe offered his views on comfort women during a joint press conference with President Bush, who expressed gratitude for Abe's candor and said, "I accept the prime minister's apology."[5] Even on these issues, the Bush administration was loath to appear to take a position contrary to Japan's. And it chose silence on the East China Sea.

Washington has the luxury of some time when it comes to disagreements between China and Japan over history or containing the Taiwan Strait tensions. These are relatively slow-moving issues on which Beijing and Tokyo can calculate their actions without serious pressure. But that luxury would not necessarily exist in an East China Sea contingency, in which accurate information would be at a premium, the nations' publics would quickly register their own strong responses, institutional factors would bias results, and Washington would have to weigh its obligations to Japan against the danger, even limited, of war with China, a nuclear power, especially when it and that power have a significant economic interdependence.

Susan Shirk begins her study of Chinese foreign policy with an imaginary account of an accidental clash between a plane of the People's Liberation Army Air Force (PLAAF) and one of Taiwan's air force. In her scenario, Chinese leaders execute their policy response quickly. They allege that the Taiwan side is at fault and frame the situation as an "intentional attack on China," boxing "themselves into a corner." The PLA mobilizes as protesters fill the streets of China's major cities. As for the United States, it is behind the crisis management curve.[6] Because a similar set of circumstances between China and Japan could pose a major challenge for the United States, it is in its interest to reduce the probability of a clash between Japan and China, which no one really desires.

The United States Faces China

It is worth noting that the United States is in the same fundamental position vis-à-vis China as Japan, one in which rivalry exists whether leaders like it or not. There is, to be sure, extensive interdependence between the U.S. and Chinese economies, where U.S. consumption and PRC production are two sides of the same coin. There are foreign policy issues on which Washington and Beijing seek to cooperate, the North Korean nuclear program being the most obvious example. Just as Japan seeks a "mutually beneficial strategic relationship" with its neighbor to the west, so the United States has agreed with China to "work together to build a positive, cooperative, and comprehensive U.S.-China relationship for the 21st century."

Yet Washington, like Tokyo, still faces a security dilemma driven by China's growing power and its own response. This dilemma takes the form of a capabilities race, in which China modernizes its naval, air, and missile forces in order to better project power into the East Asian littoral and the United States improves the power of the conventional military capabilities (personnel and equipment) that it deploys in the Asia-Pacific area (building up on Guam, for example). The United States also has sought to enhance its defense relationships with Japan, Taiwan, and South Korea. China views both of those trends as a constraint on its ambitions. To some extent, each is responding to the actions of the other. Because neither can be confident that the other's long-term intentions are benign, each hedges to cover downside risks.[7]

Moreover, both the United States and China interact on specific difficult issues and draw conclusions from their interactions about the long-term intentions of the other. Taiwan is the most obvious example of the entanglements. China has believed that Washington has overtly or covertly supported the purported separatist plots of Taiwan leaders Lee Teng-hui and Chen Shui-bian, through arms sales, security cooperation, political initiatives, and a refusal to crack down sufficiently on Taiwan provocations. The United States, on the other hand, has worried that the PLA's military buildup since the late 1990s is intended not only to deter "Taiwan independence" but also to create the option of coercing Taipei to settle on Beijing's terms. Moreover, it has been concerned that Beijing might overreact to Taiwan initiatives, leading to a conflict through miscalculation. In fact, the U.S.-China "capabilities race" has stemmed from mutual anxiety regarding Taiwan. In addition, from their interaction regarding Taiwan, each side has drawn inferences—well founded or not—about the other's intentions. Some Americans believe that China's actions reflect a Chinese inclination to challenge U.S. hegemony in the Western Pacific. Some Chinese believe that U.S. policy toward Taiwan serves its broader goal to contain China's revival as a great power.

Yet Taiwan is not the only issue on which China and the United States have drawn general conclusions. North Korea is another. Beijing has believed that the United States has been insufficiently flexible in its approach to Pyongyang, and Washington has believed that China has not done enough to pressure North Korea to make concessions. As a result, each doubts how much the other really wants to resolve the problem of Pyongyang's weapons program. Iran also is an issue: the United States is focused on blocking its nuclear program, and China has to balance concerns about proliferation with its commercial and energy security interests. Clashes in the South and East China Seas are yet another (see chapter 6), as are climate change and global economic imbalances and instability.[8]

Finally, China and the United States each view the power and actions of the other through their historical experience. Chinese have viewed the United States as an imperialist hegemon that today wants to keep China weak and divided. Americans focus on China's communist system, the way that it allegedly has created an unlevel economic playing field that works to the disadvantage of the United States, and its growing nationalism.[9]

Similarly, the United States, even more than Japan, has deployed air and naval forces in the maritime regions into which China now seeks to expand in order to fashion a strategic buffer and, in the case of a Taiwan crisis, block U.S. forces from coming to Taiwan's defense. Dennis Blair, the director of national intelligence, has noted that many of the PLA's improving capabilities are directed at "improv[ing] China's ability to execute an anti-access and area-denial strategy in the Western Pacific."[10] The U.S. Navy and Air Force are the prime targets of that strategy. And there have been clashes between planes and ships of the two sides. Like Japan, the United States must cope with the institutional factors that affect Chinese behavior: information distortion, civil-military relations, and so on. And Chinese nationalists blame the United States about as much as they do Japan.

There is a convincing argument to be made that the United States is pursuing a hedging strategy against China by engaging it and seeking to integrate it into the international system while conducting realist-style balancing at the same time. Because Washington is ultimately uncertain about China's long-term intentions, it hopes for the best and plans for the worst. Of course, China does the same because it is uncertain about long-term U.S. intentions. In such a relationship, the "hedgee" is often uncertain about the "hedger's" predominant policy. So from China's perspective, the issue is whether the primary U.S. policy is engagement or balancing—or is it balancing disguised as engagement?

The danger of mutual hedging is that specific problems (such as Taiwan in the case of China and the United States) can create risks that incline each side in an adversarial direction, even though both benefit from engagement. Evan Medeiros warns:

> If these risks are not carefully controlled, they could result in a gradual drift from the current status quo to adversarial competition and perhaps outright strategic rivalry between the United States and China. The balancing act that is implicit in such hedging strategies is inherently unstable and demands constant nurturing to be effective and sustainable.[11]

Chinese uncertainty is on display in Beijing's assessments of U.S. intentions. Since the Tiananmen Square incident, there has emerged the view that the U.S. goal is to contain the growth of Chinese power. It has emphasized human rights in order to undermine the Chinese regime; supported Taiwan and the Dalai Lama to "split" Chinese territory; and sought trade benefits in order to limit Chinese economic growth. This view still exists, as exhibited in the analysis of Major General Luo Yuan of China's Academy of Military Sciences,[12] who concluded that among the leading "security concerns confronting China" was that Western countries—particularly the United States—were plotting to "Westernize" and "divide" China.[13]

In spite of common economic interests and complementarity, the United States has regarded China as a "strategic competitor" and is worried about its sudden rise. As specific evidence, he noted that Washington spends $400 million a year to undermine nondemocratic systems. It has taken a number of steps to increase its military threat to China, by strengthening its alliances with Korea and Japan; enhancing its capabilities on Guam; strengthening its command and control center at the Pacific Command in Hawaii; increasing its military bases in Southeast, South, and Central Asia; and gaining a military presence in Mongolia. In short, General Luo concluded, "the American military's strategic encirclement has become the most serious and complex threat facing China's security."

Even balanced civilian scholars display caution about the United States. In a generally positive assessment of U.S.-China relations at the beginning of the Obama administration, Yuan Peng of the China Institutes of Contemporary International Relations warned his readers that negative phenomena still existed. Increasingly, the two countries were engaged in a "soft trial of strength" regarding the relative merits of their respective systems and ideologies. The Obama administration would inevitably focus on "the long-term challenge posed by East Asia's and China's rise," and mutual strategic mistrust was common. Although the United States was acting with pragmatism and caution, it was likely to try to shift some of the burden of global leadership to Beijing, create new security problems for China through its Afghan policy, and give greater salience to economic and human rights issues.[14]

External polling suggests that Chinese attitudes toward the United States are mixed at best. The Pew Global Attitudes Survey found that from 2005 to 2009, the share of Chinese surveyed who had a "favorable" view of the United States vacillated from 34 to 47 percent.[15] A survey by the Chinese Academy of Social Science in 2007 found that a bare majority of those surveyed believed that the United States was "not so good, not so bad"—that China's relations with the United States were both competitive and cooperative and not sufficiently stable. But on that question, a fraction of respondents (between 15 to 25 percent) had a more negative view of the United States.[16] Of course, the Chinese who are most vocal and take the initiative to express their views on the Internet tend to be the most hostile.[17]

The U.S.-Japan Alliance and China

Since Japan and the United States share a common structural position vis-à-vis China, how do they propose to respond to the growth of its power? Have they together sought to block the revival of China as a great power, either through balancing or containment strategies (or both)? Or have they tried engagement, to induce China to support the status quo?[18] Or, given the uncertainty about China's future course, have they undertaken a mixed approach, such as hedging (working for the best but planning for the worst)?[19] What is the place of China in the U.S.-Japan alliance?

If one looks at official documents and statements, the attitude is cautious. In February 2005, senior officials of the U.S.-Japan Security Consultative Committee issued a joint statement on alliance transformation that included three common strategic objectives specifically relevant to China:

> Develop a cooperative relationship with China, welcoming the country to play a responsible and constructive role regionally as well as globally; encourage the peaceful resolution of issues concerning the Taiwan Strait through dialogue; encourage China to improve transparency of its military affairs.[20]

In an analogous statement in May 2007, there was one reference to China with no reference to Taiwan:

> Recognizing the importance of China's contributions to regional and global security, further encouraging China to conduct itself as a responsible international stakeholder, improve transparency in its military affairs, and maintain consistency between its stated policies and actions.[21]

At the January 2010 meeting of the U.S.-Japan Security Consultative Committee, the first since the Democratic Party of Japan (DPJ) came to power, the senior officials "stress[ed] that the United States and Japan will work to advance cooperative relations with China, welcoming it to play a constructive and responsible role in the international arena."[22]

Such caution is understandable, given the need to ensure that China did not infer from such statements that the United States and Japan had negative intentions that would require a hostile response. Even so, although the language on Taiwan in the 2005 statement emphasized conflict resolution, China drew the conclusion that Japan would now intervene on the side of the United States in a Taiwan crisis. *People's Daily* questioned the motivation and effect of this move: "If the United States and Japan genuinely want to do something to preserve Asia-Pacific regional security and stability, they should abide by their commitments on the Taiwan issue, resolutely uphold the one China principle, do nothing that encourages the 'Taiwan independence' forces, and refrain from adding to the Taiwan Strait turmoil."[23]

American scholars exhibit the range of views and recommendations on the alliance and China that one might expect. A number adopt some version of engagement. I have argued that the revival of Chinese power is the central strategic challenge facing the Asian region and the world and that how it occurs will determine the shape of the international system for decades to come. Consequently, Washington and Tokyo should base the alliance not on nontraditional security or common values but on the strategic task of increasing the possibility that over the long term China will take an accommodative and constructive approach to the international system.[24] Similarly, Richard Samuels believes that it is in U.S. and Japanese interests "to reassure China that its responsible rise and constructive role will be met with restraint and cooperation," which requires that Japan's role in the alliance be more equal than heretofore and that its contributions be nonmilitary and outside of Asia.[25]

Michael Green argues for more of a balancing approach. The United States should avoid "excessive . . . accommodation" in its relationship with China and instead base its "engagement with Beijing on a close alliance with Tokyo," thereby giving Japan confidence in its bilateral dealings with China and avoiding Japanese doubts of U.S. resolve.[26] Likewise, a panel led by Richard Armitage and Joseph Nye did not abandon engagement but placed somewhat more emphasis on balancing. It argued for transforming the U.S.-Japan alliance into a more inclusive structure that encompassed other democratic countries and Vietnam and that would include on its agenda "measures to expand areas of cooperation with China, while being candid with Beijing about areas of disagreement." The hope was that Tokyo and Washington could induce China to become a "responsible stakeholder."[27]

Mike Mochizuki of George Washington University usefully identifies four contending Japanese views on how to address the challenge of China, each with implications for the U.S.-Japan alliance. The first is "cooperative engagement with a hedge."[28] Those who hold this view include some scholars, the business community, and some MOFA officials. They are not naïve about the risks and uncertainties of China's rise, but they emphasize the economic and other opportunities that it presents Japan and how Tokyo can maximize those through benign, nonprovocative behavior (such as the Japanese prime minister not visiting the Yasukuni Shrine). But there is still a need to hedge against uncertainty, and maintaining the alliance is the main way to do that. It must be a careful hedge, however; for example, the alliance must not be called a means to balance or contain China. The Japan Forum on International Relations therefore urged that Tokyo and Washington "strengthen and develop their strategic concert toward China" and encourage it to be a force for stability.[29]

The second approach is "competitive engagement with a hedge." This school emphasizes the assertive aspects of Chinese behavior as opposed to the cooperative ones and is less sanguine that China's long-term intentions will be favorable for Japan, in spite of Japanese efforts to steer China in a more positive direction. This assertive trend is likely to be more pronounced as China's power grows and the East Asian military balance tilts in its favor. The recommendations of the "harder hedge" of this school include strengthening Japan's military capabilities; changing the constitution to allow more flexibility on security policy; deepening and broadening the scope of the alliance to include joint action to meet regional and global challenges; and also expanding security ties with other like-minded countries. A team assembled by the Tokyo Foundation therefore called for a new regional security structure to address the growth of Chinese power, a structure that relies less on U.S. bilateral alliances than on "a network of alliances among all nations in the region with close security ties with one another"—an approach similar to the Armitage-Nye proposal outlined above.[30]

The third group, made up of scholars and journalists, advocates balancing and containment of China. They start with two premises that are different from those of the second group. They do not see such rosy prospects for the Chinese economy. In addition, they are less optimistic than others that the United States would be prepared, in the worst case, to use nuclear weapons to defend Japan against China. Like the second group, they favor strengthening the alliance, but they also favor supplementing it by "nurturing favorable power centers around China."[31] Nishihara Masashi, for example, adopts a power-balancing approach. The basic structure in East Asia, he believes, is "the United States and Japan versus China." He worries that Japan is too complacent and the United States too distracted—in spite of what he calls the PLA's "robust military buildup"—and he believes that Beijing will seek to "drive a wedge" between the United States and Japan to weaken the alliance. Japan, he argues, should increase its defense budget, strengthen maritime defenses, and "buttress the alliance with the United States."[32]

The fourth school favors strategic accommodation. It emphasizes the potential for bilateral cooperation, as does the first school, but it downplays any objective threat from China, except if Japan fosters Chinese hostility through its own provocative actions. On the other hand, it does not favor dropping the alliance with the United States. It instead prefers to confine its scope to the defense of the home islands and eschew, for example, joining the United States in defending Taiwan.[33] The best example of this view is presented by Terashima Jitsuro, who was an adviser to the DPJ. He writes:

One can only smile bitterly over the twisted reality of U.S.-Japan security, but what we Japanese must resolve is that the peace and security of Japan has to be secured through the exercise of the will of the Japanese people themselves. It is our responsibility to exercise a *thoroughly pacifist self-restraint* that will present no threat to our neighbors [emphasis added].[34]

Concerning China, Terashima warns that the United States itself has an ambivalent stance and cannot be counted on.

In sum, Japan's views are somewhat more diverse than those of the United States. Although engagement with some hedging is certainly the mainstream view, as it is in the United States, the voices in favor of some sort of balancing strategy are more numerous. And there is a group of right-wing strategists that has no counterpart on the U.S. side.

Dilemmas of Allies

Any alliance carries with it two liabilities: the fear of abandonment and the fear of entrapment.[35] On the Japan side, for example, Defense Minister Ishiba Shigeru stated in November 2007, with specific reference to North Korea, that "profound discussion as to what 'the maintenance of deterrence' is has not been held. . . . [We should study] what deterrence the Japan-U.S alliance should have against what kind of threats."[36] Commentator Sakurai Yoshiko drew from the U.S. Department of Defense's 2009 report on the PLA's growing capabilities the conclusion that "even if [the United States] wants to protect Japanese territory and Taiwan, [it] may not be able to do so." More significant for this discussion, Sakurai warns that "if China makes a grab for the Senkaku Islands, this would mean that the United States might not necessarily stand with Japan and be able to protect Japanese territory."[37] Two right-of-center think tanks—the Institute for International Policy Studies and the Matsushita Institute of Government and Management—both express concern about what one terms a "perception gap" between Tokyo and Washington with respect to how they view the growth of Chinese power.[38]

Japanese fears of abandonment and entrapment have stemmed from a variety of sources:

—Strategic trends such as the Sino-Soviet split and the growth of China's power after 1979. Both raised questions of whether the United States would rely less on Japan and more on China to promote its interests in East Asia and the world.

—Japanese fear that Japan might get drawn into a conflict between the United States and China over Taiwan in which Japan would have no say over the U.S. intervention but would still be expected to assist U.S. armed forces, pursuant to the 1997 defense guidelines.

—Lack of consultation on sensitive issues: Tokyo fears that Washington will neglect Japan's interests by negotiating directly with North Korea on its nuclear program and by relying on China to help address challenges like North Korea and Iran, to the exclusion of Japan.

—Reliance on the United States for key "security resources" (for example, sophisticated intelligence).

But most significant are existential doubts about the credibility of the U.S. pledge of extended deterrence. Will the United States be willing to defend Japan against attack—especially a nuclear attack—by China or North Korea when China already can hold the U.S. homeland hostage to a nuclear attack and North Korea seeks to be able to do so? China's nuclear forces are the one area where Japan does not have an equivalent offensive or defensive capability, and China's current modernization in this area is more likely to fuel Japanese anxieties than conventional improvements.[39] If Japan lost confidence in the U.S. commitment to protect it against nuclear attack, at least some Japanese would argue that their country needed its own nuclear deterrent. Periodically, therefore, Washington seeks to reaffirm its commitment, at least rhetorically. In May 2007, in the joint statement of the U.S.-Japan Security Consultative Committee, the United States "reaffirmed that the full range of U.S. military capabilities—both nuclear and non-nuclear strike forces and defensive capabilities—form the core of extended deterrence and support U.S. commitments to the defense of Japan."[40]

So far, Japan's default response to its nuclear anxiety has been to seek greater clarity regarding U.S. extended deterrence. As China's capabilities grow and if the denuclearization of North Korea proves impossible, Japan's sense of uncertainty will deepen. Consequently, "Japan will expect more of the United States in terms of information about and management of the extended nuclear deterrent and will be less easily satisfied."[41]

The United States has its own fears. The first North Korean missile crisis was a wake-up call that Japan's legalistic approach to what it could and should do with respect to defense could well limit its actions to a level well below U.S. expectations. Agreements reached thereafter calmed the specific concerns, but the general problem prevails. The long-standing Japanese position that helping to defend the United States if it was under attack (collective self-defense) was inconsistent with provisions of the Japanese constitution continues to rankle. Moreover, the emergence of a DPJ government in 2009 caused anxiety that Japan's cooperation on out-of-area threats to international peace and security—in Afghanistan, for example—would decline.[42] U.S. fear of entrapment is fairly new, but it would certainly surface in any Japan-China clash in the East Asian littoral. Bernard Cole of National Defense University has warned of the significant possibility of U.S. involvement in a Senkaku dispute that would result from the "national hubris" of China and Japan.[43]

Little in the current anxieties about abandonment and entrapment is related at all to the narrow definition of the alliance, which reflects the early cold war bargain that the United States would defend territories under Japanese administration; that Tokyo would permit U.S. access to bases in Japan, from which U.S. armed forces could contribute to "the security of Japan and the maintenance of international peace and security in the Far East"; and that both countries would "maintain and develop . . . their capacities to resist armed attack."[44] Some of the problems of the post–cold war era, at least for the United States, relate to the precise terms and conditions under which it may use its bases for its East Asia missions. Yet they quickly broaden to a question of burden sharing, of what the Self-Defense Forces (SDF) will do not only to contribute to the defense of Japan—one measure of its alliance commitment—but also to help to pursue U.S. security priorities in the region and beyond. Burden sharing by Japan entails a definition of the alliance that is broader than the legal clauses of the treaty. It is a matter of policy, and policy can be plastic, subject to contending forces within the Japanese political system.

There was some hope on both sides that Japan's leaders after 2000, particularly Koizumi Junichiro and Abe Shinzo, would break through long-standing barriers and turn the security relationship into a more capable alliance. Koizumi had secured Diet authorization for using the Self-Defense Forces outside the East Asian region and for a more flexible approach to the defense of Japan. Both Koizumi and Abe hoped to end or modify the taboo against collective self-defense. In 2003, the two defense establishments launched the Defense Policy Review Initiative (DPRI) in order to "evolve the relationship to a more strategically and operationally relevant point."[45] The DPRI process achieved a lot on paper: a statement of common strategic objectives; agreements on roles and missions; an emphasis on missile defense; and consensus on the relocation of some U.S. units out of Japan to accommodate the resentment of local communities (particularly on Okinawa). However, Japan's implementation of the measures was "incomplete and often grudging, particularly in the post-Koizumi period," in part because elements of the bureaucracy that had favored the initiatives lost interest in the face of political resistance.[46]

The United States was especially disappointed that Japan did not take steps to meet the operational implications of its commitments. Doing so would have involved activities such as jointly devising contingency plans (including for regional contingencies); jointly developing crisis action procedures; combining planning and operations; and, on the part of Japan, acquiring capabilities that would add net strength to the alliance. But little happened on those fronts.[47] Inaction led in turn to suspicion that Tokyo lacked the political will and capacity to fulfill the commitments that it had made on paper.

U.S. disappointment evolved into nascent despair once the Democratic Party of Japan and its allies came to power in September 2009. To be sure, there was nothing wrong with the formal rhetoric. Prime Minister Hatoyama and his senior officials referred to the alliance as the "cornerstone" of Japan's foreign and defense policies.[48] The problem was the campaign promises that the DPJ had made to the Japanese public and its leftist coalition partners, all of which focused on lightening the burden on Japan of the U.S. presence. In particular, the coalition promised to move the Futenma Marine Air Station off of Okinawa, even though the two countries had agreed in 2006 that the facility would move elsewhere on the island. By and large, the Obama administration conveyed patience in the hope that Hatoyama and his colleagues would arrive at a mutually acceptable solution. Behind the façade, however, there was anxiety that the whole interlocking arrangement would fall apart. In the end, Hatoyama gave up trying to change the Futenma agreement significantly and resigned.

Japan has its own unmet expectations. They include its desire that the United States make its pledge of extended deterrence absolutely credible, that it mount sustained efforts for nonproliferation on a global scale, and that it ensure that its capabilities and deployments in East Asia are sufficient to deter attacks on Japan. Finally, "Japan has raised expectations about U.S. support in territorial disputes such as . . . the Senkaku Islands."[49]

The possibility of a China-Japan clash in the East China Sea brings these general alliance dynamics and unmet expectations —"operational doubts on the U.S. side and doubts of commitment on the Japanese side"[50]—into sharp relief. Japan's concern about whether the United States would in fact come to its defense gives rise to its fear of abandonment. The knowledge that Japan has made insufficient preparations to fight alongside the United States underlies the U.S. worry that Japan may entrap it in an unnecessary conflict. China anticipates that the United States would assist Japan, confirming its suspicion that, despite continual reassurances to the contrary, Washington's China policy was containment after all. Washington, having to make a choice between its ally and a rising power from which it sought global cooperation, would face one of its worst nightmares. Should the United States ever face this challenge, it will require a clear sense of U.S. interests, plus the resolve and skill to avoid temptations to escalate the conflict. Avoiding escalation also requires an effort on all sides to reduce the probability that conflict will occur in the first place.

14

What to Do?

The previous chapters identify a mix of factors that, taken together, create a policy problem for China, Japan, and the United States. The problem may move under the radar of the officials in those countries who make foreign and national security policy, but it is present all the same. And it is likely to get worse as China's People's Liberation Army Navy (PLAN), Marine Surveillance Force (MSF), and People's Liberation Army Air Force (PLAAF) expand their areas of operation in the service of China's strategic goal of widening the nation's eastern strategic buffer.

That being the case, it is in the interest of the three nations to recognize that a problem indeed exists and that it is worthy of attention. The chance of a clash between Chinese and Japanese forces is not trivial. Nor are the consequences. Whatever reward Tokyo and Beijing gain from their military operations in the East China Sea, they run a greater risk in terms of potential damage to bilateral relationships and stability in East Asia. What is more, the lessons learned from their interaction on specific maritime issues will reinforce the broader assessments that each makes about the long-term intentions of the other, for good or ill. Finally, like most policy problems, this particular problem is complex in that its manifestation—in military operations—is linked in complex ways with other factors. One factor cannot necessarily be addressed without addressing others.

The challenge facing Japan, China, and the United States is to reduce the probability of conflict. That first requires identifying the different parts of the policy problem and clarifying their character. The next step is to identify possible solutions to the various problems, knowing that the obstacles to each may be daunting. A different type of solution will be appropriate to each problem. Moreover, this may be a case in which the *process* of considering and adopting solutions may be as important as their content—the best substantive proposal can fail if the process is defective. This is in part a matter of sequencing (which problems are addressed when); it also is a function of the degree of mistrust involved. Trying to solve too much when mutual trust is low usually does not work.

Problems and Solutions

Previous chapters identify the variety of issues that converge to compose the policy problem for Japan and China:

—military and law enforcement operations in the East China Sea
—command and control and strategic culture
—security goals
—differences in interpretations of international law
—the capacity of civilian decisionmaking structures to conduct crisis management
—civil-military relations
—politicization of the bilateral relationship in both countries
—the security dilemma that each country faces in relation to the other
—the U.S.-Japan alliance.

These elements of the problem fall into three basic categories. One has to do with the institutions in each country, both military and civilian. Should there be some sort of clash, those institutions are likely to exacerbate the problem rather than contain it. A second concerns politics: public responses to an incident would be worse than the incident itself, particularly in China. And third are aspects of the security dilemma identified in chapter 4.

Regarding the security dilemma, three issues are in play. First and most important is the interaction between Japan and China on specific issues, including military operations, and the inferences drawn about the future intentions of the other. Second is the role of the past in shaping national identity, which in turn affects how each views the present and the future. And third is the capabilities race produced by the anxiety that each feels about the other's growing strength and future intentions. China increases its capabilities mainly through its own efforts, and Japan has done so by trying to strengthen its alliance with the United States (which itself creates dilemmas).

There is a repertoire of measures that two states in such a conflicted relationship might deploy to address the various types of problems listed above.

Two states, seeing that the prolongation of a specific dispute will increasingly undermine their respective interests in a cooperative relationship, may attempt through diplomacy to resolve the dispute in a way that both suits their respective interests and does not arouse such internal political opposition that the effort is unsustainable. China's resolution of a number of border disputes is a case in point.[1]

Two states that have had deeply entrenched, fractious relations sometimes recognize that changes in the international environment have rendered continued hostility and mistrust increasingly counterproductive. So they attempt a major and general rapprochement that brings about the resolution of more specific, embedded issues and facilitates cooperation. The Nixon opening to China from 1969 to 1972 and Anwar Sadat's initiative to Israel later in the decade are examples. Obviously, a major rapprochement can be more or less equal or one-sided; in the latter, one state makes a strategic accommodation of the other.

Such a grand rapprochement may require special attention to bitter episodes that occurred during the period of hostility. The states and their publics may begin a process of reconciliation to loosen the brakes that the past can place on future forward movement . Germany's reconciliation with France, Poland, and Israel is the most compelling example.[2]

The two states may create and/or join security institutions or regimes in order to facilitate cooperation and avoid conflict. They may be bilateral or multilateral, and they may include military confidence-building measures (CBMs). One example is the Helsinki Final Act of 1975 and the Document of the Stockholm Conference, which stemmed from it; together they created a variety of CBMs in Central Europe.[3]

A state also may recognize that the domestic institutional arrangements that it traditionally employed are no longer commensurate with changes in its power and in the international system. It therefore undertakes reforms in its security and foreign policy establishment so that it may better employ the tools of national power. In the United States, the National Security Act of 1947—which reorganized the Pentagon, created the Central Intelligence Agency, and centralized decisionmaking in the White House—were all a response to the emergence of the United States as a hegemon with global responsibilities and to Franklin Roosevelt's dysfunctional approach to policymaking (characterized by confused lines of authority, secrecy, playing subordinates off against each other, and so forth). An attendant development was a new approach to civil-military relations, whereby a much larger military establishment was granted significant operational autonomy on the condition that it maintain professional standards. After Deng Xiaoping set China on the policy of reform and opening up in 1979, the PRC significantly reengineered its foreign policy process and institutions in order to better address the new external environment and the decline of one-man rule.

Leaders also may come to understand that too much domestic political divisiveness undermines the pursuit of national interests abroad and that they must "demobilize" the politics of national security. That occurred in the United States after World War II, first in the late 1940s with the emerging consensus on bipartisanship in foreign policy on everything but China, and then in the early 1950s, when Congress and the Eisenhower administration eventually "defanged" Senator Joseph McCarthy, who had exploited the issue of "who lost China" for his own political gain. This process also occurred in Finland after World War II, when the elite and the public decided that their country's national independence vis-à-vis the Soviet Union required them to limit internal debate on policy toward the Soviet Union, even when Moscow's behavior made such restraint very difficult.

Obviously, some solutions may be used to address different problems. CBMs and settlement of disputes can reinforce the momentum of a grand rapprochement. Both bilateral diplomacy and multilateral institutions can work together to resolve specific disputes. More broadly, security regimes, dispute settlement, and historical reconciliation all can mitigate a security dilemma. Institutional reform and political demobilization both can reduce the probability that situations of stress and near crises become full crises.

Untangling the China-Japan Complex: The Security Dilemma

This section explores in more detail the ways in which each of the specific factors in play might be addressed. As shown, the convergence and interaction of these factors means that solutions that make sense in the abstract often do not work well in practice.

Grand Rapprochement

As unlikely as a grand rapprochement between China and Japan seems, it has been considered. Prime Minister Fukuda Yasuo of Japan hinted at such an outcome during his visit to China at the end of 2007:

> The time has come for the nations of Japan and China each to examine squarely the political and economic importance of the other and discuss how we can cooperate in order to resolve the various issues facing our region and international society. . . . [This] represents a

tremendous opportunity for both nations. . . . At the same time, there are also issues between our countries that still need to be overcome. . . . What is important as we face such issues is for us to make efforts to understand the other country in a true light, while discussing the issues sincerely and deepening our mutual understanding as we recognize that differences do exist. . . . It is important to adopt an approach under which both parties together search for ways to solve the issues, never losing sight of their shared objectives.[4]

Almost five years earlier, Shi Yinhong, one of China's most independent foreign policy thinkers, recommended just that. In March 2003, Shi wrote a provocative article that first described the growing hostility of countries on China's periphery toward China and then explained the economic, political, security, and psychological reasons why Japan might desire a fundamental improvement in relations with Beijing. He advocated new Chinese approaches on the major issues: showing "confidence and patience" in working toward the ultimate resolution of problems of history; approaching Japan's military power with a combination of inward vigilance and external magnanimity; and taking the initiative to welcome Japan to participate in the East Asian region "as a great power." Writing at the height of the George W. Bush administration's unilateralism, Shi in effect was urging just the sort of strategic realignment that Beijing had executed in the early 1970s, reducing its vulnerability by aligning with the United States.[5]

No sooner had Shi published his views than he came under "heavy and sustained attack." Critics ridiculed the idea that Beijing could drive a wedge between the United States and Japan and that the latter would ever leave its "master-servant" relationship with the United States to join with China to effectively balance U.S. power. Conciliation with Japan with respect to history was anathema.[6]

Despite the criticisms, Shi's strategic logic reflected the kind of "out of the box" thinking that sometimes is required to escape the trap of a security dilemma. Making that escape would require Chinese and Japanese leaders who have not only the vision to take the initiative but also the power to ensure that a breakthrough is sustainable. Japanese prime ministers have never had that kind of freedom of action, and Chinese foreign policy is no longer the monopoly of one or two officials. The U.S.-China rapprochement was successful, first of all, because Mao Zedong was an unchallenged decisionmaker, even in his dotage. Second, public opinion did not exist in the China of that time. Third, Beijing and Washington could conduct their diplomacy in absolute secrecy. Unlike Mao, China's paramount leader must now operate within a collective leadership, as must Japan's prime minister. In both countries, public opinion is a vital and sometimes virulent force (as Shi quickly learned). And while not impossible, conducting secret diplomacy between Tokyo and Beijing would be difficult. Today, institutional and political factors would likely impede implementation of even the most brilliant foreign policy initiatives.

In addition to those constraints, a diplomatic breakthrough does not necessarily dissolve the conflict of interests that created division in the first place. Nor does it end the reasons for the security dilemma, whether it is caused by a capabilities race, negative lessons learned on specific issues, or views seen through lenses ground by history. The Nixon opening to China may have allowed Beijing and Washington to act on their shared interest concerning the Soviet Union, up to a point. Expanding mutually beneficial economic relations gave each a stake in their bilateral ties. But concerns in each country about the power of the other were never completely allayed. The two governments could only paper over the conflict regarding Taiwan, their most serious specific issue. Conflicting identities, shaped by history and other forces, still distorted how each side saw the other, particularly on the Chinese side. And new problems exacerbated old fears: for example, the Tiananmen tragedy in 1989, Taiwan from 1995 to 2008, and China's growing power today. To make matters worse, the U.S.-China relationship has become politicized in each country.

There is no question that sometimes it is easier to address a capabilities race, specific divisive issues, and the scars of history when leaders create a completely new framework. But often crafting a new framework is not possible, particularly when domestic politics intrudes.

Resolving Specific Issues

Because specific issues can aggravate a security dilemma if they are allowed to fester, resolving those issues in a mutually acceptable way may, in theory, mitigate the way that they contribute to the fears that each side has about the long-term intentions of the other.

In the case of Japan and China, two issues foster such suspicions and lead them both to conduct military operations that are potentially dangerous. The first is the question of which nation possesses sovereignty over the Senkaku/Diaoyu Islands. The second is how the two countries should draw boundaries marking their claims to the continental shelf that extends from China's coast and to exclusive economic zones (EEZ). Note that drawing a boundary for the continental shelf is different from doing so for an EEZ. Each has a different basis in international law, and because the UN Convention on the Law of the Sea is vague, delineation is subject to conflicting interpretations. Not surprisingly, China and Japan each cite principles that serve their respective interests (see chapter 6).

Diaoyu/Senkaku Islands. The dispute over the islands' sovereignty is important in two ways. On one hand, there are long-standing but unverified estimates of undersea oil and gas deposits in the islands' vicinity. On the other hand, the ownership issue is highly relevant for resolving the delineation problem. If the islands are Japan's, then Japan has rights to the continental shelf and can claim that the boundary for EEZs in the East China Sea should be equidistant between China and Japan. If the islands are China's, then China can claim the entire continental shelf out to the Ryukyu Trench and establish an EEZ that extends 200 kilometers from its coastal baseline.

Because both of these matters are not only pending but also have consequences for the two countries' access to energy resources, it seems highly unlikely that Beijing and Tokyo would be willing to resolve finally the territorial issue regarding the Diaoyu/Senkaku Islands—and complicating matters further is that Taiwan also claims the islands. Japan would be reluctant to cede sovereignty if doing so meant giving up energy resources in the islands' vicinity and further north in the East China Sea. China would be unwilling to give up its claim for the same reason.[7] Indeed, the only circumstances under which the two sides could reach a final resolution of the issue would be *if* they worked out a mutually acceptable agreement on delineation of the continental shelf and their EEZs and *if* the projected reserves prove not to have enough commercial value to make them worth developing.[8] To make matters worse, the islands are a political issue in each country, particularly in China. Even if those two conditions were met, a deal that made substantive sense might be politically impossible.

There is another approach, one proposed by Deng Xiaoping in 1978. That is to shelve the dispute over sovereignty and engage in joint resource development. That remains Beijing's position. Tokyo, however, has hewed to the position that economic cooperation can be addressed only after sovereignty of the islands is resolved (that is, China must concede). Under the Deng approach, the interested parties (China, Japan, and Taiwan) would exploit whatever energy resources are there without regard to their claims of ownership and share proportionately the relevant costs and benefits.[9] For such a solution to be possible, however, Japan would need to be fully reassured on two points: first, that a cooperative approach on the issue of sovereignty of the Senkaku/Diaoyu Islands would not undermine its interests on the matter of EEZ delineation; second, that joint development would be a truly equal partnership, not a case of Japanese companies participating commercially in projects that are essentially Chinese ventures.

One advantage of setting aside the sovereignty issue and engaging in joint development is that it may be the only approach that is politically palatable in China. Just as some in China charged that the June 2008 China-Japan political framework regarding the East China Sea was a sellout, such elements might oppose a mutually acceptable outcome regarding the Diaoyu/Senkaku Islands. But if the basis of the agreement is a formula enunciated by Deng Xiaoping, his demigod status might be enough to carry the day. The People's Liberation Army Navy might also be skeptical of the arrangement, because the area in question is regarded as a portal to the Pacific Ocean.[10] Again, the previous blessing of Deng, a former chairman of the Central Military Commission, might negate military opposition.

DELINEATING THE CONTINENTAL SHELF AND EEZS. Cases in international law offer some guidance on possible approaches to the question of delineation. Peter Dutton of the Naval War College identifies three.

The first (based on the 1984 *Gulf of Maine* case between the United States and Canada) is to define a single boundary for both the continental shelf and the EEZ. Here the International Court of Justice chose not to use either continental shelf or EEZ arguments as a basis and instead used relevant geographical features of the area and took into account certain special circumstances. Such an approach is theoretically feasible in defining a single boundary between China and Japan, and the Diaoyu/Senkaku problem might be treated as a "special circumstance" for purposes of delineation. Yet Dutton finds that mutual suspicion between Tokyo and Beijing would reduce the chances of turning what is feasible in the abstract into a mutually acceptable agreement.[11]

The second approach (based on a 1978 treaty between Australia and Papua New Guinea) is to create one boundary for the continental shelf and another for the EEZ. Thus the principle of "natural extension" would define the boundary of the shelf and the principle of equidistance would be used for delimiting the two countries' EEZs. Negotiators could take into account the special circumstances of the Senkaku/Diaoyu Islands, geography, and past activities by Chinese and Japanese nationals. Such an outcome would facilitate exploitation of hydrocarbon resources. But again, the fact of mutual mistrust becomes an obstacle. Japan and China would not necessarily expect that this formula would be mutually beneficial, as was the case with the United States and Canada and with Australia and Papua New Guinea.[12]

A third approach would be for the two countries to give up on reaching a substantive agreement themselves and submit the case to an international tribunal. Yet the outcome would probably be more acceptable to one side than the other. Indeed, it appears that Japan would welcome international arbitration, expecting that it would win more than China; hence, China has preferred bilateral negotiations, even if they make no progress. Because an adjudicated outcome would likely exacerbate relations rather than improve them, it is not a good option.

Dutton himself proposes a three-step process that would produce a substantive outcome that is sufficiently satisfactory to both parties in the medium term while simultaneously building trust. The first step is to set aside the Senkaku/Diaoyu issue through an agreement that, no matter how the issue of ownership of the islands is resolved, would not affect EEZ delimitation. Second, the two sides would reaffirm adherence to their East China Sea fisheries agreement and institute joint enforcement patrols. Third, they would agree to joint development of the oil and gas resources in the disputed portion of the sea for a specified period, perhaps adapting the commercial, sovereignty-neutral arrangement developed by China, Vietnam, and the Philippines for the Spratly Islands area.

While joint development proceeds, the two governments would negotiate the delimitation of boundaries, considering various models. They would pledge that if a boundary agreement cannot be reached, they would submit the issue to an international tribunal.[13] Such an approach provides some benefits to each side and the opportunity to build trust during the period of implementation. The key question, Dutton recognizes, is that Chinese leaders might conclude that the benefits do not justify the costs to its strategic objectives in the East China Sea and to its reputation in the eyes of a nationalistic public. Indeed, they might conclude that overcoming the resistance of China's national oil companies and the PLAN would be impossible.

TAIWAN.   The Taiwan Strait is a third specific issue that has shaped the thinking of China and Japan about each other. China has feared that Japan will intervene in a hypothetical Taiwan conflict in support of the United States and help facilitate the permanent separation of the island from China. Japan fears, on one hand, that it will be attacked by Chinese missiles if it were to fulfill alliance obligations to the United States and, on the other, that PRC incorporation of Taiwan would threaten sea lanes of communication. Those mutual fears grew from 1995 through 2008, while Lee Teng-hui and Chen Shui-bian were Taiwan's presidents.

Fortunately, the chances of a conflict have declined since Ma Ying-jeou succeeded Chen Shui-bian in May 2008. Coupled with PRC president Hu Jintao's more creative approach to the island, Ma has pursued a policy of accommodation and cooperation with China, arguing that it is a better way to ensure Taiwan's prosperity, security, and dignity than Chen's strategy of provocation.[14] As long as Ma's party, the Kuomintang, stays in power and continues a policy of improving and stabilizing cross-Strait relations, the chances of war are low, benefiting Japan-China relations. Yet that requires that Beijing continue with steps that prove to the Taiwan public that Ma's policy of accommodation will yield the promised rewards. Whether it is willing to do so in the areas of security and the island's international participation is an open question. The worst outcome for China-Japan relations, as well as cross-Strait relations, would be a return to the tensions and mutual fears of the pre–Ma Ying-jeou period.

Japan has developed another concern: that Taipei may move quickly to resolve its fundamental dispute with Beijing peacefully. Some Japanese believe that that would give the PLAN access to Taiwan's naval bases and so endanger Japan's sea lanes of communication. Yet two erroneous assumptions underlie that fear. The first is that the PLA navy and air force would actually be deployed to Taiwan. Yet China's formula for resolving the dispute has included the pledge that its military would not be on the island. Admittedly, that pledge was made some time ago, but unless Beijing drops it, Japan's fears are unfounded. The second is that if the PLAN had access to Taiwan's naval bases that it would threaten Japan's sea lanes of communication. Whether Beijing acted on its ability to mount such a threat would likely depend on the overall state of China-Japan relations.

There are ways to address each of these issues (Diaoyu/Senkaku Islands, EEZs, and Taiwan) that would reduce their impact on each side's suspicions about the intentions of the other. Yet turning those "solutions" into reality is difficult because those issues are linked to other concerns, particularly domestic politics.

Mitigating the Capabilities Race

PRC, Japanese, and U.S. operations in the East China Sea are only a concrete manifestation of the shifting balance of capabilities between Japan and the United States on one hand and China on the other. China's growing force structure reflects more than a desire to create a robust military to supplement the nation's economic and diplomatic power and so restore national pride. It also stems from a security strategy that begins with deterring separatism by Taiwan and then creating a strategic buffer east and south of China's coast. Accelerating the shift in the balance are, on one hand. the resources that rapid economic growth provides the PRC government for defense spending and, on the other, Japan's flat defense budget, anemic economy, and declining population and the economic problems and overextended military of the United States. The meta-theme here is the revival of China as a great power in Asia after centuries of weakness.[15]

This power shift raises questions in all three countries regarding the motives of the others. Chinese strategists are tempted to conclude that Washington and Tokyo seek to contain their country's rise. For example, Major General Luo Yuan of the PLA stated in presentations to American audiences in October 2008 that China's leading security concern was that Western countries—particularly the United States—were plotting to "Westernize" and "divide" China.[16] Both Japan and the United States complain about the lack of transparency concerning China's growing power. In September 2009, for example, U.S. deputy secretary of state James Steinberg observed that China's increased sea, air, and space capabilities, plus some of China's actions, "have caused the United States and China's neighbors to question China's intentions." Each side asks the other to clarify the goals that its military assets are designed to serve. Steinberg observed that "while China, like any nation, has the right to provide for its security, its capabilities and its actions also heighten its responsibility to reassure others that this buildup does not present a threat."[17]

Steinberg suggests that when countries are suspicious of each other's intentions, they must engage in dialogue to offer clarification. In addition, and more important, each should take specific steps to mitigate the other's concerns.[18] Dialogue channels exist, particularly between the United States and China. Most important for the United States is the strategic and economic dialogue that brings together senior officials from the two countries on an annual basis to address the key issues in the relationship. Most important for Japan is a periodic meeting that the administrative vice minister of the Ministry of Foreign Affairs has with his Chinese counterpart. These encounters are no substitute for day-to-day diplomacy, but they can sensitize senior officials on each side to the concerns of the other and accelerate cooperation where it has been lagging. In early 2010, Defense Secretary Robert Gates recalled the dialogue that took place within the strategic arms talks with the Soviet Union. "I'm not sure," he said, that "those talks ever actually reduced any arms, but the dialogue over a long period of time with great candor . . . played a significant role . . . in preventing miscalculations and mistakes."[19]

Dialogues between China and Japan and China and the United States are weakest in the military field. That is ironic—or perhaps intentional—because that is where the need to clarify misunderstanding is the greatest. It is, after all, the military establishments of the three countries, along with intelligence establishments, whose job it is to be skeptical of the intentions of the others in light of changing capabilities. The PLA, it seems, has yet to recognize the value that interaction among senior military leaders can have in shaping the assessment of intentions. China tends to suspend its military-to-military dialogue when the United States takes a step that it does not like (for example, selling arms to Taiwan). Beijing suspended defense and security consultations with Japan during Koizumi Junichiro's tenure as prime minister and slowly resumed them thereafter; now they are to occur on an annual basis.[20] But they too are hostage to unintended problems. And to be effective, military dialogues must get beyond the repetition of standard talking points.

On the political side, there has been hope that the three countries can develop a trilateral policy dialogue. The initial plan was that the directors of policy planning at the foreign affairs agencies of the three would meet periodically and focus initially on issues like climate change and energy, possibly adding security issues to the agenda later. If so, Japan and the United States could lay out the purposes of their alliance (presumably, containing China is not one of them) and China could explain the purposes of its military modernization (presumably, none of them is to challenge the two allies).[21] During the second term of the George W. Bush administration, China and Japan had expressed greater interest in such a mechanism than the United States. The Obama administration, however, favored the idea, and the first meeting reportedly was planned for the summer of 2009. Suddenly, however, China withdrew its support, and the meeting was postponed indefinitely. There was some suggestion that Beijing was concerned about North Korea's reaction, but that was not plausible because the dialogue was explicitly designed to address issues other than the Korean peninsula.[22]

Japan is, of course, concerned that the impact of Chinese conventional capabilities varies according to the potential target and the time frame. As discussed in previous chapters, the PLA's air and naval capabilities are most relevant now and for the foreseeable future to the security of islands that Japan claims and controls and of the maritime oil and gas fields. They also would be germane if there were a reversal of current, positive trends in relations between China and Taiwan that increased significantly the possibility of a conflict in which the United States and Japan might intervene.

But China lacks the ability to project power in a way that would seriously threaten the Japanese home islands. To do so, it would require a fleet of aircraft carriers, amphibious landing capability, and a large complement of precision-strike systems (ballistic and cruise missiles). China is making progress in those areas but at a pace that will leave the home islands invulnerable for decades. And Japan has the United States and its treaty commitment on which to rely. The point at which Japan is likely to worry is when it concludes that the U.S.-China military balance in the East Asia region has tilted in China's favor, placing Tokyo in a dilemma with respect to how to respond. But that day is still long in the future.[23]

If China's peaceful intentions are serious, as it says, it would be in its interest to show some restraint in acquiring capabilities that can truly threaten the home islands, including long-range precision strike assets (ballistic and cruise missiles), aircraft carriers, and amphibious landing ships. China can also reinforce its restraint through dialogues with Japan's defense establishment on the purposes of the systems that it still decides to acquire, such as aircraft carriers. Despite the changes that have occurred in Japan's security policy since the late 1990s, it poses no military threat to China. If China's buildup leads even the most reasonable Japanese observers to conclude that its intentions are malign, it would be a serious—and unnecessary—tragedy. (Complicating this equation is the reality that China's long buildup is primarily designed to target the United States, behind which it still lags, while its impact falls much more on Japan.)

There are two Chinese capabilities that cause concern in Japan now. One is its nuclear weapons and the means to deliver them. The other is cyber warfare. China is a modest but expanding nuclear power. Of the original five nuclear weapons states, China is the only one that is expanding its arsenal of nuclear weapons, which grew by an estimated 25 percent from 2005 to 2008, to about 176 deployed warheads, with around 65 in storage. It is modernizing its missile force, moving from liquid-fuel to solid-fuel systems, adding submarine-launched to land-launched missiles, and supplementing ballistic with cruise missiles. Warheads are redesigned as new missiles are developed. Some of the missiles are long range, consistent with the perceived need to have a second-strike capability to deter the United States. But some delivery systems have a range that allows for a regional mission (for example, the DF-31), including Japan and U.S. bases there.[24]

North Korea is the other Northeast Asian nuclear power that could threaten Japan. It has a variety of missile systems and sufficient plutonium for "at least half a dozen" nuclear weapons, and it is attempting to acquire uranium enrichment capability.[25] Its possession of neither warheads nor missiles has been proven, and it lacks the ability to mate weapons to delivery systems. North Korea has a reputation for recklessness that China does not.

Japan, the only country to have suffered an atomic attack, has as a matter of policy foresworn the option of becoming a nuclear power.[26] Moreover, even if it decided to change its policy, it would face several obstacles to doing so: domestic political opposition from parts of the public, fueled by a long-standing antinuclear ethos; a negative response from its Asian neighbors; and difficulties with the United States, which, among other things, would have the right to demand the return of key elements of Japan's civilian nuclear power industry.[27] So Japan has invested significantly in a missile defense system, primarily as a way of countering North Korea.

But Japan's principal defense against a nuclear attack is the alliance with the United States and Washington's pledge of extended deterrence. That is, the United States warns a country that might threaten Japan that it is prepared to punish that country as if it had attacked the U.S. homeland. The problem with extended deterrence, of course, is the credibility of the threat to punish the aggressor, both in its eyes and in the eyes of the party to be protected. Credibility is especially problematic when the party to be deterred can punish the deterring state with overwhelming force, particularly nuclear weapons. If China can deliver nuclear weapons to Japan *and* to the United States, both Beijing and Tokyo will have some doubt, in the event of Chinese aggression against Japan, about whether Washington would have the resolve to actually punish China, since that would invite nuclear retaliation against the United States. Because Japan has limited options to defend itself, its anxiety is probably greater than that of China. To allay that anxiety, the Japanese government has sought to secure greater clarity on how and under what circumstance Washington might act on its commitment should deterrence fail.[28] The Obama administration responded positively by agreeing to hold periodic discussions on the nuclear umbrella (the first meeting occurred in July 2009).[29]

For its part, China could reduce Japan's sense of insecurity in the nuclear field through dialogue on conventional and strategic forces, similar to the interchange that the United States has sought from China. Simultaneously, Japan could reassure China about its fundamental commitment to a nonnuclear posture. The premise is that *not* exchanging views fuels suspicions that are as corrosive as they are unnecessary. The combination of such a China-Japan dialogue and discussions between Washington and Tokyo on U.S. extended deterrence would help in removing these anxieties. Yet China has shown some reluctance to carry through on a pledge in principle to engage in a similar dialogue with the United States on nuclear issues. An initial meeting was held in Beijing in April 2008, but a second meeting had not yet been scheduled as of June 2010.[30]

Regarding cyber security, Japan was rather slow to respond to the danger posed by hackers and its initial defensive capabilities were not always effective. Legislation passed in 2001 enhanced institutional capacity, vested the Prime Minister's Official Residence and Cabinet Secretariat with responsibilities for coordination, and encouraged more cooperation between government and business. Indeed, this is an area where corporate efforts are especially important, since the private sector owns and operates most of the critical infrastructure. Yet the growing capability of Chinese "cyber warriors," plus the fact that they often act independently of the PRC government, means that Japan must fortify its defenses. Lacking that, a major Chinese cyber attack, like one that might be launched in response to a clash between Chinese and Japanese military or law enforcement units, could cause material damage to important computer networks in Japan and deepen the public's sense of psychological vulnerability.[31]

Although Japan is responsible for its own cyber security, it is hard to see what China's conduct of international relations gains, on balance, from tolerating and not regulating a civilian capability that can cause damage in foreign countries. If the Chinese leadership truly regarded Japan as a serious adversary, that would be one thing (the same logic applies to the United States). Encouraging or not discouraging offensive information warfare capabilities both inside and outside the regime then makes sense. But because it is not national policy to regard Japan as the enemy, tolerating independent cyber militias is potentially counterproductive. It also gives Japan and the United States reason to develop not only robust defenses against cyber attacks but also the means to conduct offensive information warfare themselves, if only as a deterrent.[32]

Reconciliation over the Past

Ideally, mitigating the China-Japan security dilemma would include adjusting their respective approaches to their tortured shared history of the first half of the twentieth century. The lens through which each views the past colors many other problems that occur between them. Yet reconciling over the past may be an insurmountable obstacle; even time may not be the key to a solution. Chapter 2 outlines the various ways in which the narrative of Japanese evil and Chinese victimhood is written and institutionalized. Those who favor a more magnanimous approach, such as Shi Yinhong, are shouted down.

Japan, for its part, has taken a complicated approach to its past aggression. In the immediate aftermath of the war, the issue was largely ignored in favor of surviving and rebuilding, an approach favored by the U.S. occupation. Over the subsequent decades, however, Japanese were gradually more willing to expose and face the past. In the 1990s, as the regime in Beijing sought to foster legitimacy by reminding people of the Imperial Army's invasion and occupation, Japanese developed a growing sense of "apology fatigue." Despite criticisms that the Japanese government has not sufficiently atoned for the past, it "has in fact apologized for a history of colonial domination [concerning Korea] and military aggression [against China, for example] and has sought to make amends for its action."[33]

Yet Japan's degree of penitence has been far less than that of Germany, the best point of comparison. In general, the Japanese believe that their country caused less human and material destruction than Nazi Germany, that it was acting in the service of an anti-imperialist mission, and that the greatest responsibility lies with the military-dominated regime. They tend to believe that the postwar allied forces war crimes tribunal was fundamentally flawed and did not render justice fairly, either in terms of process or targets. Finally, there is the view that Japan's postwar international environment discouraged contrition, since the countries that were the victims of Japanese aggression could not exert leverage on Japan on the history issue until relatively late. Then, in the 1990s, when Japan sought to respond, leaders in those countries saw no value in coming to closure and preferred to use the history for political gain, which in turn stimulated Japanese resentment.[34] Such Japanese attitudes are somewhat self-serving, of course, but they do have a basis.

The German experience is also suggestive (but only suggestive) in contemplating whether and how reconciliation might take place between Japan and China. Lily Gardner Feldman has outlined the key elements of the German case:

—Nongovernmental actors, including religious groups, were the key catalysts.

—The perpetrators of evil in the past acknowledged that past through public acts that both sides regarded as "meaningful, durable, and enduring."

—Victims were as significant as perpetrators in stimulating reconciliation actions.

—Once the reconciliation process began, leaders in countries on both sides of the issue were critical to affirming and sustaining it.

—The perpetrators regarded reconciliation as an ongoing and protracted process rather than a series of discrete acts.

—The parties treated history as something that must be confronted continually and in an increasingly institutionalized way.

—Reconciliation provided a "framework in which the two sides [were] symmetrical in terms of their rights and obligations and in which difference [could] be negotiated."

—Sustained, binational institutions were created at the governmental and nongovernmental level.

—The perpetrator nation could have both moral and pragmatic reasons for reconciliation.

—A favorable international environment was conducive to reconciliation.[35]

Clearly, many of the elements of a "German solution" are missing in the case of China and Japan. So far, the two governments have focused on apologies by Japanese leaders (Do they say enough? Are they uttered sincerely?) while ignoring the need for nongovernmental engagement. Nongovernmental institutions of the sort that drove German reconciliation are weak in Japan and scarce in China (the "private" organizations that do exist are not necessarily private). And if there is institutionalization, it works against reconciliation. Chinese textbooks, museums, and memorials all reinforce the narrative of victimization at the hands of Japanese aggressors and occupiers.

The Japanese scene is more ambivalent. Some Japanese deflect responsibility for pre-1945 events by emphasizing their country's own victimization at the hands of the United States. But the Yasukuni Shrine and its fourteen enshrined Class A war criminals have become an obstacle to reconciliation, as have, in the Chinese view, textbooks that "whitewash" the past, even though the problematic texts are a small minority of those used.[36] Yet the most serious impediment to reconciliation is the reality that sustaining the history issue has been good for domestic politics in both countries. The Chinese Communist Party (CCP) under Jiang Zemin promoted it as a new source of legitimacy in the 1990s, while Japan's right wing has benefitted by asserting that the past should no longer be an issue in Tokyo's international relations.

The history issue, therefore, may be the hardest part of the security dilemma for Beijing and Tokyo to address in the foreseeable future. It will likely require the decisive initiative of leaders on both sides to even begin to reduce the salience of history. There are, to be sure, reasons for doing so. The Japanese right wing is in at least temporary eclipse after the August

2009 lower house elections, replaced by a ruling coalition that might be more amenable to reconciliation. Anti-Japanese nationalism in China is a double-edged sword for the communist leadership, simultaneously stimulating support for the CCP and provoking opposition if the public believes that the regime's policies toward Tokyo are too weak. So even if Chinese leaders want to take the initiative on history, it is far from clear that they could depoliticize the issue or create the institutions that could sustain reconciliation rather than obstruct it.

That being the case, the sensible approach to mitigating the Japan-China security dilemma is to start with easier matters first and move toward more difficult ones later. As hard and complex as issues of force structure or resolution of the Diaoyu/Senkaku Island dispute may be, they pale in relation to the history issue. If they can be successfully addressed, it will build mutual trust and confidence that success is possible on the more difficult problems. Yet even this approach to sequencing will run aground without reinforcing and promoting key political points: that the national interest is different from and more important than the visions of individual agencies and that the two countries have too much to lose by denying the past (in the case of Japan) or dwelling on events that ended sixty-five years ago (in the case of China).

Military Operations: Security Regimes and Confidence-Building Measures

Instead of reaching for what probably cannot be grasped—a grand rapprochement, settlement of the Diaoyu/Senkaku dispute, or reconciliation on the past—Japan and China may find a more productive approach in setting limited objectives that address directly the proximate manifestation of their complex of problems. Such an approach recognizes the difficulty of fostering cooperation in an environment of mistrust: each side fears that the other will cheat on its commitments in order to gain a marginal advantage. That being the case, a more iterative process that addresses smaller matters but builds mutual confidence can create a better environment for tackling more difficult challenges.[37]

Such a process could address the operational interaction between the Maritime Self-Defense Force (MSDF), the Air Self-Defense Force (ASDF), and the Japan Coast Guard (JCG) of Japan with the People's Liberation Army Navy (PLAN), People's Liberation Army Air Force (PLAAF), and Marine Surveillance Force (MSF) of China. Their interaction is the potential trigger of some kind of crisis; if that trigger can be disabled in some way, the other factors would never come into play. The obvious way to disable the trigger is to establish some type of security regime.

International regimes (or institutions; scholars use the terms interchangeably) are a set of implicit or explicit principles, norms, rules, and decision-making procedures that lead each actor to have complementary expectations about others' behavior in a given area of international relations.[38] The result is cooperation rather than the discord that preceded creation of the regime. Thus, cooperation implies a process of mutual policy adjustment by two parties that share interests in the abstract but are not able to act on them for whatever reasons and so end up at odds. It is only through mutual adjustment that they can act on those interests. Regimes or institutions are especially useful in reducing difficulties in communication and enhancing the credibility of commitments. They can reduce the fears of one party that a cooperative stance on its part will give the other an advantage at its expense.[39]

It is important to clarify distinctions between regimes and other phenomena. A regime does not exist when states exercise mutual restraint through reciprocal and ad hoc unilateral actions but do not develop reinforcing principles, norms, rules, and decisionmaking procedures. The decline in tensions in the East China Sea after 2006, for example, was a welcome development, but it was not rule-based.

Multilateral groups or organizations that essentially are mechanisms for dialogue are not regimes. Some groupings in East Asia may be useful forums for interaction and communication among countries, but again, they are not rule-based institutions. Evan Feigenbaum and Robert Manning offer the cogent critique that these groupings

> lack functionality or a comprehensive template to . . . assess results. They have developed habits of dialogue, but social interchange and political rhetoric dominate. Lingering suspicions and historical anxieties remain. Asian concerns about maintaining "face" have typically meant that the most sensitive topics, from human rights to territorial disputes, are avoided.[40]

Nor does regional community building necessarily result in a regime. For example, former senior Japanese diplomat Tanaka Hitoshi has proposed an East Asia security forum as one form of community building. The focus would be on functional issues on which cooperation serves the interests of all parties, such as piracy and counterterrorism, not on "divisive issues." The hope is that work on specific problems will enhance a sense of regional identity, mitigate the force of nationalistic sentiment, and foster a more secure regional environment, effects that dialogue mechanisms lack. Tanaka understands that if the forum is to succeed, it should have some rules and that conducting "specific and pro-active operations are necessary." At the same time, he acknowledges that China's and Japan's conflicting threat perceptions would be an obstacle. That and an emphasis on nondivisive issues raise questions of whether such a forum would truly increase the regional sense of security.[41]

For a security regime to be truly useful, it should in some manner reduce the security dilemma between parties, but it is the security dilemma that makes it so difficult to establish and maintain a security regime. Each side fears that if it shows good will and a desire to cooperate, the other will renege on its commitments, leaving it in a more vulnerable position. The costs of cheating are more consequential than they are for a nonsecurity regime, such as a trade agreement. Moreover, competition in the realm of security often is more intense than in other realms. The stakes are higher and the information that actors need to reassure themselves about others' intentions is harder to acquire and assess. That being the case, Robert Jervis postulates four hurdles that must be cleared to create and preserve a security regime:

—The parties must want one and the more regulated, less competitive environment that comes with it.

—Each party must believe that the other shares its desire for security and cooperation (that it will not defect).

—No party can believe that expansion best ensures its security.

—Each party must see conflict and independent action as costly.[42]

Assuming that China and Japan both met those conditions, the most immediate way to disable the East China Sea trigger is a security regime in the form of confidence-building measures. These are especially useful when two militaries operate in close proximity. CBMs may be construed broadly or narrowly. Broadly, they are any measure, either political or military, taken to reduce uncertainty; a narrower definition restricts the discussion to measures that make military intentions more predictable and transparent, thus reducing the chances of accident and miscalculation.[43]

Military CBMs can take a variety of forms, and they probably are best established in a phased manner because of the environment of mutual mistrust in which they generally are undertaken. They may begin with unilateral declarations by one side to reassure the other of its intentions. Obviously, the declarations will have the desired impact only if they are credible. Even then, they must be followed by more specific undertakings of a more bilateral sort, which can and should come in phases.

Steps in phase 1 include the gradual development of military-to-military contacts, building cooperation where the two sides share common interests, setting up direct communications links, establishing codes of conduct for military activities, setting up communications measures to take in the event of dangerous incidents, and agreeing on explicit rules of engagement.

Measures in phase 2 might include regular military exchanges, data and information exchanges, a joint military communications link and hotline for leaders, expanded military cooperation, and risk-reduction centers.

Possible steps in phase 3 are establishment of "keep-out" zones, limits on military exercises and deployments, and verification measures.[44]

Both Japanese and Chinese leaders have made unilateral political statements designed to reassure the other of their long-term intentions. During his December 2007 visit to China, Fukuda Yasuo told an audience at Peking University that "I would like . . . to convey to all the Chinese people that I am of the firmest conviction that Japan and China should become creative partners who establish a bright future for both Asia and the globe." To address the greatest source of Chinese doubt, he said, "It is only when we look squarely at the past with the courage and the wisdom to feel remorseful for actions towards which remorse is appropriate that we become able to ensure that such mistakes do not happen again in the future."[45] Speaking to students at Waseda University, President Hu Jintao promised that

China will steadfastly take the course of peaceful development. This is a strategic choice made by the Chinese government and people. . . . China will firmly carry out an independent foreign policy of peace. . . . China pursues a defensive defense policy [to] never engage itself in any arms race, never pose military threats to any country, never seek hegemony, and never seek expansion.[46]

In an early policy address, Hatoyama Yukio, prime minister of the Democratic Party of Japan–led government that took power in September 2009, said that "the seas surrounding Japan must never again be made into seas of conflict. It is important that we should continue our efforts to maintain these waters as fruitful seas of friendship and solidarity. I consider this to be in the interest of not only Japan but also the Asia-Pacific region."[47] The problem, of course, is that neither side can totally believe the other's unilateral pledges, in part because many of the other's actions seem inconsistent with its pledges.

Moreover, progress on bilateral CBMs has been modest at best. Most activity has occurred in the area of military-to-military exchanges: visits to one country by the officers of the other, which began following the visit of Defense Minister Gao Gangchuan of the PRC to Japan in August 2007:

—In September 2007, members of Japan's Ground Self-Defense Force observed an exercise in China and senior officers of the PLAAF went to Japan.

—In November 2007, the Chinese destroyer *Shenzhen* made a ship visit to Japan.

—In February 2008, the Japanese chief of the joint staff visited China and the Chinese deputy chief of general staff went to Japan.

—In March 2008, Japan's vice minister of defense visited China.

—The heads of the PLAAF and PLAN went to Japan in September and October 2008 respectively. Also in September, Chinese company grade officers were in Japan.

—Japanese defense minister Hamada Yasukaza made a return visit to China in March 2009.[48]

During the return visit of the Japanese defense minister, the two sides concluded a ten-point memorandum on exchanges. They agreed to continue visits by senior officials and service chiefs, field and junior officers, and members of military academic institutions, to continue naval port calls, and to discuss an annual defense affairs exchange program. They pledged to hold a consultation on defense affairs and security between China's Ministry of National Defense (MND) and Japan's Ministry of Defense (MOD) and, on the basis of that meeting, to strengthen communications between the policy departments of the two countries on issues like international peacekeeping, fighting natural disasters, and combating pirates. Finally, they agreed to hold or continue consultations on dialogues between their military staffs, on exchanges between their ground forces, and on building a maritime liaison mechanism between MOD and MND.[49]

The maritime liaison mechanism is the CBM most relevant to the focus of this volume. It could develop into a security regime for the East China Sea, regulating the operations of maritime vessels and air force planes operating in the same geographic space. Such a regime might include direct communications links, codes of conduct, communications measures for dangerous incidents, and explicit rules of engagement. The MSDF is apparently in favor of such measures for maritime interaction; China reportedly is not.[50] Prior to March 2009, the two sides had held one consultation among experts on the maritime liaison mechanism and pledged to hold the second one in the first half of 2009. Yet by the time of PRC defense minister Liang Guanglie's visit to Japan in November, the meeting had not occurred, and the two sides merely agreed to hold it "at the earliest possible date."[51]

One precedent for such an arrangement is the U.S.-Soviet agreement on incidents at sea (INCSEA). During the 1960s and 1970s, the Soviet and the U.S. navy and air force engaged in games of "chicken" on the high seas, increasing the risk of clashes with no strategic purpose that could strain the political relationship. After serious incidents in 1967, the two sides realized the need for restraint and negotiated an agreement that

> gave each side a mechanism to report dangerous conduct, thus deterring many risky and provocative actions. . . . When violations did occur, they were resolved smoothly because a mechanism was in place to adjudicate, review procedures, and correct transgressions.[52]

An INCSEA agreement between China and Japan could encourage restraint on both sides and give pilots and ship captains reasons to eschew risky behavior. Of course, such a pact also should apply to the Japan Coast Guard and China's Marine Surveillance Force, which are on the front lines of this interaction.

China and Japan are in fact capable of creating bilateral regimes. They did so regarding the subject of fisheries in 1997,[53] when Japan took the lead and China responded positively by proposing maritime security initiatives, which resulted in the North Pacific Coast Guard Forum.[54] They also agreed on a security CBM concerning scientific research in the exclusive economic zone disputed by the two countries. Each would notify the other when research ships entered waters "near the other." However, as discussed in chapter 6, China increasingly failed to meet its obligations during the first half of the 2000s decade.

Moreover, China has been willing to reach understandings with countries besides Japan that operate in its neighborhood. It agreed to a code of conduct with the countries of ASEAN regarding activities in the South China Sea, and no major incidents occurred thereafter.[55] China has begun a security regime with South Korea governing their naval and air forces by establishing a communications interface. The two countries agreed in November 2008 that their navies and air forces would maintain telephone links at the fleet and regional air command levels and that they would exchange information by fax and by telephone in the following circumstances:

—when an unidentified object is in the maritime and air space of the two countries

—when there is a disaster in their maritime and air space that requires a search-and-rescue operation

—in an emergency

—in order to inspect the communications facilities on a quarterly basis.

Those measures are somewhat limited in that the two navies and air forces communicate only when the unexpected is already happening, but it is better than nothing.[56] Creating communications links can be the first step to broader CBMs, and the fact that they are being done at a more operational level (as opposed to just headquarters communications) provides an element of flexibility. China could easily take such measures in an agreement with Japan.

In 1998, China agreed with the United States, at least on paper, to a military CBM in the form of a military maritime consultative agreement (MMCA). Designed to regulate activities in the East and South China Seas, it established working groups on safety. Yet the MMCA has not worked as the United States had hoped. Washington sought to convene a meeting after the clash in April 2001 between a U.S. reconnaissance aircraft and a PLAN jet (see chapter 12). But Chinese officials made clear that they had "no interest in the agreement that they had signed" and suspended the talks. Again, China uses CBMs to reflect how it regards the overall relationship rather than to achieve their ostensible purpose: to reduce risk and build confidence and trust. As one observer put it: "the Chinese are not particularly interested in a rules-based, operator-to-operator approach to safety on the high seas. They have other (probably strategic) objectives in play."[57]

And that is the rub. Each side conducts military operations in the service of broader objectives. China seeks to expand its strategic buffer toward the east and south, both to protect itself and to prepare for a Taiwan contingency. Japan intends to protect its territory as it defines it. Each side sees a way to promote its own energy security in the East China Sea oil and gas fields. Because these larger objectives are in play, there is a greater willingness to accept risk, especially on the Chinese side and particularly with the PLAN. Whether it is vis-à-vis the United States or Japan, Beijing has little interest in agreeing to mechanisms to reduce risk and avoid conflict if it has to sacrifice important interests at the same time.

Instead, Beijing regards the state of mutual strategic trust as the fundamental variable. Military CBMs should result from greater trust rather than serve as a means of creating it. It will use them only if the other party is taking steps unilaterally to reduce mistrust, not as concrete measures in the context of mutual mistrust to address specific security problems.[58] Major General Qian Lihua made this point regarding the United States as follows:

The course of the development of military relations between China and the United States shows that military relations can only develop healthily and steadily when both sides respect each other's core interests and concerns. On [these], there is no room for China to make concessions.[59]

In some cases, China prefers to increase an adversary's sense of insecurity and mistrust rather than reduce it.[60]

As a corollary, China appears to manipulate CBMs to deter behavior by Japan that it regards as provocative. As long as the broader political relationship is going well, exchanges continue, for good or ill. If Japan took an action that in the PLA's eyes was hostile to China, exchanges would be suspended as a form of punishment. For example, Beijing suspended military exchanges while Koizumi Junichiro was prime minister, as it has done repeatedly to the United States over a variety of issues. The specific dangers that CBMs might mitigate are ignored. For Japan, this on-again-off-again phenomenon, plus China's poor performance with respect to giving Japan notice of Chinese scientific research expeditions, would not inspire great confidence.

Even though CBMs like a Japan-China INCSEA make obvious sense, territorial issues would likely complicate the effort to achieve one. Would China agree to an INCSEA if it implied that Japan possessed sovereignty over the Diaoyu/Senkaku Islands? What would new rules of the road in the gas and oil fields of the East China Sea say about competing claims to exclusive economic zones? Similarly, the operations of the two air forces would be more predictable if each gave the other advance word of the air patrols that it planned in the expectation that the other air force would not scramble its interceptors. One reason, however, that intercepts are potentially dangerous is that Japan's air defense identification zone is so large—and equivalent to its claimed EEZ, which overlaps China's. What would each side believe that this conflict-avoidance practice says about its claims?

Finally, in any CBM that Japan undertook, it would want to take its own and U.S. security interests into account. It should not conclude an agreement that undermines its own ability to dissuade and deter, either by limiting the capabilities that it acquires or by restricting the ways that it exercises its forces. It should avoid CBMs that are only symbolic in their impact in a context in which the PRC's buildup renders Japan more vulnerable. Steps to reduce the risk of accidents should not affect the SDF's readiness and appropriate rules of engagement. When it comes to exchanges, Japan should ensure that it protects sensitive information relevant to the United States. And it should not reach agreements that undermine U.S. security elsewhere in the region—for example, in the Korean peninsula.[61]

There was progress of a sort in late May 2010. Premier Wen of China and Prime Minister Hatoyama of Japan agreed to set up a leaders' "hotline" to discuss important issues in bilateral ties and to avert emergencies. They also announced that they would establish a "maritime crisis management mechanism" involving their two militaries. If created and used effectively, the crisis management mechanism could be a useful tool to avoid conflict. It remains to be seen whether it will ever materialize or be effective. The fact that the hotline will be between the two premiers and that the Chinese premier is not in the military chain of command will limit its value in regulating the interaction of the two militaries.[62]

Security Dilemma: Summing Up

Clearly, each route to reducing the multifaceted security dilemma between China and Japan is strewn with obstacles. However sensible, any approach comes with difficulties, some of which have to do with institutional and political factors. Even assuming that the problems can be overcome, unwinding the factors that contribute to mutual fear is a fairly daunting challenge. The discussion so far does suggest a scenario for reducing the possibility of a clash between the two countries' units in the East China Sea and the attendant consequences. The process is incremental, which can foster the mutual trust necessary to take further steps.

STEP ONE.   To reduce the chance of an accidental clash, China and Japan should institute military CBMs that would regulate the operations of their ships and aircraft in the East China Sea, particularly in the area of the Diaoyu/Senkaku Islands. In particular, they should conclude an agreement, like an incidents-at-sea accord, to establish rules of interaction and robust communications procedures to maintain a degree of separation. That would place a "safety" on the trigger of an unnecessary conflict. Appendix 14A provides a proposal for a U.S.-China arrangement that could be adapted to the issues between Japan and China.

For such an agreement to occur and be effective, several other things must happen. China must abandon its view that trust must be established before military cooperation of this sort can proceed. It is because mistrust exists that procedures such as CBMs are necessary to reduce it. Second, China must be prepared to end the challenges that its Marine Surveillance Force makes to the Japan Coast Guard in the Senkaku/Diaoyu area. Although actions by Chinese nationalist groups concerning the islands may continue to be an irritant, decades of experience makes them manageable. It is the MSF's probes that are changing the status quo. Third, Japan must revise the rules of engagement for its coast guard to eliminate excessive use of force. All of these actions will require political leadership on both sides, but especially in China. Whatever the thinking that drives East China Sea operations, China's interest in avoiding serious clashes with Japan should outweigh it. The same is true of China's interests with respect to the United States: an agreement to regulate operations is needed here too.

STEP TWO.   Based on the trust engendered through repeated positive interaction in air, naval, and law enforcement operations, China and Japan should next seek to address as much as possible their specific disputes in the East China Sea. Even if resolution is not possible, it may be possible to make some progress.

There is, of course, a political agreement pending regarding oil and gas development in the East China Sea. The two sides reached agreement in June 2008, but because China had been unwilling to open even working-level talks, they have made no progress on a follow-up pact to implement the understandings already set forth. The PRC government came under public criticism for concluding the 2008 agreement, even though viewed objectively, the agreement favored Beijing over Tokyo. It has therefore claimed that it is up to Japan to "create an environment to realize last year's agreement."[63] For its part, Beijing's foot dragging was creating the impression in Japan that the 2008 agreement was meaningless, that China's word could not be trusted, and that its intentions in the area were not benign.

In their May 2010 summit, Premier Wen and Prime Minister Hatoyama agreed to launch formal talks to implement the principles agreed to two years before.[64] But once negotiations begin, there is no certainty that they will result in a mutually acceptable arrangement, given the reluctance of the PLAN and the China National Offshore Oil Corporation (CNOOC) to accept any restraints on their respective activities. Again, narrow bureaucratic interests might impede any significant improvement in bilateral relations. It was not a good sign, moreover, that China reportedly asked Tokyo to supervise the reporting of the Japanese media concerning the East China Sea.[65]

Assuming that China is prepared to take a more strategic approach and an implementing agreement is reached, approaches exist to drafting a resolution to delineate a boundary for the continental shelf and EEZs. One, described above, would link joint development to postponement of the Diaoyu/Senkaku issue, reaffirmation of the fisheries regime, and a promise that boundaries would be delineated in a finite period of time or that the boundaries question would be submitted for international adjudication.[66] Such an arrangement is mutually beneficial and would build trust during the period of implementation.

The Senkaku/Diaoyu issue is more intractable, because it presents an either-or choice (the islands are either China's or Japan's). Yet it becomes more manageable if its impact on delineation of the continental shelf and EEZ is reduced. The option of joint development while setting aside the sovereignty dispute has a strong political legacy. At the same time, both sides maintain unyielding positions because of a little-examined assumption: that the area is indeed rich in oil and gas deposits. Perhaps they might jointly sponsor exploration to assess the value of the energy resources and the commercial viability of developing them. If the reserves are abundant, that will increase the incentive for cooperation; if they are not, the salience of the sovereignty issue recedes.

Again, political leadership is required to secure progress, especially on the Chinese side. Without directives from the top, based on a broad definition of PRC interests, negotiations to implement the 2008 agreement are unlikely to begin or to bear fruit and creative solutions to the delineation and sovereignty issues will never be explored. Even if CBMs do not reduce the risk of an accidental clash, China would be missing an opportunity to put its relations with Japan on a significantly better footing. The emergence of the Democratic Party of Japan (DPJ) government, with its more moderate view of China, presents a golden opportunity to foster Japanese confidence in China's peaceful intentions.

Untangling the China-Japan Complex: Institutions and Politics

As is obvious from the previous discussion, institutional and political factors constrain any effort to resolve or mitigate substantive disputes. In theory, changing those factors may have a positive impact on the disputes over time; conversely, reducing mistrust by addressing disputes would provide a reason for change in institutions and political attitudes. Yet because institutions and politics affect both countries' broader security and foreign policies, improving them is worthwhile for its own sake. Doing so will improve Japan's and China's capacity as international actors—even if East China Sea disputes did not exist.

Just as obvious, it is not easy to alter institutions and the politics of external policy. They have a long history, and actors in each system, with their entrenched interests, have an interest maintaining the status quo. So change is difficult. Yet preserving the status quo entails risks. Moreover, times have changed. Some arrangements and attitudes may have been appropriate in the past, but that does not mean that they are useful in a new era. Indeed, as China revives itself as a great power and as Japan faces a post–cold war security environment, institutions and politics must change as well.

So if I could wave a magic wand and make just a few changes in Japan's and China's institutions and politics, what would I choose to change?

Institutions

THE INFORMATION PROBLEM.   First of all, I would improve the information that underlies Chinese and Japanese leaders' policy choices. Both countries suffer from dysfunctional intelligence communities. Each is stovepiped, with insufficient mechanisms for coordinating views among different agencies. Each—and particularly China—suffers from analytical weaknesses in assessing the capabilities and intentions of the other. Japan's intelligence units suffer from lack of resources. As a result, policymakers are ill-served.

Japan has taken some steps to increase coordination, but more is required. Efforts to strengthen both the capacity and role of the Cabinet Information Research Office and thereby facilitate a more centralized system should continue. Although one agency may have far greater expertise than others on some intelligence matters, there are a number of issues on which community consensus would be more useful to decisionmakers than the individual views of each agency (the security challenge posed by China is certainly one of those).

Reportedly, Japan is building such a consensus-creation mechanism by establishing the post of cabinet intelligence officer. The key is whether such officers have the power to push toward meaningful consensus on important issues. The process of reaching consensus would not only yield a better analytical product, since agencies would have to reconcile their views with those of others, but it also would foster greater cooperation among organizations. Finally, even as the Cabinet Information Resource Office is strengthened, it is probably time to end the practice of appointing its director from the National Police Agency. The principal challenge to the Japanese state no longer comes from within, as it did when the practice began, but from outside.[67]

China's intelligence system probably is even more segmented than Japan's, and segmentation appears most serious between the military and civilian sectors. As it is, with respect to questions of external policy on which the PLA can properly assert its expertise, differences between the PLA's intelligence agencies and those of the ministries of foreign affairs and state security are likely to surface only at the highest levels of the system. At that point, one of two problems can occur. Either a specific official gains a monopoly on interpretation, thus denying policymakers exposure to contrary views, or the information is filtered by high-level staff (as in the General Office of the Communist Party's Central Committee) who do not have sufficient expertise to evaluate what is significant and what is not. A more formal mechanism that both ensures sufficient expertise in the filtering process and an information delivery system that exposes and, if possible, reconciles all significant points of view would better serve decisionmakers.

Enhancing the quality of analysis requires at least two reforms. The first is to draw a sharp line between policy and interpretations of the reality that policy is trying to shape. That goal is never reached by even the best intelligence systems. Individual agencies will still shade their interpretations to suit their own interests. But the ideal is still worthy of aspiration. It requires instituting norms and incentives that encourage intelligence agencies to call the shots as they see them, not as they think policymakers prefer. The second is to create standards of analytic "tradecraft" to ensure that interpretations are based on sound assumptions and are justified by available evidence. To trigger such reforms, the two countries might appoint independent panels to evaluate past intelligence analyses to see whether explanations and predictions were borne out in reality most of the time. If they were not, it suggests a structural flaw.

The most important step that Japan can take is to place effective controls on information, including by deterring potential leakers with the prospect of severe punishment. No one intelligence agency will share its exclusive information with other organizations if it lacks confidence in their ability to keep that information secret. Fostering stricter controls will also ensure better sharing of intelligence and policy proposals with the United States. There are signs that this is beginning. The Cabinet Information Resource Office issued a manual for employees with the goal of reducing the passage of classified information to foreign spies and journalists. The Ministry of Defense has begun to do background checks on personnel who handle classified information and require them to be available for polygraph tests.[68] The key, however, will be to increase and enforce penalties for unauthorized exposure to create a deterrent.

By creating checks on the way that intelligence analysis is delivered to policymakers, institutional reform can better ensure that they have the best possible analysis. But it is the leaders in both systems who must promote these reforms. It is they whom the current arrangements handicap. It is only they who can ensure that the flow of information serves their interests.

Civil-Military Relations. The second area in need of reform is civil-military relations. Here, there is a striking asymmetry between the two systems. Arguably, the PLA has too much autonomy, particularly when it comes to operations, while the SDF has too little. In China, the Communist Party and its civilian leadership command the political loyalty of the PLA, but it tends to defer to the military regarding matters on which the latter can claim its professional prerogatives. That, combined with certain features of Chinese strategic culture, increases the chances that the PLA will take action without considering diplomatic and other implications, all the time believing that it has the authority to do so.

In Japan, it is true that the SDF's loyalty to civilian norms is occasionally called into question. At the same time, constraints on the SDF's operational autonomy and participation in policymaking should be relaxed. The legal and policy framework limits the military's ability to do its job. Because senior officers do not always get access to central decisionmaking institutions, civilian policymakers do not always get the benefit of their expertise and operational insights. Neither constraint raises the incentives for the SDF to act in accord with civilian policy preferences.

What steps should be taken to rectify the situation? In Japan, there is need for a new bargain on the role of the SDF in Japan's security policy that places less emphasis on the purported danger that the military poses to the Japanese people and state (a legacy of the twentieth century) and stresses how the SDF can reduce the external dangers to Japan and enhance the country's contributions to international society. Elements of such a bargain might include the following:

—Continued education of officers and troops regarding the reasons for and consequences of Japan's aggression in the past (why the military has a bad reputation in the first place) and the role of the military in a democratic state that does face potential external threats.

—Greater independence for the SDF in its various operations. Among the possible steps are a shift from requiring mission-specific laws governing the deployment of the SDF overseas to programmatic approval; greater flexibility on the potential use of force by deployed forces; reinterpretation of the constitution to allow collective self-defense; restricting civilian oversight to broad policy; and deferring to the judgment of senior officers on operations.

—Enhanced training of officers and troops in the field to ensure that they show good judgment in exercising greater operational autonomy.

—Greater coordination between the Maritime Self-Defense Force and the Japan Coast Guard, both in the field and at the headquarters level.

—Establishment of an institutionalized role for senior officers in policy deliberations to ensure that their operational expertise is factored directly into policy decisions rather than being filtered through civilian bureaucrats.

In China, the task is different. It is to ensure that the military's strategy, procurement, and operations reflect an approach that is consistent with China's national interest, not the PLA's view of China's national interest. If China's strategic objective is to reassure other powers that its long-term intentions are benign and that it will not overturn the existing order (as it says), then its actions must match its rhetoric. Otherwise, Japan, the United States, and others will base their assessments and their actions on China's behavior. The actions of the PLA should be a key element in a strategy of reassurance. In some cases, what the PLA does is consistent with what Beijing says (as in peacekeeping operations and contributions to multilateral anti-piracy missions). In other respects, its actions are cause for concern rather than confidence (aggressive operations in the East China Sea, the anti-satellite test, the continued buildup of military capabilities relevant to Taiwan, and so on). Just as clearly, the other powers, particularly the United States, must be sure to align the activities of their militaries with their stated policies of engaging and cooperating with China.

How might Chinese leaders achieve greater consistency between the PLA's actions and the government's stated intentions? Generally, it requires closer integration of the PRC's three hierarchies: party, government, and military. Segmentation may have been appropriate for China's strategic situation in the past, when the PLA played a greater role in ensuring domestic security and maintained a purely defensive posture externally. At that time having the primary locus of integration be the paramount leader, with his positions at the top of all three hierarchies, may have been sufficient. Today, however, the PLA's external role is no longer purely defensive. It is creating the capacity to act beyond China's borders and is slowly acting on that ability. Moreover, there is the recent case of split leadership, with Hu Jintao holding the top positions in the party and government hierarchies and Jiang Zemin retaining chairmanship of the Central Military Commission for two more years. And there is the possibility that Hu Jintao will follow that pattern when he gives up his civilian positions.[69] What that requires, probably, is for the PLA to become a national army rather than a party army, with the national command authority vested in the civilian president and not the CMC chairman.[70]

The chances of that transformation occurring are rather slim, given the current power configuration within the PRC regime and the general public support for building China's power, including its military might. It is more likely to occur as a consequence of a significant mistake whose cause is traced to the segmentation of the civilian and military hierarchies. Consequently, change is more likely in the policymaking process and in how the PLA participates.

Policymaking Structure.   The discussion of intelligence and civil-military relations indicates that even if policymakers have good information available, they will not be able to use it well if the institutions that define policy options, weigh risks and rewards, and choose a course of action do not work well. Both systems have collective leaderships, rather independent line agencies, and overloaded mechanisms for interagency coordination. From historical experience, each is wary of vesting too much power in one individual; hence their collective leaderships. But those leaderships either cannot reach consensus on what to do or, if they can, cannot force their policies on line agencies and hold those who pursue their own course accountable. The resistance of the PLA and oil companies to a true agreement on joint development of oil and gas fields is a case in point.

Each system has a fairly formal approach to the interface between leaders and agencies. In China, the system works to insulate the top leadership from agencies; in Japan, it works to preserve agency autonomy. There is, of course, no perfect solution to balancing the need for decisive executive authority and maximizing the value of agency expertise. But in both Japan and China, the current systems produce outcomes that are sometimes suboptimal.

Those imbalances come into special play in situations of stress. For different reasons, each system is unable to cope with the unexpected. Reliable information is at a premium. Response time is slow. There are two dangers: that the PLA will have too much influence in a crisis, imposing a "military logic" on decisionmaking and reducing the foreign policy logic, while the SDF will have too little influence, denying civilian leaders the sort of military viewpoint that they need.

One way of reducing the dangers is to increase the flow of information from the other country. The best method is to create and use hotlines between leaders, relevant civilian agencies, and defense establishments. Yet it is important that the two sides actually use the hotlines. The limited experience between the United States and China shows that leaders in Beijing are least likely to use a hotline when tensions are rising.[71] The collective nature of the Chinese leadership is a factor here: the members of the Politburo Standing Committee do not wish to delegate authority to the paramount leader. That is another reason to create a more specialized arrangement for making decisions on national security.

The bigger problem, it seems, is that the decisionmaking structure at the top suffers from too little division of labor and specialization. The collective leadership in each system is ultimately responsible for everything. In China, the Politburo Standing Committee must address all major decisions, domestic and external. The membership of the Foreign Affairs/National Security Leading Group in China, which is where specialization occurs, is based on a broad definition of security and includes economic and domestic security agencies. The same breadth is true for Japan. The Japanese Cabinet is the constitutionally designated agent of executive power. The Security Council includes economic ministers, which may be one reason that it meets irregularly.

Those arrangements may have functioned well in earlier times, when China had a deeper sense of vulnerability and Japan had little autonomy with respect to its national security and when both conflated domestic and external security. Yet for each, the security environment today is different, and, arguably, institutions have not caught up with the times. Interestingly, beginning in the late 1990s individuals in each system saw the need for a more specialized mechanism to address national security issues.

After the Belgrade embassy bombing, which produced severe tensions in U.S.-China relations and spurred protests within China, Jiang Zemin had pushed for a U.S.-style National Security Council as a mechanism for providing a more timely and coherent response in a crisis (he also may have wished to create a position for himself as head of the council after he had to retire from other positions). There was an extended debate, during which existing institutions apparently resisted the proposal because it would intrude on their turfs. Of particular concern in the Communist Party was the possibility that the new crisis management body would become a decisionmaking mechanism separate from and superseding the Politburo Standing Committee. Ultimately, Jiang had to accept the compromise of creating a National Security Leading Group, which was responsible for addressing both domestic and external crises. Its membership was exactly the same as that of the Foreign Affairs Leading Group, which took care of more routine external policy issues.[72]

When Abe Shinzo became prime minister of Japan in September 2006, he wished to strengthen the function of the Prime Minister's Official Residence as the government's "control tower" for national security policy. Two months later, he formed a panel composed of individuals who shared his views. It decided on combining the size of the British cabinet committee for foreign policy and national defense with the legal mandate and policy formulation role of the U.S. National Security Council. But the Foreign Ministry and Japan Defense Agency were wary that the new *kantei* body would undercut their authority (the SDF hoped that it might include former uniformed officers).[73] Still, in February 2008, the panel presented its proposal, which was turned into legislation that the LDP and Cabinet approved one after the other in early April.[74] The reform then became a casualty of politics. The Democratic Party of Japan won control of the upper house of the Diet in July, and Abe Shinzo resigned as PM. His successor, Fukuda Yasuo, lacked Abe's sense of urgency on the matter. As he said, "It's not that everything will not work if there is no NSC. There is a need to further consider whether it is necessary."[75]

In each case, the existing power centers thwarted efforts to remedy the deficiencies of the existing system because they would infringe on their power. Perhaps the time has come for both Tokyo and Beijing to revisit those proposals. In each system, the collective leadership would have to cede some power to the top leader (the paramount leader in China and the prime minister in Japan) and to those ministerial-level officials who are most relevant to external security (similar to the informal "war cabinet" in Japan). In China, a national security council would make the leading groups for foreign affairs, national security, and Taiwan unnecessary.

In each system, the manner and degree of the military's access to the decisionmaking structure would change. In China, the primary venue for the PLA's influence on policy would shift from the party's Central Military Commission to this national security mechanism. The positions of its representatives would have to be of a higher level than that of the PLA members of the current leading groups. In Japan, a representative of the SDF leadership would be a member of the national security mechanism.

As with civil-military relations, it is not likely that such significant changes would be made in the established order under normal circumstances. It probably requires some policy failure to force leaders to recognize the need for restructuring and keep at bay the bureaucratic interests that would lose out. Policy failures were the impetus for the proposal for a national security council in China and the Hashimoto reforms of the late 1990s in Japan. Hypothetically, the chances for change are greater in Japan, where the new leadership has never been in power and may be able to look at existing arrangements with a fresh eye. It already is applying a new perspective to the relationship between bureaucrats and politicians. It has the opportunity to do the same with respect to decisionmaking in the national security sphere.

POLITICS OF EXTERNAL POLICY.   In both Japan and China politics creates a difficult environment in which to conduct sound bilateral relations.

Yet it is not in the bilateral relationship alone where a shift in public attitudes would be salutary. Both nations, and especially China, would benefit generally. Yet securing that dividend will occur only if political leaders take the lead.

Here again, Japan probably is in a better position. The DPJ government has a more positive attitude toward China, and it is not associated with the policies that created tensions from 1995 to 2006. It will succeed in improving the low regard in which the Japanese public views China only if it balances engagement with defense of Japan's interests. Otherwise, it will be seen as naïve and lose support as a result.

The recent political change in Japan is beneficial in another way. It creates the possibility that the right wing of the LDP and related groups, which have been the main agents for provoking anti-Japanese sentiment, may be marginalized. They also have been most responsible for denying Japan's aggression toward and harsh occupation of China before 1945 and so have been an obstacle to some reconciliation concerning history. Yet the leaders of the LDP will have to recognize that retaining this part of the LDP posture will probably impede any effort to revive their party and act on that recognition.

China's leaders have the tougher job. Anti-Japanese and anti-foreign nationalism is stronger in China than nationalism is in Japan, and it is arguably harder to mitigate. On one hand, institutionalized channels through which nationalistic sentiment might flow and dissipate are lacking in the authoritarian political system. On the other, the energized members of the public do not lack means to vent their anger.

Here again, it makes sense to move from simple to difficult, by, for example, emphasizing the reform of institutions before trying to drain the poison from politics. In this case, however, putting off the problem of politics may undermine everything that leaders are trying to do to improve relations. Here, the approach should perhaps be dialectical: taking modest steps to improve the politics of the relationship; then, on that basis, making progress on substantive issues; then enhancing the political environment even more; and so on.

Untangling the China-Japan Complex: The U.S.-Japan Alliance

The victory of the Democratic Party of Japan in the August 2009 lower house elections cast a dark cloud over the U.S.-Japan alliance, but it was not because Japan's new leaders have a starkly different view of Japan's strategic environment and what to do about it. On the contrary, they have said that the alliance remains the foundation of their country's security. Nor was it because they favor positive Japan-China relations. Even recent LDP leaders like Abe Shinzo and Fukuda Yasuo sought to restore some balance between relations with the United States and relations with Asia. The concern about the DPJ stems more from the apparently political motivations behind the changes that they have proposed for the alliance and the lack of thought given to them. To call for a "more equal" alliance is one thing. To define equality as the United States altering its presence in Japan in order to benefit local communities and to reduce Japan's participation in international security projects is another, particularly when Japan had been unwilling to rectify the imbalance between the fundamental mutual defense obligations of Japan and the United States. But that is precisely what the new Hatoyama administration sought to do, by insisting initially on a new location for the U.S. marine air station to replace the Futenma facility at Ginowan on Okinawa. Yet focusing on narrow issues related to the U.S. military presence in Japan delayed serious consideration of the broader purposes of the alliance, which is urgently required.

In late May 2010, Hatoyama threw in the towel and abandoned his effort to secure a significant change in the agreement of which Futenma was a part; soon thereafter, he resigned as prime minister. The price of his reversal was a deepening of resentment on the part of the people of Okinawa and some bruised feelings between Tokyo and Washington. But pushing Futenma to a back burner only raises the salience of more fundamental questions, such as

—How do DPJ leaders assess Japan's security environment? Is it benign or potentially dangerous?

—How will they define Japan's international role? Should it be a civilian middle power that focuses on the country's economy and does global "good works" on the side? Or should it be one that makes real contributions to international peace and security?

—Does Japan's defense establishment have the ability to address perceived threats, both in terms of deterrence and of defense if deterrence fails? This question is especially pressing in light of a stagnant military budget that emphasizes only one mission area—missile defense—and the legal framework within which the SDF operates. If the current limits are too great, how should legal and operational flexibility expand?

—What purposes does the DPJ believe that the alliance should serve, based on the answers to the questions above? Should it be a robust alliance like the U.S. alliance with South Korea, which combines the capability to deter and defend against aggression plus cooperate in the preservation of regional security? Should it have only limited goals, as the U.S.-Philippine alliance does? Or should it be somewhere in between?

—Depending on the goals of the alliance, what degree of operational cooperation is necessary—the cold war or post–cold war configuration or something different?

In recent years, some Japanese and Americans have favored expanding the role of the alliance to give it a strategic purpose for the twenty-first century. They have talked of a multifaceted focus: defense of Japan, traditional security issues like proliferation, nontraditional security issues like cross-border crime and climate change, and projects that reflect common values like freedom and democracy. Whether the DPJ government will move in that direction is an open question. And some observers question whether expansion is justified in light of the belief of each government that the other has not met its expectations for the alliance.[76]

Yet some of these discussions ignore the central challenge facing both the United States and Japan: the revival of China as a great power. If any challenge is strategic in the true sense of the term, this is it. It is in both Washington's and Tokyo's interest that China's revival occur in a way that contributes to the stability of the international system rather than disrupts it. Working together to increase the probability of a positive outcome should be the strategic task of the alliance, because both countries (and China) have too much to lose from a negative one. The United States and Japan are likely to disagree over how to carry out this task. Each has reasons (particularly economic) to accommodate China, but each also has reason to fear. The DPJ government displays a preference for accommodation, but China's growing power is a reality that cannot be ignored.

Rising and reviving powers always present complicated challenges. Japan and the United States cannot be certain about the long-term goals of China, which is growing fast economically, is expanding its military arsenal steadily, and is usually diplomatically skillful. Will it accommodate the international system or upset it? Increasing the complexity is the reality that, understandably, a rising power is often cautious in the early stages of its rise and accumulation of power and does not reveal its intentions until later. So far, China has accommodated the international system in a number of ways, but that may be just part of a cautious strategy. Indeed, China may not know whether it will want to challenge the order in East Asia.

The answer most likely will emerge from an interactive process over the short and medium terms regarding the three countries' military capabilities and how they handle specific issues like Taiwan and North Korea. The danger is that China on one side and the United States and Japan on the other will each act on the basis of its fears of the other and create a set of interlocking vicious circles. Therein lies a potential tragedy. On one hand, even though Tokyo and Washington are prepared to accommodate a reviving China in the hope of integrating the nation into the international system, China's actions require them to act to balance against China. On the other hand, even though China may be willing to accommodate the international system, Japanese and U.S. actions lead it to challenge the existing order. The adage that two tigers cannot lie on the same mountain apparently will receive confirmation, even if the outcome is not inevitable.

The alternative is for the United States and Japan to set as their alliance's strategic task the creation of circumstances that allow all the countries of East Asia to coexist and avoid the tragedy of competing for power, thereby increasing the possibility that China will continue to take an accommodative and constructive approach to the international system. (Note that this more positive approach to China is very different from assuming that China's intentions are hostile and using the alliance to contain it.) How might such an approach be carried out? Eleven items for U.S.-Japan joint action come to mind.[77]

—*First, the two allies should foster a clear and hopefully common understanding of the nature of China's revival as a great power, one that is neither naïve nor alarmist.* If the United States has a relatively benign view of China's accumulation of power and Japan a relatively skeptical one, it will be hard to agree on a common strategic focus for the alliance. Tokyo and Washington should continue to encourage Beijing to be more transparent but also recognize that China gives a lot of clues about its intentions that can be exploited.

—*Second, the two allies should have a shared vision of China's role in the international system.* In recent years the United States has adopted the view that the problems of the system are most feasibly addressed through the cooperation of great powers, including China and Japan. If Japan, on the other hand, adopts the view that competition for power with China is an inescapable reality, then cooperation with the United States in facing China becomes less possible.

—*Third, the two allies should challenge negative Chinese interpretations of their intentions.* Even if China takes an accommodative and cooperative approach, if its institutions for assessing their intentions are flawed and produce negative misperceptions, the chances for hostile PRC actions do not decline.

—*Fourth, the two allies should find and exploit opportunities for positive engagement and cooperation with China—bilaterally, regionally, and globally.*

This is both for the substantive benefits involved and the building of trust with Beijing.

—*Fifth, the two allies should try hard to solve specific problems with China, such as North Korea's nuclear program.* Otherwise Beijing will draw negative conclusions about Tokyo and Washington and vice versa.

—*Sixth, the two allies should develop mechanisms to regulate their interaction with China if the issues that draw the three together cannot be solved.*

—*Seventh, the two allies should work on the premise that there is a happy medium between military capabilities.* They should not be so robust that China perceives a containment strategy or so modest that Beijing is tempted to exploit what it regards as weakness.[78]

—*Eighth, the two allies should ensure that individually and together they have the capacity to carry out the task of maintaining a China-focused alliance.*

—*Ninth, the two allies should educate their publics on what China is and what it is not.*

—*Tenth, the two allies should create a trilateral track-one dialogue mechanism with China.* Such a mechanism would allow them to reassure China regarding the objectives of the alliance and Beijing to convey the purposes of its growing military power.

—*Eleventh, the two allies should push for better channels of dialogue with the Chinese military.* The military is the part of the Chinese system that is most suspicious of their intentions.

Obviously, these steps overlap with the recommendations of this chapter regarding what Japan should do on its own to address its security dilemma with China. They also overlap with the steps that the United States should take to mitigate its own security dilemma with China. Yet joint action by the two allies will reinforce their respective unilateral actions.

Final Thoughts

Although some of these measures are harder to adopt than others, none is especially easy. Had they been easy, they might have been done before. None would be terribly popular in some quarters of either society. Even if a certain action makes policy sense in the abstract, policymakers often prefer doing nothing rather than doing what is difficult and unpopular. But when it comes to the perils of China's and Japan's proximity, the costs of doing nothing are not zero. By continuing to do business as usual, despite those perils, the two governments risk creating large problems in their relationship, fueled by politics and institutional weakness. Reducing those risks can begin with modest cooperative actions that both encourage mutual trust and create the possibility of more ambitious efforts to resolve disputes and build even more trust. In that regard, the arrival of a new Japanese government creates opportunities that should not be missed.

There is, of course, a tension among these various recommendations. On one hand, there are modest measures designed to address specific problems. On the other hand, there is the reality of the big picture: China's power is growing and Japan's is either stagnant or declining. Aggravating that reality are the institutional features of the Chinese system that condition how power is used. So China's large strides toward major-power status may negate any small steps toward progress that the two sides achieve. For Japan, it may mean little in the long run to create specific bilateral conflict-avoidance mechanisms for the East China Sea if the number of ships in the PLA Navy and the number of aircraft in the PLA Air Force constantly increase and confidence in the United States declines. Two tigers will still find it difficult to coexist on the same mountain.

That is certainly true. Hypothetically, there are ways of ameliorating the security dilemma between the two countries. China might exercise restraint in its acquisition of military capabilities and in how they are used. Regional institutions might mitigate their rivalry. Historical animosities may fade. But it is hard to see China stopping its buildup as long as the possibility exists that some Taiwan leader in the future might pursue de jure independence. Even if the Taiwan problem did not exist, China would still have a reason for creating strategic depth for itself in the East China Sea. And the record of regional institution-building efforts over the past twenty years does not inspire hope of their efficacy in the future. The shadow of the future that China creates for Japan will force it to choose between accommodation, which will come with some degree of humiliation, or growing dependence on the United States, which will work only if both Japan and the United States rebuild the foundations of their postwar power.

Yet there is another truth. That is, if China and Japan do not manage the perils of proximity, they increase the inevitability of rivalry. Military arsenals can certainly create mutual insecurity. But so can the lessons that are drawn when two countries do a bad job of handling specific problems. For Japan, these include North Korea and Taiwan as well as interaction in the East China Sea. Here again, institutions and politics will exacerbate tensions rather than contain them. Even if Japan and China cannot resolve *all* their problems, solving those that can be solved now will create some confidence that the shadow of the future will not be so dark.

Appendix 14A
Conceptual Outline for U.S.-China Military Maritime Coordination Procedures Agreement (MMCPA)

Based on the concept, as described by Eric McVadon, of an agreement to facilitate conflict avoidance between U.S. and Chinese forces based on the 1972 U.S.-Soviet Incidents at Sea Agreement (INCSEA).[79] The language from the U.S.-Soviet document appears in regular type; new suggestions appear in boldface type. McVadon's explanatory comments are in italics and in brackets.

Geographic Scope

Navigation of the high seas, including EEZs, and flight over the high seas [*thus effectively excluding territorial waters—just as in the 1972 INCSEA agreement*].

Types of Vessels and Aircraft Covered

Ships, **other vessels,** and aircraft of the naval forces, naval auxiliaries, **and other government agencies** of the United States and China—whether alone or in formation.

Bases and Premise

—International Regulations for Preventing Collisions at Sea (Rules of the Road)
—International law codified in the 1958 Geneva Convention on the High Seas
—Instructions of the commanding officers of their respective ships to observe strictly the letter and spirit of these fundamental guidelines.

Use of Signals and Communications

"**Every State shall take such measures for ships under its flag as are necessary to ensure safety at sea with regard, inter alia, to: . . . the use of signals, the maintenance of communications and the prevention of collisions**" (Article 94 (3)(c) of the UN Convention on the Law of the Sea). [*This new proposal gives emphasis to radio and other electronic means of exchanging information that seem available and appropriate for use between the United States and China today. INCSEA contemplated visual signals and communications. The suggested requirement, described below in some detail, to make a voluntary announcement of impending arrival in the vicinity also sets a better tone—collegial and professional rather than adversarial or confrontational.*]

Conduct by Ships, Other Vessels [*patrol craft and other types of vessels not called ships could be involved*], and Aircraft

—Avoid ship collisions by adhering to Rules of the Road

—Announce any intended deviation from the rules (for example, electing to stop or turn away when in the position of a privileged crossing ship and normally obligated to maintain course and speed) and receive acknowledgment.

—Avoid aircraft collisions by adhering to ICAO (International Civil Aviation Organization) visual or instrument flight rules and take extraordinary precautions when operations require deviation from such practices—for example, by operating in "due regard" status when an aircraft is responsible over the high seas for separation from other aircraft.

—Do not interfere in the "formations" of the other party.

—Avoid maneuvers in areas of heavy sea traffic where international traffic schemes exist.

—Surveillance ships are to maintain a safe distance from the object of investigation so as to avoid "embarrassing or endangering the ships under surveillance" [*consider a minimum-distance rule, possibly 500 yards or meters, unless consent is given for a closer approach*].

—Use accepted international signals, **including bridge-to-bridge radio circuits when ships maneuver near one another; after initial contact, automated position reporting means may be used as available but intentions must be announced for maneuvering in the immediate vicinity, perhaps within 2,000 yards.**

—Do not simulate attacks by actions such as pointing guns, missile launchers, or torpedo tubes; locking on with fire-control radar; or launching objects toward or illuminating with powerful lights **or lasers** the bridges of the other party's ship **or the cockpits of aircraft.**

—Inform vessels when submarines are exercising near them.

—Require aircraft commanders, **in addition to complying with ICAO rules for collision avoidance,** to use the greatest caution and prudence in approaching aircraft and ships of the other party and to prohibit mounting simulated attacks against aircraft or ships, performing aerobatics over ships, or dropping hazardous objects near them.

—**Require the ship or aircraft arriving in the vicinity of the other party's ship, vessel, or aircraft to announce its arrival on bridge-to-bridge radio, a specified radio frequency (to be monitored when surveillance is likely or observed), or other advanced reporting.**

Notes

Note: Access to the Open Source Center (OSC), the U.S. government's foreign media translation service, is restricted to government employees and certain contractors. Access to its publicly available version, the World News Connection, is by subscription only. All OSC sources noted here are available through the author.

Chapter Two

1. See PRC president Jiang Zemin's speech at Waseda University when he visited Japan on a state visit in November 1998: "Take Warning from History and Usher in the Future," November 28, 1998, Xinhua [New China News Agency] (Open Source Center [hereafter OSC] FTS19981129000092).

2. See Meng Guoxiang and Yu Dewen, *Zhongguo Kangzhan sunshi yu zhanhou suopei shi mo* [Losses in China's War of Resistance and the Full Story of Postwar Reparations Efforts] (Hefei, China: Anhui renmin chubanshe, 1995), pp. 178, 181–82.

3. On the patriotic education campaign, see Suixheng Zhao, *A Nation-State by Construction: Dynamics of Modern Chinese Nationalism* (Stanford University Press, 2004), pp. 218–23. On the victimization narrative and its relative novelty, see Peter Hays Gries, *China's New Nationalism: Pride, Politics, and Diplomacy* (University of California Press, 2004), pp. 69–85. On one museum display, where an overseas Chinese visitor was heard telling his young son, "No, Son, Japanese people are not evil," see Mark Gordy, comment on "Patriotic Education," *Here, There, and Everywhere* (blog), August 15, 2005 (www.lawrence.com/blogs/here_there_and_everywhere/2005/aug/15/nanjing/).

4. For an extract from a high school text concerning the 1937 Nanjing Massacre, see Xu Zongmao, "Zhonggong zhengquan yu Kangri qingjie" [The Chinese Communist Regime and the Anti-Japan Complex], *Zhongguo Shibao* [China Times], September 20, 1995, cited in Chang Jui-te, "The Politics of Commemoration: A Comparative Analysis of the Fiftieth-Anniversary Commemoration in Mainland China and Taiwan of the Victory in the Anti-Japanese War," in *Scars of War: The Impact of Warfare on*

Modern China, edited by Diana Lary and Stephen MacKinnon (University of British Columbia Press, 2001), p. 152. Mo Yan, *Red Sorghum: A Novel of China* [Honggaoliang Jiazu]), translated by Howard Goldblatt (New York: Penguin Books, 1988). At page 37, Mo Yan describes an episode in which the local Japanese commander orders the village butcher to skin alive the narrator's uncle, who has killed a Japanese soldier.

5. "Foolish Old Man of the Peninsula," Strong Nation Forum, *Renmin Wang*, April, 10, 2005 (OSC CPP20050411000028).

6. See, for example, Li Rong, *Zhonghua Minzu Kangri Zhangzhengshi* [The History of the Chinese Nation's War of Resistance against Japan] (Beijing: Zhongyang wenxian chubanshe, 2005), pp. 7–15, 134–41; and Shih Ding, *Riben Guandongjun Qinhua Beiwushih* [The History of the Japanese Guandong Army's Crimes of Aggression against China] (Beijing: Shehui kexue wenxian chubanshe, 2005), pp. 123–32. Shih Ding notes an apparent policy conflict within the Japanese government over the invasion of Manchuria but then dismisses it.

7. In January 2010, the Japan-China Joint History Research Committee released a lengthy report, "Rizhong Lishi Gongtong Yanjiu Baogaoshu" [Report on Joint Research on Japan-China History (hereafter "Baogaoshu")], composed of scholarly essays on different episodes in the history of the relationship. The chapter on the Manchurian incident subtly distinguished between the Japanese government in Tokyo and the Guandong Army and implicitly suggested that the latter operated independently of the former, but it never makes that crucial point explicit. See Zang Yun'gu, "Cong Jiuyiba Shibian dau Lugouqiao Shibian" [From the September 18th Incident to the Marco Polo Bridge Incident], part 2, chapter 1, in "Baogaoshu," Japan-China Joint History Research Committee, Japan Ministry of Foreign Affairs (www.mofa.go.jp/mofaj/area/china/pdfs/rekishi_kk_c.pdf), pp. 171–72. The essay on the beginning of the conflict admits that the Marco Polo Bridge incident of July 1937 "could have an accidental nature" but concludes that given the events that followed, it also had an "inevitable character." See Rong Weimu, "Riben di Chuanmian Qinhua Zhanzheng yu Zhongguo di Quanmian Kangri Zhanzheng"[Japan's Full-Scale War of Aggression against China and China's Full-Scale War of Resistance against Japan), part 2, chapter 1, in "Baogaoshu," p. 188.

8. The most impressive examples of that scholarship are found in the volumes in the *Taiheiyo senso e no michi: kaisen gaiko shi* series, translated into English under the title *Japan's Road to the Pacific War*, edited by James W. Morley, 5 vols. (New York: Columbia University Press, 1980–94). For other scholarly accounts, see Sadako N. Ogata, *Defiance in Manchuria: The Making of Japanese Foreign Policy, 1931–1932* (University of California Press, 1964); Michael A. Barnhart, *Japan Prepares for Total War: The Search for Economic Security, 1919–1941* (Cornell University Press, 1987); James B. Crowley, *Japan's Quest for Autonomy* (Princeton University Press, 1966); James W. Morley, *The China Quagmire* (Columbia University Press, 1966).

9. Tamogami Toshio, "Was Japan an Aggressor Nation?" posted on the website of APA Group, the sponsor of the essay contest (www.apa.co.jp/book_report/images/2008jyusyou_saiyuusyu_english.pdf). For another example of revisionist

history, see Higashinakano Shudo, *The Nanking Massacre: Fact versus Fiction. A Historian's Quest for the Truth* (Tokyo: Sekai Shuppan, 2005).

10. See Crowley, *Japan's Quest for Autonomy*, and Barnhart, *Japan Prepares for Total War*, for the events of this period based on Japanese sources; for the Chinese side, see Marjorie Dryburgh, *North China and Japanese Expansion, 1933–1937: Regional Power and the National Interest* (Richmond, Surrey: Curzon Press, 2000).

11. On the strategic importance of the Lugouqiao junction, through which ran all railroads from the south to Beijing, see Parks M. Coble, *Facing Japan: Chinese Politics and Japanese Imperialism, 1931–1937* (Harvard Council on East Asian Studies, 1991), p. 374.

12. See Dryburgh, *North China and Japanese Expansion*, pp. 147–63; Barnhart, *Japan Prepares for Total War*, pp. 77–90.

13. See Coble, *Facing Japan*, pp. 373–74.

14. This account is based primarily on Hsi-sheng Chi, *Nationalist China at War: Military Defeats and Political Collapse: 1937–45* (University of Michigan Press, 1982), pp. 40–51; Jay Taylor, *The Generalissimo: Chiang Kai-shek and the Struggle for Modern China* (Belknap Harvard Press, 2009), pp. 146–58; and F. F. Liu, *A Military History of Modern China: 1924–1949* (Princeton University Press, 1956), pp. 103–104. The late Lloyd Eastman, the dean of scholarship on Nationalist China, shares the view that Chiang launched a preemptive attack: see Lloyd Eastman, "Nationalist China during the Sino-Japanese War," in *Cambridge History of China*, vol. 13, *Republican China 1912–1949*, part 2, edited by John K. Fairbank and Albert Feuerwerker (Cambridge University Press, 1986), pp. 547–55.

15. Chi, *Nationalist China at War*, p. 42.

16. William C. Kirby, *Germany and Republican China* (Stanford University Press, 1984), p. 222.

17. Chi, *Nationalist China at War*, p. 42.

18. Some historians have argued that Chiang struck at Shanghai not to drive the Japanese from the Yangzi area but to secure foreign support. Chi rejects that hypothesis on the grounds that Chiang committed significant assets over a long period to the fight and that recent history had given him no reason to think that the Western powers would intervene militarily on China's behalf. See Chi, *Nationalist China at War*, pp. 43–45.

19. Japan made its own preemption miscalculation. In the latter part of 1941, as the noose of U.S. sanctions tightened, Tokyo sought relief by taking British and Dutch colonies in Southeast Asia to acquire their natural resources. Pearl Harbor was simply a flanking action for that southward advance. Tokyo did not appreciate how isolationist public opinion in the United States constrained Franklin Roosevelt. Tokyo assumed incorrectly that if it invaded Malaya and Indonesia, Washington would declare war, so it attempted to delay and disable the anticipated U.S. response by attacking Pearl Harbor. However, if it had eschewed Pearly Harbor, the United States might well have remained neutral. See Jeffrey Record, "Japan's Decision for War in 1941: Some Enduring Lessons," Strategic Studies Institute, U.S. Army War College, February 2009 (www.strategicstudiesinstitute.army.mil/pubs/display.cfm?pubID=905).

20. Kirby, *Germany and Republican China*, p. 222.

Chapter Three

1. For a brief but useful summary of the postwar history of China-Japan relations, see Christopher W. Hughes, "Japan's Response to China's Rise: Regional Engagement, Global Containment, Dangers of Collision," *International Affairs* 85 (July 2009), pp. 839–43.

2. On Japan's pragmatic bargain with the United States, see Kenneth B. Pyle, *Japan Rising: The Resurgence of Japanese Power and Purpose* (New York: Public Affairs, 2007), pp. 225–77; and Richard J. Samuels, *Securing Japan: Tokyo's Grand Strategy and the Future of East Asia* (Cornell University Press, 2007), pp. 34–59.

3. See Chae-jin Lee, *China Faces Japan: Political and Economic Relations in the Postwar Era* (Johns Hopkins University Press, 1976).

4. Consistent with the principles of the communiqué, Japan pledged that any continuing relations with Taiwan would be on an unofficial basis.

5. Lee, *China Faces Japan*, pp. 210–12.

6. Soeya Yoshihide, "Japan's Relations with China," in *The Golden Age of the U.S.-China-Japan Triangle, 1972–1989*, edited by Ezra F. Vogel, Yuan Ming, and Tanaka Akihiko (Harvard University Asia Center and Harvard University Press, 2002), pp. 210–25.

7. Ming Wan, *Sino-Japanese Relations: Interaction, Logic, and Transformation* (Woodrow Wilson Center Press and Stanford University Press, 2006), pp. 21–22.

8. Wan, *Sino-Japanese Relations*, pp. 22–24.

9. The clearest discussion of the "management" approach to China-Japan relations is in Quansheng Zhao, *Japanese Policymaking: The Politics behind Politics: Informal Mechanisms and the Making of China Policy* (Oxford University Press, 1993), which has a number of useful case studies. For another detailed discussion of the episodes in the 1980s, see Allen S. Whiting, *China Sees Japan* (University of California Press, 1989). On the economic issues, see Chae-jin Lee, *China and Japan: New Economic Diplomacy* (Hoover Institution Press, 1984).

10. Kokubun Ryosei, "Can the Gap between Japan and China Be Bridged? Toward Rebuilding Japan-China Relations in the New Era," *Gaiko Forum*, July 1, 2005, pp. 10–21 (Open Source Center [hereafter OSC] JPP20050822000033).

11. Ming Wan, *Sino-Japanese Relations*, p. 44. Wan's assessment raises the question of whether one side or both have an interest in keeping old wounds open.

12. International Monetary Fund, *Direction of Trade Statistics* (Washington: 1997, 2002, 2006, 2009).

13. Japan Economic and Trade Organization, "Japan's Outward and Inward Foreign Direct Investment by Country and Region" (www.jetro.go.jp/en/stats/statistics/).

14. "China Eclipses U.S. as Japan's Biggest Customer," *Telegraph*, August 21, 2008 (www.telegraph.co.uk/money/main.jhtml?view=DETAILS&grid=8xml=/money/2008/08/21/bcnjapan121.xml).

15. "Chinese Largest Foreign Group in Japan," *Daily Yomiuri*, June 3, 2008 (OSC JPP20080604036003). The Japanese reaction to Chinese laborers is not necessarily

positive, especially in rural areas; see Norimitsu Onishi, "As Its Work Force Ages, Japan Needs and Fears Chinese Labor," *New York Times*, August 14, 2008.

16. Koji Watanabe, "Japan-U.S.-China Relations in Asia," speech given June 3, 2009, in Kuala Lumpur (on file with the author).

17. Ming Wan makes the intriguing observation that before 1990 there was little specialized writing in either country on security or military issues. See Ming Wan, *Sino-Japanese Relations*, pp. 33–34.

18. The following summary is based on Ming Wan, *Sino-Japanese Relations*, pp. 34–43; and Michael J. Green, *Japan's Reluctant Realism: Foreign Policy Challenges in an Era of Uncertain Power* (New York: Palgrave, 2001), pp. 77–109.

19. Wan, *Sino-Japanese Relations*, pp. 262–86.

20. Green, *Japan's Reluctant Realism*, p. 82. Ming Wan notes that the Japanese may have miscalculated in thinking that aid provided effective leverage in the first place; see Ming Wan, *Sino-Japanese Relations*, p. 286.

21. These efforts are recounted in Wan, *Sino-Japanese Relations*, pp. 37–39.

22. Gilbert Rozman, *Northeast Asia's Stunted Regionalism: Bilateral Distrust in the Shadow of Globalization* (Cambridge University Press, 2004).

23. "China's Jiang Instructed Diplomats to Push History Issue with Japan," Kyodo World Service in English, August 10, 2006 (OSC JPP20060810969046).

24. Green, *Japan's Reluctant Realism*, p. 97.

25. Ibid., p. 82.

26. He Xiaosong, "Why Koizumi Runs Counter to Public Will," *Renmin Ribao* [People's Daily], July 28, 2006 (OSC CPP20060728701007). He Xiaosong is an assistant research fellow with the Institute of Japanese Studies, Chinese Academy of Social Sciences.

27. Ma Licheng, "New Thoughts for China-Japan Relations—Worrisome Problems among Chinese and Japanese People," *Zhanlue yu Guanli*, December 1, 2002, pp. 41–47 (OSC CPP20021224000140); Shi Yinhong, "Sino-Japanese Rapprochement and 'Diplomatic Revolution,'" *Zhanlue yu Guanli*, March 1, 2003, pp. 71–75 (OSC CPP20030506000224).

28. For an excellent discussion of the "new thinking" episode, see Peter Hays Gries, "China's 'New Thinking' on Japan," *China Quarterly* 184 (December 2005), pp. 831–50; cited passage is on p. 832.

29. Reinhard Drifte, "Territorial Conflicts in the East China Sea: From Missed Opportunities to Negotiation Stalemate," *Asia Pacific Journal: Japan Focus*, essay 3156, June 2009 (www.japanfocus.org/-Reinhard-Drifte/3156).

30. PRC State Council Information Office, "China's National Defense in 2004," December 27, 2004 (www.fas.org/nuke/guide/china/doctrine/natdef2004.html).

31. The Council on Security and Defense Capabilities, "The Council on Security and Defense Capabilities Report: Japan's Visions for Future Security and Defense Capabilities," October 2004 (www.globalsecurity.org/wmd/library/news/japan/2004/041000-csdc-report.pdf).

32. "National Defense Program Guidelines, FY 2005–09," approved by the Security Council and the Cabinet on December 10, 2004 (www.mod.go.jp/e/d_policy/pdf/national_guideline.pdf), p. 3.

33. Kent E. Calder, "China and Japan's Simmering Rivalry," *Foreign Affairs* 85 (March-April 2006), p. 5.

34. Yutaka Kawashima, *Japanese Foreign Policy at the Crossroads: Challenges and Options for the Twenty-First Century* (Brookings, 2003).

35. "Minshutō seisakushū Index 2009" [Policy Index of the Democratic Party 2009], June 2009 (www.dpj.or.jp/policy/manifesto/seisaku2009/img/INDEX2009.pdf); Brad Glosserman, "Back to Earth with the DPJ," *PacNet,* no. 60, Pacific Forum CSIS, September 10, 2009 (csis.org/files/publication/pac0960.pdf).

Chapter Four

1. Economic interdependence today does not guarantee mutual benefit tomorrow. Claes G. Alvstam, Patrik Ström, and Naoyuki Yoshino explore negative future scenarios in "On the Economic Interdependence between China and Japan: Challenges and Possibilities," *Asia Pacific Viewpoint* 50 (August 2009), pp. 198–214.

2. Norimitsu Onishi, "As Its Work Force Ages, Japan Needs and Fears Chinese Labor, *New York Times,* August 14, 2008.

3. Huang Fuhui, "Chinese Ambassador to Japan Cui Tiankai Comments on Promoting Good-Neighborliness and Friendliness, Building a Harmonious Peripheral Environment," Xinhua, July 27, 2009 (Open Source Center [hereafter OSC] CPP20090727172008); Zhang Tuosheng, "Sino-Japanese Relations at New Starting Point in History," *Waijiao Pinglun,* December 25, 2008 (OSC CPP20090202671005); "Forging the Future Together," speech by Prime Minister Fukuda Yasuo at Peking University, December 28, 2007, Japan Ministry of Foreign Affairs (www.mofa.go.jp/region/asia-paci/china/pmv0712/); Tanaka Hitoshi, "A Japanese Perspective on the China Questions," *East Asia Insights* 3 (May 2008), pp. 1–5.

4. Michael J. Green, "Understanding Japan's Relations in Northeast Asia," testimony before the House Committee on International Relations, *Japan's Tense Relations with Her Neighbors: Back to the Future,* September 14, 2006 (http://csis.org/files/media/csis/congress/ts060914green.pdf).

5. Christopher W. Hughes, "Japan's Response to China's Rise: Regional Engagement, Global Containment, Dangers of Collision," *International Affairs* 85 (July 2009), p. 838.

6. For example, see Ming Wan, *Sino-Japanese Relations: Interaction, Logic, and Transformation* (Woodrow Wilson Center Press and Stanford University Press, 2006); Michael J. Green, *Japan's Reluctant Realism: Foreign Policy Challenges in an Era of Uncertain Power* (New York: Palgrave, 2001), especially p. 93; Kenneth B. Pyle, *Japan Rising: The Resurgence of Japanese Power and Purpose* (New York: Public Affairs, 2007); Richard J. Samuels, *Securing Japan: Tokyo's Grand Strategy and the Future of East Asia* (Cornell University Press, 2007); Thomas J. Christensen, "China, the U.S.-

Japanese Alliance, and the Security Dilemma in East Asia," *International Security* 23 (Spring 1999), pp. 49–80; Kent Calder, "China and Japan's Simmering Rivalry," *Foreign Affairs* 85 (March-April 2006), especially p. 2; Denny Roy, "The Sources and Limits of Sino-Japanese Tensions," *Survival* 47 (Summer 2005), pp. 191–214; Mike M. Mochizuki, "Japan's Shifting Strategy toward the Rise of China," *Journal of Strategic Studies* 30 (August-October 2007), pp. 739–76; and Susan L. Shirk, *China: Fragile Superpower* (New York: Oxford University Press, 2007).

7. John H. Herz, "Idealist Internationalism and the Security Dilemma," *World Politics* 2 (January 1950), pp. 157–80; Robert Jervis, "Cooperation under the Security Dilemma," *World Politics* 30 (January 1978), pp. 186–214; Ken Booth and Nicholas J. Wheeler, *The Security Dilemma: Fear, Cooperation, and Trust in World Politics* (New York: Palgrave Macmillan, 2008).

8. See Richard C. Bush, "China-Japan Tensions, 1995–2006: Why They Happened, What to Do," Foreign Policy Paper Series 16, Brookings, June 2009 (www.brookings.edu/papers/2009/06_china_japan_bush.aspx).

9. Based on Robert Jervis, "Was the Cold War a Security Dilemma?" *Journal of Cold War Studies* 3 (Winter 2001), p. 36.

10. For more details, see Bush, "China-Japan Tensions," pp. 5–8.

11. "China's National Defense in 2006," issued by the Information Office of the State Council, December 29, 2006, Xinhua (OSC CPP20061229968070); [Japan] Defense Agency, *2004 Defense of Japan* (Tokyo: Inter Group, 2004).

12. Christopher W. Hughes, "Japan's Military Modernization: A Quiet Japan-China Arms Race and Global Power Projection," *Asia-Pacific Review* 16 (May 2009), pp. 120–21; "Japan's Defense Budget to Fall for 6th Straight Year," Kyodo World Service, December 20, 2007 (OSC JPP20071220969008).

13. Roy, "The Sources and Limits of Sino-Japanese Tensions," p. 209.

14. For an example of a focus on legal and policy prohibitions and their relaxation, see Jin Xide, "Riben Anquan Zhanlue Mianlin Shizilukou" [Japan's Security Strategy Faces a Crossroads], *Guoji Zhanlue Yanjiu* 65 (July 2002), pp. 18–25.

15. Evan S. Medeiros and others, *Pacific Currents: The Responses of U.S. Allies and Security Partners in East Asia to China's Rise* (Santa Monica, Calif.: RAND Corporation, 2008), p. 242; Hughes, "Japanese Military Modernization," p. 96. On the no-arms-race side of the debate, see also Richard C. Smith, "Military Change in Asia," *Asia-Pacific Review* 16 (May 2009), pp. 73–83.

16. In the International Relations vocabulary, building one's military capabilities to respond to a threat is termed "internal balancing;" responding by strengthening alliances is "external balancing."

17. Wang Te-chun, "Strengthening of U.S.-Japanese Alliance Explicitly Aimed at China," *Ta Kung Pao*, February 2005 (OSC CPP20050219000027).

18. See, for example, David Shambaugh, "China's Military Modernization: Making Steady but Surprising Progress," in *Strategic Asia 2005–06: Military Modernization in an Era of Uncertainty*, edited by Ashley J. Tellis and Michael Wills (Seattle, Wash.: National Bureau of Asian Research, 2005), pp. 67–103, especially pp. 94–101.

19. Christopher W. Hughes, "Japanese Military Modernization: In Search of a 'Normal' Security Role," in *Strategic Asia 2005–06: Military Modernization in an Era of Uncertainty*, edited by Tellis and Wills, pp. 112, 114.

20. On this more constructivist approach, see Alexander Wendt, "Anarchy Is What States Make of It: Social Construction of Power Politics," *International Organizations* 46 (Spring 1992), pp. 396–99; and Michael Alan Brittingham, "The 'Role' of Nationalism in Chinese Foreign Policy: A Reactive Model of Nationalism and Conflict," *Journal of Chinese Political Science* 2 (2007), pp. 147–66. For an application of this approach to foreign policy conflicts, see Alastair Iain Johnston, "Beijing's Security Behavior in the Asia-Pacific: Is China a Dissatisfied Power?" in *Rethinking Security in East Asia: Identity, Power, and Efficiency*, edited by J. J. Suh, Peter J. Katzenstein, and Allen Carlson (Stanford University Press, 2004), pp. 34–96.

21. Dai Xu, "Donghai Zhengduan shi Riben Qinlue Yichan" [The East Sea Dispute Is the Legacy of Japan's Aggression], *Huanqiu Shibao*, January 14, 2009, p. 11.

22. International Crisis Group, "North East Asia's Undercurrents of Conflict," *Asia Report* 108 (December 15, 2005), p. 19.

23. Okamoto Yukio and Tanaka Akihiko, "Can the World Exist with China?" *Japan Echo* 35 (October 2008), p. 53; this statement of Japan's frustration is provided by Tanaka. For a good analysis of how history has been an issue in China-Japan relations, see He Yinan, "National Mythmaking and the Problems of History in Sino-Japanese Relations," in *Japan's Relations with China: Facing a Rising Power*, edited by Lam Peng Er (New York: Routledge, 2007), pp. 69–91.

24. Jiang Zemin, "Take Warning from History and Usher in the Future," speech at Waseda University, November 28, 1998, Xinhua (OSC FTS19981129000092).

25. Green, "Understanding Japan's Relations in Northeast Asia."

26. On the need for an enemy, see Yu Jie, "The Anti-Japanese Resistance War, Chinese Patriotism, and Free Speech. How Can We Forgive Japan?" July 16, 2007 (www.japanfocus.org/-Yu-Jie/2654). I interviewed the retired officer in January 2008.

27. Feng Zhaokui, "Koizumi Goes Backward on Historical Issue, but Acts with Premature Haste in Bid for a Permanent Seat on UN Security Council," *Shijie Zhishi*, May 16, 2005 (OSC CPP20050606000191).

28. "Commentary: Correct Handling of History Important to China-Japan Ties," Xinhua, April 30, 2005 (OSC CPP20050430000078); Feng, "Koizumi Goes Backward on Historical Issue."

29. Shi Yinhong, "The Immediate and Remote Causes of Deterioration in Sino-Japanese Relations," *Ming Pao*, April 21, 2005 (OSC CPP20050421000089).

30. For these themes, see selected articles by Jin Xide during 2004 and 2005: "Japan's Motives in Proposing Scenarios in Which China Might Attack Taiwan Are Extremely Insidious," *Zhongguo Tongxun She*, November 9, 2004 (OSC CPP20041109000147); "Does Koizumi's New Cabinet Have Any New Policies toward China?" *Shijie Zhishi*, November 1, 2004, pp. 32-33 (OSC CPP20041110000199); "Beijing Scholar Says Sino-Japanese Exchange Visits Are to Be Far Away," *Hsiang Gang Shang Pao*,

November 23, 2004, p. A2 (OSC CPP20041123000106); and "Shrine Visit Leads to Cold Ties," *China Daily*, February 3, 2005 (OSC CPP20050203000016). See also Wang Te-chun, "Strengthening of U.S.-Japan Alliance Explicitly Aimed at China," *Ta Kung Pao*, February 19, 2005 (OSC CPP20050219000027).

31. Matthew Penney and Bryce Wakefield, "Right Angles: Examining Accounts of Japanese Neo-Nationalism," *Pacific Affairs* 81 (Winter 2008), p. 551.

32. Tamogami Toshio, "Was Japan an Aggressor Nation?" APA Group, October 2008 (www.apa.co.jp/book_report/images/2008jyusyou_saiyuusyu_english.pdf).

33. Kiichi Fujiwara, "Remembering the War, Japanese Style," *Far Eastern Economic Review*, December 2005, pp. 51–56.

34. For the civilian/middle power viewpoint, see Yoshihide Soeya, "Japan's 'Middle Power' Strategy and the U.S.-Japan Alliance," in *Asia Eyes America: Regional Perspectives on U.S. Asia-Pacific Strategy in the Twenty-First Century*, edited by Jonathan D. Pollack (Newport, R.I.: Naval War College Press, 2007), pp. 135–38. Yoichi Funabashi, "Japan and the New World Order," *Foreign Affairs* 70 (Winter 1991-92), pp. 58–74. This perspective is a post–cold war extrapolation of the Yoshida Doctrine, on which see Pyle, *Japan Rising*, pp. 225–77; Samuels, *Securing Japan*, pp. 34–59.

35. Euan Graham, *Japan's Sea Lane Security, 1940–2004: A Matter of Life and Death?* (New York: Routledge, 2006), p. 108.

36. "Japan's Rivalry with China Is Stirring a Crowded Sea," *New York Times*, September 11, 2005.

37. For example, see Okamoto and Tanaka, "Can the World Exist with China?"

38. James J. Przystup, "Japan-China Relations: Trouble Starts with 'T'," *Comparative Connections* 2 (July 2001), pp. 96–99 (www.csis.org/media/csis/pubs/0102q.pdf); James J. Przystup, "Japan-China Relations: A Volatile Mix: Natural Gas, a Submarine, a Shrine, and a Visa," *Comparative Connections* 6 (January 2005), pp. 128–29 (www.csis.org/media/csis/pubs/0404q.pdf).

39. Brian Bridges and Che-po Chan, "Looking North: Taiwan's Relations with Japan under Chen Shui-bian," *Pacific Affairs* 81 (Winter 2008), pp. 577–96.

40. Conservative Japanese scholars emphasized that the PLA's buildup was creating tensions in East Asia and changing the regional balance of power. They believed that Japan's response to China's rise had been too passive and that Japan needed to demonstrate greater firmness. See remarks of Morimoto Satoshi in Hanzawa Naohisa and others, "U.S. Military Reform, Transformation," *Sankei Shimbun*, May 3, 2005 (OSC JPP20050505000009); Kayahara Ikuo, "Military Aims of China's Ocean Foray—Objective Not Just Resources," *Chuo Koron*, October 1, 2004 (OSC JPP20040917000002); Nakajima Mineo, "Easy Compromise Will Have Contrary Effect on China Relations," *Sankei Shimbun*, December 30, 2004 (OSC JPP20050104000049); and remarks by Morimoto Satoshi in "Japan's New National Defense Program Outline Turns a Blind Eye to Threats Posed by the Chinese Military," *Shokun*, January 1, 2004, pp. 42–54 (OSC JPP20041216000008).

41. Przystup, "Japan-China Relations: A Volatile Mix," p. 127; "National Defense Program Outline for FY 2005 and After," adopted by the Security Council and the Cabinet, December 10, 2004, p. 3 (www.mod.go.jp/e/d_policy/pdf/national_guideline.pdf).

42. Przystup, "Japan-China Relations: A Volatile Mix," pp. 128–29.

43. On maritime encroachment, see "Threat of 'Marine Strategy' China Is Steadily Pushing against Backdrop of 'Anti-Japanese Uproar,'" *Yomiuri Weekly,* May 1, 2005, pp. 21–24 (OSC JPP20050421000021); and Kayahara Ikuo, "Military Aims of China's Ocean Foray," pp. 62–69. On the strategic value of Taiwan, see "Threat of 'Marine Strategy'"; "Japan's New National Defense Program Outline"; and Nakajima Mineo, "Illusion of an Immense China," *Seiron,* March 1, 2004, pp. 306–18 (OSC JPP20040225000013).

44. Ibid.

45. "Japan's Rivalry with China Is Stirring a Crowded Sea," *New York Times,* September 11, 2005.

46. The phases are explained in "Defense of Japan 2006," Japan Ministry of Defense, pp. 221–23 (www.mod.go.jp/e/publ/w_paper/pdf/2006/4-2-1.pdf).

47. Yu Shan, "The United States and Japan Should Not Add to the Taiwan Strait Turmoil," *Renmin Ribao,* February 21, 2005, p. 3 (OSC CPP20040221000049).

48. "Text of PRC Premier Wen Jiabao's News Conference after NPC Closing," March 14, 2005, *CCTV-1* (OSC CPP20050314000075).

49. "Statement by the Press Secretary/Director-General for Press and Public Relations, Ministry of Foreign Affairs, on the Anti-Secession Law," Ministry of Foreign Affairs, March 14, 2005 (OSC JPP20050315000105).

50. "Foreign Minister Machimura Expresses Concern on EU's Lifting of Arms Embargo on China," *Tokyo Shimbun,* February 9, 2005 (OSC JPP20050210000005).

51. Ministry of Foreign Affairs, *Diplomatic Blue Book 2006,* April 2005, p. 9 (www.mofa.go.jp/policy/other/bluebook/2006/02.pdf).

52. China Institutes of Contemporary International Relations, *Guoji Zhanlue yu Anquan Xingshi Pingku: 2005/2006* [Strategic and Security Review: 2005/2006] (Beijing: Shishi chubanshe, 2006), p. 144.

53. Takagi Seiichiro observes that China would react "more fiercely" to Japan's involvement in a war over Taiwan because of Taiwan's place in China's larger twentieth-century narrative; see "The Taiwan Factor in Japan-China relations," in *Japan's Relations with China,* edited by Er, p. 124.

54. See Daniel Kliman, "China: Japan's Rising Power Conundrum," *Japan Chair Platform,* Center for Strategic and International Studies, August 14, 2009 (http://csis.org/files/publication/090814_platform.pdf).

55. Shinichi Kitaoka, "Decisions or Crisis of Japan: It Cannot Be Immature Forever," *Chuo Koron,* January 2010, pp. 82–91 (OSC JPP20091210033002).

56. "Where Is Hatoyama Administration Heading?" panel discussion among Yoichi Kato, Ryosei Kokubun, Tsuneo Watanabe, *Gaiko Forum,* February 2010, pp. 50–59 (OSC JPP20100118176001).

57. Brad Glosserman, "Back to Earth with the DPJ," *PacNet* 60, Pacific Forum CSIS, September 10, 2009 (http://csis.org/files/publication/pac0960.pdf).

58. "Yang Bojiang, Director of the Institute for Japanese Studies at the China Institute of Contemporary International Relations, Views Sino-Japanese Relations after Democratic Party Takes Office," *Henan Bao Online,* September 4, 2009 (OSC CPP20090911624001). See also Yang Bojiang, "The Hatoyama Regime's China Policy May Shift to a Hard Line," *Guoji Xianqu Dabao Online,* March 1, 2010 (OSC CPP20100310671005).

59. "Asahi: Japan Gets Jitters on China Navy," *Asahi Shimbun,* April 15, 2010 (OSC JPP20100415969008).

Chapter Five

1. Euan Graham, *Japan's Sea Lane Security, 1940–2004: A Matter of Life and Death?* (New York: Routledge, 2006), pp. 123–47.

2. Ibid., p. 143, citing an article from *Far Eastern Economic Review,* February 3, 1983.

3. Graham, *Japan's Sea Lane Security,* pp. 145–56.

4. Yuki Tatsumi, *Japan's National Security Policy Infrastructure: Can Tokyo Meet Washington's Expectation?* (Washington: Henry L. Stimson Center, 2008), p. 78.

5. Bernard D. Cole, *Sea Lanes and Pipelines: Energy Security in Asia* (Westport, Conn.: Praeger Security International, 2008), p. 133.

6. Based on Cole, *Sea Lanes and Pipelines,* pp. 134–35. Richard J. Samuels, "'New Fighting Power!': Japan's Growing Maritime Capabilities and East Asian Security," *International Security* 32 (Winter 2007), pp. 84–112.

7. Takei Tomohisa, "Japan Maritime Self-Defense Force in the New Maritime," manuscript on file with the author, November 2008, pp. 3, 7.

8. *Defense of Japan 2008,* Ministry of Defense, September 2008, pp. 204, 200 (www.mod.go.jp/e/publ/w_paper/pdf/2008/29Part3_Chapter1_Sec3.pdf).

9. Ibid., pp. 181, 201.

10. Ibid., p. 181.

11. Ibid., pp. 200–01.

12. The navy participates in search-and-rescue operations in Japanese territorial waters. For a summary of the MSDF's main missions, see Tatsumi, *Japan's National Security Policy Infrastructure,* pp. 76–78.

13. Katsuyama Hiraku, "Operational Concept of JMSDF's Aegis Ships," *Sekai no Kansen,* August 1, 2007 (Open Source Center [hereafter OSC] JPP20070717465006); emphasis added.

14. Alessio Patelano, "Shielding the 'Hot Gates': Submarine Warfare and Japanese Naval Strategy in the Cold War and Beyond (1976–2006)," *Journal of Strategic Studies* 31 (December 2008), pp. 859–95; quoted passages are on pp. 879, 886 (citing Ministry of Defense, *Defense of Japan 2007*).

15. Cole, *Sea Lanes and Pipelines,* pp. 136–37.

16. Tatsumi, *Japan's National Security Policy Infrastructure,* pp. 84–86; Samuels, "'New Fighting Power!'" p. 84.

17. Samuels, "'New Fighting Power!'" pp. 85, 99–102; quoted phrase is on p. 102.

18. Ibid., p. 96. Samuels reports on p. 97 that in its publicity materials the JCG trumpets its new "fighting power." The Japanese term used for "fighting power"— *senryoku*—is the same as the one used in article 9 of the constitution for the "war potential" that Japan is never to maintain.

19. Christopher W. Hughes, *Japan's Remilitarisation,* Adelphi Series 403 (Oxon, U.K.: Routledge/International Institute for Strategic Studies, 2009), p. 42.

20. For the capabilities of the F-15s, see "F-15 Eagle," Federation of American Scientists (www.fas.org/programs/ssp/man/uswpns/air/fighter/f15.html#f15j).

21. David A. Fulghum, "Face-to-Face with Japanese Air Force Lt. Gen. Hidetoshi Hirata," *Aviation Week and Space Technology,* July 27, 2009, p. 48.

22. Tatsumi, *Japan's National Security Policy Infrastructure,* p. 67.

23. See "Japanese Air-Defence Identification Zone," Sun Bin Blog, May 2005 (http://sun-bin.blogspot.com/2006/05/japanese-air-defence-identification.html).

24. *Defense of Japan 2008* (www.mod.go.jp/e/publ/w_paper/pdf/2008/28Part3_Chapter1_Sec2.pdf).

25. Tatsumi, *Japan's National Security Policy Infrastructure,* p. 69.

26. China Institutes of Contemporary International Relations, *Guoji Zhanlue yu Anquan Xingshi Pingku: 2005/2006* [Strategic and Security Review: 2005/2006] (Beijing: Shishi chubanshe, 2006), p. 136; Richard J. Samuels, *Securing Japan: Tokyo's Grand Strategy and the Future of East Asia* (Cornell University Press, 2007), p. 168.

27. Tatsumi, *Japan's National Security Policy Infrastructure,* p. 67.

28. See Tatsumi, *Japan's National Security Policy Infrastructure,* p. 70; Hughes, *Japan's Remilitarisation,* pp. 42–45.

29. Note that it was the expansion of Soviet air and naval power in Asia that turned the Japan MSDF into a serious navy and the fall of the Soviet Union that led to PLAN's transformation from a coastal defense force.

30. See David M. Finkelstein, "China's National Military Strategy: An Overview of the 'Military Strategic Guidelines,'" in *Right-Sizing the People's Liberation Army: Exploring the Contours of China's Military,* edited by Roy Kamphausen and Andrew Scobell (Carlisle, Pa.: Strategic Studies Institute, U.S. Army War College, 2007), pp. 69–140, especially pp. 95–132.

31. On the Chinese submarine force in general, see William S. Murray, "An Overview of the PLAN Submarine Force," in *China's Future Nuclear Submarine Force,* edited by Andrew S. Erickson and others (Annapolis, Md.: Naval Institute Press, 2007), pp. 59–75. On the vulnerability of U.S. ships to quiet Kilo class submarines, see Peter Howarth, *China's Rising Sea Power: The PLA Navy's Submarine Challenge* (New York: Routledge, 2006), p. 100.

32. Bernard D. Cole, "Right-Sizing the Navy: How Much Naval Force Will Beijing Deploy?" in *Right-Sizing the People's Liberation Army: Exploring the Contours of China's Military*, edited by Kamphausen and Scobell, pp. 526–55; Eric A. McVadon, "Recent Trends in China's Military Modernization," testimony before the U.S.-China Economic and Security Review Commission, September 15, 2005 (www.uscc. gov/hearings/2005hearings/written_testimonies/05_09_15wrts/mcvadon.pdf); Cole, *Sea Lanes and Pipelines*, pp. 139–140; direct quote is on p. 140.

33. Office of Naval Intelligence (hereafter ONI), *China's Navy 2007* (Washington, 2007), pp. 1, 7; Bernard D. Cole, "The Organization of the People's Liberation Army Navy (PLAN)," in *The People's Liberation Army as Organization: Reference Volume v1.0*, edited by James C. Mulvenon and Andrew N. D. Yang (Santa Monica, Calif.: RAND Corporation, 2002), pp. 491–92.

34. ONI, *China's Navy 2007*, p. 1.

35. From the PRC 2006 Defense White Paper, cited in ONI, *China's Navy 2007*, p. iii.

36. "Hu Jintao Emphasizes When Meeting Deputies to 10th Navy CPC Congress, 'Follow the Principle of Integrating Revolutionization, Modernization, and Regularization, and Forge a Powerful People's Navy That Meets the Demands of Our Army's Historic Mission'; Guo Boxiong, Cao Gangchuan, and Xu Caihou Attend," Xinhua, December 27, 2006 (OSC CPP20061227004003).

37. Wu Shengli and Hu Yanli, "Building a Powerful People's Navy That Meets the Requirements of the Historical Mission for Our Army," *Qiushi*, July 2007 (OSC CPP20070716710027); emphasis added. Apparently there are differences of views within the PLAN on how much strategic depth China needs. Some reportedly emphasize the area within the first island chain. Others advocate a "far sea defense" that can go beyond that boundary. See Office of Secretary of Defense (hereafter OSD), "Annual Report to Congress: Military Power of the People's Republic of China 2009" (hereafter "Military Power of the People's Republic of China 2009"), March 2009 (www.defenselink.mil/pubs/pdfs/China_Military_Power_Report_2009. pdf), pp. 17–18.

38. Ma Haoliang, "China Needs to Break through the Encirclement of First Island Chain; Nansha Cannot Afford to be 'Harassed,'" *Ta Kung pao Online*, February 21, 2009 (OSC CPP20090221708020).

39. Michael McDevitt, "The Strategic and Operational Context Driving PLA Navy Building," in *Right-Sizing the People's Liberation Army: Exploring the Contours of China's Military*, edited by Kamphausen and Scobell, pp. 481–522; cited passage is on p. 490. On the anti-access/area-denial focus, see Roger Cliff and others, *Entering the Dragon's Lair: Chinese Antiaccess Strategies and Their Implications for the United States* (Santa Monica, Calif..: RAND Corporation, 2007).

40. Paul H. B. Godwin, "China's Emerging Military Doctrine: A Role for Nuclear Submarines?" in *China's Future Nuclear Submarine Force*, edited by Erickson and

others, p. 49; Nan Li, "The Evolution of China's Naval Strategy and Capabilities: From 'Near Coast' and 'Near Seas' to 'Far Seas,'" *Asian Security* 5 (May 2009), pp. 144–69.

41. OSD, "Military Power of the People's Republic of China 2009," p. 28. For a speculative exercise about the consequences of growth of the PLAN to support an anti-access strategy, see James Kraska, "How the United States Lost the Naval War in 2015," *Orbis* 54 (Winter 2010), pp. 35–45.

42. ONI, *China's Navy 2007*, p. 96. The scale can run from tactical to strategic; exercises may include an opposition force or not; they may have live maneuvers and live fire or not; they may occur indoors, in port, or at sea; the objective may be inspection, trials, or demonstration.

43. ONI, *China's Navy 2007*, pp. 96–98.

44. Ibid., p. 27.

45. M. Taylor Fravel, "China's Search for Military Power," *Washington Quarterly* 31 (Summer 2008), pp. 125–41 (quoted passages are on pp. 130, 136); emphasis added.

46. "MSDF Detected Two Chinese Submarines in East China Sea That Aimed to Threaten U.S. Aircraft Carrier," *Sankei Shimbun*, October 17, 2008; "Chinese Destroyer Sailed through Tsugaru Strait," *Yomiuri Shimbun*, October 22, 2008 (OSC JPP20081021969112); "Chinese, Russian Warships Spotted in Japanese Territorial Waters," *Nihon Keizai Shimbun*, November 4, 2008 (OSC JPP20081104044003); "Chinese Survey Ships Enter Japanese Waters," Jiji Press, December 8, 2008 (OSC JPP20081208969069); "Chinese Submarine Patrols Doubled in 2008," Federation of American Scientists Security Blog, February 3, 2009 (www.fas.org/blog/ssp/2009/02/patrols.php).

47. Chen Guangwen, "China's Maritime Security Forces," *Bingqi Zhishi* (May-June 2009) (OSC CPP20090610678001).

48. Li Ying and Yu Dong, "Directly Facing Provocations from Foreign Armed Ships: China Marine Surveillance Enhances Law Enforcement," *Guoji Xianqu Daobao*, February 1, 2010 (OSC CPP20100219671004).

49. Zhang Xinsin, "The China Marine Surveillance Force Will Soon Be Incorporated into the Reserve Force of the Chinese Navy," *Renmin Haijun*, October 27, 2008 (OSC CPP20081204318005).

50. Sun Zhihui, "Strengthening Ocean Administration and Composing Blue Brilliance," *Qiushi Online*, September 16, 2009 (OSC CPP20090918710012).

51. OSD, "Annual Report to Congress: Military Power of the People's Republic of China 2008" (hereafter "Military Power of the People's Republic of China 2008"), p. 1 (executive summary) (www.defenselink.mil/pubs/pdfs/China_Military_Report_08.pdf). For a catalogue of PLAN weaknesses, see Ronald O'Rourke, "China Naval Modernization: Implications for U.S. Naval Capabilities: Background and Issues for Congress," Congressional Research Service, November 19, 2008.

52. Cole, *Sea Lanes and Pipelines*, p. 140; Cole, "Right-Sizing the Navy," pp. 535–541, 552–553; cited passage is on p. 553.

53. OSD, "Military Power of the People's Republic of China 2009," p. 40. Not all PRC observers believe that carriers should be a high priority. As one wrote, "Compared with the other powers, China is obviously in a weak position. Having no aircraft carrier is not a major problem, but having no territorial integrity is." See Ma Xiaojun, "Is China an Ocean Nation?" *Shijie Zhishi*, April 16, 2009 (OSC CPP20090515671002).

54. On China's submarine debate, see Ian Storey and You Ji, "China's Aircraft Carrier Ambitions: Seeking Truth from Rumors," *Naval War College Review* 57 (Winter 2004), pp. 76–93; and Andrew S. Erickson and Andrew R. Wilson, "China's Aircraft Carrier Dilemma," *Naval War College Review* 59 (Autumn 2006), pp. 12–45. Erickson and Wilson's essay also appeared in *China's Future Nuclear Submarine Force*, edited by Erickson and others, pp. 229–69.

55. National Institute for Defense Studies, *East Asian Security Review 2008* (Tokyo: Japan Times, 2008), p. 103.

56. "Su-27 Air-Superiority Fighter Aircraft" (www.sinodefence.com/airforce/fighter/su27specifications.asp) and "Su-30MKK Multi-role Fighter Aircraft" (www.sinodefence.com/airforce/fighter/su30specifications.asp).

57. "China's National Defense in 2008," Information Office of the State Council of the People's Republic of China, January 2009 (http://english.gov.cn/official/2009-01/20/content_1210227.htm), pp. 35–36; emphasis added. In contrast, the basic mission was described as "airspace security and maintaining a stable air defense posture nationwide"; see "China's National Defense in 2006," Information Office of the State Council of the People's Republic of China, December 29, 2006, Xinhua (OSC CPP20061229968070).

58. Mark A. Stokes, "The Chinese Joint Aerospace Campaign: Strategy, Doctrine, and Force Modernization," in *China's Revolution in Doctrinal Affairs: Emerging Trends in the Operational Art of the Chinese People's Liberation Army*, edited by James Mulvenon and David M. Finkelstein (Alexandria, Va.: CNA Corporation, December 2005), p. 254 (www.cna.org/documents/doctrinebook.pdf).

59. Wang Ran, "Tenth Air Force CPC [Communist Party of China] Committee Holds its 11th Plenary (Enlarged) Meeting in Beijing: Firmly Take the Course of Scientific Development, Raise the Air Force's Scientific Development to a New Level," *Kongjun Bao*, December 30, 2008 (OSC CPP20090223682009).

60. Kevin M. Lanzit and Kenneth Allen, "Right-Sizing the PLA Air Force: New Operational Concepts Define a Smaller, More Capable Force," in *Right-Sizing the People's Liberation Army: Exploring the Contours of China's Military*, edited by Kamphausen and Scobell, pp. 444–45.

61. Lanzit and Allen, "Right-Sizing the PLA Air Force," pp. 438–39, 455–61, 466–70.

62. OSD, "Military Power of the People's Republic of China 2009," p. 18.

63. Feng Chunmei and others, "Take the Road of Scientific Development, Build an Iron Great Wall in the Blue Sky: Special Interview with Xu Qiliang, Member of the

Central Military Commission and Commander of the Air Force," Xinhua, November 1, 2009 (OSC CPP20091101073001).

64. Stokes, "The Chinese Joint Aerospace Campaign," p. 250.

65. Ibid., pp. 247–48.

66. "China's National Defense in 2006."

67. Phillip C. Saunders and Erik Quam, "Future Force Structure of the Chinese Air Force," in *Right-Sizing the People's Liberation Army*, edited by Kamphausen and Scobell, p. 392.

68. Ibid., pp. 401–19; Saunders and Quam provide a good analysis of various trade-offs.

69. Ibid., p. 396.

70. OSD, "Military Power of the People's Republic of China 2009," p. vii.

71. Ibid., p. 15.

72. OSD, "Military Power of the People's Republic of China 2008," March 2008. The number of more modern CSS-5s (also known as the DF-21) has grown steadily, from a minimum of nineteen in 2006, to forty to fifty in 2007, to at least sixty in 2008; see Hans M. Kristensen, "Chinese Nuclear Arsenal Increased by a Third since 2006, Pentagon Report Indicates," FAS Strategic Security Blog, March 6, 2008 (www.fas.org/blog/ssp/2008/03/chinese_nuclear_arsenal_increa.php). China's missiles for delivering nuclear weapons are to provide second-strike capability against the United States.

73. Evan S. Medeiros, "'Minding the Gap': Assessing the Trajectory of the PLA's Second Artillery," in *Right-Sizing the People's Liberation Army*, edited by Kamphausen and Scobell, pp. 167–69, 175, 177–78; cited passages on pp. 177 and 167. Still, the steady development and fielding of short- and medium-range ballistic missiles and land-attack cruise missiles could tip regional balances and deprive U.S. armed forces of their operational sanctuary in the Western Pacific—with serious implications for Japan's own threat assessments. Moreover, as Medeiros points out on p. 167, Chinese doctrine in this realm appears to stress an offensive purpose. "The PLA emphasizes using conventional missiles to strike first, strike hard, strike precisely, and strike rapidly."

74. Mara Hvistendahl, "The China Syndrome," *Popular Science* 274 (June 2009) (www.popsci.com/scitech/article/2009-04/hackers-china-syndrome).

75. Remarks by Dennis Wilder, "Beyond the Taiwan Strait: PLA Missions Other Than Taiwan," Brookings Institution event, April 30, 2009 (www.brookings.edu/~/media/Files/events/2009/0430_pla/0430_pla.pdf).

76. *Defense of Japan 2008* (www.mod.go.jp/e/publ/w_paper/pdf/2008/11Part1_Chapter2_Sec3.pdf), p. 54.

77. Anthony Faiola, "Anti-Japanese Hostilities Move to the Internet; Chinese and South Korean Hackers Blamed for Digital Barrage Designed to Cripple Web Sites," *Washington Post*, May 10, 2005, p. A12.

78. "The Clear and Present Danger Is Information Warfare," *Gunji Kenkyu*, August 2007 (OSC JPP20071214437002).

79. The National Police Agency publishes reports on cyber attacks every month. For example, see "National Police Agency Internet Security Report for Jan 09," National Police Agency, February 25, 2009 (OSC JPP20090302134004).

80. U.S.-China Economic and Security Review Commission, "Report on the Capability of the People's Republic of China to Conduct Cyber Warfare and Computer Network Exploitation," October 9, 2009 (www.uscc.gov/researchpapers/2009/Northrup Grumman_PRC_Cyber_Paper_FINAL_Approced%20Report_16Oct2009.pdf).

81. Cited in Hvistendahl, "The China Syndrome."

82. Cited in Shane Harris, "China's Cyber-Militia," *National Journal*, May 31, 2008 (www.nationaljournal.com/njmagazine/cs_20080531_6948.php). China is also vulnerable to cyber attacks; see Ellen Nakashima, "China Leads the World in Hacked Computers," *Washington Post*, February 15, 2010, p. A3; "Cyberspying Fears Help Fuel China's Drive to Curb Internet," *New York Times*, February 12, 2010, p. A1.

83. Hvistendahl, "The China Syndrome."

Chapter Six

1. Hans M. Kristensen, "US-Chinese Anti-Submarine Cat and Mouse Game in South China Sea," Federation of American Scientists Security Blog, March 10, 2009 (www.fas.org/blog/ssp/2009.03/incident.php); Michael Swaine, "The U.S.-China Spat at Sea," *Foreign Policy*, March 11, 2009 (www.carnegieendowment.org/publications/index.cfm?fa=view&id=22848).

2. On the *Bowditch*, see Xu Bingchuan, "Chinese Fishing Boat Rams into U.S. Spy Ship; Expert on International Issues Says the Incident Would Not Affect Mainstream Sino-US Relations," *Qingnian Cankao*, September 25, 2002 (Open Source Center [hereafter OSC] CPP20020926000031).

3. Swaine, "The U.S.-China Spat at Sea." See also Jin Wei, "United States Refuses to Stop Reconnaissance of China in Offshore Waters," *Guoji Siangqu Daobao Online*, September 7, 2009 (OSC CPP20090909072004). This is an account of a meeting of the U.S.-China maritime military safety consultation mechanism, at which the Chinese representative demanded that "the United States must change its ship and aircraft reconnaissance policy."

4. The U.S. intelligence community has specified China's "expansive definition of its maritime and air space with consequent implications for restricted freedom of navigation" as one of the four key ways in which the PLA poses "challenges to its neighbors and beyond Taiwan." See Dennis C. Blair, "Annual Threat Assessment of the U.S. Intelligence Community for the Senate Select Committee on Intelligence," February 2, 2010, p. 28 (www.dni.gov/testimonies/20100202_testimony.pdf).

5. Li Ying and Yu Dong, "Directly Facing Provocations from Foreign Armed Ships: China Marine Surveillance Enhances Law Enforcement," *Guoji Xianqu Daobao*, February 1, 2010 (OSC CPP20100219671004).

6. For a discussion of the international law dimension of the *Impeccable* case, see Peter Dutton and John Garofano, "China Undermines Maritime Laws," *Far Eastern Economic Review*, April 2009 (www.feer.com/essays/2009/april/china-undermines-maritime-laws).

7. The PRC's National Defense Law of 1997 states: "The state shall step up the building of frontier, coastal, and air defenses and take effective defensive and administrative measures to safeguard the security of its land, inland waters, territorial waters, territorial airspace, and the marine rights and interests of the country." "Law of the People's Republic of China on National Defense," adopted March 14, 1997, Xinhua (OSC FTS19970321001189).

8. Quan Jinfu, "The Innovations and Development of the Chinese Navy's Strategy Theory in the New Century," *Journal of PLA Nanjing Institute of Politics*, March 3, 2004 (OSC CPP20071012436001).

9. Quoted in Huang Haixia, "Rough Waves in China's Territorial Seas," *Liaowang*, April 13, 2009 (OSC CPP20090417710014).

10. Interviews with Chinese scholars specializing in Japan, January 2008.

11. To avoid appearing to endorse the claims of either country, I use "Senkaku/Diaoyu" and "Diaoyu/Senkaku" interchangeably to refer to the same set of islands.

12. Takai Mitsuo, "Will Japan's Military Resources Be Able to Defend 6,800 Islands? Senkaku Islands Defense Plan for Regional Stability and Prevention of War," *Gunji Kenkyu*, September 2006 (OSC JPP20060929326003), pp. 54–59; Nakanishi Terumasa, "Taiwan Is Japan's Lifeline: We Should Not Let Ourselves Be Taken in by China, Which Is Expanding Its Power by Using North Korea," *Voice*, April 2004, pp. 124–35 (OSC JPP20040315000014); Kayahara Ikuo, "Military Aims of China's Ocean Forays: Objective Not Just Resources," *Chuo Koron*, October 2004, pp. 62–69 (OSC JPP20040917000002).

13. Paul D. Senese and John A. Vasquez, *The Steps to War: An Empirical Study* (Princeton University Press, 2008), pp. 253–56.

14. Paul Huth and Todd L. Allee, *The Democratic Peace and Territorial Conflict in the Twentieth Century* (Cambridge University Press, 2002), p. 148. Many of the disputes that these scholars assessed were concerned with land territory, and there was no discrimination between disputes over islands and ones over land. But the findings are suggestive.

15. M. Taylor Fravel, *Strong Borders, Secure Nation: Cooperation and Conflict in China's Territorial Disputes* (Princeton University Press, 2008), p. 267.

16. Yusin Lee and Sangjoon Kim, "Dividing Seabed Hydrocarbon Resources in East Asia: A Comparative Analysis of the East China Sea and the Caspian Sea," *Asian Survey* 48 (September-October 2008), pp. 794–815.

17. "'Potential Threats from China' Reflected: Behind This Lie Territorial Row, Dispute over Ocean Resources," *Kyodo Clue II*, November 17, 2004 *(OSC* JPP20041117000055).

18. *Xihu* means "West Lake" in Chinese.

19. Zha Daojiong, "Calming Troubled Waters, China and Japan Agree to Jointly Develop Energy Resources in the East China Sea," *Beijing Review*, July 7, 2008 (www. bjreview.com/quotes/txt/2008-07/08/content_131974.htm). *Senkaku* is the Japanese name for "Pinnacle Islands," the Western name. The PRC uses *Diaoyudao* (*Diaoyu* means "fishing"; *dao* means "island"), and Taiwan uses *Diaoyutai*. At the peak of the last ice age, the extension of the Chinese mainland was a vast plain, cut by rivers. The extension of the Yangzi River probably flowed through what is now the Xihu depression, and the Okinawa trough was probably a vast lake; to get a sense of its size, search GoogleEarth (www.googleearth.com) for Okinawa. The Ryukyu Islands were a chain of mountains. See Li Guangxue and others, "Ancient Changjiang Channel System in the East China Sea Continental Shelf during the Last Glaciation," *Science in China, Series D: Earth Sciences* 48 (2005), pp. 1972–78.

20. Wenran Jiang, "East Asia's Troubled Waters," YaleGlobal Online, April 25, 2006 (http://yaleglobal.yale.edu/display.article?id=7302); Erica Downs, "China," Brookings Foreign Policy Studies Energy Security Series, December 2006, p. 1 (www. brookings.edu/~/media/Files/rc/reports/2006/12china/12china.pdf).

21. For one recent summary of estimates, see Reinhard Drifte, "Japanese-Chinese Territorial Disputes in the East China Sea: Between Military Confrontation and Economic Cooperation," Asia Research Center Working Paper 24, London School of Economics and Political Science, April 2008, p. 11 (http://eprints.lse.ac.uk/20881/1/Japanese-Chinese_territorial_disputes_in_the_East_China_Sea_(LSERO).pdf). See also "East China Sea," Country Analysis Briefs, Energy Information Administration, U.S. Department of Energy, March 2008 (www.eia.doe.gov/emeu/cabs/East_China_Sea/Background.html).

22. These differences are drawn from Drifte, "Japanese-Chinese Territorial Disputes in the East China Sea," pp. 4–8; Peter Dutton, "Carving Up the East China Sea," *Naval War College Review* 60 (Spring 2007), pp. 49–72; Peter Dutton, "Scouting, Signaling, and Gatekeeping: Chinese Naval Operations in Japanese Waters and the International Law Implications," Chinese Maritime Studies Institute (U.S. Naval War College, February 2009); Selig S. Harrison, "Seabed Petroleum in Northeast Asia: Conflict or Cooperation" (Washington: Woodrow Wilson International Center for Scholars, 2005), pp. 3–4; Li Ming, "Having an Accurate Understanding of the China-Japan Consensus on East China Sea," *Huanqiu Shibao*, June 30, 2008 (OSC CPP20080731587001).

23. On the latter point, see Jiang Xinfeng, "China-Japan: How to Develop the East China Sea's Oil-Gas Fields," *Shijie Zhishi*, July 2008 (OSC CPP20080829702012), pp. 27–29.

24. Dutton, "Carving Up the East China Sea," observes that the issues of the continental shelf and the EEZ are conceptually different.

25. Peter A. Dutton, "*Caelum Leberam*: Air Defense Identification Zones outside Sovereign Airspace," *American Journal of International Law* 103 (October 2009), pp. 1–22.

26. Katsumata Hidemichi, "Land Disputes Expose Weaknesses," *Daily Yomiuri*, April 21, 1998 (OSC FTS19980421000044).

27. See "Japanese Air-Defence Identification Zone," Sun Bin Blog, May 2005 (http://sun-bin.blogspot.com/2006/05/japanese-air-defence-identification.html). Japan is one of a few states (Canada, Australia, Iceland, and the United States are others) that have defined a very wide ADIZ. Peter Dutton, "China's Views of Sovereignty and Methods of Access Control," testimony before the U.S.-China Economic and Security Review Commission, February 28, 2008, p. 5 (www.uscc.gov/hearings/2008hearings/written_testimonies/08_02_27_wrts/08_02_27_dutton_statement.pdf). China has not designated a formal ADIZ zone, but its policy on foreign military aircraft flying above its EEZ amounts to the same thing.

28. The Diaoyu/Senkaku Islands are not the only places over which Beijing and Tokyo have legal disagreements. Japan claims that the Okinotorishima formation, located north and west of Taiwan, is a group of islands and therefore deserves its own EEZ. China disagrees, presumably, among other reasons, because it would limit the flexibility of the PLAN beyond the first island chain. See Yukie Yoshikawa, "The U.S.-Japan-China Mistrust Spiral and Okinotorishima," *Asia-Pacific Journal: Japan Focus*, essay no. 2541 (www.japanfocus.org/-Yukie-YOSHIKAWA/2541); "China Opposes Japan's Continental Shelf Claim through Okinotori," Zhongguo Tongxun She [news service], August 28, 2009 (OSC CPP20090828704002); Peter J. Brown, "China All at Sea over Japan Island, *Asia Times Online*, March 3, 2010 (OSC CPP20100304715029).

29. On this point, see Drifte, "Japanese-Chinese Territorial Disputes in the East China Sea," pp. 18–21.

30. Ren Xiaofeng and Cheng Zezhong, "A Chinese Perspective," *Marine Policy* 29 (2005), pp. 139–46; quoted passage is on p. 139. Dutton, "Carving Up the East China Sea," pp. 51–52, notes some Chinese analyses that come close to treating the East China Sea as if it were sovereign territory, not as an area over which it has sovereign rights of exploitation.

31. Geological surveys suggest that the continental shelf contains between 10 and 100 billion barrels of oil, but no test surveys have confirmed that estimate. See Erica Strecker Downs and Phillip C. Saunders, "Legitimacy and the Limits of Nationalism: China and the Diaoyu Islands," *International Security* 23 (Winter 1998–99), p. 124.

32. The discussion of historical background and legal claims is based on International Crisis Group, "North East Asia's Undercurrents of Conflict," *Asia Report 108*, December 15, 2005, pp. 4–5; and Fravel, *Strong Borders, Secure Nation*, p. 334.

33. For an exhaustive review of the competing historical claims, see Han-yi Shaw, *The Diaoyutai/Senkaku Islands Dispute: Its History and an Analysis of the Ownership Claims of the P.R.C., R.O.C., and Japan*, Occasional Papers/Reprint Series in Contemporary Asian Studies 152 (University of Maryland School of Law, 1999).

34. For episodes from 1971 to 1996, see Shaw, *The Diaoyutai/Senkaku Islands Dispute*, pp. 11–22. For a fuller discussion of the 1990 and 1996 episodes, see Downs and Saunders, "Legitimacy and the Limits of Nationalism," pp. 126–38. For more recent

cases, see Ming Wan, *Sino-Japanese Relations: Interaction, Logic, and Transformation* (Woodrow Wilson Center Press and Stanford University Press, 2006), pp. 34–43, 146–49.

35. On preserving economic ties, see Min Gyo Koo, "The Senkaku/Diaoyu dispute and Sino-Japanese Political-Economic Relations: Cold Politics and Hot Economics?" *Pacific Review* 22 (May 2009), pp. 205–32. On the "management" approach to China-Japan relations, see Quansheng Zhao, *Japanese Policymaking: The Politics behind Politics: Informal Mechanisms and the Making of China Policy* (Westport, Conn.: Praeger, 1993).

36. Krista E. Wiegand, "China's Strategy in the Senkaku/Diaoyu Islands Dispute: Issue Linkage and Coercive Diplomacy," *Asian Security* 5 (May 2009), pp. 170–93.

37. Euan Graham, *Japan's Sea Lane Security, 1940–2004: A Matter of Life and Death?* (New York: Routledge, 2006), p. 213.

38. "JCG To Boost Personnel to Reinforce Security Measures around Senkaku Islands," *Yomiuri Shimbun,* July 28, 2004 (OSC JPP20040728000007).

39. James J. Przystup, "Japan-China Relations: Not the Best of Times," *Comparative Connections* 6 (October 2004), pp. 118–20 (www.csis.org/media/csis/pubs/0403q.pdf).

40. Feng Zhaokui, "The Waters of the Diaoyu Islands: An Emergency?" *Shijie Zhishi,* March 16, 2009 (OSC CPP20090403671001), pp. 26–28.

41. Dutton, "Scouting, Signaling, and Gatekeeping," p. 11.

42. "The Law on Foreign Ship Navigation in Territorial Waters Is Enacted to Regulate Suspicious-Looking Foreign Ships in the Japanese Territorial Waters," *Yomiuri Shimbun,* June 5, 2008 (OSC JPP20080606023001).

43. Hai Tao, "China Breaks Through Japan's Diaoyu Islands' Defense Line: Careful Timing of Cruise to Declare Sovereignty Is beyond Reproach," *Guoji Xianqu Daobao,* December 12, 2008 (OSC CPP20081215005001).

44. Ibid.

45. Ibid.

46. "Two Chinese Ships Leave Japan's Territorial Waters," Kyodo, December 8, 2008 (OSC JPP20081208969059); "PRC FM Spokesman Denies China Provoking Japan over Disputed Isles," Kyodo, December 9, 2008 (OSC JPP20081209969061); Kenji Minemura, "PRC Steps Up Offensive on Territorial Dispute over Senkaku Islands; Heated Exchange during Summit Meeting," *Asahi Shimbun,* December 13, 2008 (OSC JPP20081215036002).

47. Minemura, "PRC Steps Up Offensive on Territorial Dispute over Senkaku Islands"; Hai, "China Breaks Through Japan's Diaoyu Islands' Defense Line."

48. Zhang Wenmu, "China Should Prevent Blind Leap forward of Its Sea Power," *Huanqiu Shibao,* April 1, 2009 (OSC CPP20090401710003).

49. Guo Yadong, "China Should Not Rush to Flex Its Muscles," *Huanqiu Shibao,* February 25, 2009 (OSC CPP20090313710004).

50. Liu Zhongmin, "Argument about China-U.S. Battle Misleading," *Huanqiu Shibao,* March 12, 2008 (OSC CPP20080407587002).

51. "Coast Guard Strengthening Surveillance of Territorial Waters, Stationing Helicopter-Equipped Patrol Vessel in Senkaku Islands Vicinity," *Sankei Shimbun*, February 4, 2009 (http://sankei.jp.msn.com/politics/policy/090204/plc0902040146001-n1.htm); "Japan Coast Guard Quietly Beefing Up Security around Senkaku Islands," *Foresight*, March 21, 2009 (OSC JPP20090331036005); Hai Tao, "Japan Deploys 'Powerful Vessel' to Patrol Diaoyu Island Waters," *Guoji Xianqu Daobao*, February 9, 2009 (OSC CPP20090217671001).

52. "'Do Not Irritate China.' Then How Should We Handle Them?" *Foresight*, May 1, 2009 (OSC JPP20090508164002); "'Intrusions into Territorial Waters' Still Silent since Strengthening the Crackdown," *Foresight*, August 2009 (OSC JPP2009 0803043004). The Foreign Ministry was worried that too strict enforcement would create diplomatic problems with China.

53. "'Yūai no umi' kakoikomi" [Enclosure of "Sea of Fraternity"], *Yomiuri Shimbun*, September 30, 2009.

54. Institute for International Policy Studies, "A New Phase in the Japan-U.S. Alliance," September 2009; Matsushita Institute of Government and Management, "A Critical Moment for the Japan-U.S. Alliance: The Urgent Need for Progress toward a 'Broad and Balanced Alliance,'" November 24, 2008, p. 10 (OSC JPP20090106134001).

55. Bernard D. Cole, "Right-Sizing the Navy: How Much Naval Force Will Beijing Deploy?" in *Right-Sizing the People's Liberation Army: Exploring the Contours of China's Military*, edited by Roy Kamphausen and Andrew Scobell (Carlisle, Pa.: Strategic Studies Institute, U.S. Army War College, 2007), pp. 543–44.

56. Dutton, "Carving Up the East China Sea," p. 66.

57. Reinhard Drifte, "Territorial Conflicts in the East China Sea: From Missed Opportunities to Negotiation Stalemate," *Asia Pacific Journal: Japan Focus*, essay 3156, June 2009 (www.japanfocus.org/-Reinhard-Drifte/3156).

58. Li Ming, "Having an Accurate Understanding of the China-Japan Consensus on East China Sea."

59. Drifte, "Japanese-Chinese Territorial Disputes in the East China Sea," p. 24 (http://eprints.lse.ac.uk/20881/1/Japanese-Chinese_territorial_disputes_in_the_East_China_Sea_(LSERO).pdf).

60. For general background on the development of Chunxiao, see Zha Daojiong, "Calming Troubled Waters, China and Japan Agree to Jointly Develop Energy Resources in the East China Sea."

61. James J. Przystup, "Japan-China Relations: Not Quite All about Sovereignty—But Close," *Comparative Connections* 6 (July 2004), pp. 125–26 (www.csis.org/media/csis/pubs/0402q.pdf); Przystup, "Japan-China Relations: Not the Best of Times"; "Japan-China Relations: A Volatile Mix: Natural Gas, a Submarine, a Shrine, and a Visa," *Comparative Connections* 6 (January 2005), pp. 119–21 (www.csis.org/media/csis/pubs/0404q.pdf).

62. James J. Przystup, "Trying to Get beyond Yasukuni," *Comparative Connections* 7 (April 2005), pp. 115–16 (www.csis.org/media/csis/pubs/0501q.pdf).

63. James J. Przystup, "Japan-China Relations: No End to History," *Comparative Connections* 7 (July 2005), pp. 125–27 (www.csis.org/media/csis/pubs/0502q.pdf).

64. Evidence also indicated that a pipeline had connected the fields to the east coast of China.

65. James J. Przystup, "Japan-China Relations: Summer Calm," *Comparative Connections* 7 (October 2005), pp. 119–20 (www.csis.org/media/csis/pubs/0503q.pdf); Richard J. Samuels, *Securing Japan: Tokyo's Grand Strategy and the Future of East Asia* (Cornell University Press, 2007), p. 169; and "Waiting for Chunxiao in East China Sea—Cold and Warmth between China and Japan Are Felt From an Oil and Gas Field," *Guoji Xianqu Daobao*, June 19, 2008 (OSC CPP20080801587001).

66. James J. Przystup, "Japan-China Relations: Yasukuni Stops Everything," *Comparative Connections* 7 (January 2006), n.p. (www.csis.org/media/csis/pubs/0504q.pdf).

67. "Waiting for Chunxiao in East China Sea."

68. "20,000 Times of Scrambles," in *Defense of Japan 2006*, Japan Defense Agency, October 2006 (www.mod.go.jp/e/publ/w_paper/pdf/2006/3-2-2.pdf), p. 174.

69. "China's State Oceanic Administration Director: China Is Determined to Safeguard its Sovereignty over Sea Territory," Zhongguo Tongxun She, April 29, 2006 (OSC CPP20080429004002).

70. "Gas Field Development in East China Sea; China Aims at Acknowledgment of 'Territorial Issue': Japan Exposed Its Vulnerabilities," *Sankei Shimbun*, March 17, 2006 (OSC JPP20060320016003).

71. "China Proposes Joint Gas Field Development in 'Sea Areas Near Median Line' Only on Japanese Side; Talks Break Down," *Sankei Shimbun*, January 15, 2008 (OSC JPP20080114026002).

72. *Defense of Japan 2008*, Japan Defense Agency, 2008, p. 182 (http://www.mod.go.jp/e/publ/w_paper/pdf/2008/28Part3_Chapter1_Sec2.pdf); "Hot Scrambles," Japan Air Self-Defense Force (www.mod.go.jp/asdf/en/mission/bouei.htm). Ross Liemer provided the research on this point. In the second quarter of 2009, the number of intercepts was 213, 11 percent of which were of PLAAF aircraft; see "Japan ASDF Most Active in Five Years against Unidentified Aircraft," Jiji Press, January 21, 2010 (OSC JPP20100121969043).

73. The departure of the hard-line Nakagawa Shoichi as METI minister in October 2005 may have been a factor. In early 2008 Nakagawa criticized Japan's diplomatic approach with a soccer metaphor: "We [Japan] have just been going around in circles with the ball, while our opponent [China]—while breaking the rules—has been scoring points." See Nakagawa Shoichi, "The Day the East China Sea Gas Fields Are Usurped by China," *Voice*, March 2008 (OSC JPP20080219044001).

74. Communication from a Japanese diplomat who was involved in the negotiations, October 2, 2009; "Meeting between the Japan Coast Guard and the State

Oceanic Administration of China," press release, Japan Ministry of Foreign Affairs, July 20, 2007 (www.mofa.go.jp/announce/announce/2007/7/1174543_830.html).

75. James J. Przystup, "Japan-China Relations: Spring Thaw," *Comparative Connections* 8 (July 2006), n.p. (www.csis.org/media/csis/pubs/0602qjapan_china.pdf); "Japan-China Relations: Searching for a Summit," *Comparative Connections* 8 (October 2006), n.p. (www.csis.org/media/csis/pubs/0603qjapan_china.pdf); "Japan-China Relations: Ice Breaks at the Summit," *Comparative Connections* 8 (July 2006), n.p. (www.csis.org/media/csis/pubs/0604qjapan_china.pdf).

76. James Manicom, "China's Claims to an Extended Continental Shelf in the East China Sea: Meaning and Implications," *China Brief* 9 (July 9, 2009) (www.jamestown.org/programs/chinabrief/single/?tx_ttnews%5Btt_news%5D=35243&tx_ttnews%5BbackPid%5D=414&no_cache=1).

77. "China, Japan Reach Principle Consensus on East China Sea Issue," Xinhua, June 19, 2008 (www.china.org.cn/international/foreign_ministry/2008-06/19/content_15852895.htm).

78. Ibid.; James J. Przystup, "Japan-China Relations: Progress in Building a Strategic Relationship," *Comparative Connections* 10 (July 2008), n.p. (www.csis.org/media/csis/pubs/0802qjapan_china.pdf).

79. Kristine Kwok, "Gas Field Deal Will Not Affect Territory," *South China Morning Post*, June 20, 2008 (OSC CPP20080620968047); Sudo Takashi, Hirachi Osamu, and Otsuka Takuya, "Gas Field Development under Japan-China Agreement Shunts Aside Border Line Issue," *Mainichi Shimbun*, June 19, 2008 (OSC JPP20080619045001); Fukushima Kaori, "Gas Field Agreement Causes CPC Criticism to Swamp China Websites," *Sankei Shimbun*, June 20, 2008 (OSC JPP20080620038001); "Difficult Breakthrough Brought About in East China Sea Dispute: China and Japan Reach Consensus in Principle," *Huanqiu Shibao*, June 19, 2008 (OSC CPP20080721508001). One creative activist organization later called on the National People's Congress (China's legislature) to rule that the agreement was unconstitutional; see "Zhongri Donghai Gongshi Beizhi Weixian; Minjian Baodiao Lianhui Shangshu Renda Yaouqiu Boujue" [Accusation That the China-Japan Consensus on the East Sea Is Unconstitutional; Federation for Defending the Diaoyu Islands Submits Request to the NPC Calling for Rejection], *Mingbao*, October 12, 2009 (OSC CPP20091012722015), p. A20.

80. Jia Yu, "The 'East Sea Consensus' Carries Legal and Practical Significance," *Zhongguo Qingnianbao*, July 3, 2008 (OSC CPP20080703710006). Li Ming drew a similar conclusion: "Japan has tacitly acknowledged the sovereign rights of the Chinese side over the Chunxiao . . . fields"; Li Ming, "Having an Accurate Understanding of the China-Japan Consensus on East China Sea."

81. "East China Sea Gas Field Issue: Japan-China Agreement Does Not Resolve Any Problems; Appealing Once Again for Exploratory Drilling by Japan," Japan Policy Institute, June 19, 2008 (OSC JPP20080620260004).

82. "Plan for Joint Development of Gas Field at a Standstill; Even Foreign Ministerial Meeting Fails to Make Progress—Chinese Public Opinion Is Hampering Project from Moving," *Nihon Keizai Shimbun,* August 19, 2008 (OSC JPP20080819045002).

83. Kristine Kwok, "CNOOC Official Defends Gas Deal with Japan," *South China Morning Post,* June 28, 2008 (OSC CPP2008062898058).

84. James J. Przystup, "Japan-China Relations: All about Gyoza: Almost All the Time," *Comparative Connections* 10 (October 2008), n.p. (http://www.csis.org/media/csis/pubs/0803qjapan_china.pdf); James J. Przystup, "Japan-China Relations: New Year, Old Problems," *Comparative Connections* 10 (April 2009), n.p. (www.csis.org/media/csis/pubs/0901qjapan_china.pdf); "3rd Lead: Japan, China Agree to Work Together toward Creation of E. Asia Group," Kyodo World Service, September 28, 2009 (OSC JPP20090928969070).

85. "Chūgoku ga shirakaba ni kussakushisetsu kansei nihon to kaihatsu goui yosoni" [China Completes Construction of Derrick at Shirakaba Gas Field, in Disregard of Agreement on Joint Development with Japan], *Yomiuri Shimbun,* December 9, 2009; Tanaka Miya, "2nd Lead: Japan to Take Action if China Violates E. China Sea Project Accord," Kyodo World Service, January 17, 2010 (OSC JPP20100117969012); "Secret Talks Fall Through, Joint Development of East China Sea Gas Fields Runs Aground," *Kyodo Clue III,* December 31, 2009 (OSC JPP20100102034003). These sources used the term "joint development" loosely in describing what the 2008 agreement permitted in the Chunxiao area.

86. Author's interviews with Chinese specialists on Japan, January 2008; Wang Shan, "Cong Donghai Youqi Zhengduan Kan Riben Duihua Nengyuan Zhengce" [Examining Japan's Energy Policy towards China in Light of the East Sea Oil and Gas Dispute], *Xiandai Guoji Guanxi* 194 (December 2005), p. 42; Dutton, "Carving Up the East China Sea," pp. 65–66; Wiegand, "China's Strategy in the Senkaku/Diaoyu Islands Dispute." The cited passage is from Wang, "Cong Donghai Youqi Zhengduan." For the counterargument that Beijing and Tokyo have overwhelming reasons for avoiding conflict regarding the East China Sea, see James Manicom and Andrew O'Neil, "Sino-Japanese Strategic Relations: Will Rivalry Lead to Confrontation?" *Australian Journal of International Affairs* 63 (June 2009), pp. 218–22.

87. Technically, these high-seas corridors are not the high seas, because they are still part of Japan's exclusive economic zones. See Dutton, "Scouting, Signaling, and Gatekeeping," pp. 3–5; Law on the Territorial Sea and the Contiguous Zone (Law No. 30 of 1977, as amended by Law No. 73 of 1996) (www.un.org/Depts/los/LEGISLATIONANDTREATIES/PDFFILES/JPN_1996_Law.pdf).

88. "Former Envoy Says Japan Narrowed Territorial Waters for U.S. Nuke Ships," Kyodo World Service, October 17, 2009 (OSC, JPP20091017969038). Had those straits been Japanese territorial waters, the passage of the ships would have violated Japan's nuclear principles.

89. Dutton, "Scouting, Signaling, and Gatekeeping," p. 12.

90. Ibid., pp. 1–4.

91. Peter A. Dutton, "International Law and the November 2004 '*Han* Incident,'" *Asian Security* 2 (June 2006), pp. 87–88. Dutton's essay also appeared in Andrew S. Erickson and others, *China's Future Nuclear Submarine Force* (Annapolis, Md.: Naval Institute Press, 2007), pp. 162–81.

92. Dutton, "International Law and the November 2004 '*Han* Incident,'" pp. 93–98.

93. Peng Guangqian and Yang Youzhi, *The Science of Military Strategy* (Beijing: Academy of Military Science of the People's Liberation Army, 2005), pp. 442–43. For an exhaustive and illuminating discussion of Taiwan's strategic value in Chinese eyes, see Alan M. Wachman, *Why Taiwan: Geostrategic Rationales for China's Territorial Integrity* (Stanford University Press, 2007).

94. Shigeo Hiramatsu, "After Defeat of DPP, What Are Chinese Submarines Aiming At?" *Sankei Shimbun*, January 30, 2008 (OSC JPP20080130020001). Hiramatsu ignores the fact that even if China and Taiwan were to resolve the fundamental dispute between them under the terms that China has put forward, no PLA units would be deployed to Taiwan.

95. Wendell Minnick, "Taiwan Issues Discussed Backstage at Shangri-La," *Defense News*, June 2, 2009 (www.defensenews.com/story.php?i=3558147).

96. "Japan's Rivalry with China Is Stirring a Crowded Sea," *New York Times*, September 11, 2005. Note that this anxiety exists even though China's own proposal for Taiwan unification does not seem to contemplate the PLA Navy operating out of Taiwan ports. Even if they did, Japanese ships could simply bypass the Taiwan Strait. Moreover, there are limits on how far China-Taiwan reconciliation can go; see Richard C. Bush and Alan D. Romberg, "Cross-Strait Moderation and the United States," *PacNet*, no. 17A, Pacific Forum CSIS, March 12, 2009 (www.csis.org/media/csis/pubs/pac0917a.pdf).

97. Dutton, "China's Views of Sovereignty and Methods of Access Control"; Dutton and Garofano, "China Undermines Maritime Laws."

Chapter Seven

1. On the Whig view, see Bernard Bailyin, *The Ideological Origins of the American Revolution* (Cambridge, Mass.: Belknap Press, 1967), pp. 61–63, 112–119; and Richard H. Kohn, *Eagle and Sword: The Beginnings of the Military Establishment in America* (New York: Free Press, 1975), pp. 1–16.

2. Peter D. Feaver, "The Civil-Military Problematique: Huntington, Janowitz, and the Problem of Civilian Control," *Armed Forces and Society* 23 (Winter 1996), pp. 158–60. Morris Janowitz argued that Huntington's dichotomy is too simplistic and that because officers are never politically neutral, institutional mechanisms are required to restrain them. Yet the essentials of the type are the same.

3. On praetorianism and Leninism, see Amos Perlmutter and William M. LeoGrande, "The Party in Uniform: Toward a Theory of Civil-Military Relations in

Communist Systems," *American Political Science Review* 76 (December 1982), pp. 778–89. The concept of praetorianism applies well to China and Japan in the first half of the twentieth century but differently to each country. In China, civilian authority collapsed completely after the imperial system ended in 1911, and military factions competed for territory and power essentially until the Communists' victory in 1949. In Japan, civilian institutions were stronger and were autonomous, but the military origins of the Meiji order gave senior officers substantial independence and direct access to the emperor. The Imperial Army's independence was most visible in the 1931 takeover of Manchuria and the subsequent delivery of military faits accomplis in North China. Civilians who sought to stop the China intervention were either assassinated or intimidated.

4. This paragraph and the next are based on Perlmutter and LeoGrande, "The Party in Uniform," pp. 778–89; cited passage is on p. 782. Note that there are different aspects to civil-military relations: the extent to which the military intervenes in domestic politics; the extent to which military and civilian values concur; the extent to which civilian and military leaders agree on the core issue of the use of force; and the mechanisms by which civilian authorities maintain control of the military. For an analysis that avoids mixing apples and oranges, see Peter D. Feaver, Takako Hikotani, and Shaun Narine, "Civilian Control and Civil-Military Gaps in the United States, Japan, and China," *Asian Perspective* 29 (Spring 2005), pp. 233–71.

5. Masculine forms of nouns and pronouns are used to refer to the members of the government and the armed forces mentioned here and in following chapters because overwhelmingly, those individuals are men.

6. This summary is based on Ellis Joffe, "Party-Army Relations in China: Retrospect and Prospect," in *China's Military in Transition*, edited by David Shambaugh and Richard H. Yang (Oxford: Clarendon Press, 1997), pp. 36–45.

7. Michael Kiselycznyk and Phillip C. Saunders, "Civil-Military Relations: The PLA's Role in Elite Politics," *China Strategic Perspectives* 2 (Washington National Defense University Press, 2010).

8. Ibid.

9. Lyman Miller, "The Political Implications of PLA Professionalism," in *Civil-Military Relations in Today's China: Swimming in a New Sea*, edited by David M. Finkelstein and Kristen Gunnes (Armonk, N.Y.: M.E. Sharpe, 2007), pp. 134–38.

10. David L. Shambaugh, *Modernizing China's Military: Progress, Problems, and Prospects* (University of California Press, 2002), p. 13. You Ji is another advocate of the idea that the PLA has moved "beyond symbiosis" into being "a true professional army." See his "The PLA, the CCP, and the Formulation of Chinese Defence and Foreign Policy," in *Power and Responsibility in Chinese Foreign Policy*, edited by Yongjin Zhang and Greg Austin (Canberra, Australia: Asia Pacific Press, 2001), pp. 105–31; cited statements are on p. 105.

11. Andrew Scobell, "China's Evolving Civil-Military Relations: Creeping *Guojiahua*," in *Chinese Civil-Military Relations: The Transformation of the People's Liberation*

Army, edited by Nan Li (New York: Routledge, 2006), pp. 25–39; Andrew Scobell, "Is There a Civil-Military Gap in China's Peaceful Rise?" *Parameters: U.S. Army War College Quarterly* 39 (Summer 2009), p. 18. Scobell's review of a series of recent incidents leads him to conclude that the PLA is on "a loose leash" and that civilian leaders are unaware of military operations and have poor oversight.

12. James Mulvenon, "China: Conditional Compliance," in *Coercion and Governance: The Declining Political Role of the Military in Asia*, edited by Muthiah Alagappa (Stanford University Press, 2001), pp. 317–35.

13. How effective civilians are in shaping the PLA's values is open to some question. For example, Hu Jintao initiated a "socialist core values campaign" that was meant in part to address various abuses within the PLA. But Hu stated those values in a rather general way, raising questions about the true effectiveness of the campaign. See James Mulvenon, "Hu Jintao and the 'Core Values of Military Personnel,'" *China Leadership Monitor* 28 (Spring 2009) (http://media.hoover.org/documents/CLM28JM.pdf).

14. The PRC vice president is sometimes a CMC member or vice chairman, but when the Eleventh National People's Congress named Xi Jinping as vice president in March 2008, it did not give him a CMC slot. It was expected that he would receive one in 2009, since Hu Jintao became vice chairman of the CMC at the analogous point in his succession to Jiang Zemin, to prepare for his ascension to the presidency and chairmanship of the CMC. But for reasons that are unknown, Xi was not appointed. For speculation on why, see Alice Miller, "The Case of Xi Jinping and the Mysterious Succession," and James Mulvenon, "The Best Laid Plans: Xi Jinping and the CMC Vice-Chairmanship That Didn't Happen," both in *China Leadership Monitor* 30 (Fall 2009) (http://media.hoover.org/documents/CLM30AM.pdf and http://media.hoover.org/documents/CLM30JM.pdf, respectively).

15. Moreover, the chairman of the CMC reportedly does not usually attend the weekly meetings of the CMC, which discuss policy and other major issues (he is likely represented by an aide). See Tai Ming Cheung, "The Influence of the Gun: China's Central Military Commission and Its Relationship with the Military, Party, and State Decision-Making Systems," in *The Making of Chinese Foreign and Security Policy in the Era of Reform*, edited by David Michael Lampton (Stanford University Press, 2001), p. 71.

16. Michael D. Swaine, *The Role of the Chinese Military in National Security Policymaking* (Santa Monica, Calif.: RAND Corporation, 1996), p. 32.

17. Nan Li, "Chinese Civil-Miliary Relations in the Post-Deng Era: Implications for Crisis Management and Naval Modernization," U.S. Naval War College, China Maritime Study 4 (January 2010), p. 5.

18. Qi Zhou, "Organization, Structure, and Image in the Making of Chinese Foreign Policy since the Early 1990s," Ph.D. dissertation, Johns Hopkins University, 2008, p. 122.

19. John Wilson Lewis and Xue Litai, *Imagined Enemies: China Prepares for Uncertain War* (Stanford University Press, 2006), p. 102; author's interview with a Chinese scholar.

20. Scobell, "China's Evolving Civil-Military Relations," pp. 26–28.

21. Contrast this segmented system with that in the United States, where decisionmaking is centralized in the institution of the National Security Council, whose key officials and staff lead the interagency system. In the U.S. system, the uniformed military is automatically present, if it chooses to be, at the multi-tiered policy meetings. "Suits" and "uniforms" may not always agree, but the system forces them to interact on a regular basis. During the destructive Sichuan earthquake of May 2008, tension emerged between Premier Wen Jiabao, who was the principal and intensely engaged civilian leader on the ground, and the PLA units that were involved in rescue and relief operations, because the military is under the authority of the CCP general secretary and PRC state chairman (in this case, Hu Jintao), not the premier. See Hiroki Fujita, "Rift between Premier and Military Caused by Sichuan Earthquake," *Foresight*, July 2008 (Open Source Center [hereafter OSC] JPP20080625034003).

22. This discussion is based on David M. Finkelstein's very insightful "China's National Military Strategy: An Overview of the 'Military Strategic Guidelines,'" in *Right-Sizing the People's Liberation Army: Exploring the Contours of China's Military*, edited by Roy Kamphausen and Andrew Scobell (Carlisle, Pa.: Strategic Studies Institute, U.S. Army War College, 2007), pp. 69–140. Finkelstein gives the PLA high marks for the reengineering that it has accomplished since the Persian Gulf War in the areas of hardware, institutions, and doctrine (see in particular pp. 69–74).

23. Tai Ming Cheung, "The Influence of the Gun," p. 76; author's interviews in Beijing.

24. Michael D. Swaine, "Chinese Decision-Making Regarding Taiwan, 1979–2000," in *The Making of Chinese Foreign and Security Policy in the Era of Reform*, edited by David Michael Lampton (Stanford University Press, 2001), pp. 316–17.

25. Swaine, "Chinese Decision-Making Regarding Taiwan," pp. 322–23.

26. John W. Garver, *Face Off: China, the United States, and Taiwan's Democratization* (University of Washington Press, 1997); Tai Ming Cheung, "Chinese Military Preparations against Taiwan over the Next Ten Years," in *Crisis in the Taiwan Strait*, edited by James R. Lilley and Chuck Downs (National Defense University Press, 1997); Tai Ming Cheung, "The Influence of the Gun," p. 76; Andrew Scobell, *China's Use of Military Force: Beyond the Great Wall and the Long March* (Cambridge University Press, 2003), pp. 171–91. You Ji also adopts Swaine's perspective; see his "Changing Leadership Consensus: The Domestic Context of War Games," in *Across the Taiwan Strait: Mainland China, Taiwan, and the 1995–1996 Crisis*, edited by Suisheng Zhao (New York: Routledge, 1999), pp. 77–98.

27. "Shadow of Power Struggle behind Hu's Stance," JijiWeb, April 24, 2005 (OSC JPP20050424000047).

28. Joffe, "Party-Army Relations in China," pp. 45–46.

29. Ellis Joffe, "The Chinese Army in Domestic Politics: Factors and Phases," in *Chinese Civil-Military Relations: The Transformation of the People's Liberation Army*, edited by Nan Li (New York: Routledge, 2006), pp. 12–18.

30. Peter A. Dutton, "International Law and the November 2004 'Han Incident,'" *Asian Security* 2 (June 2006), pp. 87–88.

31. Office of Naval Intelligence (hereafter ONI), *China's Navy 2007* (Washington, 2007), p. 1.

32. Dutton, "International Law and the November 2004 'Han Incident,'" p. 98.

33. On the known facts regarding the test, the possible reasons behind it, and the implications, see Phillip C. Saunders and Charles D. Lutes, "China's ASAT Test: Motivations and Implications," INSS Special Report, Institute for National Security Studies, National Defense University, June 2007 (www.ndu.edu/inss/Research/SRjun07.pdf); Ashley J. Tellis, "China's Military Space Strategy," *Survival* 49 (September 2007), pp. 41–72; Eric D. Hagt, "Testimony before the U.S.-China Economic and Security Review Commission, Hearing on Chinese Military Modernization and Its Impact on the United States and the Asia-Pacific," March 30, 2007 (www.uscc.gov/hearings/2007hearings/written_testimonies/07_03_29_30wrts/07_03_29_30_hagt_statement.pdf).

34. On the government's failure to consult its own space debris experts, see "Orbiting Junk, Once a Nuisance, Is Now a Threat," *New York Times*, February 6, 2007.

35. James Mulvenon, "Rogue Warriors?: A Puzzled Look at the Chinese ASAT Test," *China Leadership Monitor* 20 (Winter 2007) (http://media.hoover.org/documents/clm20jm.pdf), pp. 3–5.

36. Mulvenon, "Rogue Warriors?" p. 4. In January 2010, the PLA conducted a "missile defense intercept test. In this case, the regime had a communications plan in place to deflect and defuse negative international reaction. That suggests that Beijing had learned its lesson, at least on the public relations side. See James Mulvenon, "Evidence of Learning? Chinese Strategic Messaging Following the Missile Defense Intercept Test," *China Leadership Monitor* 31 (Winter 2010) (http://media.hoover.org/documents/CLM31JCM.pdf).

37. Eiichi Katahara has characterized this shift as a movement from "containment to normalization." See his "Japan: From Containment to Normalization" in *Coercion and Governance: The Declining Political Role of the Military in Asia*, edited by Alagappa, pp. 76–86. This section is based on Katahara's chapter and Feaver, Hikotani, and Narine, "Civilian Control and Civil-Military Gaps," pp. 244–55. On the slicing away of restrictions that constrained the SDF, see Richard J. Samuels, *Securing Japan: Tokyo's Grand Strategy and the Future of East Asia* (Cornell University Press, 2007), pp. 86–108.

38. Richard J. Samuels, "Politics, Security Policy, and Japan's Cabinet Legislation Bureau: Who Elected These Guys Anyway?" Japan Policy Research Institute Working Paper 99, March 2004 (www.jpri.org/publications/workingpapers/wp99.html).

39. Yuki Tatsumi, *Japan's National Security Policy Infrastructure: Can Tokyo Meet Washington's Expectation?* (Washington: Henry L. Stimson Center, 2008), p. 122.

40. During the spring and summer of 2009, the Diet debated a programmatic law to authorize international anti-piracy efforts.

41. Tatsumi, *Japan's National Security Policy Infrastructure*, pp. 133–35.

42. Ibid., pp. 136–39.

43. Ibid., pp. 139–43.

44. The MOD's annual *Defense of Japan* volumes cover the corpus of law and policy; recent volumes can be found at www.mod.go.jp/e/publ/w_paper/index.html.

45. Arthur Lord, "From Agency to Ministry: Creation of the Ministry of Defense and Implications for the U.S.-Japan Alliance," in *The United States and Japan in Global Context: 2008*, by the Edwin O. Reischauer Center for East Asian Studies (Johns Hopkins University School of Advanced International Studies, 2009), p. 78; and Feaver, Hikotani, and Narine, "Civilian Control and Civil-Military Gaps," pp. 245–49; the cited passage is from p. 245.

46. Tomohito Shinoda, *Leading Japan: The Role of the Prime Minister* (Westport, Conn.: Praeger, 2000), pp. 46–47. For example, on the proposal to change the JDA to the MOD, the New Komei would consent only if the LDP agreed, as a matter of law and policy, that "international peace cooperation" was now the SDF's "primary mission"—more important even than the defense of Japan.

47. Feaver, Hikotani,and Narine, "Civilian Control and Civil-Military Gaps," pp. 249–51; Lord, "From Agency to Ministry," p. 88.

48. Katsuyuki Yakushiji, "Japan's Evolving Security Policy," summary of a presentation at the Henry L. Stimson Center, March 7, 2002 (www.stimson.org/eastasia/?SN+EA2001111334).

49. Yakushiji, "Japan's Evolving Security Policy."

50. Sasaki Yoshitaka, "A Case of Stepping Out of Line That May Hurt Civilian Control and Japan-U.S. Relations," *Asahi Shimbun*, May 6, 2002 (OSC JPP2002 0506000013).

51. Ogawa Kazuhisa, "National Defense Crisis Moriya Scandal Exposed: Look Squarely at Limitation of Leadership by Bureaucracy," *Chuo Koron*, February 2008 (OSC JPP20030221043001), pp. 138–45.

52. "Shigeru Ishiba on 'Weaknesses of the GSDF, MSDF, and ASDF,'" *Flash*, November 11, 2008 (OSC JPP20081031043001); "Mr. Moriya Is Able, but If One Stays in Office Too Long, There Tends to Be Adverse Effects," *Shukan Bunshun*, November 2007 (OSC JPP20071102034005), pp. 151–55. Ishiba proposed such an integration after he returned as defense minister in September 2008; see "Defense Minister Ishiba Says Overlapping Operations of Defense Ministry's Internal Bureau Staff Offices Will be Integrated," *Mainichi Shimbun*, January 23, 2008 (OSC JPP20080123043001).

53. For a discussion of the council and the reform process, see "Reform of the Ministry of Defense," *Defense of Japan 2008*, part IV, pp. 360–385 (http://www.mod.go.jp/e/publ/w_paper/2008.html, chapter 4, part 4, sections 1-5). A summary of the list of recommendations appears on pp. 366–67.

54. "Bōeishō kaikaku zenseiken no kettei hakushini—Kaikakukaigimo haishi seimusanyaku aratamete giron" [Defense Ministry Reform Plan Scrapped: Defense

Counselors Abolished Advisers Created as Proposed Before], *Asagumo*, October 15, 2009 (www.asagumo-news.com/news/200910/091015/09101501.htm); "Defense Minister Kitazawa Deadlocked over 'Futenma Issue,'" *Shukan Bunshun*, October 22, 2009 (OSC JPP20091019640001).

55. Ishimatsu Hisashi, "Bunmintosei ni shoten boeishokaikaku hachigatsumadeni an" (Government Intends to Come Up With Defense Ministry Reform Plan by August: Ensuring Civilian Control in Focus), *Asahi Shimbun*, March 18, 2010, p. 4.

56. Yakushiji, "Japan's Evolving Security Policy."

57. Ishimatsu, "Bunmintosei ni shoten boeishokaikaku."

58. Iokibe Makoto, "The SDF's Future Begins with the National Defense Academy," *Mainichi Daily News Online*, March 23, 2009 (OSC JPP200903223969083).

59. Sabine Fruhstuck and Eyal Ben-Ari, "'Now We Show It All!': Normalization and the Management of Violence in Japan's Armed Forces," *Journal of Japanese Studies* 28 (Winter 2002), pp. 1–39.

60. The results are summarized in Takako Hikotani, "Japan's Changing Civil-Military Relations: From Containment to Re-engagement," *Global Asia* 4 (Spring 2009), pp. 20–24. The civilian elites were randomly selected University of Tokyo Faculty of Law graduates. Some questions asked in a government-conducted general population survey were included to enable civil-military comparisons. The questionnaire was modeled on the Civil-Military Gap Survey conducted in the United States by the Triangle Institute for Security Studies (TISS), led by political scientists Peter Feaver and Richard Kohn.

61. Tamogami Toshio, "Was Japan an Aggressor Nation?" (www.apa.co.jp/book_report/images/2008jyusyou_saiyuusyu_english.pdf); "Tamogami Essay Sparks Criticism in SDF Ranks," *Daily Yomiuri*, November 1, 2008 (OSC JPP20081101969036).

62. "Opposition Criticizes ASDF Chief over Controversial Essay," Kyodo World Service, October 31, 2008 (OSC JPP20081031969113); "OSC Report: Officials, Papers Criticize ASDF Chief's Essay Denying Wartime Aggression," OSC Report, November 3, 2008 (OSC JPP20081103023001); "Japan: New Fallout from Essay on War," *New York Times*, November 5, 2008; "Joint Staff Chief, GSDF Chief of Staff Also Criticize Tamogami: 'He Should Follow Government Decision,'" JijiWeb, November 6, 2008 (OSC JPP20081114026002); "Focus: Air Force Chief's Essay Shocks Aso, Raises Woe over Civilian Control," Kyodo World Service, November 1, 2008 (OSC JPP20081101969025); "Tamogami Misses Point on Freedom of Speech," *Daily Yomiuri*, November 12, 2008 (OSC JPP20081111969120).

63. "ASDF Backed Essay Competition; Top Officer Called for Submissions," *Daily Yomiuri*, November 15, 2008 (OSC JPP20081115969055); "Focus: SDF's Rise during 1990s behind Tamogami's Confidence," Kyodo World Service, November 15, 2008 (OSC JPP20081115969042).

64. Wakamiya Yoshibumi, "Academy Chief Irked by Tamogami's Supporters," *Asahi Shimbun*, March 27, 2009.

65. Furusho Koichi, "Present and Future of the Japan Maritime Self-Defense Forces," *Sekai no Kansen*, July 2009 (OSC JPP20090714045001), pp. 145–51.

66. "Japanese GSDF Official: Alliance with U.S. Cannot Be Maintained by Rhetoric, 'Trust Me,'" Kyodo World Service, February 10, 2010 (OSC JPP20100210969061); "Kyodo: Lead: GSDF Officer Reprimanded over Speech on Japan-U.S. Alliance," Kyodo, February 12, 2010 (OSC JPP20100212969078); "Hatoyamaseiken no nichibeidōmeihihan; rikuji ittōrikusa ga idō ni" [GSDF Colonel to Be Transferred for Critical Comment on Hatoyama], *Yomiuri Shimbun*, March 17, 2010, p. 2.

67. Garth Hekler, Ed Francis, and James Mulvenon, "C3 in the Chinese Submarine Fleet," in *China's Future Nuclear Submarine Force*, edited by Andrew S. Erickson and others (Annapolis, Md.: Naval Institute Press, 2007), p. 213.

68. Shambaugh, *Modernizing China's Military*, p. 110. Note that the missile unit, the Second Artillery, is under the jurisdiction of the CMC, not the General Staff Department.

69. Ibid., p. 111.

70. James Mulvenon, "Reduced Budgets, the 'Two Centers,' and Other Mysteries of the 2003 National People's Congress," *China Leadership Monitor* 7 (Summer 2003) (http://media.hoover.org/documents/clm7_jm.pdf), pp. 4–6. The Jiang-Hu situation was even more complicated: Jiang was chairman of the state CMC for six months after Hu became chairman of the CMC.

71. Indeed, Lewis and Xue report that the four general departments, the air force, the navy, the Second Artillery, the seven military region commands, the armed police, the Academy of Military Science, the National Defense University, and the National University of Defense Technology are all considered first-grade units. See Lewis and Xue, *Imagined Enemies*, p. 295.

72. This is the *tiao-kuai* problem in PRC institutions, which has been ably elucidated by Kenneth Lieberthal; see his *Governing China: From Revolution through Reform*, 2nd ed. (New York: W.W. Norton, 2004), pp. 186–88.

73. Lewis and Xue, *Imagined Enemies*, p. 137. In addition, the navy, air force, and missile forces were responsible for their own personnel, training, and logistics.

74. Ibid., pp. 137–38.

75. Hekler, Francis, and Mulvenon, "C3 in the Chinese Submarine Fleet," p. 217; Bernard D. Cole, "The Organization of the People's Liberation Army Navy (PLAN)," in *The People's Liberation Army as Organization: Reference Volume v1.0*, edited by James C. Mulvenon and Andrew N. D. Yang (Santa Monica, Calif..: RAND Corporation, 2002), p. 490.

76. Michael D. Swaine, *The Military and Political Succession in China: Leadership, Institutions, Beliefs* (Santa Monica, Calif..: RAND Corporation, 1992), p. 122.

77. Bates Gill, James Mulvenon, and Mark Stokes, "The Chinese Second Artillery Corps: Transition to Credible Deterrence," in *The People's Liberation Army as Organization*, edited by Mulvenon and Yang, p. 522; Swaine, *Military and Political Succession in China*, pp. 122–27.

78. Ibid., p. 123.

79. Ibid.

80. Office of the Secretary of Defense (hereafter OSD), "Military Power of the People's Republic of China 2009," March 2009 (www.defenselink.mil/pubs/pdfs/China_Military_Power_Report_2009.pdf), p. 24.

81. OSD, "Military Power of the People's Republic of China 2009," p. 26.

82. Author's interview with American specialists on the PLA, August 2009; James Mulvenon, "Straining against the Yoke? Civil-Military Relations after the Seventeenth Party Congress," in *China's Changing Political Landscape: Prospects for Democracy*, edited by Cheng Li (Brookings, 2008), pp. 269–70; Nan Li, "Educating 'New-Type Military Talent,'" in *The "People" in the PLA: Recruitment, Training, and Education in China's Military*, edited by Roy Kamphausen, Andrew Scobell, and Travis Tanner (Carlisle, Pa.: Strategic Studies Institute, U.S. Army War College, 2008), pp. 296–97. Mulvenon also notes control issues in the strategic nuclear area. In an era when missiles are mobile and the adversary has incentives to target and "decapitate" the national leadership, should that leadership give missile-base commanders authority to launch retaliatory strikes if the leadership disappears?

83. Chen Guangwen, "China's Maritime Security Forces," *Bingqi Zhishi* [Ordnance Knowledge], May-June 2009 (OSC CPP20090610678001); Sun Zhihui, "Strengthening Ocean Administration and Composing Blue Brilliance," *Qiushi Online* 18, September 16, 2009 (OSC CPP20090918710012).

84. Zhang Xinsin, "The China Marine Surveillance Force Will Soon Be Incorporated into the Reserve Force of the Chinese Navy," *Renmin Haijun* [People's Navy], October 27, 2008 (OSC CPP20081204318005).

85. Xiong Yongxin and Zhu Guangyao, "Naval Base Explores Mechanisms for Ocean Region Control," *Jiefangjun Bao Online*, July 22, 2008 (OSC CPP200807227100090).

86. Tatsumi, *Japan's National Security Policy Infrastructure*, pp. 48–49.

87. Ibid., pp. 48–49, 66.

88. "Ministry of Defense," GlobalSecurity.org (www.globalsecurity.org/military/world/japan/jda.htm); Japan Self-Defense Forces Law, chapter 2 ("Command and Control") (http://law.e-gov.go.jp/htmldata/S29/S29HO165.html).

89. Communication to the author from Yuki Tatsumi, August 10, 2009.

90. Tatsumi, *Japan's National Security Policy Infrastructure*, p. 79.

91. Takino Takahiro, "A Speedy Decision-Making in Maritime Policing Operation Is Needed," *Mainichi Shimbun*, December 18, 2004 (OSC JPP20041220000023); Takahata Akio, "'Things Have Gone Bad, Japan!'; Invisible Foes—Bureaucrats Say They 'Cannot Think Flexibly,'" *Sankei Shimbun*, July 23, 2007 (OSC JPP20070726045001).

92. Tatsumi, *Japan's National Security Policy Infrastructure*, pp. 85–86.

93. "Dispatch of Maritime Self-Defense Force to Waters off Somalia Will Bring Two 'Historic Reconciliations,'" *Foresight*, March 2009 (OSC JPP20090303164003), p. 28; Richard J. Samuels, "'New Fighting Power!': Japan's Growing Maritime Capabilities and East Asian Security," *International Security* 32 (Winter 2007), p. 97.

94. Tatsumi, *Japan's National Security Policy Infrastructure*, pp. 126, 140.

95. Ibid., p. 140.

96. Communication to the author from an ASDF officer, September 2009.

97. Tatsumi, *Japan's National Security Policy Infrastructure*, p. 69.

98. Bernard D. Cole, *Sea Lanes and Pipelines: Energy Security in Asia* (Westport, Conn.: Praeger Security International, 2008), p. 135.

99. Alistair Iain Johnston defines strategic culture as "an integrated system of symbols (i.e., causal axioms, languages, analogies, metaphors, etc.) that acts to establish pervasive and long-lasting strategic preferences by formulating concepts of the role and efficacy of military force in interstate political affairs." See Johnston, "Cultural Realism and Strategy in Maoist China," in *The Culture of National Security: Norms and Identity in World Politics*, edited by Peter J. Katzenstein (Columbia University Press, 1996), pp. 222–23; cited passage is on p. 222.

100. On the cult of the offensive, see Stephen Van Evera, "The Cult of the Offensive and the Origins of the First World War," *International Security* 9 (Summer 1984), pp. 58–107. On civil-military relations, see Jack Snyder, "Civil-Military Relations and the Cult of the Offensive: 1914 and 1984," *International Security* 9 (Summer 1984), pp. 108–46. Interestingly, Snyder demonstrates that the cult of the offensive was associated with patterns of civil-military relations that gave military establishments substantial autonomy, especially in Germany.

101. Scobell, *China's Use of Military Force*, p. 16.

102. Ibid., pp. 26–35.

103. Thomas J. Christensen, "Windows and War: Trend Analysis and Beijing's Use of Force," in *New Directions in the Study of China's Foreign Policy*, edited by Alastair Iain Johnston and Robert S. Ross (Stanford University Press, 2006), p. 52.

104. Thomas J. Christensen, "Coercive Contradictions: *Zhanyixue*, PLA Doctrine, and Taiwan Scenarios," in *China's Revolution in Doctrinal Affairs: Emerging Trends in the Operational Art of the Chinese People's Liberation Army*, edited by James Mulvenon and David M. Finkelstein (Alexandria, Va.: CNA Corporation, 2005), pp. 309–24 (www.cna.org/documents/doctrinebook.pdf). Paul Godwin observes that it is precisely because the PLA lags behind its main adversaries technologically that it emphasizes offensive operations. See Paul H. B. Godwin, "China's Emerging Military Doctrine: A Role for Nuclear Submarines?" in *China's Future Nuclear Submarine Force*, edited by Erickson and others, p. 49.

105. Lonnie D. Henley, "Evolving Chinese Concepts of War Control and Escalation Management," in *Shaping China's Security Environment: The Role of the People's Liberation Army*, edited by Andrew Scobell and Larry M. Wortzel (Washington: Carnegie Endowment for International Peace, 2007), pp. 85–110.

106. Henley, "War Control," p. 96.

107. Kevin M. Lanzit and Kenneth Allen, "Right-Sizing the PLA Air Force: New Operational Concepts Define a Smaller, More Capable Force," in *Right-Sizing the People's Liberation Army*, edited by Kamphausen and Scobell, p. 452.

108. Mark A. Stokes, "The Chinese Joint Aerospace Campaign: Strategy, Doctrine, and Force Modernization," in *China's Revolution in Doctrinal Affairs*, edited by Mulvenon and Finkelstein, pp. 250–51.

109. ONI, *China's Navy 2007*, p. 10. On the approval of "offensive defense," see Kamphausen and Scobell, *Right-Sizing the People's Liberation Army*, p. 474, note 26.

110. Sun-Zhihui, "Strengthening Ocean Administration and Composing Blue Brilliance."

111. "China's State Oceanic Administration Director: China Is Determined to Safeguard Its Sovereignty over Sea Territory," Zhongguo Tongxunshe [news service], April 29, 2006 (OSC CPP20080429004002).

112. Li Haitao, "It Is Appropriate to Struggle Rather Than Fight in Order to Defend Maritime Sovereignty," *Ta Kung Pao Online*, November 9, 2009 (OSC CPP20091109710010).

113. Thomas U. Berger, "From Sword to Chrysanthemum: Japan's Culture of Anti-Militarism," *International Security* 17 (Spring 1993), pp. 119–50; cited passage is on p. 134. See also Peter J. Katzenstein, *Cultural Norms and National Security: Police and Military in Postwar Japan* (Cornell University Press, 1996).

114. Samuels, *Securing Japan*, p. 189.

115. Thus, Samuels makes the case that Yoshida Shigeru was in fact a master strategist. His approach, which Japan pursued during the cold war, was to build national power economically while "subcontracting" defense responsibility to the United States. That was, in fact, a sensible and sophisticated response to Japan's security situation, one that used pacifist sentiment as a pretext to shift the burden of defending Japan to the United States. As a result, the Yoshida Doctrine both commanded a broad political consensus and successfully secured Japan at low cost. Kenneth B. Pyle makes a similar argument. See his *Japan Rising: The Resurgence of Japanese Power and Purpose* (New York: Public Affairs, 2007).

116. Samuels, *Securing Japan*, pp. 192–94.

117. Ibid., p. 193.

118. Ibid., p. 198. An assessment of rising leaders found that a plurality were in the normal-nation camp but that pacifists and middle-power internationalists together constituted an equal share. Neoautonomists were negligible, and the rest were ambivalent. See J. Patrick Boyd and Richard J. Samuels, "Prosperity's Children: Generational Change and Japan's Future Leadership," *Asia Policy* 6 (July 2008), pp. 15–51, especially pp. 37–38; cited passage is on p. 37.

119. Another cut at the examination of Japanese "strategic thought" toward Northeast Asia is by Gilbert Rozman and his coauthors. They focus on how Japan has sought, during periods of power transition, to balance relations with the United States on the one hand and the Asian region on the other. They find that Tokyo's efforts were moderately successful in the 1980s, less successful in the early 1990s, and most successful in the late 1990s and that they failed under Koizumi Junichiro. See Gilbert Rozman, Kazuhiko Togo, and Joseph P. Ferguson, "Overview," in *Japanese*

Strategic Thought toward Asia, edited by Gilbert Rozman, Kazuhiko Togo, and Joseph P. Ferguson (New York: Palgrave Macmillan, 2007), pp. 1–32.

120. "Outline of International Peace Cooperation Law, etc." *Defense of Japan 2008*, Ministry of Defense (www.mod.go.jp/e/publ/w_paper/pdf/2008/33Part3_Chapter3_Sec1.pdf), p. 283.

121. "Operations for Defending Japan's Territory (Response to Landing of Invading Forces)" and "Operations for the Defense of Surrounding Sea Areas," *Defense of Japan 2008*, Ministry of Defense (www.mod.go.jp/e/publ/w_paper/pdf/2008/29 Part3_Chapter1_Sec3.pdf), pp. 200, 202–03.

122. "Response to Attacks by Guerillas and Special Operations Forces," *Defense of Japan 2008*, Ministry of Defense (www.mod.go.jp/e/publ/w_paper/pdf/2008/28Part3_Chapter1_Sec2.pdf), pp. 175–76.

123. "Response to Aggression on Japan's Offshore Islands," *Defense of Japan 2008*, Ministry of Defense (www.mod.go.jp/e/publ/w_paper/pdf/2008/28Part3_Chapter1_Sec2.pdf), p. 181.

124. Dutton, "International Law and the November 2004 'Han Incident,'" p. 99.

125. "Former Japan Defense Agency Director Gen Nakatani: 'We Should Work toward an Active Missile Defense,'" *Sankei Shimbun*, May 26, 2009 (http://sankei.jp.msn.com/world/korea/090526/kor0905261824026-n1.htm).

126. Takako Nagai: "Having 'Ability to Attack Enemy Bases' Is Dangerous Game of 'Playing with Fire,'" *Shukan Asahi*, June 12–18, 2009 (OSC JPP20090608015003), pp. 30–31.

127. Hai Tao, "China Breaks through Japan's Diaoyu Islands' Defense Line—Careful Timing of Cruise to Declare Sovereignty Is beyond Reproach," *Guoji Xianqu Daobao*, December 12, 2008 (OSC CPP20081215005001).

128. Samuels, "'New Fighting Power!'" pp. 96–97, 100, 107, 111; cited passages are on pp. 111 and 107. The JCG possesses another advantage: it has the political support of the New Komei Party, which is not always supportive of the SDF (see p. 98).

Chapter Eight

1. Ye Zicheng, "Geopolitics from a Greater Historical Perspective," *Xiandai Guoji Guanxi*, June 20, 2007 (Open Source Center [hereafter OSC] CPP20070712455001). Ye Zicheng's advice does not apply only to China. Dennis Ross writes of the United States: "There is something profoundly wrong when our objectives . . . are disconnected from the means we possess or can mobilize; [and] when our understanding of the world is askew because our assessments are driven by ideology and not by reality." See Dennis Ross, "Remember Statecraft? What Diplomacy Can Do, and Why We Need It More Than Ever," *American Scholar* 76 (Summer 2007), p. 47.

2. Tomohito Shinoda, *Koizumi Diplomacy: Japan's Kantei Approach to Foreign and Defense Affairs* (University of Washington Press, 2007), p. 145.

3. This is the thrust of David Michael Lampton's conclusions in his introduction to the most comprehensive, scholarly assessment of Chinese foreign and security policymaking. See David M. Lampton, "China's Foreign and National Security Policy-Making Process: Is It Changing, and Does It Matter?" in *The Making of Chinese Foreign and Security Policy in the Era of Reform*, edited by David M. Lampton (Stanford University Press, 2001), pp. 1–16.

4. Here I follow Kenneth Lieberthal, *Governing China: From Revolution through Reform*, 2nd ed. (New York: W.W. Norton, 2004), pp. 207–12.

5. Phillip C. Saunders and Brian Harding, "The Chinese Politburo Hits the Books," *China Brief* 6, no. 15, July 19, 2006 (http://www.jamestown.org/programs/chinabrief/single/?tx_ttnews%5Btt_news%5D=3963&tx_ttnews%5BbackPid%5D=196&no_cache=1). On the relative unimportance of the Politburo under Hu Jintao, see Alice Lyman Miller, "More Already on Politburo Procedures under Hu Jintao," *China Leadership Monitor* 17 (Winter 2006) (http://media.hoover.org/documents/clm17_lm.pdf). On p. 5, Miller writes, "None of the 34 Politburo meetings reported thus far describes the Politburo making decisions in the sensitive areas of leadership appointments, foreign policy, or military affairs."

6. John Wilson Lewis and Xue Litai, *Imagined Enemies: China Prepares for Uncertain War* (Stanford University Press, 2006), pp. 86–87; Lu Ning, "The Central Leadership, Supraministry Coordinating Bodies, State Council Ministries, and Party Departments," in *The Making of Chinese Foreign and Security Policy in the Era of Reform*, edited by Lampton, p. 42.

7. Lieberthal, *Governing China*, p. 214. One uncertainty is whether retired senior leaders—"elders"—retain influence and interfere in policymaking, despite the fact that they have no position. It seemed that the current leadership of Hu Jintao and Wen Jiabao had a freer hand and were not constrained by elders like Jiang Zemin second-guessing their decisions (see Lieberthal, *Governing China*, p. 211). More recent evidence suggests that Jiang at least expects deference from his successor and may be able to intervene in policy issues to a point (the location of that point is completely unclear). See "Jiang Zemin Tells Ex-U.S. Official Brzezinski: Hu Jintao Provided Nightly Reports," *Sentaku*, February 1–29, 2008, p. 20 (OSC JPP20080207044001). A continuing role for Jiang in policymaking would be significant because of his personal contribution to the deterioration of Japan-China relations in the late 1990s.

8. Lewis and Xue, *Imagined Enemies*, pp. 97, 102. In the past, the Secretariat of the party has played an important role in implementing policy decisions; currently, it is responsible for party affairs only. And unlike sometimes in the past, there is currently no military representative on the Secretariat. See Alice Lyman Miller, "Xi Jinping and the Party Apparatus," *China Leadership Monitor* 25 (Summer 2008) (http://media.hoover.org/documents/CLM25AM.pdf).

9. Alice Lyman Miller, "Institutionalization and the Changing Dynamics of China's Leadership Politics," in *China's Changing Political Landscape: Prospects for*

Democracy, edited by Cheng Li (Brookings, 2008), pp. 64–71. For arrangements after the Seventeenth Party Congress, see Alice Lyman Miller, "The Work System of the New Hu Leadership," *China Leadership Monitor* 24 (Spring 2008) (www.hoover.org/publications/clm/issues/16610876.html).

10. Lieberthal, *Governing China*, pp. 215–19. It is worth noting, therefore, that unlike Westerners, Chinese officials would not necessarily lump the term "national security" and foreign policy together because "national security" in Chinese parlance includes internal security. The flexibility of the issue-based system is reflected in scholarly disagreement concerning which issues are most important. Lu Ning cites military affairs, legal affairs (including law enforcement), administrative affairs (which includes the domestic economy, social issues, and foreign affairs), propaganda affairs, united front affairs (including minorities, religion, Hong Kong–Macao, and Taiwan), and mass organization affairs. See Lu Ning, *The Dynamics of Foreign-Policy Decisionmaking in China* (Boulder, Colo.: Westview Press, 1997), pp. 7–8. Lieberthal draws the categories slightly differently, specifying, in a nonexclusive list, six *xitong* that he says have been important for concrete management of the country: party affairs, organization and personnel, propaganda and education, political and legal affairs, finance and the economy, and military affairs; see Lieberthal, *Governing China*, p. 219 and following.

11. Kenneth Lieberthal notes that within the CCP's top elite of around thirty-five individuals, it is generally a "bridge leader" who takes charge of a particular issue area and the relevant bureaucracies. Sometimes, however, a leader in the more senior role of "key generalist" or "CEO" may appropriate that function; see Lieberthal, *Governing China*, pp. 211–12. Hu Jintao's leadership over foreign affairs, military affairs, national security affairs, and Taiwan is a perfect example of the CEO assuming the role of a bridge leader on specific issues.

12. Erica Downs, "China," Brookings Foreign Policy Studies Energy Security Series, December 2006 (www.brookings.edu/~/media/Files/rc/reports/2006/12china/12china.pdf), p. 19.

13. "Dai Bingguo—State Councilor," Xinhua News Agency, March 17, 2008 (OSC CPP20080317968225); "Few Surprises in Delegation of Duties for New Vice-Premiers," *South China Morning Post*, April 1, 2008 (OSC CPP20080401968008). The latter item was quoting a story in the Guangzhou newspaper *Southern Metropolitan News*. When Dai Bingguo moved from the International Department to the Foreign Affairs Office, he brought some of his key staff with him. On Dai's service in the CCP's International Department, author's conversation with a Chinese scholar, April 2008.

14. On leading groups, see A. Doak Barnett, *The Making of Foreign Policy in China: Structure and Process* (Boulder, Colo.: Westview Press and the Johns Hopkins School of Advanced International Studies, 1985), pp. 43–44; Carol Lee Hamrin, "The Party Leadership System," in *Bureaucracy, Politics, and Decision Making in Post-Mao China*, edited by Kenneth G. Lieberthal and David M. Lampton (University

of California Press, 1992), pp. 95–124. See also Lu, *The Dynamics of Foreign-Policy Decisionmaking in China*, p. 12; and Taeho Kim, "Leading Small Groups: Managing All under Heaven," in *China's Leadership in the 21st Century: The Rise of the Fourth Generation*, edited by David M. Finkelstein and Maryanne Kivlehan (Armonk, N.Y.: M.E. Sharpe, 2003), pp. 121–39.

15. Lieberthal, *Governing China*, p. 214.

16. Lu, *The Dynamics of Foreign-Policy Decisionmaking in China*, p. 12; Hamrin, "The Party Leadership System"; Kim, "Leading Small Groups," especially pp. 129–35; Barnett, *The Making of Foreign Policy in China*, p. 44.

17. Tai Ming Cheung, "The Influence of the Gun: China's Central Military Commission and Its Relationship with the Military, Party, and State Decision-Making Systems," in *The Making of Chinese Foreign and Security Policy in the Era of Reform*, edited by Lampton, p. 68; Lieberthal, *Governing China*, p. 229.

18. Nan Li, "The Central Military Commission and Military Policy in China," in *The People's Liberation Army as Organization: Reference Volume v1.0*, edited by James C. Mulvenon and Andrew N.D. Yang (Santa Monica, Calif.: RAND Corporation, 2002), p. 46; and David Shambaugh, "The Pinnacle of the Pyramid: The Central Military Commission," in *The People's Liberation Army as Organization*, edited by Mulvenon and Yang, p. 95. There are actually two CMCs, one created by the party and the other by the state. This is an anomaly from the 1980s, when there was a move to separate the party from the state and perhaps an aspiration to create a truly national army. All that went by the boards after Tiananmen Square, when a mass movement threatened communist *party* rule. All that is left of the 1980s organizational re-engineering is the two "signboards." Until now, the membership of the two is exactly the same, and the party CMC is more significant.

19. The PRC vice president probably is added in preparation for his ascension to the presidency and chairmanship of the CMC. But as of mid-2010, the vice president appointed in March 2008, Xi Jinping, still had not become a member, although he may become a CMC vice chairman in the fall.

20. Michael D. Swaine, *The Role of the Chinese Military in National Security Policymaking* (Santa Monica, Calif.: RAND Corporation, 1996), pp. 41–42. Swaine's research in the mid-1990s revealed that on matters of defense policy, the top three to five members of the CMC constitute an informal executive committee. He found that Jiang Zemin deferred to the CMC vice chairmen on defense matters and that the executive committee consulted with the other CMC members.

21. Qi Zhou, "Organization, Structure, and Image in the Making of Chinese Foreign Policy since the Early 1990s," Ph.D. dissertation, Johns Hopkins University, 2008, pp. 140–41; Shao Zonghai, "Zhonggong Zhongyang Gongzuo Lingdao Xiaozu di Zuzhi Dingwei" [The Organizational Identity of the Chinese Communists Central Work Leading Groups], *Zhongguo Talu Yanjiu* [Research Regarding the Chinese Mainland] 48 (September 2005), pp. 6–11. For the institutional evolution of the Secretariat, see Alice Miller, "Xi Jinping and the Party Apparatus," *China*

Leadership Monitor, no. 25 (Summer 2008) (http://media.hoover.org/documents/CLM25AM.pdf).

22. Information provided to the author by a Chinese scholar, March 24, 2008.

23. It appears that the paramount leader has some discretion in deciding who will become members of these leading groups. Jiang reportedly shrunk the TWLG when he took over its leadership in 1993; see Michael D. Swaine, "Chinese Decision-Making Regarding Taiwan, 1979–2000," in *The Making of Chinese Foreign and Security Policy in the Era of Reform*, edited by Lampton, p. 299. Hu Jintao expanded both leading groups to include more officials than his predecessor after he replaced Jiang Zemin.

24. "Zhang Kehui, Li Yifu Are Not Found in the Members of the 11th CPPCC National Committee," *Lien-Ho Pao*, January 27, 2008 (OSC CPP20080208622001); "Transcript of PRC State Council TAO Press Conference 16 Apr 2008," Taiwan Affairs Office of the State Council (www.gtytb.gov.cn), April 16, 2008 (OSC CPP20080416075001). Some position identifications are made from the China Vitae website, www.chinavitae.org/index.php. Because the membership of these bodies is not publicized, who is actually a member is not always known. Thus it is not clear whether Ma Xiaotian, the deputy chief of staff for foreign affairs and intelligence, who has a heavy workload, continues as a member. On Ma Xiaotian, see James Mulvenon, "The 'Dawn of Heaven'?—A New Player in Sino-U.S. Mil-Mil," *China Leadership Monitor* 24 (Spring 2008) (http://media.hoover.org/documents/CLM24JM.pdf); the discussion of Ma's leading group memberships is on p. 10.

25. Bonnie S. Glaser and Phillip Saunders, "Chinese Civilian Foreign Policy Research Institutes: Evolving Roles and Increasing Influence," *China Quarterly* 171 (September 2002), p. 602.

26. Zhou, "Organization, Structure, and Image," pp. 151–52; author's interview with a Chinese scholar, November 2007; "Dai Bingguo—State Councilor," Xinhua News Agency, March 17, 2008; author's interview with a Chinese scholar, January 2008. There is some debate concerning the institutional impact of the NSLG. Lewis and Xue assert that it plays a significant role while You Ji claims that it is a "concept" that has never functioned. See Lewis and Xue, *Imagined Enemies*, pp. 91–95; and You Ji, "Imagined Enemies: China Prepares for Uncertain War" (review article), *China Journal* 59 (January 2008), pp. 236–38.

27. Author's interview of a Chinese scholar, February 20, 2008.

28. Wang Yizhou, "Who Is in Charge of China's Diplomacy?" *Dongfang Zaobao*, September 30, 2009 (OSC CPP20091006038001); author's interview of a Chinese scholar, March 26, 2008. On the Taiwan Affairs Office, see Richard C. Bush, *Untying the Knot: Making Peace in the Taiwan Strait* (Brookings, 2005), p. 200.

29. Maryanne Kivlehan-Wise, Dean Cheng, and Ken Gause, "The 16th Party Congress and Leadership Changes in the PLA," in *Civil-Military Change in China: Elites, Institutes, and Ideas After the 16th Party Congress*, edited by Andrew Scobell and Larry Wortzell (Carlisle, Pa.: Strategic Studies Institute, U.S. Army War College, 2004), p. 207.

30. David Shambaugh, *Modernizing China's Military: Progress, Problems, and Prospects* (University of California Press, 2002), p. 119.

31. Shambaugh, *Modernizing China's Military*, pp. 111–24; cited passage on p. 122; Lewis and Xue, *Imagined Enemies*, p. 116; Mark A. Stokes, *China's Strategic Modernization: Implications for the United States* (Carlisle, Pa.: Strategic Studies Institute, U.S. Army War College, 1999), pp. 45–46. This is likely the same unit that Michael Swaine, writing in 1991, termed the command-and-control headquarters. "It functions not only as a communications center, but also as an intelligence center and a combat control center." According to Swaine, the center was located in the Western Hills area west of Beijing near the General Staff Department and was staffed by the GSD's First Department, which is responsible for PLA operations. See Michael D. Swaine, *The Military and Political Succession in China: Leadership, Institutions, Beliefs* (Santa Monica, Calif.: RAND Corporations, 1992), pp. 122–23; cited passage is on p. 122.

32. "Expert Group for Revising Regulations of Headquarters, Campaign and Tactics Research Department, Academy of Military Science, Distinct Characteristics, Strategic Advantage—On the Main Characteristics of the Chinese People's Liberation Army Headquarters 'Regulations,'" *Jiefangjun bao*, February 4, 1997, cited in David M. Finkelstein, "The General Staff Department of the Chinese People's Liberation Army: Organization, Roles, and Missions," in *The People's Liberation Army as Organization*, edited by Mulvenon and Young, p. 127. In 1997, General Fu Quanyou, then the chief of the general staff and GSD head, offered a slightly different perspective of the GSD's mission by identifying five roles: acting as adviser to the Central Committee of the CCP and to the CMC; guidance for war planning; coordination; problem solving; and acting as an example (for subordinate units). See Ma Xiaochun, "Fu Quanyou on 1998 Military Work," Xinhua, December 17, 1997, cited in Finkelstein, "The General Staff Department," p. 128.

33. Finkelstein, "The General Staff Department," p. 132.

34. Ibid., pp. 141–43.

35. Finkelstein, "The General Staff Department," p. 148; Nicholas Eftimiades, *Chinese Intelligence Operations* (Annapolis, Md.: Naval Institute Press, 1994), pp. 75–85; Bates Gill and James Mulvenon, "Chinese Military-Related Think Tanks and Research Institutions," *China Quarterly* 171 (September 2002). For an evaluation of *Chinese Intelligence Operations* as a source, see Finkelstein, "The General Staff Department," pp. 147–48.

36. "Second and Third Department, PLA Staff Headquarters," FAS Intelligence Resource Program (http://fas.org/irp/world/china/facilities/pla.htm); Stokes, *China's Strategic Modernization*, pp. 45–46.

37. For an inventory of the PLAN commander's roles, see Bernard D. Cole, "The Organization of the People's Liberation Army Navy (PLAN)," in *The People's Liberation Army as Organization*, edited by Mulvenon and Yang, pp. 475–81. On the PLAN, see also Shambaugh, *Modernizing China's Military*, pp. 163–66.

38. Office of Naval Intelligence (hereafter ONI), *China's Navy 2007* (Washington, 2007), p. 8; Cole, "Organization of the People's Liberation Army Navy," p. 484. On organization at the fleet level, see ONI, *China's Navy 2007*, pp. 4–10.

39. Ken Allen, "PLA Air Force Organization," in *The People's Liberation Army as Organization*, edited by Mulvenon and Yang, pp. 370–76. On the PLAAF, see also Shambaugh, *Modernizing China's Military*, pp. 158–63.

40. Allen, "PLA Air Force Organization," pp. 402–04.

41. Allen, "PLA Air Force Organization," p. 382.

42. "Economic Policymaking in the PRC," *China Business Review*, May-June 2005, p. 22.

43. Eftimiades, *Chinese Intelligence Operations*, pp. 107–08; Zhou, "Organization, Structure, and Image," p. 49.

44. Lu, *The Dynamics of Foreign-Policy Decisionmaking in China*, pp. 108–17.

45. Zhou, "Organization, Structure, and Image," p. 64.

46. Ministry of Foreign Affairs, "Departments" (www.fmprc.gov.cn/eng/wjb/zzjg/default.htm) and "Embassies" (www.fmprc.gov.cn/eng/wjb/zwjg/default.htm) and related subpages of the website.

47. Yoichi Funabashi, *The Peninsula Question: A Chronicle of the Second Korean Nuclear Crisis* (Brookings, 2007), p. 290, citing a senior MFA official.

48. Funabashi, *The Peninsula Question*, p. 290, citing a Chinese diplomat.

49. Ministry of Foreign Affairs, "The Department of Policy Planning" (www.fmprc.gov.cn/eng/wjb/zzjg/zcyjs/default.htm).

50. This section is based on David Shambaugh, "China's 'Quiet Diplomacy': The International Department of the Chinese Communist Party," *China: An International Journal* 5 (March 2007), pp. 30–31. The English rendering of the organization's name used to be "International Liaison Department"; the Chinese name still contains the word for "liaison."

51. Shambaugh, "China's 'Quiet Diplomacy,'" pp. 31, 32.

52. Ibid., p. 46.

53. Much of this section is based on Eftimiades, *Chinese Intelligence Operations*, pp. 17–26. For an example of the internal operations of the MSS, see Zhang Liang, comp., Andrew J. Nathan and Perry Link, eds., *The Tiananmen Papers* (New York: Public Affairs, 2001). What is remarkable about the reports of the 1989 demonstrations that the MSS conveyed to the CCP leadership was their objective character and how they eschewed any conclusions regarding the motivations behind the protests. Senior leaders like Li Peng, on the other hand, were quick to jump to conclusions.

54. "China's Major Consultative and Research Institutions for Policy Decisions," *Liaowang*, January 26, 2009 (OSC CPP20090210710007), pp. 33–37. Shambaugh argued that CICIR was under the MSS for administrative and budgetary purposes only; see David Shambaugh, "China's International Relations Think Tanks: Evolving Structure and Process," *China Quarterly* 171 (September 2002), p. 582. But the bulk of the scholarly and expert opinion is that CICIR is an MSS unit.

55. Shambaugh, "China's International Relations Think Tanks," p. 583.

56. China Institutes of Contemporary International Studies, "Organization Structure" (www.cicir.ac.cn/en/institute/institute01.php).

57. Xuanli Liao, *Chinese Foreign Policy Think Tanks and China's Policy toward Japan* (Hong Kong: Chinese University Press, 2006), p. 56.

58. Gill and Mulvenon, "Chinese Military-Related Think Tanks and Research Institutions," pp. 622–23.

59. Information for this section is drawn from Shambaugh, "China's International Relations Think Tanks," and Glaser and Saunders, "Chinese Civilian Foreign Policy Research Institutes," pp. 597–600.

60. Shambaugh, "China's International Relations Think Tanks," p. 587.

61. Zhou, "Organization, Structure, and Image," p. 239.

62. Lu Ning, "The Central Leadership, Supraministry Coordinating Bodies, State Council Ministries, and Party Departments," pp. 42, 45; Kim, "Leading Small Groups," p. 128.

63. Lu Ning, "The Central Leadership, Supraministry Coordinating Bodies, State Council Ministries, and Party Departments," pp. 46–47; the cited passage is on p. 47.

64. Alexander L. George, *Presidential Decisionmaking in Foreign Policy* (Boulder, Colo.: Westview Press, 1980), pp. 155–57.

65. James Mulvenon, "China: Conditional Compliance," in *Coercion and Governance: The Declining Political Role of the Military in Asia,* edited by Muthiah Alagappa (Stanford University Press, 2001), p. 326; author's interview with a Chinese scholar, January 2008; Bonnie S. Glaser and Phillip Saunders, "Chinese Civilian Foreign Policy Research Institutes: Evolving Roles and Increasing Influence," *China Quarterly* 171 (September 2002), p. 605; Eftimiades, *Chinese Intelligence Operations,* p. 108–09; Lewis and Xue, *Imagined Enemies,* p. 101; Lu, *The Dynamics of Foreign-Policy Decisionmaking in China,* pp. 23–33. Lu reports that the foreign ministry leadership receives two GSD reports but among external sources pays attention only to *Cankao Ziliao,* a highly classified digest of overseas news, prepared by Xinhua News Agency.

66. Glaser and Saunders, "Chinese Civilian Foreign Policy Research Institutes," pp. 597–616; cited passages are on pp. 602, 612. David Shambaugh believes that think tanks have more influence than Glaser and Saunders conclude. See his "China's International Relations Think Tanks," pp. 575–96.

67. Zhou, "Organization, Structure, and Image," p. 269; emphasis added.

68. Ibid., pp. 270–71.

69. Wei Li, *The Chinese Staff System: A Mechanism for Bureaucratic Control and Integration,* China Research Monograph 44 (Institute of East Asian Studies and Center for Chinese Studies, University of California, Berkeley, 1994), p. 46–47.

70. Lieberthal, *Governing China,* p. 214; Wei Li and Lucian W. Pye, "The Ubiquitous Role of the Mishu in Chinese Politics," *China Quarterly* 132 (December 1992), pp. 913–36.

71. Lu, *The Dynamics of Foreign-Policy Decisionmaking in China,* p. 30.

72. Lu Ning, "The Central Leadership, Supraministry Coordinating Bodies, State Council Ministries, and Party Departments," p. 52.

73. Author's interview with a Chinese scholar, March 2008.

74. Author's interview with a Chinese scholar, March 2008.

75. James Mulvenon, "'Ding, Dong, the Witch Is Dead!' Foreign Policy and Military Intelligence Assessments after the Retirement of General Xiong Guangkai," *China Leadership Monitor* 17 (Winter 2006) (http://media.hoover.org/documents/clm17_jm.pdf).

76. On Lee Teng-hui, see Bush, *Untying the Knot*, pp. 335–80. Similarly, Andrew Bingham Kennedy has explored Chinese perceptions of U.S. policy toward Taiwan and concludes that "Chinese perceptions are on the whole too pessimistic" about U.S. intentions. See his "China's Perceptions of U.S. Intentions toward Taiwan: How Hostile a Hegemon?" *Asian Survey* 47 (March-April 2007), pp. 268–87; cited passage is on p. 285.

77. Alastair Iain Johnston kindly provided me the slides of both talks: Luo Yuan, "Ehrshiyi Shiji Chuqi di Guoji Zhanlue geju yu Zhongguo Zhoubian Anquan Qingxing" [The International Strategic Configuration in the Initial Stage of the 21st Century and the Security Environment on China's Periphery]; and Fan Gaoyue, "China's National Defense: Challenges and Responses." Both PowerPoint presentations are in the author's files.

78. The allegation about Westernizing and dividing does not appear in the discussion of the "first concern," but it does appear in the introduction.

79. For example, Huang Fafu, "Riben di Yatai Anquan Zhanlue [Japan's Asia-Pacific Security Strategy]," *Guoji Zhanlue Yanjiu* [International Strategic Studies] 65 (July 2002), pp. 14–17; Jia Kunji, "Riben Jinxing Fangwei Zhengce Datiaozheng [Japan Carries Out a Big Adjustment of Its Defense Policy]," *Guoji Zhanlue Yanjiu* 70 (October 2003), pp. 13–17. In a revealing article, Shi Yinhong of People's University argued that there was something wrong with the way Chinese analysts saw Japan, in that it exaggerated the influence of right-wing forces in Japan during the Koizumi period. See Shi Yinhong, "Need for New Strategic Considerations and Strategic Experiments on Sino-Japanese Relations," *Zhongguo Pinglun*, November 2007 (OSC CPP20071107710010), pp. 42–44.

80. ONI, *China's Navy 2007*, p. 30.

81. Lu, *The Dynamics of Foreign-Policy Decisionmaking in China*, pp. 31–32; George Yang, "Mechanisms of Foreign Policy-Making and Implementation in the Ministry of Foreign Affairs," in *Decision-Making in Deng's China: Perspectives from Insiders*, edited by Carol Lee Hamrin and Suisheng Zhao (Armonk, N.Y.: M.E. Sharpe, 1995), pp. 95–96. On departmental rivalry in the MFA on North Korea policy, see Funabashi, *The Peninsula Question*, p. 290, citing a senior official.

82. Lu, *The Dynamics of Foreign-Policy Decisionmaking in China*, pp. 32–33.

83. Communication to the author from a Chinese scholar, January 2008.

84. The Foreign Ministry may itself be divided on its priorities. On one hand, the Asian Affairs Department would have a bias toward an outcome that improved relations

with Japan. On the other, the Department of Treaty and Law might be more inclined to worry about the implications of any settlement for broader territorial claims.

85. Information from a Japanese diplomat.

86. "PRC Official He Yafei Expresses Regret to Japan FM Komura over Food Poisoning," Kyodo News Service, December 31, 2007 (OSC JPP20080131969061).

87. See, for example, "Japan, China Investigators at Odds over Tainted-Dumpling Probe," Nikkei Telecom 21, February 28, 2008 (OSC JPP20080228969122); "Jiji: China Denies Deliberate Contamination of Dumplings," Jiji Press, February 13, 2008 (OSC JPP20080213969114); "Anonymous Panel Discussion: Active Chinese Bureaucrats Discuss Olympics, Tibet, Poisoned Gyoza Case, etc.," *Shukan Shincho*, April 17, 2008, pp. 144–47 (OSC JPP20080421034001); "Japan-China 'Sources': Hu Jintao's Visit Likely to Take Place 'Mid-May or Later,'" Kyodo World Service, March 5, 2008 (OSC JPP20080305969048); "President Hu Jintao Furious with 'Poisonous Gyoza'; Expresses Displeasure to Quality Supervision Bureau; 'Have You Thought about International Public Opinion?'" *Zakzak*, March 5, 2008 (OSC JPP20080305026005).

88. "Anonymous Panel Discussion"; "President Hu Jintao Furious with 'Poisonous Gyoza.'" The reference to Hu being furious and to his question about international opinion is from the second source.

89. Bonnie S. Glaser and Brad Glosserman, "Promoting Confidence Building across the Taiwan Strait: A Report of the CSIS International Security Program and Pacific Forum CSIS," Center for Strategic and International Studies and Pacific Forum CSIS, September 2008, p. 4.

90. Lu, "The Central Leadership, Supraministry Coordinating Bodies, State Council Ministries, and Party Departments," p. 44; Zhou, "Organization, Structure, and Image, pp. 47–48.

91. Author's interviews with scholars, January 2008.

92. Author's interview with a Chinese scholar, January 2008.

93. Lu, *The Dynamics of Foreign-Policy Decisionmaking*, pp. 18, 33–34, 107–08; Swaine, "Chinese Decision-Making Regarding Taiwan, 1979–2000," p. 309.

94. Robert Lawrence Kuhn, *The Man Who Changed China: The Life and Legacy of Jiang Zemin* (New York: Crown Publishers, 2004), p. 204.

95. Interview with Chinese scholar, January 2008.

96. This is the principal theme of Susan L. Shirk, *China: Fragile Superpower* (Oxford University Press, 2007).

97. Bush, *Untying the Knot*, pp. 182–83.

98. Author's communication with a Chinese scholar, June 2008.

99. Funabashi, *The Peninsula Question*, p. 292.

100. Alan D. Romberg, "After the Taiwan Election: Restoring Dialogue while Reserving Options," *China Leadership Monitor* 25 (Summer 2008) (http://media. hoover.org/documents/CLM25AR.pdf), p. 27, n. 73.

101. Funabashi, *The Peninsula Question*, p. 267.

102. Interviews with Chinese scholars, January 2008.

103. Based on the observations of a number of Chinese scholars. This sort of gridlock makes China's MFA, by and large, an implementing agency. It translates the policy decisions of the leadership into action plans and operational routines and conducts China's foreign relations. For an assessment that seeks to put the best face on MFA's role but acknowledges the more important role of the FALG and the Foreign Affairs Office that staffs it, see Wang Yizhou, "Who Is in Charge of China's Diplomacy?" *Dongfang Zaobao*, September 30, 2009 (OSC CPP20091006038001).

104. Author's interview with Chinese scholar, January 2008.

105. "Shadow of Power Struggle behind Hu's Stance," JijiWeb, April 24, 2005 (OSC JPP20050424000047); "Behind Ordeal of Hu Leadership Is Shanghai Group," *Kyodo Clue II*, April 22, 2005 (OSC HPP20050424000057).

106. Lewis and Xue, *Imagined Enemies*, pp. 92, 102.

107. Lu, *The Dynamics of Foreign-Policy Decisionmaking*, pp. 12, 18, 33–34, 107–08; Hamrin, "The Party Leadership System"; Kim, "Leading Small Groups: Managing All under Heaven," especially pp. 129–35; Barnett, *The Making of Foreign Policy in China*, p. 44.

108. Interviews with Chinese scholars, January and February 2008.

109. "What If N. Korea Conducts Second Nuke Test?" Seoul *Chosun Ilbo*, January 3, 2007 (OSC KPP20070103971028); Kim, "Leading Small Groups: Managing All under Heaven," p. 128. On broadened participation concerning Taiwan, see Swaine, "Chinese Decision-Making Regarding Taiwan, 1979–2000," p. 322.

110. In this regard, one interesting point of reference is Alexander George's delineation of different modes of interaction between chief executive and senior advisers in U.S. administrations from Roosevelt to Carter, in which he differentiates the competitive, formalistic, and collegial models. See George, *Presidential Decisionmaking in Foreign Policy*, pp. 145–68.

111. On this point, see Melissa Murphy, "Decoding Chinese Politics: Intellectual Debates and Why They Matter," Report of the CSIS Freeman Chair in China Studies, January 2008.

112. For an illuminating discussion, see Guoguang Wu, "'Documentary Politics': Hypotheses, Process, and Case Studies," in *Decision-Making in Deng's China: Perspectives from Insiders*, edited by Carol Lee Hamrin and Suisheng Zhao (Armonk, N.Y.: M.E. Sharpe, 1995), pp. 24–37. Wu details the stages of document preparation: initiation, selection of drafters, directives from the top leader in charge of the project, research and drafting, revision, approval, and dissemination through the propaganda apparatus and through major meetings.

113. For accounts of two such policy conferences, see Bonnie S. Glaser, "Ensuring the 'Go Abroad' Policy Serves China's Domestic Priorities," *China Brief* 7 (March 8, 2007), pp. 2–5; Bonnie S. Glaser and Benjamin Dooley, "China's 11th Ambassadorial Conference Signals Continuity and Change in Foreign Policy," *China Brief* 9 (November 4, 2009), pp. 8–12.

114. "Full Text of Report Delivered by Hu Jintao at 17th Party Congress 15 Oct 2007," Beijing CCTV-1, October 15, 2007 (OSC CPP20071015035002).

115. "Full Text of PRC President Hu Jintao's Speech on PLA's 80th Anniversary," CCTV-1, August 1, 2007 (OSC CPP20070801050015). For a discussion of PRC defense policy that aggregates a series of verbal formulas, see Chen Zhou, "Xin Zhongguo Fangyuxing Guofang Zhengce di Fazhan" [Development of the Defensive Defense Policy of the New China], *China Daily Online*, July 30, 2007 (www.china daily.com.cn/hqzx/2007-07/30/content_5446118).

116. Information Office of China's State Council, "China's Peaceful Development Road," December 22, 2005 (OSC CPP20051222078042).

117. For the process that led up to Jiang Zemin's January 1995 statement on Taiwan policy, see Swaine, "Chinese Decision-Making Regarding Taiwan," pp. 289–336.

118. James Mulvenon, "Chairman Hu and the PLA's 'New Historic Missions,'" *China Leadership Monitor* 27 (Winter 2009) (http://media.hoover.org/documents/CLM27JM.pdf), pp. 1–11, on which this paragraph is based. The cited passage appears on p. 2.

119. Finkelstein notes that "strategic guidelines" are issued for every *xitong* in the PRC system and become the basis for policy; see David M. Finkelstein, "China's National Military Strategy: An Overview of the 'Military Strategic Guidelines,'" in *Right-Sizing the People's Liberation Army: Exploring the Contours of China's Military*, edited by Roy Kamphausen and Andrew Scobell (Carlisle, Pa.: Strategic Studies Institute, U.S. Army War College, 2007), pp. 81–82.

120. Finkelstein, "China's National Military Strategy," pp. 82–95.

121. Finkelstein, "China's National Military Strategy," p. 69.

122. "Hu Jintao Meets Junichiro Koizumi," Xinhua, November 22, 2004 (OSC CPP20041122000184); "Hu Jintao Gives Important Speech on Sino-Japan Relations," Xinhua, April 23, 2005 (OSC CPP20050423000134).

123. "Sources Say Hu Jintao Leads Moves to Improve China's Ties with Japan," Jiji Press, April 9, 2005 (OSC JPP20050409000014).

124. James J. Przystup, "Trying to Get Beyond Yasukuni," *Comparative Connections* 7 (April 2005), pp. 115–16 (www.csis.org/media/csis/pubs/0501q.pdf).

125. "Text of PRC Premier Wen Jiabao's News Conference after NPC Closing 14 Mar," Beijing CCTV-1, March 14, 2005 (OSC CPP20050314000075).

126. "Tang Jiaxuan Meets Japan's Kyodo News Agency President," Xinhua, April 15, 2005 (OSC CPP200504150000193).

127. James J. Przystup, "Japan-China Relations: No End to History," *Comparative Connections* 7 (July 2005), pp. 125–27 (www.csis.org/media/csis/pubs/0502q.pdf).

128. "Hu Jintao Gives Important Speech on Sino-Japan Relations."

129. "Hu Jintao's Five-Point Proposal Provides Basic Guide for Promoting Health and Stable Development of China-Japan relations," Xinhua, April 29, 2005 (OSC CPP20050429000242); "Hu's Proposal Establishes Framework for Sino-Japanese Relations: Experts," Xinhua, April 25, 2005 (OSC CPP20050425000222);

Jin Xide, "Always Bear in Mind Need to Take Peaceful Development Path, Strive to Create Good Surrounding Environment," *Renmin Ribao*, April, 27, 2005 (OSC CPP20050427000041); Wang Yi, "Sino-Japanese Joint Declaration Sets Up Guide to Action for New Century," *Renmin Ribao*, April 28, 2005 (OSC CPP20050428000039).

130. For a case in which a PRC leader other than the paramount leader promoted a new *tifa*, only to encounter overwhelming resistance, see Bonnie S. Glaser and Evan S. Medeiros, "The Changing Ecology of Foreign Policy-Making in China: The Ascension and Demise of the Theory of 'Peaceful Rise,'" *China Quarterly* 190 (June 2007), pp. 291–310.

131. Wang Jisi believes that for all its formulations, China lacks a serious international strategy. See his "Views on Devising International Strategy," *Shanghai Dongfang Zaobao*, January 8, 2008 (OSC CPP20080110319001). Robert Sutter rejects the common scholarly belief that China is following a clear, well-defined strategy that more or less reflects official principles and goals. Instead, he observes twists and turns, debates, and confidence in some areas and caution in others. On balance, contingency and insecurity are the order of the day. The "strategy" is merely the post hoc rationalization for the contingent behavior. See Robert G. Sutter, *Chinese Foreign Relations: Power and Principle since the Cold War* (Lanham, Md.: Rowman and Littlefield, 2007), pp. 1–12. The most prominent expression of the view that China forges and uses a coherent strategy, see Avery Goldstein in *Rising to the Challenge: China's Grand Strategy and International Security* (Stanford University Press, 2005).

132. For example, Beijing's Taiwan policy review of 1993 and 1994 started with flawed conclusions about Lee Teng-hui's intentions; Richard Bush, "Lee Teng-hui and 'Separatism,'" in *Dangerous Strait: The U.S.-Taiwan-China Crisis*, edited by Nancy Bernkopf Tucker (Columbia University Press, 2005), pp. 70–92.

133. Swaine, "Chinese Decision-Making Regarding Taiwan," pp. 318–19; Mulvenon, "Chairman Hu and the PLA's 'New Historic Missions,'" p. 9.

Chapter Nine

1. Tomohito Shinoda, *Leading Japan: The Role of the Prime Minister* (Westport, Conn.: Praeger, 2000), p. 72.

2. Michael J. Green, "Japan's Confused Revolution," *Washington Quarterly* 33 (January 2010), p. 9.

3. The DCCS-A is usually an official from one of the ministries that were spun off from the old Home Ministry after World War II. Prime Minister Aso Taro raised eyebrows when he chose as his DCCS-A an official from the National Police Administration. Although the NPA was a part of the old Home Ministry, it was an infrequent source of DCCS-As. See "Key Players at Aso's PMOR," *Sentaku*, November 2008, pp. 48–50 (Open Source Center [hereafter OSC] JPP20081120043002).

4. Matsuda Yasuhiro, "Topics and Issues in 'Japanese Version of NSC,'" National Institute for Defense Studies Briefing Memo, February 2007 (OSC JPP20070227026003).

5. Yuki Tatsumi, *Japan's National Security Policy Infrastructure: Can Tokyo Meet Washington's Expectation?* (Washington: Henry L. Stimson Center, 2008), p. 51.

6. "Organization of the Internal Bureau" (chart) (www.mod.go.jp/j/defense/mod-sdf/sosikizu/inner/index.html).

7. Tatsumi, *Japan's National Security Policy Infrastructure*, pp. 47–48. The Defense Policy Bureau has five divisions (*ka*), for defense policy, Japan-U.S. defense cooperation, international policy, intelligence, and defense planning, with an emphasis on equipment acquisition. The *ka* for defense policy contains the Strategic Planning Office.

8. Tatsumi, *Japan's National Security Policy Infrastructure*, pp. 48–49.

9. Arthur Lord, "From Agency to Ministry: Creation of the Ministry of Defense and Implications for the U.S.-Japan Alliance," in *The United States and Japan in Global Context: 2008* (Edwin O. Reischauer Center for East Asian Studies, Johns Hopkins University School of Advanced International Studies, 2009), pp. 87–88.

10. Richard J. Samuels, "Politics, Security Policy, and Japan's Cabinet Legislation Bureau: Who Elected These Guys Anyway?" Japan Policy Research Institute Working Paper 99, March 2004 (www.jpri.org/publications/workingpapers/wp99.html); Tatsumi, *Japan's National Security Policy Infrastructure*, p. 122.

11. Tatsumi, *Japan's National Security Policy Infrastructure*, pp. 107–10.

12. Ibid., pp. 111–12.

13. Ibid., pp. 105–07.

14. Ibid., pp. 114–15.

15. Kuroi Buntaro, "Special Project: What Are Japan's Foreign Intelligence Capabilities Now? (Part 2)," *Gunji Kenkyu*, September 1, 2005 (OSC JPP20051107326003).

16. Aurelia George Mulgan, *Japan's Failed Revolution: Koizumi and the Politics of Economic Reform* (Canberra, Australia: Asia Pacific Press, 2000), pp. 130, 134.

17. Ellis S. Krauss and Robert Pekkanen, "Explaining Party Adaptation to Electoral Reform: The Discreet Charm of the LDP?" *Journal of Japanese Studies* 30 (Winter 2004), p. 22.

18. For the origins and development of the defense *zoku*, see Michael J. Green, "*Boeizoku*: Defense Policy Formation in Japan's Liberal Democratic Party" (Japan Program, Center for International Studies, MIT, April 1992) (http://libaxis5.mit.edu/bitstream/handle/1721.1/17099/JP-WP-92-04-26848018.pdf?sequence=1); Aya Onami, "Four LDP Diet Members Emerge as Prominent Players in Defense Issues Debate," *Shukan Asahi*, October 19, 2001 (OSC JPP20011012000048), p. 32.

19. "Outrageous Anachronistic 'New Defense Program': 'Military Intelligence Revolution' Faces Vested Interest Barrier," *Sentaku*, October 2002 (OSC JPP20021004000083), pp. 60–61.

20. Onami, "Four LDP Diet Members"; "Mr. Moriya Is Able, but If One Stays in Office Too Long, There Tends to Be Adverse Effects" [interview with Shigeru Ishiba], *Shukan Bunshun*, November 2007 (OSC JPP20071102034005), pp. 151–55.

21. Onami, "Four LDP Diet Members."

22. Kazuki Yoshiyama, "'Heiwa Boke': Why Defense Zoku Are Furious over Merger of Three Space Bodies," *Yomiuri Weekly*, October 27, 2002 (OSC JPP20021028000067), pp. 18–19.

23. Katsuyuki Yakushiji, "'New Japan-U.S. Alliance Factionalists' Emerge in Connection with U.S. Military Restructuring : Intra-MOFA Confrontation in Connection with Japan-U.S. Relations," *AERA*, November 8, 2004 (OSC JPP20041110000010); "Japanese Media Split on Naming of China in NDPO, Export Ban Easing," OSC foreign media analysis, December 16, 2004 (OSC JPF20041216000158); Takanori Ishimori, "Potential New Problems within Ruling Parties in Connection With 'Permanent' Self-Defense Force Overseas Deployment Law," *Sande Mainichi*, June 15, 2008 (OSC JPP20080504004003), pp. 40–41; "Can the SDF Protect Japan? Tear up and Throw Away 'National Defense Taboo' to Discuss Such Issues as 'Possible Preemptive Strikes at North Korea,' 'China as a Theoretical Adversary,' and 'Tanks as Unnecessary,'" *Sapio*, July 22, 2009 (OSC JPP20090721043004); "Defense Agency Desire to Upgrade to Ministry in White Paper," *Okinawa Times*, May 5, 2002 (OSC JPP20020506000001).

24. "Jūyōhōan no taisho katameru seifu yotō kaiki enchōmo kentō" [Government, Ruling Party Settle on How to Deal with Emergencies Legislation, Considering Diet Session Extension], *Mainichi Shimbun*, April 17, 2002 (Dow Jones Factiva [www.factiva.com, maidmi0020020417dy4h00006]).

25. Krauss and Pekkanen, "Explaining Party Adaptation to Electoral Reform," p. 34.

26. This discussion draws on Mulgan, *Japan's Failed Revolution*.

27. The original membership included the prime minister (who served as chair), minister of state, foreign minister, finance minister, chief cabinet secretary, chairman of the National Safety Commission, director of the Japan Defense Agency, and director general of the Economic Planning Agency; Ronald E. Dolan and Robert L. Worden, *Japan: A Country Study*, 5th ed. (Federal Research Division, Library of Congress, 1992), p. 436.

28. Shinoda, *Leading Japan*, p. 75; Tomohito Shinoda, *Koizumi Diplomacy: Japan's Kantei Approach to Foreign and Defense Affairs* (University of Washington Press, 2007), p. 91.

29. Shinichi Kitaoka, "Insights into the World: Trim Security Council Key to Meeting New Threats," *Daily Yomiuri*, February 10, 2007 (OSC JPP20070210969075).

30. Shinoda, *Leading Japan*, pp. 16, 46–47.

31. For Japan's response to the Kobe/Hanshin earthquake, see James L. Schoff, *Crisis Management in Japan and the United States: Creating Opportunities for Cooperation amid Dramatic Change* (Dulles, Va.: Brassey's, 2004), pp. 33–41.

32. On administrative reforms, see Shinoda, *Leading Japan*, pp. 183–200.

33. Shinoda, *Koizumi Diplomacy*, p. 77.

34. For a discussion of the council and the reform process, see "Reform of the Ministry of Defense," *Defense of Japan 2008*, Part IV, sections 1–5, pp. 360–85 (www. mod.go.jp/e/publ/w_paper/pdf/2008/38Part4.pdf); a summary of the list of recommendations appears on pp. 366–67.

35. On the strengthening of the secretariat, see Tomohito Shinoda, "Japan's Cabinet Secretariat and Its Emergence as Core Executive," *Asian Survey* 45 (September-October 2005), pp. 800–21.

36. Shinoda, *Koizumi Diplomacy*, p. 77.

37. Schoff, *Crisis Management in Japan and the United States*, p. 84; Shinoda, *Koizumi Diplomacy*, pp. 10, 72; communication with senior Japanese officer, March 2010.

38. The 2001 reforms also authorized the PM to appoint a small number of special advisers (now five). For example, Abe Shinzo appointed Koike Yuriko to work on national security, but she soon got into a turf battle with the CCS, Shiozaki Yasuhiso. See "The Backstage of the Decision on the Japanese Version of the NSC," *Kyodo Clue III*, February 27, 2007 (OSC JPP20070228026003).

39. The new members included the prime minister; a minister of state; the chief cabinet secretary; the foreign minister; the finance minister; the minister of internal affairs and communications; the minister of land, infrastructure, and transport (which has jurisdiction over the Japan Coast Guard); the minister of defense; the minister of land, posts, and telecommunications; the minister of economy, trade, and industry; and the chairman of the National Safety Commission. "Anzen hosh kaigi secchi h" [Security Council of Japan Establishment Law], Showa 61 Law No. 71 as amended by Heisei 18 Law No. 118.

40. Matsuo Takashi, "Will Japan Prepare for War?: The Emergencies Legislation Is Part of a U.S. Strategy," *Sekai* (June 2003), pp. 64–72 (OSC JPP20030519000094).

41. Matsuo, "Will Japan Prepare for War?"

42. Tatsumi, *Japan's National Security Policy Infrastructure*, pp. 34–40. For example, the Policy Coordination Division played a key role in arranging for deployment of MSDF vessels for refueling operations in the Indian Ocean and of GSDF troops for assisting in reconstruction in Iraq. In the process, it worked with the JDA; with the Security Treaty Division of the North American Affairs Bureau; with the International Legal Affairs Bureau to construct a legal basis for the deployment; with the Middle East Division; and with the UN Policy Division.

43. Lord, "From Agency to Ministry," pp. 74–75.

44. Japan Ministry of Defense, "Responsibility of Chief of Staff, JS" (www.mod. go.jp/jso/e_responsibility.htm).

45. Japan Ministry of Defense, "Organization of Joint Staff" (www.mod.go.jpjso/e_ organization.htm). Conventionally in most militaries, the J-2 office is responsible for intelligence, but the SDF created a separate headquarters for intelligence, negating

the need for a separate J-2. Each of the three services has a chief of staff and a staff office with components that match those of the Joint Staff. Each branch of service has commands that reflect its various missions. Thus, the ASDF has five commands— air defense, air support, air training, air development and testing, and air materiel, of which the first two are most important. Each service has field units deployed to various places in Japan. The GSDF has five regional armies and other specialized units. ASDF air-defense assets are grouped into four different regional commands (northern, central, western, and southwestern). With its four destroyer groups, four submarine groups, one minesweeper group, and nine air squadrons, the MSDF has been organized into one fleet, five geographic districts, a command for air training, and a training squadron. See Tatsumi, *Japan's National Security Policy Infrastructure*, pp. 67–68, 78.

46. For a discussion of the scandals and the reforms, see "Reform of the Ministry of Defense," *Defense of Japan 2008*, Part IV, sections 1 to 5, pp. 360–85 (www. mod.go.jp/e/publ/w_paper/pdf/2008/38Part4.pdf). The growing standing of Japan's defense establishment, reflected in the transition from the JDA to MOD, has had three important institutional consequences. First, up-and-coming politicians now see an advantage in being appointed minister of defense. Second, key positions are no longer "reserved" for officials from other ministries. And finally, ambitious civil servants increasingly regard MOD as an agency where they may pursue an influential career. See Lord, "From Agency to Ministry," pp. 87–88.

47. Also during the 1990s, a shift in the electoral system from multimember districts to a combination of single-member districts and regional proportional representation reduced the electoral role of factions and strengthened that of the party headquarters. As a result, factions lost some of their power. They continued to contend over who should be the president of the LDP and therefore prime minister, not over policies.

48. On the constitution, see J. Patrick Boyd and Richard J. Samuels, *Nine Lives? The Politics of Constitutional Reform in Japan*, Policy Studies 19 (Washington: East-West Center, 2005).

49. Tatsumi, *Japan's National Security Policy Infrastructure*, pp. 125–39.

50. Shinoda, *Leading Japan*, p. 58.

51. John Creighton Campbell and Ethan Scheiner, "Review Essay: Fragmentation and Power: Reconceptualizing Policy Making under Japan's 1995 System," *Japanese Journal of Political Science* 9 (April 2008), pp. 89–113. Campbell and Scheiner provide a sophisticated analysis of when and why the Japanese policy process worked on a bottom-up or top-down basis in the LDP era.

52. Shinoda, *Leading Japan*, pp. 48–49.

53. Council on Security and Defense Capabilities, "The Council on Security and Defense Capabilities Report: Japan's Visions for Future Security and Defense Capabilities," October 2004 (www.globalsecurity.org/wmd/library/news/japan/2004/041000-csdc-report.pdf). On advisory councils, see Shinoda, *Leading Japan*, pp. 107–09.

54. Krauss and Pekkanen, "Explaining Party Adaptation to Electoral Reform," p. 23.

55. Shinoda, *Koizumi Diplomacy*.

56. Mulgan, *Japan's Failed Revolution*.

57. Christopher W. Hughes and Ellis S. Krauss, "Japan's New Security Agenda," *Survival* 49 (Summer 2007), pp. 157–76; cited passage is on p. 160.

58. Shinoda, *Leading Japan*, pp. 99–107; Shinoda, *Koizumi Diplomacy*, pp. 146–48.

59. A related issue is the stance of opposition parties on LDP policy initiatives. Shinoda assesses several cases of national security legislation. He concludes that the New Komei Party cooperated with the LDP in order to influence the final package, while the DPJ often staked out its own position, either to demonstrate that it was capable of governing or to establish a basis for negotiations with the LDP in the Diet. See Tomohito Shinoda, "Japan's Parliamentary Confrontation on the Post–Cold War National Security Policies," *Japanese Journal of Political Science* 10 (December 2009), pp. 267–87.

60. Tatsumi, *Japan's National Security Policy Infrastructure*, pp. 55–56.

61. Shinoda, *Koizumi Diplomacy*, pp. 70–76.

62. Shinoda, *Koizumi Diplomacy*, pp. 75–76. As of mid-2006, there were fifteen ad hoc policy rooms, five of which were in the foreign affairs and national security realm: information security, treatment of abandoned chemical weapons, Japanese citizens abducted by North Korea, Iraqi reconstruction, and continental shelf research.

63. Tatsumi, *Japan's National Security Policy Infrastructure*, pp. 56, 99–101.

64. "Appointment as Assistant Chief Cabinet Secretary for Second Time," *Bungei Shunju*, March 2010, p. 234 (OSC JPP20100212164001).

65. Matsuda, "Topics and Issues in 'Japanese Version of NSC.'"

66. Communication with a senior Japanese officer, March 2010.

67. "Japan without Security or Peace of Mind," *Shokun*, January 2004, pp. 42–54 (OSC JPP20041216000008).

68. Defense Intelligence Agency, "Introduction to DIA" (www.dia.mil/thisisdia/intro/index.htm).

69. "Agency That Got Iraq Least Wrong," *New York Times*, July 19, 2004.

70. Kotani Ken, "Current State of Intelligence and Intelligence Issues in Japan," *National Institute for Defense Studies News* 100 (May 2006), p. 2 (www.nids.go.jp/english/dissemination/briefing/2006/pdf/100.pdf).

71. Kuroi Buntaro, "Special Project: What Are Japan's Foreign Intelligence Capabilities Now? (Part 1)," *Gunji Kenkyu*, September 1, 2005 (OSC JPP20051104326002).

72. Tatsumi, *Japan's National Security Policy Infrastructure*, p. 101.

73. Schoff, *Crisis Management in Japan and the United States*, p. 28.

74. Kotani, "Current State of Intelligence and Intelligence Issues in Japan," p. 4.

75. Interview with a former Japanese intelligence analyst.

76. Kuroi, "What Are Japan's Foreign Intelligence Capabilities Now? (Part 2)"; Yakushiji Katsuyuki, "Japan's Evolving Security Policy," summary of presentation at the Henry L. Stimson Center, March 7, 2002 (www.stimson.org/?SN=JP2001111334).

77. Kotani, "Current State of Intelligence and Intelligence Issues in Japan," p. 3.

78. "Kyodo: Lead: Incoming U.S. Official Shows Discontent over SDF Data Leak," Kyodo, December 19, 2007 (OSC JPP200071219969030); Kuroi, "What Are Japan's Foreign Intelligence Capabilities Now? (Part 1)." This dependence leads to calls for greater autonomy from the United States; see Kuroi Buntaro, "Even Intelligence That Can Move a Nation Can Mostly Be Obtained from 'Open Source,'" *Interijensu no Gokui*, December 4, 2008 (OSC JPP20090209026009).

79. For an example from journalism see, "Behind Ordeal of Hu Leadership Is Shanghai Group," *Kyodo Clue II*, April 22, 2005 (OSC HPP20050424000057). For a scholarly view, see Ryosei Kokubun, "Changing Japanese Strategic Thinking toward China," in *Japanese Strategic Thought toward Asia*, edited by Gilbert Rozman, Kazuhiko Togo, and Joseph P. Ferguson (New York: Palgrave Macmillan, 2007), pp. 141–42.

80. National Institute for Defense Studies, *East Asian Strategic Review 2005* (Tokyo: Japan Times, 2005), p. 94.

81. Lyman Miller, "With Hu in Charge, Jiang's at Ease," *China Leadership Monitor*, no. 13 (Winter 2005) (http://media.hoover.org/documents/clm13_lm.pdf); Tony Saich, "China in 2005: Hu's in Charge," *Asian Survey* 46 (January-February 2006), pp. 37–48.

82. Yoshifumi Nakai, "Japan's View on the Rise of China and Its Implications: Bureaucratic Interests and Political Choices," in *Rise of China: Beijing's Strategies and Implications for the Asia-Pacific*, edited by Hsin-Huang Michael Hsiao and Cheng-yi Lin (New York: Routledge, 2009), pp. 219–34.

83. Japan Defense Agency, *Defense of Japan 2000* (Tokyo: Japan Times, 2000), pp. 43–49; quoted passage is on p. 46.

84. Japan Ministry of Defense, "China," *Defense of Japan 2006*, part 1, chapter 1, sections 2 and 3 (www.mod.go.jp/e/publ/w_paper/pdf/2006.html); and Japan Ministry of Defense, "China," *Defense of Japan 2008*, part 1, chapter 2, section 3, pp. 53, 56 (www.mod.go.jp/e/publ/w_paper/2008/html).

85. Japan Defense Agency, *Defense of Japan 2000*, pp. 43–49; quoted passage is on p. 46.

86. Japan Defense Agency, *Defense of Japan 2002* (Tokyo: Urban Connections, 2002), pp. 55–64; cited passages are on pp. 62 and 64.

87. "China," *Defense of Japan 2006*, pp. 40 to 49.

88. "Analysis: Retired Senior Japanese Officers Tout 'Offensive Defense' Concepts," OSC Feature, March 28, 2007 (OSC FEA20070329111667); Mitsuo Takai, "Will Japan's Military Resources Be Able to Defend 6,800 Islands?" *Gunji Kenkyu*, September 1, 2006, pp. 54–59 (OSC JPP20060929326003); Tomohide Murai, "Overcoming the 'China Threat Theory': Considering the 'China Threat Theory'—'Past,' 'Present,' 'Future'—From 'Supreme Ruler of the Orient' to 'Promotion of China,'" *Toa*, December 1, 2006, pp. 10–20 (OSC JPP20070725363002); Keiichi Nogi, "Hypothetical Ground Self-Defense Force Enemy and East Asian Military Force: 21st

Century Chinese Military: A Military Organization Comprising 3 Million Strong People's Liberation Army," *Gunji Kenkyu*, July 1, 2002 (OSC JPP20030220000042).

89. "Former Japan Defense Agency Head: China Seeking to Replace U.S. as Dominant Power in Asia," *Chung-Kuo Shih-Pao* [*China Times*], February 15, 2005 (OSC CPP20050214000061).

90. Schoff, *Crisis Management in Japan and the United States*, p. 8; "Japan-U.S. Foreign Ministerial Talks," *Kyodo Clue III*, October 18, 2006 (OSC JPP20061019026001); "N. Korea Nuke Situation Not Contingency in Japan's Vicinity: Kyuma," Kyodo, October 20, 2006 (OSC JPP20061020969022).

91. "'Do Not Irritate China': Then How Should We Handle Them?" *Foresight*, May 1, 2009 (OSC JPP20090508164002).

92. Tomohito Shinoda, "Japan's Top-Down Policy Process to Dispatch the SDF to Iraq," *Japanese Journal of Political Science* 7 (April 2006), pp. 71–91.

93. Ibid., pp. 72, 74–75.

94. Ibid., p. 77.

95. Ibid., pp. 75–76.

96. Ibid., p. 76.

97. Ibid., pp. 77–78.

98. Ibid., pp. 78–79. The discord within the LDP was connected to a more general conflict between Koizumi and his detractors in the run-up to an election for party president (which Koizumi ultimately won).

99. Shinoda, "Japan's Top-Down Policy Process," pp. 81–83.

100. Ibid., pp. 85–89.

101. The total number of ships attacked was 110, up from 44 the year before. Some were seized for ransom. Twelve of the vessels attacked were Japanese. "MSDF Can Protect Non-Japanese Ships If Loaded with Japanese Cargo," Kyodo, January 13, 2009 (OSC JPP20090113969080).

102. "Ensuring Safe Seas a Global Task Japan Should Play Its Part In," *Yomiuri Shimbun*, August 18, 2008 (OSC JPP20080818969079); "Antipiracy Legislation Badly Needed," *Yomiuri Shimbun*, August 19, 2008 (OSC JPP20080818969080).

103. "Ensuring Safe Seas a Global Task Japan Should Play Its Part In."

104. "Antipiracy Legislation Badly Needed."

105. "Japan Must Help Battle Piracy," *Yomiuri Shimbun*, October 5, 2008 (OSC JPP20081005969018); "Japan Eyed Sending Destroyer off Africa to Guard Luxury Cruise Ships," Kyodo, October 3, 2008 (OSC JPP20081003969021); "Government Must Tackle Rampant Piracy off Somalia," *Yomiuri Shimbun*, October 22, 2008 (OSC JPP20081023230002).

106. "Japan PM Aso Supports Proposal to Send MSDF Anti-Piracy Ships to Somalia," Kyodo, October 17, 2008 (OSC JPP20081017969056).

107. "Legal Restrictions Blocking Dispatch of MSDF Troops," *Mainichi Daily News Online*, November 25, 2008 (OSC JPP20081125969030).

108. "Government Weighing Sending SDF to Protect Ships from Somali Pirates," Nikkei Telecom 21, November 19, 2008 (OSC JPP20081119969004); "Give

MSDF Legal Base to Tackle Pirates," *Yomiuri Shimbun*, November 27, 2008 (OSC JPP20081126969073).

109. "Antipiracy Mission Needs Authorization for Use of Force: Defense Chief," Kyodo, November 21, 2008 (OSC 20081121969039).

110. "China Antipiracy Move Leaves Japan All At Sea," *Yomiuri Daily Online*, December 21, 2008 (OSC JPP20081221969029).

111. "Japan to Send Destroyer for Antipiracy Mission off Somalia in Feb," Kyodo, December 25, 2008 (OSC 20081225969077); "Japan to Consider Warship Dispatch off Somalia under Current Law," Jiji Press, December 26, 2008 (OSC JPP20081226969047); "Japan Eyes Allowing Limited Arms Use under Antipiracy Law," Jiji Press, December 26, 2008 (OSC JPP20081226969039); "Aso Orders Minister to Consider Defense Force Ship Mission near Somalia," Kyodo, December 26, 2008 (OSC JPP20081226969050); "Aso Seeks Swift SDF Dispatch to Deal With Pirates off Somalia," *Asahi Shimbun Online*, December 26, 2008 (OSC JPP20081226969052); "Government Laying Groundwork for SDF Antipiracy Mission off Somalia," Nikkei Telecom 21, December 27, 2008 (OSC JPP20081227043006).

112. "Focus: Japan's SDF to Go Abroad on Antipiracy Ops with Ambivalent Feelings," Kyodo, February 7, 2009 (OSC JPP20090207969032).

113. "MSDF May Be in Somali Waters by March," *Daily Yomiuri Online*, January 15, 2009 (OSC JPP20090115969098); "Government to Order MSDF to Prepare for Dispatch on Antipiracy Mission," Kyodo, January 16, 2009 (OSC JPP20090116969087); "Special Unit to Add Some Steel to MSDF Mission against Pirates," *Daily Yomiuri Online*, January 19, 2009 (OSC JPP20090119969064); "Ruling Parties Largely Agree on Defense Force's Antipiracy Mission," Kyodo, January 20, 2009 (OSC JPP20090120969050); "Ruling Parties Officially Agree to Seek MSDF Antipiracy Mission," Kyodo, January 22, 2009 (OSC JPP20090122969039); "'Sources' Say Minister to Instruct SDF to Prepare for Antipiracy Mission," Kyodo, January 27, 2009 (OSC JPP20090127969064).

114. "Defense Minister Tells MSDF to Ready for Antipiracy Mission off Somalia," Kyodo, January 28, 2009 (OSC JPP20090128969021).

115. "Ruling Parties Largely Agree on Defense Force's Antipiracy Mission."

116. "Defense Official Calls for Eased Weapons Rules to Engage Pirates," Kyodo, January 29, 2009 (OSC JPP20090129969063); "Government Poll Says Over 70 Percent Japanese Back MSDF Refueling Mission," Jiji Press, March 5, 2009 (OSC JPP20090305969073); "Japan to Deploy MSDF for Antipiracy Operations under Current Legal Framework," OSC report, February 17, 2009 (OSC JPP20090217020005).

117. "Ruling Coalition OKs Japan Antipiracy Mission Plan," Jiji Press, March 4, 2009 (OSC JPP20090304969072); "LDP OKs Antipiracy Bill ahead of Dispatch of Destroyers," Kyodo, March 10, 2009 (OSC JPP20090310969034); "Japan Orders MSDF Dispatch for Antipiracy Mission off Somalia," Kyodo, March 13, 2009 (OSC JPP20090313969041).

118. "Top MSDF Official Oks Force against Pirates Attacking Non-Japan Related Vessels," *Mainichi Daily News Online*, April 8, 2009 (OSC JPP20090408969079).

119. "Japan Readies P-3C Aircraft for Antipiracy Mission off Somalia," Kyodo, April 17, 2009 (OSC JPP20090417969026); "Japan to Send Ground Troops to Assist Antipiracy Mission off Somalia," Kyodo, April 23, 2009 (OSC JPP20090423969071); "Japan Dispatches Patrol Aircraft for Antipiracy Mission off Somalia," Kyodo, May 28, 2009 (OSC JPP20090528969017).

120. "Antipiracy Law Authorizing SDF Protection of Any Ship Enacted," Kyodo, June 19, 2009 (OSC JPP20090619969093). The law also placed restrictions on the government's authority to order a deployment. The defense minister was given authority to order an SDF deployment, subject to reporting the circumstances of the mission to the prime minister and gaining his approval. The prime minister was required to report on the deployment to the Diet. In emergencies, the defense minister was allowed to act first and report later. "Anti-Piracy Strategy off the Coast of Somalia; Full Text of New Anti-Piracy Law of Japan," *Sekai no Kansen*, October 2009 (OSC JPP20090923422001).

121. "Ex-Pentagon Official Warns of Japan's Decline," Kyodo, February 5, 2009 (OSC JPP20090205147003).

122. "Full Text of Prime Minister Hatoyama's Policy Speech on 26 Oct 09," Kyodo, October 26, 2009 (OSC 20091026027004).

123. "Senior Vice Ministers Required to Play More Important Role in New Administration," *Mainichi Daily News*, September 19, 2009 (OSC JPP20090919969039); Aurelia George-Mulgan, "Decapitating the bureaucracy in Japan," East Asia Forum, December 10, 2009 (www.eastasiaforum.org/2009/12/10/decapitating-the-bureaucracy-in-japan/; "Cabinet Legal Adviser To Cease Speaking in Diet," *Daily Yomiuri*, October 9, 2009 (OSC JPP20091010969019); "Official Seeks to Clarify Remarks on Constitutional Interpretations," Kyodo, November 5, 2009 (OSC JPP20091105696076).

124. "Mainichi: Hatoyama Sidesteps Bureaucratic Involvement in Creation of Policy Speech," *Mainichi Daily News*, January 30, 2010 (OSC JPP20100130969021).

125. "Nikkei: Prime Minister to Name Top Bureaucrats; Prosecutors Office Excepted," Nikkei Telecom, February 6, 2010 (OSC JPP20100206969064). Ozawa Ichiro, the DPJ's secretary-general, also considered a plan to foster policy interactions between senior party and agency officials; Takayama Yu and Kondo Daisuke, "DPJ: Ozawa Gradually Increasing His Involvement in Policymaking, Undermining Effort To Centralize Policymaking in Cabinet, Causing Concerns Over Ozawa's Growing Power," *Mainichi Shimbun*, February 15, 2010 (OSC JPP20100219038004).

126. Information from a Japanese diplomat, November 2009.

127. "The Strengths and Weaknesses of Mr. Hatoyama's Government," *Observing Japan*, September 15, 2009 (www.observingjapan.com/2009_09_01_archive.html).

128. Of course, the Japanese system of government did not change overnight in all respects. Reportedly, bureaucrats were able to retain a significant role in some issue areas, and although officials from some ministries were getting minimal "face time" with the new prime minister, senior career people from the Foreign Ministry

saw him frequently to discuss a range of issues. See Shiraishi Hitoshi, "'Post-Bureaucracy' Controlled by Bureaucrats," *Foresight* [Tokyo], October 17, 2009 (OSC JPP20091023004002); "Ministry Bureaucrats Getting Less Face Time with Hatoyama," Nikkei Telecom, November 4, 2009 (OSC JPP20091104969009).

129. "Gaimushō burēn ga nihontaishikan shusai seminā de Hatoyamashushō hihan wo daitenkai" [Policy Adviser to Foreign Ministry Criticizes Prime Minister Hatoyama at a Seminar Sponsored by Japanese Embassy], *Shukan Asahi*, March 5, 2010, p. 128.

130. Uesusgi Takashi, "Hatoyama's 'Haphazard PMOR' Straying Toda, Too," *Shukan Bunshun*, February 11, 2010 (OSC JPP20101212020013).

131. "Bōeishō kaikaku zenseiken no kettei hakushini—Kaikakukaigimo haishi seimusanyaku aratamete giron" [Defense Ministry Reform Plan Scrapped—Defense Counselors Abolished Advisors Created as Proposed Before], *Asagumo*, October 15, 2009 (www.asagumo-news.com/news/200910/091015/09101501.htm); "Defense Minister Kitazawa Deadlocked over 'Futenma Issue,'" *Shukan Bunshun*, October 22, 2009 (OSC JPP20091019640001).

132. "Jiji: Hatoyama Negative on Easing Rules on Peacekeepers' Arms Use," Jiji Press, March 17, 2010 (OSC JPP20100317969031).

133. "Kan Mends Fences with Bureaucracy, Pledges New Era of Cooperation," *Mainichi Daily News Online*, June 11, 2010 (OSC JPP20100611969063).

134. When the DPJ came into office, work was well under way on a new National Defense Program Guidelines. Fearing that the document would have an LDP and bureaucratic bias, the Hatoyama administration scrapped the process and started over. See "Kyodo: Panel to Launch Discussions on Revision of Defense Policy Platform," Kyodo, February 16, 2010 (OSC JPP20100216969018).

135. Initial reports about the Hatoyama administration were that the *kantei* did not function well; author's conversation with a long-term observer of the Japanese system, December 2009.

136. Of course, it is not just in Japan and China that personalities are important; see Peter W. Rodman, *Presidential Command: Power, Leadership, and the Making of Foreign Policy from Richard Nixon to George W. Bush* (New York: Alfred A. Knopf, 2009).

137. This summary is based on Uri Bar-Joseph and Jack S. Levy, "Conscious Action and Intelligence Failure," *Political Science Quarterly* 124 (Fall 2009), pp. 461–88.

138. Alexander L. George, *Presidential Decisionmaking in Foreign Policy* (Boulder, Colo.: Westview Press, 1980), pp. 155–57.

Chapter Ten

1. Interview with a Chinese scholar, January 2008.

2. See Susan Shirk, *China: Fragile Superpower* (Oxford University Press, 2007). Whether government officials can agree on a definition of the national interest is another matter.

378   Notes to Pages 192–93

3. John Wilson Lewis and Xue Litai, *Imagined Enemies: China Prepares for Uncertain War* (Stanford University Press, 2006), pp. 107–08.

4. The growing autonomy of subnational governments and companies (other actors in China-Japan relations) has led to complaints about actors who do not understand that there is a close connection between the domestic and foreign chessboards on which the government plays ("*guonei, guowai, liangge daju*"). That occurs even though some companies are promoted by central government agencies and provinces are in the middle of the administrative hierarchy. One diplomat complained about the actions of companies overseas: "Chinese businesses are going out into the world and they lack knowledge about the world. They have demonstrated bad behavior. They ignore the local conditions. People have criticized their behavior as representative of the Chinese government's behavior." Chinese scholars have used the word "hijacked" to describe the impact of companies on PRC diplomacy. See Bonnie S. Glaser, "Ensuring the 'Go Abroad' Policy Serves China's Domestic Priorities," *China Brief* 7 (March 8, 2007), pp. 2–5; cited passages are on pages 2 and 3. See also "Chinese Diplomacy 'Highjacked' by Companies," *Financial Times*, March 17, 2008, p. 2.

5. Edward Gu and Merle Goldman, "Introduction: The Transformation of the Relationship between Chinese Intellectuals and the State," in *Chinese Intellectuals between State and Market*, edited by Edward Gu and Merle Goldman (New York: RoutledgeCurzon, 2004), pp. 1–17.

6. Joseph Fewsmith and Stanley Rosen, "The Domestic Context of Chinese Foreign Policy: Does Public Opinion Matter?" in *The Making of Chinese Foreign and Security Policy*, edited by David Michael Lampton (Stanford University Press, 2001), pp. 158–69; cited passage is on p. 153.

7. Suisheng Zhao, "Chinese Intellectuals' Quest for National Greatness and Nationalistic Writing in the 1990s," *China Quarterly* 152 (December 1997), pp. 725–30; cited passage is on p. 728.

8. Based on Yongnian Zheng, *Discovering Chinese Nationalism in China: Modernization, Identity, and International Relations* (Cambridge University Press, 1999), pp. 97–100; Edward Friedman, "Chinese Nationalism: Challenge to U.S. Interests," in *The People's Liberation Army and China in Transition*, edited by Stephen J. Flanagan and Michael E. Marti (National Defense University Press, 2003), pp. 92–98.

9. Zhao, "Chinese Intellectuals' Quest for National Greatness," pp. 738–43.

10. Zhao, "Chinese Intellectuals' Quest for National Greatness," pp. 730–35.

11. Ibid., pp. 735–38. Yongnian Zheng offers a convergent analysis in *Discovering Chinese Nationalism*. See pp. 46–66 on opposition to Western approaches to modernization and pp. 67–86 for a discussion of cultural nationalism.

12. Suisheng Zhao, "Chinese Nationalism and Its International Orientations," *Political Science Quarterly* 115 (Spring 2000), pp. 5–10. Joseph Fewsmith and Stanley Rosen identify a similar trichotomy: cosmopolitanism, a residual readiness to embrace the capitalist and democratic West; nativism, a desire to reject it; and the

intermediate stance of self-strengthening, the desire to build up China's power so that it can meet the West more on the basis of parity and without jettisoning Chinese values. Fewsmith and Rosen, "The Domestic Context of Chinese Foreign Policy," pp. 158–69.

13. "Shadow of the future" is a common term in international relations, used to refer to the uncertainty that a country must face in conducting its relations with others.

14. Peter Hays Gries, "China's 'New Thinking' on Japan," *China Quarterly* 184 (December 2005), pp. 831–50.

15. Ma Licheng, "New Thoughts for China-Japan Relations—Worrisome Problems among Chinese and Japanese People," *Zhanlue yu Guanli*, December 1, 2002, pp. 41–47 (Open Source Center [hereafter OSC] CPP20021224000140).

16. Shi Yinhong, "Sino-Japanese Rapprochement and 'Diplomatic Revolution,'" *Zhanlue yu Guanli*, March 1, 2003, pp. 71–75 (OSC CPP20030506000224).

17. Feng Zhaokui, "On the New Thinking on Sino-Japanese Relations," *Zhanlue yu Guanli*, July 1, 2003, pp. 1-17 (OSC CPP20030821000188).

18. Quoted in Sun Yafei, "Is 'New Thinking' Needed on Japan?" *Nanfang Zhoumo*, June 12, 2003 (OSC CPP20030617000011).

19. Bai Jingfan, "Luoji hunluan di 'xin siwei'" [The Confused Logic of the "New Thinking"], *Kang Ri Zhanzheng Yanjiu* [Journal of the War of Resistance against Japan] 3 (2003), pp. 198–202; summarized in Gries, "China's 'New Thinking' on Japan," pp. 837–38.

20. Feng Zhaokui, "More Discussion of New Thinking on Sino-Japanese Relations," *Zhanlue yu Guanli* 5 (2003), p. 78; as cited in Gries, "China's 'New Thinking' on Japan," p. 838.

21. Gries, "China's 'New Thinking' on Japan," pp. 838–39.

22. Michael Alan Brittingham, "The Role of Nationalism in Chinese Foreign Policy: A Reactive Model of Nationalism and Conflict," *Journal of Chinese Political Science* 12 (2007), p. 150.

23. James Townsend, "Chinese Nationalism," *Australian Journal of Chinese Affairs* 27 (January 1992), p. 114; Frank Dikotter, "Racial Identities in China: Context and Meaning," *China Quarterly* 138 (June 1994), pp. 404–12; Lei Yi, "Xiandai de 'Huaxia zhongxingguan' yu 'minzhu zhuyi'" [Modern "Sinocentrism" and "Nationalism"], in *Zhounguo Ruhe Miandu Xifang* [How China Faces the West], edited by Xiao Pang (Hong Kong: Mirror Books, 1997), pp. 49–50, cited in Peter Hayes Gries, *China's New Nationalism: Pride, Politics, and Diplomacy* (University of California Press, 2004), p. 8; "China Gives No Ground in Spats over History," *Washington Post*, September 22, 2004.

24. On humiliation and victimization, see Suisheng Zhao, "Chinese Nationalism and Its International Orientations," pp. 5, 7; and Gries, *China's New Nationalism*, pp. 45–52, 69–85. For the quoted passage, see Geremie Barmé, "To Screw Foreigners Is Patriotic: China's Avant-Garde Nationalists," *China Journal* 34 (July 1995), p. 233.

Chinese history, as presented for popular audiences, is often selective and distorted, and it ignores cases in which China's difficulties were the result of its own leaders' mistakes; see "China's Textbooks Twist and Omit History," *New York Times*, December 6, 2004, p. A10.

25. Peter Hays Gries, "Tears of Rage: Chinese Nationalist Reactions to the Belgrade Embassy Bombing," *China Journal* 46 (July 2001), pp. 25–43; cited passage is on p. 26.

26. Gries, *China's New Nationalism*, pp. 43–53.

27. There are, to be sure, exceptions to the basic themes. One is that resentment of past victimization has a flip side: a yearning for acceptance by the very powers that caused China's humiliation. See "Nationalist Fervor in China Is Backed by Anger," *New York Times*, June 27, 2008 (www.nytimes.com/2008/06/27/world/asia/27iht-rchinat. 1.14041557.html). Another is the ambivalence with which some young people view their country. They are realistic and even frustrated about China's backwardness relative to the world's most advanced countries. They prefer to go and live abroad for a time for the sake of a better education and quality of life. But their love of country is a "filial nationalism," "in which China was identified with a long-suffering parent who, despite her flaws, deserved the filial devotion of her children." See Vanessa Fong, "Filial Nationalism among Chinese Teenagers with Global Identities," *American Ethnologist* 31 (November 2004), pp. 631–48; cited passage is on p. 632.

28. Shirk, *China: Fragile Superpower*, pp. 79–80.

29. Ma Jiuqi, "Simple Hatred Made Us Overlook Japan's 'Terrific' Aspects," *Zhongguo Qingnian Bao* [China Youth Daily], July 20, 2007 (OSC CPP20070724455002).

30. Xiao De, "Discovering 'Another Japan': Do the Chinese People Begin to Have a New Thinking on Japan?" Xinhua Wang, June 3, 2008 (OSC CPP20080605071001); "Government Shelves Dispatch of SDF Planes in Consideration of Opposition within PRC, Leakage of Information Is One of Miscalculation," *Nihon Keizai Shimbun*, May 30, 2008 (OSC JPP20080530045002).

31. Zxhm [pseudonym], "An Updated Ranking List of Contemporary Chinese Traitors," Sino-Japanese Forum, *Renmin Wang*, October 11, 2005 (OSC CPP200510175020001).

32. On gratitude for Japanese aid after the May 2008 Sichuan earthquake, see "Discovering 'Another Japan': Do the Chinese People Begin to Have a New Thinking on Japan?" Xinhua Wang [online service of the Xinhua News Agency] (OSC CPP20080605071001). For criticism of Chinese netizens cheering an earthquake in Japan, see Ma Jiuqi, "Simple Hatred Made Us Overlook Japan's 'Terrific' Aspects."

33. Fewsmith and Rosen, "The Domestic Context of Chinese Foreign Policy," pp. 171–72.

34. Suisheng Zhao, "China's Pragmatic Nationalism: Is It Manageable?" *Washington Quarterly* 29 (Winter 2005–06), pp. 131–44. On the point that the regime's propaganda has fostered the very nationalistic attitudes that now constrain it, see Nicholas D. Kristof, "The China Threat?" *New York Times*, December 20, 2003, p.

A19. Gries, *China's New Nationalism,* is especially effective in demonstrating the authenticity of popular sentiments.

35. Shirk, *China: Fragile Superpower,* pp. 84–85; cited passages are on p. 84.

36. This paragraph is based on Guobing Yang, "China since Tiananmen: Online Activism," *Journal of Democracy* 20 (July 2009), pp. 33–36. See also Xu Wu, *Chinese Cyber Nationalism: Evolution, Characteristics, and Implications* (Lanham, Md.: Lexington Books, 2007).

37. Wu, *Chinese Cyber Nationalism,* p. 75.

38. Wu, *Chinese Cyber Nationalism,* pp. 74–82. The Internet is also a means by which Chinese nationalists mobilize boycotts of Japanese companies with which they have a grievance; see Emily Parker, "The Burden of Being Japanese," *Asian Wall Street Journal,* April 25, 2005, p. A13 (http://awsj.com.hk/factiva-ns).

39. "PRC: Communist Party Paper's Website Allows Criticism of Hu Jintao's Japan Trip," Strong Nation Forum, *Renmin Wang,* May 6–7, 2008 (OSC CPP20080508611001).

40. Wu, *Chinese Cyber Nationalism,* pp. 180–87.

41. "General Secretary Hu Jintao Arrives at Renmin Wang's Qiangguo Luntan and Chats with Netizens Online," Strong Nation Forum, *Renmin Wang,* June 20, 2008 (OSC CPP20080620701003).

42. Yu Jie, "The Anti-Japanese Resistance War, Chinese Patriotism, and Free Speech. How Can We Forgive Japan?" *Japan Focus,* February 2, 2008 (www.japan focus.org/products/details/2654). In August 2009, a government adviser warned about the growing phenomenon of "cyber-vigilantism," in which netizens unfairly attack individuals and officials; see "China's Internet a Major Concern to Officials: Govt Adviser," Agence France-Presse, August 10, 2009 (OSC CPP20090810968190).

43. For Genron NPO's "Japan-China Joint Opinion Polls" for 2005, see www.genron-npo.net/forum_pekintokyo/000897.html and www.genron-npo.net/forum_pekintokyo/000895.html; for 2006, www.genron-npo.net/forum_tokyopekin/001580.html; for 2007, www.genron-npo.net/forum_pekintokyo3/002757.html; for 2008, http://tokyo-beijingforum.net/index.php?option=com_content&view=article&id=345:canvass4th2008&catid=83:canvass4th2008&Itemid=160; and for 2009, http://tokyo-beijingforum.net/index.php?option=com_content&view=article&id=439:5-&catid=110:20095&Itemid=160. In the 2007 survey, for example, 1,609 urban residents were divided more or less evenly among Beijing, Shanghai, Xian, Chengdu, and Shenyang. Ages ranged from twenty to sixty years. Around 90 percent of those polled had at least a junior high school education. The occupations were varied, including senior management, freelance workers, physical laborers, retirees, laid-off workers, and unemployed persons.

44. Genron NPO, "2007 Japan-China Joint Opinion Polls."

45. Genron NPO, "2007 Japan-China Joint Opinion Polls."

46. Genron NPO, "2007 Japan-China Joint Opinion Polls." I am grateful to Yasushi Kudo of Genron NPO and Iwashita Akihiro of Hokkaido University for clarifying some points on some of the graphs in this study.

47. Peter Hays Gries and others, "Historical Beliefs and the Perception of Threat in Northeast Asia: Colonialism, the Tributary System, and China-Japan-Korea Relations in the Twenty-First Century," *International Relations of the Asia-Pacific* 9 (May 2009), pp. 245–65.

48. Gries's *China's New Nationalism* takes the 1999 demonstrations as its point of departure.

49. David M. Finkelstein, "China Reconsiders Its National Security: The Great Peace and Development Debate of 1999" (Alexandria, Va.: CNA Corporation, December 2000), p. i. This section is based on Finkelstein's monograph.

50. Finkelstein, "China Reconsiders Its National Security," pp. 5–7.

51. Ibid., pp. 16–18.

52. The leadership's effort to manage the response to Belgrade was complicated by Taiwan president Lee Teng-hui's "special state-to-state" announcement that happened to come in the summer of 1999, because it raised questions about the effectiveness of Jiang Zemin's relatively moderate and patient policy toward the island. See Robert L. Suettinger, *Beyond Tiananmen: The Politics of U.S.-China Relations 1989–2000* (Brookings, 2003), pp. 384–85.

53. Jiang's handling of these incidents is consistent with the results of scholarly analysis of the CCP leadership's handling of nationalistic political forces. Suisheng Zhao concludes that its pragmatic approach treats nationalism in an instrumental, reactive, and state-centered way: "Being instrumental and state-led, nationalism may be used to flex China's muscles in international affairs if it is deemed desirable by Chinese leaders to enhance their political power. But being reactive to international currents, nationalist sentiments may decrease if perceived external pressure diminishes and if China's confidence in international affairs increases." See Zhao, "Chinese Nationalism and Its International Orientations," p. 23.

54. This section is based in part on James J. Przystup, "Japan-China Relations: No End to History," *Comparative Connections* 7, no. 2 (July 2000) (www.csis.org/media/csis/pubs/0502q.pdf); and Wu, *Chinese Cyber Nationalism*, pp. 82–86. For a Japanese account, see Ryosei Kokubun, "Changing Japanese Strategic Thinking toward China," in *Japanese Strategic Thought toward Asia*, edited by Gilbert Rozman, Kazuhiko Togo, and Joseph P. Ferguson (New York: Palgrave Macmillan, 2007), pp. 139–42.

55. "Propaganda Toned Down to Cool Anti-Japanese Sentiment," *South China Morning Post*, April 6, 2005 (OSC CPP20050406000028).

56. Xinyugong, "Protests against Japan Should Not Be Limited to the Textbook Issue: There Should Be All-Out Countermeasures," Strong Nation Forum, *Renmin Wang*, April 7, 2005 (OSC CPP20050407000163).

57. "Propaganda Toned Down to Cool Anti-Japanese Sentiment."

58. "China Expresses Regret over Violence During Demonstrations," Kyodo, April 9, 2005 (OSC JPP20050409000072); "As Various Localities Staged Anti-Japanese Demonstrations Today, Japan Lodged Protest, Urging China to Protect Japan-Funded

Firms," *Ping Kuo Jih Pao*, April 10, 2005 (OSC CPP20050410000016). One Japanese media report alleged that the PRC public security authorities had worked to facilitate the demonstrations and that the police had no choice but to accommodate them. "'Anti-Japanese Sentiments' Going Dangerously out of Control," JijiWeb, April 9, 2005 (OSC JPP20050410000091). A Chinese contributor to an Internet chat room asserted that many of the protesters in Shenzhen were members of the People's Armed Police in plain clothes; see Requiem, "Shocking Inside Story of Mainland's Anti-Japanese Demonstrations," Boxun, April 11, 2005 (OSC CPP20050412000222).

59. "Shadow of Power Struggle behind Hu's Stance," JijiWeb, April 24, 2005 (OSC JPP20050424000047); "Behind Ordeal of Hu Leadership Is Shanghai Group," *Kyodo Clue II*, April 22, 2005 (OSC HPP20050424000057).

60. Satoshi Saeki and Masahiko Takehoshi, "Chinese Government Fears Criticism," *Daily Yomiuri*, April 12, 2005 (OSC JPP20050411000187).

61. "Behind Ordeal of Hu Leadership Is Shanghai Group."

62. "Web Site Launching Anti-Japanese Demonstration Is Closed Up," *Ping Kuo Jih Pao*, April 13, 2005 (OSC CPP20050413000100); Cindy Sui, "China on Alert for Further Protests, University Students Boycott Japan Goods," Agence France-Presse, April 12, 2005 (OSC CPP20050412000119); "Beijing Public Security Warns against Demonstrations without Permission," Kyodo, April 15, 2005 (OSC JPP20050415000062); "Tang Jiaxuan Meets Japan's Kyodo News Agency President," Xinhua, April 15, 2005 (OSC CPP20050415000193).

63. "Tang Jiaxuan Meets Japan's Kyodo News Agency President."

64. "Increase in Articles Criticizing Government; PRC Authorities Fear Spread of Disturbances," *Kyodo Clue II*, April 18, 2005 (OSC JPP20050419000022). There were no protests allowed in Beijing, where security was tight in advance of the visit of the Japanese foreign minister.

65. Tetsu Shiraishi, "China: Publicity Team to Improve Relations with Japan," *Tokyo Shimbun*, April 22, 2005 (OSC JPP200504220000280).

66. "Under Siege: Internet Intruders," *Asahi Shimbun*, April 14, 2005 (OSC JPP20050414000048); "Foreign Ministry's Homepage Goes Down Due to Concentrated Access," *Yomiuri Shimbun*, April 9, 2005 (OSC JPP20050411000008); "NPA, SDF Web Sites Hit by Cyber Attacks," *Daily Yomiuri*, April 15, 2005 (OSC JPP20050414000168); "Japanese Firms, University under Cyber Attack with Anti-Japan Messages," Kyodo, April 15, 2005 (OSC JPP20050415000086).

67. Cyber Force Center, National Police Agency Japan, "Wagakuni ni okeru internet chianjyōsei nitsuite" [Internet Security in Japan], March 2005, April 2005, May 2005 (www.cyberpolice.go.jp/detect/pdf/H170413.pdf, http://www.cyberpolice.go.jp/detect/pdf/H170513.pdf, www.cyberpolice.go.jp/detect/pdf/H170608.pdf).

68. Ayumi Otani, "China: Anti-Japan Demonstration Leaders Lose Control over Participants," *Mainichi Shimbun*, April 12, 2005 (OSC JPP20050412000036); the quote is from this article.

69. Interview with a foreign resident of Beijing, October 2009.

Chapter Eleven

1. Karel van Wolferen, *The Enigma of Japanese Power: People and Politics in a Stateless Nation* (New York: Vintage Books, 1989).

2. Aurelia George Mulgan, *Japan's Failed Revolution: Koizumi and the Politics of Economic Reform* (Canberra, Australia: Asia Pacific Press, 2000).

3. Gerald L. Curtis, *The Logic of Japanese Politics: Leaders, Institutions, and the Limits of Change* (Columbia University Press, 2000), pp. 59–60.

4. Populism is not a new phenomenon. As early as the 1920s, Japan had a mass culture and mass participation, and the mass media generated strong support for the 1931 takeover of Manchuria. See Marius B. Jansen, *The Making of Modern Japan* (Harvard University Press, 2002), p. 577.

5. For results of the polls, see Genron NPO, "Japan-China Joint Opinion Polls: Reference Material" (in English), August 17, 2007 (www.genron-npo.net/pdf/20070817_e_press.pdf); GenronNPO, "2008 Japan-China Joint Opinion Polls" (http://tokyo-beijingforum.net/index.php?option=com_content&view=article&id=345:canvass4th2008&catid=83:canvass4th2008&Itemid=160); Genron NPO, "2009 Japan-China Joint Opinion Polls" (http://tokyo-beijingforum.net/index.php?option=com_content&view=article&id=439:5-&catid=110:20095&Itemid=160).

6. Patrick L. Smith, "Uncertain Legacy: Japanese Nationalism after Koizumi," *International Herald Tribune*, September 11, 2006 (www.nytimes.com/2006/09/11/world/asia/11iht-national.2767320.html?scp=1&sq=japan%20nationalism%20shinzo%20abe&st=cse). On Japan's "identity crisis," see Brad Glosserman and Scott Snyder, "Confidence and Confusion: National Identity and Security Alliances in Northeast Asia," *Issues and Insights* 8, September 2008 (http://csis.org/files/media/csis/pubs/issuesinsights_v08n16.pdf), pp. 4–7.

7. Hitoshi Tanaka, "Nationalistic Sentiments in Japan and their Foreign Policy Implications," *East Asia Insights* 2 (January 2007), pp. 1–5; cited passage is on p. 1.

8. For a brief summary, see Colum Murphy, "Do or Die for Japan's Radical Right," *Far Eastern Economic Review*, April 2007, pp. 15–20.

9. National Police Agency, *White Paper on Police 2008*, August 2008 (www.npa.go.jp/english/kokusai9/WhitePaper2008-7.pdf), p. 161.

10. This segment of the Japanese public both affirms Japan's role before 1945 and rejects the idea that Japan should contribute constructively to international security. See Kitaoka Shin'ichi, "Goodbye Tanaka-Style Politics, Hello New Center," *Japan Echo* 36 (August 2009), pp. 15–19.

11. Glosserman and Snyder, "Confidence and Confusion," p. 7. The love of country is higher among the elite cohort, even over 90 percent.

12. Matthew Penney and Bryce Wakefield, "Right Angles: Examining Accounts of Japanese Neo-Nationalism," *Pacific Affairs* 81 (Winter 2008), p. 551.

13. Nobuhiro Hiwatari, "Japan in 2005: Koizumi's Finest Hour," *Asian Survey* 46 (January-February 2006), p. 27.

14. Penney and Wakefield, "Right Angles," pp. 547–51.

15. Penney and Wakefield, "Right Angles," p. 555.

16. Brian J. McVeigh, *Nationalisms of Japan: Managing and Mystifying Identity* (Lanham, Md.: Roman and Littlefield, 2004), pp. 33–37, 56–80. And young people do not exhibit anti-foreign nationalism any more than do their elders; see Hironori Sasada, "Youth and Nationalism in Japan," *SAIS Review* 26, no. 2 (Summer-Fall 2006), pp. 109–22.

17. Denny Roy, "The Sources and Limits of Sino-Japanese Tensions," *Survival* 47 (Summer 2005), p. 204.

18. Ellis S. Krauss, "Has Japanese Politics Really Changed?" *Japan Economic Currents* 66 (October 2007) (www.kkc.or.jp/english/activities/publications/economic-currents68.pdf), pp. 1–2. On the basics of the Japanese electoral system, see "Election 2009 Factbox: Electoral System for Japan's House of Representatives," Kyodo, August 14, 2009 (Open Source Center [hereafter OSC] JPP20090814057001).

19. J. Patrick Boyd and Richard J. Samuels, "Prosperity's Children: Generational Change and Japan's Future Leadership," *Asia Policy* 6 (July 2008), pp. 15–51, especially pp. 37–38; cited passage is on p. 37.

20. Leif-Eric Easley, Tetsuo Kotani, and Aki Mori, "Electing a New Japanese Security Policy? Examining Foreign Policy Visions within the Democratic Party of Japan," *Asia Policy* 9 (January 2010), pp. 45–66.

21. "Scanner: Bōeitaikōkaitei giron kaishi minshu towareru anpokan" [Scanner: Attention Focused on DPJ's Views of National Security in Discussion on Revising National Defense Program Guideline], *Yomiuri Shimbun*, February 19, 2010, p. 3.

22. Wang Yang, "The Dragon Spruce Can Bear Witness: The International Liaison Department of the CPC Central Committee Replies to 21 Shiji Jingji Baodao and Analyzes Interparty Exchange History between the CPC and Democratic Party of Japan," *21 Shiji Jingji Baodao*, September 9, 2009 (OSC CPP20090915624001).

23. "Foreign Policy Speech by Minister for Foreign Affairs Katsuya Okada to the 174th Session of the Diet," January 29, 2010 (www.mofa.go.jp/announce/fm/okada/speech1001.html).

24. "Kyodo: Lead: Ozawa Expressed Concern over China's Military Buildup," Kyodo, December 11, 2009 (OSC JPP20091211969044).

25. "Opposition Leader Ozawa Says Japan Could Produce Nuclear Weapons, Surpass China," Kyodo, April 6, 2002 (OSC JPP20020406000056).

26. Kyodo: Kitazawa Rejects Idea of Transferring All Okinawa Marines to Guam," Kyodo, February 21, 2010 (OSC JPP20100221969015).

27. "Chugoku ni taisuru shinkinkan" [Affinity toward China], *Gaikō ni kansuru yoronchōsa* [Public Opinion Poll on Japanese Diplomacy] (Cabinet Office, Government of Japan, December 2008), diagram 10 (http://www8.cao.go.jp/survey/h20/h20-gaiko/index.html).

28. "Genzai no Nihon to Chugoku to no kanke" [Current Japan-China Relations], *Gaikō ni kansuru yoronchōsa* [Public Opinion Poll on Japanese Diplomacy]

(Cabinet Office, Government of Japan, December 2008), diagram 12 (http://www8. cao.go.jp/survey/h20/h20-gaiko/index.html).

29. Susan J. Pharr, "Introduction: Media and Politics in Japan: Historical and Contemporary Perspectives," in *Media and Politics in Japan*, edited by Susan J. Pharr and Ellis S. Krauss (University of Hawaii Press, 1996), p. 6.

30. Dentsu Communication Institute, *Joho media hakusho: 2008* [News Media White Paper: 2008]—*A Research for Information and Media Society* (Tokyo: Daiyamondosha, 2008), p. 16.

31. Tomohito Shinoda, "Becoming More Realistic in the Post–Cold War: Japan's Changing Media and Public Opinion on National Security," *Japanese Journal of Political Science* 8 (August 2007), p. 175.

32. D. Eleanor Westney, "Mass Media as Business Organizations: A U.S.-Japanese Comparison," in *Media and Politics in Japan*, edited by Pharr and Krauss, pp. 77–79.

33. Shinoda, "Becoming More Realistic in the Post–Cold War," p. 189. Moreover, the media did not always discuss potential military threats and the role of the SDF in Japan's security policy. They have done so since the late 1990s. See Sabine Früstück, *Uneasy Warriors: Gender, Memory, and Popular Culture in the Japanese Army* (University of California Press, 2007), pp. 5–6.

34. Shinoda, "Becoming More Realistic in the Post–Cold War," p. 190.

35. Susan J. Pharr, "Media as Trickster in Japan: A Comparative Perspective," in *Media and Politics in Japan*, edited by Pharr and Krauss, pp. 19–44. For a critique that assumes that the media are the servant of the state, see Nobuyuki Okumura, "The Backwardness of Japanese Political Journalism: Nonestablished Ethics and Unwritten Rules," CSIS Japan Chair Platform, May 7, 2008 (http://csis.org/files/media/csis/pubs/080507_okumura_.pdf).

36. Okazaki Hisahiko, "Media Role Helps Inflame the Yasukuni Issue," *Daily Yomiuri*, September 3, 2006 (OSC JPP20090902690028).

37. John Creighton Campbell, "Media and Policy Change in Japan," in *Media and Politics in Japan*, edited by Pharr and Krauss, p. 208.

38. Janice Tang, "Japan Vows to Prevent Data Leak, Asks U.S. for Info on F-22A Fighter," Kyodo, April 30, 2007 (OSC JPP20070430969059).

39. "Security Order Issued to MSDF for Unidentified Submarine in Japan's Water," NHK General Television, November 10, 2004 (OSC JPP20041110000008).

40. "NHK Airs Special News Bulletin on Submarine Found in Territorial Waters," NHK General Television, November 10, 2004 (OSC JPP20041110000055); Furumoto Yoso, "Suspicious Submarine: Intrusion of Territorial Waters; JDA Sends AWACS to Surrounding Ocean; Watch Out for Chinese Fighter Jets," *Mainichi Shimbun*, November 13, 2004 (OSC JPP20041113000004).

41. "Chinese Official Tells Kyodo PRC Foreign Ministry Has No Knowledge of Submarine," Kyodo, November 11, 2004 (OSC JPP20041111000013); "Further on Suspected Chinese Nuclear Submarine Entering Japanese Waters," Kyodo, November 10, 2004 (OSC JPP20041110000051); "NHK Carries Photos of Chinese Ships

Spotted Near Japan since 5 Nov," NHK General Television, November 10, 2004 (OSC JPP20041110000013); "Japan Identifies Intruding Sub as Chinese, to Lodge Protest with China," Kyodo, November 12, 2004 (OSC JPP20041112000079).

42. "Japanese Media Speculate on Motives behind PRC Submarine Incursion," Foreign Broadcast Information Service (FBIS) Report, November 29, 2004 (OSC JPP20041129000153); "Japanese Articles on Submarine Intrusion 10, 11 Nov 04," FBIS Report, November 10, 2004 (OSC JPP20041110000019).

43. "Government Beset by Criticisms from LDP on Submarine Intrusion Incident," *Kyodo Clue II*, November 12, 2004 (OSC 20041115000027); "Officials Criticized for Response to Submarine," *Asahi Shimbun*, November 12, 2004 (OSC JPP20041112000044); "Government Maintains Cautious Stance; Test of Diplomacy toward China," *Sankei Shimbun*, November 11, 2004 (OSC JPP20041112000055); "Non-Disclosure for a Certain Period Considered: Making Security Operations Public May Affect SDF Operations: Government to Consider Issue for Future," *Asahi Shimbun*, November 13, 2004 (OSC JPP20041115000031); "Intrusion into Territorial Sea: Chinese Submarine Identified; Public Reaction Stronger Than Expected," *Sankei Shimbun*, November 13, 2004 (OSC JPP20041115000007).

44. "Tokyo Editorials on Alleged PRC Sub's Intrusion into Japanese Waters," FBIS Report, November 11, 2004 (OSC JPP2004111200003).

45. "Japan: Editorials on PRC Submarine Intrusion 13 Nov 04," FBIS Report, November 13, 2004 (OSC JPP20041114000059); "China's Apology for Intrusion into Territorial Sea Commendable," *Nihon Keizai Shimbun*, November 17, 2004 (OSC JPP20041117000020); "Chinese Submarine's Intrusion: We Demand the Punishment of Officials Concerned," *Sankei Shimbun*, November 18, 2004 (OSC JPP20041118000014).

46. "Anti-Japanese Protests in China: Explosive Situation," *Asahi Shimbun*, April 7, 2005 (OSC JPP20050407000005); "Deep-Rooted Nature Not to Be Underrated," *Mainichi Shimbun*, April 8, 2005 (OSC JPP20050408000002); Ito Tadashi, "Deep-Rooted Criticisms on Historical Issues; 'Anti-Japan' Rallies Become Venues to Vent Dissatisfaction," *Sankei Shimbun*, April 5, 2005 (OSC JPP20050407000015).

47. "Japan: Editorials on Anti-Japan Demonstrations in China, 10–11 Apr 05," FBIS Report, April 11, 2005 (OSC JPP20050410000084).

48. Source: "Nichibei kyōdō yoronchōsa teimeisuru nihonkeizaini kibishiime/ Yomiuri shimbunsha gyarappu sha" [Japan-U.S. Joint Public Opinion Poll: Foundering Japanese Economy Eyed Critically/Yomiuri Newspaper–Gallup], *Yomiuri Shimbun*, December 5, 2002, p. 26; "Nichibei kyōdō yoronchōsa chūgokujūshi, senmeini 'iraku' kageotosu/Yomiuri Gyarappu sha" [Japan-U.S. Joint Public Opinion Poll: China's Importance Becomes Clear, Iraq Casts a Shadow/Yomiuri–Gallup], *Yomiuri Shimbun*, December 12, 2003, p. 14; "Nichibei kyōdō yoronchōsa nichibei 'ryōkō' ninshikiwa kyōtsū/Yomiuri shimbunsha gyarappu sha" [Japan-U.S. Joint Public Opinion Poll: Japan-U.S. 'Favorable' Perception Is Mutual/Yomiuri Newspaper– Gallup], *Yomiuri Shimbun*, December 16, 2004, p. 14; "Nichibei kyōdō yoronchōsa

'nichibei ryōkō' sōhōde zōka chūgokueno fushin senmeini" [Japan-U.S. Joint Public Opinion Poll: 'Japan-U.S. Favorable' Increases on Both Sides, Mistrust toward China Becomes Apparent], *Yomiuri Shimbun*, December 15, 2005, p. 16; "Kyōdō yoron-chōsa 'kitachōsen no kaku' kenanni nichibeikankei ryōkō, sōhōde zōka – tokushū" [Joint Public Opinion Poll: 'North Korean Nuclear Weapons' Remain Unresolved, Japan-U.S. Relations Favorable Perception Increases on Both Sides–Special Edition], *Yomiuri Shimbun*, December 16, 2006, p. 14.

Chapter Twelve

1. "Sino-Japanese Rivalry: Implications for U.S. Policy," INSS Special Report (Institute for National Strategic Studies, National Defense University, April 2007) (www.ndu.edu/inss/Research/SRapr07.pdf), p. 3.

2. Bernard D. Cole, "Right-Sizing the Navy: How Much Naval Force Will Beijing Deploy?" in *Right-Sizing the People's Liberation Army: Exploring the Contours of China's Military*, edited by Roy Kamphausen and Andrew Scobell (Carlisle, Pa.: Strategic Studies Institute, U.S. Army War College, 2007), p. 543–44.

3. Sato Masaru, "Senior Chinese PLA Official Expresses Concern about Japan-China Friction over East China Sea Gas Fields, 'Small-Scale Conflict Conceivable,'" *Nihon Keizai Shimbun*, November 3, 2009 (Open Source Center [hereafter OSC] JPP20091103176001).

4. Cole, "Right-Sizing the Navy: How Much Naval Force Will Beijing Deploy?" pp. 543–44. Kenneth Allen presents a useful scenario of an escalating interaction between the air forces of China and Taiwan in his "Air Force Deterrence and Escalation Calculations for a Taiwan Strait Conflict: China, Taiwan, and the United States," in *Assessing the Threat: The Chinese Military and Taiwan's Challenge*, edited by Michael D. Swain, Andrew N. D. Yang, and Evan S. Medeiros (Washington: Carnegie Endowment for International Peace, 2007), pp. 153–84.

5. "Military Power of the People's Republic of China 2009," March 2009 (www.defenselink.mil/pubs/pdfs/China_Military_Power_Report_2009.pdf), p. 20.

6. On the relevance of competing interests to crisis management, see Jack S. Levy, "The Role of Crisis Management in the Outbreak of World War I," in *Avoiding War: Problems of Crisis Management*, edited by Alexander L. George (Boulder, Colo.: Westview Press, 1991), pp. 62–102.

7. "Sino-Japanese Rivalry: Implications for U.S. Policy," p. 3.

8. Jonathan Wilkenfeld, "Concepts and Methods in the Study of International Crisis Management," in *Managing Sino-American Crises: Case Studies and Analysis*, edited by Michael D. Swaine, Zhang Tuosheng, and Danielle F. S. Cohen (Washington: Carnegie Endowment for International Peace, 2006), p. 104.

9. Alexander L. George, "A Provisional Theory of Crisis Management," in *Avoiding War*, edited by George, pp. 22–23.

10. George, "A Provisional Theory of Crisis Management," pp. 22–23; Alexander L. George, "Findings and Recommendations," in *Avoiding War*, pp. 545–50.

11. Wilkenfeld, "Concepts and Methods in the Study of International Crisis Management," pp. 110–11; Michael D. Swaine, "Chinese Crisis Management: Framework for Analysis, Tentative Observations, and Questions for the Future," in *Chinese National Decisionmaking under Stress,* edited by Andrew Scobell and Larry M. Wortzel (Carlisle, Pa.: Strategic Studies Institute, U.S. Army War College, 2005), pp. 6–7.

12. Scobell and Wortzel, *Chinese National Decisionmaking under Stress,* also takes a broader approach.

13. George, "Findings and Recommendations," p. 562.

14. Swaine, "Chinese Crisis Management," p. 6. Much of the discussion that follows comes from George, "Findings and Recommendations," pp. 553-560.

15. Michael D. Swaine, "Understanding the Historical Record," in *Managing Sino-American Crises,* edited by Swaine, Tuosheng, and Cohen (Carnegie Endowment for International Peace, 2006), pp. 11–12; cited passage is on p. 11.

16. Alexander L. George, "Strategies for Crisis Management," in *Avoiding War,* edited by George, pp. 377–93.

17. Alexander L. George, "The Tension Between 'Military Logic' and Requirements of Diplomacy in Crisis Management," in *Avoiding War,* edited by George, pp. 13-27.

18. John Wilson Lewis and Xue Litai, *Imagined Enemies: China Prepares for Uncertain War* (Stanford University Press, 2006), pp. 89–91, 86, 93. Lewis and Xue say that the decision is passed through the Secretariat to the leading group, but generally, they place far too much emphasis on the Secretariat; see, for example, pp. 80–82. For some time the Secretariat has been responsible only for party affairs; see Alice Miller, "Xi Jinping and the Party Apparatus," *China Leadership Monitor* 25 (Summer 2008) (http://media.hoover.org/documents/CLM25AM.pdf).

19. Lewis and Xue, *Imagined Enemies,* pp. 87–116; cited passages are on pp. 90, 97, and 93. Glaser and Saunders observe that a crisis can make analysts risk averse in offering recommendations that are outside what they think is the mainstream. See Bonnie S. Glaser and Phillip Saunders, "Chinese Civilian Foreign Policy Research Institutes: Evolving Roles and Increasing Influence," *China Quarterly* 171 (September 2002), pp. 597–616; cited passages are on p. 612.

20. Swaine, "Understanding the Historical Record," pp. 13–14.

21. Ibid., pp. 23–26.

22. Ibid., pp. 28–30.

23. Ibid., pp. 33–35.

24. Michael D. Swaine, "Conclusion: Implications, Questions, and Recommendations," in *Managing Sino-American Crises: Case Studies and Analysis,* edited by Swaine, Tuosheng, and Cohen, p. 423–24.

25. This description of context is based on James L. Schoff, *Crisis Management in Japan and the United States: Creating Opportunities for Cooperation amid Dramatic Change* (Dulles, Va.: Brassey's, 2004).

26. Ibid., p. 79.

27. Ibid., pp. 39–40.

28. Ibid., p. 84; Tomohito Shinoda, *Koizumi Diplomacy: Japan's* Kantei *Approach to Foreign and Defense Affairs* (University of Washington Press, 2007), pp. 10, 72. In routine circumstances, the DCCS-CM heads a situation room in which information is collected and distributed to relevant agencies. Both centers are in the basement of the *kantei*.

29. Schoff, *Crisis Management in Japan and the United States*, p. 86.

30. Koike Yuriko, "What Will Become of Security Strategy? Crisis Management, Prevention Strategy Is Key," *Ryuku Shimpo*, January 20, 2007 (OSC JPP20070120015001).

31. Schoff, *Crisis Management in Japan and the United States*, pp. 87–89; cited passages are on pp. 87 and 89.

32. Tomohito Shinoda, *Leading Japan: the Role of the Prime Minister* (Westport, Conn.: Praeger, 2000), pp. 46–47.

33. "Japan's New National Defense Program Outline Turns a Blind Eye to Threats Posed by the Chinese Military," *Shokun*, January 1, 2005 (OSC JPP20041216000008), pp. 42–54.

34. Mori Akio and Hidaka Tetsuo, "Defense Procedure Said Flawed," *Daily Yomiuri*, June 7, 2003 (OSC JPP20030608000010).

35. "Did Japanese Government Depend on the United States for Information Gathering on North Korea's Missile Launches?" *Kyodo Clue III*, July 7, 2007 (OSC JPP20070709043005). There was some hope that the elevation of the Japan Defense Agency to ministry status in January 2007 would improve crisis response, but that aspiration has yet to be realized. See Arthur Lord, "From Agency to Ministry: Creation of the Ministry of Defense and Implications for the U.S.-Japan Alliance," in *The United States and Japan in Global Context: 2008*, by the Edwin O. Reischauer Center for East Asian Studies (Johns Hopkins University School of Advanced International Studies, 2009), p. 76.

36. "Missile Launches Reveal Flaws in Nation's Crisis Management," *Daily Yomiuri*, July 6, 2006 (OSC JPP20060706969104); "Fukuda Comments on 'Laxness' of MOD's Crisis Management System," NHK General Television, February 19, 2008 (OSC JPP20080220004001); "Defense Ministry to Review Communication; Notification Sent by Administrative Vice Minister; Ishiba Will Conduct Surprise Training," *Sankei Shimbun*, March 8, 2008 (OSC JPP20080310043001); "'Ripples of Missile Launch'; Fragile Crisis Management Exposed," *Kyodo Clue III*, April 7, 2009 (OSC JPP20090410036007); Tetsuya Harada, "Political Pulse/Can SDF Become Real Tiger?" *Daily Yomiuri*, April 9, 2009 (OSC JPP20090410036006).

37. For example, the Cabinet Office's Disaster Management Bureau has fifty people; the headquarters of FEMA has between 500 and 1,000; see Schoff, *Crisis Management in Japan and the United States*, pp. 113–44, n. 66.

38. Schoff, *Crisis Management in Japan and the United States*, p. 8; "Japan-U.S. Foreign Ministerial Talks," *Kyodo Clue III*, October 18, 2006 (OSC JPP20061019026001); "N. Korea Nuke Situation Not Contingency in Japan's Vicinity: Kyuma," Kyodo, October 20, 2006 (OSC JPP20061020969022).

39. Schoff, *Crisis Management in Japan and the United States*, pp. 25–27.

40. Michael D. Swaine, "Chinese Decision-Making Regarding Taiwan, 1979–2000," in *The Making of Chinese Foreign and Security Policy in the Era of Reform*, edited by David M. Lampton (Stanford University Press, 2001), p. 319.

41. Swaine, "Chinese Decision-Making Regarding Taiwan," p. 322; fn. 95 on p. 458. Swaine doubts that the elders had much impact.

42. Robert L. Suettinger, *Beyond Tiananmen: The Politics of U.S.-China Relations, 1989–2000* (Brookings, 2003), pp. 224–25, 245–46, 262–63; John W. Garver, *Face Off: China, the United States, and Taiwan's Democratization* (University of Washington Press, 1997); Tai Ming Cheung, "Chinese Military Preparations against Taiwan over the Next Ten Years," in *Crisis in the Taiwan Strait*, edited by James R. Lilley and Chuck Downs (National Defense University Press, 1997); Tai Ming Cheung, "The Influence of the Gun: China's Central Military Commission and Its Relationship with the Military, Party, and State Decision-Making Systems," in *The Making of Chinese Foreign and Security Policy in the Era of Reform*, edited by Lampton, p. 76; Andrew Scobell, *China's Use of Military Force: Beyond the Great Wall and the Long March* (Cambridge University Press, 2003), pp. 171–91. You Ji also adopts Swaine's perspective; see his "Changing Leadership Consensus: The Domestic Context of War Games," in *Across the Taiwan Strait: Mainland China, Taiwan, and the 1995–1996 Crisis*, edited by Suisheng Zhao (New York: Routledge, 1999), pp. 77–98.

43. Swaine, "Chinese Decision-Making Regarding Taiwan," pp. 323–24.

44. See the items cited in note 4 plus Robert S. Ross, "The 1995–96 Taiwan Strait Confrontation: Coercion, Credibility, and the Use of Force," *International Security* 25 (Fall 2000), p. 118; and Allen S. Whiting, "China's Use of Force, 1950–1996, and Taiwan," *International Security* 26 (Fall 2001), pp. 120–23.

45. Eric A. McVadon, "The Reckless and the Resolute: Confrontations in the South China Sea," *China Security* 5 (Spring 2009), pp. 4–5.

46. Dennis C. Blair and David B. Bonfili, "The April 2001 EP-3 Incident: The U.S. Point of View," in *Managing Sino-American Crises*, edited by Swaine, Tuosheng, and Cohen, pp. 378, 412.

47. John Keefe, "Anatomy of the EP-3 Incident, April 2001" (Alexandria, Va.: CNA Corporation, January 2002), pp. 4–5. At the time of the incident, Keefe was a special assistant to the U.S. ambassador to the PRC, Joseph Prueher.

48. James Mulvenon, "Civil-Military Relations and the EP-3 Crisis: A Content Analysis," *China Leadership Monitor* 1 (Winter 2002), p. 4 (http://media.hoover.org/documents/clm1_JM1.pdf).

49. Zhang Tuosheng, "The Sino-American Aircraft Collision: Lessons for Crisis Management," in *Managing Sino-American Crises*, edited by Swaine, Tuosheng, and Cohen, p. 409.

50. Zhang, "The Sino-American Aircraft Collision," p. 395.

51. Ibid., p. 418, n. 10.

52. See Keefe, "Anatomy of the EP-3 Incident, April 2001," p. 20, for the text of the PACOM statement.

53. Mulvenon, "Civil-Military Relations and the EP-3 Crisis," pp. 4–5.

54. "CCTV Carries FM Spokesman's Comments on U.S. Military Plane Incident," April 1, 2001 (OSC CPP20010401000065. The broadcast was at 10:20 p.m. It is sometimes said that the Chinese stance on the incident was a response to a statement by Admiral Dennis Blair, the U.S. commander in the Pacific. But Blair's statement came *after* the first Zhou-Prueher meeting, by which time the Chinese had locked in their basic position.

55. Zhang, "The Sino-American Aircraft Collision," p. 395; Keefe, "Anatomy of the EP-3 Incident, April 2001," p. 5.

56. Zhang, "The Sino-American Aircraft Collision," p. 415. Zhang himself believes that the quiet diplomacy approach would have been impossible given the state of the bilateral relationship at the time.

57. Blair and Bonfili, "The April 2001 EP-3 Incident," p. 379.

58. Mulvenon, "Civil-Military Relations and the EP-3 Crisis," pp. 7–8.

59. On the debate on U.S. policy, see David M. Finkelstein, "China Reconsiders Its National Security: The Great Peace and Development Debate of 1999," Project Asia (Alexandria, Va.: CNA Corporation, December 2000), pp. 5–7.

60. Wu Baiyi, "Chinese Crisis Management during the 1999 Embassy Bombing Incident," in *Managing Sino-American Crises*, edited by Swaine, Tuosheng, and Cohen, p. 355.

61. Wu Baiyi, "Chinese Crisis Management during the 1999 Embassy Bombing Incident," p. 355.

62. Qi Zhou, "Organization, Structure, and Image in the Making of Chinese Foreign Policy since the Early 1990s," Ph.D. dissertation, Johns Hopkins University, 2008, p. 345. Zhou based her account of the Belgrade bombing episode on Zong Hairen, *Zhu Rongji zai 1999: diyishou cailiao jiekai gaoceng juice guocheng* [Zhu Rongji in 1999: First-Hand Materials Reveal the High-Level Policymaking Process] (Hong Kong: Mingjing Chubanshe, 2003), pp. 74–88; Robert Lawrence Kuhn, *The Man Who Changed China: The Life and Legacy of Jiang Zemin* (New York: Crown Publishers, 2004); and Yu Qingsheng, "Jiang Zemin shi neizheng waijiao fangzhen de sanci neibu jiang hua" [Three Internal Talks on Domestic and Foreign Policies during Jiang Zemin's Period], in *Jiang Zemin: Yunzhou Weiwo* [Jiang Zemin: Devising Strategies] (Hong Kong: Jingbao wenhua qiye youxian gongsi, 1999), pp. 286–87.

63. Wu Baiyi, "Chinese Crisis Management during the 1999 Embassy Bombing Incident," p. 356.

64. Zhou, "Organization, Structure, and Image," pp. 345–48. The quote is from Deputy Foreign Minister Wang Guangya; cited in Kuhn, *The Man Who Changed China*, p. 5. On China's accommodationist foreign policy, see Avery Goldstein, *Rising to the Challenge: China's Grand Strategy and International Security* (Stanford University Press, 2005).

65. Zhou, "Organization, Structure and Image," pp. 348–53.

66. "Xinhua Cites Clinton Remarks on Embassy Bombing," May 8, 1999 (OSC FTS19990508000903); "Clinton Sends Letter of Apology to Jiang Zemin," May 10, 1999 (OSC FTS19990510001965). When the United States is in daylight savings time, as it was in May 1999, Beijing is twelve hours ahead of the U.S. East Coast.

67. Kurt M. Campbell and Richard Weitz, "The Chinese Embassy Bombing: Evidence of Crisis Management?" in *Managing Sino-American Crises*, edited by Swaine, Tuosheng, and Cohen, pp. 335–38.

68. Peter Hays Gries, "Tears of Rage: Chinese Nationalist Reactions to the Belgrade Embassy Bombing," *China Journal* 46 (July 2001), p. 31.

69. Glaser and Saunders, "Chinese Civilian Foreign Policy Research Institutes," p. 602. The AMS analysis may have been similar to that provided by missile experts from the China Aerospace Industry Corporation in an interview to Xinhua over the weekend. They offered technical evidence to reject DOD's initial explanation of collateral damage and to assert that the attack was "absolutely premeditated no matter how it is analyzed." See "PRC Missile Experts Say Embassy Attack 'Premeditated,'" May 10, 1999 (OSC FTS19990510000407). China, which saw the Kosovo operation as a U.S. operation conducted under the superficial aegis of NATO, went further, claiming that the United States hit the Chinese embassy not in error but *because* it was the Chinese embassy.

70. "Renmin Ribao Commentator on Embassy Bombing," May 9, 1999 (OSC FTS19990509000110); "Commentary Condemns NATO Attack on Embassy," May 10, 1999 (OSC FTS19990510000141); "Commentary on NATO Explanation on Attack," May 10, 1999 (FBIS FTS19991510000169). Generally, the Xinhua commentator articles were harsher than those of *People's Daily*, perhaps because the news agency lost personnel in the bombing.

71. Zhou, "Organization, Structure and Image," pp. 354–57; "Ministry Spokesman Announces Decisions on Ties with US," May 10, 1999 (OSC FTS19990510000725); "Further on Tang Jiaxuan 'Representations' to Sasser," May 10, 1999 (OSC FTS19990510000806); "Qin Huasun Addresses Press Prior to UNSC Meeting on NATO," May 10, 1999 (OSC FTS19990510001988). The Foreign Ministry also announced that it was "postponing" bilateral dialogues with the United States on human rights and nonproliferation of weapons of mass destruction and suspending exchanges between the two military establishments.

72. Wu Baiyi, "Chinese Crisis Management during the 1999 Embassy Bombing Incident," p. 356–57.

73. Zhou, "Organization, Structure, and Image," p. 357.

74. Wu Baiyi, "Chinese Crisis Management during the 1999 Embassy Bombing Incident," pp. 358–59.

75. See Finkelstein, "China Reconsiders Its National Security."

76. Wu Baiyi, "Chinese Crisis Management during the 1999 Embassy Bombing Incident," p. 357.

77. David Kang and Ji-young Lee, "Japan-Korea Relations: Missiles and Prime Ministers May Mark a Turning Point," *Comparative Connections* 8 (October 2006) (http://csis.org/files/media/csis/pubs/0603qjapan_korea.pdf), n.p.

78. "Declaration by a 'Politician Who Will Fight,'" *Bungei Shunju*, September 2006 (OSC JPP20060816016003).

79. The members of the Security Council are the prime minister; the chief cabinet secretary; the foreign minister; the defense minister (the head of JDA before 2007); the ministers of internal affairs and communications, of finance, and of land, infrastructure, and transportation; and the chairman of the public safety commission.

80. "Declaration by a 'Politician Who Will Fight.'"

81. "Government to Issue Destruction Order by End of Month, to be on Standby to Intercept DPRK Missile," *Nihon Keizai Shimbun*, March 22, 2009 (OSC JPP20090323026004).

82. "Scoop! 'Taepo Dong Hits Japan Archipelago' at 11:00 a.m. 4 April," *Shukan Gendai*, April 4, 2009 (OSC JPP20090324026001), pp. 16–19; "Interception of N. Korean Rocket Could Be Ordered By Defense Minister," *Mainichi Daily*, March 24, 2009 (OSC JPP20090324969061).

83. The prime minister has the authority to issue the order unilaterally; see Yuki Tatsumi, *Japan's National Security Policy Infrastructure: Can Tokyo Meet Washington's Expectation?* (Henry L. Stimson Center, 2008), pp. 126–27.

84. Michael J. Green, "Japan's Confused Revolution," *Washington Quarterly* 33 (January 2010), p. 11.

85. "Government May Issue Order Friday to Ready for N. Korean Rocket Intercept," Kyodo, March 24, 2009 (OSC JPP20090324969121); "Japan Orders N. Korean Rocket Destruction in Event of Launch Failure," Kyodo, March 27, 2009 (OSC JPP20090327969014). The cited passage is from the first item.

86. "Public Will Be Alerted Quickly after Launch," *Japan Times*, April 3, 2009.

87. "Japan Issues Wrong Info on N. Korean Rocket Launch," Kyodo, April 4, 2009 (OSC JPP20090404969026); Katsumata Hidemichi and Nakayama Shozo, "Performance of Missile Defense System during Tense Tracking of DPRK Missile," *Yomiuri Shimbun*, April 5, 2009 (OSC JPP200906004002); "Background behind Uproar about 'Erroneous Missile Detection,'" *Bungei Shunju*, June 2009 (OSC JPP20090622043003), pp. 234–35.

88. Hiroyuki Noguchi, "Ground SDF's Full-Blown Activities for Tsunami-Hit Areas: Slow Political Decision, Poor Equipment, Limit Revealed in Urgent Dispatch Overseas," *Sankei Shimbun*, January 29, 2005 (OSC JPP20050201000007).

89. On the political motivations for the operation, see Kinya Fujimoto, "Complicated Mixture of Ulterior Motives; the U.S. Wants to Ease Anti-U.S. Sentiments, China Wants to Calm Down View of China as 'Threat,' Japan Hopes to Form East Asia Community," *Sankei Shimbun*, January 6, 2005 (OSC JPP20050106000160); Hidetoshi Ikebe, "Japan Aims for Leadership Role," *Yomiuri Shimbun*, January 6, 2005 (OSC JPP20050205000125); and Takeshi Sato, "Largest-Ever SDF Overseas Relief Mission:

Aimed at Adding Momentum to Make This Regular Duty—With Cooperation of U.S. Forces in Mind," *Asahi Shimbun*, January 8, 2005 (OSC JPP20050110000004).

90. "Japan Sets up Crisis Office to Deal with Quake-Triggered Tsunamis," Kyodo, December 26, 2004 (OSC JPP20041226000073); Ikebe, "Japan Aims for Leadership Role."

91. "Japanese Media Highlight Tokyo's Unprecedented Relief for Tsunami Affected Areas," FBIS Report, January 10, 2005 (OSC JPP20050112000117), disseminated January 20, 2005.

92. "Koizumi Vows to Help Tsunami-Hit Areas, 43 Japanese Missing," Kyodo, December 27, 2004 (OSC JPP20041227000043).

93. "MOFA Spokesman on Assistance for Tsunami-Hit Nations, Aid for Iraq," Ministry of Foreign Affairs, December 28, 2004 (OSC JPP20040104000018); Ikebe, "Japan Aims For Leadership Role"; "Japan Eyes Sending over 800 Troops for Tsunami Relief," Kyodo, January 4, 2005 (OSC JPP20050104000079). To secure such a radical increase, MOFA required the approval of the prime minister and the minister, which was not so easy during the end-of-year holiday.

94. Ikebe, "Japan Aims for Leadership Role"; "Japanese Media Highlight Tokyo's Unprecedented Relief for Tsunami Affected Areas."

95. Ikebe, "Japan Aims for Leadership Role"; "Japan Sends Navy to Thailand to Help Rescue Work," Agence France-Press, December 28, 2004 (OSC JPP20041228000114); "JDA Says Japan's MSDF Ends Tsunami Relief Activities in Thailand 1 Jan," Kyodo, January 1, 2005 (OSC JPP20050101000030); and "Two Japanese Aid Helicopters Arrive on Phuket," Kyodo, January 2, 2005 (OSC JPP20050102000009).

96. Noguchi, "Ground SDF's Full-Blown Activities for Tsunami-Hit Areas."

97. "Japanese Media Highlight Tokyo's Unprecedented Relief for Tsunami Affected Areas."

98. "Japan to Send Ground, Maritime, Air Forces to Thailand for Relief," Kyodo, January 2, 2005 (OSC JPP20050102000027).

99. "Japan Eyes Sending Over 800 Troops for Tsunami Relief"; "Japan: Defense Minister Orders SDF to Prepare for Tsunami-Hit Indonesia," Jiji Press, January 4, 2005 (OSC JPP200501014000081); "SDF Team Departs Japan to Prepare Japan's Biggest-Ever Aid Mission," Jiji Press, January 4, 2005 (OSC JPP200501040000115). Within three days of approval of the deployment, on January 7, JDA head Ono would raise the authorized number of troops to 1,000; "Japan to Send 1,000 SDF Members for Relief in Tsunami-Hit Areas," Kyodo, January 7, 2005 (OSC JPP20050107000061). The process for securing that change is unknown; nor is it clear that the number of troops dispatched ever reached that level.

100. "Japan Sends Plane to Airlift Supplies to Tsunami-Hit Indonesia," Kyodo, January 6, 2006 (OSC JPP20050106000012); Noguchi, "Ground SDF's Full-Blown Activities for Tsunami-Hit Areas"; "Japan MSDF Transport Ship Leaves Kure on Relief Mission," Jiji Press, January 7, 2005 (OSC JPP20050107000041).

101. "Japan MSDF Transport Ship Leaves Kure"; "2 MSDF Ships Head to Sumatra for Relief Mission," Kyodo, January 12, 2005 (OSC JPP20050112000045); "Destroyer, Plane Leave for Sumatra to Help Tsunami Victims," Kyodo, January 14, 2005 (OSC JPP20050114000051); "Japan's GSDF Medical Team Arrives in Aceh," Kyodo, January 16, 2005 (OSC JPP20050116000016).

102. "MOFA Spokesman on Assistance for Tsunami Disaster," Ministry of Foreign Affairs, January 4, 2005 (OSC JPP2005010405000043).

103. Noguchi, "Ground SDF's Full-Blown Activities for Tsunami-Hit Areas"; "Japanese Troops Board MSDF Ship in Singapore, Head to Aceh," Kyodo, January 22, 2005 (OSC JPP20050122000009). Noguchi reveals that Japan also faced problems in securing overflight and landing rights for ASDF aircraft en route. Singapore was a particular problem, for reasons that were not explained.

104. Noguchi, "Ground SDF's Full-Blown Activities for Tsunami-Hit Areas."

105. Ibid.

106. Cole, "Right-Sizing the Navy: How Much Naval Force Will Beijing Deploy?" in *Right-Sizing the People's Liberation Army*, edited by Kamphausen and Scobell, pp. 543–44.

Chapter Thirteen

1. "Treaty of Mutual Cooperation and Security between the United States and Japan," Japan Ministry of Foreign Affairs, January 19, 1960 (www.mofa.go.jp/region/n-america/us/q&a/ref/1.html).

2. Yoichi Funabashi, "Maintain the Armitage Doctrine Quietly," *Asahi Shimbun*, February 10, 2004 (Open Source Center [hereafter OSC] JPP20040210000034).

3. The general discussion of the Taiwan Strait issue is based on my *Untying the Knot: Making Peace in the Taiwan Strait* (Brookings, 2005). For an exploration of escalation dynamics under a conflict scenario, see Richard C. Bush and Michael J. O'Hanlon, *A War Like No Other: The Truth about China's Challenge to America* (New York: Wyley Publishers, 2007).

4. Communication with a senior official of the Bush administration, October 1, 2009. See also Hiroshi Ito and Tsutomu Watanabe, "Koizumi's Risky Way of Placing Top Priority on Japan-U.S. Relations," *Asahi Shimbun*, November 17, 2005 (OSC JPP20051117016001; "Japan's Asian Relations Important to Ties with U.S., Bush Says," Nikkei Telecom 21, November 16, 2005 (OSC JPP20051117036007).

5. Michael J. Green and Shinjiro Koizumi, "Steadying the Alliance and Bracing for Elections," *Comparative Connections* 9 (July 2007) (http://csis.org/files/media/csis/pubs/0702qus_japan.pdf), pp. 23–24.

6. Susan L. Shirk, *China: Fragile Superpower* (Oxford University Press, 2007), pp. 1–3.

7. See Hugh White, "The Geostrategic Implications of China's Growth," in *China's New Place in a World in Crisis: Economic Geopolitical and Environmental*

Dimensions, edited by Ross Garnaut, Ligang Song, and Wing Thye Woo (Australian National University, ANU E Press, July 2009) (http://epress.anu.edu.au/china_new_place/pdf/ch05.pdf); Evan S. Medeiros, "Strategic Hedging and the Future of Asia-Pacific Stability," *Washington Quarterly* 29 (Winter 2005–06), pp. 145–67; Richard C. Bush, "The Revival of China as a Great Power and What It Means for the United States," speech at Towson State University, November 17, 2008 (www.brookings.edu/~/media/Files/rc/speeches/2008/1117_china_bush/1117_china_bush.pdf); Jia Qingguo, "Learning to Live with the Hegemon: Evolution of China's Policy toward the U.S. since the End of the Cold War," *Journal of Contemporary China* 14 (August 2005), pp. 395–407.

8. For a clash over the South China Sea, see Dennis C. Blair and David V. Bonfili, "The April 2001 EP-3 Incident: The U.S. Point of View"; and Zhang Tuosheng, "The Sino-American Aircraft Collision: Lessons for Crisis Management," both in *Managing Sino-American Crises: Case Studies and Analysis*, edited by Michael D. Swaine, Zhang Tuosheng, and Danielle F. S. Cohen (Washington: Carnegie Endowment for International Peace, 2007), pp. 377–90, 391–423.

9. See the discussion of the EP-3 incident of 2001 in chapter 12 and that on maritime incidents in 2009 in chapter 6.

10. Dennis C. Blair, "Annual Threat Assessment of the U.S. Intelligence Community for the Senate Select Committee on Intelligence," February 2, 2010 (www.dni.gov/testimonies/20100202_testimony.pdf), p. 29.

11. Medeiros, "Strategic Hedging and the Future of Asia-Pacific Stability"; quoted passage is on p. 158.

12. Alastair Iain Johnston kindly provided me the slides of Luo's talk—Luo Yuan, "Ehrshiyi Shiji Chuqi di Guoji Zhanlue geju yu Zhongguo Zhoubian Anquan Qingxing" [The International Strategic Configuration in the Initial Stage of the 21st Century and the Security Environment on China's Periphery]—and that of Fan Gaoyue, "China's National Defense: Challenges and Responses." Presentations are in the author's files.

13. The allegation about Westernizing and dividing does not appear in the discussion of the "first concern," but it does appear in the introduction of Luo's talk.

14. Yuan Peng, "The Direction of the Obama Administration's China Policy and Prospects for Sino-U.S. Relations," *Waijiao Pinglun*, February 25, 2009 (OSC CPP20090506671002), pp. 1–6.

15. "Opinion of the United States," Pew Global Attitudes Project, Key Indicators Database (http://pewglobal.org/database/?indicator=1&country=45).

16. "Chinese View of Americans: A Survey and Analysis," presentation by Zhou Qi at the Brookings Institution, November 9, 2009; data in author's files.

17. See Xu Wu, *Chinese Cyber Nationalism: Evolution, Characteristics, and Implications* (Lanham, Md.: Lexington Books, 2007), particularly pp. 45–58.

18. See Randall Schweller, "Managing the Rise of Great Powers: History and Theory," in *Engaging China: The Management of an Emerging Power*, edited by Alastair Iain Johnston and Robert Ross (New York: Routlegde, 1999), pp. 1–31.

19. On U.S. and Chinese mutual hedging, see Medeiros, "Strategic Hedging and the Future of Asia-Pacific Stability," pp. 145–67.

20. "Joint Statement U.S.-Japan Security Consultative Committee," February 19, 2005, Ministry of Defense (www.mod.go.jp/e/d_policy/dp10.html).

21. "Joint Statement of the U.S.-Japan Security Consultative Committee: Alliance Transformation: Advancing United States–Japan Security and Defense Cooperation," May 1, 2007, Ministry of Defense (www.mod.go.jp/e/d_policy/dp16.html).

22. "The U.S.-Japan Security Consultative Committee Marking the 50th Anniversary of the Signing of the U.S.-Japan Treaty of Mutual Cooperation and Security," January 19, 2010 (www.state.gov/secretary/rm/2010/01/135312.htm).

23. Yu Shan, "The United States and Japan Should Not Add to the Taiwan Strait Turmoil," *Renmin Ribao*, February 21, 2005 (OSC CPP20040221000049), p. 3. Christopher Hughes has a more balanced assessment: Tokyo and Washington were trying to hedge against a possible crisis without designating China as a threat; see Christopher W. Hughes, *Japan's Re-emergence as a 'Normal' Military Power*, Adelphi Paper 368-9 (Oxford University Press for the International Institute for Strategic Studies, 2006), p. 101.

24. Richard C. Bush, presentation on the "U.S.-Japan Alliance and the Rise of China," at the conference "The U.S.-Japan Alliance: Beyond Northeast Asia," Center for Northeast Asian Policy Studies, Brookings Institution, May 9, 2009, pp. 23–29 (www.brookings.edu/~/media/Files/events/2009/0508_us_japan/20090508_japan_full.pdf).

25. Richard J. Samuels, "Wing Walking: The U.S.-Japan Alliance," *Global Asia* 4 (April 2009), pp. 14–19.

26. Michael J. Green, "Japan Is Back: Why Tokyo's New Assertiveness Is Good for Washington," *Foreign Affairs* 86 (March/April 2007), p. 144.

27. Richard L. Armitage and Joseph S. Nye, *The U.S.-Japan Alliance: Getting Asia Right through 2020* (Center for Strategic and International Studies, 2007), pp. 14, 23. The panel rejected both a U.S.-China condominium over East Asia at Japan's expense or a bipolar structure (U.S. and Japan versus China) that would force Japan to choose. Christopher Preble argues for a loosening of the alliance: shedding to Japan the responsibility of defense of its homeland and leaving it up to the littoral countries of Asia, Japan included, to decide whether and how to balance China. See his "Two Normal Countries: Rethinking the U.S.-Japan Strategic Relationship," Policy Analysis 566 (Washington: Cato Institute, April 18, 2006), especially pp. 19–21.

28. Mike M. Mochizuki, "Japan's Shifting Strategy toward the Rise of China," *Journal of Strategic Studies* 30 (August-October 2007), pp. 759–62.

29. "Positive Pacifism and the Future of the Japan-U.S. Alliance," Policy Council, Japan Forum on International Relations, October 2009 (www.jfir.or.jp/e/pr/pdf/32.pdf), p. 11. See also Hitoshi Tanaka, "A New Vision for the U.S.-Japan Alliance," *East Asian Insights* 4 (April 2004) (www.jcie.org/researchpdfs/EAI/4-1.pdf); and "Is Japan a UK of the Orient?" interview with Akio Watanabe, *Gaiko Forum* (May 2006), pp. 8–10 (OSC JPP20060419124002). Tanaka is a former MOFA official, and Watanabe is the president of the Research Institute on Peace and Security.

30. Mochizuki, "Japan's Shifting Strategy toward the Rise of China," pp. 762–65; Okazaki Hisahiko, "Time to Change Our National Security Strategy," *Daily Yomiuri*, April 22, 2006 (OSC JPP20060422969032); Policy Research Division, Tokyo Foundation, "New Security Strategy of Japan: Multilayered and Cooperative Security Strategy," October 8, 2008 (www.tokyofoundation.org/en/additional_info/New%20 Security%20Strategy%20of%20Japan.pdf).

31. Mochizuki, "Japan's Shifting Strategy toward the Rise of China," pp. 765–66. See also "China Would Surely Try to Seize Taiwan and the Senkaku Islands" (a conversation between the conservative Kyoto University scholar Nakanishi Terumasa and the commentator Shi Ping), *Seiron*, January 2008, pp. 46–59 (OSC JPP20071217043005).

32. Masashi Nishihara, "What to Expect from the New U.S. Administration #4—Have Closer Consultations with Japan, Please!" AJISS-Commentary 53, Japan Institute of International Affairs, January 9, 2009 (OSC JPP20090112134001); Henry Shinn, "Seoul and Tokyo Need Closer Cooperation" (an interview with Masashi Nishihara), *Korea Herald Online*, January 21, 2009 (OSC KPP20090126049001).

33. Mochizuki, "Japan's Shifting Strategy toward the Rise of China," pp. 766–67.

34. Terashima Jitsuro, "The Will and Imagination to Return to Common Sense: Toward a Restructuring of the U.S.-Japan Alliance," *Asia-Pacific Journal*, March 15, 2010 (http://japanfocus.org/-Terashima-Jitsuro/3321).

35. The classic statement is Glenn H. Snyder, *Alliance Politics* (Cornell University Press, 2007), especially pp. 165–99.

36. "Defense Minister Ishiba Notes Need to Verify Japan-U.S. Alliance Deterrence; 'Nuclear' Capability Is Also Subject to Verification," JijiWeb, November 9, 2007 (OSC JPP20071113032001).

37. Sakurai Yoshiko, "U.S. Military Report Suggests United States May Not Be Able to Protect Japan," *Shukan Daiyamondo*, April 11, 2009 (OSC JPP20090410040001), p. 155.

38. Research Group on the Japan-U.S. Alliance, Institute for International Policy Studies, "A New Phase in the Japan-U.S. Alliance," September 2009; Matsushita Institute of Government and Management, "A Critical Moment for the Japan-U.S. Alliance: The Urgent Need for Progress toward a 'Broad and Balanced Alliance,'" November 24, 2008 (OSC JPP200901061340010).

39. For a statement of the problem by the Institute for International Policy Studies, see "A New Phase in the Japan-U.S. Alliance," p. 10.

40. "Joint Statement of the Security Consultative Committee: Alliance Transformation: Advancing United States-Japan Security and Defense Cooperation," May 1, 2007, Ministry of Foreign Affairs (www.mofa.go.jp/region/n-america/us/security/scc/joint0705.html).

41. Michael J. Green and Katsuhisa Furukawa, "Japan: New Nuclear Realism," in *The Long Shadow: Nuclear Weapons and Security in 21st Century Asia*, edited by Muthiah Alagappa (Stanford University Press, 2008), pp. 349–68; cited passage is on

p. 365. Ironically, U.S. initiatives during the Bush administration to improve command and control, missile defense, and advanced conventional strike weapons may have spurred Beijing to increase its numbers of warheads and missiles, which would then only increase Japanese fears. For a general survey of Japan's assessment of its nuclear dilemma, see Mike M. Mochizuki, "Japan Tests the Nuclear Taboo," *Nonproliferation Review* 14 (July 2007), pp. 303–28.

42. See, for example, Bruce Klinger, "America's New Japan Challenge," September 2, 2009 (www.heritage.org/Press/Commentary/ed090209c.cfm); Leif-Eric Easley, Tetsu Kotani, and Aki Mori, "Japan's Foreign Policy and the Alliance: Transcending Change with Trust," *PacNet* 64, September 22, 2009 (http://csis.org/files/publication/pac0964.pdf).

43. Bernard D. Cole, "Right-Sizing the Navy: How Much Naval Force Will Beijing Deploy?" in *Right-Sizing the People's Liberation Army: Exploring the Contours of China's Military*, edited by Roy Kamphausen and Andrew Scobell (Carlisle, Pa.: Strategic Studies Institute, U.S. Army War College, 2007), p. 543.

44. "Treaty of Mutual Cooperation and Security between the United States and Japan," articles 3, 5, and 6.

45. Michael Finnegan, "Managing Unmet Expectations in the U.S.-Japan Alliance," Special Report 17, National Bureau of Asian Research, November 2009 (www.nbr.org/publications/specialreport/pdf/SR17.pdf), p. 9.

46. Ibid., pp. 9–10.

47. Ibid., p. 11.

48. See "Policy Speech by Prime Minister Yukio Hatoyama at the 174th Session of the Diet," January 29, 2010 (www.kantei.go.jp/foreign/hatoyama/statement/201001/29siseihousin_e.html); "'Beigun wa jūyō' de icchi" [Japanese, Singaporean Defense Ministers Agree on Importance of Presence of U.S. Troops], *Yomiuri Shimbun*, December 17, 2009, p. 4.

49. Finnegan, "Managing Unmet Expectations in the U.S.-Japan Alliance," p. 12.

50. Ibid.

Chapter Fourteen

1. On China's efforts to resolve territorial disputes, see M. Taylor Fravel, *Strong Borders, Secure Nation: Cooperation and Conflict in China's Territorial Disputes* (Princeton University Press, 2008).

2. See Lily Gardner Feldman, "German-Polish Reconciliation: How Similar, How Different?" (http://csm.org.pl/fileadmin/files/csm/SPOTKANIA/Dr%20Lily%20Gardner%20Feldman_German%20Polish%20Reconciliation%20How%20Similar%20How%20Different.pdf), based on a lecture by Feldman at the German Historical Institute, Warsaw, Poland, February 25, 2008.

3. Robert O. Keohane and Lisa L. Martin, "The Promise of Institutional Theory," *International Security* 20 (Summer 1995), pp. 39–51; Bonnie S. Glaser, "Cross-Strait

Confidence Building: The Case for Military Confidence-Building Measures," in *Breaking the China-Taiwan Impasse*, edited by Donald S. Zagoria (Westport, Conn.: Praeger, 2003), pp. 155–72.

4. Fukuda Yasuo, "Forging the Future Together," speech at Peking University, December 28, 2007 (www.mofa.go.jp/region/asia-paci/China/speech0712.html.)

5. Shi Yinhong, "Sino-Japanese Rapprochement and 'Diplomatic Revolution,'" *Zhanlue Yu Guanli,* March 2003 (Open Source Center [hereafter OSC] CPP20030506000224), pp 71–75.

6. Peter Hays Gries, "China's 'New Thinking' on Japan," *China Quarterly* 184 (December 2005), pp. 840–42.

7. In addition, Japan fears that flexibility on the islands would undermine its position in its territorial dispute with Russia concerning the islands that make up the Northern Territories; see Selig S. Harrison, "Seabed Petroleum in Northeast Asia: Conflict or Cooperation?" in *Seabed Petroleum in Northeast Asia: Conflict or Cooperation?* edited by Selig S. Harrison (Asia Program, Woodrow Wilson International Center for Scholars, 2005), p. 6.

8. Indeed, the amounts involved probably are not great, and whatever Japan might extract would probably be sold to China anyway because the cost of transport back to Japan is too great. Communication from Itoh Shoichi, Economic Research Institute of Northeast Asia, December 13, 2009.

9. The technical term for such an approach is unitization. See Thomas J. Schoenbaum, "Resolving the China-Japan Dispute over the Senkaku Islands," *Asia Pacific Journal: Japan Focus*, essay 1734, February 18, 2005 (www.japanfocus.org/-Thomas_J_-Schoenbaum/1734); Andrew B. Derman, "Unitization," FindLaw for Legal Professionals, Thompson and Knight LLP, January 30, 2003 (http://library.findlaw.com/2003/Jan/30/132512.html).

10. Feng Zhaokui, "The Waters of the Diaoyu Islands: An Emergency?" *Shijie Zhishi*, March 16, 2009, pp. 26–28 (OSC CPP20090403671001).

11. Peter Dutton, "Carving Up the East China Sea," *Naval War College Review* 60 (Spring 2007), pp. 54–58.

12. Dutton, "Carving Up the East China Sea," pp. 58–62.

13. Dutton, "Carving Up the East China Sea," pp. 62–67.

14. From 1995 on, Taiwan and China were trapped in their own security dilemma, in which each felt increasingly vulnerable because of the other's actions and responded in ways that only fostered a deeper sense of vulnerability.

15. On China's reemergence, see Richard C. Bush, "The Revival of China as a Great Power and What It Means for the United States," speech at Towson State University, November 8, 2008 (www.brookings.edu/speeches/2008/1117_china_bush.aspx).

16. Luo Yuan, "Ehrshiyi Shiji Chuqi di Guoji Zhanlue geju yu Zhongguo Zhoubian Anquan Qingxing" [The International Strategic Configuration in the Initial Stage of the 21st Century and the Security Environment on China's Periphery], October 2008 (PowerPoint presentation in the author's files).

17. James B. Steinberg, "Administration's Vision of the U.S.-China Relationship," address at the Center for a New American Security, September 24, 2009 (www.state. gov/s/d/2009/129686.htm). Those who suggest that China's intentions are completely opaque underestimate what may be inferred from Beijing's behavior. For an example of skillful inference, see M. Taylor Fravel, "China's Search for Military Power," *Washington Quarterly* 31 (Sum. 2008), pp. 125–41.

18. Steinberg, "Administration's Vision of the U.S.-China Relationship." The 2010 quadrennial defense review by the Department of Defense urged that "the United States and China should sustain open channels of communication to discuss disagreements in order to manage and ultimately reduce the risks of conflict that are inherent in any relationship as broad and complex as that shared by these two nations." See Department of Defense, Quadrennial Defense Review Report, February 2010 (www.defense.gov/QDR/QDR%20as%20of%2029JAN10%201600.pdf), p. 60.

19. "Press Conference with Secretary Gates from India," News Transcript, Department of Defense, January 20, 2010 (www.defense.gov/transcripts/transcript. aspx?transcriptid=4540).

20. "Chinese and Japanese Defense Departments' Joint Press Communiqué," Xinhua, November 27, 2009 (OSC CPP20091127354001).

21. "Japan, U.S., China to Hold 1st Trilateral Policy Dialogue," Kyodo, June 6, 2009 (OSC JPP20090606969001).

22. "1st Trilateral Talks among U.S., Japan, China Postponed: Yonhap," Kyodo, July 20, 2009 (OSC JPP20090720969024).

23. Mike M. Mochizuki, "Japan's Shifting Strategy toward the Rise of China," *Journal of Strategic Studies* 30 (August-October 2007), pp. 771–72.

24. Robert S. Norris and Hans M. Kristensen, "Chinese Nuclear Forces, 2008," *Bulletin of Atomic Scientists* 64 (July-August 2008) (www.thebulletin.org/files/06400 3009.pdf), pp. 42–45.

25. Dennis C. Blair, Office of the Director of National Intelligence, "Annual Threat Assessment of the Intelligence Community for the Senate Select Committee on Intelligence," testimony before Senate Select Committee on Intelligence, February 12, 2009 (www.dni.gov/testimonies/20090212_testimony.pdf), p. 24.

26. According to the conventional interpretation of the constitution, Japan has the legal right to possess nuclear weapons as long as they would be used in self-defense.

27. Mike M. Mochizuki, "Japan Tests the Nuclear Taboo," *Nonproliferation Review* 14 (July 2007), pp. 303–28; Llewelyn Hughes, "Why Japan Will Not Go Nuclear (Yet): International and Domestic Constraints on the Nuclearization of Japan," *International Security* 31 (Spring 2007), pp. 67–96.

28. Sato Yukio, "Reinforcing American Extended Deterrence for Japan: An Essential Step for Nuclear Disarmament," Japan Institute of International Affairs, commentary 57, February 3, 2009 (www.jiia.or.jp/en_commentary/200902/03-1.html).

29. "Japan, U.S. Should Talk More on Nukes: State Dept Official," Nikkei Telecom, July 17, 2009 (OSC JPP20090717969001). For a more lengthy discussion on

this issue, see Richard C. Bush, "The U.S. Policy of Extended Deterrence in East Asia: History, Current Views, and Implications," an essay to be posted in fall 2010 on the Brookings Institution website (www.brookings.edu).

30. Bonnie Glaser, "U.S.-China Relations: Chock-full of Dialogue: SED, Human Rights, and Security," *Comparative Connections* 10 (July 2008) (http://csis.org/files/media/csis/pubs/0802qus_china.pdf), n.p.

31. James L. Schoff, *Crisis Management in Japan and the United States: Creating Opportunities for Cooperation amid Dramatic Change* (Dulles, Va.: Brassey's, 2004), pp. 63–73, 95–97; Masao Tatsuzaki, "Cyber-Crime: Current Status and Countermeasures in Japan," in *Cyber-Crime: The Challenge in Asia*, edited by Roderic Broadhurst and Peter Grabosky (Hong Kong University Press, 2005), pp. 169–81; "Big Gaps Found in Japanese Cyber Security," UPI Security and Terrorism, July 27, 2006 (http://search.ebscohost.com/login.aspx?direct=true&db=tsh&AN=1HTP1024475664&site=ehost-live); Steve Sin, "Cyber Threat in Northeast Asia," United Forces Korea J2, Joint Intelligence Operations Center–Korea, December 15, 2008, on file with author; "Japan System That Protects against 10-Gigabit-Per-Second Cyberattacks Developed," FujiSankei Business, February 21, 2007 (OSC JPP20070223134003).

32. Shane Harris, "The Cyberwar Plan," *National Journal*, November 14, 2009 (www.nationaljournal.com/njmagazine/cs_20091114_3145.php).

33. Thomas U. Berger, "Different Beds, Same Nightmare: The Politics of History in Germany and Japan," AICGS Policy Report 39 (American Institute for Contemporary German Studies, Johns Hopkins University, October 2009), p. 17.

34. Ibid., p. 20, 24, 29–30.

35. Lily Gardner Feldman, "Germany's External Reconciliation as a Defining Feature of Foreign Policy: Lessons for Japan?" *AICGS Advisor*, American Institute for Contemporary German Studies, April 28, 2006 (http://aicgs.org/analysis/c/lgf042806.aspx, http://aicgs.org/analysis/c/lgf042806two.aspx).

36. Matthew Penney and Bryce Wakefield, "Right Angles: Examining Accounts of Japanese Neo-Nationalism," *Pacific Affairs* 81 (Winter 2008), pp. 547–51. Local school districts pick their textbooks from a list approved by the Ministry of Education.

37. Ken Booth and Nicholas J. Wheeler, *The Security Dilemma: Fear, Cooperation, and Trust in World Politics* (New York: Palgrave Macmillan, 2008), pp. 83–93; Robert Axelrod, *The Evolution of Cooperation* (New York: Basic Books, 1984); Kenneth A. Oye, *Cooperation under Anarchy* (Princeton University Press, 1986), especially Oye, "Explaining Cooperation under Anarchy: Hypotheses and Strategies," pp. 1–24.

38. Robert O. Keohane, *After Hegemony: Cooperation and Discord in the World Political Economy* (Princeton University Press, 1984), p. 57. Principles are "beliefs of fact, causation, and rectitude." Norms are "standards of behavior defined in terms of rights and obligations." Rules define specifically what is and what is not allowed. Decisionmaking procedures are "prevailing practices for making and implementing collective choice." See also Stephen D. Krasner , "Structural Causes and Regime Consequences: Regimes as Intervening Variables," in *International Regimes*, edited by Stephen D. Krasner (Cornell University Press, 1983), p. 2.

39. Keohane, *After Hegemony*, pp. 12–13; Keohane and Martin, "The Promise of Institutional Theory." On the credibility of commitments, see Andrew Moravcsik, *The Choice for Europe: Social Purpose and State Power from Messina to Maastricht* (Cornell University Press, 1998).

40. Evan Feigenbaum and Robert Manning, *The United States in the New Asia*, Council on Foreign Relations Special Report 50 (Council on Foreign Relations, November 2009), p. 9.

41. Hitoshi Tanaka, "East Asia Community Building: Toward an 'East Asia Security Forum,'" *East Asia Insights* 2 (April 2007) (www.jcie.or.jp/insights/2-2.html).

42. Robert Jervis, "Security Regimes," in *International Regimes*, edited by Stephen D. Krasner (Cornell University Press, 1983), pp. 173–78.

43. Glaser, "Cross-Strait Confidence Building," pp. 157–59.

44. Based on Glaser, "Cross-Strait Confidence Building."

45. Fukuda, "Forging the Future Together."

46. "Hu Jintao's Speech at Japan's Waseda University," Xinhua, May 8, 2008 (OSC CPP20080508074009).

47. "Full Text of Prime Minister Hatoyama's Policy Speech on 26 Oct 09," Kyodo, October 26, 2009 (OSC 20091026027004).

48. Also in March, Japanese company grade officers visited China; *Defense of Japan 2009*, Ministry of Defense, 2009 (www.mod.go.jp/e/publ/w_paper/2009.html). Exchanges refer to military visits; dialogues, which are much less common, refer to discussions to address general or specific issues.

49. "Joint Press Communiqué of Defense Affairs Departments of China and Japan," Xinhua, March 20, 2009 (OSC CPP20090320136021).

50. Based on interviews with Japanese military officers, February 2009.

51. "Joint Press Communiqué of Defense Affairs Departments of China and Japan," Xinhua, March 20, 2009 (OSC CPP20090320136021); "Chinese and Japanese Defense Departments' Joint Press Communiqué," Xinhua, November 27, 2009 (OSC CPP20091127354001).

52. Eric A. McVadon, "The Reckless and the Resolute: Confrontations in the South China Sea," *China Security* 5 (Spring 2009), pp. 7–8. At the end of his article, McVadon offers detailed suggestions for a U.S.-China INCSEA.

53. Mark Valencia and Yoshihisa Amae, "Regime Building in the East China Sea," *Ocean Development and International Law* 34 (April 2003), pp. 193–96.

54. Gaye Christoffersen, "Japan and the East Asian Maritime Security Order: Prospects for Trilateral and Multilateral Cooperation," *Asian Perspective* 33 (October 2009), pp. 107–49; Mark J. Valencia, "A Maritime Security Regime for Northeast Asia," *Asian Perspective* 32 (October 2008), p. 162. That China and Japan would participate in a coast guard forum is somewhat ironic, since each country has that type of organization on the front lines in the East China Sea.

55. International Crisis Group, "North East Asia's Undercurrents of Conflict," Asia Report 108, December 15, 2005, p. 26. The International Crisis Group proposes a similar code of conduct for the East China Sea.

56. Yi Kwo'n-p'yo and Hwang Chae-ho, "The Significance of the 'Memorandum of Understanding on ROK-PRC Navy/Air Force Direct Telephone Link Establishment and Operation,'" Weekly Defense Forum 1240, Korea Institute for Defense Analyses, January 26, 2009 (OSC KPP20090508024001). According to a retired Korean officer, the phone links were not fully operational as of late 2009, a full year after the signing of the memorandum of understanding.

57. McVadon, "The Reckless and the Resolute," p. 7. In the ASEAN Regional Forum (ARF), the longest-running multilateral "regime" in East Asia, China has resisted Japanese efforts to use the forum to develop tools for serious objectives like preventive diplomacy and conflict resolution; see Takeshi Yuzawa, "The Evolution of Preventive Diplomacy in the ASEAN Regional Forum: Problems and Prospects," *Asian Survey* 46 (October-November 2006), pp. 785–804.

58. Bonnie Glaser and Brad Glosserman, "Promoting Confidence Building across the Taiwan Strait," Report of the CSIS International Security Program and Pacific Forum CSIS, September 2008 (http://csis.org/files/media/csis/pubs/080910_glaser_promotingconfidence_web.pdf), pp. 9–10.

59. "Xu Caihou's Visit to the United States Will Further Advance the Development of China-U.S. Military Relations," *Jiefangjun Bao, October* 24, 2009 (OSC CPP20091024718001). From the PLA's point of view, the obstacles to decent military-to-military relations are U.S. arms sales to Taiwan; "the activities of U.S. warships and aircraft in China's exclusive economic zones"; congressional legislation restricting military contacts; and the absence of strategic trust; see "China Strongly Urges the United States to Stop Selling Weapons to Taiwan," Zhongguo Tongxun-she, October 28, 2009 (OSC CPP200910280660170).

60. Glaser, "Cross-Strait Confidence Building," p. 164.

61. Adapted from a presentation by Michael J. Green, "Building Trust across the Taiwan Strait: Cross-Strait Relations: A Role for Military Confidence-Building Measures," Center for Strategic and International Studies, January 10, 2010 (http://csis.org/event/military-confidence-building-measures-taiwan-strait).

62. "Kyodo: Japan, China Agree to Launch Hotline between Leaders to Avert Emergencies," Kyodo World Service, May 31, 2010 (OSC JPP20100531969077); "Xinhua: China, Japan Establish Prime Minister Hotline," Xinhua, June 13, 2010 (OSC CPP20100613968080).

63. "3rd Lead: Japan, China Agree to Work Together toward Creation of E. Asia Group," Kyodo World Service, September 28, 2009 (OSC JPP20090928969070). James J. Przystup, "Japan-China Relations: All about *Gyoza*: Almost All the Time," *Comparative Connections* 10 (April 2008) (www.csis.org/media/csis/pubs/0801qjapan_china.pdf), n.p.; James J. Przystup, "Japan-China Relations: The *Gyoza* Caper: Part II," *Comparative Connections* 10 (October 2008) (www.csis.org/media/csis/pubs/0803qjapan_china.pdf), n.p.; James J. Przystup, "Japan-China Relations: New Year, Old Problems," *Comparative Connections* 11 (April 2009) (www.csis.org/media/csis/pubs/0901qjapan_china.pdf).

64. "Kyodo: Japan, China Agree to Launch Hotline between Leaders to Avert Emergencies."

65. Kyodo: China Urges Japan to Supervise Media over Gas Row Reports," Kyodo World Service, May 12, 2010 (OSC JPP20100412969082).

66. Dutton, "Carving Up the East China Sea," pp. 62–67.

67. Yuki Tatsumi, *Japan's National Security Policy Infrastructure: Can Tokyo Meet Washington's Expectation?* (Henry L. Stimson Center, 2008), pp. 115–20.

68. "Government Drafts Counter-Intelligence Manual Focusing on Spying Measures; Prepared by Cabinet Information Resource Office for Ministry, Agency Leaders," *Sankei Shimbun*, December 26, 2009 (OSC JPP20091225038001); "Defense Ministry Calls on SDF Personnel to Submit to Polygraph Tests, *Mainichi Daily News*, January 20, 2010 (OSC JPP20100120969046).

69. James Mulvenon, "The Best Laid Plans: Xi Jinping and the CMC Vice-Chairmanship That Didn't Happen," *China Leadership Monitor* 30 (Fall 2009) (www.hoover.org/publications/clm/issues/70522442.html).

70. David Shambaugh, for example, envisages the possibility of such a development; see Shambaugh, *Modernizing China's Military: Progress, Problems, and Prospects* (University of California Press, 2002), p. 14–17. See also Andrew Scobell, "China's Evolving Civil-Military Relations: Creeping *guojiahua*," in *Chinese Civil-Military Relations: The Transformation of the People's Liberation Army*, edited by Nan Li (New York: Routledge, 2006), pp. 25–39.

71. "Statement of Admiral Robert F. Willard, United States Navy, Commander, United States Pacific Command, before the House Armed Services Committee on Recent Security Developments," January 13, 2010, House Armed Services Committee (http://armedservices.house.gov/pdfs/FC011310/Willard_Testimony011310.pdf).

72. Qi Zhou, "Organization, Structure and Image in the Making of Chinese Foreign Policy since the Early 1990s," Ph.D. dissertation, Johns Hopkins University, 2008, pp. 151–52; interview with a Chinese scholar, November 2007; "Dai Bingguo: State Councilor," Xinhua News Agency, March 17, 2008; interview with a Chinese scholar, January 2008.

73. "Japanese Version of the NSC to be Modeled after British Cabinet Committee; Authority Equivalent to That of the U.S. NSC," *Sankei Shimbun*, November 18, 2006 (OSC JPP20061122069002); "The Official Residence's Security Organization; Mulling the 'UK's JIC-Type' Organization," *Tokyo Shimbun*, October 26, 2006 (OSC JPP20061027033001); "Government Eyes Creating Japanese National Security Council by '09," Nikkei Telecom 21, November 13, 2006 (OSC JPP20061130045003); "Japanese Version of NSC: Role Definition at Issue; MODA, JDA Look for Ways to Maintain Influence," *Mainichi Shimbun*, Nikkei Telecom 21, November 15, 2006 (OSC JPP20061115026001); Schoff, *Crisis Management in Japan and the United States*, p. 27.

74. The proposal recommended that the new national security council be composed of the PM, chief cabinet secretary, foreign minister, and defense minister to discuss important diplomatic and national security policies and the ministers of finance, land, trade, and communications plus the chairman of the Public Safety

Commission to discuss long-term defense policies and emergency response to foreign attacks on Japan. The council was to have a secretariat headed by a secretary general and staffed by ten to twenty people, some of whom could be drawn from the SDF or the private sector. The new body would essentially displace the Security Council of Japan, which had only a nominal role.

75. "Abe Calls for Launching Japanese Version of U.S. NSC," Kyodo World Service, February 27, 2007 (OSC JPP20070227969068); "LDP Approves Bill to Set up Japanese National Security Council," Kyodo World Service, April 3, 2007 (OSC JPP20070403696023); "Japanese Cabinet Approves Bill to Set Up NSC," Kyodo World Service, April 6, 2007 (OSC JPP20070406696022); "Japan Decides to Scrap Plan to Establish National Security Council," Kyodo World Service, December 24, 2007 (OSC JPP20071224696041).

76. Michael Finnegan, "Managing Unmet Expectations in the U.S.-Japan Alliance," Special Report 17, National Bureau of Asian Research, November 2009 (www.nbr.org/publications/specialreport/pdf/SR17.pdf).

77. For a similar proposal, see Joseph S. Nye Jr., "An Alliance Larger than One Issue," *New York Times*, January 7, 2010, p. A31.

78. Thomas J. Christensen, "Fostering Stability or Creating a Monster: The Rise of China and U.S. Policy toward East Asia," *International Security* 31 (Summer 2006), pp. 81–126.

79. From Eric A. McVadon, "The Reckless and the Resolute: Confrontations in the South China Sea," *China Security* 5 (Spring 2009), pp. 10–11 (www.chinasecurity.us/pdfs/mcvadon.pdf).

Index